Pauline Frommer's

COSTA RICA

SPEND LESS SEE MORE™

*Adventure Inn (in San J.)
stayed there
(canadian hosts)

1st Edition

by David Appell & Nelson Mui

Series Editor: Pauline Frommer

1807
WILEY
2007

Wiley Publishing, Inc.

Published by:

Wiley Publishing, Inc.

111 River St.
Hoboken, NJ 07030-5774

ISBN: 978-0-470-05227-3

Editor: William Travis
Production Editor: Jana M. Stefanciosa
Cartographer: Elizabeth Puhl
Photo Editor: Richard Fox
Anniversary Logo Design: Richard Pacifico
Interior Design: Lissa Auciello-Brogan
Production by Wiley Indianapolis Composition Services

For information on our other products and services or to obtain technical support,
please contact our Customer Care Department within the U.S. at 800/762-2974,
outside the U.S. at 317/572-3993 or fax 317/572-4002.

Contents

iii

List of Maps

About the Authors

Currently based in Miami, "Latino by adoption" **David Appell** is the former editor of *Arthur Frommer's Budget Travel* and *Caribbean Travel & Life*; co-author of *Access Gay USA*; and has written for lots of other publications including *National Geographic Traveler, Travel+Leisure, The International Herald Tribune,* Spain's *El País, GQ, Men's Fitness,* and *Out.* Dave's an alum of Georgetown University's School of Foreign Service and Columbia University Graduate School of Journalism, and apart from

Spanish, gets by in a half-dozen other foreign languages. In fact, these days he's also the publisher and author of the internationally successful *Hot! Spanish* and related series of foreign-language phrasebooks devoted to love, dating, and the sundry naughtiness likely to ensue there from (www.HotBabel.com).

Pauline Frommer started traveling before she could speak, seeing the world at a young age with her guidebook writing parents Arthur Frommer and Hope Arthur. She went into the "family biz" over a decade ago, serving first as the editor of Frommers.com and then the travel section of MSNBC.com. Her articles have appeared in numerous publications including *Budget Travel,* the *Dallas Morning News, Marie Claire* and the upcoming book *The Experts Guide to Babies.* In 2006, Pauline Frommer's New York

City won "Best Guidebook of the Year" from the North American Travel Journalism Association. In 1999, she was awarded a Lowell Thomas Medal from the Society of American Travel Writers for her magazine work. She currently appears every Wednesday night on CNN's Headline News to discuss the latest travel trends. Pauline is married to physical therapist Mahlon Stewart and the mother of two very well-traveled daughters, Beatrix (age 4) and Veronica (age 8).

A former editor at *Travel + Leisure,* **Nelson Mui** has written on a variety of topics for publications such as the *New York Times, National Geographic Traveler, Men's Journal* and *San Francisco.* A native of Hong Kong who's lived in Europe and South America, Nelson inherited the travel gene from his mother, an overseas Chinese who grew up in colonial Hanoi, speaks four languages, and packs a bag at the slightest provocation. He finds comfort in the fact that virtually everywhere in the world he's visited—

including the remotest parts of Costa Rica—there's a Chinese restaurant nearby where he can gather intelligence in his mother tongue.

Additional contributions by: Eliot Greenspan, Maggie Jacobus, Rogelio Martinez, E.Z. Weaver, and Jenna Wortham.

An Invitation to the Reader

In researching this book, we discovered many wonderful places—hotels, restaurants, shops, and more. We're sure you'll find others. Please tell us about them, so we can share the information with your fellow travelers in upcoming editions. If you were disappointed with a recommendation, we'd love to know that, too. Please write to:

Pauline Frommer's Costa Rica, 1st Edition
Wiley Publishing, Inc. • 111 River St. • Hoboken, NJ 07030-5774

An Additional Note

Please be advised that travel information is subject to change at any time—and this is especially true of prices. We therefore suggest that you write or call ahead for confirmation when making your travel plans. The authors, editors, and publisher cannot be held responsible for the experiences of readers while traveling. Your safety is important to us, however, so we encourage you to stay alert and be aware of your surroundings. Keep a close eye on cameras, purses, and wallets, all favorite targets of thieves and pickpockets.

Star Ratings, Icons & Abbreviations

Every restaurant, hotel and attraction is rated with stars ★, indicating our opinion of that facility's desirability; this relates not to price, but to the value you receive for the price you pay. The stars mean:

No stars: Good
    ★ Very good
   ★★ Great
  ★★★ Outstanding! A must!

Accommodations within each neighborhood are listed in ascending order of cost, starting with the cheapest and increasing to the occasional "splurge." Each hotel review is preceded by one, two, three or four dollar signs, indicating the price range per double room. Restaurants work on a similar system, with dollar signs indicating the price range per three-course meal.

Accommodations
   $ Up to $50/night
  $$ $51–$100
 $$$ $101–$150
$$$$ Over $150 per night

Dining
   $ Meals for $6 or less
  $$ $7-$12
 $$$ $13-$18
$$$$ $19 and up

In addition, we've included a kids icon 🧒 to denote attractions, restaurants, and lodgings that are particularly child friendly.

Frommers.com

Now that you have this guidebook to help you plan a great trip, visit our website at **www.frommers.com** for additional travel information on more than 3,500 destinations. We update features regularly to give you instant access to the most current trip-planning information available. At Frommers.com, you'll find scoops on the best airfares, lodging rates, and car rental bargains. You can even book your travel online through our reliable travel booking partners. Other popular features include:

- Online updates of our most popular guidebooks
- Vacation sweepstakes and contest giveaways
- Newsletters highlighting the hottest travel trends
- Online travel message boards with featured travel discussions

A Note from Pauline

I STARTED TRAVELING WITH MY GUIDEBOOK-WRITING PARENTS, ARTHUR Frommer and Hope Arthur, when I was just 4 months old. To avoid lugging around a crib, they would simply swaddle me and stick me in an open drawer for the night. For half of my childhood, my home was a succession of hotels and B&Bs throughout Europe, as we dashed around every year to update *Europe on $5 a Day* (and then $10 a day, and then $20 . . .).

We always traveled on a budget, staying at the mom-and-pop joints Dad featured in the guide, getting around by public transportation, eating where the locals ate. And that's still the way I travel today, because I learned—from the master—that these types of vacations not only save you money, but give you a richer, deeper experience of the culture. You spend time in local neighborhoods and you meet and talk with the people who live there. For me, making friends and having meaningful exchanges is always the highlight of my trip—and the main reason I decided to become a travel writer and editor as well.

I conceived these books as budget guides for the next generation. They have all the outspoken commentary and detailed pricing information you've come to expect from the Frommer's guides, but they take bargain hunting into the 21st century, with more information on how you can effectively use the Internet and air/hotel packages to save money. Most importantly, we stress the availability of "alternative accommodations," not simply to save you money but to give you a more authentic experience in the places you visit.

In this Costa Rica book, for example, we tell you about the dozens of home-rental opportunities that put you in real Costa Rican neighborhoods (not tourist enclaves), for the same or less money than you'd spend on a hotel.

In the following chapters, our sections on "The Other Costa Rica" immerse you in the life that residents of a place enjoy; the "only in Costa Rica" experiences that go beyond the usual zipline tours, surfing, and volcano hikes. Page through this guide and you'll read about tours that take you to the studios of contemporary Costa Rican artists working in San José (p. 35); volunteer opportunities with the many scientific organizations that are studying the complex and changing ecosystems here (p. 37); and language schools that arrange homestays and other activities so that you'll learn as much about the culture here as you will Spanish (p. 36), among dozens of other experiences.

The result, I hope, is a valuable new addition to the world of guidebooks. Please let us know how we've done! I encourage you to e-mail me at editor@frommers.com or write me care of Frommer's, 111 River St., Hoboken, NJ 07030.

Happy Traveling!

Pauline Frommer

Pauline Frommer

1 The Best of Costa Rica

From lush rainforests and tropical beaches to spectacular hiking and breathtaking ecoadventures, where do you start?

by David Appell

FOR SUCH AN ITTY-BITTY COUNTRY (SMALLER THAN WEST VIRGINIA, ABOUT two-thirds the size of Scotland, and three-quarters the size of Newfoundland), Costa Rica's jampacked with enough sights and experiences to keep you busy for weeks and reminiscing (not to mention make your friends and family green with envy) for years. But although point-to-point air flights are quick, distances on the ground that look short on the map can take a lot longer where the rubber meets the road.

You probably have only 1 or 2 precious weeks of vacation time, and we suspect you have your own ideas about how to spend it. That's why we're going to cut through the brochure-speak and help you home in on the best of the best, right from the start.

A QUICK LOOK AT COSTA RICA

SAN JOSE & THE CENTRAL VALLEY

Climate comfy at 1,050 to 1,500m (3,500–5,000 ft.) above sea level, this is the heart and soul of Tiquicia (the local name for Costa Rica). It's home to the country's capital and a mix of city, suburbia, rolling countryside—including lots of coffee-growing areas—and a surprisingly big chunk of wilderness where you can thrill to volcanoes, quetzals, and lots more. San José, meanwhile, may not be the most lovely city in the world, but it's definitely well worth a stop for its quality museums, dining, and nightlife. And the fetching cities and towns of Alajuela, Heredia, and Cartago that ring the capital also make excellent bases for seeing a good bit of the rest of the country.

NORTHERN ZONE

North of the Central Valley between the jungly lowlands stretching east to the Caribbean and the dry plains going westward to the Pacific, this rich, rolling region is not only Costa Rica's farming breadbasket but also a playlist of its greatest eco- and soft-adventure hits. World-famous Arenal volcano still regularly belches glowing lava, and nearby Lake Arenal is a primo windsurfing magnet. Farther east and north, the wetlands of Caño Negro Wildlife Refuge serve up world-class birding, the Venado caves spectacular spelunking, and Sarapiquí riproaring rafting on Class IV and V whitewater.

MONTEVERDE

On a mountaintop in the Tilarán range between Arenal and the Guanacaste coast, this extension of the northern zone is such a singular spot that it rates its own chapter. Home to Costa Rica's most famous cloud forest (misty, riotously green, and wildlife-rich), this mountaintop also has a remarkable, quirky community of Ticos (as Costa Ricans call themselves) and gringo expatriates who have turned it into one of the "greenest," most conservation-minded communities in the world. Digs range from humble/no frills to full-scale resorts. If you can handle the rocky drive along steep mountain roads, it's well worth the trip.

CENTRAL PACIFIC COAST

An easy drive from San José, this stretch is home to Costa Rica's first beach resorts. It's also the most easily accessible coastline in Costa Rica. Playa de Jacó is a popular destination here, not only for its beach but also for its party-hearty bar and club scene. Manuel Antonio shows off its spectacular views and the country's most popular national park (and, sure, some partying, too, especially in Quepos right next door). More low key are the beach areas like Dominical, Punta Uva, and Esterillos. But the region isn't just about the beach; there's also some amazing nature here, from the scarlet macaws of Carara to the whales, dolphins, and sea turtles of Ballena Marina park, which also protects the country's biggest coral reef.

OSA PENINSULA

For truly hardcore ecoseekers, here's the Holy Grail. In many ways the country's last and wildest frontier, this remote 1,619-sq.-km (625-sq.-mile) chunk of land jutting out into the Pacific way down south has very little development and is home to primeval rainforests, including the legendary Corcovado National Park, where wildlife-spotting is tons easier than pretty much anywhere else in Costa Rica. Meanwhile, the coasts around Matapalo, Carate, and Drake Bay have some wonderful ecolodges, surfing, whale-watching, and countless ways to be amazed at the lushness of nature on land and sea.

CARIBBEAN COAST

Costa Rica's sometimes funky "left coast" is less famous and popular than the Pacific side. But it has some truly lovely beaches along with groovy beach towns, both laid-back and buzzing (thanks in good measure to the reggae vibe brought in by the Jamaican expats who settled here). You can also visit indigenous communities in the hills just inland or head to the northernmost section of coast for an Amazon-like experience at ecolodges on the jungle-lined canals of Tortuguero. Puerto Viejo's "Salsa Brava" is one of the most famous waves in the world, which helps make the area a surfer magnet. There's also some killer whitewater just a little ways inland.

GUANACASTE & NICOYA PENINSULA

Once a land of cowboys and fishermen, this is Costa Rica's go-go cutting edge of tourism, with golf courses and gated condo complexes threatening to overrun the laid-back coastal towns of old. But though towns like Tamarindo and Playa del Coco have become party central, others such as Nosara have managed to keep the honky-tonk at bay—especially down the Nicoya coast, with villages like Malpaís and Montezuma. Surfing's big all along this stretch, but you can also see marine turtles down south, volcanoes up north, and inland traditional villages producing ages-old pottery and other crafts.

BEST NATURAL SIGHTS & ATTRACTIONS

VOLCANO-WATCHING   Volcanoes, dead and alive, dot the entire country. Most active and thus most thrilling to view are Arenal in the Northern Zone (p. 90), Rincón de la Vieja in Guanacaste (p. 292), and Poás in the Central Valley (p. 56). Of the three, Arenal gives it up the most (you can actually see lava on clear days), while at the other two you can catch some geyser and other sulphuric action.

HOT SPRINGING   With all those volcanoes come geothermal springs, and in various parts of the country you'll find "spas" to loll around in, from the Orosi Valley near San José up to Rincón de la Vieja near Guanacaste's border with Nicaragua. But the most elaborate are in Arenal, Las Fuentes, Baldi, Eco Termales, and especially Tabacón, an elaborately landscaped hot-water park you've got to see to believe (p. 102).

BIRD-WATCHING   This birders' paradise is home to nearly 900 species, some unique to this part of Central America. The top spots to see them include La Selva, way up north near Puerto Viejo de Sarapiquí (p. 110), a bio-research station where the (concrete) paths are excellent and 500 species live (especially toucans, various parrot varieties, flycatchers, hummingbirds, and dacnis). Others include national parks like Carara, on the Pacific just north of Jacó (p. 155), known for its scarlet macaws but also harboring various trogons, manakins, and birds like the golden-naped woodpecker and fiery-billed aracari. Up the coast in north Guanacaste, in the tropical dry forest of Santa Rosa (p. 290), you can spot various hummingbirds and parrots, and species like the roadside hawk and white-throated magpie-jay. Closest to San José, the best part of the Central Valley's Braulio Carrillo (p. 72) for birding is the Quebrada González trail, whose wet foothill forest harbors all manner of tanagers, antshrikes, and woodcreepers; you'll also spot tweeters here you probably won't elsewhere, like the streak-crowned antvireo, lattice-tailed trogon, and yellow-eared toucanet.

SEA TURTLE NESTING   Several species of huge marine turtles use Costa Rican beaches as annual mating, nesting, and hatching grounds, and watching these ancient creatures return year after year to answer their ancient instincts is incredibly moving, and quite a learning experience. The best places to witness them in action at various times of year are Guanacaste's Playa Ostional (p. 318), Nancite (p. 291), and Grande (p. 303); Playa Tortuga near Dominical (p. 187) along the Central Pacific; and Tortuguero (p. 235) and Gandoca (p. 253) on the Caribbean coast. You'll probably see the biggest number (a mix of four species) at Tortuguero because this entire stretch of coast is off limits to the big development that scares them away, but it's also one of the most inaccessible viewing spots—you'll ideally need to devote at least 2 to 3 days to a visit here.

WHALE- & DOLPHIN-WATCHING   Humpback and sperm whales, orcas, various dolphins—they're all here, usually seasonally and sometimes permanently.

Top spotting spots include Ballena Marina national park in the Central Pacific (p. 177) and off Drake Bay in the Osa Peninsula (p. 194).

OTHER WILDLIFE-SPOTTING   Practically anywhere you go offers great possibilities, but we'd say the pick of the litter is the Osa Peninsula's Corcovado National Park (see p. 196), whose larger-than-usual chunk of primeval forest harbors more than a dozen micro-climates and ecosystems, along with ocelots, margays, tapirs, peccaries, exotic tree frogs, jaguars, and pumas. For crocs, the Central Pacific's Carara and Bijagual (p. 155) are pretty sure bets.

BEST ACTIVE EXPERIENCES

CANOPY TOURS & ZIPLINES   Now it's catching on from Mexico to Jamaica, but it's here that this uniquely thrilling way of touring the upper reaches of the rainforests originated. Firmly strapped into a harness, you zip from tree to tree hanging from a reinforced steel cable. Monteverde has some of the zippiest ziplines (p. 129), and Nosara now has the longest lines in the country (p.315) but you can find them all over Costa Rica.

WHITEWATER RAFTING   Spectacular scenery and H_2O that'll get your adrenaline surging are found in the Central Valley's Pacuare and Reventazón rivers near Turrialba (p. 86), and way up north on the Peñas Blancas, Toro, and Sarapiquí (p. 106).

RIDING THE SURF   Costa Rica's coasts have some of the gnarliest waves on earth. On the Caribbean coast, near Puerto Viejo, is Playa Pirriplí's world-famous "Salsa Brava" break (p. 266). On the Pacific side, in Guanacaste, it's Playa Naranjo (p. 291), Tamarindo (p. 303), Guiones, and Nosara (p. 316); in southern Nicoya, it's Santa Teresa, Los Cedros, Carmen, and Mar Azul (p. 337). The Central Pacific has Jacó, Hermosa, and Esterillos (p. 139), and farther south Dominical (p 140). Down in the Osa, check out Matapalo, Pan Dulce, and Backwash beaches (p. 211).

DIVING & SNORKELING   With two *costas ricas* (rich coasts) and pair of reefs, Tiquicia has as much to see under water as on land. On the Caribbean side, check out Cahuita (p. 245) and Manzanillo (p. 252), where you'll get some of your best reef action, visibility, and riots of tropical fish. Pacific hot spots include Guanacaste's Catalina and Bat Islands in Santa Rosa Park (p. 290), which also have loads of fish, great visibility most of the year, and harbor manta rays and sharks (bull, tiger, and whitetip) to boot.

Possibly the country's best scuba/snorkel spot, though, is way down in the Osa Peninsula: Caño and Coco islands, off Drake Bay (p. 225), with crystalline H_2O and a Jacques Cousteau special's worth of very varied marine critters, including mantas, morays, barracuda, reef sharks—you'll probably spot dolphins, too. *FYI:* Caño's much closer in and less pricey.

BEST PEOPLE-WATCHING BEACHES

Starting out on the Caribbean side, the biggest "scene" is Playa Cocles, just south of Puerto Viejo, which in spite of a good crowd on the sands in season has a verdant tropical backdrop. Things really get hopping out on the Pacific coast, along strands like Guanacaste's Tamarindo (p. 278), Flamingo (p. 295), and Coco

(p. 280), backed up by towns with something of a honky-tonk flavor—Jacó down on the Central Pacific (p. 139) also falls into this category. For a certain amount of action plus a slightly less hopped-up town accompanying it, try Montezuma on the southern Nicoya (p. 330), or the Central Pacific's Playa Espadilla in Manuel Antonio (p. 172).

BEST BEACHES FOR THAT CASTAWAY FEEL

On the Caribbean side, we're fans of the Robinson Crusoe–like feel at Punta Uva (p. 260), while Pacifically speaking Guanacaste's Santa Rosa National Park has several that are lovely but hard to get to, including Playa Naranjo (p. 291) and Nancite (p. 291). Down in Guanacaste's resortier areas, try Playa Panamá (p. 280), Playa Grande near Tamarindo (p. 303), and the Sámara area's slightly more off-the-beaten path playas Buena Vista and Barrigona (p. 327). Farther south still, along the Central Pacific, we like Playa Arco in Ballena Marina National Park (p. 185), or if you want to be a little closer to a town, Manuel Antonio's Playa Biesanz and La Macha (p. 173). And as far south as you can go, on the Osa, it doesn't get much wilder than Sirena beach in Corcovado National Park (p. 196), though much of the sands along Drake Bay (p. 221) also do the trick, and are a bit more accessible

BEST BEACHES FOR KIDS & FAMILIES

Mixing both calm waters and lots of stuff to do, Cahuita's Puerto Vargas (p. 250), and Chiquita, south of Puerto Viejo (p. 266), is the kid-friendliest along the Caribbean. Over on the Pacific, for the same reasons, we like Playa Pelada in Nosara (p. 316), with its great beach-shack eatery and tire swings hanging from trees, and south of Nosara in Sámara, at playas Sámara and Carrillo (p. 326). There's also Playa Herradura (p. 153), north of Jacó.

BEST MUSEUMS & HISTORIC SITES

The Central Valley is the star in this area, San José is the star in the Central Valley, and the stars in San José are the Precolumbian Gold Museum (p.32), followed by the Jade Museum (p. 33) and National Museum (p. 33), the last set in an old fort on a rise east of downtown. Art lovers, meanwhile, will find a lot of talent on display at the Museo de Arte Costarricense (p. 34). Historic spots are few and far between down here, but a pair not to miss are San José's elegant National Theater (p. 32) and the smaller nearby city of Cartago's large, fetching pilgrimage church, Nuestra Señora de Los Angeles (p. 46). If you're up in Guanacaste, don't miss La Casona in Santa Rosa National Park, site of a 19-century battle that was a defining moment in Tico history (p. 291).

BEST CULTURAL EYE-OPENERS

Although Costa Rica is a Spanish-speaking Latin American country, parts of it provide peeks at other cultures. There's the reggae/rasta flava of the Caribbean coast's Limón, Puerto Viejo, and Cahuita, where blacks descended from Jamaican immigrants still speak English with an island lilt (p. 230). Then there are the indigenous tribes that used to run the place before the Spaniards pushed them out into the hills and jungles. You can meet their descendants the BriBri near the

Caribbean coast (p. 232) and the Guaymí on the Osa Peninsula (p. 217). In inland Guanacaste, you can see the handiwork of the vanished Chorotegas, whose striking pottery the locals still craft in the town of Guaitil (p. 305).

BEST PLACES TO EAT

Though far from a culinary hot spot, Costa Rica does have some world-class dining. Bright spots include the tropical Latin fusion of La Luz and Grano de Oro in San José (p. 31) and Sofia in Monteverde (p. 125). Up in Arenal, under the volcano, you can dig into the nouvelle Latin and international at Acuarelas and Tabacón (p. 100).

Out on the coasts, stop in the *stupendo* Italian at La Pecora Nera, just outside Puerto Viejo (p. 265), on the Caribbean. On the Pacific side, the pick of the Guanacaste resorts includes the Med-Asian fusion and polished ambience at Ginger in Playa Hermosa (p. 289); La Laguna del Cocodrilo Bistro in Tamarindo (p. 302), serving French cuisine with local twists overlooking a *cocodrilo*-filled lagoon; La Luna in Nosara, with an elegant open-air vibe and fab seafood (p. 314); and sophisticated Asian-inflected continental at Nectar in Malpaís (p. 335).

Down in Manuel Antonio, the must-nosh is La Hacienda, serving nouvelle Latin-Med-Asian amid open-air elegance. Finally, down in the Osa, you won't want to miss the international fare with fresh local ingredients at Jade near Puerto Jiménez (p. 209).

WEEKLONG ITINERARIES

HITTING THE HIGHLIGHTS

For a reasonably representative Tico city-mountain-beach sampler, here's a four-stop itinerary you can squeeze into a week (if you don't mind hitting the road and changing hotels a fair bit). Having a car on this one helps with flexibility, but it's not a must-have; there are plenty of transport options between and at each stop.

Day 1   San José

After flying in, you can take in the major downtown attractions in a day. Get a sense of what this country was and is all about with visits to sights like the Precolumbian Gold Museum (p. 32), National Museum (p. 33), Mercado Central (p. 28), and National Theater (p. 32). They're close and compact enough to do them all in a full day, depending on your level of interest. Also, to get more of that old-time vibe, consider a bite along the way at the historic Cafetería 1830 in the Gran Hotel de Costa Rica (p. 29), the cafe in the National Theater, or the old-time-Tico-farmhouse-style Nuestra Tierra (p. 29).

Day 2   San José to Arenal/La Fortuna

Leave early in the morning for the 3½- to 4½-hour bus or car ride to the town of La Fortuna (you can take a half-hour flight, too). After settling in and having lunch, head up to Arenal Volcano National Park (p. 102) on your own or with a guide (a good idea for getting the most out of the wildlife-spotting) and hike trails both short and long, through forest and lava fields. Many trips take place to hit their halfway mark at sunset so that trekkers can hike up to where they can clearly see glowing lava snaking down the volcano. Afterward, soak your weary feet and other body parts at Tabacón or other local volcanic hot springs (p. 102); if you take a guided tour, hot springs will usually be included in the package (p. 102).

Day 3   Arenal to Monteverde

Feel free to soak up more of Arenal in the morning, and ideally take an adventure tour like whitewater rafting, caving, canyoning, or hiking down to the lovely La Fortuna waterfall (p. 104). Then after lunch, drive around Lake Arenal to Monteverde, which will take a good chunk of the afternoon. Stroll around the town of Santa Elena.

Day 4   Monteverde

Get up at dawn and hit the famous Monteverde Cloud Forest Reserve (more critters are out first thing in the A.M.). You'll spend the rest of the morning roaming 13km (8 miles) of trails and trying to spot some of the thousands of animal species—including the magnificent, elusive quetzal. You can go on your own, but spending a little extra on the savvy local guides will pay off big time, and you'll spot lots more that way (p. 129). In the afternoon, check out one of a trio of famous canopy tours (p. 129), which will strap you into a harness and send you careening down steel cables through the treetops. The Original Canopy Tour is the tamest—good for beginners, small kids, and seniors—while Selvatura has the biggest circuit and longest lines, plus a slew of other on-site attractions like canopy suspension bridges and great butterfly, hummingbird, and insect exhibits.

Day 5   Monteverde to Manuel Antonio

In the morning, either take an early tour of a local coffee plantation (p. 131) or, for something a little low-key, pay a visit to the local Quakers at their cheese/ice cream factory (p. 131). Around midday, drive out to the Pacific coast and head south to Manuel Antonio. Leave early enough to get settled and still get in some afternoon beach time on Playa Espadilla (p. 172). Around sunset, drinks or a nosh at any of the hilltop cafes, restaurants, and hotels to ogle the dazzling display is practically de rigeur.

Day 6   Manuel Antonio

Get up early and head to Manuel Antonio National Park, where you can spot monkeys and other various varmints (with or without a guide), then head to one of four bodacious beaches. In the afternoon, you've got a choice of two nearby canopy tours, a nature refuge where you stroll through the canopy on suspension bridges, or a reserve right in Manuel Antonio's Sí Como No resort, which includes a nice butterfly garden (p. 174).

Day 7   Leaving San José

Leave early from Manuel Antonio and head to the capital; it's 3 to 3½ hours by road, 25 minutes flying. Use any spare time you have before your flight out of San José to buy last-minute souvenirs and gifts, or catch things you missed. If you can't—hey, there's always next time. . . .

GETTING THE ADRENALINE PUMPING

Along with eco comes adventure, and hurling you down rivers and waterfalls, into caves, and through the treetops has become quite the growth industry, with scores of adventure outfitters and attractions throughout the country. Here's an itinerary that'll let you sample most of the highlights in a week—and it promises to leave you breathless with excitement.

Day 1 San José

After flying in, you'll probably need to overnight in the capital before tomorrow's early-morning whitewater, so rest up—and while you're here, take part of the afternoon to check out a couple of the highlights downtown, like the Precolumbian Gold Museum (p. 32), National Museum (p. 33), Mercado Central (p. 38), and National Theater (p. 32). But if you get in early enough, and really want to squeeze in a thrill right off the bat, zip 39m (130 ft.) over a river canyon on a wire at Canopy Adventure (p. 72), which borders Braulio Carrillo National Park.

Day 2 San José to Turrialba

Up 'n' at 'em, you're off to have a whack at the whitewater on the Pacuare River near Turrialba, in nearby Cartago province (p. 86). Any one of a bunch of outfitters we list will pick you up, and you can do it as a day trip or an overnighter. Either way, they'll provide your eats and extras.

Day 3 San José or Turrialba to Arenal/La Fortuna

In Turrialba, your river outfitter can get you a transfer up to Arenal; from San José, you'll probably rent a car, or take a bus or shuttle van; it should take you about 4½ hours (if you must rush, a flight from SJ's takes half an hour). Drop your bags and head for an afternoon soak at one of the hot springs (p. 102), then an evening hike for a closer peek at the lava-spewing volcano (some outfits running the volcano tours end up with a hot-spring soak; if yours does you might want to skip the afternoon visit).

Day 4 Arenal/La Fortuna

Head off with one of the local adventure outfitters for a morning of canyoning—that is, hiking along mountain canyon rivers and streams, floating down a little whitewater, jumping off a huge boulder into the water, and—coolest of all—rappelling down several waterfalls (p. 106). (You'll probably need to book this at least a day in advance). Grab a quick lunch, catch your breath, then head out on your afternoon jaunt, 45 minutes north of La Fortuna in the Venado caves (p. 92), complete with plenty of stalactites, stalagmites, streams—and bats. After all that exertion, another soak, this time at night, could be just the ticket.

Day 5 Arenal to Monteverde

Maybe you're raring for another full day of Arenal-area *adrenalina*. But if you'd rather move on to mountaintop Monteverde, don't go via the same-old same-old car or bus around Lake Arenal. Instead, do a 2½-hour jeep-boat-jeep or jeep-boat-horse trip (p. 118). You'll get there by lunchtime, then in the afternoon you can hit one of the trio of canopy tours (p. 129), which will strap you into a harness and send you careening down steel cables through the treetops. If you're the type who prizes a rush, go with Selvatura, where the lines are so long you'll swear you were flying (the canopy suspension bridges are fab here, too). While the Original Canopy Tour is the most famous, it may be a bit too slow for someone who chooses this adrenaline itinerary.

Day 6   Monteverde to San José

Today you get up at dawn and hit the famous Monteverde Cloud Forest Reserve (more critters are out first thing in the morning). You're on the hunt for the elusive quetzel (with binoculars not bullets, of course—you wouldn't want to slaughter one of these splendid rare birds). Hire a guide to help you track one down and also help you identify the other slithering or cuddly creatures you'll be passing on the trail. After lunch, do another zipline or take a horseback ride and hike out to a waterfall and swimming hole with a local outfitter (p. 133). If you have an early flight, make your way back to San José in the late afternoon.

Day 7   Leaving San José

Back to the airport—with lots of cool pix and memories, right?

BEACHY FAMILY FUN

More than a few parts of Costa Rica can be a tricky for families traveling with kids (especially little ones). But here's a week that's doable for most ages. By basing yourself at one beach resort and taking day trips, you'll get to mix sun 'n' fun with a good dollop of the eco-wonder the country's famous for.

Day 1   Arrive Playa Hermosa, Guanacaste

Mamá, are we there yet? You'll skip San José and fly right into Liberia, then drive or take a bus (40 minutes to an hour) out to the Pacific coast's Papagayo Gulf. We especially like the trio of horseshoe beaches at Playa Hermosa, Panamá, and Coco, and our pick hereabouts is Playa Hermosa's Villa del Sueño (p. 285), especially great for families because of its bevy of services and extras. This'll be your base.

Day 2   Hang Out & Chill

Enjoy the weather, hit the pool and beach, and get out a bit to explore the Playa Hermosa area, which has volleyball and a good selection of watersports and other stuff to do out on the sand.

Day 3   Raft the Corobicí, Do a Canopy Tour, Check Out the Turtles

For a nice gentle float down a nearby river where you'll see lots of critters, hook up with Safaris Corobicí (☎ 669-6191; www.nicoya.com) for a couple of hours to a half day; it's a winner for all ages. You might also have time to zip through the treetops on a canopy tour (perfectly safe and okay for most kids older than 6; p. 294). And if you're around between late September and late February, take a nighttime tour to see the awesome sight of leatherback turtles laying eggs and later the babies racing to the water at Playa Grande (p. 304); this can run late into the night and involve a good bit of standing and walking on sand, so make sure your little guys and gals are up for it.

Day 4   Explore Nearby Towns & Beaches

The big "action" around here is the booming beach town of Playa del Coco, popular with Tico families and with a festive vibe a bit on the Coney Island side (p. 280). There's lots of stuff to do and places to eat—and if you're here the last weekend in March, you'll get to see the festivities surrounding the sand-sculpture competition called Papagayo Sand Fest (p. 290).

Day 5   Rincón de la Vieja National Park & Hacienda Guachipelín

Head a little farther afield today, northward up to a national park where you'll spend the whole day seeing some way-cool (er, actually hot) bubbling mud pots and geysers, checking out an awesome waterfall swimming hole, and doing some fun activities at a resort called Hacienda Guachipelín, with wall climbing, tubing, horseback riding, rappelling, cattle round-ups, and thermal springs (p. 293).

Day 6   Tamarindo—Surf Lessons, Anybody?

A short drive south of Playa Hermosa, Tamarindo (p. 303) is another rockin' beach town with a lot of fun stuff to do, including a bunch of surfing schools where any child older than 6 can learn to ride surf or boogie boards (and they'll even snap pics of you doing it!).

Day 7   Leaving Liberia

Have one last morning by the water, then head to the airport. On the flight back, have the kids work on their presentations for show-and-tell.

2 San José & the Central Valley

Crammed with both nature and culture, Costa Rica's heartland and capital set the country's tone.

by David Appell

THE MAGNETIC ATTRACTIONS THAT PULL SO MANY VISITORS TO COSTA Rica—the country's rainforests and beaches—mean that few spare much thought to the Central Valley. Considering this is the place that's home to more than two-thirds of all Ticos and where the national soul was forged, that's a real shame. If they'd stick around a couple of days before or after rushing off to the coasts or the farther reaches of the country, they'd find they can do a lot of the same stuff—wander primeval wilderness, zip through the treetops, raft some adrenaline-pumping whitewater, spot a zooful of critters, or watch a volcano do its thing. And at the same time they could learn about its culture and history in the many sites, museums, churches, and performance spaces of towns and cities like Alajuela, Heredia, Cartago, and especially San José.

Ah, much-dissed San José. Admittedly it's no great looker (the downtown's grubby and much of the "fancier" suburbs are strip-malled), traffic can be smelly and chaotic, and you've sometimes gotta watch your wallet. But on the other hand, most larger cities in Central America are dumps. And not only is "Chepe," as many locals call it, nicer than most, but it has a comfy climate, some very appealing neighborhoods, interesting museums, a vibrant cultural scene, and a collection of surprisingly good restaurants, nightspots, and hotels.

And furthermore, gaze up into the distance around you: All that puffy-cloud-wreathed purple mountains' majesty is a promise that the surrounding Central Valley is a pretty special spot in its own right. A good 900m to 1,500m-plus (3,000–5,000 ft.) above sea level, the valley ranges from areas densely populated with homes, businesses, and light industry—closer between San José and the nearby cities of Alajuela and Heredia—to spectacular open country along the lines of lightly populated subvalleys like Orosi to the southeast or wilderness national parks like Braulio Carrillo farther north. One thing I've noticed about a lot of other parts of the country, as marvelous as they are, is that they tend to be one-dimensional (okay, maybe sometimes two). That's why one of the things we most like about the Central Valley and San José is the fact that this region's an entire symphony, and enough to keep you ecologically, culturally, and all-around happily enthralled by the music for a week, or two, or more.

DON'T LEAVE SAN JOSÉ & THE CENTRAL VALLEY WITHOUT . . .

VISITING SAN JOSÉ'S GOLD, JADE, AND NATIONAL MUSEUMS
Besides exquisitely worked metal and stone, you'll learn about the sometimes surprisingly rich cultures of ancient Mesoamerica through modern-day Costa Rica's occasionally weighty role in the history, politics, and eco-movement of the Americas.

STOPPING BY THE NATIONAL THEATER FOR A SHOW (OR AT LEAST A CUP OF JOE) Like a world-class jewel gleaming in downtown's dime-store setting, one of Central America's most elegant buildings still draws top-notch international talent, and its inexpensive cafe sure makes for one glitzy pit stop.

MOTORING UP TO A VOLCANO   There are three within an hour's drive of San José—Poás (Alajuela), Barva (Heredia), and Irazú (Cartago), all in national parks—and each a knockout in its own way, whether you're into lush rainforest or lunar landscape.

VISITING A COFFEE PRODUCER   At the source of some of the world's most bodacious beans, several operations have opened their doors to the public, like Doka in Alajuela (which grows and roasts), Britt in Heredia (roasts, puts on a heck of a tour), and Café Cristina in Cartago's breathtaking Orosi Valley (quirky mom-and-pop organic). *We did this in MonteVerde*

OGLING THE WATERFALLS AT LA PAZ WATERFALL GARDENS   This elaborate eco–theme park in Alajuela has a lot of cool bells and whistles, but they pale in comparison to its quintet of crashing cataracts, each more awesome than the last, and the last three giving the cool illusion of pouring into each other.

EXPLORING THE BIG-CITY CENTRAL MARKETS   Downtown San José, Alajuela, Cartago, and Heredia all have historic covered markets, taking up an entire city block each. Their warrens of colorful stalls and eateries are roamed by locals shopping for everything from daily groceries and household cleaners to pets and saddles (in the San José one you'll find some souvenirs, too). *HUGE!*

A BRIEF HISTORY

Once upon a time, going back thousands of years, the only inhabitants of these forested hills were the Huetars, animists living in circular thatched dwellings who, when not subsistence farming, were often fighting, killing, kidnapping, and enslaving their neighbors, all under the rule of *caciques* (chieftains) and priests. One town you can still visit today, Guayabo, out in present-day Cartago province, was advanced enough to have cobblestone streets and aqueducts.

   Christopher Columbus spotted the Talamanca coast on his last Caribbean cruise, in September 1502. Then, 4 years later, gold-greedy conquistadors started pushing inward from the coasts until Costa Rica officially became part of Spain's "kingdom" of Guatemala in 1548. Then in 1562 Juan Vásquez de Coronado and company found their way to the Central Valley, bringing "civilized" colonists to settle Cartago, which became the territorial capital a year later. They didn't mix much with the folks they invaded, who weren't all that many to begin with; those few survivors that weren't then wiped out by the usual Euro-diseases, conscripted into slave labor, or engaged in failed uprisings escaped to more remote parts of the country.

The colonists bumped along barely above subsistence level for more than a century, but gradually they started spreading through the valley, founding Heredia in 1706, San José (originally Villa Nueva de la Boca del Monte) 30 years later, followed by Alajuela in 1782. Things were miserable for years—mostly muddy roads and wooden shacks—but little by little, this shaped up into a society of merchants and peasant farmers, who had a go at various export industries, like mule raising, sugar cane, tobacco, and—finally, *ka-ching*—coffee and bananas (by the early 19th century). What little truly gracious old architecture you'll see throughout the Central Valley was paid for mostly by *café*, and fields of the stuff still blanket square mile after mile.

Politically, after Mexico overthrew the Spaniards in 1821, Costa Rica ended up in the new Central American federal republic. In the meantime Cartago was challenged for top-dog-city status by Alajuela, Heredia, and San José—and we know who won that one, right? After the federation also bit the dust, the Republic of Costa Rica was born in 1848, and things were going along smoothly enough, with the coffee industry booming. Then gringo William Walker from the Confederate States of America (remember, the U.S. Civil War was going on), took over Nicaragua during its own civil war and made a bid to annex all of Central America to Dixie. In 1856, it was Costa Rica's government that finally beat Walker back by winning battles in Guanacaste and southern Nicaragua, commemorated by statues and museums you can visit today (this campaign also created the country's official national hero; p. 47).

Even so, recession, a cholera epidemic, and governments with dictatorial tendencies plagued the country for the next few decades, but in the early 20th century the ideas of reform were starting to catch hold, picking up speed once the Great Depression hit. Then, after World War II ended, political turmoil developed and built to the point that in 1948, a 5-week civil war killed 2,000 people. The junta and Second Republic that took over abolished the army, boosted social reforms, nationalized the banks, gave women and blacks the right to vote, and led to a run of economic growth and improved social welfare. It was far from perfect, but it was in these next few decades that Costa Rica picked up its rep as the "Switzerland of Central America."

In more recent years, what's left of the welfare state has taken some hits, thanks to rising energy prices in the '70s; the pullout of United Fruit plus upheavals in Nicaragua and El Salvador in the '80s (then and now president Oscar Arias nabbed the '87 Nobel for peace by brokering a regional settlement); and globalization and the collapse in coffee prices. Drug trafficking rose and governments went in for free-market "shock therapy," social spending sank, and poverty shot up again, as did corruption and tax evasion by the rich (three recent presidents have been investigated—no wonder the roads never got fixed!). Since 1985, call centers, the CAFTA trade agreement, and especially tourism have helped the economy grow, but this has also helped Americanize the country, creating cheesy sprawl in the Central Valley as it has on the Pacific coast, and putting huge tracts of land into gringo hands. Yes, we gringos have been trying to invade Costa Rica ever since William Walker—and it looks like we're finally making some headway.

SAN JOSÉ

First the basics: population 310,000, not counting suburbs; 1,100m (3,690 ft.) above sea level; founded 1736; national capital since 1823.

In terms of tourism, Costa Rica's Big Banana is also something like its Rodney Dangerfield—it doesn't get much respect. In a land for whose visitors nature and the great outdoors rule, San José is too homely and chaotic to bother with—not exactly the best fit for the national tourism flacks' current come-on: "No Artificial Ingredients." Many people fly in and then immediately fly or drive right to the coasts, or the north (these days, some even wing it directly into Liberia up in Guanacaste). If they do stay here, it's a few hours or an overnight at most.

But really, no town in Costa Rica is what you'd call well, attractive. And to us, among the cool things about this country isn't just all that riotous nature, but also the interplay of nature, culture, and history. And that's where "Chepe" shines, with its good to very good museums; pretty parks; appealing old architecture (surprise!) paid for by riches brewed by the coffee biz; and a quite happening arts and performance scene. It doesn't hurt that there are some very good restaurants (not exactly thick on the ground out in the boonies and even on the coasts), a diverse nightlife, and a number of good hotels, including some that mix charm with real history (also rare outside the Central Valley).

LAY OF THE LAND

In this sprawling patchwork of *barrios* and suburbs, a lot of what there is to see and do revolves around downtown. This is where you'll find the fab **Precolumbian Gold Museum,** the **Belle Epoque–era National Theater,** the covered maze of market stalls that is the **Mercado Central;** heading out east and west are good museums devoted to Tico art, history, and pre-Columbian jade. A good share of hotels, restaurants, casinos, museums, historic sites, parks, and plazas are also concentrated here in downtown, whose main drag here is Avenida Central, which is also pedestrian-only along the 4 blocks between calles Central and 7 (heads-up: some of the side streets can get a little seedy and/or deserted at night).

But a block or two north of downtown, you shouldn't miss pretty **Morazán Park** and the colonial, neoclassical, neo-Moorish, and Art Deco mix of **Barrio Amón** and **Barrio Otoya;** just watch the occasional holes in the sidewalk and those yawning storm drains that run along some sidewalks—in several places you've got to hop over 'em to cross the street! Some of these old buildings have been turned into restaurants and lodgings, and Amón also has a bit of a gallery scene. Nearby **Barrio Aranjuez** has some nice architecture and several good places to stay.

West of downtown, you may find yourself staying or eating in the area anchored by main drag Paseo Colon, or visiting the **Museum of Costa Rican Art** at its end, in Parque La Sabana. East of downtown, both **Barrio California** and quiet but up-and-coming **Barrio Escalante** next door have some nice dining, clubbing, and architecture, while farther eastward you'll find more restaurants, nightspots, and hotels in the upper-middle-class neighborhoods of **Los Yoses** and student-filled **San Pedro,** home to the University of Costa Rica.

San José

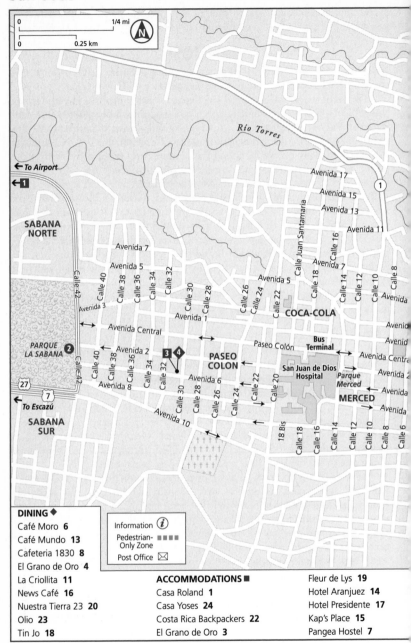

DINING ◆
Café Moro **6**
Café Mundo **13**
Cafeteria 1830 **8**
El Grano de Oro **4**
La Criollita **11**
News Café **16**
Nuestra Tierra 23 **20**
Olio **23**
Tin Jo **18**

Information ⓘ
Pedestrian-
Only Zone ▪▪▪▪
Post Office ✉

ACCOMMODATIONS ■
Casa Roland **1**
Casa Yoses **24**
Costa Rica Backpackers **22**
El Grano de Oro **3**

Fleur de Lys **19**
Hotel Aranjuez **14**
Hotel Presidente **17**
Kap's Place **15**
Pangea Hostel **7**

To Heredia   **To Limón**

Calle Cipres

109

5

108

EL PUEBLO

TOURNON

Calle Central

Avenida 13
6
Avenida 11
7

OTOYA

14

Avenida 9

Avenida 7

Calle 1

Calle 3

Calle 5

Calle 7

Calle 9

Calle 11

Calle 13

Calle 15

13

BARRIO AMÓN

12

11

Avenida 5

Calle 2

Avenida 3

Avenida 1

Plaza de la Cultura

Parque Morazán

Calle 17

Calle 19

Calle 21

Calle 23

Calle 25

Calle 29

Calle 31

Calle 33

Calle 35

Calle 37

15

Parque Nacional

8

Parque Central

Avenida 4

9

10

i

17

16

Avenida Central

Avenida 2

21

20

Paseo Ruben Dario

23

To San Pedro →

Avenida 6

Avenida 8

Calle 3

Calle 5

Calle 7

SOLEDAD

19

Calle 9

18

Calle 11

Calle 13

Calle 15

Calle 17

Calle 19

Calle 21

22

Calle 27

Calle 29

Calle 33

LOS YOSES

Calle 39

24 →

Avenida 10

Calle 1

Avenida 12

Avenida 14

Paseo de los Estudiantes

Avenida 16

Avenida 18

Calle 37

Calle 35

ATTRACTIONS ●

Museo de Arte Costarricense **2**

Museo de Jade **12**

Museo de los Niños **5**

Museo del Oro Precolombino **10**

Museo Nacional de Costa Rica **21**

Teatro Nacional **9**

Caribbean Sea

COSTA RICA

✱**San Jose**

PACIFIC OCEAN

0   50 mi

0   50 km

Finally, switching from east to west, the neighborhood just beyond Sabana Park is **Rohrmoser** (named after its German developer, FYI), where you'll find fancy residences including the current president's, embassies, restaurants, and hotels. **Escazú** (4.8km/3 miles west) and slightly more rural and artsy **Santa Ana** (14km/8½ miles west) are nestled in the hills with upscale condo communities, dining, shopping malls, and small lodgings (especially B&Bs). There are so many expats living out here that some people dub it "gringo gulch."

The rest of the metro area and its immediate suburbs are more residential, commercial, or a mix of both. But you might find yourself staying or dining out in "gringo gulch," or partying in San Pedro, where the University of Costa Rica is located. There are, of course, shabbier and more dangerous parts of town you won't want to wander at night, but no out-and-out horrific slums like I've seen so much of in Central and South America. And petty theft like car break-ins, pick-pocketing, and purse snatching has been a nuisance, but take it from a Miamian and a New Yorker: as in all big cities, a little alertness and common sense go a long way toward defeating the evildoers. With all that in mind, I'm sure you won't be sorry to have given Chepe a chance.

GETTING TO & AROUND SAN JOSE
By Air

Costa Rica's main gateway is **Juan Santamaría International Airport (SJO; ☎ info 437-2626, offices 437-2400; www.alterra.co.cr)**, a small, easily manageable but mod and comfy airport that handles not only domestic flights on **Sansa (☎ 290-4100; www.flysansa.com)** and **Nature Air (☎ 299-6000, or 800/235-9272 in the U.S.; www.natureair.com)** but also daily international connections from North America on Air Canada, American, Continental, Delta, Martinair, United, USAirways, and the Central American airlines Copa, Taca, and Lacsa. Gateways include Chicago, Dallas/Fort Worth, Houston, Los Angeles, Miami, New York, Orlando, Washington/Dulles, San Francisco, and Toronto. There's also a good bit of service from Mexico, Central and South America, and key airports in Europe and the Caribbean.

SJO is on the outskirts of the city of Alajuela, and a 20-minute ride into San José, 25 minutes to Heredia, and 85 to Cartago. **Tuasa (☎ 442-6900)** buses run every 5 minutes daily from 5am to 10pm into Alajuela and San José, the latter dropping off in the western part of downtown along the main drag Paseo de Colón/Avenida Central or on Parque de La Merced; the fare's 65¢ each way. **Station Wagon (☎ 441-1181)** is another company that makes this run. For door-to-door service, a ride in an orange cab from **Taxis Unidos Aeropuertos (☎ 222-6865; www.taxiaeropuerto.com)** will run you $18 downtown and Escazú, $13 to Santa Ana; you pay your money—dollars are fine—and you get your voucher from a kiosk outside the arrivals area (regular city and gypsy cabs here will also vie for your attention). **Interbus (☎ 283-5573; www.interbusonline.com)** runs plush buses to various San José-area hotels every half-hour for $6. A few charter and domestic flights (especially on **Nature Air**) go through the single-runway **Pavas aka Tobías Bolaños Airport** (MRPV; ☎ 232-2820) in a closer-in suburb called Pavas.

By Bus

There's good bus service connecting the capital with the rest of the Central Valley as well as various farther-flung parts of the country at rates that are affordable (for fancier private lines) to downright cheap (the more standard domestic lines); travel times range from a 30 minutes (Alajuela or Heredia) to 8 hours (Puerto Jiménez on the Osa Peninsula). The two fanciest are **Gray Line Costa Rica** (☎ 220-2126; www.graylinecostarica.com) and **Interbus** (☎ 283-5573; www.interbusonline.com), which will pick you up at your hotel up to three times a day for runs to and from most major tourist areas for varying one-way fares in the $20 to $40 range.

Bevies o' buses with fares of $6 or less leave for points north from **Terminal Atlántico Norte** (Av. 9 at Calle 12) and for the Caribbean coast out of the **Gran Terminal del Caribe** (Calle Central at Av. 13); various other stops and stations are scattered all over downtown, depending on the destinations. Lines and destinations include **Arenal/La Fortuna** (**Autotransportes San José-San Carlos;** ☎ 255-0567), **Cahuita/Puerto Viejo/Tortuguero** (**Mepe;** ☎ 257-8129), **Drake Bay/Osa Peninsula** (**Tracopa;** ☎ 223-7685), **Jacó/Quepos** (**Transportes Quepos;** ☎ 777-0734), **Liberia/Guanacaste** (**Pulmitan;** ☎ 222-1650), **Monteverde** (**Transportes Tilarán;** ☎ 222-3854), **Playa Hermosa/Panamá** (**Traslapa;** ☎ 680-0392), **Puerto Jiménez/Osa** (**Blanco Lobo;** ☎ 771-4744), **Puerto Viejo de Sarapiquí** (**Transportes Guapileños;** ☎ 710-7780), **Quepos/Miguel Antonio** (**Transportes Morales;** ☎ 223-5567), and **Tamarindo** (**Tracopa-Alfaro;** ☎ 222-2666). You can get more details on schedules and fares from your hotel or at www.visitcostarica.com.

If you're rolling in from elsewhere in Central America, **Tica Bus** (☎ 221-0006; www.ticabus.com) runs daily service complete with A/C and videos between its fairly new terminal on Paseo Colón (200m/656 ft. north/100m/328 ft. west of Torre Mercedes, in front of Magisterio Nacional funeral home), as well as a couple of other downtown locations, and to the capitals of El Salvador (from $38), Guatemala ($49), Honduras ($25), Nicaragua ($13), and Panama ($25).

By Car

Do you know the way to San José? In Costa Rica—most of the main roads lead to it; the biggest highway, the Interamerican Highway, runs from Nicaragua through Liberia, south to the city of Puntarenas, east to Alajuela and Santamaría airport, through San José, then onward through Cartago and snaking down into southern San José and Puntarenas provinces past the Osa Peninsula before going into Panama a bit south of Golfito. Another big artery is the Guápiles Highway, which heads north from San José through Braulio Carrillo National Park before swinging east out to Limón on the Caribbean coast. These roads and, from what I've been able to tell, a fair number of the ones in the Central Valley are in decent shape and have reasonably helpful signage. But once you get onto the smaller byways and the farther from San José you get—oy. Dirt or gravel roads, potholes the size of Belize, bad or zero signs—and don't forget few named roads and almost no house numbers or precise addresses—make navigating a crap shoot. At the very least, you'll want to factor in extra time for wrong turns and the like, and avoid driving after dark.

Getting Around

If you're staying in or around downtown, walking and the occasional cab should get you most everywhere you want to go, since so much falls inside the stretch between the National Museum and La Sabana Park, a half-dozen blocks wide and a couple dozen long. Areas east of downtown, like Los Yoses and San Pedro, are also reasonably walkable, but mostly sidewalkless Escazú and Santa Ana are walkable for only certain stretches. Don't bother with renting a car in town here—traffic, parking, and possible break-ins are too much of a pain when you can get around town on foot as well as pretty cheaply and easily by taxi, bus, and train.

Licensed cabs are red, and their rates are fairly reasonable; at the time of writing, the official rate was about 70¢ for the first kilometer—just over a half mile—then 66¢ per kilometer. Cabs are pretty much safe to take, but a few bad apples have been known to pull fast ones like setting their meters *(marías)* to the higher night rate during the day, or not putting them on at all. So in that case ask your *taxista* to put it on *("ponga la maría, por favor"),* or at the very least get a rate before you pull away from the curb. Your best bet is to ask workers at hotels, restaurants, and clubs to call you reliable cabs, or do it yourself. I've had good luck with **Coopeirazu** (☎ 254-3211), **Coopeguaria** (☎ 227-9300), and **Coopetaxi** (☎ 235-9966).

There's a fair-size fleet of buses tooling around San José day and night, most costing about 39¢ or less (keep coins handy). One that can help you get around the key central area is the **Sabana-Cementerio** line out to Sabana park (where the Spanish colonial–style art museum is), with stops near the main post office on Avenida 3 near Calle 2, on Calle 22 between avenidas Central and 1, and all along Avenida 2. Another good one to keep in mind is the bus running eastward to **San Pedro/Los Yoses** from Avenida Central between calles 9 and 11, in front of the Cine Capri. If you're staying a bit away from the center, such as in San Pedro or Escazú, learning which ones go to downtown will help cut your back-and-forth costs and save you money for a cab for that last return home at night. Printed bus schedules are in short supply, though; try your hotel and the tourism office in the Precolumbian Gold Museum off Avenida Central under Plaza Democracia. If they can't hand you a piece of paper, they can at least tell you where to go, so to speak.

Another potential leg up in navigating this central area is the recently opened **Ferrocarril Eléctrico al Pacífico** (☎ 221-0777), a single commuter-train line running from Pavas out west to San Pedro in the east, stopping along the way near downtown and the university. They're infrequent (every 2 hr., 5am–6pm) but cheap (20¢–45¢). My opinion: It might be worth a stab, but almost no one seems to know about or use this train, and info is hard to come by. Par for the course in Costa Rica, actually.

ACCOMMODATIONS, BOTH STANDARD & NOT

Compared to the Pacific coast and Costa Rica's other magnets for beach and eco-tourism, there aren't all that many vacationers who spend much time in the capital. Most people come on business or are just passing through on their way to the coasts or the interior. But they create enough business, along with folks who find it useful to set up base in the big city while making day trips into the hinterland. Thus, the city offers a nice variety of digs at most price points, with the exception of extremely upscale properties (the **Four Seasons** is out in Guanacaste). They run the gamut from simple hostels and B&Bs to historic boutique hotels, corporate chains, vacation rentals (see below), and even several bigger, fancier resorts (these last, like the **Marriott** and the **Meliá Cariari,** in outlying areas).

You've also got a decent variety of settings to choose from. There's the hurly-burly and action of downtown and more urban-feeling nearby areas, where many of the museums, restaurants, and nightspots are concentrated, and where you can pretty much get around on foot or by short taxi hops. Surrounding these, a handful of nabes like Aranjuez, Escalante, and Amón combine nice architecture with peace and quiet. Now, if you don't mind a bit more of a schlep in to town, you could head farther out to upscale suburbs like Escazú and Santa Ana, which aren't walkable but do offer loads of dandy dining and shopping, plus places to stay ranging from interesting B&Bs to hotel charmers like the **Alta** (p. 27). If you want to stay out even farther, the province of San José reaches out a few miles to the east, west, and especially the southeast, where you'll find a mix of suburb and countryside, including some country inns and resorts. In all cases, keep in mind that air-conditioning isn't the norm around here, because it usually just doesn't get that hot. Also don't forget that you've got several great options in nearby Alajuela (p. 46) and Heredia (p. 63), some as convenient a commute as areas like Escazú and Santa Ana.

In the selection below, I've focused mostly on affordability (with one notable splurge) and convenience (meaning I've tended to stick closer to downtown and Escazú/Santa Ana); if the idea of more of a country setting tickles your fancy, have a look in Central Valley. And if you really need to keep your bunking budget as low as possible, there are several rock-bottom options I've found to be clean, friendly, and convenient. In downtown's quiet, historic Barrio Amón, check out the **Pangea Hostel** (Av. 11 at Calle 3, across from Amstel Amón Plaza Hotel; ☎ 221-1992; www.pangea.hostel.com; MC, V), where you can get dorm beds for $10, and private rooms from $25; it even has a pool with swim-up bar. Toward the east end of downtown, a hop and a skip from the hopping Barrio California nightlife (p. 42), **Costa Rica Backpackers** (Av. 6 between calles 21 and 23, 100m/328 ft. east of Corte Suprema; ☎ 221-6191; www.costaricabackpackers.com; cash only) is another newish, very good hostel with an inexpensive restaurant and a pool of its own, too. Dorm beds start at $10, and rooms at $22. Or over in Los Yoses, close to the Mall San Pedro and student nightlife areas, check out **Casa Yoses** (Av. 8 at Calle 41, 250m/820 ft. west of Spoon; ☎ 234-5486; www.casayoses.com; MC, V), with especially roomy beds, well-lighted rooms, Wi-Fi, and 24/7 reception in a colonial-style stand-alone house. Dorm beds here are $10, with doubles going for $28.

Vacation Rentals & Homestays

Few methods of travel give you a better insight into the local scene than a homestay. You get to see up close and personal what people's homes and lives are like, and you'll get their honest, warts-and-all takes on local culture and doings. (And if you speak with most of them, ask what they think about the ol' U.S. of A. These days—hold on to your *sombreros.*)

In Costa Rica, homestays are usually an option open to you only if you're signing on with some volunteer outfit or Spanish-class program. But even as a free agent, you still have a chance to be placed in local homes by checking the classifieds at www.ticotimes.com or contacting **Bell's Home Hospitality** (☎ 225-4752; www.homestay.thebells.org), which charges $30 for a single and $45 for a double per night for living with your choice of a dozen middle-class families mostly in and around San Pedro, a relatively short hop east of downtown. What you get is a room, typically, in a stand-alone single-family home: concrete block with ceramic-tile floors, corrugated metal roofs, whitewashed walls, and a mix of homey plush and tropical wood furniture. Kansas-born owner Vernon Bell has lived here since 1972, and he and his Tica wife Marcela know lots of great locals; they've made sure that most of the host families have at least one member who speaks English. The mix of hosts is wide-ranging and includes a lawyer, a secretary, a teacher, a physical therapist, and a retiree. The Bells arrange to have you picked up at the airport, then they and your Tico family will help you out with just about anything you could want. Amenities and degrees of privacy run the gamut from quite private to right under the noses of your hosts, so just let them know what you need—say, a household with an English speaker and a private entrance and bathroom—and they'll match you up. Breakfast is part of the deal, and other add-ons like laundry and dinner ($7) are yours for the asking.

If homestays are a bit too up close and personal for you, but you still want to feel like you're living right out there in the community, some B&Bs do fit the bill, but you might also give a thought to short-term house and condo rentals. In Costa Rica this market has been heating up like a house on fire (um, let us rephrase that). Most, however, are along the Pacific and to a lesser extent the Caribbean coasts. The pickings in and around San José tend to be longer-term rentals (a month or more) aimed at expats and/or concentrated in the outskirts of the city, in the areas dubbed "gringo gulch" (including Santa Ana, Escazú, and Bello Horizonte). And though out on the coasts you'll find agencies that rep a stable of properties, in and around the capital most realtors seem to stick to sales and long-term rentals, and owners tend to rent through their own websites or clearinghouses like **RentCostaRica.com**, **Vacation Rental by Owner** (www.vrbo.com), **Vacation Rentals.com**, and **Villa4Vacation.com**. You can also check listings on sites like **www.amcostarica.com** and **www.govisitcostarica.com**.

One outfit that *does* rep a handful of San José–area apartments and houses (a half dozen, covering dozens of units, if you *must* know) for short-term rentals is Isabela Brown's **Costa Rica Valley Properties** (☎ 288-4680; www.costaricavalleyproperties.com), whose rates start from $55 a day or $300 a week (for a cute little cottage on a secluded 2 hectares/5 acres in Santa Ana, for example, sleeping two, with satellite TV, phone, washer/dryer, and so forth). At the upper end, $110 daily or $650 weekly will bag a big, luxe one-bedroom (sleeping up to four) in a building with pool and Jacuzzi out in the genteel Rohrmoser neighborhood, a hop and a skip from where the country's president Oscar Arias lives; $120 daily or $700 weekly will fetch a palatial two-bedroom condo in Escazú.

Over in Barrio California, an easy stroll to downtown yet right around the corner from a key nightlife hub (p. 42), a pair of cream-color three-story buildings called **Scotland Apartments** (Av. 1 at Calle 27, 100m/328 ft. east of parking lot behind Cine Magaly; ☎ 223-0033; www.hotels.co.cr/scotland.html) rent out 25 one-bedrooms sleeping two, done up in a low-key style (white walls and tile floors, homey but contemporary furniture in blues, grays, and earth tones), for $200 to $350 weekly (you can only rent for a week or more). Ranging from 37 to 56 sq. m (400–600 sq. ft.), they've got full kitchens, private terraces or gardens, cable TV, and high-speed Internet connections; washers and dryers are on the premises.

A handful of blocks northwest of California in quiet, historic Barrio Otoya, Tomás de la Ossa has got a deal for you: his **Casa Don Tomás** (☎ 258-1847; www.villa4vacation.com/vacation-rental/san-jose/439386.aspx) is a fairly stylish two-bedroom/one-bath penthouse sleeping up to six, with extras like stereo, cable TV, DVD, Wi-Fi, maid service, and outdoor Jacuzzi in a bougainvillea-filled garden. For $75 a night or $500 a week (3-night minimum)—way to go, Tom.

There's also a category called "apartotels," aimed mostly at business travelers staying in town for more than a couple of overnights and looking for something a little roomier and serviceable than a standard hotel unit. The bastard child of apartment complexes and hotels, apartotels aim to offer the best of both worlds— condo-style units usually on the bland side but roomier than hotel rooms, with kitchens and livings rooms, plus hotel-like perks like breakfast in the morning, maids to clean up after you, business services, and often pools. Several worth looking into include **El Sesteo** (☎ 296-1805, or 877/623-3198 in the U.S. and Canada; www.sesteo.com) in La Sabana, at the western end of downtown near the art museum; with a double-decker motel-resort feel, arranged around a central pool, 21 of its 36 rooms have full kitchens and separate dining/living areas (the rest are more standard-hotel-like). Rooms start at $46, and apartments begin at $55. In that same area, we find **La Sabana** (☎ 220-2422; www.apartotel-lasabana. com) similar but even more inviting, with colorful touches like warm folkloric murals and tile work in the dining room, plus a sauna in addition to a pool. Room rates go from $45, with apartments starting at $59. The **María Alexandra** (☎ 228-1507; www.mariaalexandra.com), out in the Trejos Montealegre section of Escazú, has, again, a similar setup (throwing in a small gym); one of its main advantages in my opinion is as a base for getting out into the surrounding Central Valley, because you're already halfway out of town. Here rooms cost $90 and up. Finally, **Los Yoses** (☎ 225-0033; www.apartotel.com) might be worth a look if you're interested in being in a commercial area just east of downtown, right amid a whole bunch of bars, restaurants, and shops (including the San Pedro Mall), with the university campus right down the street. Rooms start at $64.

Hotels

$ Right across the street and very similarly priced (doubles $32), the **Hotel Aranjuez** (Calle 19 between avs. 11 and 13, 200m/656 ft. west and 25m/82 ft. south of Santa Teresita church; ☎ 256-1825, or 877/898-8663 in the U.S.; www. hotelaranjuez.com; MC, V) is pretty with-it socially, this time on the green front— recycling trash (not yet widespread in Costa Rica), solar-heating water, and biodegradables detergents, and so forth. It's five houses jammed together into a homey, picturesquely rambling compound owned by Oscar Torres and family. It's got *mucho* neat little nooks and crannies for exploring and hanging out, including cozy lounging areas, a bar, and a lush, tropical courtyard where you get the complimentary breakfast plus snacks and drinks (it feels kind of like a rainforest greenhouse, with orchids, ferns, and other exotics). The 35 rooms (doubles $32–$36) vary a bit in size and look but are all comfy and attractive, with wood floors and sometimes paneling, nice tile work, local art, orthopedic mattresses, and halogen lights. Most also have private baths (some with skylights), but if you can do without, go for it—you'll whack around $10 off the rent. Other perks: free Wi-Fi and local faxes, parking, laundry, free local calls, and a good tour desk.

IN & AROUND DOWNTOWN

$ In an old townhouse in Aranjuez, a quiet neighborhood that is just a 10-minute stroll northeast of downtown, **Kap's Place** 🧒 (Calle 19 between avs. 11 and 13, 200m/656 ft. west and 50m/164 ft. north of the Shell station; ☎ 221-1169; www.kapsplace.com; AE, MC, V) is an understated gem run by young Karla Arias with 11 seriously colorful (sometimes even downright whimsical) rooms and an apartment; some are on the small side, but the website lays out the pros and cons of each so you don't get any surprises—and for rates starting at $31 (including breakfast), well, the place is quite frankly a steal. Rooms have perks like cable TV, fans, and hair dryers, and on-premises extras include yoga, massage, Spanish lessons, free Internet stations, and a small roof terrace. There's also a back patio with hammocks, a trampoline, and a playground, and there's access to a common kitchen (apart from the included breakfast, you're otherwise on your own feeding yourself, but there's plenty in the neighborhood to take care of that). By the way, if you're expecting to find "Kap" (sounds kinda like some 1940s movie bartender, don't it?), that's a nonstarter—the word's supposedly an acronym for "Knowledge, Accommodation, and Personalized Service." A little forced, yeah—but at these prices, we're forced to say, "Whatever you want, Karla *querida*."

No Such Number, No Such Zone

You might wonder why the heck I almost never list street numbers and instead am constantly putting things like "100m north and 50m west of the Magaly Cinema." Well, welcome to Costa Rica, where that's the way locals have dealt with addresses since forever (I remember back in the 1970s writing to a penpal in Alajuela at "125m east of Coopatenas"). What really kills me is when the landmark in question *no longer exists*, as in such-and-such-many meters south of the old fig tree, the former Coca-Cola bottling plant, or the ex-general store. That's one reason why trying to find addresses on your own can be as tricky as tracking down WMDs in Iraq. At least San José and the larger Central Valley cities have numbered streets and avenues, and usually we're able to tell you someplace is on such-and-such avenue between these two streets (though most cabbies will need to know the "Tico-style" address). But the majority of cities and towns in Costa Rica have no formal street names; it's all done by landmarks. Some people find all of this cute and quaint. I'm not among them.

$$ For about the same outlay (or for the top suite, quite a bit less), just a step removed from action without being exiled to the burbs, **Casa Roland** (100m/ 328 ft. from end of Bulevar Rohrmoser; ☎ 520-1900; www.casa-roland.com; MC, V) is a pretty fab find at $85 per double. It's over in mansion- and embassy-filled Rohrmoser, west of La Sabana park at the end of Paseo Colón and one of San José's most gracious and pretty neighborhoods (don't take just our word for it—the country's prez lives over here), The service is friendly, the public areas snazzy—the reception area and bar/lounge, for example, woody with colorful nature murals and lots of plants—and the 20 plush rooms a nice mix of traditional and mod— white walls with dark-wood accents, plus perks like A/C, cable, fridge, and Wi-Fi (there are also two Internet stations in the lobby). A half dozen of them also have access to semi-private Jacuzzis in a plant-filled atrium; for your own private soak, plus a separate entrance, go for the three-bedroom top suite at $190.

$$ Really into historic charm? Give a thought to shelling out just a smidgeon more ($89 double, including breakfast) for one of my local favorites, the French-owned **Fleur de Lys** ★ (Calle 13 between avs. 2 and 6, 50m/164 ft. north of Clínica Drs. Echandi; ☎ 223-1206; www.hotelfleurdelys.com; AE, MC, V). It's con- veniently located, too, in an early-1900s, pink-painted clapboard off Plaza Democracia below the national museum. Service is friendly and quite good, and the rambling manse is chockablock with fetching, sometimes surprising nooks and crannies, plus great details like mosaic floors and Arts and Crafts windows (it's got kind of a Key West–guesthouse vibe, actually). There's a nice restaurant with updated Tico cuisine and a twice-weekly happy hour with live music. The 31 flower-named rooms each look different but they share warm, rich woods, soft colors, and original local artwork: and in some cases they include minibars and (tiny) terraces—just no A/C, since the ceiling fans usually do the trick just fine. And I like the bathrooms, too, with granite counters and bidets (plus tubs in the original house), *muchas gracias.* The suites are a pretty good deal, too, for $104 (junior) to $135 (master); the one they call the Daisy is a doozy, with a Jacuzzi, glass details everywhere, and even a cute little bridge to get from one part of the suite to the other.

$$ As luck would have it, one of San José's best full-service hotel values is also one of its most central. Owned for the last 7 years by a Tico family of Polish ori- gin and right smack on downtown's pedestrian main drag, just a handful of blocks from most of the downtown museums, the eight-story **Hotel Presidente** (Av. Central at Calle 7; ☎ 222-3022; www.hotel-presidente.com; AE, MC, V) has as its highest-profile feature the News Café (p. 28), one of the street's most hap- pening eateries (you'll spot gaggles of gringos hanging out at the high streetside tables). The main hotel entrance right to it is actually kind of easy to miss. One floor up from the cafe and the attractive marble lobby, you'll find a fairly popular video bar/lounge as well as the Fiesta casino; there's also a good little gym with a view of cloud-swathed mountains in the distance. As for the 100 units, for $85 you get a clean, attractive, double of decent size, with tile floors and done in Indonesia-flavored rattan and nicely understated earthtones like beige, khaki, and burnt ochre (great mattresses, too). If you really want some major elbow room, the $125 junior suites are just the ticket, and if you feel like a splurge, the nearly 186-sq.m (2,000-sq.-foot) master suite has two bedrooms sleeping four, and includes an eight-person Jacuzzi and 57-inch flat-screen TV. I'd definitely give this *presidente* more than one term.

$$$ Another historic clapboard, though a little less central (off Paseo de Colón in the Nomosco neighborhood west of central downtown), **El Grano de Oro** ★★ (Calle 30 between avs. 2 and 4; ☎ 255-3322; www.hotelgranodeoro.com; MC, V) may just be *the* prettiest and most service-oriented of San José's Victorian coffee-planter-manses-turned-inns (the name means "bean of gold," which is sure what java turned out to be for those folks). The original house is a maze of hallways and little courtyards, crammed with tropical plants, gorgeous tile fountains, bird cages, and walls full of art and old photos. Its 37 rooms and three suites are each individually decorated, tastefully done up with rich fabrics and dark-wood furniture, their blue-and-white, good-size baths with oversize tubs or walk-in showers. Some are on the smallish size (those would be the $100 jobs), while the "superior" rooms (from $120) are more spacious and some have private patios. One recent addition I could do without is a mod, out-of-place-looking entryway of blocky black stone, metal, and smoked glass (on the other hand, I did finally get used to that glass pyramid thingie at the Louvre). The perks pop, too—not just minibars and room service but a boutique, rooftop terrace with two Jacuzzis, and one of the best destination restaurants in town, set in a lushly landscaped courtyard, mixing international classics and fancified local fare.

IN THE SUBURBS

$$ If you're okay with basing yourself outside downtown, out in the gringo-heavy suburb of Escazú, try **The Fountains Guesthouse** (Santa Ana-Escazú road, across from Plaza del Río mall; ☎ 378-6679, or 866/673-5869 in the U.S.; AE, MC, V via Paypal). In 2007, Vicki Skinner, a chatty, jovial transplanted Californian, reincarnated a roomy but nondescript middle-class family house as an orange-sponge-painted New-Agey oasis replete with cascades of candles, tiki torches, and fountains, on a secluded-feeling .8-hectare (2-acre) spread tucked off of a road lined with myriad but less than spiritual dining and shopping options. The half-dozen rooms ($60–$100, breakfast included) have high wood-paneled ceilings and individual decor (sometimes colorful—the room full of blue and red pillows is something), and the master suite throws in a big, lavish bath, cute interior courtyard, and extra-swell closet space (TVs are available upon request). It's really a peach of a place to hang—watch the birds, hummingbirds, and butterflies; laze in the hammock; have a massage in the gazebo; tap into the Wi-Fi; fix yourself something in the large kitchen. Self-styled "sarong goddess" Vicki's a trip and a half—she's the queen of the fruit smoothies, has a collection of sarongs to wear while you're staying, and is plugged into the local "alternative" scene. She includes 10 minutes' daily of free phone calls in-country or to North America, and another neat perk is a spin in her fancy-schmancy massage chair.

HOTEL WORTH A SPLURGE

Though it's definitely up there for San José ratewise (standard rooms $167, junior suites $197, master suite $390), to park yourself at such dreamy digs as Santa

The Way to Stay Gay in San José

For you nonstraights (and you know who you are), Costa Rica's become one of Latin America's top meccas for *maricones*—especially out on the Pacific Coast in Manuel Antonio (p. 161), but also here in the capital, where you've got a sprinkling of lodgings catering to you.

The most central and least pricey is the quaint, long-standing, and German-owned **Kekoldi** (Av. 9 between calles 5 and 7, 70m/300 ft. east of INVU; ☎ 248-0804 or 786-221-9011 in the U.S.; www.kekoldi.com; high-season doubles from $55 including breakfast; AE, D, MC, V), in Barrio Amón, right above downtown. It's a whitewashed, very homey feeling Deco-style spot up a stairway from street level, with 10 rooms and a very cute little garden courtyard running down a hillside. (There's another branch out on the coast in Manuel Antonio, by the way.)

A couple of notches up in amenities but a little farther from downtown, out west in genteel Rohrmoser, the 20-room, Spanish-colonial-style **Colours Oasis** (200m/656 ft. from end of Bulevar Rohrmoser; ☎ 296-1880; www.coloursoasis.com; AE, D, MC, V) is a great coed deal—from $79 double in high season, breakfast included—for upscale-resort-like bells and whistles such as a nice-size pool, Jacuzzi, bar, and small workout room.

Ana's American-owned **Alta Hotel** ✪✪✪ (Carretera Vieja Santa Ana, Alto de las Palomas; ☎ 282-4160, or 888/388-2582 in the U.S. and Canada; www.thealta hotel.com; AE, D, MC, V) could be second-mortgage territory in many other countries, or even some of the more exclusive stretches of Costa Rica's Pacific coast. It's a hacienda-flavored, spectacularly *romántica* collection of arches, ramps, catwalks, and spiral stairs layered across a lush hillside out in the ritzy (well, ritzi*er*) western burbs. The glass-tiled oval pool out back shares sweeping valley views with a nearby Jacuzzi, a small spa, a pretty good little gym, and La Luz, a nouvelle-fusion destination restaurant that is among the very tippy-top dining experiences I've had in Costa Rica. All the above makes it sound like the Alta's some big, sprawling resort, when it's actually got all of 23 rooms, which are much cozier than the public spaces, with an upscale-rustic feel and earth-tone palette: terra-cotta floors, old-fashioned tile counters in the bathrooms, and arches all over, from windows to alcoves. With the exception of air-conditioning, they've got all the main "mod-cons," as the Brits say: satellite TV, minibar, robes, room service, and high-speed Internet hookups; breakfast is included in your rate.

DINING FOR ALL TASTES

There's surprising quality and diversity in Chepe's chow, and it's scattered all over the city and its immediate suburbs (and you can even find a few spots open 24/7). The wide variety of choices runs from the usual fast-food chains and those cheap, humble rice-and-beans joints called *sodas* to some truly fine world cuisine I'd stack up against nearly any in, say, New York or London. On the lower end, one neat way to combine sightseeing, shopping, and getting a decent bite to eat is a meander through the warren of stalls and shops inside downtown's historic covered market, the **Mercado Central** (between avs. Central and 1, calles 6 and 8) where two- or three-course daily specials can run as little as $2 (check out **Soda La Típica,** on the closest corridor parallel to Av. Central—I'll bet it's got the teeniest tables you ever did see). Other particularly good, cheap *sodas* include **Chelles** (Av. Central at Calle 9; ☎ 221-1369; daily 24 hr.) near the Gold Museum, a small, simple spot with a bit of a late-night bar scene, and the spiffy **Tapia** (Calle 23 at Paseo de Colón; ☎ 222-6734; Sun–Thurs 6am–2am, Fri–Sat 24 hr.), a bit west, across from the Museo de Arte Costarricense. You can also grab light and inexpensive noshes in the sumptuous **National Theater cafe** (p. 32). And if you must do fast food, good Tico chains to look for include **Rústico** *(comida típica),* **RostiPollo** (chicken), and **Spoons** (light cafe-style fare).

The farther you get from downtown, the more international the dining tends to get; especially out in "gringo gulch," the western suburbs of Escazú and Santa Ana, where you'll find not only good moderate options but most of the upscale ones along with a United Nations of gastronomy, from Cuban to Lebanese and Brazilian to Indian (all right, all right—and Hooters). Anyway, here's a good cross section from cheap to moderate, but you can find plenty more depending on your tastes and where you're staying, by asking around and keeping your eyes open (some of my nightlife and hotel listings also serve food). If you're a real foodie or going to be in San José for more than a couple of days, **7th Street Books** (p. 39) sells a local restaurant guide in English; and *Sibarita,* an annual guide to more than a hundred quality eateries in San José and beyond, is free for the grabbing at various hotels and shops.

In & Around Downtown

$–$$$ Several blocks east and also plenty atmospheric but in a very different way, **Café Mundo** (Calle 15 at Av. 9, 200m/656 ft. east and 100m/328 ft. north of INS/Jade Museum; ☎ 222-6190; Mon–Thurs 11am–11pm, Fri 11am–midnight, Sat 5pm–midnight; AE, MC, V) is set in a colonial clapboard manse that manages to feel cozy and hip at the same time. Inside amid all kinds of groovy Tico modern art, or outside on the wraparound porch, you'll find some of Chepe's younger, more artsy/boho crowd (including a good smattering of gays) having a feed on a nice multi-culti array of pizzas, mains ($5–$16), and pastas like the popular penne with shrimp and grilled veggies in white sauce, plus desserts like its crowd-pleasing choco cake.

$–$$$ For possibly the biggest gringo scene downtown, your best bet would pretty much have to be the Hotel Presidente's **News Café** (Av. Central at Calle 7; ☎ 222-3022; daily 6am–11pm; AE, MC, V), where said news might be a mite on the stale side (framed newspapers on the beige brick walls with headlines in English announcing the end of World War II and the like), but the place is usually abuzz (try to nab a streetside table if you can, to watch the passing parade on Av. Central), and the grub is tasty and reasonably varied, from sandwiches, burgers, quesadillas, and wraps to nicely done entrees like *arroz con pollo* ($3.95), fish and chips ($6), tilapia with tomato relish ($10), and Argentine-style *churrasco* steak with chimichurri sauce ($13). Don't miss the thick, tangy, tasty tortilla soup with guacamole.

$–$$$ A very similar kind of cookery corner a little closer to downtown's museums and hotels—cater-corner from the national museum and right around the corner from the Fleur de Lys, for example—**Nuestra Tierra** ★ (Av. 2 at Calle 15; ☎ 258-6500; daily 24 hr.; cash only) is open round the clock and has that same rough-farmhouse thing down pat, with even more and varied doodads hanging all over (Indian masks, saddles, enamel cups) and tabletops varnished with old black-and-white shots of San José back in the day; there's even an antique marimba in here. Prices on some of the "house specialties" at the front of the bilingual menu tip the scales at $13 to $17, but after that comes plenty of affordable homestyle cooking—for $6.75, tuck into the *Alforja Tica,* a banana-leaf-lined wood platter with strips of beef, grilled sausage, fried cheese, *gallo pinto,* fried sweet plantain, and tortillas. It's boffo for breakfast, too—for just $3.85, you'll get stuffed to bursting by the *Gallo Pinto Completo* of rice, beans, tortilla, fried plantain, sour cream, corn on the cob, with a choice of beef in tomato-based sauce, eggs as you like 'em, fried cheese, bacon, pork chop, steak, or *chicharrones.* Try washing it down with the yummy, cinnamony rice drink *resbaladera* ($1.95), and afterward order some of that great Tico coffee, if only to watch them brew it right at your table the old-fashioned way: in a cloth sock. And while you're waiting for your grub, feel free to check your e-mail at a handful of comp Internet stations.

$$ My pick for Ye Olde Worlde *élégance* (not to mention nifty people-watching and views of the historic National Theater) is **Cafeteria 1830** (Plaza Mora Fernández; ☎ 221-4000; www.granhotelcostarica.com; daily 24 hr.; AE, D, MC, V), on the portico of downtown's classic Gran Hotel Costa Rica. The hotel was actually built a century later, in 1930, but you get the idea: graceful white Corinthian columns under high arches, antique tile floors in interlocking browns, beiges, and creams—it really is kind of like eating in a sepia *fin de siècle* photo, very Hemingway/Kipling (the slightly cheesy tables and chairs break the spell a tad, but hey, you can't have everything). It's especially magical at night, what with the ornate theater across the way awash in floodlights. The menu offers decent quality and variety, from crepes and sandwiches ($3–$9.45) to pastas and international entrees ($10–$12) that are nicely executed but don't leap off the beaten path—stuff like filet mignon and pork chops with apple sauce. Afterward, check out the major selection of tasty coffee drinks. Minor gripes: service on the pokey side, and that live piano's swell, but we gotta say, "Havah Nagilah" just does not do it for us as a dinner mood-setter.

$$ Speaking of atmospheric, I heartily recommend an alfresco dinner amid the "1,001 Nights" thing going on at Barrio Amón's **Café Moro** ★ (Calle 3 between avs. 11 and 13, 450m/1,476 ft. north of Automercado; ☎ 223-3116; Mon–Thurs 11:30am–10pm, Fri 11:30am–10:30pm, Sat 5pm–10:30pm; AE, D, MC, V). Opened in 2004 in the tiled courtyard of an old, castlelike neo-Moorish *(moro)* townhouse built in 1910, it's also got a small inside dining room, deep blue with Arabic calligraphy running as a frieze along the ceiling and modern art on the walls (another theme—in fact, Thursdays are "gallery nights" here). The food's pretty good, too, a mix of Latin and Middle Eastern with entrees usually running about $8.50 to around $10; tasty and filling wraps with a side salad $6.60 to $7.15, and couscous is $7.15 to $9.45. If you dare and your insulin shots are in order, have a peck at the *pollo a la miel,* fried chicken sautéed in honey sauce. And it would be a crime not to make room for the pistachio flan ($3.50) afterward—honestly one of the best variations on this old standby I've yet put to mouth.

$$ Up in laid-back, historic Barrio Amón, just north of central downtown, I really like **La Criollita** (Av. 7, 50m/164 ft. west of Jade Museum/Plaza de España; ☎ 256-6511; Mon–Fri 7am–9pm, Sat 7am–4pm; AE, D, MC, V) for both its good, affordable international menu and an ambience that's both friendly and even a little upscale-feeling. There are actually three distinct spaces here: Just inside the door, it's all cozy and wood-paneled; then there's an outdoor covered patio with plants; and in between, our favorite, a long soaring room with semitransparent rounded roof, green-stucco walls piled with paintings both traditional and mod, and a trio of boob tubes perched at either end (unfortunately, this is also a smoking area, but at least it's well ventilated enough that it hasn't yet really bugged me). This is a good place to order critters with fins, gills, and scales—the fish soup ($5.50) is a winner, as is the shrimp (spicy *a la diabla* $11, in garlic sauce $7.45) and the sea bass, served up five ways ($6.95). But there are plenty of meats and veggies, too, plus a decent selection of sandwiches and desserts (save room for the strawberry mousse, $1.75), and last but not least, very nice fruit smoothies and shakes, in water or milk.

$$ In another quiet little nabe called Barrio Escalante, a $1 cab ride northeast of downtown, **Olio** ✦ (200m/656 ft. north of Bagelmans; ☎ 281-0541; Mon–Fri noon–5pm, Sat–Sun noon–2am; AE, D, MC, V) is a classy little spot named after olive oil and is all about Mediterranean fare (heavy on Spanish and Italian), from simple to pretty darn sophisticated. The 19th-century red-brick building with graceful wrought-iron window grates was a railway office in the days when Costa Rica's Atlantic and Pacific rail lines intersected right at this spot, and the travel theme's picked up by the inside's bric-a-brac decor yielded by the globetrotting of owners Federico and Fernando; they've got something of a gay following but the clientele really is all over the map. Start out with some classic Spanish tapas ($4.35–$7.80) like potato omelette, cured Serrano ham, and *patatas bravas* (potato chunks with spicy sauce), before moving on to pasta ($4.55–$9.15) or main ($8.20–$12). Our fave: "New World" chicken, wrapped in a tortilla, stuffed with mozzarella, tomato, and basil, all doing the backstroke in a tasty, roasted, red-pepper sauce. For dessert, they make *un bel tiramisù,* and the expresso is the top-of-the-line Italian brand Illy (always a good sign in a restaurant, in our opinion). If you'd rather do lunch, the sandwiches are good and inexpensive ($4.75), as is the buffet for all of $2.90.

$$ Actually, we kinda wish we had more restaurants in the States like **Tin Jo** ✦ (Calle 11 between avs. 6 and 8, across from Teatro Lucho Barahona; ☎ 221-7605; www.tinjo.com; Mon–Thurs 11:30am–3pm and 5:30–10pm, Fri–Sat 11:30am–3pm and 5:30pm–11pm, Sun 11:30am–10pm; AE, MC, V), near central downtown. With more than a decade of business under its belt, not only do owners Maria

Hon and Robert Faulstich offer good service and understated but very appealing decor (exotic floral arrangements, bamboo placemats, and fascinating masks, sculptures, and kites), but also an eight-page menu that takes you on a terrifically tasty tour through at least a half-dozen Asian cuisines—Chinese, Filipino, Indian, Indonesian, Japanese, and Thai. The quality's top-notch (organic veggies, for example) and the preparation and presentation creative (check out the bowls made out of noodles that some dishes are served in). Some of the libations are pretty interesting, too, like the Burbujas de Japón (plum wine spritzer with mint) or the balsamic vinegar soda (nice dry bite to it). Tin Jo's a lifesaver for vegetarians, too, thanks to a good 15 choices, conveniently summarized on one page of the menu. Entrees run $5.15 to $9.75.

$$–$$$$ Moving on up to the level of bona fide fine dining, whether the eponymous restaurant at **El Grano de Oro** ✹✹ (Calle 30/avs. 2 and 4; ☎ 255-3322; daily 6am–10pm; AE, D, MC, V) is *the* best in San José or not is obvious a matter of opinion. But I can sure make a good case; the inside part has a casual, woody elegance to it, and out in the lush courtyard you could almost pretend you're chowing down in the rainforest, except that rainforest chow tends to be mostly raw food, and the stuff you get here is usually pretty well cooked. Entrees run $11 to $28 and include a contingent of classics—filet mignon, rack of lamb, duck *à l'orange*—along with snazzier, tropical concoctions like chicken breast stuffed with dried tropical fruit or bathed in a coconut cream sauce. The house specialty on the decadent dessert list, meanwhile, is Pie Grano de Oro, with chocolate cookie crust and coffee cream. And you'll be happy to know that a cut of your check goes to a local home for poor single *mamás* that's run by the hotel.

IN THE SUBURBS

$–$$ Way out west in Santa Ana, there are loads and loads and loads of eateries, so you might wonder what in tarnation would makes us plump for **Rock & Roll Pollo** 🧒 (Santa Ana-Escazú road, 25m/82 ft. west of Servicenter Herreri; ☎ 282-9613; daily 8am–1:30am; AE, MC, V), 2 minutes down the hill from the Alta Hotel. Run since 2006 by bearded San Francisco ex-restaurant guy Bill Russi and his pretty Tica wife Lizette, this bamboo-lined roadside spot is like a traditional thatched *rancho*-meets-sports bar, except that it's usually more laid-back than your average sports bar (still, when there's a big game on in the States, the gringos come a flockin' to the pair of big-screen TVs here). Whatever—the fact is that if you need a break from *comida típica* (oh yeah, we all do after a certain point) and have a hankerin' for some red-white-and-blue comfort grub like barbecue ribs, meatloaf, wings, burgers, Southern fried chicken, eggs Benedict, brownie a la mode, and banana cream pie ($2.40–$9.55), this is the place to pull up a rattan chair at one of the varnished tables and have at it (this kind of food also makes it a prime pick for parents trying to placate homesick kids). I especially dig the chicken, roasted to a T with coffee wood. And by the way, the chef is Tico, so the *arroz con pollo*, ceviche, and other local standards are very good, too. Also, if you want to lug your laptop along, you can Wi-Fi while you wait.

$$$ Out in Santa Ana, **La Luz** ✹✹ (Carretera Vieja Santa Ana; ☎ 282-4160; daily 6:30am–3pm and 6–10pm; AE, D, MC, V), the dining room at Santa Ana's

Hotel Alta, is just as strong a contender for top table, thanks to all its pluses: elegant yet not stuffy surroundings, very correct service, and killer valley views through floor-to-ceiling windows. Then of course there's the main event, New York chef Carlos Zuñiga's ambitious nouvelle fusion of tropical, European, Latin, and Californian elements and ingredients that can be so creative that even its occasional misfires are worth the price. I'm talking about starters ($6–$12) like feta tart with oven-dried tomato, sweet peppers, caramelized onions, and honey cilantro vinaigrette, and mains ($14–$21) along the lines of grilled beef tenderloin with strawberry sauce and balsamic vinegar with champagne risotto, Parmesan slices and white truffle pesto. This is world-class stuff, folks. Keep in mind that jackets are "recommended" for dudes, and reservations are often a good idea.

WHY YOU'RE HERE: THE TOP SIGHTS & ATTRACTIONS

There's more interesting stuff to see and do in Chepe than many people realize, and the pick of the litter is laid out below. But it still goes without saying that what most people come to Costa Rica for is ecotourism, which you just ain't gonna find in the capital. Nearby, though, is another story—if you want to be able to make the most of San José's dining and nightlife, you can still base yourself here while taking advantage of the volcanoes and whitewater and wildlife and all that good stuff out in the surrounding areas of the Central Valley. To see the stuff to do in easy striking distance, check "Why You're Here" for Alajuela (p. 55), Heredia (p. 71), and Cartago (p. 83). But in the capital, don't make the zoo or the butterfly farm a priority (you'll find much better flora and fauna out of town). Instead, here's the major stuff that's unique and you don't want to miss, listed in order of not wanting to miss it.

Most people seem to be fascinated by gold, and there's plenty of it under the plaza right in the middle of downtown between the National Theater and Avenida Central. Run by the Banco Central, the **Museo del Oro Precolombino** ✪✪ (Plaza de la Cultura at Calle 5; ☎ 243-4202; Mon–Sun 9:30am–5pm; www.museosdelbanco central.org/eng/museo_del_oro/informacion_general.html; $7; students/kids $3) is a trove of 1,600-ish pieces of the shiny yellow stuff, dating from 500 to 1500 A.D. And it also gives one of its two floors over to a survey of this swath of Central America's indigenous cultures before our old pal Chris Columbus happened by, including exhibits about metalworking, history, and customs (check out the mock-up of an ancient tomb from down south). It's attractive and expertly lit, and you'll be amazed at some of the intricate workmanship on the mostly small to downright teeny gold items. All the minute detail needs a certain amount of focus, so it might be a little boring for kids, even with the sprinkling of dioramas and mock-ups of guys 'n' gals in loincloths. But for thinking people curious about what was going on around here before the Euros crashed the party, it can be pretty cool—we find it especially interesting comparing the similarities and differences with indigenous societies closer to home, in North America. If you're a really diehard coin fan, the attached numismatic museum, which just might float your boat (keep in mind it's just Costa Rica–oriented). And the longtime no-pictures-no-video rule is now just no-video.

Probably the fanciest historic building in the whole country is right next to the Plaza de la Cultura: the **Teatro Nacional** ✪ (Av. 2 at Calle 5; ☎ 221-3756 www. teatronacional.go.cr; Mon–Sat 9am–4pm; guided tours hourly 9am–3pm, $5), or as we like to call it, "the house that joe built." This handsome theater was tacked together in 1891–97 by Belgian architects and Italian artists financed by a coffee export tax so that the local java barons could prove that they weren't uncultured provincial hicks (they were obviously tax-and-spend plutocrats, instead of borrow-and-spend). And it's true that all the Belle Epoque marble, gilt, and frescos makes a pretty good stab at aping the famous European big-leaguers like the Opéra de Paris and La Scala. There are (mostly but not only classical) performances and exhibitions here pretty regularly—check out the website above. But you can also just get an eyeful by taking a 40-minute guided tour (*en español* only, unfortunately); browsing the baubles, books, and music in the gift shop at right when you enter; or having a sip, crepe, salad, or sandwich at the cafe ($3.60–$6.60) across the lobby.

Up the hill a few blocks east, you'll get a good overview of this country's history at the **Museo Nacional de Costa Rica** ★ (Calle 17 between avs. 2 and Central, at Plaza de la Democracia; ☎ 257-1433; Tues–Fri 8:30am–4:30pm, Sat-Sun 9am–4:30pm; $4, students $2, under 12 free), in the pockmarked, mustard-color Cuartel Bellavista, a 19th-century fortress that used to be the army's HQ till it was deep-sixed after the 1948 civil war—actually, you can get a pretty good look at the city from the ramparts here. It helps to be a history buff to enjoy this place, but if you aren't, it's well designed and gets to the point. One side is all about pre-Columbian art and artifacts including musical instruments, recreated tombs, pottery, and gold pieces. One of our favorite parts here is the dramatically lit *metates* (carved volcanic stones for grinding corn and grain—some pretty elaborate and evocative). The wing across the courtyard covers the colonial period onward, with recreated interiors, paintings, furniture, and dioramas (lots of the explanations are in English, you'll be relieved to know, and reasonably informative). At the south end there's a room for temporary exhibits (cool indigenous tribal photos last time we were here), and in the courtyard you'll spot a bunch of huge round stone spheres—they're from the Osa Peninsula, made by ancient tribes for nobody-knows-what reason. Once you're done with the museum, hang a left outside and follow the pleasant paved promenade covering this stretch of Calle 17 to the Parque Nacional, which features a big statue commemorating the Battle of Rivas (April 11, 1856), the south Nicaragua town where Costa Rica's national hero Juan Santamaría (p. 47) got that way by getting killed while burning the HQ of William Walker, whose mercenary army from the U.S. was trying to invade the country (p. 14).

The Spanish conquistadors may have been gaga over gold, but the folks they conquered were more into jade, and several blocks northwest of here, across from the lush Plaza de España, we think it's well worth ducking into the **Museo de Jade** ★ (Av. 7 at Calle 9, northwest corner of plaza; ☎ 287-6034; http://portal.ins-cr.com/social/museojade; Mon–Fri 8:30am–3:30pm, Sat 9am–1pm; $2, under 12 free), at the corner of the ground floor of the mod-ugly National Insurance Building. It's Central America's biggest pre-Columbian collection of the stuff, even if most of what you'll see here is actually pottery and artifacts of wood and other types of stone. Whatever—there's some pretty neat items in here, including mysterious stone spheres from the southern reaches of the country, and one of the most striking pieces in the whole museum is a terra-cotta incense burner in the shape of a mythological crocodile. The jadework you do see just rocks, so to speak—many reflecting Olmec and Maya influences, they're almost modern-looking in their elegant simplicity, and include a couple of cases worth of erotic piece. There are also plenty of other cool members of mineraldom here, including jadeite, nephrite, serpentine, lapis lazuli, obsidian, and quartz.

A bit west of downtown at the edge of La Sabana park—San José's ex-airport—its ex-terminal has since 1978 been on duty as the **Museo de Arte Costarricense** ★ (Calle 42 at Paseo de Colón, on eastern edge of Parque Metropolitano La Sabana; ☎ 222-7155; www.musarco.go.cr; Tues–Fri 9am–5pm, Sat–Sun 10am–4pm; $5, students $3, Sun free), which comes across more like a Spanish colonial manse, complete with soaring ceilings and stairs, balconies, and beams of dark, handsome wood. Costa Rica has produced some top-notch fine artists, and many of them, from the 19th century to the present, have works here—names like Juan Manuel Sánchez, Alexander Jiménez Matarrita, Margarita Berteau, and Luis Daell. Yeah, we know you don't know who any of these characters are, and yeah, a lot of it tends to ape and echo European art (in fact, one recent exhibition was blatantly titled "Homage to Rembrandt"). But there's a whole bunch of real talent in here, and it's also worth a stop for the pretty outdoor sculpture garden and the second-floor Salón Dorado ★, the old diplo VIP room, with more than 150 sq. m (1,600 sq. ft.) worth of stucco bas-reliefs carved in 1940 by a French expat named Louis Feron (who later designed for Tiffany and Cartier), showing scenes from Costa Rica's history.

Finally, this one's for the mamas and the papas: Give a thought to hauling the gang off to jail. Oy, such a kidder I am—actually, that would be the **Museo de los Niños** 🧒 (Av. 9 at Calle 4; ☎ 258-4929; www.museocr.com; Tues–Fri 8am–4:30pm, Sat–Sun 9:30am–5pm; weekends $2.15, kids/students $1.55, weekdays $1.95/$1.35), in La Peni, a 1909 ex-penitentiary with castlelike crenellations that since 1994 has been home to a swell little collection of hands-on exhibits that are both fun and educational. You can experience a simulated earthquake, explore a real helicopter, and take a simulated jaunt inside the human body. There's a cafeteria here if you want to catch lunch, and FYI the National Auditorium is also here, worth checking out for concerts and other events.

THE "OTHER" SAN JOSE

Museums and statues and fancy buildings are all swell and good, but the way to get under the surface of Tico culture and better get what makes it tick is to be on the lookout for "alternative," not necessarily touristy, things to see and do—especially when they let you mingle more meaningfully with locals. Since Costa Rica's capital is its biggest metro area, it naturally serves up the country's biggest and most varied menu of stuff along these lines, and the fact that so many expats live and work here means that they've organized more groups, activities, and specialized tours for you to take advantage of than most anywhere in the country (there's a lot along the Pacific coast, but it tends to be more spread out). Also consider planning your trip around holidays and festivals when you can rub shoulders with locals—just keep in mind that during the really big ones, like Semana Santa (Easter week), prices can shoot up and room availability drops like a stone. In the capital area, good bets include Costa Rica's Independence Day on September 15; the week between Christmas and New Year's when locals celebrate the country's horsey heritage downtown in El Tope (Dec. 26), followed by a big street carnival

(Dec. 27) and various festivities and fun at the Zapote fairgrounds southeast of downtown; and Escazú's Día del Boyero, the second Sunday in March, when processions of colorful folkloric oxcarts spotlight Costa Rica's most famous symbol.

The following are a few more ongoing options to consider. An excellent source for lots more ideas is the English-language *Tico Times* (www.ticotimes.com), where on my last visit down I got turned on to events given by, for example, Democrats Abroad of Costa Rica, the International Gay and Lesbian Association, Coffee-Pickin' Squares Dance Club, the Quilt Guild of Costa Rica, the Tibetan–Costa Rican Cultural Association, and the Women's Club of Costa Rica. You can also pick up leads from a raft of active online boards and discussion groups we've come across like Yahoo's "Costa Rica Living," "Costa Rica Central Valley Living," and "Escazu News" groups. Otherwise, here are a few more leads:

Sports

I often find that rooting—especially for *fútbol* (as soccer is called in this soccer-besotted land)—and playing together can do wonders for getting under the surface of the local scene. The soccer season is September through June, and the finals stretch into early July. The main San José teams play at the **Estadio Nacional** (☎ 221-7677) in Sabana Park and at the home of the "Purple Monster," the **Estadio Ricardo Saprissa Ayma** (☎ 240-4034 or 206-7770; www.saprissa. co.cr) in suburban Tibás (to which regular buses leave from the downtown San José corner of Av. 5 and Calle 2); check local papers for details. You think U.S. sports fans can be rabid? Down here they wear team colors, chant and cheer themselves hoarse, paint their faces, the whole bit—plus on occasion get worked up enough to clobber each other (Costa Rica's neighbors El Salvador and Honduras once actually fought a shooting war with armies over a soccer game back in 1969).

Culture & the Arts

There's some world-class art being made down here, and you can see it being made and make some interesting connections on **Molly Keeler's art tour** ✪ (☎ 359-5571; www.costaricaarttour.com; $95). She ferries groups of up to 10 people around to the studios of 5 of the local (mostly Tico) artists in her 300-artist database, and you'll get to watch them working, chat them up (with Molly as interpreter; most of her folks *no habla inglés*) and buy pieces—sans sales pressure. Molly will pick the artists according to your specific interests; in fact, she finds that many of them get as much out of the deal as the tourists.

If you find Molly's tab a bit too steep, you could try asking around at the galleries if any of their artists would be available for visits. Or head to **TEOR/éTica** (Calle 7 at Av. 11, 400m/1,312 ft. north of Morazán Park; ☎ 233-4881; www.teor etica.org) in Barrio Amón, a nonprofit gallery/foundation (keep an eye peeled for the massive snowflakes painted on the side) that holds regular discussions, recitals, concerts, and exhibits where you're sure to meet lots of interesting characters. For current details, check the website, call, or stop by. In the past they've had guest artists from places like Argentina and Puerto Rico to discuss their work; hosted a Cuban dinner in the gallery to go along with an exhibition from the island; and had musicians playing everything from chamber music to electronica.

Or come and meet those dancing feet over in Barrio Escalante, where the old railroad customs house is now the **Taller Nacional de Danza** (250m/820 ft. south of Iglesia Santa Teresita; ☎ 257-3017 or 222-9398; www.mcjdcr.go.cr/artes_escenicas/tnd.html), which offers classes to all comers (Mon–Thurs $7.75, Fri–Sat $12) in Latin and Afro-Caribbean dance among lots of others (belly dancing or hip-hop, anybody?). The Ticos do like to get down when they go out, and after a session or three here, not only will you pick up some local buddies, but you'll be able to hold your own with them out on the dance floor. An excellent spot to put your new moves into practice and meet more locals is up on the northeastern outskirts of town at the enormous club **El Tobogán** (200m/656 ft. north and 100m/328 ft. east of Diario La República, off Guápiles Hwy.; ☎ 223-8920), packed on weekend evenings, especially Sundays.

Language Schools

San José is one of the top spots in Costa Rica for Spanish schools, thanks to the bigger pool of teaching talent, choice of facilities, and local demand that goes along with being the country's biggest city. And in most cases these programs not only bolster your *español* but serve up a host of ready-made entrees into local society, through homestays and extracurricular programs. You'll want to research the following main programs in the capital area to see which would be the best fit.

The **Centro Cultural de Idiomas** (☎ 256-8981; www.spanish-in-action.com) on Paseo Colón just west of downtown makes a point of focusing on conversational skills beyond textbook learning, and in small groups (up to just four). Regular programs of four 5-day weeks run $630 to $860, including room and board, but there's also a 2-week "survival course" ($330–$440), as well as private classes for as few or as many hours as you need. Extras like gym membership, Internet access, tours, and dancing/cooking/scuba classes are provided at discounted rates. And if you bring a second student along with you, you'll get 20 percent off on your own set-up.

From $1,015 per month (you can also do it for less—1 week is $270), the **Costa Rican Language Academy/CRLA** (☎ 280-5164, or 866/230-6361 in the U.S. and Canada; www.spanishandmore.com), east of downtown near the Mall San Pedro in Barrio Dent, includes textbooks, half-board homestay, and extras like classes in cooking (weekly) and Latin dancing (daily), tours, gym membership, airport transfers, Internet/Wi-Fi, and coffee and juice on premises. And for you do-gooders, CRLA will also help arrange a local stint as a volunteer after you're done studying.

Southeast of downtown just below Los Yoses and San Pedro, the **Costa Rica Spanish Institute/COSI** (☎ 234-1001, or 800/771-5184 in the U.S. and Canada; www.cosi.co.cr) charges from $425 for a week to $1,480 per month for tuition, texts, airport pickup, and half-board homestay (you can also opt for an apartment, or no room/board at all). Some extras like tours, dance and cooking classes, are thrown in, as are volunteer/internship opportunities (for an $80 placement fee), and you can even get in a little beach time by splitting your classes between the school here and a sister school in Manuel Antonio.

In Los Yoses, the **Forester Instituto Internacional** (☎ 225-3155 or 305-767-1663 in the U.S.; www.fores.com) starts at $480 per 5-day week of classes ($1,180 for 4 weeks), including textbooks, half-board homestay, daily Latin dance classes, and Internet/Wi-Fi. One perk that stands out here is an on-campus swimming pool; other highlights include imaginative activities like learning about tropical fruits, theater outings, and nights out to local hotspots.

Oh dear, at $305 per week and $1,300 per month for tuition and half-board homestay, the **Instituto Británico** (☎ 225-0256; www.institutobritanico.co.cr) is a more serious school, and doesn't have all the jolly activities many of its competitors offer. But it does have one big advantage: It teaches the Queen's English to locals.

Volunteering

Helping build a house or replant a hillside can be a hugely rewarding way to spend at least part of your vacation. You'll not only do some good, but meet locals and maybe even learn a bit about carpentry or botany or whatever. Loads of local and international NGOs (Non-Governmental Organizations) accept international volunteers for projects in Costa Rica—some for as little as a week, some for a minimum of a month—but most of this tends to go on not right in San José but out in the countryside, small town, or national parks, spread throughout the Central Valley and beyond (see also entries in this chapter for Alajuela, Heredia, and Cartago, p. 46, 63, and 77).

Several that do offer options in and around the capital include the **Association for the Conservation and Sustainable Development of the Escazú Mountains/CODECE** (☎ 228-0813; www.codece.org), where you'll help Tico volunteers plant native trees, clear pathways and brush, fix fences, pick up trash, and provide support to programs to get local farmers with the organic program in and around the village of San Antonio; CODECE also runs events and fundraisers they could use help for, like April's 21km (13-mile) race, for example. It runs social and cultural events at night, too, and will set you up with a host family, who provides all meals, at a cost typically of $400 to $480 for an 8-day stint.

Then there's the local branch of **Habitat for Humanity** (☎ 296-3436; www.habitatcostarica.org), which accepts volunteers in its administrative offices as well as building projects in San José and throughout Costa Rica for a $100 contribution; for construction, the minimum's a week, whereas for office work it's 6 weeks plus reasonably strong Spanish; you cover your own expenses, and homestays can be arranged for $15 a day.

Finally, for a $150 program fee plus $120 a week for lodging, the **Costa Rica Spanish Institute/COSI** (☎ 234-1001, or 800/771-5184 in the U.S. and Canada; www.cosi.co.cr) will also arrange placements in San José and beyond without making you take its Spanish courses. Local gigs include teaching English, reading to the blind, caring for animals and doing office work at the zoo, helping with recreational activities at an orphanage, and more. Time commitment ranges from 1 to 3 weeks, and among the many jobs available are several that require minimal experience and Spanish.

ATTENTION, SHOPPERS!

We wouldn't exactly call San José (or Costa Rica in general) a retail-therapeutic paradise, but you can actually pick up some nifty, distinctively Tico products especially when it comes to crafts, coffee, and fine art, and there are a few good galleries, shops, and markets in and around this town that might be worth your while. In fact, in many cases if you're traveling around the country but passing through San José on your way home, you're better off shopping here in terms of

El Médico Is In: "Health Tourism" Catches Tico Fever

Beaches, rainforests, volcanoes—check. Care for a nip and tuck with that? Jeez, talk about cutting-edge travel.

As health care costs in the United States continue to zoom disgracefully out of control, "medical tourism" has turned into a booming biz, and Costa Rica lately has turned into quite the *Costa Médica*. Medical training and standards here are generally top-notch; in fact, many of the fully certified, English-speaking docs have also trained in North America and Europe. Thousands of mostly U.S. residents a year come down here for things like face-lifts, nose jobs, liposuction, laser eye surgery, varicose vein removal, root canal, and dental and breast implants (this last of which, by the way, California-based Allergan has just started manufacturing down here). In fact, Costa Rica's one of the top five countries in the world that Americans travel to for medical treatment, according to the book *Patients Beyond Borders*. San José plastic surgeon Arnoldo Fournier, for example, estimates he treats around 200 gringos a year in his own practice alone.

But why go through all that trouble? *Dinero, amigos*—50 to 70 percent less of it. A laser eye zapping can easily run you $5K in the States, while down here the same procedure, equipment, and training level would run just $1,600. A spot o' lipo that'd suck up four grand here can be had for $1,200. A $900 crown up north takes just a $350 bite down south, Combined with the relative nearness—close in time zone and less than 3 hours by plane from Miami, 3½ from Houston, 4 from Charlotte, 5½ from New York and Los Angeles—and the country's vacation appeal, and a trip here adds up to a winning choice.

And this may still be a "third-world" country, but at least some of the facilities catering to foreigners (many but not all in the Central Valley) are way modern and impressive, such as San José's big **Clínica Bíblica** (☎ 221-0645; www.clinicabiblica.com) and **Hospital CIMA San José** (☎ 208-1000; www.hospitalsanjose.net). Not only that, but a post-op cottage industry has sprung up to coddle you after you're off the table or out of the chair. **Las Cumbres Inn** (☎ 228-1011; www.surgery-retreat.com) in Escazú

---

selection, quality, and sometimes even price than in many touristy parts of the coast. The airport has several good gift shops, but prices tend to be higher than here in town—for a couple of bucks for a package of local coffee to a sometimes significant bundle for craft-y types of things.

IN & AROUND DOWNTOWN

For sightseeing even more than shopping, you shouldn't miss downtown's 128-year-old **Mercado Central** (Av. Central between calle 6 and 8; Mon–Sat 6:30am–5:30pm), where amid the stalls hawking detergents, produce, flowers, tourist tchotchkes, pets, and clothes you'll also spy artesanal pottery and leather goods

offers full daily room and board for $115 for you and a companion, while all-inclusive rates at comfy **CheTica Ranch** (☎ 268-6133; www.cheticaranch. com) in the northeastern suburb of Moravia run as little as $75 per patient, as does Escazú's **Paradise Cosmetic Inn** (☎ 252-3530; www. paradisecosmeticinn.com).

So, if you've got an inconvenient tooth, or maybe a double chin you'd like to slice, could this be for you? For starters, is it *really* safe? Well, I don't make any endorsements, and I don't think we'd want to come down for brain surgery or heart transplants or anything like that. But consider this: Britain's National Health Service is reimbursing operations abroad (growing numbers of U.S. companies are considering or doing it, too), and some programs also provide for follow-ups in patients' home countries, which is also a worry critics always trot out. So for some elective operations—and certainly check-ups and diagnostics—it may be worth a look. Know that the pros doing the treating don't always speak English; be sure to check into this and be ready to bring along someone fluent in Spanish if yours isn't so hot. There are other, more serious issues, too; my doctor friend J. Thalia J. Cunningham, a New York emergency department director and part-time travel writer tells me, "I'm still worried about informed consent, litigation, patients' rights and advocacy, what happens when and if things go wrong, from hospital administrators to government bureaucracy. These don't exist in Europe and Latin America the way they do here." Translation: nobody to sue.

Bottom line: this isn't something you want to take lightly; you'll have to do your homework, ask around, get references, and make up your own mind. Start with websites like www.costarica-surgeons.com, www.edenia. com/medical, www.arrivacostarica.com, www.theswancr.com, www.med retreat.com, and www.treatmentabroad.net. The book we mentioned above, Josef Woodman's *Patients Beyond Borders,* is another fab resource, as Woodman visited hospitals across the globe, rating them on a number of different treatments.

like wallets, sandals, even saddles. And unlike other places in town you'd typically head to buy mementos, this atmospheric maze has a much more "real" feel to it—you'll be shoulder-to-shoulder with housewives, students, and all sorts of regular Ticos doing their regular shopping; sometimes it can almost feel like you've stepped into an anthropology article from *National Geographic.*

Parenthetically, a good, central spot for locally published books about Costa Rica in English, plus novels for the beach, nights in, or the plane back is **7th St. Books** (Calle 7 between avs. 1 and Central; ☎ 256-8251; Mon–Sat 9am–6pm, Sun 10am–5pm), just off downtown's main pedestrian drag; it's also got a nice little cafe.

On the *típico*-Tico-products front, various brands of the excellent local coffee (p. 58) are sold not only at some food stores but at various tourist shops and the airport concourse. But if you have the time, we'd really recommend heading out of town a little ways out to a producer like **Britt** (p. 73), **Doka** (p. 56), or **Café Cristina** (p. 78) and buying it in situ while learning how it's made.

When it comes to crafts, there are certainly countries that do them better than Costa Rica, but as long as you're here, you'll find the best selection downtown at a couple of markets. In a yellow building behind and owned by a church called Iglesia de la Soledad, the **Mercado Nacional de Artesanía** (Calle 11 between avs. 4 and 6; daily 10am–6pm) sells works from 700 or so artisans. Prices are negotiable, but you might find repros of pre-Columbian terra cotta for the equivalent of $12; colorful scarves for $8; hand-embroidered peasant blouses $21; carved wood boxes $18; paintings $30 to $350; an elaborately carved wood table $90; even an entire, rustic-style living room set (love seat, a pair of armchairs, and coffee tables) for $830.

Just a hop and a skip away, a blocklong stretch has been put under a tin roof and turned into the **Calle Nacional de Artesanía y Pintura** ✹✹ (Calle 13 between avs. 2 and Central; daily 9am–6pm), with a head-spinning array of coffee, hammocks, sandals, paintings, jewelry, bags, caps, colorful *carreta* (oxcart) replicas, and more. Things that jumped out at me on my last swing through here included the cute little wood froggies and crickets ($5–$12) sold by **Miriam Hildalgo** (stand 44; ☎ 388-3618)—they come with little sticks that when you scrape them make sounds surprisingly close to the real critters. Meanwhile, **Juan Carlos Solorzano** (stand 62; ☎ 254-9980) sells his wife Ana's renditions of a popular local art form: delicate paintings of everything from flowers to entire country scenes on real feathers ($8–$75) from birds like parrots, cranes, peacocks, and toucans.

There are also a handful of stand-alone shops downtown carrying this kind of thing, and one of the best selections is at **Suráska** ✹ (Calle 5 at Av. 3, on Parque Morazán; ☎ 222-0129; daily 9am–6pm), where you might nab an exotic wood cutting board for $9 to $22 or bowls from $45, a small *carreta* for $15, feather paintings as low as $4. You might also try checking out the similar goods across the street at the two-story **Galería Zukia** (south side of Morazán Park between calles 5 and 7; ☎ 258-2404; Mon–Sun 9am–6:30pm), which also sells art and sculpture (negotiable prices from about $100); pick up the gallery brochure in here and you will nab an automatic 15 percent discount. And one of our favorite kinds of crafts in Costa Rica (or anywhere else for that matter) is indigenous masks—which are such a hoot on Halloween—so we really like Aisling and Conall French's **Galería Namu** ✹✹ (Av. 7 between calles 5 and 7, 200m/656 ft. west of INS/Jade Museum; ☎ 256-3412; www.galerianamu.com; Mon–Sat 9am–6:30pm), which stocks an excellent selection of masks from the Borucas of the Osa peninsula ($65), along with crafts from the Guaymí, Bribri, and Huétar. There's other neat stuff, too, including modern Tico folk art, pre-Columbian replica jewelry, and Guanacaste's bold, distinctive Chorotega pottery; prices start around $7 (for handmade fauna "eco-pens").

There are several modern art galleries worth a gander, too, and a good chunk of them are concentrated in Barrio Amón. One of the newer ones, set in an impeccably maintained 1937 house, is Ohioan Robert Griffith's welcoming **Galería Amón** ✹ (937 Calle 7, 250m/820 ft. north of Parque Morazán; ☎ 223-9725;

www.amon937.com; Tues–Wed 1–6pm, Thurs and Sat 10am–6pm, Fri 10am–5pm), with work from a wide range of artists, from young unknowns to established names like Miguel Hernández, Adrián Arguedas, and Adolfo Siliézar; prices start at $50 for a small Siliézar woodblock print. Nearby, **Galería Amir** ★★ (Calle 5 at Av. 5, on Parque Morazán across from Hotel Aurola Holiday Inn; ☎ 256-9445; www.amirart.com; Mon–Sat 9am–6:30pm) is another eclectic collection of mostly Tico painters sprinkled with a few other Latin Americans, with prices from $20; a flyer you get right in the gallery gets you 10 percent off. A third spot with reasonable prices and a broad range of local artists is the smallish **Galería Andromeda** (Calle 9 at Av. 9, across from Hotel Don Carlos; ☎ 223-3529; weekdays 9am–7pm, Sat noon–6pm), with items from $10. If you *still* can't get enough, consider signing on to the **art tour** ★ run by Molly Keeler (☎ 359-5571; www.costaricaarttour.com), who will squire you around various artists' studios for a day for $95, which includes lunch (p. 35).

Away from Downtown

A little farther afield, one single-artisan shop worth checking out is expat Midwesterner Barry Biesanz, a naturalized Tico whose **Biesanz Woodworks** ★★ (800m/2,624 ft. south of church/school; ☎ 289-4337; www.Biesanz.com; Mon–Fri 8am–5pm, Sat 10am–4pm), in a garden setting out in the Escazú neighborhood of Belo Horizonte, is filled with beautiful hardwood boxes (including humidors), vases, bowls, and indigenous masks and crafts. You can find a good number of items here for $5 to $20. A little farther still, if you have the time and the wheels, consider a jaunt up north to the crafts town of **Sarchí** ★★ in Alajuela (its biggest specialties are *carretas* and furniture; p. 62) and out east to the **Calle de las Artesanía** in **San Vicente de Moravia** ★★ (p. 76).

Finally, if you're a dyed-in-the-wool mall rat (or are just after some primo people-watching), one of the coolest of the centrally located ones is the four-story **Mall San Pedro** (Av. Central at Fuente de la Hispanidad; daily 10am–9:30pm) east of downtown out by the university campus—it's where a lot of the young 'uns hang out and there are several nightspots on site—among whose more than 200 stores you'll also find a couple of galleries and craft shops.

NIGHTLIFE

Okay, it obviously ain't New York, London, Berlin, or Buenos Aires. But San José's *vida nocturna* is actually not half bad; there's *un poco* for everyone, whether your tastes run to laid-back lounge, hectic headbanging, casinos, techno-fueled boogie fever, whatever, and scattered throughout the city. Downtown, it's heavy on casinos (the one inside the Hotel Presidente, p. 25, is pretty good, if you like that sort of thing) and "gentlemen's" clubs (like Key Largo, that genteel-looking manse on the southeast corner of Morazán Park); many of the gay clubs are in this area, too. Here's a rundown of the capital's various vibes and scenes.

Swell 'n' Mellow

Starting on the low-key end, up in a quiet but up-and-coming area called **Barrio Escalante,** a mellow spot to start an evening out (perhaps before or after dinner at nearby **Olio;** p. 30) is the **Café Arte** at the **Academia de las Artes** (Av. 5; ☎ 278-3594; Tues–Wed and Sun 2pm–midnight, Fri–Sat 2pm–2am; no cover). Here in an appealing colonial building, a grab-bag of acts from magicians, storytellers, and musicians (including a well-known student classical ensemble called Editus) do their thing at 9pm most evenings. Then, around the corner, head for a drink at Rafa Rojas and Carlos Montalban's small **Ancora Lounge** (Calle 7 at Negritos, 575m/1,886 ft. north of Bagelmans; ☎ 224-7116; Mon–Thurs 9pm–midnight, Fri–Sun 9pm–1am), with a cool, alternative vibe, *minimalista* decor (modern art, a waterfall wall in back), and a soundtrack that might mix, say, chill-out, flamenco, and jazz.

Higher-Energy Watering Holes

West of downtown in Escazú/Santa Ana (especially the Escazú strip mall **Trejos Montealegre,** with bar-restaurants like **Five, Órale, Frankie Go,** and **La Cantina/ Fandango**) there are concentrations of buzzier, sometimes Americanized-feeling joints. You'll also find them north across the Torres River in the mall/entertainment complex **El Pueblo,** where party places include **Cocoloco** and **Twister.** But a good chunk of the game these days lies eastward, between toward and beyond the University of Costa Rica campus, in **Barrio California, Los Yoses,** and **San Pedro.** You can find updated listings in the *Tico Times* (and *La Nación,* if you read Spanish), but in the meantime, here's a good sampling of the spots where (mostly young) Josefinos and Ticos from the provinces are livin' *la pura vida loca.*

In **Barrio California,** a hot mini-nightlife district sprouts from the corner of Calle 23 and Avenida 1 (cabbies know it as just down from the Cine Magaly). The big kahuna, going strong since the 1970s, is right on that corner: the famous **El Cuartel de la Boca del Monte** ★ (☎ 221-0327; daily 6pm–2am or later; $3.85– $5.80 cover for performances). It's actually on the no-frills side—several darkish rooms with tables and chairs, plus a covered outdoor bar area with a handful of trees; on some nights the young, hip, and hot are just a-spillin' out onto the street—Ticos, expats, a few tourists, a little bit of everything. The bar staff slings some funky libation concoctions, and the tunes tend toward '80s and '90s new wave and rock. Or go artsy over on Calle 23: next to El Cuartel in a 70-year-old townhouse, the **Bar La Esquina** (no phone; Tues–Sat 7pm–whenever; varying cover for special events) is heavy on alt rock and modern art, while at the roomy, high-ceilinged **El Observatorio** (☎ 223-0725; Mon–Sat 6pm–2am; cover usually $4.85 for performances), owned by a local filmmaker, the schtick is movies—sometimes they do screenings—but the hook is more probably the three-beers-for-$2.90 specials.

From here, if you're still standing, you can always stumble down to the main drag (the continuation of Av. Central, right here it's also called Paseo Rubén Darío) and point yourself eastward toward the **Los Yoses** area (where some then refer to it as Bulevar Los Yoses). On your right, just before the Kentucky Fried Chicken, on one roof you'll spot a bunch of wire thingies shaped like onion domes, glowing in different colors. That would be **El Sultán** (☎ 884-8546; www. elsultanpub.com; Mon–Sat 11:45am–2pm and 5pm–2:15am; $2–$3), run by a big, bald, goateed Lebanese dude called Nabil. The music leans toward Latin pop, and all the Aladdins and Scheherezades are more focused on coaxing a buzz out of the bottle than a genie. A couple of blocks along, hang a right at the Subaru dealership, and a few doors down you'll come to **Qbico** (25m/82 ft. south of Subaru dealer; ☎ 225-5696; daily 11:30am–2am; Fri–Sat cover $3.85) a big, angular-roofed, '60s-type house—can't miss it thanks to all the cars out front. Argentine owner Gabriel Gallini has created a scene that's like the hippest house party in San José, with three bars, a chill/electronica soundtrack (DJs Thurs–Sat), and a fab new landscaped area out back with South Beach–style beds and such; most partiers are in their early 20s to early 30s, with a smattering of older folks; there's a Mediterranean-Argentine menu, too.

Another several blocks east, on the south side of Bulevar Los Yoses, you'll come to a neighborhood classic since the 1980s: **Rio** (150m/500 ft. west of Automercado; ☎ 225-8371; riobar@ice.co.cr; daily noon–2am), an indoor-outdoor cafe-bar with a sports-bar feel, due to the slew of screens big and small, usually with some game or other going full-throttle. It's a festive, unpretentious, mixed-age bunch, just hanging and listening to the Latin pop and '80s tunes (or chowing down on sandwiches and bar food, if they're hungry like the wolf). For happy hour and big soccer matches, of course, it's a friendly mob scene.

On the other side of the highway in San Pedro itself, another nightlife cluster 4 blocks east of the mall, just north of the Church of San Pedro and south of the university campus, is the place to see college kids letting loose. A 3-block stretch dubbed **La Calle de Amargura** ("Bitterness Street") is *the* big student hangout, bopping nightly and on weekends positively packed with sometimes rowdy young 'uns blowing off steam and tying one on at spots like **Omar Khayyam** (☎ 253-8455), **Terra U** (☎ 225-4261), and **Tavarua** (☎ 225-4279); generally hours run Monday through Saturday noon till 1 or 2am. Now, on my last visit, folks told us they though things were getting a little *too* rowdy and rough. If you want to wade in, chances are you'll be fine—just use your noggin, please, and you'll keep the bitterness on the street to a minimum.

Dance Clubs

Right above **Rio,** with its entrance just around the corner, the small, attitudinous **Nova Rio Lounge** (☎ 283-1548; Tues–Sat 8pm–4am, later Fri–Sat; gals $1.95, guys $3.85) is the cutting-edge urban-chic dance lounge of *el momento,* bathed in icy-blue light and packed with under-30 hotties both male and female; the soundtrack is house and electronica, Latin on Fridays and Saturdays, and there's a menu of bocas and a few sophisto entrees like Katmandu salmon.

If that's a little too rarefied for you, head down the road apiece to the San Pedro mall and join the krazy kidz in the basement-level **Touch** (☎ 280-1777 or 280-7717; Fri–Sat 8pm–4am; cover $3.85), as they pick each other up to the throb of Latin and reggaetón beats and ogle the eye-candy girls and boys of a singing/dancing group deeply irritatingly named Grupo Swingy Boom.

Or kick it up a few notches and go all the way at San José's premier big-boom-boom dance club west of downtown. **Vértigo** (Edificio Colón, Paseo Colón between calles 38 and 40; ☎ 257-8424; www.vertigocr.com; daily 10pm–sunrise; cover $3.85–$8.70) is cavernous (it "officially" holds 850) and specializes in electronica well on the far side of midnight.

Live Music

A number of the above nightspots have live music on a regular or semiregular basis, such as **Bar La Esquina** and the **Cuartel de la Boca del Monte** (see above), whose next-door annex **El Cuartel,** quieter most nights, on Mondays is packed to the rafters for the live music (mostly Latin, or as one manager described it to us, *"chiki-chiki"*). But personally, my favorite venue—still hot but slightly more sophisticated—is out east in San Pedro. Behind a gabled brick facade and big revolving neon sign, **Jazz Café** (Av. Central, next to Banco Popular; ☎ 253-8933; www.jazzcafecostarica.com; daily 6pm–2am; cover $4.85–$5.80) has since 1999 been one of Chepe's most killer live-music venues—not just jazz, but blues, R&B, salsa, Latin pop, world music from Ireland to Senegal, and a smattering of alternative sounds (sometimes the names are pretty darn big, à la Juanes and Chucho Valdez). Shows start at 10pm, and the energy bouncing off these exposed brick walls and concrete floor can be incredible—and the menu ain't half bad, either.

Gay Nightlife

And finally, San José boasts the best gay nightlife in Central America—even if that's not saying a whole helluva lot. Costa Rica is the region's least bigoted country, and San José has the most queer nightspots and lodgings (even a sauna) of probably any burg between Mexico City and Rio de Janeiro. Two spots we find particularly festive are **Bochinche** (Paseo de los Estudiantes, Calle 11 between avs. 10 and 12; ☎ 221-0500; Wed–Thurs 8pm–3am, Fri–Sat 8pm–5am; cover $3.85–$7.75), a sleek split-level video bar that gets so packed that last time it set the mezzanine floor vibrating and we admit we were getting a touch worried; and the cavernous, two-story **La Avispa** (Calle 1 between avs. 8 and 10, 250m/820 ft. south of Banco Popular; ☎ 223-5343; www.laavispa.co.cr; Thurs–Sun 8pm–3am; $2–$4, Sun 5–6pm free), which recently got a face-lift after a quarter-century and is lookin' better than ever. It's got three bars, two dance floors, an eclectic playlist, a big bunch of palms right in the middle of things, and tables/chairs on an upstairs catwalk from which you can check out all the action from on high. At both these clubs you'll see more boys than girls, but Avispa does have ladies-only nights twice a month (usually a Wed or Fri). Meanwhile, southwest of downtown, **Club Oh!** (Calle 2 between avs. 12 and 14, under the Clínica Bíblica; ☎ 248-1500 and 248-1424; www.clubohcr.com; Mon, Wed, and Fri–Sat 9pm–4am; cover $7.70, VIP lounge $12), the former Déjà Vu, is airport-hangar huge (holds 2,000) and its bone-rattling sound system outputs heavier on house and electronica. The cover's on the steep side for San José, but it does buy you open bar 9pm to midnight or 1am, and there's still a line of cute guys out the door most nights. Get info on other spots at www.gaycostarica.com.

THE CENTRAL VALLEY

Want to get to know the real, quintessential Costa Rica? Dumb question, you're reading this book, right? Well, it's not out at the beach, even if that's where most of the tourists flock. It's here in the Valle Central, aka the Meseta Central—9,000 rolling to mountainous sq. km (3,500 sq. miles) 900 to 1,500m (3,000–5,000 ft.) above sea level, ringed by spectacular mountain ranges like the Cordilleras Central, de Talamanca, and Tilarán. Tiquicia's heartland is the country's mini-me,

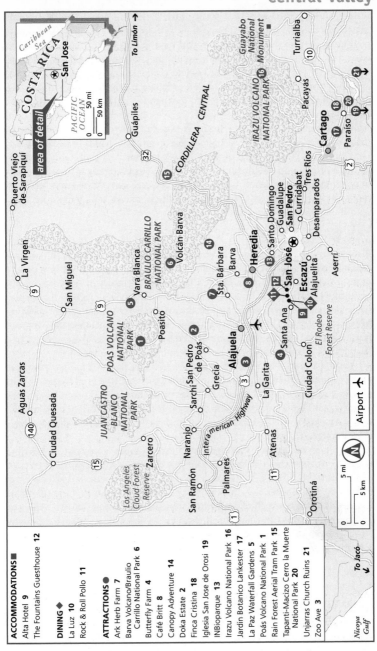

ACCOMMODATIONS ■
Alta Hotel **9**
The Fountains Guesthouse **12**

DINING ◆
La Luz **10**
Rock & Roll Pollo **11**

ATTRACTIONS ●
Ark Herb Farm **7**
Barva Volcano/Braulio
  Carrillo National Park **6**
Butterfly Farm **4**
Café Britt **8**
Canopy Adventure **14**
Doka Estate **2**
Finca Cristina **18**
Iglesia San Jose de Orosi **19**
INBioparque **13**
Irazu Volcano National Park **16**
Jardin Botanico Lankester **17**
La Paz Waterfall Gardens **5**
Poás Volcano National Park **1**
Rain Forest Aerial Tram Park **15**
Tapanti-Macizo Cerro la Muerte
  National Park **20**
Unjarras Church Ruins **21**
Zoo Ave **3**

a microclimate-filled mix of fetching little cities and towns, rolling farmland (especially coffee), and wild preserves full of rainforests, whitewater rivers, and volcanoes. Besides the historic spots that have helped make Costa Rica's identity what it is, here you can also catch most all the kinds of eco-wonders the country is famous for (well, except maybe the mass turtle nestings on the beaches) within a 2-hour drive of the capital. And you can base yourself in its charming bigger cities: Alajuela (historic cradle of Tico independence), Heredia (beautiful downtown, lots of college kids), and Cartago (former capital, site of one of Central America's top pilgrimage churches). Or you can opt to stay out in countryside that can be as spectacular and memorable as any you'll find in Guanacaste, the Osa Peninsula, Monteverde, or what have you—but lots easier going, roadwise. In the morning you could be crashing down Class IV rapids or spotting quetzals in a primeval-feeling cloud forest, visiting a coffee estate that afternoon, and at night catch a play or concert, down a world-class meal, then party your butt off with hundreds of young Ticos.

LAY OF THE LAND

Roughly in the middle of the country, the 9,000-sq.-km (3,500-sq.-mile) Valle or Meseta Central has San José just below its center, and includes sections of several other provinces, all of which have their provincial capitals in the valley. A dozen or so miles northwest of San José, **Alajuela** is Costa Rica's second biggest city, a lively burg with the national airport on its outskirts, a great central park, some history (hometown of Costa Rica's national hero and the museum devoted to him), and neat nearby attractions like Poás Volcano, Doka coffee estate, La Paz Waterfall Gardens, and Sarchí, the crafts and furniture capital of the country.

Around 11km (7 miles) both east of Alajuela and north of San José, the eponymous capital of **Heredia** province is another charmer, and even livelier thanks to all the students at the Universidad Nacional and various other local schools. Heredia, too, has a local volcano (Barva) and coffee icon (Britt), plus one of the major national wilderness parks and some of the better Central Valley dining outside San José.

The third major area, **Cartago,** is 23km (14 miles) southeast of San José, a sleepier city than the first two. Darned if it doesn't have its very own volcano as well—Irazú—but some folks know it more for its elaborate basilica Nuestra Señora de los Angeles, which pulls in pilgrims from all over Central America. Nearby, visitors in search of ancient mysteries should check out the Indian ruins at Gayabo and nature and adrenaline junkies won't want to miss Turrialba with its fab whitewater rafting, or the gorgeous Orosi Valley with its small town/rural vibe and great B&Bs.

ALAJUELA

If you've flown into Santamaría International Airport, you've already been to the outskirts of Costa Rica's second largest city (pop. 43,000), just over a 19km (12 miles) northwest of San José. On a hillside at the base of Poás volcano, the 226-year-old "City of Mangos" was the national capital for a year in the 19th century, and has been paying its bills for much of its existence thanks to coffee and sugar cane, but it's also famous because of an *"erizo"* (hedgehog). That would be Juan Santamaría—the dude the airport's named after—a drummer boy with a hedgehog-like bristle-cut who became the country's top national hero back in 1856, getting killed while foiling U.S. mercenaries under William Walker (see sidebar). There's a plaza named after Santamaría complete with statue; the main "sight" in town is the museum on him and his period in history; and every April 11 the city becomes ground zero for the big national holiday, El Día del Erizo. As with every other Tico city and town, Alajuela (pronounced "ah-lah-HWAY-lah") is built around its central park—in this case the Parque de Los Mangos, which does indeed sport some large, lush, and lovely fruit trees of this ilk. It's an easy place to like—the climate's sweet (rarely above 85°F/29°C or below 62°F/17°C), the people friendly, and even though it's maybe not the most exciting burg around, it does have some nice and even historic lodgings both in and out of town, and makes a pleasant base to explore the rest of the Central Valley and even up through the Arenal area and out to the Central Pacific coast. If you're not crazy about overnighting in San José, it's an easy commute to there, too.

Alajuela is also Costa Rica's second largest province, beautiful and vividly varied, with more than 700,000 people. In this chapter, however, we're just covering the highlights of its southernmost reaches, the Central Valley part surrounding the provincial capital. But the rest of its nearly 9,800 sq. km (3,800 sq. miles) just goes on and on and on, north up to the Nicaragua border and westward along borders with Puntarenas and then Guanacaste, including Arenal (p. 92), Rincón de la Vieja National Park (p. 292), and the Caño Negro Wildlife Refuge (p. 106)— there's so much, in fact, that we couldn't fit it all into a single chapter. In the area

The Tale of the Heroic Hedgehog

Statues were built to him; plazas, a museum, and the national airport named after him; his death's commemorated every April 11 as "Hedgehog Day"; and he's been idolized by generations of Tico schoolkids. He's Costa Rica's official national hero, Juan Santamaría, a poor kid in the Alajuela militia who was part of the campaign to keep William Walker and his merry band of mercenaries from taking over Costa Rica and the rest of Central America and annexing it all to the U.S. slave states. (The whole "hedgehog" thing, by the way, was because of Johnny's spiky hairdo.) Walker and Co. tried to invade Guanacaste in 1856, but a makeshift army of Costa Rican peasants marched up, kicked their butts (p. 14), and chased them over the border into southern Nicaragua. Here, during the famous Battle of Rivas, the gringos holed up in a wood fort and kept firing away at the Ticos, who couldn't pry them out. The captain asked for volunteers to set the fort afire, and supposedly it was Santamaría to the rescue, running and throwing a torch, even as he was getting shot to death by the Walker gang.

Is any of it true? Who knows, maybe some. What's clear is that until the 1890s, practically nobody'd heard of the dude, until the grand poobahs in the régime of the time needed a hero figure to help pull its disgruntled, disorganized subjects together. So it was a convenient mix of fact and fib that got turned into national myth. Not so different from anywhere else in the world, really.

within easiest striking distance of San José, there's Poás (p. 56) as well as attractions like the Doka coffee estate (p. 56); the touristy but still amazing La Paz Waterfall Gardens complex ★ (p. 57); wildlife attractions like Zoo Ave (p. 57) and the Butterfly Farm (p. 58); and the crafts and woodworking up in the towns of Sarchí. You could easily spend a week just seeing and doing all there is within a couple hours' drive of Alajuela city. And while you're at it, you'll come away with an especially good sense of what Costa Rica and the Costa Ricans are all about. Get more info online at www.alajuelavirtual.com.

Getting to & Around Alajuela

Downtown is 2.5km (1½ miles) from the airport and 20km (13 miles) from San José; driving, take the Interamerican Highway toward the airport, then after passing through the toll booth, take the exit marked ALAJUELA after the first light. Between 4am and 10pm, **TUASA buses** (☎ 442-6900) leave San José from La Merced park west of downtown every 5 minutes for the 45-minute trip to Alajuela, with a fare equal to 60¢. The city itself is laid out in a straightforward, easily walkable grid.

Accommodations, Both Standard & Not

There's a reasonably good variety of digs, both in town, in the countryside, and of course out by the airport (many of them cookie-cutter chains, if you're into that—but if you were, you wouldn't be reading this book). If you're looking to keep it cheap, cheap, cheap, there's a simple but clean hostel in town, the **Villa Real** (Av. 3 at Calle 1; ☎ 441-4022; villarealcr@hotmail.com; $9 per bed). And keep in mind that after what you read about Alajuela's climate in the intro above, air-conditioning is not usually necessary, and quite a few places don't have it.

VACATION RENTALS

Out in the Central Valley there's a smattering of houses and condos for rent by the day or week, but as it's not a vacation destination, it's practically nowheresville compared to what's available on the coasts (especially the Pacific). The choices here, as in San José (p. 21), are far more limited, and few agencies handle multiple properties. Mostly you'll be dealing with individual owners, either through their own websites or clearinghouses like **RentCostaRica.com**, **VRBO.com**, **VacationRentals.com**, and **Villa4Vacation.com**. Others are units owned by inns or B&Bs. You can also check the real estate classifieds on local websites like **www.amcostarica.com**. But there are a handful of worthy options.

Right near the center of downtown, the **Hotel 1915** (☎ 441-0495; 1915Hotel@ice.co.cr) rents out a trio of cozy two-bedroom/two-bath apartments off a quiet interior courtyard, with tile floors, full kitchens, cable TV, phones, and a homey, comfy, low-key (some might even say nondescript) decor for $100 a night for up to four people.

If you feel green acres is the place to be (where, of course, you'll really need your own wheels), head a half-hour's drive southeast of the city to the town of Atenas, where the country inn **El Cafetal** (☎ 446-5785; www.cafetal.com; p. 51) maintains a pair of fetchingly woody two-bedroom/two-bath houses tucked amid greenery. They've got tile floors; new, fully equipped kitchens; outdoor patios, and lots of windows and French doors. And we especially like the blue-and-white-tile

Alajuela

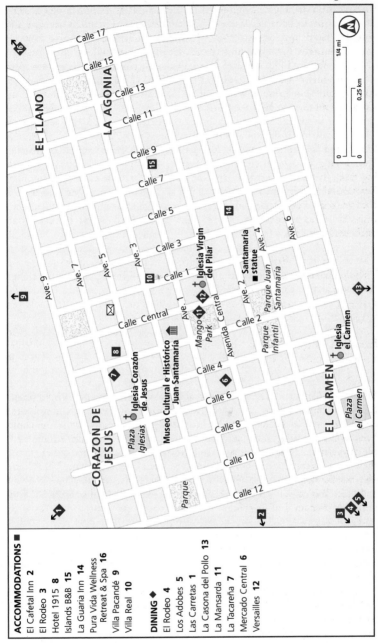

ACCOMMODATIONS ■
El Cafetal Inn **2**
El Rodeo **3**
Hotel 1915 **8**
Islands B&B **15**
La Guaria Inn **14**
Pura Vida Wellness
  Retreat & Spa **16**
Villa Pacandé **9**
Villa Real **10**

DINING ◆
El Rodeo **4**
Los Adobes **5**
Las Carretas **1**
La Casona del Pollo **13**
La Mansarda **11**
La Tacareña **7**
Mercado Central **6**
Versailles **12**

bathroom in the main house because of its sunken Jacuzzi tub and picture window looking out into a landscaped minicourtyard. The house by the river sleeps four for $80 daily or $500 to $550 weekly, and the other sleeps six for $100 a day or $600 to $650 a week (both have a 2-day minimum).

Over east of Alajuela city in La Garita, near the eco-attraction **Zoo Ave** (p. 57), the three pink **Villa Rita Country Cottages** (☎ 487-7566; www.villaritacountry cottages.com), on a gated spread with pool and tennis court, are yours for $215 to $255 per week in high season (if available, they also rent by the day for $50), including breakfast. Sleeping up to three, they're fully equipped, well kept, and the decor comfy, if slightly on the old-fashioned side (turned wood bed spindles, rustic night tables; owners Rita and Jennifer run a quilting circle, if that floats your boat).

Some 17 miles (30 km) west of the city, outside the town of Palmares not far from Sarchí, Canadian **Robert Smith** (☎ 453-3844) rents several one- and two-bedroom villas with cable TV, DSL, ceiling fans, and a common hot tub and pool, for $75 to $125 per day ($395–$495 per week, and $925–$1,250 per month). All the units have wood-beam ceilings but otherwise vary a bit in feel, from woody to white stucco to a bit more colorful, from old-fashioned to slightly more contemporary. They're adorned with nice homey details, like floral arrangements and touches of art on the walls, and dark woods are a theme throughout, from the kitchen cabinets to the platform beds.

HOTELS

$ A good in-town option, the **Islands B&B** (Av. 1 between calles 7 and 9, 50m/164 ft. west of Iglesia La Agonía; ☎ 442-0573; IslandsBB@hotmail.com; AE, MC, V) is a comfy but not fancy place to crash right near the center of things. Fabio and Lorena Quesada's two-story place around the corner from the mighty impressive Agonía church offer nine clean, basic rooms with rustic tile floors, private baths, a clothes rack, ceiling fans, and that's it. But the price is right (doubles $39, including breakfast), the staff friendly, and the place cute and homey; a common TV room overlooks a plant-lined courtyard with a mossy stone fountain and pond with goldfish. Cute, cheap, and friendly—but that "Islands" thing, we just don't get it (the owners say they bought the place already named).

$ With its gracious arched windows and red-tile roof, white-stucco **Villa Pacandé** (road to Poás volcano, 2.5km/1½ miles north of Parque de los Mangos; ☎ 441-6795; www.villapacande.com; AE, MC, V) is one of the better countryside deals, and one that's an easy 2.5km (1½ mile) away from town to boot. On a good-size spread out in the country, it's got a lovely backyard great for bird-watching, plus six rooms that're on the simple side, but fresh and attractive, with TVs, private baths, and lots of light. Digs start at just $33 for a double (breakfast included); $43 snags you two queen beds, more space, and a balcony (and breakfast, of course). One nice perk here is Internet access (connections in rooms and a station outside). Owner Cecilia Tamayo and her family also run an even cheaper (but still nice and clean) eight-room place downtown, the **Hotel Pacandé** (www.hotel pacande.com; doubles $17–$39), and they'll spring for your taxi from the airport to either property.

$–$$ A sucker for the atmosphere of a bygone era? At downtown's **Hotel 1915** ★★ (Calle 2 between avs. 5 and 7, 275m/902 ft. north of central park; ☎ 441-0495; 1915Hotel@ice.co.cr; AE, MC, V), welcome to nostalgiaville. Owner Adela Vargas grew up in this stucco-and-brick house built (guess when?) by her cattle-and-coffee-farmer grandpa, and the old-timey touches make this one of Alajuela's prettiest places to park your buggy: antiques, stone arches, cement mosaic-tile floors, a grand staircase, cathedral ceiling, two parlors, and fetching gardens and fountains. The 17 rooms have the same feel (bamboo, wood-beam ceilings), yet they're also tricked out with all the amenities—A/C (well, in 90 percent of them), cable, phone, Wi-Fi, hair dryer, safe, and skylit bath; two also have fridges. There's now a roof terrace with hot tub, and the included breakfast, served in the pretty garden area, is a cut above the usual, with hot treats like omelettes and French toast. Considering the perks, location, and history, I'd say $45 for a double is darn fine; admittedly, that gets you one of the smaller rooms, either with viewless windows or none at all, but you can upgrade for a still very reasonable $65. *One caveat:* Because Doña Adela refuses to pay kickbacks to taxi drivers, some will tell you 1915 is closed or whatever. They're lying, the buggers.

$–$$ You also get considerable kick for your *colones* at the three-story **La Guaria Inn** ★ (Av. 2 between calles 1 and 3, 225m east of Parque Santamaría; ☎ 440-2948; LaGuariaHotel@netscape.net; AE, MC, V), in a green-and-yellow, semicolonial house with wrought-iron balconies just south of Mango Park. Not only do the 25 rooms offer a significant soupçon of style (colorful bedspreads and prints on the blue walls, white-iron headboards), but 10 have air-conditioning (the rest just ceiling fans), 8 have their own balconies, and all have cable TV. On top of that, they've recently put in a swell free-form pool with bar and outdoor shower, have Internet stations in the lobby ($2 for a half-hour), and on-site parking. Especially considering it's right in town, well, it ain't too shabby for $45 double, including breakfast ($53 if you want A/C); you could bump yourself up to a junior suite for $64, which is still pretty sweet. All this, and they're suspiciously friendly, too.

$$ Java junkies might cop a nice buzz from **El Cafetal Inn** ★ (next to Bar-Restaurant El Rincón del Indio Rómulo; ☎ 446-5785; www.cafetal.com; AE, MC, V), run by Romy and Lilián Cortes Saavedra since 1997 in Santa Eulalia, outside the town of Atenas. The inn is set right in the middle of the 2.4-hectare (6-acre) family-owned coffee plantation *(cafetal),* but don't expect old and quaint—it's more on the modern side, but warmly and *very* tastefully done. I just love the semi-open-air lobby adorned with pre-Columbian artifacts; the huge glass alcoves with sweeping views; the good-size pool; the poolside restaurant (great breakfast buffet, included in the rate); and the hiking trails to a river and waterfall. You can get a tour of the coffee operation and sample and/or buy their house-brand joe, La Negrita. And if you still haven't had enough of the bean, have Norma the masseuse give you a coffee scrub (that and a massage will run you $40). The 10 units are gorgeously decorated in earth tones and stylish murals, and have fabulous baths with raised Jacuzzi tubs, but no TV or A/C. They range from the smaller Cafetal rooms for $90 double ($80 if you take it for at least a week) to

$150 for a two-story poolside bungalow; you can knock 17 percent off the rate if you pay in cash or travelers' checks. Dog lovers will have a ball romping with Panda, Chuy, and Loli.

$$–$$$ It's not PC to say this, but in Costa Rica you'll hear the phrase *"pura vida!"* so much it you might start wanting to slap people—the literal translation ("pure life!") doesn't quite convey the meaning, an all-purpose ejaculation of wonderfulness along the lines of "way awesome!" Well, we've gotta say, **Pura Vida Wellness Retreat & Spa** (700m/2,296m from Cantina Apolo 15; ☎ 483-0033, or 888/767-7375 in the U.S.; www.puravidaspa.com; MC, V) has been around since the mid-'80s and is in fact pretty awesome if you're focused on a serene (if gringo-flavored) getaway—and especially if you're into yoga. On a hilltop near the town of Carrizal, just under 8km (5 miles) north of Alajuela city, 3.2 lush hectares (8 acres) of gardens and rainforest have been turned into a lovely full-service resort—a fair-size pool, big hot tub, boutique, spa, bar, restaurant, and rec room—which also happens to have five yoga halls and a "meditation tower." The 50 units range from tent cabins (sorry, "tentalows") up to luxe, Japanese-pagoda-style bungalows. Keep in mind that the cheaper rooms have shared baths—so you might think $95 for the tent cabins and $103 for the standard rooms seems a bit of a ripoff (rooms with private baths start at $116). But at least that includes all meals (which are mostly vegetarian, but also include fish and chicken), and the folks in the kitchen will do their best to work with your food preferences, allergies, and so forth. Another thing we like: We're not into the overly touchy-feely stuff some New Age-style retreats are so fond of—and neither is Pura Vida. The spirituality is there, for sure, but it's nicely balanced by the resort side of things. Oh, what the hey—*pura vida, mae!*

$$$ Down south of the airport, between Alajuela city and San José, the Jiménez-family-owned **El Rodeo** ★ 🧒 (Carretera Belén, diagonally across from Panasonic; ☎ 293-3909; www.elrodeohotel.com; MC, V) is a real find in the town of San Antonio de Belén. It's got just 29 rooms but the look and feel of a bigger resort—lush landscaping, trellis-screened pool with waterfall (and volcano views), hot tub, kids' pool, tennis court, room service, playground, spa, outdoor lounging areas, and two eateries (including a steakhouse that's popular with Ticos all over the area; p. 54). Wi-Fi, too. We dig the spacious rooms at least as much, with their polished wood-plank floors, high ceilings, wonderful closet space, and elegant look—lots o' green—and it goes without saying they deliver the extras you'd expect, like A/C, cable, etc; most also have some kind of balcony or porch. Units can sleep up to three and start at $105 and junior suites at $112 (double occupancy), including breakfast in a dramatic eatery/bar with a soaring ceiling and huge wrought-iron chandelier.

Dining for All Tastes

We've found Alajuela to be a decent eating town—maybe not quite as good and varied as Heredia, but certainly inexpensive for the most part (most of the better and more upscale restaurants are outside the city). As with every Costa Rican city, you'll find scads of inexpensive *sodas* lining the streets, with solid fare that's pretty interchangeable. Actually, one of our favorite places for a feed is the traditional covered market a block west of Mango Park, the **Mercado Central** (between Av. 1 and Central, calles 4 and 6; Mon–Fri 7am–7pm, Sat 7am–5pm). Not only can you get oodles of noodles and other good, inexpensive fare at all the sodas and lunch counters in here, but you get to eat it while doing some primo people-watching. One of our favorites in here is over near the southeast corner, **Delicias Marinas** (☎ 443-4270; Mon–Sat 7am–5pm; cash only). Yep, that means "marine delicacies"—this may be up in the Meseta Central, but the coast is close, and here the ceviches and sea bass really rock (they also have nonmarine stuff), and we didn't notice a thing for more than $3.65. And now for our other top picks in and out of town:

$ Marie Antoinette would've gotten her knickers in a bunch and had the owner's heads lopped off for christening their downtown eatery **Versailles** (Calle Central, between Av. 2 and Central, 50m/164 ft. south of cathedral; ☎ 443-0667; daily 8am–7pm; cash only). Fluorescent lights? *Mais non, parbleu!* But so what if the joint is just a couple of notches above a *soda?* The *comida típica* is nicely executed, and the prices unbeatable—the 11am–2:30pm lunch buffet is $3.10, *casados* (meat or fish plus several sides) $3.50, and main dishes at dinner average $6.75 (try the pork chops, in mushroom sauce or *à l'orange*). And talk about "let them eat cake"—them pastries in the glass case by the window (68¢–77¢) are definitely worth leaving room for, as is the nice, cinnammony *arroz con leche* (rice pudding). And Marie be darned—I do kinda like the homey terrazzo floors, nice wood tables, and leather-and-wood chairs.

$–$$ If you do make it up to the crafts towns of Sarchí, **Las Carretas** (next to Joaquín Chaverri oxcart emporium; ☎ 454-1633; daily 9am–7pm; AE, MC, V) is admittedly a teensy bit touristy (tour groups stop in for lunch on a regular basis). But it's cute—beamed ceilings, wooden window bars, wagon-wheel chandeliers, and a salad bar made out of the colorfully painted oxcarts that is Costa Rica's biggest icon. It also has beautiful views over the valley, and it's convenient—right next door to the main maker and seller of the oxcarts and other tourist tchotchkes that most people make the trip up here for. And oh yeah, the food is actually pretty darn good; I like the chicken in heart-of-palm sauce ($7.50), veggie burrito ($5.60), the fresh-cut french fries, and especially the flan ($1.15), one of the best I've had anywhere, period. And filling *casados* for four bucks? Not bad.

$–$$ Ticos do love their chicken, and **La Casona del Pollo** 🅺🅸🅳🆂 (200m/656 ft. north of Balneario Ojo de Agua; ☎ 442-1359; www.lacasonadelpollo.com; daily 10am–10pm; AE, MC, V), between the airport and a popular water park, is a family favorite for its ambience, prices, and setting (amid coffee fields; there's also a little playground). A big, open-air place with faux brick columns and red-tile floors, it does a fine job of serving up our feathered friends every which way— barbecue, grilled, in lasagna, with lemon or mushroom or white-wine sauce—for around $3.85 to $4.85; the specialty, though, is fried ($1.85 per portion, $7.35 for a whole bird). There are plenty of non-*pollo* dishes, too; *casados* will set you back $3.40; and don't miss the *tres leches* ($1.25), a sopping-wet Nicaraguan cake topped with whipped cream. Then top it off with some fab homemade molasses candies, on the house. The joint gets jumping on weekends, when local bands serenade; otherwise, the music comes from a jukebox that's a virtual Latin music hall of fame.

$–$$ A couple of blocks north of Mango Park, **La Tacareña** (Av. 7 at Calle 2; ☎ 441-2662; daily 11am–midnight, later on weekends; V) is a little three-room place founded in 1961 on the corner of a popular food stand that'd been there more than 40 years. But be it ever so pedigreed, it's still unpretentious and intensely local-feeling, with a big-screen TV and wood-plank walls plastered with old soccer posters and record-album covers (Andy Gibb and Rod Stewart— *nooooo!*). You can stop in for a light nosh or a full meal; *casados* cost $3.50 and entrees up to $7.75; I'm particularly partial to the *pollo al cazador* (chicken in pepper sauce with just a hint of sweetness). Folks seem to like the pizza here, too.

$$ Another downtown Alajuela favorite, **La Mansarda** (Calle Central between avs. 2 and Central, 25m/82 ft. south of Mango Park; ☎ 441-4390; daily 11am–1am; AE, MC, V) is run by an expat from Sicily, and it's a little unusual in that it's on the second floor of a nondescript building, over a general goods store called Karnaval. It still has an old-fashioned vibe but also a bit more of an upscale feel than some of the other eateries nearby (pink-and-ochre tablecloths, green iron cafe chairs with plaid upholstery, colonial-Spanish-style lanterns). There are local dishes here, but much of the menu tends toward international—give a thought to the seafood pasta ($6.50), the sea bass in white mushroom sauce ($7.45), or the lemon chicken ($6.60). In the evening there's a bit of a low-key bar scene. All in all, a nice place for a bite or a sip.

$$ Where's the beef? South of Alajuela city, in the town of San Rafael, keep an eye peeled for the blue-and-white stucco front of the longstanding **Los Adobes** (200m/656 ft. west of Panasonic; ☎ 239-0957; Mon–Fri 11am–9:30pm, Sat 11am–midnight, Sun 11am–6pm; AE, MC, V), which has developed quite a local following thanks to its laid-back, semiopen atmosphere; its live music on Fridays and Saturdays; and its *lomito* (beef). Mostly around $9, the steak here comes grilled, breaded, with onions, in jalapeño sauce, filet mignon, you name it (there's other stuff on the menu, too, of course). You chow down out back on a polished-concrete terrace screened by thick tropical vines and bushes. And you'll probably be the only gringo here. By the way, it's just up the road apiece from the **Butterfly Farm** in La Guácima (see below).

$$–$$$ Normally we wouldn't plug a steakhouse so close by when we just finished going mad for the cow at Los Adobes, but just down the road a piece, **El Rodeo** ★ 🛈 (Carretera Belén, diagonally across from Panasonic; ☎ 293-3909; www.elrodeohotel.com; Mon–Sat noon–10pm, Sun noon–4:30pm; AE, MC, V) is a case apart. Long before it was the resort we've touted above, El Rodeo was one of the Central Valley's best-known steakhouses, founded by the Jiménez family more than a quarter century ago. It's a little pricier than most other places (outside San José, at least)—most of the top-quality cuts run about $10 to $16 and max out at $18 for the "super T-bone"—but it's whither locals mosey when they want a special night out. Part of the fun is the cowboy decor (hey, Costa Rica has its *sabaneros*—jes' canter on over to our Guanacaste chapter), which stops just short of hokey: crowned with a high-pitched wood-plank roof, the huge room features saloon doors, cowhide sofas, and saddles all over the place. You can also get fish and chicken, by the way, but vegetarians need not apply.

Why You're Here: The Top Sights & Attractions
ALAJUELA

You'll want to start with the **downtown core,** which shouldn't take you too long to do—it's a nice way to spend a couple of hours. The obligatory main plaza, the *parque central,* is often referred to as the **Parque de los Mangos** (Mango Park) because just guess what it's full of? On any given day, and above all weekends, it's also full of *alajuenses* relaxing and hanging out; you'll see a lot of retired old guys sitting on benches chewing the fat; kids feeding pigeons, eating shaved ice, and being jollied up by clowns; the inevitable Andean music group (if we hear "El Cóndor Pasa" one more time . . .). I'm not a big fan of that cheesy '70s-looking bandstand, or of the McDonalds on the south side of the square, but for the most part the architecture around the park is a fetching mix of Art Deco (like the theater that's now a MegaSuper supermarket) and colonial—especially the whitewashed **cathedral** built in 1854. It's a stately neoclassical with two bell towers, a red cupola toward the back, and a simple interior (a couple of ex-presidents are stashed in here). But partly because it's not part of the square but behind a fence across the street, and partly because of all those mango trees, it doesn't dominate the plaza quite like you see in most other Costa Rican cities and towns. In a way, the building that catches the eye the most is the Ministry of Education on the north side. With a castlelike notched roof parapet and painted drab brown, it used to be the local jail, but now the main reason for visitors to give a hoot is around its backside.

Here, a block above the park and around the corner, several rooms and a pretty little courtyard have been turned into the **Museo Cultural e Histórico Juan Santamaría** (Av. 3 between calles 2 and Central, 1 block north of Mango Park; ☎ 441-4775; www.museojuansantamaria.go.cr; Tues–Sun 10am–5:30pm; free), named after the young hedgehog we mentioned above (p. 47). It's a moderately interesting look at the mid-19th-century beginnings of Costa Rica as a country, including U.S. soldier of fortune William Walker's stab at taking over and the resistance of Ticos including their doughty hero Juan Santamaría. The old printing presses are cool, as are the paintings of Mango Park during that era. But the exhibits are in Spanish, so unless you *habla español,* you will likely miss a good chunk of it, and won't be able to take advantage of the guided tours between 9am and 4:30pm Tuesdays through Fridays.

And that, friends, is pretty much it. Sure, you can and should take a stroll a couple of blocks south of Mango Park to check out the **statue of Juan Santamaría** in the recently remodeled plaza named for him. The covered **central market** a block west of the park (see intros for the dining and shopping sections, above) is definitely worth a wander. And you shouldn't pass up the 4-block detour due east of Mango Park to take in the excruciatingly named but striking **Iglesia de la Agonía,** another large whitewashed church but more impressive than the cathedral on the main plaza, with a more elaborate baroque feel, including graceful curlicues and an elegant central tower. But once you're through with these, you've pretty much done "the sights" of Alajuela city.

OUTSIDE ALAJUELA

Of the rest of what's worth seeing in the southern sector of this sprawling province, the biggest deal is the 6,400-hectare (16,000-acre) **Poás Volcano National Park** ★★ ✱ (☎ 482-2165; www.costarica-nationalparks.com/poasvolcanonationalpark. html; daily 8am–4pm). Of the three big Central Valley volcano parks (the others being Barva in Heredia and Irazú in Cartago), this park is our fave for several reasons. One is that it's still active (don't worry, not dangerously) and lets you know it with geysers and fumaroles shooting up all over the place (though no lava, like up at Arenal). Another is that not only is the drive up fairly short from San José (64km/40 miles) and Alajuela city (30km/19 miles) and scenic as the dickens, but the road in takes you practically up to the rim of the crater; you pile out at a mod-looking visitors' center with a shop, eatery, and exhibits, then stroll 10 minutes up to the main crater of the volcano (which maxes out at 2,670m high (8,900 ft.); the Escalonia trail leads from here through mossy, bromeliad-crammed cloud forest down to a second lake, but that's it for trails in this park). It's popular with locals, so we advise avoiding weekends, when lots of families and others drive up for an outing. The drive up, which takes you past coffee and strawberry fields, and fern and flower plantations, gets more pulchritudinous the higher you get—the scenery (and sometimes the architecture) turns Alpine and the fog creeps in on little cat feet, and the craggy profile of Poás looms above, appearing to issue clouds to billow out over the valley. In the park itself, you walk past prehistoric-looking "poor man's umbrella" plants, with red-veined leafs a half-dozen feet wide, up to the blue-greenish main lake, 4,330 feet (1,320m) wide, 985 feet (300m) deep, and an average temperature of 104°F (40°C). Dress warmly and bring rain gear—the mist can get so wet they call it "horizontal rain." And don't be surprised, as happened on our last visit, if it's *so* darn foggy you can't see the lakes at all; sometimes Mother Nature can be damn uncooperative. If you're coming out here from San José, you might also consider doing it as an escorted tour; one local outfit we like is **Expediciones Tropicales** (☎ 257-4171; www.costaricainfo.com), whose 5-hour tour ($36) includes La Paz Waterfall Gardens and the Doka coffee estate.

If you're a caffeine fiend—er, coffee aficionado—you'll definitely want to make time to check out what's brewing at the Vargas Ruiz family's **Doka Estate** ✱ (in Sabanilla, 4km/2½ miles west of San Isidro; ☎ 449-5152; www.dokaestate. com; weekdays 9am–3:30pm, weekends 9am–2:30pm). Some 9½ miles (15km) north of Alajuela city and 16 miles (26km) from San José, this 16-sq.-km (6-sq.-mile) spread makes a superb stop on the way to or from Poás or La Paz Waterfall Gardens. Doka grows, roasts, mills, and markets, unlike the slicker Britt operation in Heredia (p. 63), which is mainly a roaster. Here there's less of a song and dance and it just feels a bit more authentic; highlights include a peek at Costa Rica's oldest water-powered coffee mill. Naturally there's a shop where you can buy the goods—not only beans and grinds ($5–$7 per 350-gram bag) but also coffee candies, booze, and Doka logo stuff. And by the way, you're probably drinking Doka's output already; 90 percent goes right to Starbucks. Many local tour operators include this on their itinerary, but you can arrange it directly: the 90-minute tour, run three times in the morning and three times in the afternoon, costs $21 ($8 for ages 6–12) including lunch; they have a $37 package ($42 with lunch) including transportation from hotels throughout the Central Valley. FYI, if you want to sample but can't make it up here, there's an affiliated cafe in downtown Alajuela called **Casa de Café La Begonia** (4 blocks south of La Agonía

Church; ☎ 442-9846; Mon–Sat 11am–7pm). Also, the Vargas family runs a four-bedroom B&B nearby called **Siempreverde** (doubles from $60—nothing special architecture-wise but comfortable and with a nice setting and view overlooking the coffee fields).

About 22 miles (35km) north of Doka and 14 miles (22 km) from Poás on its northeast slope, the elaborate **La Paz Waterfall Gardens** ★★ (kids) (4km/2½ miles north of Vara Blanca gas station; ☎ 482-2720, or 954-727-3997 in the U.S.; www.waterfallgardens.com; daily 8am–5pm; $29, ages 12 and under $18, with lunch buffet $41/$24), is frankly touristy. But despite the cutesy replica village and the glitzy signage and large souvenir shop, it's a worthy visit as it offers an in-depth and often thrilling look into the local ecology, not to mention a smidgeon of history. How? Well, the owners, the Leebanks family from Miami, have taken the usual butterfly garden, froggery, hummingbird garden, and serpentarium that are a dime a dozen in Costa Rica and super-sized 'em. The butterfly exhibit is the largest in the country, a two-story atrium filled with flutterers and English-speaking docents who will explain life-cycle issues and even place a newly hatched butterfly on your forefinger for a spell. The hummingbird garden literally buzzes with hundreds of tiny birds; nowhere else in Costa Rica will you see these beauties in such abundance. Extras include a recreated old-style Tico farmhouse, complete with a "farmer" standing out front with a live ox pulling a cart for the kiddies. But what really blows you away about the place is what awaits below all that, along a mile's worth of cement, wood, and metal walkways and stairways following the river. Winding your way through the rainforest, the only sound you hear is the rush and thunder of wild H_2O, and soon you find out why: a string of five waterfalls, one more spectacular than the next. Get up right next to the 36m (120-ft.) Magia Blanca ("White Magic"), or check out the view from the bridge below, where you can see three waterfalls appearing to pour into each other; it's all great for kids, but for the very young ones, keep in mind that this last part involves a lot of steps and schlepping. You can have a nice buffet lunch in a beautifully constructed dining pavilion, pick up souvenirs galore, and if you want to splurge on an overnight, the Peace Lodge next door has swell amenities and digs (with standard doubles from $255 a night, I'd certainly hope so). The gardens' 28 hectares (70 acres, including the La Paz River) are 45km (28 miles) north of Alajuela city and 5km (3 miles) from San José.

As we never shut up about, Costa Rica is tops for bird-watching, and Zoo Ave (kids) ★ (2.5km/1½ miles east of Puente Manolos; ☎ 433-8989; www.zooave.org; daily 9am–5pm; $15) makes it a downright cinch even for the bird-brained. While tromping around birding hot spots like Sarapiquí and the Osa Peninsula, trying to spot our feathered friends can be hit or miss, and rarely do you get to see them up close and personal. In the town of La Garita, a 45-minute drive from San José, this 59-hectare (145-acre) open-plan zoo has the largest bird collection in Central America, all donated, rescued from poachers and smugglers, or nursed back to health after being injured. There are a good hundred species, including more than a dozen kinds of raptors, 16 types of parrots, and 5 toucans. So while coming here won't give you quite the rush of spotting them in the wild, you're sure to get a good, close look. Oh, and did we mention they've got a prized quetzal? Most of the birds are Costa Rica natives, but a few exotics from elsewhere, are also sprinkled in, like ostriches and peacocks. Plenty of critters without wings here, too—for

Bean There, Done That

What countries do you think of when it comes to coffee? Colombia, right? Maybe Brazil—and if you're really up on the good stuff, Ethiopia, Hawaii, Indonesia, Jamaica. Smaller than all of them, Costa Rica has more of its land per capita planted with the little brown bean—and this even though it's not nearly as much as it used to (these days just 15 percent of exports). Though the country's small size means it can only contribute just a few drops to the global pot, Tico coffee is some of the best in the world, and in a real sense it helped bring into bean—er, being—Costa Rica of today. You'll see the stuff sold and referred to everywhere you go down here (beginning with the big ol' coffee-pickers statue right in front of the airport), so you just might find this quickie primer on *el grano de oro* (the golden bean) handy.

Originally discovered around Kaffa, Ethiopia, *qahhwa* made a splash on the Arabian peninsula, was first brewed as a drink in Turkey, and percolated over to be grown in Asia, then the Americas. It was brought to Costa Rica from Jamaica in 1791, and Ticos started exporting it in 1820, eventually branching out to Europe. The sales igniting a boom here that minted many a mustachioed plutocrat, created class divisions, and after 1840 dominated the national economy, all the while remaking the ecology of the Central Valley. It was taxes on coffee profits that built San José's National Theater and other institutions, and in 1897 made this city only the third in the world to get that crazy newfangled thing called *electricidad*. The fall in prices in recent years means that nowadays yearly production is almost half of what it was 20 years ago—yet still, practically anywhere you go in the valley you'll still see endless hectares of bushes, their rows sprawled across rolling hills and up steep mountainsides.

example, at least 20 species of mammal (monkeys, leopards, pumas) and 15 of reptiles (land tortoises, big snakes like boas, caimans, and crocs—whoa, dude, check out that 12-footer). You can spend a good couple of hours here, and there's a little snack bar with chips, soda, and so forth

For those really loony for lepidopterans, this country's also a paradise—sometimes it seems like every two-bit B&B has some kind of *mariposario* (butterfly garden). But Joris Brickerhoff and María Sabido's 1.6-hectare (4-acre) **Butterfly Farm** (La Guácima Abajo, 400m/120 ft. south of Los Reyes Country Club; ☎ 438-0400; www.butterflyfarm.co.cr; daily 8:30am–5pm; $15, students $10, ages 5–12 $7) in the town of La Guácima is worth a trip in itself, because the 900-sq.-m (9,700-sq.-ft.) screened-in garden here not only gives an up-close look at about 80 of the 1,000 species found in Costa Rica (the *mariposario* at La Paz may be fancier, but all it's got is a measly 20 species), but also provides you one of the most in-depth looks you'll get down here of these beautiful bugs—for starters, a 2-hour tour of its labs and nurseries, with all the eggs, cocoons, pupae, and caterpillars.

See, the Central Valley's got a climate and conditions that *coffea arabica* plants *really* love—starting with rich volcanic soil, comfy temps between 64°F and 73°F (18°C–23°C) and altitudes 984m to 1,686m (3,280–5,620 ft.) above sea level. All that, plus the fact that a good bit of them are shade-grown, makes for hard, slow-maturing, flavor-filled beans which in turn adds up to hearty brews with lots of body and robustness (as opposed to *robusta*, the second-class grade of coffee—that crap's actually illegal to grow in Costa Rica). Plants usually last a little over 20 years, but the first 4 of those years don't bear fruit, which look like little green cherries that turn red as they ripen. Most Tico growers have just a dozen acres or less (though bigger operations take up more total land), and they're spread across seven main districts. The best are probably Tarrazú in southern San José province and Tres Ríos to the east, near Irazú volcano in Cartago (some call this one the "Bordeaux of Costa Rica"). Not far away in Cartago, the Orosi Valley is another top-grade district, and nearby Turrialba is pretty good, too. The classic traditional coffee areas lie around Poás and Barva volcanos in Heredia and Alajuela, known as the Valle Central zone.

To get a firsthand feel for what the whole coffee thing is all about while you're down here, check out our Central Valley entries for **Café Britt** in Heredia (p. 73), **Doka Estate** in Alajuela (p. 56), and **Finca Cristina** in Cartago's Orosi Valley (p. 78). A couple of others in southern San José province include **Finca Don Evelio** near San Marcos de Tarrazú (☎ 546-5010; www.tarrazucafe.com) and **Coopedota** in Santa María de Dota (☎ 541-2828; www.dotacoffee.com). If you're heading up to Monteverde, see our entries (p. 131) for the **Don Juan Coffee Tour** (p. 131), **Finca Cielo Verde** (p. 132), and **Coope Santa Elena/Café Monteverde** (p. 132).

And there's nothing like strolling along and having an electric blue morpho or a brown owl butterfly alight on your shoulder. The farm is 7½ miles (12km) southwest of Alajuela city and 16 miles (26km) from San José; three times a day it runs buses and tours from some 20 hotels in the area for an extra $10 for adults and students, $6 for kids.

The "Other" Alajuela

Everybody's gotta shop, Tico or gringo, so one good way to rub shoulders with locals is to browse with them at the very picturesque covered **Mercado Central** (p. 38), which does double duty by providing a peek into how important this traditional style of market still is to many people in Costa Rica. Sure, most locals these days are going the usual modern supermarket and big-box-store route, but these old-fashioned covered mazes hark back to the formative era of Tico culture and society, when everybody would come here to do their daily marketing, socialize with their neighbors, maybe have lunch at one of the *sodas;* our own grandparents

Pick a Peck of Tico Parks

The Central Valley has more than its share of expansive parks, bio-reserves, and wildlife refuges, public and private. Throughout this chapter we've pointed you toward a handful of the top and most interesting ones, but even so, we thought this "quick 'n' dirty" 411 on what we've included might help you keep things straight:

- **Braulio Carrillo/Barva Volcano National Park, Heredia** More fauna and dense flora than Irazú or Poás, but Barva crater tougher to get to (it's a mile-long hike); an enormous wilderness park with many miles of trails, its depths are best for harder-core hikers who really know what they're doing; 26km (16 miles) from Heredia city. See p. 72.

- **Guayabo National Monument, Cartago** Main attraction is ancient indigenous ruins, takes up to an hour to walk the trails; 19km (12 miles) outside Turrialba, 64km (40 miles) east of Cartago city. See p. 87.

- **Irazú Volcano National Park, Cartago** Here, everyone's gone to the moon (as in lunar-looking landscape); four craters, some fumaroles, not much flora/fauna, few trails; quickly/easily accessible from Cartago city. See p. 84.

- **Poás Volcano National Park, Alajuela** The best of the Central Valley volcano parks for geysers and fumaroles; short, easy stroll to crater, not a lot of trails/walking involved; 64km (40 miles) from San José, 31km (19 miles) from Alajuela city. See p. 56.

- **Tapantí-Macizo Cerro la Muerto National Park, Cartago** Lots of flora/fauna, rivers, streams, waterfalls, and swimming holes; three trails, the longest a 90-minute walk; less than 24km (15 miles) from Cartago, via the Orosi Valley. See p. 86.

used to have similar places, but in North America that's mostly a thing of the past. Occupying an entire city block, the Mercado has been an integral part of small-town life for generations, and still is for enough people that it still manages to thrive even in our standardized, plasticized, cellophane-wrapped era.

You might also try breaking the ice by joining *alajuelenses* at two other traditional venues. Help them cheer on their top-notch soccer team (Costa Rica's most popular) at the **Estadio Alejandro Morera Soto** in Llano de Alajuela (☎ 443-1617; http://ldacr.org); *fútbol* is so bred into the national soul by now that this is a great way to see Tico passion (sports-fan version) at full throttle. Or consider taking a dip with them at the popular and classic natural-spring water park **Ojo de Agua** (just south of Santamaría airport; ☎ 433-8989; daily 9am–4pm; $1.15), in San Antonio de Belén near the airport. Yes, it's essentially a public pool, but one that's been a famous favorite with Tico families for generations, and we've found it's easy to talk to folks here and even make a friend or two here.

Taking classes is another winning way to meet people, and at the same time learn about local culture. Over west of Alajuela city in the town of Atenas, since

2005 local expats have been running a community center called **Su Espacio** (☎ 446-7735; www.suespacio.org), where weekdays from 8am to 9pm plus Saturday mornings expats and Ticos alike take dance, fitness, crafts, and Spanish/English classes for practically nothing (sometimes as little as $10 for a whole month). In a town with this few evening activities, the night courses here can get very social.

Then there are the local language schools, which can arrange homestays with families and field trips and activities that get you involved with locals in various ways. A trio worth checking into:

Right downtown, the **Centro Cultural de Idiomas** (☎ 441-9202; www.spanish in-action.com) makes a point of focusing on conversational skills beyond textbook learning, and in small groups (up to just four). Regular programs run four 5-day weeks for $630 to $860 including materials, and room and board (independent or through a family homestay), but there's also a 2-week "survival course" ($330–$440), plus private classes for as few or as many hours as you need. Extras like gym membership, Internet, tours, and dancing/cooking/scuba classes are provided at discounted rates. Hey, and bring a second student in with you and you'll get 20 percent off your own costs.

There's also **IMAC** (☎ 866/306-5040 in the U.S. and Canada; www.spanish-school.com.mx/costarica/alajuela.html), part of a six-country network of Spanish-language schools. Based outside downtown in the small town of La Guácima (not far from the Butterfly Farm we mentioned above), it, too, offers dancing and cooking class options. Four weeks here runs $1,450 to $1,750, down to a single week for $410 to $510 (whether the higher numbers or the lower ones depends on the number of hours of class you want per day) including books, homestay with three meals a day, and airport transfers. There's a pool on campus for goofing off, plus extracurricular stuff like field trips, cooking/dancing classes, and volunteer work with poor kids.

The third, downtown's **Intensa** (☎ 281-1818; www.intensa.com) sets you up with cooking/dancing classes; hosts get-togethers with the Tico students to whom it teaches English; and helps with tours and volunteer opportunities working in one of the national parks, an orphanage, old-age home, school, and animal shelter, and so on. The fees of $390 to $480 per week up to $1,305 to $1,665 per month cover classes, books, and activities plus a half-board homestay and airport transfers.

Speaking of volunteering, it's a great way to really make your vacation meaningful by doing good, learning a thing or two, and meeting locals—and you don't have to take a Spanish course in order to do it. For example, the U.S.-based **Institute for Field Research Expeditions** (☎ 800/675-2504; www.ifrevolunteers. org) will get you into projects mostly in and around the town of Atenas, including teaching English and other subjects; clearing trails in national parks; helping out at daycare centers and orphanages (where, for example, you'll help with janitor duties but also help the kids directly by playing with them, teaching English, serving meals, and helping with homework). The minimum time commitment is a week, which includes room, board, and Spanish lessons if you want them for $599; 2 weeks run $688, and so on (there's also an additional one-time fee of $349).

You can try several locally based nonprofits, too. There's a rescue and breeding program for scarlet and great green macaws called **Amigos de las Aves** (☎ 441-2658; www.HatchedtoFlyFree.com) in Rio Segundo, just under 2 miles southeast of Alajuela city, which accepts volunteers for a minimum of a month to help maintain aviaries, feed and tend to the birds, farm crops on the estate, and community outreach, as well as lend a hand with other chores 6 days a week; the cost starts at $5 a day for room, $12 for room and board. Another outfit called the **Nature Restoration Fund** runs Zoo Ave (see above) and an animal rescue center in Alajuela (along with other projects around the country). Jobs include cleaning cages, feeding animals, and helping with repairs and janitorial stuff. Minimum periods vary but can be as little as a week; if you stay a couple of weeks or longer, they'll put you up and maybe feed you (depending on space availability). For more info and to apply, call ☎ 433-8989, ext. 10 or check www.zooave.org.

For volunteering that's more social than eco-oriented, over in the town of Atenas the community center we plugged above, **Su Espacio** (☎ 446-7735; www.suespacio.org) accepts teaching volunteers for subjects like English, aerobics, yoga, Pilates, swimming, and dance. And if you have a skill they don't teach—ventriloquism? Ichibana?—they just might let you start a new class. The folks here can also arrange cheap homestays—$250 a month cheap enough?—as well as volunteer work out in the community, with local kids, seniors, and others. And they like to share the wealth—the wealth of visitors, that is—so director Tina Newton can also help set you up in volunteer situations outside her center.

Attention, Shoppers!

Let's be blunt: There's very little shopping of note in Alajuela itself. One of the very few places in town is a tiny hole in the wall called **Elipse** (Av. 3, 1 block north of central park and 50m/164 ft. east of Juan Santamaría Museum; ☎ 440-7052; Mon–Sat 9am–6pm), selling handmade albums, wood puzzle boxes, and ceramic mobiles; we especially like the tribal masks (from $13) and paintings on bird feathers (from $2.90). Also, southwest of downtown over in Atenas, check **El Mirador** shop (☎ 446-7361; daily 6am–6pm) for pre-Columbian art (there's a restaurant attached, too).

But when it comes to shopping, the name of the game in Alajuela is **Sarchí** ★★. It's a small town, about 22km (14 miles) from the city. It's a pretty drive, and at the end of it you'll find yourself at the **Fábrica de Carretas Chaverri** (☎ 454-4411; daily 7am–6pm), the most famous maker of the traditional, distinctively Tico painted oxcarts *(carretas)*, in business since 1903. These colorful contraptions were used in the old days to haul coffee, other merch, and their owners, and in an artistic arms race of keeping up with the Sanchezes, naturally people started pimping their rides. So the decorative versions you'll see here at Chaverri are plastered with all kinds of parrots, butterflies, flowers, and abstract designs. Last we checked, the largest (1.2m long × .6 high × .6m wide/4 ft.×2 ft.×2 ft.) was $406 plus $106 if you want to have it shipped; there are, however, lots of smaller sizes, down to minicarts for $6.40. There's plenty of other neat stuff here, too—the place feels about half-a-football-field big, and gets a lot of cruise-ship tours—such as caneback and embossed leather rockers, and various other leather and wooden tchochtkes (on the low end, you can pick up a cute little animal figurine for $2.60). My faves are sinuous, artsy bowls, carved out of the gnarly trunks of *cocobolo* trees ($43–$152); I've seen them on sale at the Santamaría airport gift shop for around $215. Out back is a garden area with antique oxcarts and a woodshop off to one side, where you can watch them being cobbled together.

A little farther along, across the bridge in Sarchí Norte, the artisans' cooperative **Coopearsa** (next to Clínica CCSS; ☎ 454-4050; daily 8am–6pm) offers a similar selection of intriguing goodies. If you're in the market for something a little larger, Sarchí is also where a lot of Costa Rica's furniture comes from, fine or otherwise. As you drive along, you'll find store after store, many of them attached to the workshops where the stuff is actually cobbled together. One that we like, **Muebles Finos Sarchiseños** (800m/2,624 ft. north of Plaza de las Artes, next to Casa del Bastón; ☎ 454-4934; daily 9am–5pm) sells, for example, a very classy dining room set of Guanacaste wood (with cabriolet legs and upholstered chairs with elegant simple rose carvings) for just $1,379.

Nightlife

Sorry to report not all that much to do in Alajuela after dark. For one thing, it's so close to San José that most partiers head south to the big city (p. 41) or east to Heredia, which at least has a university-student scene to support a handful of nightspots (p. 76). What little there is around here is mostly along the lines of small watering holes along with several restaurants that have sprouted a halfway decent bar scene, such as **La Mansarda** (see above) and **Cugini** (Av. Central at Calle 5; ☎ 440-6893; Sun–Thurs 4am–10pm, Fri–Sat 11am–1am).

For the boogie-feverish too lazy to schlep into San José, it can't hurt to give it a go at **Spectros Disco** (Carretera Radial, across from Perimercado; ☎ 440-6287; daily 7pm–6am; cover Fri–Sat $1.95–$2.90), just south of central downtown. Above a grubby minimall, it's a cavernous, semi-industrial-looking bit of business—the dance floor sports black-steel girders—that attracts a mostly under-25 crowd. Last we checked, ladies got open bar Friday till midnight, Saturdays featured live dancers and a 1am fashion show, and Sunday was about karaoke and then as of 1am *las chicas vaqueritas*—"little cowgirls" (use your imagination).

Since 2005, another spot that has developed some pull is the **Fiesta Casino** (across from Santamaría airport; ☎ 380-0573; open 24 hr.), attached to a Denny's in a complex of airport hotels. It's about the size of a medium Indian casino in the States, but better done—well, in a Disneyish kind of way. You've got your clouds on the ceiling, à la Caesar's Palace and The Venetian in Vegas, and the theme is pre-Columbian, with faux stone walls and columns, all loomed over by gargantuan Olmec-style heads. Apart from the usual money-pits (rummy, blackjack, dice, and lots and lots o' slots), the "Pirates" bar-lounge here brings in live music and dancers every night from 10pm to 2am, and has two giant TV screens along with a handful of smaller ones. Gringos flock here when there's a big game and also tend to hang out on weekdays, whereas the weekends pull in more Ticos.

HEREDIA

A diverse, svelte slice of Costa Rica between Alajuela to its west, Limón stretching to the Caribbean out east, and San José just south, Costa Rica's smallest province (2,657 sq. km/1,026 sq. miles, pop. 355,000), we've gotta say, punches above its weight touristically speaking. It serves as a good base for hitting some of the great national parks (including volcanoes and rainforests), San José's culture and dining, and even some of the beach areas of the Central Pacific. The feel of

Heredia ("eh-REH-dee-ah") ranges from suburban and light-industrial (the provincial capital's just 11km/7 miles from San José, and between the two are a string of towns that pretty much run together) to countryside to downright wild (at least 85 percent of it, farther north in Braulio Carillo National Park/Barva Volcano and the Sarapiquí region—the latter covered in Chapter 3). The Central Valley part of Heredia province came into its own as a big coffee-growing center, and though residential and other development has pushed a lot of this out, Heredia's far from a has-bean (had-bean?). Driving around, you'll still spot plenty of fields, and the country's most famous name in java—Café Britt—is based here (and puts on a damn good tour, by the way).

Founded in 1706 at the foot of Barva Volcano, the province's eponymous capital and single biggest burg today is quite the charmer—in fact, of the "Big 3" Central Valley cities outside San José, we find Heredia the most fetching, thanks to its architecture and street life. Ticos know it as the City of Flowers (some say because of the flora, others the fauna), but what really puts its stamp on the place is UNA, the parklike **Universidad Nacional de Costa Rica,** with a student body of around 12,000—out of a city population of 20,000! And that's not the only school—there are *colegios* and *institutos* and language schools (see "The Other Heredia") up the wazoo; there's even one called the "Instituto Parauniversitario Richard Nixon" (motto: *"Yo no soy criminal"*—ha, ha, we *kid* the Instituto Parauniversitario Richard Nixon). Nonetheless, all of this gives the town a pretty youthful feel—not to mention keeps prices under control. As with most Tico towns and small cities, Heredia also picks up maja-flava from its *parque central,* the gracious, shady central plaza dominated by a blocky white church on its east side and on the north side by a pretty distinctive-looking old tower that's the city's symbol, called **El Fortín.** It's a pretty neat place that makes a good base of operations—less congested (and, some would say, dumpy) than San José, yet pretty cosmopolitan. Plus it's close to tons of cool stuff, from the capital just to the south, Arenal and Sarapiquí to the north, the Central Pacific coast out west, and even the Caribbean coast, several hours east.

Getting To & Around Heredia

It's a fairly easy drive here from San José—take Route 3 to the airport and turn right at the Uruca rotunda past the Best Western. Buses include No. 400, which leaves from San José at Calle 4 between avenidas 5 and 7, leaving every 5 to 7 minutes from 5am to 11:30pm. A commuter train was slated to start service in late 2007, but as we went to press, no choo-choo yet. If you're coming from the airport, you'll need to take a cab through **Taxis Unidos Aeropuertos** (☎ 222-6865; www.taxiaeropuerto.com); the fare should run $12 to $15.

Downtown's grid is easy to navigate on foot, and slightly outlying spots like Paseo de las Flores Mall and Plaza Heredia shouldn't cost more than a buck or so by cab. If you're planning to explore the rest of the province and Central Valley, though, a car is definitely the way to go—bus service hereabouts is pretty darn good, but to cover a lot of ground, you'll end up spending too much time making connections.

Accommodations, Both Standard & Not

Heredia's actually a pretty swell city to bunk in—there ain't a whole lot of tourists, but there are plenty of students and other folks coming and going, so you'll find

Heredia

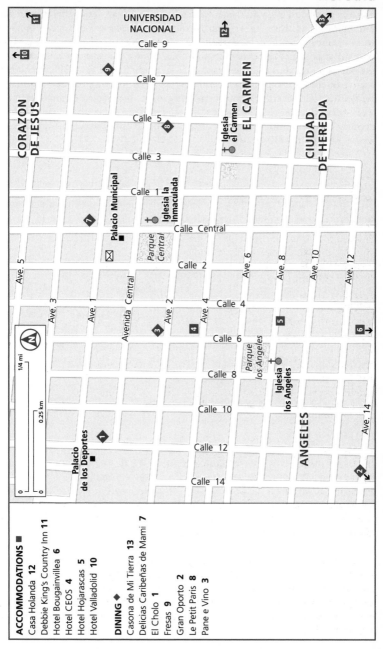

ACCOMMODATIONS ■
Casa Holanda **12**
Debbie King's Country Inn **11**
Hotel Bougainvillea **6**
Hotel CEOS **4**
Hotel Hojarascas **5**
Hotel Valladolid **10**

DINING ◆
Casona de Mi Tierra **13**
Delicias Caribeñas de Mami **7**
El Cholo **1**
Fresas **9**
Gran Oporto **2**
Le Petit Paris **8**
Pane e Vino **3**

65

a choice of decent, affordable options in and around town. Those flying in to San José Airport and planning on going on towards Arenal and other points north without hitting San José, may want to consider staying in Heredia instead as it's near the airport and can slice a good 40 minutes off the drive to Arenal. Out in the surrounding towns and countryside, meanwhile, you get more B&Bs and resorts catering to tourists, often run by ex-pat gringos, and pretty reasonably priced, for the most part. Not all lodgings have air conditioning (even some of the nicer ones), but the Central Valley climate is usually cool enough that you don't need it. For rock bottom in town (from $12 per person) take a bed at the cozy, newish **Dream Place** hostel (2½ blocks east of central park; ☎ 560-1111; www. costaricatravel.ch; cash only), which has perks like Wi-Fi and cable TV.

VACATION RENTALS

Properties in Costa Rica (☎ 844-5431, or 888/607-6772 in the U.S. and Canada; www.propertiesincostarica.com) reps rentals in a gated community of cute, two-story, stand-alone two- and three-bedroom villas in San Rafael, a 10-15-minute drive away from downtown. Ranging in size from 1,776 to 2,637 square feet (165-245 square meters), they're nice middle-class Tico homes, with upscale but not extravagant furnishings, full up-to-date kitchens, furnished terraces, and amenities like cable, DSL, and washing machine. The catch is, there's a 2-week minimum; monthly rates are $1,200 to $1,400. For something a little more short-term, just north of the city toward the town of Barva, Tina Newton and Nolan Quirós rent out their nice, 125-sq.-m (1,350-sq.-ft.) **Villa Verde** (☎ 386-8103; www.suespacio.org/villaverde.html), with three bedrooms, 2½ baths, full kitchen, washing machine, backyard, and great mountain views (and the garage even has an automatic door opener, woo-hoo!). Inside the feel is a mix of spare (tile floors) and plush (living room furniture), with nice art on the walls and cheerful touches like the blue-and-yellow bedspreads. It sleeps up to eight, and the cost is $80 a night or $500 a week for four, plus $10 per night per additional person; there's a 3-night minimum.

HOTELS & B&BS

$ You sure wouldn't spot any high-off-the-hog CEOs dead at the **Hotel CEOS** (Av. 1 at Calle 4, 100m/328 ft. north and 100m/328 ft. east of central park, next to BAC bank; ☎ 262-2628; www.hamerica.net; AE, MC, V), but the next-to-rock-bottom rates—$23 per double—would definitely warm the bean-counting heart of a CFO. One of four properties of a locally owned budget-hotel group, this old two-story white house, just a couple of blocks away from the main plaza, has an antique but not shabby look to it, with blue trim and wrought-iron gates, and a balcony upstairs for hanging out. The 10 rooms are on the basic side, but they're clean and have pleasing pluses, like private baths, high ceilings, old-fashioned tile floors, and cable TV. You can get more than adequately fed at the inexpensive restaurant downstairs (breakfast isn't included).

$$ You could split the difference between city and countryside at the elegant suburban **Casa Holanda** ✦ (500m/1,640 ft. south and 100m/328 ft. east of the Municipalidad; ☎ 238-3241; www.casaholanda.com; AE, D, MC, V), on a quiet street in San Pablo, a town between Heredia and San José and a quick, easy hop to both. Talented 30-something pianist and composer James Holland fled the concrete jungle of New York City to continue composing while he runs a B&B with gracious personalized service and three rooms done up very tastefully and individually, with mosquito-netting-swathed beds, cable TV, and Wi-Fi (the two $65 doubles share a bath, though; the $150 "honeymoon suite" has its own, with an oversize Jacuzzi tub). The guy's a great cook, too, very into Tico culture, and has a grand piano whose ivories he'll be happy to tickle for you or let you play (sometimes he even puts together concerts with local musicians). By the way, for an extra 3-percent off the rate, just pay in *colones.*

$–$$ Up in the countryside with double volcano views, **Debbie King's Country Inn** (500m/1,640 ft. south of Pulpería El Trapiche; ☎ 268-3084 or 380-8492; www.freewebs.com/debbieking; cash only) is a no-nonsense but appealing wood-and-stucco house on a 3-acre coffee and fruit farm on a hillside just outside the town of San Rafael, 5½ miles (9 km) from Heredia city and 7½ (12 km) from San José. A Liverpudlian by way of L.A., where she did a little of this and a little of that (most relevantly, concierge at the Century Plaza), Debbie's a hoot, and has run the place since 1992. The views are pretty special (among other things you can see Irazú volcano), and the digs are cozy—four wood-paneled rooms upstairs with balconies (but a shared bath) for $42, a couple of stand-alone guesthouses with kitchens and their own baths for $76 (longer stays get 10-percent discounts). There's no phone or A/C, but Debbie will be happy to stick a TV in your room if you stay at least 3 days. There's also a three-bedroom house that rents by the month.

$$ Back in the "big city," several blocks south of the main plaza, the **Hotel Hojarascas** (Av. 8 between calles 4 and 6, across from Más X Menos parking lot; ☎ 260-7783; www.hotelhojarascas.com; AE, D, MC, V) set up shop in 2005, and it's quite the deal for $51 per double (breakfast included). All of its dozen rooms are on a skylit inside courtyard, so there's a lot of light bouncing off a lot of white walls and tile floors; plus they come with touches you wouldn't expect at this price level, like halogen lights, music, cable TV, coffeemaker, and Wi-Fi. The Arias family—two brothers and two sisters, no relation to the current president—are just that kind of amazingly friendly folks (enough smiling already!); they even throw in airport transfers, laundry service, and a kitchen for guests to use. And another 10 bucks gets you a fab apartment with its own full kitchen. The only "but" we can think of at the moment is that it's a little tough to sleep in on Sundays because it's near a church. The bells! The bells!

$$ If you're in the mood for a little more of a hotel-like feel in the city, the four-story **Hotel Valladolid** (Av. 5/Calle 7, across from L'Antica Roma pizzeria; ☎ 260-2905; www.hotelvalladolid.net; AE, MC, V), on the eastern end of downtown near the university, is an attractive choice with perks like a rooftop bar (opens at 5:30pm) and sundeck with great views, plus Jacuzzi and a sauna. Dating from the early 1990s, its ochre exterior is kind of cubelike and minimalist (though the atrium lobby does sport some nice wildlife murals), and its 11 whitewashed rooms certainly aren't overdecorated (nice prints, soft colors), but they do have nice architectural touches (columns, arches), along with good drawer and closet space, kitchenettes, and spic-n-span white-tiled bathrooms (No. 8, 10, and 11 also have oversize tubs). And depending on your personality, you might prefer that the service is good, yet a little more distanced than our other medium-range option in town, Hojarascas. Doubles run $73, including breakfast.

$$ Tennis courts, a large pool, sauna, business center, a nice gift store, a bar, a business center—for those hankering for a real "resort" experience, the Dutch-owned, three-story **Hotel Bougainvillea** ★ 🧒 (1km east of Farmacia Nopal; ☎ 244-1414, or 866/880-5441 in the U.S.; www.hb.co.cr; AE, D, MC, V) is the ticket. It's not fancy by any means—its endless corridors and spacious but kind of dated, blah rooms make it look and feel more like a Holiday Inn than a Ritz-Carlton—but the lovely landscaping of the grounds (there's even a hedge maze that the kids will have a ball in), the unusually attentive service, and the fact that there's a top-notch restaurant on-site, make up for a lot. Each of the 81 rooms comes with either a balcony or a terrace; ask for one overlooking the gardens—they're much quieter and sport nicer views. Recently, the hotel put in Wi-Fi in addition to its Internet stations. Another helpful perk is a free shuttle to San José. Considering doubles start at $90, we'd have to call that Dutch treat enough.

Dining for All Tastes

Heredia boasts one of the Central Valley's better and more varied dining scenes. At the bottom end, as always, there's no shortage in this city and province of humble *sodas* for a cheap, decent feed. For one downtown spot that's open 24/7, try **Soda La Modelo,** right next to the **Mercado Central** (Av. 6 at Calle 4; Mon–Sat 6am–6:30pm, Sun 6am–12:30pm). And by the way, this large traditional covered market itself has a slew of them where you can get combination plates for as little as $2.60 while getting in some great people-watching as locals bustle around shopping; we especially like **Soda La Rústica** (☎ 237-1559), with tasty corn tortillas, and **Soda Paco Alfaro** (☎ 237-1173). There are also plenty of inexpensive Chinese places around town (look for the pagoda façades). And we very much like a two-room corner place called **Café Scarlett** (Av. 2 at Calle 5, 2 blocks east of the central park; ☎ 260-1921; Mon–Sat 8am–6:30pm), run by a cool black lady from the Caribbean coast, Ana Loletti Scarletti—she only turns out about three pastries and one main dish a day, but it's a great little spot to hang for a while.

We should also mention one more spot that's popular, especially with students: the spiffy 3-year-old **Paseo de las Flores** mall (☎ 261-9898; www.paseodelas flores.com; Mon–Sat 10:30am–9pm, Sun 11am–8pm), one of the country largest, just south of downtown on the road to San José. Normally we'd rather chew glass than recommend a food court, but downstairs here you'll find some good inexpensive grub at Tico names like **Oliva Verde, Cevichería,** and **Rústico.** Our favorite here, though, is **Maredo,** run by a French Arab with tasty North African dishes like *merguez* (a savory sausage; combo platter $4.35). Upstairs are other more conventional restaurants that are still good deals by U.S. standards, including Peruvian at the elegant **Inka Grill** and more upscale Costa Rican at **Bruno's.** And one final note: remember the **Hotel Bougainvillea** (above) may also be worth a trip for lunch or dinner if you happen to be in the area.

$ For a slight change of pace downtown, get your mouth around some Tico with an Afro-Caribbean twist at the Foulkes-Brown family-run **Delicias Caribeñas de Mami** (Calle Central, 2 blocks north of central park; ☎ 262-0359; Tue–Sat

A Honeymoon-Worthy Splurge

It may not be quite as amenity-packed as the Bougainvillea, but if you're a fan of art, architecture, or just plain old want some real charisma in your sleeps, the eco-friendly **Finca Rosa Blanca** ✪✪✪ (.8km/½ mile north of Café Britt distribution center; ☎ 269-9392; www.fincarosablanca. com; AE, MC, V), a half-mile north of Santa Bárbara, is one of Costa Rica's most special places to stay. A vision in white tucked amid 20 acres of coffee fields and orchards, it has an Antoni Gaudí-meets-Georgia-O'Keeffe ambiance, what with the sinuous lines of its whitewashed stucco, quirky windows, and the artwork all over the place (50-something ex-Californian Glenn Jampol and his wife Terri run the place with their daughters Lily and Olivia, and his art's mixed with pieces by Ticos both contemporary and pre-Columbian). As you'd expect, each of the nine rooms is unique, from "Las Máscaras" ($200), lined with masks *(máscaras)* from around the globe to "El Cafetal" ($250), whose most distinctive adornment is a mural of the coffee plantation outside for which it's named (we love the blue-and-white bathroom and big Jacuzzi tub, too), to the Rosa Blanca tower suite ($300), a duplex with 360-degree windows and balcony in the upstairs bedroom, a wooden staircase that's a work of art, and a rain-forest style bathroom whose "tub" is practically a pool. Speaking of which, the spring-fed infinity pool with its dozen-foot waterfall is one of the dreamiest we've seen in this country, and the food's a major yum-fest; breakfast is included, but you should also have dinner ($37) here at least once—it's a concerto of creative Latin fusion, heavily organic. And if you like dogs (guilty as charged), you'll love the trio of friendly family pooches. Funny, we'd always heard of the White Rose as a group that was a beacon of anti-Nazi resistance in wartime Germany; here, I guess you can say it's a beacon against the tyranny of hotel mediocrity.

11am–8pm, Sun noon–7pm; AE, MC, V). It's essentially a notch or two above a *soda*, but with a more festive feel—waitresses in bright orange-yellow uniforms, painted beach scenes on the wall, and a "beach shack" that's an open kitchen where you can watch *mami* (mom) or maybe *papi* cooking the house specialty, *rizanbin*, which is jerk-style chicken with rice and beans simmered in coconut milk and allspice ($6.75). Most of the rest of it is good but fairly standard *comida típica*, with all main dishes $6.95 or less and weekday lunch specials going for $2.30. And service is no-nonsense rather than warm, but whatever—for that you've got your own *mami*, right?

$ Though this spot is slightly off the beaten path, if you're a seafoodie, it's well worth the picturesque drive several miles northwest from downtown Heredia, to make a mouthwatering withdrawal at the "seafood bank"—**El Banco de los Mariscos** ✪✪ (600m west of downtown Santa Bárbara; ☎ 269-9090; Mon–Sat

11:30am–10pm, Sun 11:30am–9pm; AE, MC, V), a cavernous, 500-person space with skylights, chunky varnished-wood tables, and all kinds of sharks and anchors and stuff hanging from the sloping ceiling. Here everything is fresh from the coast—the ceviches (10 kinds, $1.85–$4.35) are awesome, and they also do wonders with sea bass *(corvina)*—grilled, breaded, in garlic sauce, whatever—served with fries and a salad ($3.85–$4.85). There's also plenty of stuff for non-fish-eaters, and for dessert we do kinda like the creamy orange flan ($1.75). On weekends, a word of advice: go early—on Sundays, you literally need to take a number, though things are a little quieter on Saturdays. And if you're thinking of going to the Ark Herb Park, it's right nearby.

$ For another swell change of pace, this time from the "mother country" (Costa Rica's, of course, i.e. Spain), we're always up for tapas and Rioja at **El Cholo** ★ (Calle 12, across from Palacio de Deportes; ☎ 862-6810; 5pm–midnight; AE, MC, V). The crowd and vibe are social and friendly; the red-and-yellow walls full of appropriately themed paraphernalia; and the fare pretty authentic (David's lived in Spain, so we should know, right?). Potato omelet, Serrano cured ham, manchego cheese, Asturian bean stew, sautéed calamari—all the classics are here, the portions are decent-size, and at $1.90 to $3.55 each you can piece together a pretty dandy and varied meal for minimal outlay (there's also one single and not-the-most-Iberian-sounding main dish, pork steak flambéed with rum and raisins, accompanied by potato chunks with spicy sauce, $4.35). Wine starts at $2.40 a glass or $8.70 a bottle.

$ Several generations of *heredianos* have made big, double-decker **Fresas** (Av. 3 at Calle 7, 100m/328 ft. east of UNA; ☎ 262-5555; Mon–Thurs 8am–11pm, Fri–Sat 8am–midnight, Sun 8am–10pm; AE, MC, V), with its huge red-and-white-striped awnings, something of a local institution for the past 20 years or so. You'll find a mix of students (the university's a block away), families, and 20-somethings with jobs enjoying ice cream ($1.55) or the house special chocolate-strawberry *(fresa)* cake ($2.40), or sometimes ticking off the paper menu's boxes for something a little heartier (combo platters start at $4.75, entrees like *arroz con pollo* at $3.50). So what is it about the joint—the retro '70s/'80s-style feel of the wood booths and formica tables, or maybe the pink-white-red color scheme? It sure ain't the cuddliness of the serving staff (think Greek diner, but in Spanish). But what do we know—the Carmiol Jiménez family has opened three more of these babies throughout the Central Valley, so they've gotta be doing something right.

$–$$—It's only been open since 2005, but San Pablo's **Casona de Mi Tierra** (1½ km east of UNA, across from MABE refrigerator factory; ☎ 261-9645; daily 10am–10pm; AE, MC, V) feels like your grandma's cute little yellow farmhouse if your grandma were Tica: cobblestone and antique-tile floors, elegant-rustic leaf stenciling, hanging kitchen tools, split-log planters, the works. The kitchen of friendly henna-haired owner Flor Marina Franco turns out some nice takes on local cookery, her entrees come with salad, mashed potatoes, rice, beans, sweet plaintains, and tortillas starting at $5.60; I especially approve of her *chicharrones de la casona* (tender pork chunks, $6.75). It's a great place for breakfast, too, and vegetarians will be happy to know that she does a nice *almuercito vegetariano* featuring tofu ($4.25). If you happen to be staying at Casa Holanda, it's right down the road.

$–$$ I was happily surprised at how tasty the pizza is at downtown Heredia's **Pane e Vino** (☎ 263-3550; Mon–Sat noon–midnight, Sun 11:30am–10pm), not just because it's a Costa Rican restaurant but especially because it's a Costa Rican *chain* restaurant, with eight other locations in the Central Valley. And it gets double honorable mention because here you'd never know it's a chain from the setting, a handsome 19th-century house, creamy yellow with brown trim and with beautiful old patterned cement-tile floor; it makes for a nice peek into the past while you eat a more than passable repast. The pizza comes 45 ways, from $4 for a personal-size tomato-and-oregano to a 19-inch *gigante* with the works ($7.50); they also do a scrumptious chicken or beef lasagna ($6.15); and we're fans of the "Pane e Vino" dessert ($2.80), which is kind of like a tiramisu jacked up *(hic)* with amaretto and marsala wine. And you might even get it for free—that's the deal if your table drops about $12.

$$ One of the finer standalone restaurants in the area, **Gran Oporto** ★ 🧒 (road to Aurora, near Hipermas; ☎ 263-2059; Mon–Wed 11:30am–9pm, Thurs–Sat. 11:30am–9:30pm; AE, MC, V) is just west of the city, in the village of San Francisco, but feels like it could be in, say, California wine country. Gracefully run since 2003 by the three Gara sister (two identical twins plus another who's a ringer for Penélope Cruz), it's a tad pricier than most other eateries around here, but seems to the one the local expat gringos—and better-off Ticos—seem to love for international classics ($7.60–$8.45) like chicken cordon bleu, parmesan, or teriyaki, baby back ribs, steak with chimichurri sauce, and pies like lemon meringue and pecan ($2.30–$2.95); the menu's bilingual, and there's even a kids' section. The joint has a classy look, too—outside a wall of French doors, inside an elegant gray room with high ceilings and a pyramidal skylight over a bubbling fountain.

$$ Tasty as *comida típica* can be, at some point you'll definitely need a change of pace, so what have you got "Toulouse" by trying **Le Petit Paris** (Calle 5 between aves 2 and Central, 200m/656 ft. east and 50m/164 ft. north of Los Tribunales; ☎ 262-2564; Mon–Sat noon–10pm; AE, MC, V)? Sorry about that the pun—but at least Cyril the owner really is from Toulouse. Anyway, it's not what it used to be (hey, after a dozen years, what is?), but I still really enjoy sitting out on the greenhouse-roofed back patio, and the woody interior plastered with antique French posters is *très* cozy at night if a little dim in the daytime. The big thing here is crêpes ($2.20–$4.90)—one of our faves is the "Siciliana" ($4.55), with chicken, sweet pepper, tomato sauce, mushrooms, and cheese. But you can also get main dishes ($6.95–$8.30), pastas ($4.25–$4.85), and even a big pot of fondue ($25). It's also the spot to quaff some artesenal Belgian beer, like cherry-flavored Belle Vue or Leffe Abbey ale ($2.70–$3.50). Sometimes you'll find art exhibitions or live jazz here, too. *Voulez-vous?*

Why You're Here: The Top Sights & Attractions

Starting at downtown's ground zero, the **Parque Central,** is a leafy plaza that around noon on Sundays gets pretty festive—you'll usually catch a band and maybe even *payasos* (clowns) and *mascaradas* (folks in colorful papier-maché masks); I also love hanging out here at sunset. On the east side, don't miss a duck into the **Iglesia de la Inmaculada Concepción** (☎ 237-0779; weekdays 8am–11am and 2pm–6pm, Saturday 8am–noon, Sunday 6am–7pm), the blocky, whitewashed church that looms over the square. It's a clean, neoclassical bit of business dating from 1797 (the second oldest church in Costa Rica) and declared a national monument in 1963. The inside's fetching—neither stark nor overdone, with fluted columns and plasterwork, gold-painted trim, and crystal-drop chandeliers. You can catch masses here Saturdays at 4 and 7pm and Sundays at 9am, 11am, 4pm, and 7pm. On the north side of the plaza, you'll spot the distinctive **El Fortín,** a 43-foot circular tower of an 1876 fort, not open to the public though (and just check out all those holes—not the smartest design, folks). Across from it, the **Casa de la Cultura** (☎ 261-4485; 9am-9pm; free) is the handsome, single-story house of an early-20th-century president named Alfredo González Flores, with lovely old tile floors and courtyards. What's it all about, Alfie? Well, there's no furniture left; it's all been given over to art exhibitions, along with a big, skylit central hall, which hosts music and other performances; the last Friday of every month is a particularly big day for all sorts of special events here. Out on the balustraded street-level veranda, the local culture and tourism **Info Center** (☎ 260-9452 or 393-0993; InfoCenterCR@yahoo.com; weekdays 9am-2pm, Sat. 8am-noon) not only hands out maps, schedules, and all sorts of other helpful stuff but also runs tours of the city (weekends, $50) and province up to Sarapiquí (Sundays, $75).

It seems like every major city in the Central Valley has its very own pet volcano, and the one outside Heredia, the nearly 2-mile-high **Volcán Barva,** happens to be Costa Rica's oldest as well as the most accessible part of one of the country's biggest chunks of protected nature, 183-square-mile **Barva Volcano/Braulio Carrillo National Park** ✚ (Puesto Barva station on Rte. 114, 3km/2 miles north of the town of Sacramento; www.costarica-nationalparks.com/brauliocarrillo nationalpark.html; ☎ 268-1038; daily 7:30am–3:30pm; $6). Some 26km (16 miles) north of downtown, it's higher than Poás in Alajuela and more crammed with flora and fauna that either Poás or Cartago's volcano, Irazú. Though it doesn't get the crowds those two sometimes do, mainly because you can't just drive right up—from the ranger station there's a mile-long trail to the main lake in the crater, Laguna Barva, 690m wide (2,300 ft.). But if you're up for the hike, what a magical experience—it's a riotously dense, mossy green wonderland of cloudforest, rainforest, rivers, and waterfalls, with something like 6,000 plant species (especially oodles of ferns, heliconias, and orchids), 515 kinds of birds (including toucans, eagles, even the legendary quetzales), and mammals including monkeys, mountain goats, pumas, jaguars, and honeybears. If you want more than a peek at the crater lake, there are plenty of other trails, ranging from .8km (less than a half-mile) up to 48km (30 miles). Just keep in mind it's a wilderness in here, and really geared to hardcore hikers who know what they're doing. It can get cold—dress in layers—muddy and slippery (rains a lot, too; it's driest in March and April). You can book a day trip to Barva through the **Info Center** in downtown Heredia's **Casa de la Cultura** (see above); if you're driving on your own, though, a four-wheel drive is a good idea, especially for that last rugged couple of klicks.

Slightly more manageable forms of eco-fun are on tap at several smaller reserves bordering Braulio Carrillo. One, 560 hectares (1,400 acres) in all near the town of San José de la Montaña, is home to **Canopy Adventure** (11km/7 miles north of downtown Heredia; ☎ 394-9222; www.canopycr.com; daily 7am–5:15pm, by reservation), where you can try what's become a signature of Costa Rica adventure travel: the zipline. This one involves 13 platforms built around giant oak trees, connected by 10 cables up to 200m long (660 ft.) that zoom you a good 39m (130 ft.) over the Porrosati river canyon, complete with waterfalls. There are three 2-hour tours a day, in the morning and early afternoon, and rates range from $40 adults/$30 kids if you get yourself up there on your own, to $73/$51 with transfers and lunch included. Oh, and a dog-lover alert: lots of 'em here.

Over on the eastern side of Braulio Carrillo, the **Rain Forest Aerial Tram Park** (Guápiles Hwy., 5km/3 miles north of Río Sucio bridge; ☎ 257-5961, or 866/ 759-8726; www.rfat.com; Mon 9am–4pm, Tues–Sun 6:30am–4pm) is a beautiful 480-hectare (1,200-acre) reserve that offers an eco-experience more on the prepackaged side than the national park. Its centerpiece is an 80-minute air-conditioned cable-car ride 50m (170 ft.) up in the rainforest canopy, which some people like and some find less than informative (not to mention pricey—a full-day tour, including lunch and hotel transfers, goes for $85 for adults, $58 for kids). There are also viewing platforms; hanging bridges; video/information room; a shop; a couple of eateries; butterfly, frog, and snake exhibits ($10 each), and a small (seven platforms, six lines) canopy tour that'll set you back an extra $45 (kids $30). And if you want to overnight, the 10-bungalow ecolodge will rent you a double from $109 (including meals, guided walks, and a couple of cable-car rides). It's not a bad choice especially if you're looking for something a little lower impact for your kids, seniors, or even yourself.

A lot closer in, java junkies should get a kaffeinated kick out of **Café Britt** ★ (500m/1,640 ft. north and 400m/1,312 ft. west of Automercado; ☎ 260-1456, or 800/462-7488 in the U.S. and Canada; www.cafebritt.com or www.coffeetour. com; daily 9am–5pm), a coffee roaster and marketer owned by short, bearded ex-Bronxite Steve Aronson, in business since 1985 and running tours since 1991. The country's best-known brand name (in coffee or anything else), Britt now pulls in more than 50,000 visitors a year to its 8-hectare (20-acre) spread just west of downtown Heredia. The 2-hour tour ranges over handsome stone pathways, some coffee bushes, and the processing facilities—but they go the extra mile to make it fun and friendly (some might say heading toward hokey), and throw in a little video presentation in a 180-seat theater. The basic price tag is $19 (kids $14), but there are lots of add-ons, natch: lunch; hotel transfers (from San José; if you're coming from Heredia you'll need to take a cab); coffee tastings; visits to plantations; combos with other attractions like butterfly garden, Poás volcano, and so forth. If on the other hand you want to show yourself around, it's free; if you want to save the bucks, that's fine, but if you can swing the tour, go for it—there really are some interesting moments. At the end, there's an elaborate shop crammed with packages of ground and whole-bean coffee and candy at good prices (about $2 less than at the airport, for example), including bulk discounts ($1 off per pack if you buy 20), plus free samples galore and free Internet terminals. Plus the breezy, bamboo-lined restaurant serves an organic buffet lunch that's tops but a little pricey ($18) if you buy it separate from a tour. And by the way, the theater also does artistic stuff on weekends from June through December (some in English), from *Macbeth* to the *The Vagina Monologues* ($7.75).

Another kind of neat but admittedly prepackaged nature attraction, **INBioparque** ★ (Calle 1 and Av. 7, 150m/492 ft. north of Radiográfica Costarricense; ☎ 507-8107; www.inbio.ac.cr; Tues–Sun 8am–6pm; last admission

4pm; adults $20, students $14, kids $8) is located outside the town of Santo Domingo de Heredia, 7 miles (11 km) from downtown in the direction of San José. The 5.5-hectare (14-acre) spread is part of the National Biodiversity Institute, and the 2-hour guided tour doesn't include a whole lot in the way of actual live critters, but does a good job of giving you a sense of Costa Rica's biodiversity and topography; it starts with a 15-minute video and then off you go on a three-trail walk through outdoor trails and indoor pavilions with exhibits including a butterfly garden and a lagoon you peek at through an underwater window. There's a restaurant and souvenir shop, and you can also opt for a full-day package including a jaunt to the Rain Forest Aerial Tram Park (see above). Very much worth a stop, just as long as you're not expecting the rainforest.

This last one might sound like it's mostly of interest to hardcore gardeners (which we're not), but we were still pretty impressed by the **Ark Herb Farm** (Cerro de Rosales, 2km/1¼ mile north of San Pedro de Santa Bárbara; ☎ 846-2694 or 239-2111; www.lospatitos.com/arkherbfarm/index.htm; Mon–Thurs 6am–3pm, Fri–Sat 6am–noon; $31), 7.2m (4½ miles) northwest of Heredia, west of the town of Santa Bárbara. Run by Tommy Thomas from Texarkana, Texas, it's a 6.8-hectare (17-acre) "ethno-botanical garden" that not only grows for export but also gives highly interesting (well, to some, anyhow) 2-hour tours of its more than 300 medicinal plants from all over the world. Take birthwort, for example—a plant with a long history of controlling bacterial infections, helping healing, and use by midwives to coax babies out of mommies—some studies even hint it has anti-cancer properties (now *that's* what we call flower power). Anyway, the folks here recommend you call the day before, and get up here early, between 9 and 9:30am.

The "Other" Heredia

The **Info Center** (☎ 260-9452 or 393-0993) at the **Casa de la Cultura** on the north side of the central park can fill you in on all kinds of doings around town, both in that same building and elsewhere. And this being a university town, there's often something going on up—a concert, a play, a lecture (sometimes even in English). At **UNA** (☎ 237-5929 or 277-3224; www.una.ac.cr/hoycampus), the national university, you can get the latest events bulletin online, though it's in Spanish only; another way of getting clued in is to get in touch with Paula Vargas Segnini (☎ 277-3822; PVarga@UNA.ac.cr), the lady in charge of the exchange-student program.

As we implied above, you can't throw a brick in Heredia without hitting a school of some sort—and a good bunch of them are language schools. And even if you don't want or need to take an actual Spanish class, one school, called **IPAI** (behind Liceo de Heredia, in front of the bus stop to University of Costa Rica in San José; ☎ 260-2100 or 826-2226; www.ipailanguageschool.com), has a fun and interesting "conversational club," where you can get together with the school's students Fridays and Saturdays 3 to 5pm so they can practice their English (and, if you want, you your Spanish). *One catch:* For nonstudents of the school there's a slightly steep fee of $19; it's good for a year, but for a pretty foolproof way of meeting Ticos, it could well be worth it.

If you want to go all the way and sign up for *español*, that, too, is a swell way to make instant connections in town here, especially if you take the option most schools offer of living with a local family. Following is a quality threesome to start with:

Spanish Abroad Heredia (☎ 244-2713, or 888/722-7623 in the U.S.; www. spanishabroad.com/cpi.htm) is the least expensive. Set in a small town near Santo Domingo, it offers dance classes and other cultural activities, and throws in the option to spend part of your time at its sister schools out on the Pacific at Tamarindo, Jacó, Sámara, and Manuel Antonio. Or maybe you'd prefer one of the pair in San José or yet another one up in Monteverde. The rate schedule including homestays starts at $290 for 1 week, up to $ 1,570 for a month; a private apartment will run you a bit more.

Based in the town of San Joaquín de Flores, the **Centro Panamericano de Idiomas** (☎ 265-6306, or 877/373-3116 in the U.S.; www.cpi-edu.com) also has locations in Monteverde and in the Pacific coast's Flamingo Beach, so you can divide your classes up between the three locations for a bit of a Costa Rica sampler experience. There are other cool CPI programs in Heredia, too, like a soccer camp, cooking/dance classes, field trips, and volunteer slots teaching English or helping poor local girls and adults with disabilities. Rates including books and homestays (and two meals a day) with local families run $415 to $520 for a week, up to $1,580 to $1,870 for a month; there's also an independent apartment option ($300 weekly up to $600 monthly).

Intercultura (☎ 260-8480, or 866/363-5421 in U.S. and Canada; www.inter culturacostarica.com) has another location you can split time between; this one, in the Guanacaste beach town of Sámara, offers a similar menu of music/dance/ cooking classes, cultural activities, and volunteer opportunities; one major difference is that it's located downtown rather than in a small town in the countryside. Here a half-board homestay with a week of classes and activities would run $370; for 4 weeks you'll pay $1,215.

The short-term volunteer opportunities in Heredia not directly connected with Spanish-language schools seem to be more limited than in other areas of the Central Valley, but there are several. For program fees starting at $900, for the minimum of 2 weeks, **Experiential Learning International** (☎ 303-321-8278; www.eliabroad.org) will have you pitching in at day camps for underprivileged kids, soup kitchens, clinics, and conservation work in Braulio Carrillo National Park. You'll have to speak some Spanish, though, but if you need help the program includes some language training. Also, at private reserves such as **Cerro Dantas Refugio de Vida Silvestre** (☎ 354-9271; www.cerrodantas.co.cr) you can give the botanists/biologists/researchers a hand and help with maintenance, but it's on a case-by-case basis; there's no structured program and no lodging provided.

For something a bit less formal, a good place to rub *codos* with the locals beyond lifting a few at the watering holes in town is to stop at downtown's traditional covered market, the **Mercado Central,** especially at the various companionable *soda* lunch counters (see "Dining for All Tastes," p. 68); there's also a Saturday-morning street market on Avenida Central (200m/656 ft. west of central park, in front of Banex), where locals and expats alike come to shop for greens, mangos and other tropical fruits, Turrialba cheese, flowers, and so on. In both of these cases, this is the kind of traditional market scene that has been part of Costa Rica culture and society for generations, and you'll be glad to see it hasn't been totally squeezed out of existence by soulless, sterile supermarkets and big-box stores. The market is also somewhat unique to the Central Valley with its larger cities and towns; you won't find these kinds of markets if you're going towards the beach, so check them out in this region before moving on.

Attention, Shoppers!

Like Alajuela's and also Cartago's, Heredia's shopping is overwhelmingly local rather than tourist-oriented. Locals have taken a shine to a big, modern mall just south of town on the road to San José called **Paseo de las Flores** (☎ 261-9898; www.paseodelasflores.com; Mon–Sat 10:30am–9pm, Sun 11am–8pm), crowned by a stylized version of El Fortín, the historic downtown tower that's Heredia's symbol. Especially on weekends, you'll also find artisans, sometimes music events, and attractions like a bungee jump, merry-go-round, and rock-climbing wall.

In terms of spots selling stuff you might actually want to take back home with you, one of the few shops in town is Marco Vinicio Vilchez' **Artesanía Pancho** (Calle 6 at Av. 12, 100m/328 ft. east of city hospital; ☎ 260-8281; Mon–Sat 8am–7pm, Sun 9am–2pm), with wood puzzles and animal boxes from $6.65, delicate paintings on feathers from $3.75, folkloric oxcarts also from $6.65 (if you can, though, get them at the source, in the Alajuela province town of Sarchí; p. 62), and indigenous tribal masks $12 and up.

For a much larger and more interesting selection, head to Moravia. Technically part of San José but just as convenient to Heredia if not more so, this town's crafts-shop district, the **Calle de las Artesanías,** is a couple of blocks on Calle 1 off Avenida 63 (look for a Shell station), and 3 blocks east of the main square, just north of the MegaSuper (drive through Tibás, then turn left at big AutoMercado stoplight that will lead you right into Moravia); it's a sliver under 3km (2 miles) past AutoMercado. The biggest of the shops over here are **Souvenir World** and the especially imposing **Souvenir el Gran Brunca.** But my favorite is **La Rueda** (☎ 297-2736; Mon–Sat 8am–7pm, Sun 9am–6pm), marked by a giant toucan and parrot on its roof. It's got a good-quality array not only of the usual stuff you'll see everywhere, but also some more unusual stuff. Highlights include clever little jewelry boxes made from irregular, polished hunks of tree trunk (a small two-drawer job runs $15), and rosewood jewelry boxes overlaid with real butterflies under glass (from $104); there's maybe 10 to 12 percent haggle room on those prices. Oh, and if you're jonesin' for some real Cuban cigars, they'll reband them for you to get past Customs. You might also want to make time for a tour of the leatherworking shop in the back. For paintings along this street, there's a small stretch of several shops, the best of which are both owned by Cuban Julio Ernesto Triana: **Souvenir Guayacán Real** and **Galería Orisha** (☎ 297-5074; Mon–Sat 8:30am–6pm, Sun 9am–5pm), where, for example, an 18×12 in acrylic would run around $80.

Nightlife

Frankly, a good bit of downtown Heredia's pretty dead at night—plus, it's so close to San José that most folks looking for a little action just hop into a car or onto a bus down to the big bad city. But on the other hand, the many students guarantee a certain amount of decent nightlife right here in town, more so than Alajuela or Cartago, certainly. There's your standard assortment of local watering holes in the wall, of course (look for any Imperial beer sign out front), but nightlife ground zero in town is the mini-student-bar-quarter, Avenida Central about a block and a half in from Calle 9 (road from San José, eastern edge of town near UNA), there seems to always something be going on over here at night, unlike elsewhere in town. First up is a 24-hour juice/sandwich joint called **La Guarapera** (touting its "Ticoburgers"); followed by the bakery-cafe **Trigo Miel;** a three-story bar-restaurant called **La Choza** (☎ 237-1553) with a nice, breezy upstairs balcony; and most especially the two-story **Bulevar Relax** (☎ 237-1832; daily 11am–1am) with its metal tables, glass-brick bar, pool tables, and foosball. At this last one, big mugs of beer run $4.60, and there's live *trova* (a type of easy listening) music Thursday through Saturday 8 to midnight.

Meanwhile, over on a block of Avenida 2 just west of the central park, there are a couple of other spots worth a gander. **Miraflores Disco** (☎ 237-1880; Fri–Sun 8pm–3am; cover $1.95) is a favorite that's been packing them in since 1971, and just below it in the same building, **Taberna Tropical** (daily 7pm–3am; no cover) brings in live bands on Tuesdays and Thursdays. Also over here is the popular **Bar Océano** (Calle 4 between avs. 2 and 4; ☎ 260-7809; daily 11am–midnight; no cover), which pumps out mostly classic and alt rock.

Finally, just down the hill from the university on the road to San José, a double-decker strip mall called **Plaza Heredia** (Av. 4 at Calle 9) is also something of a student hangout, thanks especially to a popular trio of bars out back. One is **Speed 7** (☎ 865-0051; Fri–Sun 7pm–2am; cover $2.90), a small, very loud, race-car-themed video bar where ladies drink free on Friday and Saturday. And a hop and a skip away in a ugly brown building, **2-cos Place** (☎ 341-6336; Tues–Sun 7pm–2am; cover $1.95–$2.90), a music club known for cheap beer (96¢! 77¢ on Sun!), gets especially crankin' on Tuesday and Thursday when *las chicas* get in free 7 to 11pm, Friday for reggaetón night (when EXA radio 92.3FM broadcasts), and Saturday when DJs crank up the hip-hop and dance hall. Right next door, red-lit-dungeon-flavored **Champs Disco** (☎ 391-8181; Thurs–Sun 7pm–2:30am; girls $2.90, guys $3.50) draws a very young crowd and goes more tropical, as in salsa, merengue, and cumbia; Saturday's open bar is, *hic,* nasherally a biiig draw.

CARTAGO

Some Ticos will tell you there ain't all that much to make Cartago (pop. 27,000) worth the 9.3km (15-mile) drive from San José. Yeah, once upon a time it was a big deal hereabouts—founded in 1563, it logged 260 years as Costa Rica's first capital and for a good chunk of that, its only real city. The *cartaginense* mucky mucks not only held the reins of government but pretty much had a lock on the colony's trade, Caribbean cacao plantations, the Guanacaste ranches, you name it. But once Tico independence from Spain arrived in 1821, Cartago lost out to the new capital, San José (though not without a fight, dammit), and settled into life as the quietest of the Central Valley's three main provincial cities, surrounded by rich farmland where coffee was becoming ever the bigger deal.

Over the generations, earthquakes and fires took their toll on the colonial architecture, and though in town there are still some old stone sidewalks, a pretty above-ground cemetery on the western edge of town, and cute little houses and buildings here and there (gingerbread Victorian, neoclassical, and so forth), more typical is downtown's Plaza Mayor, dominated by the atmospheric **Santiago Apóstol ruins,** a 1562 church flattened twice by quakes before they finally left the darn thing alone after 1910. Try to come see it, if you can, on Sunday around 10am or Thursday around 5:30pm, when the town band gives concerts in the square (info ☎ 260-3092); just ignore the charm-killing Papa John's and Burger King on the south side. It's also interesting to take a stroll through the **Mercado Central,** a covered market with restaurants and stalls selling everything from meat and produce to hardware and toothpaste (no tourist souvenirs here, unlike the one in San José). But the city's main claim to fame these days, even more so than being the gateway to nearby **Irazú Volcano National Park** (see below), is as home to Costa Rica's most impressive church, the fanciful **Iglesia de la Virgen de los Ángeles** (see below), a pilgrimage site that's the Tico version of Lourdes or Santiago de Compostela.

So while the city of Cartago itself is not everybody's idea of a thrill a minute, the real knockouts out this way are actually found out of town, in Cartago province, with areas flaunting some of the Central Valley's most spectacular scenery; it's a wonderful place to hang out for a few days if what you're looking for is peace, quiet, and nature. There's Irazú, of course, but also the nearby **Orosi Valley** (pop. 8,900), where the local Tico community has been supplemented in recent years by a gang of gringos who've opened B&Bs and such. The drive from Cartago to this steep-walled, 60-sq.-km (23-sq.-mile) valley—especially once you get past the town of Paraíso—is nothing short of breaktaking, with mountains, several rivers, a manmade lake, pine forests, and fields of coffee and chayote (like a cross between potato and squash, chayote grows on supports above the ground, so the fields have a really cool 3D look to them).

The valley's main town has the same name, and that's where most of the restaurants and some of the lodgings are; it's tiny and *extremely* laid-back—in fact, you come here to get away from it all and get up close and personal with local natural beauty by hiking, horseback riding, and watersports on the Cachí reservoir (fed by the Reventazón river, which has a great name—"explosion"—no doubt due to the flash floods that still happen every once in awhile). There are a few modest attractions scattered around the valley, connected by a road that loops around the reservoir (or, you might say, makes a ring around Orosi); they include the oldest church in Costa Rica and the oldest one still operating; but one of the highlights for me is **Café Cristina,** a mom-and-pop organic coffee farm that offers a very different take on the country's java industry than you'll get at Britt in Heredia and Doka in Alajuela. Farther east, 53km (33 miles) from San José and 40km (25 miles) from Cartago, Turrialba is a cute hill town that can be used as a base for some of Costa Rica's best whitewater rafting, as well as its top pre-Columbian archeology site, the **Guaynabo National Monument.**

Getting to & Around Cartago

LUMACA Route 300 buses (60¢) make the 45-minute run from San José to Cartago weekdays 6am to midnight, weekends 6am to 2am, leaving every 15 minutes from the corner opposite the Teatro Nacional. **Route 339** buses to Orosi from Cartago leave every 20 to 30 minutes from the terminal behind the Iglesia de los Padres Capuchinos between 4:45am and 10pm; it takes about a half-hour and the fare is 65¢. To Turrialba, **Route 302** buses leave hourly every day between 4am and 10:30pm from the southeast side of the Tribunales de Justicia (city courthouse); it costs $1.05 and takes 45 minutes. Some Orosi innkeepers will shuttle you from San José and the airport for an extra fee.

You won't need a car within the city of Cartago, but for everything else in the area, it makes more sense to rent wheels than depend on public buses. In that case, you'll take the Panamerican Highway on a pretty much straight shot east to Cartago in about a half-hour to 45 minutes, depending on traffic. To drive to Orosi from Cartago, take the road that goes east out of town to Paraíso, then hang a right at the central park and head south; you'll hit Orosi town just over 7km (4 miles) southeast of Paraíso; it does get a little twisty and turny, so watch it, especially at night. For the road to Turrialba, instead of turning right in Paraíso keep going straight and you'll see a sign pointing left toward Turrialba; from here it's 38km (24 miles), passing through the towns of Birrisito, Cervantes, and Juan Viñas.

Accommodations, Both Standard & Not

There's not much in Cartago itself, since most people come to get out into the countryside, but whether in town or out in the sticks, most digs tend to be small and on the inexpensive side. For rock-bottom ($6.50–$25), your best bet's probably **Montaña Linda** (☎ 533-3640; www.montanalinda.com), a hostel and language school in Orosi town.

VACATION RENTALS

The Orosi Valley is the main place for rentals, though they're fairly scarce. I have but one pick in the area but it promises a real Bali high: Steve and Nancy Riley's Indonesian-flavored **Paradise Peak** (☎ 533-1453, or 800/867-5761 in the U.S.; www.paradisepeak.com), on a coffee/citrus farm and 1.2 hectares (3 acres) of botanical gardens. For $60 a night ($360 a week) it sleeps up to four in a two-bedroom/one-bath with some nifty details (check out the spiral staircase and the whimsical frog sink in the kitchen) and perks (like an outdoor Jacuzzi and a DVD player with a hundred or so late-run flicks—though no TV reception, because, says Steve, "the news was always bad.")

HOTELS

$ Out in Orosi town, the **Hotel Reventazón** (300m/984 ft. south and 25m/82 ft. west of soccer field; ☎ 533-3838; AE, D, MC, V) is a great little place with a great big view to the north of the Turrialba and Irazú volcanoes and seven comfy rooms in a double-decker block; for just $40 a night, they're cheerful (sponge-painted yellow walls, blue-tile floors, nice friezes) and surprisingly crammed with amenities (private baths, ceiling fans, small TV, phone, minifridge, safe, even room service). Try to score one of the units on the upper floor, which have the volcano views along with higher ceilings. Other pluses include a nice 24/7 bar; an open-air restaurant (daily 7am–9pm) that's something of a gringo hangout and serves up a mean chocolate cheesecake, and a holding tank so you won't run out of H_2O as can happen in the valley on occasion. Your hosts are Frank Bynum and his wife, Tiffany Carroll, who moved down here from Orlando in 2005; they're very nice but very white—by that we mean so gringo they still, for example, barely speak Spanish. Fortunately, they've got a great staff which will take care of you to a T.

$ You don't necessarily have to schlep way out of the city for some dandy topographic eye candy. **Las Brumas** (2km/1¼ miles east of Puente Bailey, carretera al

Volcán Irazú; ☎ 553-3535; MC, V), in the hillside community of San Rafael de Oreamuno just above Cartago on the road to Irazú volcano, is a little inn with a woody, Alpine flavor, very friendly staff, and 13 clean, homey, and fresh-feeling rooms at $47 for a double, including breakfast. They all have private bath, 10 have cable TV, and a half-dozen "B rooms" add phones and open onto a common balcony that'll give you a nice eyeful over a sloping meadow toward the mountains in the distance. Internet access is also offered here, but the coolest perk is the fact that you're right above a big, country-style restaurant called Mi Tierra, with great grub and even better prices (p. 83).

$ If you're up for a night or two smack in the city of Cartago, Paulina Mora Sáenz' seven-room **Los Ángeles Lodge** (Av. 4 between calles 14 and 16, on the north side of Plaza Santuario Nacional; ☎ 829-6279; AE, MC) may just be the best game in town. It's certainly got one of the best locations: on the second floor of an early-20th-century red-brick building right next door to Puerta del Sol restaurant—and a quick 'n' easy crawl to the Los Angeles basilica just across the street (some of the faithful make the last part of their pilgrimages on their knees, you'll see). For $22 per person or $35 for a double, you get homey quarters with painted wood-plank walls, newish green-tiled baths, and cable TV (there's no phone). In the rear, a skylit newer wing has larger units for a couple of bucks more a night; their beige-tiled baths do sport slightly roomier showers, but personally, give us rooms no. 2 and 3 upfront because of their basilica views. Breakfast is included in a comfy lounge area with picture windows.

$ Just a skip up the street from the Hotel Reventazón, on a small rise at the southern edge of Orosi town, the 7-year-old **Orosi Lodge** (25m/16 miles east of Balneario Termal Orosi; ☎ 533-3578; www.orosilodge.com; AE, MC, V) is just a smidgeon pricier (doubles are $48 in high season, $40 in low), and it has a little more architectural charm but no TVs or phones in its half-dozen white rooms, crisply furnished in rattan and each sporting an excellent orthopedic bed, minifridge, private bath, and balcony or terrace. Even if you don't stay here, definitely stop by the cafe (daily 7am–7pm) upfront for an organic cuppa; to check e-mail; buy Costa Rican artworks or music CDs; play foosball; or have a listen to the genuine 1959 Wurlitzer jukebox, complete with its original 45s (tutti frutti, baby!). Bavarian owners Andreas Veit and Cornelia Neck also rent out canoes and mountain bikes.

$ Perched along the road down to town, the **Orosi Valley Farm** ✵ (800m/2,624 ft. before Puente Negro; ☎ 533-3001, or 866/369-7871 from the U.S. and Canada; www.orosivalleyfarm.com; MC, V) has just three rooms on a steep 2-hectare (5-acre) plot filled with fruit trees draped in Spanish moss; a superbly high-up version of the boffo valley vista; and a superfriendly boxer terrier named Gretel (we're dog people, so sue us). We love the high-ceilinged common room, which feels like it's floating over the valley and is quirkily appointed with colorful paintings, clay flowers, and papier-mâché heads made by local artists (check out the cabinet filled with indigenous pottery, too). Our favorite room's the upstairs unit of "Las Cabinas," lined with bamboo and offering excellent closet space and a great tree-house flavor (no exaggeration—you can step out on your balcony and pluck a mandarin orange right from the tree). The damage? Just $39 a night, including a breakfast heavy on fresh fruit. Co-owners Ray Reynolds, Chad Edwards, and Jimmy Nichols—Kentuckians all—take turns hosting.

$–$$ Another small inn perched along one of the valley's walls (and with a great view of one of the local waterfalls, 225m/750 ft. high), the **Orosi Jungle Villa** (3km/2 miles toward Ujarrás past bomberos de Paraíso; ☎ 574-5213, or 770/889-4846 in the U.S.; www.costaricavalleyhotel.com; AE, DC, MC, V) offers perks that'll please folks who just can't let go of their high-tech toys. There's a "media room" with a flat-screen TV equipped with DVD player and satellite Internet hookup, plus CD/DVD players in all four rooms, and two also throw in flat-screen TV/DVD and iPod boom box (those go for $69, otherwise the rate's $49; breakfast included). The rooms are a spiffy mix of white and woody, and eclectically appointed with local artists' objects and murals (the Mango Room delivers the best gawk at the falls). Innkeeper Cray Palmer is an old Costa Rica hand who first came here from New Orleans in 1970 and knows the area cold; he also offers all-inclusive tours of the Central Valley's highlights.

$$ With one of the valley's highest and most spectacular vantage points, just off the road as you drive down from Paraíso, **Sanchiri Mirador & Lodge** (2km/1¼ miles south of Paraíso central park; ☎ 574-5454; www.sanchiri.com; AE, MC, V) also has the local distinction of being run not by gringos but by Jorge Luis and Claudio Mata, since 1991, on land that's been in their family for generations. At $52 for a double, you have your choice of five stand-alone two-story cabins with balconies, private baths, and lovely wood-paneled interiors but not much else in the way of amenities (just a phone), or a dozen slightly more mod-feeling hotel-style rooms. One of the big draws here is the large and mighty good restaurant, serving up some great local and international dishes along with that amazing view (daily 7am–9pm).

$$–$$$$ The Orosi's largest, fanciest, and bells-and-whistliest digs, the **Hotel Río Perlas** ✹ (2½km west of Puente Negro; ☎ 533-3341, or 866/794-6478 in the U.S. and Canada; AE, DC, MC, V) is tucked up in the hills on a 108-hectare (270-acre) spread with a couple of restaurants (daily 7:30am–10:30pm), several pools, full-service spa ($57 Swedish massage, anybody?), bar, souvenir shop, babbling brook and waterfall, trout-fishing lakes and ponds—even a wedding chapel (lovebirds R us, evidently). The 69 units—mostly split among lowslung whitewashed, red-tile-roofed *casitas* and spiffy stand-alone log cabins—are similarly plush, with terraces or balconies and extras you won't find anywhere else in the valley (minibar, hair dryer, satellite TV, that sort of thing). Naturally, all this'll cost ya; out of season the $87 isn't so bad, but it hits splurge territory in season at $169 (that's rack rate, though; give it a try and there's a decent chance you'll catch a break).

Dining for All Tastes

As in every other Tico city and town, your first line of pocketbook defense when it comes to filling your belly are the *sodas,* and in Cartago they're found on and around main plazas and streets, plus several inside the colorful **Mercado Central** (between avs. Central and 6, and calles 3 and Nacional; Mon–Sat 6am–6pm). You can also grab sandwiches and lighter fair at quite a few *panaderías* (bakeries) and *reposterías* (pastry shops) around town; one particularly good chain you'll spot here and there is **Trigo Miel.** Several spots listed under "Nightlife" also have pretty decent menus, such as **Iguana Sports Café** and **Bar-Restaurante Sunset.** North of town, there are several little hillside eateries on the road to **Irazú** volcano, such as **Mi Tierra** (p. 83); there's an eatery up at the park, too. Out in Orosi, in addition to the options listed below, see also "Accommodations"; **Sanchiri Mirador & Lodge, Hotel Reventazón,** and **Hotel Río Perlas** are also good picks for grub.

$ Good, solid home cooking on the front porch of a Tico home pretty much sums up Orosi's **Soda Luz** (150m/500 ft. north of church; ☎ 533-3701; weekdays 7am–4pm, weekends 7am–9pm; cash only). Luz Coto Quesada, a friendly little slip of a lady, has run this unpretentious eatery out of her blue-and-white in-town family home since 1995. The big thing here is breakfast ($1.90) and *casados* ($2.50), those typically Tico combo plates which here usually mean beef, pork, or chicken in a tomato-based sauce, with rice, beans, pasta, salad, a veggie soup or fish stew, and a simple dessert (à la flan or a fresh orange). For something even lighter, burgers and sandwiches run a mere $1.45, and refreshing *licuados* (pureed blackberry and other fruits in water) just 75¢. The little woodburning stove, the red-white-and-blue tablecloths, the no-nonsense grub—it's all just simple home-spun perfect.

$–$$ For us, one of the best things about **Bar-Restaurante Coto** ★ (north side of soccer field; ☎ 533-3032; daily 8am–midnight; AE, DC, MC, V) is its dining-room view (Great!) of the valley's steep southern walls. But Orosi town's biggest, longest-running (1952) eatery has plenty else to recommend it, too. An open-air, rancho-flavored space with terra-cotta-tile floors, rustic rough-hewn wood columns and beams, it's run by Manuel Coto Picado and sons, who're doing a bang-up job of slinging high-quality local cuisine at very reasonable prices (most mains run $3.45–$7.70); order a *tabla* from the *menú especial* ($7.30–$7.70), like our favorite, No. 7: the *tabla de surtido* with fried pork chunks, chicken fajitas, and *churrasco*-style steak, accompanied by chimichurri sauce, beans, and tortillas. The clientele's half foreigners and half locals, and there are menus in English. The bar area turns into a bit of a nightspot especially on weekends, and you can also pick up some local art ($3–$140).

$–$$ Back in downtown Cartago, meanwhile, **La Puerta del Sol** (Av. 4 between calles 14 and 16, north side of Plaza Santuario Nacional; ☎ 551-0615; Mon–Fri 8am–11pm, Sat–Sun 8am–midnight; AE, MC, V) is a split-level local classic right across from the Los Angeles pilgrimage church, of which it has ringside views through picture windows. In business since 1957, the place has a fittingly anti-quated air, with wood paneling and fluted columns, green-padded wood booths, and old black-and-whites of the famous church and vicinity. The good-size bill of fare (with English translations) is loaded with the rib-sticking and the affordable (entrees run $3.75–$7.15, *casados* $3.50–$4.15). The house specialties are mahimahi or tenderloin in seafood sauce (both $6.35), and if you're really feeling adventurous, have a gander at the priciest dishes, in the "tongue" section (in mushroom sauce, tomato sauce, and the like). They can keep their tongues to themselves, personally—but I must say, I do like their coconut flan ($1.85).

$–$$ For a break from local fare, that's-a nice-a pizza pie at **Pizzeria Luz de Luna** (125m/410 ft. from soccer field, next to Banco Nacional; ☎ 533-3825; Mon–Thurs 2–10pm, Fri–Sat 11:30am–10pm; cash only), a stylishly rustic spot (hewn wood columns, burlap-fabric chairs, hanging wicker light fixtures at each table, local art on the walls) run by friendly locals Emilio and Rosa, it tosses a good 10 types of pizza ($2.90–$11), with light tasty crusts and something for everyone, carnivorous or herbivorous (in fact, one of the faves is the veggie pizza, with thin-sliced tomatoes and a good dusting of oregano). On weekend nights the joint can get kind of mobbed, so you might even find yourself waiting for a table.

$–$$ Around here, nothing says a fun family meal out better than **Restaurante Mi Tierra** ★★ 🅺 (2km/1¼ miles east of Puente Baily, carretera al Volcán Irazú; ☎ 553-3838; daily 8am–10pm; V), a quick drive up the hill toward the volcano, in the small community of San Rafael de Oreamuno. It's a huge place with a rustic log-cabin decor, with all kinds of hanging onions, bananas, yokes, wagon wheels, and plows (try to snag one of the handful of tables with a view of the mountains, in the back). Especially on weekends, Mi Tierra is jammed with *cartaginenses,* including lots of families (it's especially kid-friendly because of its indoor playground and small kids' menu, with entrees all $3), being serenaded by a marimba band. Corn—soups, tamales, breads, ears—is big, some of it savory, some candy-sweet (slurp down some *pozol,* chunky corn in chicken broth). But the Spanish-only menu is huge, with something for everybody—as are portions, served on wood platters covered with banana leaves; main dishes run up to $9, *casados* are $4.50 to $5.60. One of my favorites here, though, is *resbaladera* ($1.35), a drink made from milk, rice, cinnamon, sorrel, and peanuts—like a yummy rice pudding, only liquid.

$–$$$ The king of both cookery and class in Orosi—and very possibly all of Cartago—is surprisingly pretty affordable at **La Casona del Cafetal** ★★★ 🅺 (2km/1¼ miles south of Cachí dam; ☎ 577-1414; www.lacasonadelcafetal.com; daily 11:30am–6pm; AE, MC, V), whose entrees top out around $15 (for jumbo shrimp) but start at just $5.60 for chicken dishes; *casados* are an even better bargain at $5.30 to $6.65. Yet the quality and gracious atmosphere at this idyllic red-brick restaurant—a local institution since 1994, it has a spectacular view over the Cachí reservoir—is top-dollar. The skylit interior is handsome and high-ceilinged, but the spot to sit is out on the terrace, gazing through vine-draped bowers at the water. Because of that, and its little landscaped island with a moat you can rent boats on, it's particularly ravishing for romance-hounds, and moms and dads will also appreciate the playground and Sunday pony rides. Sunday, in fact, is the big day here, because of the locally famous noon to 6pm *boulevar* (all-you-can-scarf buffet), a gastro-extravaganza that's $15 per person (kids $5.95–$8.25); it's also the best day for the on-premises artisans' market.

Why You're Here: The Top Sights & Attractions
IN & AROUND CARTAGO
How can we not start with Cartago's big kahuna? The **Basílica de Nuestra Señora de los Ángeles** (between avs. 2 and 4, and calles 14 and 16, east side of Plaza Santuario Nacional; daily 5:30am–8pm; free), "Our Lady of the Angels," is the turf of Costa Rica's patron saint—its Lourdes, Fatima, and Santiago de

Compostela rolled into one. The 1635 original was, of course, flattened by an earthquake, so the tin-roofed confection you behold today—gray with graceful white angels, belltowers, and trim—dates from the 1920s. All the fuss is about an 8-inch black stone statue of the Virgin Mary (dubbed *La Negrita*, "the little black lady"), which, as the story goes, was found by a peasant girl on a rock on this site. So the padres had built what became the country's top pilgrimage church, and every August 2 thousands of Ticos and other Central Americans trek here from San José, many on their knees over the last stretch across the plaza (and a few of the superzealous all the way from the capital, ouch). Other times of the year, you can catch some knee-shuffling up the central nave at any given Sunday mass, in a soaring interior like some fanciful English Victorian pavilion or railway station plastered with colorful Tico folk designs. La Negrita's in there somewhere—just tough to spot amid all the baroque altar's gilded curlicues—and on the church's east side you can go down into an "ex-voto" museum built in 2001 to display all the stuff folks have dedicated to her over the years (including sports trophies and lots of charms in the shape of "miraculously" healed body parts); you can also see a diorama portraying her founding, along with the reknowned rock itself. Nearby there's a circular ramp to a grotto where a natural spring spouts conveniently pre-blessed water (fork over less than a couple of bucks for a little plastic La Negrita jug right on the spot and fill 'er up).

Costa Rica's sure has no shortage of volcanoes, but its tallest active one (3,432m/11,257 ft.) is just north of the city, in the 2,309-hectare (5,700-sq.-acre) **Irazú Volcano National Park** (27km/17 miles north of Puente Bailey; www.costa rica-nationalparks.com/irazuvolcanonationalpark.html; ☎ 200-5025; daily 8am–3:30pm; $7, kids $1). Don't worry, it hasn't seriously blown its top since 1965 (the last little burp was in '94), and folks smarter than we—though surely not you—are still keeping an eye on things even as you read this. In fact, compared to **Arenal** (p. 92) and even **Poás** up in Alajuela (p. 56), Irazú doesn't provide as much in the way of fireworks; the main point here is to ogle the eerie, sulphur-scented lunar landscape and the awesome views (on a good day you can see as far as the Caribbean, Pacific, and the Lago de Nicaragua). There are four craters, but the main pair are Diego de la Haya and the only active one, Cráter Principal—1,505m (3,445 ft.) wide, 300m (985 ft.) deep—are both filled with greenish lakes; along the northwest rim of Principal you'll spy some fumaroles a-spouting. The road up to the park (actually, practically up to the rim) is nicely paved, and there's not much in the way of hiking trails or flora/fauna to see; just a short path to the craters from the visitor center. There's a small eatery with picture windows up here (claims to be Central America's highest restaurant). *Some tips:* Try to make it up during the dry season (Dec–Apr); get here as early as possible (clouds can set in as early as noon); avoid Sundays, when Tico families like to make excursions up here; and always have a jacket or sweater with you—it does get chilly, billy. If you're coming out here from San José, you might also consider doing it as an escorted tour; one local outfit we like is **Expediciones Tropicales** (☎ 257-4171; www.costaricainfo.com), whose 5-hour visit ($36) includes a swing around Cartago city.

For about as much tropical flower power as you can handle, head about east of Cartago toward the town of Paraíso, where the 11-hectare (27-acre) **Jardín Botánico Lankester** ✦ (3km/2 miles east of Cartago, near Casa Vieja restaurant/across from the AMANCO factory; ☎ 552-3247; jbl@cariari.ucr.ac.cr; 8:30am–4:30pm; $5, students $3.50) showcases exotic-looking blooms, specializing in epiphytes—plants that grow on top of other plants. At this University of Costa Rica research project and botanical garden, founded in 1973 on the spread of expat Brit coffee magnate Charles Lankester, the star of the show is an impressive 800-species orchid collection, but the greenhouses and gardens and well-marked forest pathways are also chockablock with more than 3,000 other types of bromeliads, heliconias, cacti, ferns, bamboo, palms, and other *Land Before Time*–style flora up the wazoo (and where there are flowers and trees, there are lots of birds and butterflies). You'll get the best show during the February to April blooming season, especially March and April. There's a little shop in here selling coffee, books, paintings, crafts, and tchotchkes, along with a picnic area.

IN & AROUND OROSI

Starting in town, the main "attraction" would be the adobe **Iglesia San José de Orosi** (west side of soccer field; ☎ 533-3051; Tues–Sun 9am–5pm, but hours can vary). Founded in 1743 by Franciscan friars burned out of their original digs on the Talamanca coast by ticked-off indigenous tribes, this is Costa Rica's oldest still in business. It's a colonial charmer, with three naves; ornate wooden altars; cedar columns and struts; and 17th-century paintings from Guatemala and Mexico of stations of the cross and other religious scenes. At the southeast side is the **Museo de Arte Religioso** (Tues–Sat 1–5pm, Sun 9am–5pm; adults 60¢, kids 30¢), which once used to be a monastery and then a trade school for indigenous people. The first couple of rooms have panels in Spanish and English detailing the history of the area and the church, and in the rest you'll find various furnishings (including an antique pulpit and confessional); 18th-century Mexican religious paintings; vestments and bibles; indigenous pottery and other artifacts; and altarpieces from other churches (including the one at Ujarrás, now in ruins; see below). Also check out the recreation of a monk's cell—just a leather cot, a chest, and a rosary, it's an eye-opener for the iPod generation.

San José may be Costa Rica's oldest still-operating church, but make a point of taking a short drive out of town to the **Ujarrás Church Ruins** (7km/4⅓ miles east of Paraíso on road to Cachí, across from public pool complex; daily 7am–5pm; free), the country's oldest church still (more or less) standing—it dates almost 2 centuries earlier, to 1575. On a shady, parklike little plot of land surrounded by chayote fields, it's a sweet little spot where you'll often find Tico families hanging out before or after a dip in the public pool across the way, punctuated by the gorgeous little ruin of Nuestra Señora de la Purísima Concepción del Rescate de Ujarrás, which was beyond most pure rescue after the surrounding town was wiped out by a flood in 1833. It was built to commemorate yet another "miraculously" discovered Virgin Mary figurine, and if you show up here on April 16, you'll find all sorts of hoopla around a procession of this little statue to this church from its current home in the town of Paraíso, just north of the valley.

Be sure to make time for caffeinated peek at another kind of bygone Costa Rica history up on slopes north of Orosi town, where Ernest Carman, Linda Moyher, and their three kids kept **Finca Cristina** (Birrisito, 3km/2 miles east of Paraíso on Turrialba Hwy.; ☎ 574-6426, or 800/355-8826 from the U.S. and Canada; www.cafecristina.com; by appointment; $10; MC, V) going on 12 hectares (30 acres) of mountainside since 1977. We've done the better known coffee tours at places like Britt and Doka, but what Linda and Ernest provide visitors with is totally different: a look at an intimate mom-and-pop operation that's an ecofriendly throwback—growing, grinding, and roasting just 50 to 100 pounds a day of fabulous shade-grown organic Arabica. In fact, unless you have 2 or 3 hours to kill (which is how long the tour can take), you might want to mention you need the abbreviated version. In either case, it's a superfascinating up-close-and-personal look at java from plant to cup, ending up in the small roasting shed, where you can taste the luscious brew and buy bags of the stuff at wholesale prices ($5 for 14 oz.) along with chocolate-covered coffee beans, shirts, aprons, and so forth. Some great bird-watching here, too (280 species)—and if you're a dawg-lover, they've got a friendly bunch of mutts romping around.

If you've got some extra time to kill, you can always head 12km (7½ miles) south of Orosi for another nature fix at the 57,600-hectare (144,000-acre) **Tapantí-Macizo Cerro la Muerte National Park** (at end of road; ☎ 200-0090; www.costarica-nationalparks.com/tapantinationalpark.html; daily 7am–5pm; $7), whose claim to fame is H_2O, and lots of it: for starters, Costa Rica's highest average rainfall (280 in. a per year), along with swimmin' holes, waterfalls galore, and 150-plus rivers and streams, the biggest of which is the Río Grande de Orosi. As you can guess, that means a lot of green—hundreds of tree species—plus a cavalcade of critters (a good four dozen kinds of mammals, including jaguars), almost as many amphibians and reptiles, and hundreds of birds (including the rare and legendary quetzal). You take the main road in 1.6 km (1 mile) to the ranger station, then branch out on three trails, the longest of which should take no more than an hour and a half. It's darn pretty in here, and you might be tempted to overnight—in which case at La Esperanza del Guarco Biological Station for a coupla bucks you can rent a cabin that's basic but does have showers 'n' power.

IN & AROUND TURRIALBA

Speaking of water, thanks to a bunch of gorgeous gushers including the Reventazón (Class III), Pacuare (Class IV), and Pascua (Class IV), the Turrialba area's one of Costa Rica's rip-roaringest for year-round **river-running** ★★ in rafts, kayaks, and canoes (not a few Olympic kayaking teams train here). The scenery's breathtaking as you float (or careen) through steep-walled gorges punctuated with lush rainforest and spectacular waterfalls; in the quieter moments there's some amazing wildlife-spotting.

A number of local outfitters offer tours covering the area's highlights, specializing in whitewater. One of the biggest, best and oldest (1985) is Fernando Esquivel and Rafa Gallo's **Ríos Tropicales** (☎ 233-6455, or 866/722-8273 in the U.S. and Canada; www.riostropicales.com). Other good ones include another pioneer, Michael Kaye's **Costa Rica Expeditions** (☎ 257-0766; www.costarica expeditions.com), as well as **Costa Rica Rios** (☎ 556-9617, or 888/434-0776 in the U.S. and Canada; www.costaricarios.com), **Rio Locos Tropical Tours** (☎ 556-6035; www.whiteH20.com), and **Tico's River Adventures** (☎ 556-1231; www. ticoriver.com). Come to think of it, with all these outfits converging on just a small handful of rivers, you'd half-expect aquatic traffic jams—but somehow *no problema.* Anyway, costs and times vary, depending on which river you're on, where you're leaving from (here in Turrialba or being picked up in San José), and how fancy you wanna get (some outfits now offer fancy-schmancy cooking, Wi-Fi, and other frills). But most basic 1-day trips fall in the $65 to $100 per-person range; there are also overnighters, and for hardcore adrenaline junkies, even week-long packages.

And more ruins, anybody? A little older, this time—Costa Rica was inhabited by tribal peoples before the Spaniards barged in, and though they didn't leave cinematic cities like the Maya, Inca, and Aztecs did, there are a few spots where they left their mark—the most interesting and impressive (excavated so far, anyway) being the 220-hectare (550-acre) **Guayabo National Monument** ✦ (10km/6¼ miles after Santa Teresita bridge; ☎ 559-1220; www.costarica-nationalparks.com/guayabo nationalmonument.html; daily 8am–3:30pm; $4, kids $1), about a dozen miles northeast of town. Nobody knows why the Guayabos suddenly hightailed it out of here around 1400 A.D. (some think they headed south to Colombia for some reason), but in the town as many as 10,000 of them inhabited for a good 2,400 years, archeologists have been hacking away since 1968, and they've dug up about 4 hectares (10 acres) of cobblestone roads, aqueducts and bridges, temple and circular house foundations, and petroglyphs. It takes about 40 minutes to an hour to stroll the paths; you can do it either on your own with a pamphlet from the ranger station or with a guide (for just $5.75, a good bet). If you're moved to overnight, there's a campsite.

The "Other" Cartago

Los Ángeles church, with its stream of pilgrims from all over the country every day and especially on weekends and above all Sundays, is very much the heart of Cartago and should be visited, if you're interested in learning about life here. All are welcome at masses. And there seems to be something about the pilgrim/ "seeker" experience that invites camaraderie and sharing; of course, it helps to have some rudimentary Spanish.

For something a little more physical, how about a yoga class east of the city at the **Centro de Balance Integral Arco Iris** (road to Paraíso, 700m/2,300 ft. south of Casa Vieja restaurant; ☎ 551-7566; $19 per month, call for individual class rates/times; Mon–Sat 8am–9pm)?

There are plenty of chances around here for volunteering, too. In the Orosi Valley, **Tropical Adventures** (☎ 800/832-9419 in the U.S. and Canada; www.my tropicaladventure.com), run by gringo psychologist and former USAF chaplain Scott Pralinsky and his Tico partner Isaac García, puts you into the small town of La Flor to help teach things like recycling, English, or computers. Or maybe you'd like to direct kids' activities or help out with upkeep, gardening, and repairs at the town orphanage. The minimum commitment is 2 weeks, and the cost is $597 a week (then $195 for each additional week), and it's well organized and tries to be as full service as possible, including not just room and board but stuff like airport pickups, free cell phones, and guided tours.

Cross-Cultural Solutions (☎ 800/380-4777 in the U.S.; www.crosscultural solutions.com) also runs a program in the Cartago region, where choices include teaching English in poor communities; working in daycare for seniors, disabled people, and poor kids; and AIDS-related work (like helping doctors treating patients, counseling and education, caring for kids whose families are affected by the disease); an all-inclusive 2-week program is $2,489, then $272 for each extra week.

In the Orosi/Paraíso area, at **Finca La Flor de Paraíso** (☎ 534-8003; www.la-flor-de-paraiso.org), a 14-hectare (35-acre) nonprofit environmental school and organic farm, you can for example help with the farming and animal-raising (time to slop the hogs, pa!), plant trees for reforestation, and lend a hand with local environmental education efforts—all for $12–$15 per day, including eats and sleeps. And this is one that you can simply do for a day or two, an unusual option with volunteer vacations. Over in Turrialba, **CATIE,** aka the **Centro Agronómico Tropical de Investigación y Enseñanza** (☎ 558-2000 or 558-2201; www.catie.ac.cr), accepts volunteers for a minimum of 2 weeks at its botanical gardens, where they receive and guide visitors, work in the nursery, and if they know anything about botany, sometimes tackle more advanced stuff like seed analysis. There's no program fee, but CATIE will put you up on premises starting at $25 a night; tack on $15 daily if you want all your meals here, too.

Attention, Shoppers!

In Cartago, most stuff to buy tends toward local-targeted household goods or pilgrim-targeted religious tchotchkes (check out the little window on the ramp leading down to the trophy room of the **Los Angeles** church—an adorable little brown jug for holy water, in the shape of the Little Black Virgin, is yours for a mere $1.75!). One exception is **Creaciones ABBA—Arte en Cuero** (225m/738 ft. east of the Plaza Mayor, next to Banco Costa Rica *sucursal* Los Angeles; ☎ 552-8190 and 356-3684; daily 9am–7pm), a tiny storefront with some beautifully worked leather, much of it from artisan José Manuel Bonilla Solano in nearby Paraíso. Handbags run $34 to $40, fanny packs $11 to $13, wallets $13 to $17, and belts $9 to $15.

Meanwhile, down in the valley, the valley so low, a couple of establishments in town hawk some nice stuff, notably **Bar-Restaurant Coto** and **Orosi Lodge** (p. 82 and 80). There's a crafts market (daily, but especially good on weekends) on the grounds of **Casona del Cafetal** (p. 83), with wonderful wood and stone carvings, jewelry, and even marimbas of all sizes (try explaining *that* at Customs). My favorite spot here, though—a standout in the whole Central Valley, actually—is a short drive east of town, in Cachí: **Casa del Soñador** ★★ (1km/⅔ mile from Cachí dam bridge; ☎ 577-1186; daily 9am–6pm). A hop and a skip from the Casona del Cafetal, the "dreamer's house" looks like some ramshackle Brothers Grimm hovel, built out of coffee wood over a rocky outcropping by the side of the road, across from towering, Spanish-moss-draped cypresses. Founded in 1987 by Macedonio Quesada, it's now run by his sons Miguel and Hermés, who carve all kinds of rustic canes and figurines out of recycled or found wood (mostly coffee) for as little as $9 each; bigger pieces, like a neat-o chess set, are pricier but negotiable. They'll even do commissions, in as little as a half-hour or for more complicated stuff up to a week. Miguel's branched out into colorful, Modiglianesque paintings, too ($150–$300). While here, you can check out the upstairs room full of bric-a-brac and framed newspaper clippings about Macedonio, give a scratch to house dog Perrín, or even ask for free woodcarving lessons. Last visit, I walked out of there with an armful of canes carved with owls and long-bearded wizards.

Nightlife

Cartago probably has some of the Central Valley's more "so-what" nightlife, but it is there. For starters, you can pretty much locate some kinda party by spotting the Imperial beer signs out on the street. But I've found the best in-town bets include the newish **Iguana's Sport Café** (Av. Central, 50m/164 ft. north and 25m/82 ft. east of María Auxiliadora church, across from El Pochote; ☎ 551-5318; Tues–Thurs 5pm–12:30am, Fri–Sat 5pm–1am, Sun noon–midnight), out toward the western end of downtown. It's got the requisite video screens and jockish paraphernalia on the walls (cute kayak, dudes), but with a more "homespun-slick" Southern California feel (wrought-iron chandelier—nice), along with popular cocktails like massive margaritas ($4.75–$5.15) and the 4×4 Mudslide ($5.15). Besides a pretty decent local and international menu, it's hopping around happy hour and on weekend nights; when I was here, Thursday had become "gringo night" thanks to a bunch of employees from a nearby industrial park.

Several blocks south, the **Bar-Restaurante Sunset** (Av. 2, across from Licorera Persépolis, a block and a half west of María Auxiliadora church; ☎ 551-0451; Mon–Thurs 5pm–midnight, Fri–Sat 11:30pm–1am) is a tad less Americanized and a little more popular with (middle-class) Ticos, a good bunch of them under 40. It's red bricks, woodwork, and '70s and '80s tunes and videos in the ground-floor bar-restaurant area, and on weekends there's a wood-beamed disco space open upstairs.

A little more down and dirty without quite hitting sleazy, it sure smells like teen (and early-20-something) spirit at **Bar La Reforma** (100m/328 ft. south of Tribunal, across from Soda Pamperito; no phone; daily 11am–midnight). This blue corner joint several blocks southwest of Los Angeles church flaunts a grimy college dive feel and a mostly under-30 crowd that spills out on the sidewalk most evenings, thanks to cheapo drink specials like Monday through Saturday brewskis for $1.90, $1.50 afternoons Monday through Wednesday, and Sunday all tipples 95¢. Between this and a similar bar a block south called Aquel Lugar #2, you'll get a suds-soaked peek at how Cartago's kids let off steam.

In Orosi, things are of course a lot quieter (hey, you don't come out here to party). But **Bar-Restaurante Coto** (p. 82) has a somewhat lively scene some nights, especially weekends. So does **Bar El Nido** around the corner (125m/410 ft. north of the soccer field; ☎ 533-3793; daily 11am–1am), a hole in the wall run by José Sánchez (aka "Calimán"), which slings *casados* and bar food along with cheap drinks (a half-liter bottle of booze will set you back just $2.90; shots just 75¢–$1.15). On weekend nights, the local young 'uns into lasers and strobes tend to party these days at an otherwise simple spot called **Bar Ekos** (300m/984 ft. south of the Orosi gas station; no phone; hours vary), up a gravel road on the right as you head south out of town.

3 Arenal & the Northern Zone

Costa Rica's agro-powerhouse now also packs an eco-punch for volcano-watching and soft adventure.

by David Appell and Nelson Mui

IF SUCH A THING AS A "GREATEST HITS OF COSTA RICA" EXISTS, THE Northern Zone would be among them. That's all due to the fame of **Arenal** ★★, a perfectly conical volcano that belches plumes of smoke and day-glo lava almost as regularly and reliably as Old Faithful. Like Mount Kilauea for Hawaii, Arenal has become a Costa Rican icon and, along with nearby **Lake Arenal,** is now the centerpiece of a popular adventure destination that includes hot-springs bathing pools, canopy tours, and all kinds of action and educational activities. And the Ticos are beyond proud to share Arenal with you: In a land where road signs are often lacking or misleading, all roads seem to lead to the volcano. The Central Valley is blanketed with arrows and signposts (with just the silhouette of the volcano, and no name) leading the way.

Arenal's popularity and dominance as a tourist destination, though, obscures the ecological diversity and richness of the surrounding lowlands and river valleys. Fertile plains are carpeted with hectares and hectares of banana, sugar cane, and pineapple plantations, earning the region the moniker of "Costa Rica's bread basket." Cloud forests surround the volcano, stomping grounds for dozens upon dozens of species of plants and animals. In the far north are marshy wetlands, home to a large number of migrating bird species, crocodiles, caimans, and the odd-looking garfish, a unique, endemic specie to the area. Out east in the sweltering rainforest, just inland from the Caribbean coast, you can almost imagine you're in the Amazon. A drive through the Northern Zone is among the most scenic ones in Costa Rica—a lush tropical paradise with volcanic landscapes, verdant green pastures with grazing cattle, and fields that seem to go on forever.

And up here you get a choice of how much of the "trimmings" you want. Around Arenal, swoop through forest canopy and hike volcanic badlands by day, then by night down tasty, even gourmet meals and go disco dancing. Or head more off the beaten path at remote ecolodges, which let you go birding in the wetlands of the **Caño Negro Wildlife Refuge** ★, spelunking in the **Venado caves** ★★, or rafting and rainforest hiking in **Sarapiquí.** If you want to get right to the heart of Costa Rica's eco-allure and can only visit one area, the Northern Zone is a damn good candidate to be the one.

DON'T LEAVE THE NORTHERN ZONE WITHOUT . . .

WATCHING LAVA FLOW DOWN ARENAL AT NIGHT   Staring mesmerized at bright orange lava oozing out of one of the world's most active volcanoes—complete with tumbling rocks and gurgly explosions—is truly a trip and a half.

GOING ON A NATURE HIKE   Whether you hit the trails through the rainforests of Arenal National Park or stroll high amid forest canopy along the Arenal Hanging Bridges, the whole Northern Zone is bursting with tropical flora and fauna for you to spot.

GETTING YOURSELF IN HOT WATER   Treat yourself to a dip in Arenal's thermal pools and streams, naturally heated thanks to the nearby volcano. They range from simple streams and elaborately landscaped stepped waterways and waterfalls to waterpark-like extravaganzas with slides and swim-up bars.

RAFTING OR KAYAKING DOWN THE TORO OR SARAPIQUÍ RIVERS
Get a thrill of a soaking on a Class III or IV rapid through lush tropical scenery—you might even spot a tiger heron or toucan along the way.

A BRIEF HISTORY

The Arenal area has long been defined by both the mile-high volcano's eruptions and by farming. The earliest known instances of Arenal blowing its top have been traced back 7,000 years, and even back then, prehistoric farmers were working the land around it. A 1984 University of Colorado study used fancy NASA remote-sensing tech to uncover trails around the volcano dating back to 500 B.C. They also discovered that nomads probably settled near the lake around 2,000 B.C. but had been floating around the area for another 8,000 years before that, farming corn and beans on the slopes. After each big eruption, these tribes would move on maybe another 15 miles or so, then go back when their crops made a come-back. It wasn't the volcano that finally wiped them out but an epidemic, courtesy of their friendly neighborhood Spanish conquistadors. The area remained a low-key farming community through colonial times, and with the volcano mostly dormant, some locals even built small farms on its slopes.

But this all changed in a big way on July 9, 1968, when Arenal erupted with such a hullabaloo that tremors were measured as far away as Colorado Springs. The villages of Tabacón and Pueblo Nuevo were essentially wiped off the map by shockwaves, poison gases, superheated rocks, and lava; almost 80 people died. Today's top local resort, also called Tabacón, is built on top of that '68 lava flow.

But far from killing the region, it actually gave it a shot in the arm, economically if not ecologically. Farming moved to the fertile lowlands east of La Fortuna, toward San Carlos and the Caribbean coast, where whole forests were chopped to make way for sugarcane, pineapples, bananas, and oranges. San Carlos (aka Ciudad Quesada) turned into an agro-hub, and to this day you'll see *campesinos* (farmers) hawking produce at its Saturday market. La Fortuna, meanwhile, went from a dusty, dirt-street farmville to tourism central, with dozens of tour operators, adventure outfitters, and travel agencies squeezed into a 3-odd-block radius. In peak season it can feel like everybody here is either a tourist or caters to tourists.

And the trend is still going gangbusters; in fact, practically every *cabina* and hotel in town is expanding or planning to expand.

Nearby Lake Arenal, meanwhile, was for millennia barely more than a swampy puddle. Then in the 1970s, an ambitious hydropower project and dam were set up to divert water to Guanacaste farms and crank out electricity for Costa Rica, Nicaragua, and Panama. The village that stood on the shore was moved, and an aquatic addition to the local tourism industry was born in the form of freshwater fishing and a kickin' windsurfing/kiteboarding scene (especially Dec–Mar), both mostly based out of the town of Tilarán, on the lake's south shore toward its western end.

LAY OF THE LAND

The Northern Zone is a big and varied area with lots of very different things to see and do, from superb windsailing on Lake Arenal and nearby volcano-watching to ogling the tropical flora and fauna of the rainforests toward the Caribbean coast.

ARENAL–LA FORTUNA

Of the nearly two million tourists that pass through Costa Rica each year, a million and a quarter make it up to Arenal, one of the world's most active volcanoes. It's not quite as dramatic as some in, say, Hawaii—where you don't have the problem of deep clouds sometimes cutting off the view (hey, it's in a rainforest, so it gets cloudy here)—but Arenal's perfect conical shape and regular bursts of steam and lava make for an awesome show. Around the volcano there are tropical rainforests rich in plant and animal life, and a town called La Fortuna, home to an "eco-industrial complex" determined to get you up to the volcano, onto/into the water, and through the forests, via canopy attractions, ATV tours, hikes, horseback rides, and lots more. The nearby Toro, Sarapiquí, and Peñas Blancas rivers provide some world-class rafting and kayaking for all skill levels through scenery that can sometimes take your breath away.

LAKE ARENAL

A dinky little lagoon before a hydroelectric project turned it into Costa Rica's biggest lake (32km/20 miles long and up to 4km/2½ miles wide) in the early 1970s, **Lake Arenal** ✸ is picture-postcard pretty, with upscale Alpine-chalet-style lodges on its hilly shores and some fine fishing and wicked windsurfing (considered some of the world's best), thanks to surface winds that can hit 111 kmph (69 mph). Some even claim a Tico version of the Loch Ness Monster is slithering around in its depths.

THE FAR NORTH

Up by the border with Nicaragua, near the town of Los Chiles, the wetlands of the **Caño Negro Wildlife Refuge** ✸, along the Río Frío, are from January to April aflutter with migratory birds—roseate spoonbills, jacanas, herons, cormorants—nesting and breeding among the sloths, iguanas, and caimans (much harder to spot is the garfish, dubbed a "living fossil" because of its hard exoskeleton). Close by are the **Venado Caverns** ✸✸, with underground streams and limestone stalactites and stalagmites carved out over millions of years.

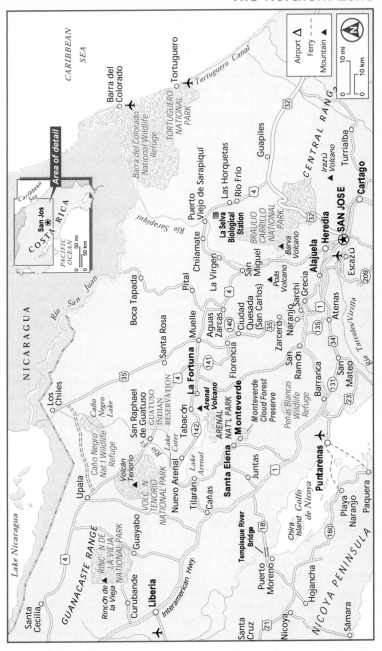

THE SARAPIQUI RAINFORESTS

This lush area lies along the Sarapiquí River, just north of the **Braulio Carillo National Park** and west of watery coastal **Tortuguero.** Its climate is hot and humid, and its rainy season is more or less year-round. Too much of the forest has long been cleared for growing bananas, pineapple, and palms, but there's still plenty for you to experience. Be sure to check out the **La Selva Biological Station** ★★, a 16-sq.-km (6-sq.-mile) park and research center run by the Organization for Tropical Studies. Seventy percent of the park is rare primary forest, home to over 400 species of migratory and resident birds along with such mammals as jaguars and ocelots. Several other top private reserves and ecolodges here include **Rara Avis** ★, **Selva Verde** ★, and **Centro Neotrópico Sarapiquís** ★. Adrenaline junkies can get a world-class jolt of whitewater rafting from the Sarapiquí's class III/IV rapids.

GETTING TO & AROUND ARENAL & LA FORTUNA

Getting up here from San José is pretty straightforward. You can rent a car and drive up on some of the country's better paved roads. Taking the bus is another fine option, as the service is frequent. Plus once you're here, taxis and organized tours can take you most anywhere you want. From San José, the drive takes 3 to 4½ hours (maybe about 45 minutes less if you come right from the airport); if you want to cut it down to a half-hour (plus airport time, of course), you can always fly.

BY BUS

Starting at 6am, intercity buses leave San José's **Atlantico del Norte** terminal (Av. 9 at Calle 12; ☎ 255-4318; $4) for La Fortuna every 2 hours or so. The bus that passes through Ciudad Quesada is the most direct route (roughly 4½ hours).

For a mite more comfort and convenience, air-conditioned **Gray Line** coaches (☎ 220-2126; www.graylinecostarica.com) headed for the Pacific coast beaches will pick you up from your San José hotel and drop you in La Fortuna for $27 to $38; check the website for current times, locations, and prices.

BY CAR

There are several routes from San José, depending on whether you plan to stop at Central Valley sites such as the **Los Angeles Cloud Forest, La Paz Waterfall Gardens** (p. 57), or the scenic towns of **Grecia, Sarchí,** and **Heredia** (p. 63). The most direct route is to take the Interamerican Highway west. Then turn north at San Ramón de Alajuela, about an hour northwest of San José, and follow signs for the Hotel Villablanca. You'll end up on the scenic La Tigra Road, which passes through a private reserve and dead ends into La Fortuna. It should take you 3 to 4 hours, depending on driving conditions.

You can also take the Interamerican Highway (Hwy. 1) west, and turn north at Naranjo and pass through **Zarcero**—a picturesque town with a topiary garden in a downtown park—San Carlos (aka Ciudad Quesada), and Florencia. Head out in the early morning to catch the volcano in **Poás National Park** before the clouds move in (you can drive practically right up to the summit); just follow signs for the town of San Miguel before cutting back west through Aguas Zarcas.

If you're coming from Liberia or the Pacific Coast, head east on the Interamerican Highway, passing through Cañas, Tilarán, and Nuevo Arenal before getting to La Fortuna 3½ to 4 hours later. The last stretch from Nuevo Arenal to La Fortuna is on the bumpy side, with potholes making the driving a bit like an obstacle course.

BY PLANE

Nature Air (☎ 299-6000, 800/235-9272 from the U.S. and Canada; www.nature air.com) flies from San José's Pavas airport daily at noon, with returns at 12:40pm; flight time is a half-hour, $65 each way. There are also daily departures from Liberia, Tamarindo, and Quepos that involve layovers at Pavas.

GETTING AROUND

If you don't have your own ride, taxis are plentiful hereabouts. If you can't flag one down you can usually find them lined up at the central park in front of the church in downtown La Fortuna. A trip from town up to the Tabacón Resort or hot springs, for example, will run about $7. Keep in mind that if you're bunking outside La Fortuna, the meter starts from the moment the taxi leaves town to pick you up. Most tour operators provide hotel pick-ups, but you can shave a fraction off the price by showing up at their offices in town. (By the way, there are car rental companies in La Fortuna, but if you've already made it here without one, don't bother—you'll end up saving more with guided tours including transport.)

✳   ‸**Monteverde or Bust!**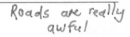

Roads are really awful

While it can make sense to combine neighboring Monteverde and Arenal on a single visit, getting from one to the other around Lake Arenal can take 4 to 8 hours by car or bus. And the roads—the one from Arenal to Nuevo Arenal is riddled with potholes, and the rocky, 34km (21 miles) gravel road that runs along steep drops in and out of Monteverde—can be white-knucklers and kidney rattlers (sometimes at the same time).

A good way to save both time and a few white hairs is the **jeep-boat-jeep transfer.** A number of local outfits have come up with a service that ferries you across the lake in the morning in a half-hour and gets you to Monteverde by noon with a total trip time of about 2½ hours. Prices range from $19 to $25 each way (going on horseback instead of jeep will bump it up to $65-plus)—just don't try it during rainy season). Most hotels can book this, but in La Fortuna you can try the main outfits directly. **Sunset Tours** (☎ 479-9800; www.sunsettourcr.com) has both jeeps ($25; $50 if you want a jeep to yourself) and horses ($65); **Desafío Expeditions** (☎ 479-9464; www.desafiocostarica.com) weighs in with one of the better equine options, also $65. (If you already have a rented car, many local agencies will allow you to drop it off in La Fortuna.)

ACCOMMODATIONS, BOTH STANDARD & NOT

Unlike many other areas of Costa Rica, the Zona Norte doesn't have too much in the way of nonstandard digs. Why not? It's still mostly agricultural, and while tourism has taken off in certain parts, there's no beach and little flashy dining or nightlife to help bring in the kinds of folks who set up B&Bs or build vacation rentals. So most of what you'll find leans toward traditional hotels, resorts, or ecolodges.

LA FORTUNA

With a looming view of the volcano some 5.5km (3½ miles) uphill, former farming town La Fortuna de San Carlos is now the main base for excursions up to Arenal; the dormant volcano next door, Cerro Chato; and other local sites. Increasingly honky-tonk and crowded, La Fortuna itself is small and simply laid out: At the center is a *parque central* (central park/plaza), and most of the town's lodgings, eateries, and tour operators are found within 3 blocks of here, making it a cinch to shop around for you-name-it. During high season (Dec–Apr), travelers seem to outnumber residents, and you can overhear them swapping tips and tales in the open-air *sodas* ringing the park. We're not fans of staying in La Fortuna though, as it's easy to find affordable digs with better views of the volcano, and quicker access to it, along the road leading uphill west of the town toward the volcano and the lake. Most of these hotels will pick you up in town for no extra charge and all double as travel agencies if you decide to book a tour (you can also book with any of the agencies recommended in the chapter, often for less, and they will pick you up at your hotel for only a tiny bit more—trust me, it all works out in the end). You are here to commune with the volcano after all, and the views upslope (volcano and otherwise) are way more inspiring; these properties are also closer to most of the stuff you've come all this way to see and do.

If you're without a car and nervous about being captive to shuttles, taxis, and the whims of your hotelier, you can stay in town among its many restaurants and shops (and their noise and grit). The best of the in-town lodgings are **Las Colinas** (99m/330 ft. south and 50m/165 ft. west of central park; ☎ 479-9305; www.lascolinasarenal.com; $15 single/$30 double with breakfast and Internet access; MC, V), a simple place, run by the helpful and locally plugged-in Flor Fernández; the **Hotel Monte Real** ✹ (99m/330 ft. south and 296m/985 ft. east of central park; ☎ 479-9357; www.monterealhotel.com; $40 double; AE, DC, M, V) which will be a bit quieter and has a pool; or the **Hotel Arenal Jireh** (147m/490 ft. west of central park; ☎ 479-9004; www.arenaljireh.com; $52 double with breakfast; MC, V), which has more of the "up-the-hill" amenities than the other two, including cable TV, lush landscaping, Internet, air-conditioning, and a pool.

Along the road west out of La Fortuna that climbs toward the volcano and lake is where you'll find the higher-end resorts and lodges, but a couple of real bargains, too.

$ The cheapskate's choice, **Cabinas Loma Real** ✹ (7km/4⅓ miles west of La Fortuna; ☎ 479-9227; MC, V) isn't actually cabins, but a recently built (2005) block of five motel-like rooms fronting a small swimming pool. Up the hill is the home of the non-English-speaking but very friendly owners, and behind it the volcano itself, looming in the background (the views are deluxe, even if the hotel

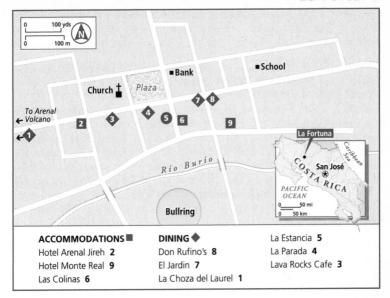

isn't). Between the house and the rooms is a small, open-air kitchen where the guests can store food in the large fridge, dine at the long table, and even cook a simple meal. While the rooms are nothing special—no TV or phone, ultrafirm beds (read: hard), lime-green walls, a framed print here and there, tile floors, private bathrooms—they're lovingly kept up and white-glove clean. And the kicker: just $35 per night for a double, pretty much year-round. Through sign language and lots of pointing, the owners will book tours for you, and they don't go over the top with their commissions. ***One word of warning:*** To get here, you'll have to endure one of the bumpiest, most rustic side roads in the area, lined with run-down shacks and barns slowly sinking into the soil. But once you're past the 10 minutes of relentless jolting, you'll feel as if you're in the middle of the countryside, far from the crowded town and mountain road.

$–$$$ Yeah, "home away from home" may be a cliché, but it's hard to avoid that description of the **Posada Colonial** ✪✪ (10km/6¼ miles west of La Fortuna; ☎ 460-5955; leif@yahoo.com; cash only) because this is actually somebody's home, namely Canadian ex-pat Leif Carlson. He lives in the swank main house when nobody's renting it, and moves out to allow parties of up to six to move in for a pretty darn reasonable $150 per night. For that they get a full and very modern kitchen (used by Leif's helper Miriam to whip up different breakfasts each morning at no extra charge); a large living room filled with family-reunion-friendly gadgets and amenities like big-screen TV, CD player, and board games; and beautifully appointed bedrooms up top, with high sloping ceilings, pretty quilts, and the kind of design-forward furnishings (carved headboards, plush chairs) you'd want in your own home. Above the garage is another room with its own private entrance, sleeping up to three (in queen-size and single beds) with the same sorts of furnishings and a huge plate-glass window facing the volcano. This one goes for $50 a night, including breakfast; another small, more rustic house for up to four is also available, also for just $50. As for the views, Leif says "you'll feel like you can reach out and touch the volcano." Nice, but—er, ouch.

$$ Another of the best value in resorts with Arenal as its backyard (lava views, baby!) is the **Hotel Lavas Tacotal** (about 10km/6¼ miles west of La Fortuna; ☎ 460-9998, 800/793-0597 in the U.S. and Canada; www.tacotal.com; V), which sits next to a farm with grazing horses and cows. The decor is vaguely indigenous— the Italian-Costa Rican dining room's a large, soaring *rancho* with thatched roof— and the 47 units woody. You can choose from cabins starting at $47 and spacious rooms from $79 (breakfast included), with A/C, whirlpool baths, fridges, a safe, and so forth (but not all have TV and none have a phone, so you gotta book tours through the hotel—devious, eh?). Views vary, but all have private terraces facing the volcano. On the grounds are hiking trails and a pair of pools (just keep in mind that depending on the season, you might end up wallowing with students on spring break).

$$ I also must include the cute, 10-room **Roca Negra Inn** ✖ (about 5km/3 miles west of Fortuna; ☎ 479-9274; rocanegrainn@yahoo.com; MC, V), which for $50 a night you're in walking distance to a couple of the mountain road's best restaurants/nightspots (giving you some of the pluses of living in town without the grit and bustle). It looks like many of the other budget lodgings in the area, but a couple of caring touches set it apart: The tile floors are painted to look like the wood ceilings, the bathrooms are slightly larger than usual, the bedspreads are colorful and downright pretty, and each room has a small veranda with a rocking chair for eruption watching. It has also set aside one room for folks with disabilities, keeping all surfaces level, adding doors wide enough to accommodate wheelchairs and creating a special driveway so that cars can pull right up to its door. My only disappointment is the teeny-tiny pool.

$$ It's a hotel! No, a canopy tour! No, hot springs! If soft-adventure bells and whistles get your juices going, have a gander at the **Hotel Arenal Paraíso** ✖ (8km/5 miles west of La Fortuna; ☎ 460-5333; www.arenalparaiso.com; AE, D, MC, V), with the best ziplines in the area, including a dozen 78m-high (260-ft.) platforms. It also has its own landscaped thermal springs, too (or you can stick to the regular swimming pool), as well as gardens, hiking trails (with two waterfalls), and a modest spa with sauna. The complimentary breakfast is a lavish spread, with an omelet station, rice and beans, pancakes, cereals, fruits—you name it. And the price is right—$70 for a double, breakfast included—given all the perks and the proximity to the national park. The downside? The 42 rooms are plain looking and thin-walled, so if you get a *cabina* that shares a wall with another, you may find yourself up late into the night, trying not to eavesdrop on your neighbors (try and snag one of the free-standing cabins if you can). Plus the on-site steakhouse is overpriced and mediocre. But there's no other place around here that has as many on-site amenities at these rates.

$$–$$$ For *really* up close and personal, the **Arenal Observatory Lodge** ✖✖ (about 6km/3¾ miles west of La Fortuna; ☎ 290-7011; www.arenal-observatory. co.cr; AE, MC, V) is actually inside the national park, on a ridge a mile and a half from the Big Guy. Originally the HQ for volcano researchers from the Smithsonian, it's got an Alpine look and fabulously forested setting, a half-dozen trails (guided walks included), and volcano and lake views approaching orgasmic—from the spring-fed infinity pool and Jacuzzi, through the restaurant's picture windows, and from most of the airy, rustic rooms. However, be ready to give up phones, TV, and Internet (hey, there's a Ping-Pong table, okay?). In-season rates start at $68 for doubles with shared showers and go up to $137 for suites with terraces (breakfast included).

$$$ On the other hand, if you're looking for more pampering and a classier feel, you might do better at the Villegas family's **Montaña de Fuego Hotel & Spa** ★★ (11km/6¾ miles west of La Fortuna; ☎ 460-1220; www.montanadefuego.com; AE, D, MC, V), on a graciously manicured hillside with a couple of nice pools (one with Jacuzzi and swim-up bar), the requisite boffo volcano vista, and a 30-hectare (75-acre) forest out back for hiking and birding. But what especially sets Fire Mountain apart is a spa that's probably the area's best (two stories, glass-walled treatment rooms, and a pretty respectable menu of treatments both classic and trendy), along with one of its top fine-dining spots (Acuarelas, with a nouvelle Latin menu). The 66 units are spread among a bunch of pricier pointy-roofed bungalows and a double-decker building with the rustically varnished all-wood standard doubles for $100 a night, including A/C, cable TV, private glassed-in terrace for volcano gawking, and breakfast.

DINING FOR ALL TASTES

LA FORTUNA

By far your best values are the *sodas* slinging typical Tico fare (and unsurprisingly, these are where you'll rub shoulders with the locals); if there's a counter to sit at, that'll save you even more dough. These are places like the popular, alfresco **El Jardín** ★ (50m/165 ft. southeast of central park; ☎ 479-9360; MC, V) or **La Parada** (across from west side of central park; ☎ 479-9547; no credit cards), which serves food all day and all night. La Parada is unusual in its hours, though. Unless we mention otherwise, the restaurants below are open till 11pm; many of the *sodas* open as early as 7 or 8am. All accept dollars as well as local *colones*.

$ A great place for breakfast, the groovy **Lava Rocks Cafe** ★ (99m/330 ft. west of central park; ☎ 479-9341; MC, V; 7am–10pm) serves hefty portions of both typically American scrambled eggs, bacon, and hash browns ($3–$4) as well as local *gallo pinto* combos ($5). You eat on a sunny patio surrounded by heliconias and other tropical flora—it feels a little like chowing down in a greenhouse. Folks drop in throughout the day for yummy *batidos* (fruit shakes, $2) in a dozen flavors from papaya and pineapple to mango and *guanábana* (soursop). The rest of the day, the restaurant serves the usual array of pastas, hamburgers, and chicken dishes for $5 to $6, but there are better places to score these foods.

$ On the very edge of the town proper, **La Choza del Laurel** ★★ (on road to volcano, on the western edge of town; ☎ 479-9231; AE, MC, V; daily 7am–10pm) is the best place for typical Costa Rican food in a town where most other eateries are trying to channel Italian trattorias or Argentine steakhouses. You've got your thatched roof, your colorful staff costumes (red bandanas and sashes for the fellas, ruffled shirts and full skirts for the gals), your table settings (complete with jars of pickled who-knows-what), and your decor, which basically consists of chickens roasting on a spit, no walls, picnic-style tables, and here and there bunches of hanging bananas. And it certainly tastes Tico, especially if you slather your food with the scrumptious homemade salsas (red for hot, green for savory). We recommend a "typical plate" mixing rice, beans, and some sort of meat (chicken, grilled pork, or steak; $5–$6) with a chayote and ground-beef stew, a salad, and a hardboiled egg. One dish can easily be shared, and the meats are carefully cooked and well seasoned. Come after 1pm if you want to try one of the succulent chickens you'll see slowly turning on a spit before a wall of fire as you arrive; they're terrific. La Choza closes earlier than most of the other restaurants in town (10pm), but it's open for breakfast—a definite plus.

$–$$ A recent, more upscale-feeling addition to the scene—some say now the best restaurant in town—is **Don Rufino's** ★★ (across from La Fortuna gas station; ☎ 479-9997; www.donrufino.com; MC, V; daily 11am–11pm). With a comfy-cozily lit interior wrapped in blond wood, it's a relaxing place to order a casual and still affordable meal off an Italian/American/Tico menu (a 7-oz. hamburger or *casado* with beef, chicken, or fish costs $4). From breakfast stuff to fettucine, French onion soup to roast beef and pastrami sandwiches, it's honestly pretty hard to go too wrong. At night, the bar (which opens to the street) perks up into something of a "scene," with all manner of tourists and even a few locals.

$$ Another stylish Juanito-come-lately, **La Estancia** ★ (173m/575 ft. south of Banco Nacional; ☎ 479-7132) is an open-air Argentine-style *parrilla* (steakhouse)—and hands-down the most romantic and chic dining experience right in town (love the wood tables and the tea candles along ochre walls). It's a bit more of a splurge; a steak will run $10 to $15. But if you're jonesing for a little refinement (not to mention a good wine list), here's the beef.

UPHILL NEAR THE VOLCANO

There are a number of options just west of La Fortuna on the road to Arenal volcano and lake. As with the hotels up here, the view is the draw, and you may get a show with your meal if your cafe's an open-air one—and if the volcano decides to oblige. Beyond the restaurants listed here, you can get gourmet but pretty overpriced meals at **Tabacón Resort** (☎ 519-1900; www.tabacon.com) or Acuarelas restaurant at **Montana de Fuego** (☎ 460-1220). If it's a special occasion, then splurge; otherwise, you'll have a darn good feed at the options below.

$–$$ All that being said, at **Il Vagabondo** ★ (3km/1¾ miles west of La Fortuna; ☎ 479-9565; MC, V) the volcano views are slightly marred by the curtain of twinkly Christmas lights that hang throughout this pretty open-air restaurant. Pizza's the lure here, and it's surprisingly good—thin crusted, charred just enough by the on-site brick oven, and slathered with a robust tomato sauce. A pie is $5 to $10, and since it helps the wallet by being sharable, many families come here—in fact, the last time we visited, there was only one table in the place that *didn't* have kids at it. **One warning:** If you're in a rush, don't go for a pasta dish

($6–$9)—they're cooked from scratch, meaning it's about a half-hour from ordering time to table (pizza? 10 min. and you're chowing down).

$$ The steakhouse **El Novillo** ✯✯ (10km/6¼ miles west of La Fortuna; ☎ 460-6433; cash only; open until midnight) doesn't have the ambiance of La Estancia (see above), but what it lacks in looks, this concrete-floored, zinc-roofed, oversized shack makes up in terrific eats. The steaks are the best in the area, and the lemony, juicy pork chops ($6) may well be tops in Costa Rica. Sure, you're eating on a plastic table, sitting on a plastic chair, but get over it—you can dine like a king. In fact, because the setting's so basic and open, you get a great look at the volcano; last time we were here, the Big Guy started to lava up so good the owner turned off all the lights to help us see better. For 10 minutes we munched in the dark, staring spellbound as rivers of red slithered down the mountain.

WHY YOU'RE HERE: THE TOP SIGHTS & ATTRACTIONS

VOLCANO-WATCHING

No doubt about it: **Arenal** is quite a sight, and you can behold it from practically the whole surrounding area. It regularly belches out gray-brown clouds of steam and gas, and sends boulders tumbling down its slopes. But the most dramatic views are at night when you can make out the flame-orange fireworks and glowing red lava flows. For the real lava-licious money shots, your best bets are Arenal's western and southwestern slopes. That's the advantage of staying at a hotel along the road to Tabacón on the northwest side, or along the lakeshore—you can sit back and wait for the Big Guy to do his thing while sipping a cocktail in the pool or hanging out on your private terrace. There aren't any better views, even from the trails nearest to the cone.

A Couple of "Buts" . . .

Número uno: It's not easy to get onto Arenal itself, and there's a reason for that—every once in a while, somebody gets hurt or killed trying. As recently as 2000, a guide and tourist died during a particularly strong blow-up near Los Lagos, an area nobody had thought was particularly dangerous. So don't expect to get too close.

Número dos: Yes, Arenal's one of the world's most active volcanoes, with eruptions sometimes every few hours. But it can still go through quiet periods for months at a time. And since the peak's surrounded by cloud forests, it can get socked in by fog and all you'll get to do is listen to the rumbling. The best times to visit are September, October, and November, when daily rainstorms help to disperse the clouds. Lousiest times of the year: December through February, when the clouds can get thick. But even at these times of the year, have your camera ready as you may get a peek. And if you do spot some action, get your shot right away—views can come and go in seconds.

Getting into Hot Water

An Arenal visit wouldn't be complete without a soak in one of the various local volcanic hot springs that've been turned into attractions, from simple to spectacular. The best bargains are the nighttime packages, which combine a trip to watch the eruptions with a 2-hour stop at one of the pool complexes (often Baldi). Below we've listed the main contenders. (A couple of tips: Down in La Fortuna you can often prepay for less than you'd get at the pool entrance. And once you're into the resort of your choice, you can prepay or leave a deposit at the sap so you in your bathing suit don't have to carry cash around inside for drinks and such.)

The most famous and upscale of the lot is **Tabacón Hot Springs ★★** (9km/14 miles west of La Fortuna; ☎ 519-1900; www.tabacon.com/hot-springs; daily 10am–10pm; $29). Owned by the resort of the same name—and only a quick stroll down the road from the resort itself—a dozen hot pools are connected with stepped waterways, waterfalls, paths, and lavish landscaping—all with va-va-voom volcano views. There's also a water slide, restaurant, and a chichi spa where you can get a "volcanic mud-wrap" and other treatments for less than you'd shell out in the States ($55 for a 50-min. "tropical massage," $45 for 40 min. of "coffee sugar exfoliation"). The spa, which was totally revamped in 2006, also has a gringo "shaman" performing sweat lodge ceremonies (call for rates), if you want an experience to tell the grandkids about. Reservations are a good idea in season; if you're staying at Tabacón resort, it's no extra charge.

Also popular is **Baldi Aguas Termales ★** (5km/8 miles west of La Fortuna, next to the Volcán Look disco; ☎ 479-9651; www.infoturistica.com/tours/baldi.html; daily 10am–10pm; $17), with 10 pools of varying temperatures (some with waterfalls, slides, and other nifty stuff), a Jacuzzi and sauna, a pair of restaurants, and several swim-up bars. Baldi's geared to more of a party scene, so its look is more bar-centric and not as landscaped with greenery like Tabacón. Since it's part of many volcano tours and even several hotel packages, it can get crowded. But it's sure fun in its own way!

The newer, family-owned **Eco Termales ★** (5km/8 miles west of La Fortuna, across from Baldi; ☎ 479-8484; 10am–9pm; $19) is probably the best option if you're not doing a tour, want to avoid crowds, and/or are looking for a Tabacón-style experience for less. It's as big as Baldi, but with pools and waterfalls swathed in tropical flora like Tabacón. The downsides are it has no spa services or volcano views. Call ahead to reserve.

If you're staying down in La Fortuna, where the volcano is visible but not as flashy, consider signing onto a **night tour** to **Arenal Volcano National Park ★** (14km/8¾ miles west of La Fortuna; ☎ 461-8499; www.costarica-nationalparks.com/arenalnationalpark.html; $7), hawked by practically every hotel and outfitter

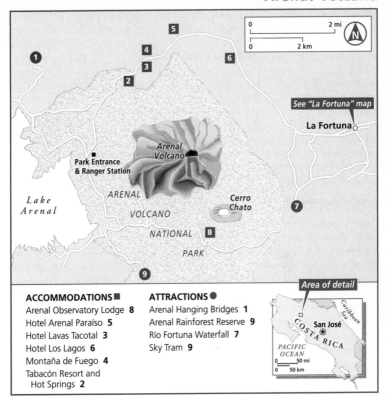

ACCOMMODATIONS ■
Arenal Observatory Lodge **8**
Hotel Arenal Paraíso **5**
Hotel Lavas Tacotal **3**
Hotel Los Lagos **6**
Montaña de Fuego **4**
Tabacón Resort and
   Hot Springs **2**

ATTRACTIONS ●
Arenal Hanging Bridges **1**
Arenal Rainforest Reserve **9**
Río Fortuna Waterfall **7**
Sky Tram **9**

in town. For starters, the park's closed after 4pm except for these tours, and bus service to the park is spotty (you'd have to catch one headed to Tilarán), while a cab can easily run you $15 each way. The cheapest jaunts start at $15 to $20 for a drive up to the park's edge for some oohing and aahing, followed by a soak in one of the nearby thermal pools (p. 102)—not a bad deal since getting into the pools alone can cost $20 a head. It's definitely worth getting up to the 119-sq.-km (46-sq.-mile) park by day, too. The scenic, well-kept trails cross through lava fields and forests, which were flattened by lava flows from the big eruption of '68 (especially the 4km/2.5-mile **Tucanes Trail** ✷✷). You can tackle it on your own (and save a few bucks) if you've got wheels, which also helps big time if you have a sharp eye for wildlife-spotting. The easiest way to see some hot lava is the 1.3km/.8-mile **Lookout Point Trail,** which will take you to a *mirador* (overlook) where you can watch it ooze. If you're hoping to check out some critters along the way, do the 1.2km (.75-mile) **Los Miradores Trail** in the direction of Lake Arenal. Another option is to get onto the trails on the property of the **Arenal**

Observatory Lodge (but that'll be another $3, *muchas gracias*). One of the best is the **Cerro Chato Trail,** a 4-hour toughie that gets you right up to the crater of the dormant nearby Cerro Chato volcano. Here you can check out a cool vista of an emerald-color lagoon ringed by green, green forest. Bring your binoculars or, even better, a telescope.

A word of advice: If you're like most of us, not attuned to the rainforest, you could wander the trails till the *vacas* come home and your feet fall off without so much as a glimpse any of the sometimes skittish animals who live up here. So we'd splurge on the $35, usually plus park admission fee, for a guide who'll help you see spider monkeys, oropendolas, agoutis, blue morpho butterflies, and toucans, plus explain the basics of the ecosystem. Try **Desafio Expeditions** (☎ 479-9494; www.desafiocostarica.com), which employs some of the most experienced naturalists in the vicinity.

OTHER NATURAL HIGHLIGHTS

There's plenty to see outside of the volcano park, as well. High on our list would be a visit to the scenic **Río Fortuna Waterfall** ★★ (daily 8am–4pm; $6)—a neat way to spend a morning. The 74m-high (246-ft.) waterfall lies amid lush greenery some 5.6km (3½ miles) south of La Fortuna. Signs for LA CATARATA are posted around town, but basically, you start from the west end of town and head south over the little bridge. Then after a half-mile or so, look for a gravel road, which you take west through the woods to a lookout's entrance where you'll pay an entrance fee. You can swim near the base of the falls. A couple of things to keep in mind: There's a wicked undertow right at the falls themselves, and the trail down to the water is pretty steep (meaning you'll have to clamber back up it after your dip). If you're not feeling up to hoofing it, or it's rainy and the trails are muddy, a fun option is a $25 horseback ride (no experience necessary), sold by various local outfitters (go to any local travel agent to book).

The **Arenal Hanging Bridges** ★ (kids) (3km/1¾ miles west of Tabacón, near the Arenal dam; ☎ 253-5080; www.hangingbridges.com; daily 6am–7pm; $20 adults, kids under 12 free) are a nifty and easy way to get close to the spectacular nature around the volcano. Most hikes will take you along the forest floor, where you'll spend half your time craning your neck up toward the canopy—here you tiptoe through the treetops, along a half-dozen suspension bridges connecting a 3km (2-mile) trail. Up here is where most of the birds and howler monkeys are—but again, we recommend a guided tour ($10 extra per person) to make sure you spot them. Desafio Tours (see above) is, once again, a top choice for tours. All in all, your hike through and above the trees will take about 2 hours, and with the exception of one steep climb, it's on fairly level ground, making this one of Arenal's best activities for young kids.

A newer but pricier option is the **Sky Tram** (El Castillo, 20km/12 miles west of La Fortuna, near Arenal Observatory Lodge; ☎ 645-6003; www.skytrek.com; hours vary by season; $50 adults, kids $26), part of a collection of attractions and trails (one a canopy tour, see below) in a private reserve. You basically stand in open cages that are hauled through the canopy on a cable 39m (130 ft.) up, ending in a lookout platform from where you can hike trails and hanging bridges; do the zipline; check out snake and butterfly exhibits; and/or take the tram back. We have mixed feelings about this attraction—you can get just as much out of the hanging

Kool for Kids

Schlepping the kids around Costa Rica isn't for wimps, which is why moms and dads will be thrilled to find **Hotel Los Lagos** ✪ 🆒 (3km/1¼ miles west of La Fortuna; ☎ 461-1818; www.hotelloslagos.com; farms 8am–4pm, pools 8am–8pm; day pass $10). This square-mile-and-a-half spread is well worth considering as a place to stay, but can also deliver a super-duper afternoon's worth of fun for toddlers through teens (and what the heck, well beyond). There are thermal pools, plus one with a volcano-shape waterfall designed for little ones, and another bigger pool with a bunch of waterslides. And if that isn't enough, there's a crocodile zoo, butterfly garden, frog farm, zipline, hiking trails, and horseback riding ($25 extra for 3 hr.). The restaurant, meanwhile, serves small-person faves like quesadillas and french fries. Los Lagos also runs a shuttle to and from town; call ahead for current prices.

bridges above, for less money—unless you're in a wheelchair or have trouble getting around, in which case it can be a real plus. Also, some eco-purists think these trams are gimmicky and "Disneyfy" nature—and maybe they have a point.

MORE OUTDOOR ADVENTURES

There's a ton of ways to get your *adrenalina* a-flowing around Arenal. The most popular are canopy tours (which are really more like thrill rides than ways to get close to nature—after all, how likely are you to notice a chestnut-mandibled toucan while whizzing through the treetops?). Monteverde has the area's biggest and arguably its best, but if you're not headed up there, the top Arenal option is probably in the 64-hectare (161-acre) reserve of the **Arenal Paraíso Resort** ✪✪ (7km/4½-miles west of La Fortuna; ☎ 460-5333; www.arenalparaiso.com; $45; ages 7 and up). The ziplines here are strung up to 78m (260 ft.) above ground between a dozen platforms, and even pass through a couple of waterfalls. Real daredevils should ask the guides to let them do a few lines upside down (trust me, it's a blast). There are a couple of 2-hour tours a day (8am/1pm/3pm), and hotel pickups are included.

Up the road apiece, on the grounds of the eponymous resort, the **Tabacón Canopy** (☎ 257-5149; www.tabacon.com) has a setup that includes bird-watching platforms and rappelling down trees, though you won't get quite the same "George of the Jungle" feel since you'll be fairly close to the road and it's hard to feel completely lost in nature here. Two-hour tours run four times a day, for $45.

The third and priciest option is the "SkyTrek," which is run by the **Sky Tram** and **Arenal Rainforest Reserve** ✪ (9km/5½ miles west of Tabacón; ☎ 645-6003; www.arenalreserve.com; daily 7:30am–3:30pm). This one offers eight cables up to a half-mile long, with some of the highest drops in the area (up to 200m/656 ft.); gorgeous lake views; and a comfier and safer handle bar. But it's $60, including entrance to the reserve and a Sky Tram ride to the ziplines ($68 if you need a hotel pick-up).

If canopy tours are already old hat and you're looking to kick it up a notch, how's about rappelling down a waterfall? **Pure Trek Adventures** ★ (☎ 479-9940, 866/569-5723 in the U.S. and Canada; www.puretrekcostarica.com; $85; daily 7am–noon) will have you rappelling like nobody's business a half-hour outside of La Fortuna. The 4-hour jaunt includes lunch and five rappels and is fine for kids over 6—everybody just has to be in decent physical shape. There's a good chance you'll spot a sloth or a parrot along the way, and Pure Trek runs plenty of other adventures and trips hereabouts, too.

Another great way to take in the scenery and wildlife around you is to go on one of the area's top-notch **rafting or kayaking tours,** which usually takes only half a day, leaving you time for another tour or to just kick back. Depending on your experience level, outfitters take you down the **Peñas Blancas,** south of La Fortuna, or the **Toro or Sarapiquí rivers,** out east toward the Caribbean coast. Both Toro and Sarapiquí are Class III and IV rapids, but the Toro has more stretches that are Class IV and whitewater, so if you wanna really kick butt, go with the bull (which means *toro* in Spanish). As you float down the river through rainforests, lowland swamps, and rippling green pastures, you'll see herons, warblers, wrens, and other fine feathered friends, and at the end you get to dive in the water, followed by an onshore snack.

The two largest outfits running the rivers are **Desafío** ★ (☎ 479-9464; www.desafiocostarica.com), whose half-days start at $85, and **Aguas Bravas** (☎ 292-2072; www.aguas-bravas.co.cr), which charges $70; both are fine, but Desafío has more skilled guides. To shave a little off those prices, try **Adventure Center** ★★ (☎ 479-8585; www.adventurecenterarenal.com), a newish outfit run by a local family, which does runs down the Sarapiquí's Class III rapids for $65, but knocks off $20 if you'll meet your group at the La Fortuna office. Its guides are enthusiastic but careful. The last time we signed on with this company, we pulled a guide raised in La Fortuna who attended a nearby university, so he knew a ton about the area's history and offered an insider's tour en route to the Sarapiquí.

SIDE TRIPS FROM ARENAL & LA FORTUNA

If you're planning on more than 2 or 3 days in the area, there are several easy side trips an hour or two's drive away. If you're fit and have a dash of *cojones,* take a tour or drive yourself the 45 minutes to an hour from La Fortuna to **Venado Caverns** ★★ (45km/28 miles north of La Fortuna; ☎ 384-9616; $5). Under a local farm, this network of limestone caves, tunnels, stalactites, and streams was formed some 7 million years ago; it's more than a mile-and-a-half long, but just over a third of a mile is open to visitors. It's not for the claustrophobic—some parts are massive chambers 6m high (20 ft.), but others narrow down to a crawl space. It's also not for the squeamish—bats fly around and spiders and crickets are aplenty. But the reward is plenty of cool stuff to gape at, like the "papaya," a 5,000-year-old rock formation that grows just over an inch a decade. You can come down here on your own, but you'll get more out of it with a morning or afternoon guided tour (not to mention gear like boots, flashlights, and hardhats). You can book in La Fortuna at any hotel or outfitter.

Up toward the Nicaragua border, about 2½ hours north of La Fortuna, the 100 sq. km (39 sq. miles) of marshes and wetlands in **Caño Negro National Wildlife**

Refuge ☆ (☎ 661-8464; www.costarica-nationalparks.com/canonegrowildlife refuge.html) are packed with sloths, iguanas, monkeys, even a croc or caiman or two. But they're best known for truly bodacious birding; besides the biggest known concentration of Neotropical cormorants, you've got aquatic birds such as the endangered jabiru, northern jacana, anhinga, and light-pink roseate spoonbill (peak birding season is Jan–Apr). And if you're lucky enough to spot a rare garfish, the "living fossil" with a hard exoskeleton, well, *yee-ha!*

You can only get in here by boat—and though plenty of outfitters will bring you up from La Fortuna as a day trip (from $45), you will leave early (around 7:30am) and get taken only up to the area around the Frío River on the refuge's edge. It's a long way to go for a few hours on a canopy-covered boat tour down the river. If you really want to do it right, get a car, drive to Caño Negro village, and overnight at one of the lodges. Our picks are **Albergue Caño Negro** (☎ 461-8442; doubles from $55) or **Hotel de Campo Caño Negro** (☎ 471-1012; www. canonegro.com; doubles from $55). You'll be able to get up early for the best birding, hire a park guide ($50 per person), and get a bonus glimpse of life in a rural Costa Rican village. Most day tours route you through the bustling tourist town of Los Chiles, just south of the Nica border.

Okay, now for Lake Arenal. From December to April, the reliably consistent windy conditions (average speeds of 40kmph/25 mph but gusts up to 111kmph/69 mph), warm water, and gorgeous views of volcano and undulating hills make Lake Arenal spectacular for **windsurfing and kiteboarding.** Most outfitters and lodges are based around Nuevo Arenal and Tilarán, and all offer beginner to advanced lessons and gear rental by the hour or day. The **Tilawa Windsurf Center** ☆ (☎ 695-5050; www.windsurfcostarica.com) at the Hotel Tilawa is ground zero for this crowd; lessons start at $100 for a half-day, including board rental (gear alone is $45)—you can have a blast learning various loops, rotations, and flips. There's also a skate park, with a large "dish" or half pipe, pool tables, tennis courts, and a spa—all of which helps makes it great for families. The other major windsurfing/kiteboarding outfit is **Tico Wind** (☎ 692-2002; www.ticowind. com), which rents equipment ($38 per half-day) and can arrange windsurfing packages with nearby inns **Rock River Lodge** and **Mystica.**

Yodel-adee-tee, Paging Heidi . . .

Settled by a number of Mittel-European ex-pats, many of the lodges on the shores of Lake Arenal have a Teutonic, Swiss-cheesy flavor. Exhibit A is **Hotel Los Héroes, aka La Pequeña Helvecia** ("Little Switzerland," ☎ 692-8012; www.pequena helvecia.com; doubles from $55). Thirty-two kilometers (20 miles) west of Tabacón on the lake's eastern shore, it's a chalet-style resort complex with 13 rooms, a chapel, and—a railway station. What's up with that? There's also a revolving restaurant, which is only reachable via a half-hour train ride through green pastures, a trio of tunnels, and even a viaduct. You get off at the other end at a station displaying artifacts and costumes of pre-Columbian Costa Rica—then you go in for fondue.

Despite the fact that the tiny town of Nuevo Arenal is only 47km (29 miles) of scenic driving from La Fortuna, the state of the road between Arenal Hanging bridges and Nuevo Arenal would make for a bumpy commute. So better than a day trip, make it a stopover en route to somewhere else like Monteverde or Guanacaste. If you don't have a car, you can always take the bus ($4) to Tilarán from La Fortuna around 8am or 5pm; you can ask to be dropped off anywhere along the 3-hour route. From Tilarán, you can snag buses onward to Guanacaste and Monteverde.

ATTENTION, SHOPPERS!

The itty-bitty shopping scene of La Fortuna mostly boils down to a handful of souvenir shops and a couple of galleries, and you'll find goods are more expensive here than in San José or the Central Valley. On the other hand, the small size of La Fortuna's artisan community gives you a higher chance of getting to see artists finishing a painting or a ceramic bowl—a touch that just might be worth the few extra *colones.*

You'll find pottery made in the tradition of Costa Rica's pre-Columbian Chorotega Indians at **Artesanía Chorotega** ★ (main street near police station; ☎ 479-9738; daily 7am–8pm). Pick up an earth-toned fertility or power sculpture pigmented with local sands, and keep an eye out for work by José Luis, the area artist best known for Chortega-style pottery.

Don't miss meeting the lively eponymous owner of **Neptuno's House** (right next to La Fortuna waterfalls; ☎ 479-8269; daily 7am–8pm), whose hammocks are painstakingly hand-woven from cotton and recycled materials, and are available in a wide choice of fabrics and sizes. You can test-drive the merchandise on the open-air veranda that wraps around the shop.

Possibly the only shop in Fortuna where you can walk out with a freshly painted hand-carved Boruca mask and a pierced nose is the **Toji Shop** (296m/985 ft. east of central park, in front of the high school; ☎ 479-9884; daily 9am–9pm). The specialties here are earrings, bracelets, and necklaces of bamboo, coconut, and leather. Those who partake of "herbal remedies" will also appreciate exquisite hand-blown glass pipes, along with rolling papers and various other paraphernalia.

Artists like to get together at the **Mercado de Artesanías** ★ (behind the church; ☎ 479-8687; daily 8am–8pm) to chat, catch up on news, use the work-stations, and sell their stuff. The prices are good, but in our opinion just as fab is the chance to watch these folks work, and talk to them about their work, inspiration, and lives. Afterward, wander next door to the **Galería Aguas Verdes** (next door to the Mercado and behind the church; ☎ 479-9805; daily 8am–8pm), with wood sculptures, watercolors, and some standard crafty souvenirs. You might even run into local artist Rodrigo Luzano, famous for his breathtaking volcano paintings. For indigenous tribal art, check with Francesa Machi, the chatty owner of **Lunática** (345m/1,150 ft. east of the church; ☎ 479-8255; Mon–Sat 8:30am–8pm), who's always willing to guide you through her vibrant collection of local and non-local pieces, from Maleku masks to art from a local women's co-op.

If you're out towards Lake Arenal, **Toad Hall** ★★ (road between Nuevo Arenal and La Fortuna; ☎ 692-8020; www.toadhall-gallery.com; daily 7:30am–5pm), sells ceramics, paintings, woodworks, jewelry, gourds, and banana-paper art, many done by some of the bigger names in Costa Rican handicrafts. After browsing, grab a bite in the cafe next door, which specializes in American-style fare, except that it's organically homegrown.

NIGHTLIFE

As in rural towns the world over, there's not all that much to do even on weekend nights in La Fortuna and Arenal, beyond a nice meal out and knocking back a beer or cocktail alfresco while taking in the views of the volcano (if it's not too cloudy, of course). Locals tend to congregate by the central square, and some of the *sodas* fill up when there's a game on TV. And chances are there'll be a bit of a (gringo-heavy) crowd at the on-street bar at **Don Rufino's** (p. 100). Things might get a little livelier on karaoke nights (most recently Mon and Thurs) at **Chela's Bar** (near the main gas station in town; daily noon–1am; no phone), which keeps it hoppin' till 1am. If it's a dance floor you're after, head uphill to the **Pizzería Il Vagabondo** (☎ 479-9565; 1km/⅔ mile west of La Fortuna; daily 6pm–2am), which has an open-air bar, music nightly, and on some nights karaoke.

Weekends perk up a little, of course. Besides the stuff above, on Friday nights at the **Twins Bar** (50m/165 ft. from central park, next to El Jardín; daily 8pm–midnight; no phone) the house band, The Gypsies, cranks out classic-rock chestnuts to a crowd of tourists mixed with a few Ticos. Not long on decor—faux-wood paneling, industrial tables/chairs, and a long wooden bar with stools—it's got an oddly down-at-heel charm not unlike your average roadside bar in the States. To put in your mouth, Twins has a *boca* menu and a decent booze selection.

Most locals, however, head for the long-running **Volcán Look Discoteca** (5km/3 miles west of La Fortuna; ☎ 479-6961; hours vary), a cavernous, nondescript box of a disco just outside town popular with a younger crowd of locals and gringos (put 200 people on the dance floor and it'll still look empty, but on some weekend nights, or New Year's Eve, it's wall to wall). And we're not kidding about the "younger" part; locals tend to get hitched by their early 20s, and mostly stop going out; besides, the macho culture makes it less fun for women to hit the scene on their own. So all that tips the balance toward young tourists, with a sprinkling of older gringos (often in search of sex). *FYI:* Since the erratic schedule seems to change all the time, we'd call before heading over.

PUERTO VIEJO DE SARAPIQUI

This swath of the eastern end of the Northern Zone, often called simply as Sarapiquí, is home to some of Costa Rica's last remaining bits of lowland rainforest, thanks to local environmentalists and conservationists who pushed to have huge tracts set aside instead of getting turned into banana and papaya plantations. Today, a patchwork of private reserves of primeval rainforest form kind of a biocorridor from **Braulio Carrillo National Park** up to the Nicaraguan border.

For you, that adds up to lots and lots of nature-tourism experiences and lodges to visit and/or overnight at. These are among Costa Rica's most organized operations, with well-trained guides, excellent gardens, nature trails, and exhibits, plus all sorts of educational stuff for researchers, students, and plain old tourists. Most aren't as cheap as you might think, though—a room can easily set you back more than $100.

Most of the reserves and lodges, though, are within a 1- or 2-hour drive from San José and the Central Valley, so you can even stop over on an affordable day pass before moving on to, say, Arenal or Tortuguero. If you're looking to hang out here for a few days here, consider taking a rafting or kayaking jaunt down one of the rivers. Base yourself in more modest digs in the area and, again, do the day-pass thing.

GETTING TO SARAPIQUI

By Bus

Buses to the area's main town, Puerto Viejo de Sarapiquí, leave San José's **Gran Terminal del Caribe** terminal (Calle Central at Av. 11; ☎ 257-6854) every 90 minutes daily between 6am and 6pm; the fare's $3.60. This route is the quickest—an hour and a half up the Guápiles Highway and around through **Braulio Carrillo National Park** (p. 72). Or go a more scenic way through **Heredia, La Virgen,** and past the **Poás and Barva volcanoes,** with **Empresarios Guapileños** (☎ 710-7780), whose buses leave at 6:30am, 1pm, and 5:30pm, taking from 3½ to 4 hours ($2.15).

By Car

From San José, take Calle 3 downtown to the Guápiles Highway north toward the Caribbean coast. After cutting through the rainy but scenic **Braulio Carrillo,** keep going until you see a turnoff for Río Frio/Carretera 4. Another half-hour north on Highway 4 and you'll reach Puerto Viejo de Sarapiquí.

THE RESERVES

The serious science and myriad trails through one of Costa Rica's biggest lowland rainforest reserves are what draw in-the-know ecotourists to **La Selva Biological Station** ✦ (4km/2½ miles south of Puerto Viejo de Sarapiquí; ☎ 524-0607; www.ots.ac.cr). With 73 percent of the area primary rainforest, La Selva's bursting with more than 2,000 tree and plant species, and 436 types of birds including a razzle-dazzle rainbow of toucans, parrots, and trogons. About 250 or so scientific researchers come here each year to do research in the field and the state-of-the-art labs—churning out 240 scientific papers a year.

We civilians can go out on guided walks (full day $36, half-day $28; MC, V) at 8am and 1:30pm, along with 5:30am birding tours and 7pm night walks; the paths are paved and pretty flat, and guides are friendly and know their stuff cold. On our last visit we spotted an orendopola, a keel-billed toucan, a couple of sloths, and a few lizards trying to camouflage their horny little selves. As you're walking, researchers bike past, sometimes carrying specimens and equipment, which makes it feel like a kind of tropical university campus. (Sometimes it's an especially good thing they're around; during our tour, one had spied a poisonous pit viper coiled just off a trail, and told us where it was, so we could give it a wide berth.)

Researchers and students get first dibs on digs, but no big loss—the plain dorm-style rooms are no great shakes, especially considering that per person La Selva wants $86 for single occupancy and $78 double. And it's unlikely you'll get to chat up any of these cliquish folks in the cafeteria, anyway, so might as well save your money and stay in or around Puerto Viejo, 10 minutes away.

Heading in the other direction out of Puerto Viejo, the **Centro Neotrópico Sarapiquís** ★ (16km/10 miles west of Puerto Viejo; ☎ 761-1004; www.sarapiquis. org) is also a serious research center, but goes more out of its way to be accessible and entertaining to visitors (an especially good thing for little kids and older folks). First off, there's more to do: a pre-Columbian dig, smallish ethnography museum, and canopy, birding, even chocolate tours. The museum is good, but we'd save the $12 and instead spend $7 on the archeological park: grab an orange from the orchard and make your way around its 600-year-old burial field (unearthed in 1999), petroglyphs, and reconstructed 15-century indigenous village. Beyond that, the canopy tours and river rafting here cost just $45 each, a good bit less than most commercial outfitters charge, and you can be sure you're getting guides who know the rainforests like the proverbial backs of their proverbial hands. You can do a motorboat trip down the Sarapiquí River (from $20) and other guided tours (from $15) that cover birding, local organic chocolate making (and, yep, tasting!), bat netting/feeding, and more.

The center will put you up in some style, too, in thatched-roof *palenques* with open verandas and ceiling fans (don't worry, at night you won't miss the A/C). Mostly nestled in perfumed gardens with clear views out into the rainforest, the 36 pretty rooms ($70) have hardwood furniture, stone floors, and *beaucoup* bouquets of tropical blooms. Buffet meals (breakfast $5, lunch/dinner $20) are good and even include a decent choice of veggie options; you can also get a price break on food if you do two or more activity packages.

A reserve that stands out by being particularly well plugged into local communities is **Selva Verde Lodge** ★ (7km/4⅓ miles west of Puerto Viejo; ☎ 766-6800, 800/451-7111 in the U.S. and Canada; www.selvaverde.com; day pass $5; AE, MC, V), on 190 hectares (475 acres) of primary rainforest reserve next to **Braulio Carrillo National Park.** The paths are well kept, and guided hikes with naturalists cost just $15 for 2 hours. There's wildlife all over, especially for birders (jacamars, oropendolas, mot-mots, parrots, you name it). You can drop your bags in a towering complex on stilts over the Sarapiquí river, with hammock-draped verandas all round. The 40 rooms here ($70; $56 without meals) are gorgeously woodpaneled and have private baths and a polished resort feel (though of course no TV, A/C, and such); for the same rate, you can try to snag one of five air-conditioned bungalows down nearby forest trails (*FYI:* these might be a little tricky for little kids or seniors). There's a pool, Jacuzzi, and complimentary twice-daily birding walks, as well as a slew of extra-charge boating excursions, guided hikes, canoeing, rafting, and mountain biking. Finally, a conservation learning center open to locals runs a variety of community projects, as well as a program that lets you spend time, and even stay overnight, with locals (p. 112). Be sure to reserve as far ahead as you can—this place is popular with tour groups.

For a reserve with another twist, check out 13-sq.-km (5-sq.-mile) **Rara Avis** ★★ (30km/19 miles from Las Horquetas; ☎ 764-3151; www.rara-avis.com; AE, MC, V), a fascinating progressive experiment in commercial—as opposed to nonprofit—conservation. Founded by ecologist Amos Bien in 1983, its goal is to produce profits from the rainforest without messing it up (which in the long run is probably the only way to make sure it gets saved around the world). The fullbore research station works on sustainable canopy-orchid farming, butterfly export, and other projects that could show the way for future landowners and farmers. To bankroll it all, they let us unwashed masses come to experience its amazing biodiversity—outstanding even for Costa Rica. The weather conditions and rainfall here attract more than 360 bird species (like tanagers, green macaws, kingfishers, trogons, and more than a dozen different types of hawks) plus mammals such as tapirs and jaguars. There are miles of hiking trails, canopy observation platforms, swimming in waterfalls, giant tree climbing, a butterfly farm, and orchid house.

All rarin' for Rara? First, listen up. It's only open to overnight guests, and I'd recommend staying at least 2 nights, since getting and staying here isn't exactly a walk in the park, so to speak. From the village of Las Horquetas, it's a bumpy 3½-hour ride via tractor-pulled cart (leaving at 8:30am); the grub is simple (sometimes just rice and beans); and digs are bare-bones (as in no electricity, mostly). But if you're willing to put up with all of that, this can be a hugely rewarding experience. There's a lodge near a 60m (200-ft.) double waterfall ($60–$80), riverside cabins with private baths and solar-powered electricity ($70–$90), and shared-bath *casitas* with bunk beds ($45). Those rates include guides, meals, and the ride from Las Horquetas.

THE "OTHER" NORTHERN ZONE

This part of Costa Rica is mostly wilderness or farming-oriented countryside where people stay mostly focused inward, on themselves and their families; you'll find it much easier to gain entree into Tico life, for example, in the Central Valley and San José. You can always try heading down to a local bar some night, but even this may not always do the trick, especially if you *no habla español*.

But . . . there are ways, there are ways. First of all, try volunteering on one of the many local projects; almost all of the private reserves in the Sarapiquí area, for example, accept volunteers (check their websites for details).

There's also Selva Verde Lodge's Sarapiquí Conservation Learning Center (p. 111), a local community center that arranges a slew of activities that bring visitors together with Sarapiquí residents: learning salsa, merengue, and cumbia dancing ($10 per person); cooking patacones, empanadas, and other typical Tico dishes; visiting schools; and performing community service like tree planting or cleaning up rivers and roadsides. The SCLC will also pair you with a family for a homestay ($12 a person per night); most will be pretty basic by overfed North American standards, but to get a glimpse of local life most tourists will never see, it's an amazing, even life-changing, opportunity.

4 Up in the Clouds: Monteverde

Costa Rica's most famous "cloud forests" are home to the razzle-dazzle quetzal—and the fascinating local communities harbor some pretty colorful characters, too.

by David Appell and Nelson Mui

"CLOUD FOREST" IS SUCH A ROMANTIC-SOUNDING TERM, ISN'T IT? IN Spanish, too: *bosque nuboso*. The reality lives up to the magic of the name—high in the mountaintops, a mystical mist has turned the wooded hills into a lush green tangle roofed by dense canopy. Toucans and other exotic birds flit through (and if you spot one of the spectacular, elusive quetzals, shimmering red, green, and blue—jackpot!). Monkeys swing through the trees, snakes and lizards wend their ways across the forest floor, and tarantulas tuck themselves into little nooks in the soil. You feel enveloped in exuberant, primordial nature, in ways our increasingly hectic, paved-over lifestyles doesn't easily allow anymore. It's kind of a no-brainer, then, that the **Monteverde Cloud Forest Reserve** ✪✪✪ should be one of Costa Rica's most popular ecotourist attractions.

The colorful cast of characters out in the woods is matched by the one peopling Monteverde's three communities (Santa Elena, Cerro Plana, and Monteverde)—an 8,000-strong mix of Ticos, expats from Europe and North America, and the descendants of Quakers who moved here from the U.S. a half-century ago (many have intermarried, so this is one of the few places in this country where you'll see blond Ticos). It has a way of breeding some eccentric characters, too—sometimes it feels to us vaguely like that bizarre old TV show *Twin Peaks*. But most of all, it's turned into a cool little microcosm illustrating the challenges facing Costa Rica as a whole: folks of different origins nurturing conservation and bonding to live sustainably off the land. Granted, the eco-balancing act isn't always easy with a tourism industry that's pulling in close to a quarter million visitors a year. But despite complaints that tourism has "ruined" Monteverde (and yes, you'll see some crowds in high season), we're happy to report that, for the most part, things are still under control.

If you're thinking about becoming one of those quarter million, keep in mind that as breathtaking as the nature up here is, there are plenty of more accessible parts of Costa Rica where you can drink your fill of it (the roads into and out of here are hairy, believe me). And some people who've blown into town for a couple of days, tromped through the woods and rode a zipline, actually leave disappointed at how little there was to "see." But it takes more than a couple of days for Monteverde to fully unfold for you. Come for the cloud forest, of course, where the guides are among Costa Rica's best. Come, too, for the canopy tour. But in some ways, the real treat is that this is one of Costa Rica's most distinctive communities, with a great arts scene. You can catch a concert at the mammoth Monteverde Amphitheater, spend a day at the art center, or drop in for a chat with the ladies at the native arts-and-crafts co-operative. Way up here on the mountaintop there's a surprisingly dynamic, progressive community for you to discover.

DON'T LEAVE MONTEVERDE WITHOUT . . .

TAKING A GUIDED CLOUD FOREST TOUR Both the famed Monteverde and less trafficked Santa Elena cloud forests employ some of Costa Rica's best naturalist guides. Without them, the untrained eye will mostly see green, green, and more green.

NIGHTTIME ANIMAL-SPOTTING The general rule is bird-watching by day, other-critter-watching by night, when they're most out and about. You'll get a chance to see bats, two-toed sloths, caimans, tarantulas, snakes, and more.

TRYING TO GLIMPSE A QUETZAL Witnessing this majestic bird swoop through the canopy with its long red tail feathers and iridescent green coat is an electric thrill not just for birders. The odds are better here than anywhere, since a hundred pairs of quetzals are known to nest in the Monteverde area.

ZIPPING THROUGH THE TREES ON A CANOPY TOUR The birthplace of the canopy tour is now home to three different operations; with Costa Rica's highest platforms and longest cables, they're still reckoned the best. Attach yourself to a holster, and zip down a cable from platform to platform through the forest canopy 90m (300 ft.) up.

DABBLING IN THE ARTS No visit to this artists' colony–cum–conservationist mecca would be complete without taking in live music at the outdoor amphitheater or Bromeliad's cafe, or dropping in at one or more art galleries.

A BRIEF HISTORY

We know practically nothing about the Monteverde area's early history except that Corobici Indians once lived and hunted around here. Thanks to its remoteness, Ticos didn't get around to settling until very late in the game. The first to arrive were a handful of families who homesteaded up here in 1918, farming and raising cattle. Back then there weren't even poor roads—there were none, so these folks lived pretty isolated lives with practically no commerce or infrastructure beyond a *trapiche* (sugar cane mill) and a two-grade schoolhouse in the flyspeck that was Santa Elena. Apart from that village, the area didn't even have a name.

Then one fine day in 1951, 44 members of 11 Quaker families from Alabama showed up. Unhappy with the Korean War and the draft, these pacifists came to Costa Rica because it made a point of staying neutral in world affairs and having no army. They bought up about a half-dozen square miles, divvied it up, and got to work clearing forest for dairy farming. More importantly, they also set aside part of their land for preservation, and this tract later became the famous cloud forest reserve. It was these Quakers who gave the area its straightforward moniker: *monte* (mount) *verde* (green).

The Quakers immediately launched a handful of low-key development projects, building a school, a Friend's Meeting Room to meet weekly for prayer, and a cheese factory, which before too long had become the backbone of the local economy. Family and friends visiting them from the States planted the seeds of a tourism industry, which really took off once scientists got wind of the biodiversity—and especially rare species like the golden toad—in the 1960s.

When some of the Quakers noticed that homesteading was crowding out the nature, they raised money to fix the situation. Those sums, along with grants from the World Wildlife Fund, bought up huge hectares of the cloud forest and subsequently set up the Monteverde Cloud Forest Biological Reserve in 1972. Bright move! Before long, the preserve became one of Costa Rica's top ecotourism draws, not just for its own sake but also these communities' special flavor.

The numbers making the trek up here have lately swelled to more than 200,000 a year, and the "gentlemen's agreement" to keep growth from getting out of control has started to fray. Business interests have tried to get the road in paved, even trying to get authorization to develop a local reservoir, supposedly for an all-inclusive resort. But locals fought back to keep their laid-back small-town vibe from getting steamrollered. They know their fortunes are now tied to tourism. Thus new hotel rooms and restaurants are still opening at a brisk pace despite a couple of recent lean seasons. But Monteverdeans realize that keeping an industry like this in balance with nature in the face of greed and tunnel vision means constant watchfulness. Up to now they've managed to pull it off.

LAY OF THE LAND

Part of the province of Puntarenas, Monteverde sits atop a 1,350m-high (4,500-ft.) plateau on the Cordillera de Tilarán, in what's known as the cloud forest belt. There are three up here: the Santa Elena Cloud Forest Reserve, Monteverde Cloud Forest Reserve, and the Bosque Eterno de Niños cover nearly 363 sq. km (140 sq. miles). There are also a handful of private reserves. But development pressure has

What Is a Cloud Forest?

In some of the mountaintop tropical rainforests of nearly 40 countries, dense clouds and close to 100 percent humidity combine to create explosions of biodiversity, both animal and especially vegetable (there are more than 2,500 plants species in Monteverde). Part of what makes these forests so otherworldly is all the epiphytes, plants that grow on top of other plants. It's a misty tangle in here, with moss carpeting everything including the trees, profusions of ferns, and vines looping around the canopy (some of the vines are stranglers, wrapping themselves around trees until they're completely suffocated and die, leaving hollow cores).

taken its toll, and the numbers of species found around here—especially wildcats like jaguars and pumas that require lots of territory—are a fraction of what they used to be. But what's left is still impressive enough. If you have limited time, the one not to miss is the largest, Monteverde Cloud Forest (though it can get crowded in peak season).

As you'd expect for a damp, fog-blanketed high-altitude area, the climate up here is much cooler than most anywhere else in Costa Rica. Temps can drop down to the 50s (low teens Celsius) even during the day, so don't forget those light jackets and sweaters (but local microclimates mean you could be warm one moment, chilly the next, so dress in layers).

GETTING TO & AROUND MONTEVERDE

Driving is the only way up here, and one of these days, somebody's gonna make a T-shirt that says, "I survived the road to Monteverde." The 2-hour drive from the main roads in and out of Monteverde is nothing short of spectacular—sweeping valleys, craggy peaks, vibrant blue sky, and sometimes even views out over the Nicoya Gulf. But the road is dusty gravel all the way, strewn with big, sharp rocks and sometimes careening around sheer drops from hundreds of feet high. Take it from us: Tackle it by day only, and empty your bladder before starting.

BY BUS

Bus travel time from San José is 4 to 4½ hours. **Express buses** (Transportes Tilarán; ☎ 222-3854) leave Atlántico del Norte Terminal (Calle 12 at Av. 9) for Santa Elena daily at 6:30am and 2:30pm; the fare's about $5. If you're headed to a hotel outside of Santa Elena, you can stay on the bus as far as the cheese factory in Cerro Plano, but then you'll have to catch a taxi or arrange ahead to be picked up. From La Fortuna, you can catch the 8am bus for Tilarán, which takes 3 hours. In Tilarán, you can stop for lunch before catching the 12:30pm bus for Santa Elena, which takes 2 hours and costs $2.

Interbus (☎ 283-5573; www.interbusonline.com) out of San José is pricier ($29, kids $15) but comfier, and will pick you up from your hotel; daily departures are around 8:15am and 2:30pm. The similar **Grayline** (☎ 220-2126; www.graylinecostarica.com) charges $38 and leaves San José every day at 7am. If you're in a group, the folks at **Monteverdeinfo.com** can set up transfers in air-conditioned minibuses between Monteverde and San José ($109) or anywhere else in the country ($130) for up to six people.

Don't Buy the Map

If you're driving up, make sure to watch out for "government representatives" who flash makeshift municipal permits or clipboards. They'll try to make you buy a Xeroxed map for the road to Monteverde for 2,000 *colones* ($4). Not only do you not need the damn thing, but giving in only encourages a cottage industry of graft.

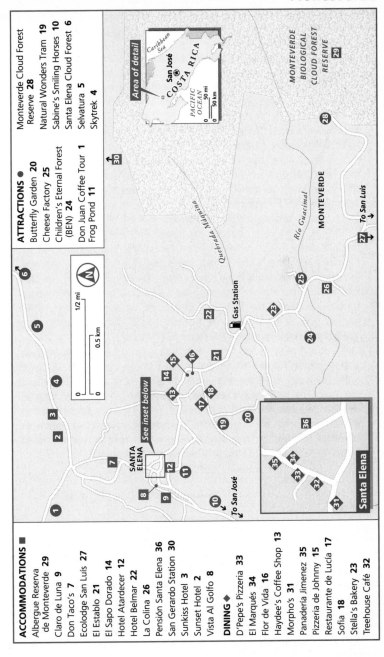

ACCOMMODATIONS ■

Albergue Reserva
de Monteverde **29**
Claro de Luna **9**
Don Taco's **7**
Ecolodge San Luis **27**
El Establo **21**
El Sapo Dorado **14**
Hotel Atardecer **12**
Hotel Belmar **22**
La Colina **26**
Pensión Santa Elena **36**
San Gerardo Station **30**
Sunkiss Hotel **3**
Sunset Hotel **2**
Vista Al Golfo **8**

DINING ◆

D'Pepe's Pizzería **33**
El Marqués **34**
Flor de Vida **16**
Haydee's Coffee Shop **13**
Morpho's **31**
Panadería Jimenez **35**
Pizzería de Johnny **15**
Restaurante de Lucía **17**
Sofia **18**
Stella's Bakery **23**
Treehouse Café **32**

ATTRACTIONS ●

Butterfly Garden **20**
Cheese Factory **25**
Children's Eternal Forest
(BEN) **24**
Don Juan Coffee Tour **1**
Frog Pond **11**
Monteverde Cloud Forest
Reserve **28**
Natural Wonders Tram **19**
Sabine's Smiling Horses **10**
Santa Elena Cloud Forest **6**
Selvatura **5**
Skytrek **4**

117

My Dinner with a Young Monteverdean

by Nelson Mui

On my last visit to Monteverde, I had the luck to become fast friends with a young local named Gema Cantillano. Having spent all her 19 years in Monteverde, she was among the first crop of students to attend the foreign-run Escuela Creativa, the area's first bilingual school, which builds environmental education into its daily curriculum. Everyone in town seemed to know her, and she them.

Like many of her neighbors, Gema seemed excited that so many people find her home such an enchanting place—and she was proud to show it off. On any given day she was seemingly everywhere at once—one moment volunteering at a restaurant, the next working at a tourist information booth, and in between helping out friends at some of the lodges.

But she was also torn about her hometown's extreme makeover from tranquil, dusty mountain hamlet into international tourist hub. "See that big tree right there?" she sighed, motioning at a 6m (20-ft), concrete-engulfed ficus on Santa Elena's main drag. "On lazy afternoons, we local kids would climb the tree and hang out on its branches." In 2005, it was turned into part of the Treehouse Restaurant, an open-air eatery where tourists now sit under branches festooned with Christmas lights and a gaudy sign promising FREE INTERNET WITH EVERY MEAL!

"Four or five years ago, there wasn't any of this," Gema said wistfully. A taste of the future? Maybe, but even if things look a little different today, the spirit of Monteverde is still in pretty good shape. It's not just the nature that's safe in the reserves, but Gema herself and others who call Monteverde home: the multi-culti brew of frontier culture; Quaker pacifism and dairy farming; the more recent injection of artists, conservationists, scientists, ecotourists, and downshifting expats from around the world. Sorta like Tanglewood, Texas, and Berkeley rolled into one.

BY CAR

From San José, get on the Interamerican Highway and head west to the Sardinal, which will take roughly 2 hours. There's an earlier turnoff at Río Lagarto, but the Sardinal route is paved as far as Guacimal, plus you'll spend less time navigating the unpaved roads and large stones. From here it's only about 35km (22 miles), but due to the roughness of the gravel, it will take 1½ to 2 hours, depending on driving conditions.

BY JEEP & HORSEBACK

If you're moving on from Monteverde to La Fortuna, consider one of the jeep-boat-jeep or horseback trips that go via Lake Arenal (p. 95).

Tough Wheels

While you don't absolutely need a 4WD to make it up here, it's an excellent idea. If not, make sure at least to rent a bigger-than-average car with a higher clearance. Also check to see that you've got a jack and a spare on board, since it's easy to get a flat from the roads in and around Monteverde. And lastly, check with your car-rental agency to see if you're insured for Monteverde—the roads up here are so rough that some of them don't.

GETTING AROUND

Local taxis are pretty inexpensive. Trips between Santa Elena and the communities of Cerro Plano and Monteverde will usually run between $5 and $10. If you don't spot one cruising around, your hotel or lodge will call for you. Most of the cloud forest and canopy tours include pick-ups and drop-offs at various hotels. Buses leave Santa Elena at 6:15am and 1pm for the Monteverde Cloud Forest Reserve, returning at noon and 4pm; fare is $2. A cab from Santa Elena will run $8 to $9.

Walking between Santa Elena and some of the outlying areas is also not a big deal (both locals and tourists do it), but it can get hilly in parts. There's a lot of dust blowing around out here, too. And at night, it's pitch black.

ACCOMMODATIONS, BOTH STANDARD & NOT

Scores of hotels and *cabinas* (cabins) spread through Santa Elena, Cerro Plano, and Monteverde cater to all levels of tourists. There are fewer "alternative" options than you might expect—limited vacation rentals (check general vacation rental websites, p. 341), few true B&Bs, and a working farm that accepts guests. If you're interested in a homestay, your options are to take a course at the **CPI** Spanish-language school or volunteer with one of the many local groups (p. 136), which will probably involve more time in Monteverde than you may have budgeted.

The more popular conventional digs fill up quickly during the December to March high season, so don't let it slide too close to your departure date. On the other hand, given how many new rooms are available online every year, even if you breeze into town last minute without reservations, chances are you'll snag something—most arriving buses are greeted by shills just itching to steer you to various hotels. It's usually a crap shoot, but we've heard from enough satisfied travelers who had no problems. Still, these guys work on commission, so it's probably safer to make arrangements ahead of time or look around on your own, starting with a couple of reputable info centers (see below).

Keep in mind that Santa Elena, Cerro Plano, and Monteverde each has its own character, pluses, and minuses, which we've summed up below. The sampling of accommodations is just that, a sampling; you can check out plenty of other options at **Monteverdeinfo.com**, or in person at its office right next to the

Treehouse Café (ask for Zack Smith). These folks know everything and everybody around here, and can arrange reservations at lodgings, restaurants, and tours that are right for you. *One note:* There's no point in comparing hotels based on whether they have air-conditioning or not. Very few have it because at this elevation, you really don't need it—honest!

IN & AROUND SANTA ELENA

Santa Elena is the only community that looks much like a traditional town, with a main street, services (bank, cybercafes, supermarkets, pharmacy, all that). If you don't have a car, staying here in town is your best option thanks to the slew of good, lower to midrange places to drop your bags. It's also ideal if you like to be near the "action." Unlike slightly more out-of-the-way Cerro Plano and Monteverde, Santa Elena has a bar-restaurant strip and people stroll the streets day and night. The only drawback is that Santa Elena is the farthest option from the Monteverde Cloud Forest Reserve. But that doesn't have to be a deal breaker, since most people on their single forest visit get picked up as part of a tour. At any rate, it's only 10 to 15 minutes by car, cab, or bus (which has fairly frequent service). Plus, Santa Elena is the closest community to the Santa Elena Cloud Forest, not to mention the canopy tours.

Since the town is, like, 4 square blocks, you can check out the lodging choices yourself. Many are owned and run by Ticos, so you'll usually get a warm welcome, plus personal touches like home cooking, laundry service, and friendly, chatty advice. And remember, though you'll be able to find a room somewhere, even if you show up without a reservation in high season, the best spots fill up quickly, so plan ahead if at all possible.

$ Among backpackers and college kids, certain places on the hostel circuit develop towering word of mouth. One of them is the **Pensión Santa Elena** (24m/80 ft. east of the Banco Nacional; ☎ 645-5051; www.pensionsantaelena.com; cash only). Ex-owner Jacques Bertrand, a talkative character who founded Monteverdeinfo.com (see above), created a funky, community-oriented spot always abuzz with activity, and the spirit lives on. Young guests hang out on hammocks and bond with other travelers, and hip, outgoing staffers (including the sibling owners, Ran and Shannon Smith) just might invite you to a party, art opening, or other happening. Most of the 25 well-worn rooms ain't much to write home about, but the bathrooms are tidy, and choices range from single-sex or coed dorm-style rooms ($8 a head) to private doubles with bath ($15).

$ For hostel rates with more of a hotel feel, head to the **Vista Al Golfo** (300m/ 984 ft. south of Morpho's; ☎ 645-6321; MC, V). What a find: $6 a person for a shared-bath private room, $21 for a double with private bath, plus the (Nicoya) gulf view promised by the name. The 14 rooms are fairly no frills, a cross between *cabina* and beach shack (for the view, ask for one on the upper floor). The overall vibe is relaxed and social—lots of note comparing and tale trading over beers in the communal kitchen or lounge areas. Owners Anali López and Jorge Campos live on-site and are enthusiastic about helping book tours—even tours elsewhere in Costa Rica, by calling on their many friends and family throughout the country.

$ Peace, quiet, and living in a residential neighborhood instead of tourist ghetto—yet still walking distance to town—that's what we like about the **Hotel Atardecer** ★ (375m/1,230 ft. south of Morpho's; ☎ 645-5685; cash only). It feels a little like some faded old frontier-style inn, with 20 rustic, wood-paneled rooms on two floors (on the upper floor you get gulf views). Doubles go for $35, including breakfast. The friendly owners are Ticos and the dining room serves cheap, tasty *casados* (heaping plates of rice, beans, fried plantains, avocado, and meat—usually chicken but sometimes fish or beef) if you're feeling too lazy for the stroll into town. In this price range, this is among Santa Elena's top values, quieter and better maintained than the first two we mention (the location's tops, too).

$ **Don Taco's** (300m/984 ft. north of the Banco Nacional; ☎ 645-5263; www.cabinasdontaco.com; MC, V) is in the same price range as Atardecer but it's even closer and boasts a livelier, more social atmosphere. In fact, many guests would just as soon chow down here as go into town. Taco, the eponymous owner, is the dude who pioneered the jeep-boat-jeep thing between Arenal and Monteverde, and he knows the scene backwards and forwards, so be sure to pick his brain as to which tours are the best. The 23 rooms are standard Motel 6–style affairs on two levels, with industrial tile floors, wooden walls, TV, and verandas or open terraces with chairs. All in all, a good deal at $40 to $50 for a double, with breakfast.

$ A little bit out of town, the peaceful forest setting and warm hospitality are the best things **Sunset Hotel** ★ (4km/2½ miles from Santa Elena and 1km /⅔ mile from Skywalk; ☎ 645-5048; www.monteverdeinfo.com/monteverde-hotels/sunset-hotel.htm; cash or barter only) has going for it. From this hill above Santa Elena on the way to the reserve, the views of the sunsets (along with the valley and gulf) are panoramic. The decor is rustic wood 'n' whitewash, and the seven rooms are pretty decent in size and comfy enough (though the too-springy mattresses might be an issue for some), especially at $23 for a single, $29 for a double. German host Vitalis Mengel and his Tica wife Carmen Blanco will whip up split-pea soup and grilled fish and meats if you ask them before 5pm. They'll also go out of their way to accommodate people who want to pay by credit card, by going with you to the local grocery store and charging the room amount there (you get to use your card, they pay off their grocery bill). But there are drawbacks: You'll need a car or cab to get in and out of town; you'll also be the farthest you can be from Monteverde Cloud Forest. On the other hand, it's almost like living in a cloud forest here (and there's a birding trail right on property).

$$ Just down the road, Vitalis and Carmen also run the newer and slightly more upscale **Sunkiss Hotel** (3km/2 miles from Santa Elena, 1km/⅔ mile from the Skywalk; ☎ 645-6984; cash or barter only, see above), with a European-inn feel: fancy carved headboards, pink walls, suede furniture, latticed windows. Four of the half-dozen spacious rooms are doubles staring at $59, including breakfast. As at the Sunset, you get great views from the veranda outside the rooms and from the homey dining room with picture windows. Get up close and personal with nature (and save major bucks) by camping out back for $11 per person. Between the Sunset and the Sunkiss, we'd try for the Sunset first; but for an extra $25 a night the decor's a little nicer here.

$$ A large, Alpine-style wood chalet in pastel blue with a dollhouse feel, the **Claro de Luna** ⭐ (200m/656 ft. south of Santa Elena; ☎ 645-5269; www.claro delunahotel.com; MC, V) is probably the area's most strikingly charming midpriced lodges. With nice gardens out front and nine cozy, simple rooms with floral duvets and polished wooden floors, it brings to mind a B&B with funky little flourishes like wrought-iron wall art, Art Deco lamps, and other bric-a-brac. It's a little on the high side for budget digs at $55 to $62 for doubles (breakfast included), but apart from the overly springy mattresses, the "Clair de Lune" has romantic ambiance and is just a stone's throw away from town.

IN & AROUND CERRO PLANO & MONTEVERDE

Over in these two communities east of Santa Elena you'll find the area's plushest lodges along with a few midrange options. There's definitely an Alpine flavor here; the hills and woods are alive with chalet lodges—one is actually called the Trapp Family Lodge. Of the two, Cerro Plano is closer to Santa Elena and has more restaurants and hotels within walking distance of each other—in other words, a compromise between being right smack in town and being way out in the woods. Out toward Monteverde, you'll need to drive or cab it almost anywhere except maybe the cloud forest reserve and a couple of attractions such as the cheese factory. But for a get-away-from-it-all vibe, there is no place better.

Within the Reserves

Though it's not much advertised, and researchers, students, and volunteers get first dibs, you can try for inexpensive—and very basic—dorm-style accommodations or cabins with shared and private baths in both the **Monteverde Cloud Forest Reserve** and **Children's Eternal Rainforest,** or Bosque Eterno de Niños (BEN). You'll want to be seriously into the nature thing, not be hung up on "amenities," and not mind that it can be a chore to get into town. If you're cool with that, these places can be kind of fun, what with a chance to really interact with the interesting people studying the amazing biodiversity out here. In Monteverde, the best options may be one field station's dorm-style **Albergue Reserva Biológica de Monteverde** (at reserve entrance; ☎ 645-5122; www.cct.or. cr), at $12 a head or $27 with all meals; they also charge $4 to $5 for primitive cabins deep in forest. In the BEN, the **San Gerardo Station** (3km/2 miles from Santa Elena reserve; ☎ 645-5200, fax 645-5104) charges $45 per person, dropping to $34 a head for groups of six or more.

Along the Road to Monteverde Reserve

$ An unpretentious lodge close to the reserve, **La Colina Lodge** (main road between Stella's Bakery and Friends Meeting House; ☎ 645-5009; www.lacolinalodge.com; MC, V) is run by a friendly American couple. Most of its 11 rooms (7 in the main lodge, 4 in a former carriage house) are charmingly rustic, with wooden antiques and Guatemalan bedspreads. Now, for the money ($38 per double with shared bath, $45 with private bath, including breakfast) you could do better in and around Santa Elena (it's also not the quietest place, especially at night), but this is a good deal for something both close to the reserve and a selection of shops, restaurants, and attractions like the cheese factory and arts-crafts co-op. Friends have complained about room cleanliness and decor, but we've never noticed a problem—just ask to see another room if you're not happy with the first one. There's a rock-bottom option here, too: camping for $5, which includes shared bathrooms.

$$ Design-lovers will dig the **Hotel Belmar** ✹✹ (100m/328 ft. northeast of the Cerro Plano gas station; ☎ 645-5201; www.hotelbelmarcostarica.com; V) for its chicer-than-your-average-chalet-lodge look. The 32 rooms have spiffy varnished hardwood floors and walls, potted ferns, gauzy white curtains, and nice big mirrors in the roomy baths. The *pièce de résistance:* French doors open up to private terraces with knockout valley and Nicoya Peninsula vistas. There's plenty of stuff to do at the Belmar, too, including a pool table, Jacuzzi, a kids' playground, and volleyball court. And the setting is secluded, set back from the road between Cerro Plano and Monteverde (yet it's just a $2 cab ride into Santa Elena). In season doubles run $85 to $95, including a hearty buffet breakfast. As always, you'll pay less when fewer folks are visiting.

$$$ For a real deal of an upscale lodge, Cerro Plano's Quaker-owned **El Establo** ✹✹ (5km/3 miles east of Santa Elena; ☎ 645-5110, or 877/623-3198 in the U.S. and Canada; www.hotelelestablo.com; AE, MC, V) is a beaut, sprawling across landscaped slopes set back from the road on a lovely 60-hectare (150-acre) spread. No, really: lawns, gardens, forest trails, lake, pool, lookouts with stupendous views, humongous restaurant—it's all good. The Campbell family's been renovating up a storm, and of its 120 rooms, the older ones are cozier, wood-paneled, and closer to the road and restaurant; the newer units sport balconies, nice stonework, and peaked timber roofs (though some are so far uphill they have to run shuttle service). A double with perks like cable TV and a fridge will run approximately $104 (including breakfast).

$$$ The drop-dead views from the private decks of the "sunset terrace suites" are a big draw at **El Sapo Dorado** ✹✹ (3km/2 miles east of Santa Elena, Cerro Plano; ☎ 645-5010; www.sapodorado.com; MC, V), named after the unique local "golden toad," now thought extinct. Though it's a short stroll to restaurants, galleries, and such, the 30 wood-paneled bungalows (some with fireplace) have a secluded feel, nestled in bucolic hills with a nature trail out back. On top of that, the on-site restaurant is a jewel and its creative Mediterranean-inspired fare one of Monteverde's fabbest. In season, double-occupancy rates start at $112 without breakfast and go up to $122 for the sunset terrace suites—on the pricy side hereabouts, but compared to the area's other similarly priced Alpine-style lodges, this would be our first pick given its ideal location, gorgeous views, and seclusion.

IN & AROUND SAN LUIS

$$ Though 45 minutes outside of Monteverde, you might find the **Ecolodge San Luís** ✹ (about 8km/5 miles past Sardinal-Lagartos intersection; ☎ 645-8049; cash only) worth it for the unusual experience of living on a working farm that doubles as a scientific station. Run by the University of Georgia, the 61-hectare (153-acre) spread includes a coffee plantation, fruit trees, and scenic woods for hiking. Besides getting to rub elbows with researchers and farmers from the agricultural community of San Luís (for meals and parties at the 80-person

dining hall, example), you can take outdoor classes in the natural sciences. All this doesn't come particularly cheap: Comfy cabins with private baths, balconies, and covered terraces overlooking the San Luís river will set you back $80 to $85 per person (but that at least includes meals); knock $20 a night off that if you're willing to sleep in bunk beds in dorm-style rooms.

DINING FOR ALL TASTES

Besides what we've listed below, most of the larger hotels in the area have restaurants open to nonguests—**El Sapo Dorado** ✸✸ (p. 123) is especially good for both food and sunset views. But there are plenty of stand-alone choices, too—in fact, more every year. Along with a couple of *sodas* in Santa Elena, you've got your pick of a decent variety of international offerings from humbler fare (burger, pizzas, veggie/crunchies) to pretty high-quality chic-nouvelle-fusion-what-have-you. Interestingly, especially given the remoteness of the place, prices aren't as inflated as in other tourist-popular areas. Keep in mind that restaurants close on the early side—usually 9 to 10pm. Finally, to keep outlays to a bare minimum, stock up on groceries and lunch sandwiches at Santa Elena's central **Supermercado La Esperanza** (☎ 645-5068).

BREAKFAST/SNACKS

While most people tend to breakfast at their hotel, many other spots serve a pretty good *desayuno* for a couple of bucks or so. In Santa Elena, the bookstore **Chunches** (around corner from the Santa Elena bus stop; ☎ 645-5147; daily 8am–6pm) has nice homemade pastries and espresso or latte, and the **Panadería Jimenez** (across from Banco Nacional; ☎ 645-5035; daily 4am–6pm) is a typical Tico bakery where you can get fresh bread, sandwiches, and pastries. In the Cerro Plano/Monteverde neck of the woods, old fave **Stella's Bakery** (across from CASEM co-op; ☎ 645-5560; www.stellasbakery.com; daily 7am–5pm) is tops to start out the day or for a snack at any point. Goodies include donuts, milkshakes, and homemade pancakes, bread, and yogurt with granola; the outdoor patio here is a great for catching your breath in the afternoon. **Haydee's Coffee Shop** (across from El Sapo Dorado; ☎ 645-5586; daily 7am–6pm) also serves a good selection of coffees and sweets on Cerro Plano's busy business strip. Besides these, a couple of other spots worth checking out are **Flor de Vida** and **Restaurante de Lucía** (see below).

RESTAURANTS

In addition to the listings below, there are a few *sodas* in town. Of these we'd head to the **El Marqués** (☎ 645-5918; daily noon–10pm; AE, MC, V) which, though basic with its plastic tables and chairs, serves tasty fish dishes. You can get a fresh sea bass with fries and salad or a large plate of prawns, each for $6.

$ D'Pepe's Pizzeria ✸ (across from the church, Santa Elena; ☎ 645-5133; daily 11am–10pm; MC, V) makes the best down-home, wood-oven pizzas ($5) in town, generously proportioned and served up on wooden platters. Mains like chicken in heart of palm sauce ($4.85) are good, too, as is the wine list (short though it is). The decor's cozy, with linen tablecloths, wood paneling and beams, and funky hanging wood light fixtures. Best of all, you can watch the world go by through the large picture windows right onto the main drag.

Fab Fusion Worth a Splurge

$$–$$$ Opened by Californian Karen Nielsen in 2004, **Sofia** ★★★ (just off Cerro Plano road, 200m/656 ft. west of Hotel Heliconia; ☎ 645-7017; daily 11:30am–9:30pm, AE, D, MC, V) isn't just Monteverde's top dining spot, but flat-out one of the most exciting restaurants in all Costa Rica, focusing on local produce and fresh seafood in serving up nouvelle Latin fare, creatively goosed with Asian and Caribbean influences.

Get your juices flowing with a signature Sofia Colada (passion-fruit juice, white rum, and coconut milk topped with a splash of dark rum and fresh coconut) or mango-ginger mojito ($4.50 each), then start with *enyu-cados* (yucca croquettes with mango aioli, $4), tangy sea bass ceviche ($4.50), or salad of locally grown organic greens tossed with hearts of palm, tangerine, and guava vinaigrette ($4). Entree hits includes fig-roasted pork loin with mashed sweet potatoes ($11) or plantain-crusted sea bass with coconut rice and chayote (kind of like squash; $11). Desserts (all $3.50) include banana bread pudding, chocolate rum flan, and watermelon granizado (with an optional spritz of tequila). There's a good wine list, too, heavy on Argentina and Chile.

The edibles are matched by the elegance of the large, airy room, with a decor that—surprise, surprise—wouldn't be out of place in California wine country: Spanish colonial–style arches, aqua walls, and glowing stone sconces. The big communal table in the center is great for striking up friendships, local or otherwise. Local bands drop by occasionally, especially in high season (when, by the way, we definitely recommend reservations).

$–$$ Giant, juicy, all-beef burgers (just try finishing one) and shakes are big stars at **Morpho's** ★ (across from La Esperanza supermarket, Santa Elena; ☎ 645-5607; daily 11am–10pm; AE, D, MC, V), a hip little second-floor eatery owned by a young Quaker fellow named Matthew Stuckey. The menu covers the waterfront, from good Tico *casados* (plates heaped with rice, beans, plantains, and usually shredded beef or chicken, from $3.10) to fancier pastas and entrees like sea bass ($7.50) and pork chops ($6). The decor is fun (check out the namesake blue morpho butterfly art on the walls and hanging from the ceiling), as is the clientele (be ready to wait, though—the place is popular, tiny, and doesn't take reservations).

$–$$ The big appeal of Santa Elena's <u>Treehouse Cafe</u> ~~Very good~~ (across from the church; ☎ 645-5751; daily 6:30am–10pm; AE, D, MC, V) is less in its good but unexceptional menu of sandwiches and international fare than the lovely setting—an open-air patio under a big old ficus festooned with lights. But even if you don't eat here, do stop in for a drink.

$$ Outside of town, another good, affordable pick for pasta, pizza, and Italian favorites in a classy ambiance is the usually bustling **Pizzería de Johnny** ★ (2km/1¼ miles east of Santa Elena on the road to Monteverde preserve; ☎ 645-5066; daily 11am–10pm; MC, V). The big selection of thin-crust wood-oven pizzas is the main draw, but I found the pastas wonderfully prepared and more authentic tasting than in most Costa Rican restaurants that call themselves Italian; most everything is under $10. The warm-yellow walls, wood tables, and soft lighting in the large open dining area make it feel like a very civilized affair, but on a nice night we like the tables out on the veranda. In season you'll definitely want to reserve ahead.

$$ Go vegetarian with a Mediterranean accent at the **Flor de Vida** (2km/1¼ miles east of Santa Elena on road to Monteverde preserve; ☎ 645-6328; www.flordevida.net; daily 7am–10pm; AE, D, MC, VC), a cafe with a funky vibe (walls covered with silk batiks, local handicrafts for sale), and great *casados*, salads, veggie burgers, and pizzas (plus, they tell us it's the only place in Monteverde where you can get bagels). Our own faves include the veggie lasagna and a mango pie that's nothing short of *delicioso*. Whatever you choose, a meal will set you back less than $10. Snag a window table for nice forest and garden views.

$$ While the menu changes nightly at the **Restaurante de Lucía** (200m/656 ft. south of Hotel Heliconia; ☎ 645-5337; daily 7am–9pm; AE, D, MC, V), a good selection of grilled meats, seafood, and sandwiches served with homemade tortillas have made it one of the most popular restaurants in Monteverde. Among the choices, the filet mignons are a standout (although a little pricey at $12), as is the vegetarian lasagna ($6). While the dining room is spacious and relaxed, the best tables here are out on the terrace, where you can watch hummingbirds flit around feeders. *A good Tico street joint : Taco to Go Go Good Burritos*

WHY YOU'RE HERE:
THE TOP SIGHTS & ATTRACTIONS
THE CLOUD FORESTS *┌ beautiful*

You are, of course, not going to haul yourself all the way up here and not check out the cloud forests, the natural wonder that's made Costa Rica famous. There are three main ones up here: the **Santa Elena Cloud Forest Reserve** ★, the **Children's Eternal Forest** ★, and the one you really shouldn't miss, **Monteverde Biological Cloud Forest Reserve** ★★★.

The first (1973), and still the biggest and best, is the **Monteverde Biological Cloud Forest Reserve** ★ (☎ 645-5122; www.cct.or.cr; daily 7am–4pm; $13, students $6.50, $15 with guided tour). The reserve holds some 142 sq. km (55 sq. miles) of varying microclimates and ecosystems 1,500m (4,987 ft.) above sea level, and is considered one of the world's premier wildlife sanctuaries. Thanks to the Tropical Science Center of Costa Rica, it's also one of the most well run, with 13km (8 miles) of great trails and some of the country's best-trained and -informed guides, who'll point out some of the hundred mammal species (many of them bats), 1,200 types of amphibians, 400 of birds, and more than 2,500 of plants.

Birds of a Heckuva Feather

by Nelson Mui

Although close to 400 avian species have been spotted in these cloud forests, there's one that's always held up as the Holy Grail: the famous, flighty **quetzal**. Yeah, yeah, I know what you're thinking: Do the green buggers actually live up to the hype?

This fan says: totally! The birds (the males, anyway) are nothing short of dazzling. Direct sunlight makes their plumages shimmer like you wouldn't believe, into glistening emerald-green and gold—it's like trying to track a flying hologram. Toss in a glowing red underbelly and tail plumes up to .6m long (2 ft.), and you've got yourself a bona fide spectacle. I'm not usually easily impressed or hyperemotional, but when my guide directed my eye toward a quetzal flitting overhead, I literally felt a visceral rush. The bird won me over on the spot.

These birds have been impressing humans for centuries, of course. The Aztecs worshipped the "plumed serpent" Quetzalcoátl, depicted with a headdress made of quetzal feathers. To the Mayans, these feathers were sacred and more valuable than gold, so they made hunting the bird a capital crime, and only high muckamucks could wear quetzal plumes. After a quetzal was caught on film in the 19th century, hunters rushed to supply the demand for their feathers destined for fashionable women's hats all over Europe. That demand, plus humans damaging natural habitats, has led to a dwindling of quetzal populations across Central America. But Monteverde is blessed with an unusually high concentration—about a hundred nesting pairs—so you may very well achieve that Holy Grail.

Your best chance to see one is during mating season, February to May, and early in the mornings. Guides are a big help, since they to know where and how to look for them—though there are never any guarantees, of course. I've also talked to travelers who've spotted them on their own, in some tree by the parking lot outside the entrance. You can get more info on quetzal nesting activity, updated every half-hour, on **www.cloudforest alive.org**.

There's a field station, called La Casona, where you can get food, drinks, buy crafts and coffee, and even bunk overnight (bring your sleeping bag).

Going in with a guide will cost you a bit more—$28, not including the cost of getting out here—but not only will you have a better stab of spotting some of the cloud forest's most compelling characters (such as the quetzal, above, or the three-wattled bell-bird, p. 131), you'll also get an expert primer on cloud forest ecology, which will make your experience of nature in Monteverde and elsewhere much more meaningful (think of it as learning a bit of a country's language and customs before visiting). If you do skip the guide, at least make sure to check out

Leading the Way

Consider hiring a private guide to take you through the reserves. You get a little more privacy, plus the chance to tailor more to your interests (for example, if you've got more birds on the brain than affinity for amphibians). The **Asociación de Guías de Monteverde** can hook you up; just ask your hotel to recommend a guide, or you can check out bios on www.cloudforestalive.org (look for expertise and experience, keeping in mind that some guides may just be farmers familiar with the forest rather than trained naturalists). Prices start at $30 for one person, dropping to $15 per person for groups.

We did this one. It was awesome.

the hummingbird gallery at the preserve entrance, where you'll see a variety of the gem-colored little guys up close and personal, flitting from feeder to feeder.

Since the Monteverde reserve is so popular, the neighboring **Santa Elena Cloud Forest** ★ (☎ 645-5390; www.monteverdeinfo.com/reserve; daily 7am–4pm; adults $10, students $6) ends up taking a lot of the spillover. But this newer (since 1992) and smaller (6 sq. km/2⅓ square miles, compared with Monteverde's 142 sq. km/55 sq. miles) reserve, owned and operated by the Santa Elena High School, has a lot going for it on its own right. You'll find many of the same species as next door, but also a distinct local ecology with varying microclimates and three separate ecosystems (that's partly because it straddles the Caribbean-side slope, instead of the drier Pacific slope). Another plus: flora and fauna such as African violets, begonias, and spider monkeys, which the Monteverde preserve doesn't have. What's more, during the green season (Aug through early Feb), you're more likely to see quetzals here than over in Monteverde. Most of the forest is secondary—it was farmed, and has been growing back since only 1989. Thus, the trees are smaller and the growth on the ground denser; you'll notice that trunks and branches are almost entirely covered with epiphytes like lichens, liverworts, bryophytes, and mosses.

The idea behind the third adjacent cloud forest, the **Bosque Eterno de Los Niños** ★ 🧒 (Children's Eternal Cloud Forest; entrance just past CASEM co-op; ☎ 645-5104; 8am–5pm, Sun 9am–4pm; adults $7, students $4) is in some ways more interesting than the reserve itself. Run by the Monteverde Conservation League, the BEN was born in 1988 thanks to a group of tree-hugging Swedish school kids who wanted to do their part to save the rainforest. They raised $1,500 to buy 6 hectares (15 acres), and as word got out, donations flooded in, letting the BEN expand to more than 21,600 hectares (54,000 acres), making it the largest private reserve in Central America.

Despite its size, the only trail open to the general public is the self-guided **Bajo del Tigre Trail,** just over 3km (2 miles). It makes a relatively easy hike, great for birding, and takes you to the edge of a canyon for some swell sunset views over the Gulf of Nicoya. If you are staying on for a few days, it's definitely worth a visit, certainly inexpensive and easy to get to. The Children's Nature Center here is a fun, colorful way to introduce kids to conservation and rainforest ecology. An especially good option is the $15 twilight/night walks.

CANOPY TOURS

Besides the cloud forests themselves, Monteverde is most famous for its canopy tours, or ziplines (you can book through your hotel or with the CETAM, p. 132). Costa Rica's very first canopy tour was founded here in 1997: the **Original Canopy Tour** (at Cloud Forest Lodge; ☎ 645-5243; www.canopytour.com; adults $45, students $35, ages 11 and under $25; tours daily 7:30am, 10:30am, and 2:30pm). This operation, consisting of 11 platforms and two rappels, has since been copied and souped up by countless competitors, but it's still one of the most unique around, thanks to touches like climbing up inside of an enormous hollow tree to get to the first platform, and rappelling down the last tree at the end of the 2½ hours. Still, of the three canopy tours now in the area, this is the shortest and has the tamest runs, so it'd probably be my last choice (on the other hand, it might be the best bet for seniors and smaller kids—they allow youngsters as young as 5). Transfers from your hotel are included.

More thrilling and higher altitude, **SkyTrek** ✦✦ (one in Santa Elena across from the National Bank, the second in Santa Elena Cloud Forest; ☎ 645-5238; www.skytrek.com; $44, students $35, kids $31; tours at 7:30am, 9:30am, 11:30am, and 1:30pm) also has 11 platforms but no rappels. The lines get gradually higher and longer until by the end you're zipping across 750m (2,500-ft.) stretches more than 120m (400 ft.) over the ground. Unlike its two competitors, the set up here involves parallel handlebars over your head instead of a single handle, which some find less comfortable. You have to be at least 10 years old to tackle this one. Also here is **Skywalk** (7am–4pm; adults $15, kids $6), a 2.4km (mile-and-a-half) series of suspension bridges 36m (120 ft.) up in the cloud forest canopy. It's a great option for those not quite up to a zipline, or more interested in the view without the adrenaline (go early to catch more of the wildlife and birds; the $15 guided tour you probably don't need in this case). You can combine both Skytrek and Skywalk for $50 (adults), and throw in a visit to the fascinating snake exhibit here for another $8.

Everything is moist *Ponchos*

Cloud Forest Preplanning *Bring WARM stuff. Rain gear*

When visiting the cloud forests, bring a light sweater or jacket. Thanks to the altitude and dampness, it can get pretty chilly, especially on a cloudy day, when temperatures can drop to the 50s (low teens Celsius). During the rainy season, trails can get muddy, too, and you might also want to think about renting boots or bringing your own (ask at your hotel about conditions the day before you head out). Lastly, in high season, get there early: No more than 120 people are allowed on the trails at any given time, so if you show up too late in the day—especially if you're on your own— you may get turned away. Wouldn't want that, right?

The Best *Spend your time here*

The Selvatura complex (office across from the church in Santa Elena; ☎ 645-5929; www.selvatura.com; canopy tour for adults $40, students $30, kids $25) is a one-stop shop that brings to mind an eco-Disneyland, with a canopy tour, butterfly and hummingbird gardens, a bodaciously bugged-out insect collection, suspension bridges through the treetops, and even a restaurant. Prices vary depending on attraction, and discounts for packages combine different exhibits and tours (for example, admission to the bridges is $20 but you can combine it with the zipline for $55; check at the in-town office or on the website for the full menu and tour times). The canopy tour has more platforms (14) and longer cables than its competitors, and there are eight bridges through the canopy (one of them a great birding trail). The **Jewels of the Rainforest** ★ 🧒 museum has more than 50,000 insects collected by world-famous entomologist Richard Whitton: a rainbow array of bugs in shimmering greens, reds, blues, silvers and golds, beautifully displayed against velvet in glass-case, art masterpieces. Kids will love the interactive exhibits and the chance to see the creepy-crawlies up close and personal (though dead).

TOURS & OTHER ATTRACTIONS

Stuff to do and ways to do it have been multiplying at such a clip that sifting through it all can be overwhelming. Frog ponds and butterfly farms; all sorts of private reserves touting trails and waterfalls; a tour of a *trapiche;* not one but three coffee tours—oy, it can make your head spin. Brochures for all of the above are floating through area hotels and other businesses, but we've boiled down a selection of greatest hits.

If you haven't overdosed on nature during the day, sign on for a **night tour** ★ in the Santa Elena, the Bosque Eterno de Ninos, or the Finca Ecológica private reserve (600m/1,968 ft. south of the Hotel Heliconia, on the Cerro Plano Road; ☎ 645-5554; www.fincaecologicamonteverde.com). Apart from the fact that you see a different cast of characters than you would during the day—tarantulas, coatimundis, snakes, bats—there's something even more otherworldly about the cloud forest at night than in broad daylight. These night tours run around $15 per person.

Volcano Views

If you haven't visited Arenal and don't plan to, you can still catch sight of the famous volcano on a clear day from the Santa Elena Cloud Forest. One of the trails leads to a *mirador* (lookout) with an observation tower with boffo Arenal views.

Though Santa Elena makes a wonderfully tranquil counterpart to Monteverde—its four trails get an average only 20 to 30 people a day—we'd recommend coming here in addition, not instead of. Try this on for size: Spend 1 full day in Monteverde (guided tour in the morning, hike on your own in the afternoon), then a self-guided visit to Santa Elena the next morning followed by an afternoon at the nearby canopy tour (p. 128).

The Varmints of Monteverde

The cloud forest reserves are jam packed with wildlife, most blending pretty thoroughly into the tangles of green. While you're not likely to spot a jaguar or other wild cats, below are a select and subjective list of critters you do stand a decent chance of seeing.

Birds In addition to **quetzals** (p. 127) and scores of **hummingbird** species, the endangered **three-wattled bell-bird** is truly magnificent to behold, with its chestnut-brown plumage, white crown, and three wattles dangling over its beak (from a distance they look like pieces of string). On a recent visit, we were lucky enough to see a pair of males perched on a branch, opening their beaks wide, chests heaving, to emit a thunderous, metallic "BONK!" Sometimes when there are several in the area, you'll hear a perpetual echo, like a bunch of bell towers pealing. Other prime sightings include the large **black guan,** which looks like a wild turkey with shiny black plumage and bright-blue facial markings, and the sleek **emerald toucanet,** like a smaller, blue-throated version of the related toucan.

Amphibians and Reptiles As recently as 1987, there were more than 100 species of reptiles and 60 kinds of amphibians around here, and scientists still aren't sure why the numbers have dropped drastically (global warming is high on the suspect list, though). Sad to say, one of the casualties seems to be the legendary **golden toad** *(sapo dorado),* which helped put Monteverde on the map and gave conservation such a boost around here in earlier years. The size of a quarter and reportedly both deaf and dumb, the males were glossy, starburst orange and the females yellow and black. For the moment, the only way to catch sight of them is in the slide show before the guided tour.

Blessed are the cheesemakers, as Monty Python would say. It's well worth stopping in for a tour of the **Lechería,** aka **the cheese factory** ★★ (300m/984 ft. southeast of CASEM; ☎ 645-5436; Mon–Sat 9am and 2pm; $8 adults, $6 students/kids), not just for a neat look at the world of curds, but also for the history of the Monteverde Quakers who started the factory in 1953. Now it makes 17 different kinds of cheese, including Gouda, cheddar, Emmentaler, and mozzarella, sold all over Central America. When it comes time for the samples, be sure to snag a chunk of low-fat Monte Rico, unique to Monteverde, and Bon Salut, a blend of Emmentaler, Dambo, Parmesan, and other European cheeses. If you're short on time or cash, there's an observation room where you can watch the workers and, of course, buy products both cheesy and freezy.

Java hounds will notice that coffee is a big deal hereabouts, and there's a growing cottage industry in tours to bring you out into the fields. The relatively new **Don Juan Coffee Tour** ★★ (☎ 645-7100; www.donjuancoffeetour.com) takes you out to a plantation just outside Santa Elena and does a good job explaining

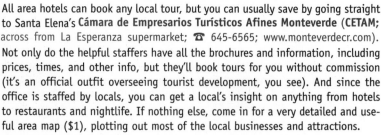

Tours: A Cheaper One-Stop Shop

All area hotels can book any local tour, but you can usually save by going straight to Santa Elena's **Cámara de Empresarios Turísticos Afines Monteverde (CETAM;** across from La Esperanza supermarket; ☎ 645-6565; www.monteverdecr.com). Not only do the helpful staffers have all the brochures and information, including prices, times, and other info, but they'll book tours for you without commission (it's an official outfit overseeing tourist development, you see). And since the office is staffed by locals, you can get a local's insight on anything from hotels to restaurants and nightlife. If nothing else, come in for a very detailed and useful area map ($1), plotting out most of the local businesses and attractions.

the production cycle, from germination beds to depulping, roasting, and packaging (along the way you'll also get plenty of insight into Costa Rica's history, economy, and culture). The 2½-hour tour even sends you off with free samples and Don Juan hats, but at $31 a person (including hotel pick-up), it's one of Monteverde's pricier tours. Comparable but cheaper ($17) is the coffee tour at the **Finca Cielo Verde,** which you can arrange directly (☎ 645-5641), or through Tina at **Tina's Casitas** (☎ 348-8770). Actually, the tour we most recommend is given daily at 8am and 1pm at the Coope Santa Elena at **Café Monteverde** (main road across from Stella's Bakery/next to CASEM women's artist co-op; ☎ 506-645-5182; www.cafe-monteverde.com; $25 adults, $23 students/kids); it's 2½ hours long, and you can book directly or through CETAM. You start out on-site, then you're taken to the Finca La Bella in the San Luis Valley.

Butterflies are free (well, kinda sorta) at Cerro Plano's **Jardín de Mariposas de Monteverde** ★ (600m/1,968 ft. south of Hotel Heliconia; ☎ 645-5512; daily 9:30am–4pm; $8 adults, $6 students, including tour). This local institution of more than a decade has four net-covered gardens designed to let different colors and species flutter past you. It's a really cool experience, like something out of Alice in Wonderland or My Little Pony. It's plenty educational, too, thanks to exhibits on insects (75 percent of the animal kingdom!) and medicinal plants (especially check out the live "bug cams" and the leaf-cutter ant colony under glass). Make sure to flit in around midmorning, when the butterflies are perkier.

The big worldwide amphibian die-off has taken hold here, too—meaning your chances of spotting some of Costa Rica's frog species in the wild aren't great, even at night when they're more active. Instead, see them at the impressive **Ranario de Monteverde (Monteverde "Froggery,")** (300m/984 ft. north of Monteverde Lodge; ☎ 645-6320; daily 9am–8:30pm; adults $8, students $2) just outside Santa Elena. No, you won't see the almost extinct golden toad, but you will get an eyeful of red-eyed tree frogs, colorful poison-dart frogs (darn things look like they've been dipped in nail polish), transparent frogs, and mammoth marine toads, along with a few snakes thrown in for good measure. Come by after dark, when things really get—ahem—hopping.

Exploring on horseback is truly one of the niftiest ways to take in Monteverde's natural beauty. Several stables rent *caballos* by the hour (around $15) and also offer guided tours, most of which take you through the San Luís Valley, followed by a hike to a big waterfall with a swimming hole. Prices vary, so it's worth comparing among stables, but we recommend the more established **Meg's Stables** (☎ 645-5419), **Sabine's Smiling Horses** (☎ 645-6894; www. horseback-riding-tour.com), and **El Rodeo** (☎ 645-5764) for their well-trained and well-cared-for horses; a typical 3-hour ride might run $40. You can also get over to Arenal/La Fortuna by horseback, and though some have said it's abusive of the horses, that's not true if you go with a reputable operator like **Desafío** (☎ 479-9464; www.desafiocostarica.com) or the jeep-boat-jeep operations mentioned on p. 95.

A final bit of business worth mentioning for those who want to take in the scenery with less exertion, or have small kids in tow, is a slow-moving ride on the **Natural Wonders Tram** (☎ 645-5960), a suspended-cable gondola through the forest that takes about an hour and costs $15 a person. Each gondola fits two people, and there are no guides to tell you what you're seeing.

ATTENTION, SHOPPERS!

Thanks to its artistic and farming scenes, Monteverde has more interesting stuff to buy than many other tourist spots in this country. Prices vary, of course (from $3 keychains to $50 and above for wooden sculptures, boxes, and jewelry), but on the whole are pretty reasonable.

An excellent first stop would be the area around **CASEM** ★ (just east of the gas station on the road to Monteverde reserve; ☎ 645-5190; Mon–Sat 8am–5pm, Sun 10am–4pm), where you're within walking distance of a number of stores. CASEM is an arts-and-crafts shop run by a co-operative of female artisans; it has a good selection of embroidered and handmade clothes, as well as wooden sculptures. Across the parking lot, at **Café Monteverde** (☎ 645-5006; Mon–Sat 7:30am–6pm, Sun 9am–4pm), sample and buy java grown by local farmers ($2 a pound). Just up the road, **Las Bromelias** (☎ 645-6272) sells arts, natural soaps, and natural history books. Even if you don't go on the tour, stop at the **cheese factory/La Lechería** (300m/985 ft southeast of CASEM; ☎ 645-5436; Mon–Sat 7:30am–5pm, Sun 7:30am–noon) to sample and buy some of the best cheeses in Central America, along with ice cream and other stuff from cows.

Joe to Go

You've sampled the Monteverde coffee and now you're hooked. But your suitcase is overflowing and already past the weight limit. So why not have it delivered? **Montana Coffee Traders** (www.cafemonteverde.com; 800/ 345-5282) will get it shipped right to you. If you do buy coffee while here, make sure it's authentic Café Monteverde, grown from the Monteverde Cooperative Farms—just look for the quetzal logo (some vendors sell look-alike varieties using inferior beans grown in the lowlands).

Arte-a-Rama

One of the most enticing galleries to set up shop in Monteverde in recent years is the **Casa de Arte** ✹✹ (200m/656 ft. north of Cerro Plano school; ☎ 645-5275; daily 9am–6pm). Stop in check out the range of styles and media of artists from all over Costa Rica: brightly colored flora and fauna sculptures, tribal masks, ceramics, paintings, and more. Some great pieces that caught our eye included Rodolfo Uder's sculptural wood cylinder, burnished to high gloss—it looked like it'd be right at home in a chic loft. Fernando Páramo weighed in with a wooden tribal mask, crafted in collaboration with the indigenous Boruca community, fiercely beautiful, at once primitive and modern. And Talía Chamorro Calvo's "Taligramas" jewelry in jade and silver were striking, inspired by both games like dominoes and tic-tac-toe and pre-Columbian motifs. You can even try your own hand at creating art through the workshops held here (you'll need to contact them in advance).

There are also a number of galleries where you can pick up unique pieces that make great additions to your decor gifts for family/friends. The **Atmosphera Art Gallery** (kitty-corner from the Cerro Plano school; ☎ 645-6555; daily 9am–6pm) has a permanent exhibition of wood sculptures from artists from around Costa Rica. This isn't your usual mass-manufactured, souvenir-grade wood tchotchke, but high-quality artistic works made from exotic woods and recycled materials.

Right next door, the **Galería Extasis** (☎ 645-5548; daily 9am–6pm) is worth a visit for the space alone. Nestled up against the forest, the three-level gallery has balconies on each floor for ogling the scenery in between the art. You'll see the works of the talented Marco Tulio Brenes, a local artist who grew up in the foothills of Monteverde and once trained under Costa Rica's famed wood sculptor Barry Biesanz. Brenes takes unconventional materials such as old fence posts or wood from decaying or insect-ravaged trees, and creates amazing sculptures, boxes, jewelry, and bowls.

The framed wildlife photographs of Michael and Patricia Fogden are the highlight at the **Hummingbird Gallery** (100m/328 ft. from the entrance of Monteverde Reserve; ☎ 645-5030; daily 7am–5pm). Their vivid images of sloths, snakes, frogs, and birds are stunning—if you went on a guided tour, you saw these same photos in the slide show before you headed out. Okay, they aren't for sale, but you can buy slides and postcards of them, plus local artist Sarah Dodwell's winsome watercolors and a wide array of souvenirs including batiks, textiles, and posters.

NIGHTLIFE

Beyond the "action" in the cloud forests that you might catch on night hikes, small Monteverde has a pretty active after-dark scene from the human standpoint, too, thanks to all the expats and visitors, sprinkled with a few appreciative Ticos—it's not quite San José or the beach towns along the Guanacaste coast, but it's far from the back of beyond. As with most Costa Rica tourist spots, live music tends to bring out the crowds. From January to April, the **Monteverde Music Festival** ★★ (☎ 645-5053; www.mvinstitute.org) brings in some of the country's best musicians—classical to jazz, folk to Latin, New Age to pop. Concerts are held at the **Monteverde Institute** every Thursday, Friday, and Saturday around 5 or 6pm. Also check the schedule at the nearby **Monteverde Amphitheatre** (☎ 645-6272). In either case, dress warmly, because nighttime can get downright chilly; tickets generally run $10 ($5 for students).

On weekends year round, the **Moon Shiva Café** (at Bromelia's Art Gallery, ☎ 645-5270; Fri-Sun 11am–11pm; movie nights free; dancing $3, for students $2) in Monteverde has live music with a festive but relaxed vibe that pulls a mix of tourists and locals. People are friendly and out to have a good time, so it's a great place to meet and chat over beer. There's a (limited) menu of Mediterranean–Costa Rican fusion fare, so many start with dinner and stay for the music or the twice-weekly movies.

In downtown Santa Elena, pretty much everybody heads to **Bar Amigos** (25m/ 82 ft. north of the church; ☎ 645-5071; daily noon–midnight; no cover), a good-size joint with a dance floors in the middle and a handful of pool tables in the back. There's usually a packed crowd of Ticos on Fridays, when live cumbia bands play, though on any given night there's always a decent bunch in for the cheap $1 *bocas* (snacks), an Imperial, or a game of pool. On weeknights, another bar with dancing, popular after 9 or 10pm, is the recently renovated **La Taberna** (☎ 645-5883; daily noon–1am), with salsa, merengue, and cumbia sprinkled with Latin and gringo pop. The two-story **Bar Unicornios**, aka **Domingo's** (opposite the Santa Elena soccer field; ☎ 642-6282; daily noon–midnight; $2 cover) draws a mostly Tico crowd; there's occasional live music and dancing, and Thursdays are karaoke nights (hmm, know any Paulina Rubio?). There's an out-and-out disco up here, too: **La Cascada** (300m/984 ft. east of the gas station, Cerro Plano; ☎ 645-5186; weekends 7pm till there is no one left; $6 cover when there's live music, otherwise free). Go *late*.

THE "OTHER" MONTEVERDE

The number of visitors to Monteverde in high season can feel a little overwhelming, even if you're one of them. So, many locals tend to be shy about giving up what privacy they can carve out. Now, a night out at the Bar Amigos or Unicornios might do the trick (even if the locals in question are likely to be three sheets to the wind), but a better quality way to tap into the local community starts with asking people what's going on around town, or paying attention to the many flyers in circulation advertising impromptu or scheduled art openings, movie nights (very popular), fundraisers, or fiestas.

On our last visit, a nondescript flyer posted at one of the shops on the main drag announced a no-cover shindig involving a dance and the chance to support the local school by buying items made by students. **Yoga classes** are popular with locals (particularly expats); they're usually held at various galleries, private homes, and other venues, and advertised via flyer.

If you're not getting word of anything, just head over for a morning art class at the **Community Arts Center** (just off the road to the preserve, right next to the Monteverde Institute; ☎ 645-6121; www.monteverdearthouse.com). There are

painting and crafts workshops, a ceramics studio, and Saturday-afternoon kids'
classes. The CAC can also arrange for a guided tour of the arts scene by one of its
artists; call directly for offerings and prices, or check with the info office in Santa
Elena (see CETAM, p. 132). Prices vary widely, but a full 1-day class would be
about $100 (shorter ones are less, longer more). The **Casa de Arte** (☎ 645-5275)
also offers art workshops.

Or just do as the locals do. If you're in town on a Sunday, both the church in
Santa Elena and the Friend's Meeting House welcome all visitors. **Church services** are held at 6 and 11am, and are pretty popular with Ticos (masses will be in
Spanish, of course); you're welcome to share in a simple lunch held here after wor-
ship. You can also head over to the **Monteverde Friends School** (300m/984 ft.
south of the cheese factory in Santa Elena; www.mfschool.org), where at 10am
many days a mixed bunch of Ticos and gringos regularly have **pick-up basketball
games** for a couple of hours, and welcome visitors. It's also worth checking with
the Friends school (or the Cloud Forest School, p. 137) to see if any of their regular fundraisers, walkathons, and holiday fairs are being held during your stay; a
lot of the community come out and mix at these things (and a good number—
perhaps 80%—speak English).

If you're hanging around for at least a week, may we suggest taking a local
Spanish course packaged with a homestay? The **Centro Panamericano de Idiomas**
(**CPI;** just west of Cerro Plano gas station; ☎ 645-5441; www.cpi-edu.com) looks
like a big Southern California–style house, with a large grass courtyard and fountain, open-air dining area, even a hot tub and tiny gym. Weeklong programs cost
$520 for 5½ hours of instruction daily and a homestay (it's $415 per week if you
opt to study for just 4 hours a day). You'll also have your own room, two meals a
day, and laundry service. Perhaps the best part of enrolling in CPI is that you'll
find yourself immediately plugged into the community—the school arranges outings into town, volunteer gigs, dance and cooking classes, and other ways of rub-
bing shoulders with locals.

Monteverde could very well be the volunteer capital of Costa Rica, and the
country's most interesting spot to try your hand at it. There are a lot of schools,
reserves, and organizations that always need extra help, and the colorful, diverse
community genuinely embraces visitors and especially volunteers. You'll get an
instant social network, pick up some Spanish if you don't speak it already, and leave
with a piece of Monteverde in your soul. You can just go and ask at the places that
interest you, or try an established program like the one at the **Ecolodge San Luís**
(p. 123). Most volunteer stints require a commitment of at least a week (sometimes two), but the **Cloud Forest School** (see below), for example, holds occasional afternoon tree-planting excursions you can sign up for (just reserve a spot
by e-mailing ahead).

The following are the most popular volunteer programs:

The **Monteverde Institute** (☎ 645-5053; www.mvinstitute.org) is a nonprofit
educational and research outfit best known for running the Monteverde Music
Festival. The institute also hosts academic and scientific groups, and offers courses
in tropical ecology, conservation, sustainable development, and suchlike (if you
want to just enroll in the courses, they run $250 for a week to $1,000 for a
month). The institute accepts volunteers for stints from 2 weeks to 3 months, and
will put you up in on-premise *cabinas* or arrange homestays. What you end up

working on depends on both your interests and what they've got going. One of their most established community projects, the **Finca La Bella** in nearby San Luís, is a 48-hectare (120-acre) community farm where volunteers stay, helping out there (picking coffee, and so forth) or in local schools.

Give a thought, too, to the bilingual **Centro de Educación Creativa,** aka the **Cloud Forest School** (☎ 645-5161; www.cloudforestschool.org), a pillar of the community where practically all the students are Ticos taking a K-12 curriculum grounded in the environment. Kids learn both the three Rs and conservation, and pitch in with growing seedlings and other reforestation projects around the beautiful 48-hectare (120-acre) campus on a hill above Santa Elena. The school takes volunteers (3 weeks to 3 months), and most of the volunteer work is pretty physical, from trail maintenance to planting gardens, along with other miscellaneous stuff on campus; you also get Spanish classes a couple days a week if you want them. When we visited, a group from Connecticut called Builders Beyond Borders were swarming all over and putting up a new school building. Homestays with local families cost $10 a day, including three meals and laundry service, and are arranged through the Centro.

The **Butterfly Garden** (p. 126) also regularly accepts volunteers, for a minimum of a month. At any given time, three to five volunteers help out maintaining the facilities and exhibits, and after some training can even lead guided tours. Room (shared bath/communal kitchen) and board are provided—Marta the gracious co-owner whips up home-cooked dinners every night (past participants say they've never been fed so well!). The director suggests that the volunteer program is probably "better suited for young people," although when we were there recently, an American gent in his 60s who globetrots on the volunteer circuit told me he was back for the third time, and it's been one of the best experiences he's had.

Both the **Monteverde Cloud Forest** and **Santa Elena Cloud Forest** reserves take on volunteers from time to time (call ☎ 645-5390 or surf to www.monteverde info.com), though it's not a structured program, and you'll have to contact them directly (p. 128). Unless you've got some specific skills or scientific training, chances are you'll be doing mostly grunt work—maintaining facilities and trails, and so forth. At Santa Elena you stay in a cabin in the reserve—great if you really want to be surrounded by nature, but a little isolated and inconvenient if you're hoping to sample the local restaurants and social life. In the Monteverde reserve, volunteers can opt to stay at the reserve's field station for $17 per person, including meals, and visit any of the shelters deep in the reserve for free. As with other programs, homestays are available for the ridiculously low cost of $10 a day including all meals and laundry.

Serpentarium
Frog Pond — really good

5 The Central Pacific Coast

Sun, surf, and scuba are what it's all about along Costa Rica's most famous shoreline.

by David Appell & Nelson Mui

THE MOST ACCESSIBLE STRETCH OF COAST FROM THE CENTRAL VALLEY (just an hour's drive from San José), Costa Rica's first resort area has been pulling in sun worshippers from around the world for decades. **Jacó** and **Manuel Antonio** are the main draws, thanks to their great surfing, snorkeling, and scuba diving. But despite the fact that the Guanacaste coast to the north is now the country's main beach destination, many visitors—and Ticos—still prefer the Central Pacific, especially for its lush, tropical feel (unlike Guanacaste's dusty deserts—think Florida versus Southern California). The roads in these parts are decent and well marked, services are everywhere, and English is widely spoken.

Like most regions in the country, the Central Pacific coast is diverse, and jammed with things to see and do. The main thoroughfare is the scenic **Costanera** (coastal route), which backs up against rainforested slopes. It starts in the north at **Carara National Park**—home to crocodiles, scarlet macaws, and monkeys—and passes through one beach town after another, each with its own distinctive vibe. Then there's bustling, honky-tonk Jacó, whose main strip is lined with sports bars, souvenir shops, and taco stands, and is usually thronged with Tico families, sunburned gringos, and a handful of hookers. An hour south is Manuel Antonio, famous for its steep hillside vistas, spectacular white-sand beaches, and an appealing national park. And as development creeps southward along the Costanera, the area around **Dominical** and **Punta Uva** are seeing high-end hotels, B&Bs, and vacation homes springing up to cater to rich gringos looking for a little more seclusion. Almost everywhere along the way, though, you'll still find beaches great for surfing or just soaking up sun—many of them almost deserted. Whatever you want, you'll be able to find on this stretch of coast, at a price that works for you.

DON'T LEAVE THE CENTRAL PACIFIC COAST WITHOUT . . .

CATCHING A WAVE   Unless you're just physically incapable of it, if you've never surfed before, giving it a try could be a highlight of your life. The smokin' waves, plus the many surf schools hereabouts, make it easy and not too pricey.

CATCHING THE SUNSET AT VILLAS CALETAS OR RONNY'S PLACE
Watch the sun go down over the Pacific in style—and for free—from the steps of the amphitheater at Caletas, a chichi boutique hotel (you also might end up watching someone get married), or this Manuel Antonio bar.

HAVING A "CROCODILE DUNDEE" MOMENT   Get up close and personal with the crocs on a tour of the local waterways, and watch 'em snap a piece of meat out of your guide's hands.

HIKING IN MANUEL ANTONIO NATIONAL PARK   The park is one of only two places in Costa Rica where squirrel monkeys can still be found, and they're not hard to spot. Some of the Pacific's best beaches are also here, so grab your swimsuit and sunblock.

HAVING A WHALE OF A TIME IN UVITA   Depending on the season, you can get out on the bay and watch humpbacks breed and play with their young.

EXPLORE THE GROTTOES IN BALLENA MARINE NATIONAL PARK
Whether you wade in or kayak through these tunnels carved out of limestone cliffs, it's an otherworldly experience.

LAY OF THE LAND

The Central Pacific coast is broken up into five distinct regions with varied topography and levels of development.

PUNTARENAS

This port city on a spit of land in the gulf of Nicoya marks the northernmost end of the Central Pacific coast. While there's a boardwalk that's popular with Ticos on a cheap beach weekend, Puntarenas is mostly a jump-off point for ferries to the Nicoya Peninsula or excursions to the beautiful Isla Tortuga, an island known for its snorkeling, immaculate sands, and turquoise waters (p. 338). There are some okay resorts along the beach here, but the city itself can be gritty and even a bit rough—there are better spots to spend your hard-earned vacation time.

JACO & VICINITY

The area's most accessible beach resort, both geographically and financially, has a frenetic, sometimes schizo vibe. You'll see loads of middle-class Tico families playing at the beach and kids slurping ice cream at the local amusement park during the day. But a party-till-you-puke scene jammed with surfers, backpackers, and sportfishermen spills out of bars and discos as transvestite hookers in skintight skirts and heels trawl the main drag (so to speak) at night. Just 10 minutes south, Playa Hermosa's gorgeous, more mellow stretch of beach is a hit with surfers (a big international wave-riding competition is held here every August, woo-hoo!) and folks looking for something more laid-back yet not too far from the action. Most people combine a visit to Jacó with a trip to the Carara National Park

THE ESTERILLOS

Halfway between Jacó and Manuel Antonio, the beach communities of Esterillos Este, Centro, and Oeste mark a long stretch of coastline with pounding surf, popular with people not into crowds—at times you might be the only one on the beach. Restaurants, shops, and tourist attractions are still on the sparse side here, but a number of family-run hotels and inns have sprung up in recent years.

MANUEL ANTONIO & QUEPOS

With stretches of white sand tucked into coves and steep, forested hills as a backdrop, Manuel Antonio plays picture-postcard tropical paradise to the hilt. There are all sorts of outdoor stuff to do—ziplines, rafting trips, mangrove kayaking, horseback riding—but the biggest deal of all is, of course, Manuel Antonio National Park. Though one of Costa Rica's smallest national parks, it's one the most popular, thanks to the area's stunning ocean views at the top of Point Cathedral, gleaming beaches, and the chance to spot the rare squirrel monkey. Its fame has translated to high prices and touches of overdevelopment, but you'll still be enchanted by the place. You can still find score affordable digs, and in a pinch, the nearby town of Quepos is not only home to most of the locals but also has developed an extensive number of budget sleeps and eats.

DOMINICAL & UVITA

An hour or two south of Manuel Antonio, these towns were once where surfers and backpackers went in search of castaway paradise. And they still have a laid-back vibe today, along with some limited development such as new B&Bs, lodges, spa resorts, and restaurants catering to more sophisticated beach bunnies. The area around Uvita, also referred to as the Brunca Coast, is home to the Parque Nacional Ballena Marina, with Costa Rica's largest Pacific coral reef and nesting humpback whales at various times of the year.

A BRIEF HISTORY

When the Beach Boys' "Surfin' Safari" hit the top of the charts in 1962, the Central Pacific coast was already catching the wave—*norteamericano* surfers had descended in search of bodacious breaks and warmer waters. As word spread about Costa Rica's "righteous" waves, so did the gringo influence on some of these coastal towns, transforming fishing villages like Jacó into their surf meccas.

While Puntarenas, the port at the northern edge of the coast, had always been a thriving hub of commerce, Jacó—the next town down, and close to San José—was the first to be touched by tourism's magic wand. Suddenly, hordes of Canadians discovered the place, not just sun-starved tourists who roam the hemisphere in search of the Next Tropical Paradise (now Cuba! The Dominican Republic! Roatán!), but also missionaries, biologists, and NGOs. To this day, you'll see the Maple Leaf all over Jacó, and Canadians still make up a big chunk of the ex-pat population.

Down the coast, Quepos has a much longer history as a settlement—it was named after the Quepoa tribe that once lived around here—but the Quepoas disappeared by the 19th century, and the local population didn't really grow until the

arrival of the United Fruit Company in the 1930s, after a plague wiped out its banana plantations on the Caribbean coast. Much of the area from Palo Seco to Matapalo was cleared for *plátano*-growing, and the UFC imported workers from Nicaragua and other Central American countries to build bridges, a railroad, and docks. Quepos turned into a company town, and the de facto feudal lord UFC supplied pretty much all of the housing, schools, hospitals, and churches. Many of the original *campamentos* (camps) built for its workers still stand along the roads in and out of town, while the Zona Americana, on the water just east of town, was where the mostly U.S. managers set up their little plot of paradise (they even had their own country club, with tennis courts, a bar, and a bowling alley— very unlike, of course, the workers they commanded). By the late '50s, though, it was "yes, we have no bananas"—year after year, crops were destroyed by floods, blights, and exhausted soils. So the UFC hit upon the African palm, which produced an oil that was dandy for making soap, chocolate, candles, makeup, and other neat-o stuff. To this day, on your way down and past Quepos you'll drive past acres upon acres of palm plantations . . . which were once banana fields . . . which were once rainforest. Today, the UFC is owned by a San José–based company called Palma Tica, and it's still one of this area's largest employers.

Tourist resorts didn't arrive until much later, after the coastal roads built in the '60s and early '70s were finally extended to San José in 1978. In 1979, when Manuel Antonio National Park was created and a paved road put in, some 29,000 people flocked to the park. These days, it gets around 150,000 per year, and there are hotels and homes all up and down along the main road to it, as well as up on the lush hillsides—anywhere there are multimillion-dollar views to be had. Yet it still feels more discreet and genteel than, say, Jacó or up in Guanacaste coast towns like Tamarindo.

Now that a paved coastal road has been extended southward to Dominical and Uvita, development has been following, and of course it ain't always pretty. For example, indigenous tribes living near the beach (how dare they!) have been thrown off their ancestral lands to make way for beachfront hotels, condos, and villas; a couple of luxe resorts are already operating, complete with fancy spas and services. But at least there's some hope that this new development may not repeat the mistakes made farther up the coast, and new residents and businesses are making an effort to strike a more even balance between conservation, ecotourism, and development—and not to kill the proverbial goose that lays the golden egg.

JACO Cool little town

We'll say this for Jacó (pronounced "ha-KOH"): It's a heck of a town for people-watching. Park yourself in one of the strip's open-air seafood restaurants, bars, or cafes, and you'll see young Tico singles, families licking ice-cream cones, sunburned gringos, and working girls (some of whom aren't even girls) in skintight tops and big-hoop earrings. At night, in the November through May high season, Ticos cruise down the main drag with big noisy motorcycles or trucks, music cranked high, even as the traffic grinds to a halt. If this isn't your cup of tea, you might find Jacó synonymous with low-rent overdevelopment and seedy nightlife rife with drugs and crime.

But that's not the only story, as the place does have some saving graces. For starters, it is one of the few spots where Ticos themselves vacation alongside

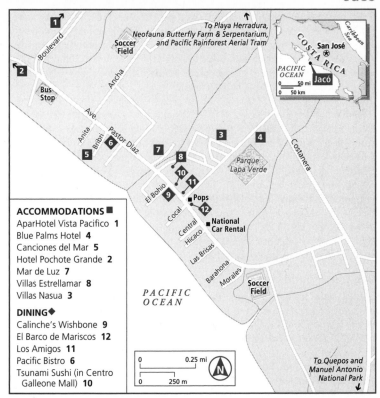

To Playa Herradura,
Neofauna Butterfly Farm & Serpentarium,
and Pacific Rainforest Aerial Tram

Soccer Field

Bus Stop

Parque Lapa Verde

Pops

National Car Rental

PACIFIC OCEAN

Soccer Field

ACCOMMODATIONS ■
AparHotel Vista Pacifico **1**
Blue Palms Hotel **4**
Canciones del Mar **5**
Hotel Pochote Grande **2**
Mar de Luz **7**
Villas Estrellamar **8**
Villas Nasua **3**

DINING ◆
Calinche's Wishbone **9**
El Barco de Mariscos **12**
Los Amigos **11**
Pacific Bistro **6**
Tsunami Sushi (in Centro Galleone Mall) **10**

To Quepos and Manuel Antonio National Park

0   0.25 mi
0   250 m

gringos, so if you're interested in a peek at how regular middle-class Ticos live and have fun, Jacó is far more authentic than the gated communities, golf courses, and country clubs that rule big swaths of the coast farther north. If you're looking to meet and chat with locals, it's easy enough to do right on the beach—just use common sense, especially if you're a guy trying to hook up; we've heard reports of scams and of hookers who'll lift your wallet, or worse. The nightlife, meanwhile, is one of the country's buzziest outside of San José.

And guess what? There's still some pretty impressive natural beauty here—including some fine volcanic-sand beaches and the consistent waves that brought people here in the first place (surfers and surf schools abound). From the nearby hills outside town, the views are downright grand—a symphony of clear blue sky, lush coastline, and white surf.

GETTING TO & AROUND JACO
By Bus

Buses (**Transportes;** ☎ 223-1109) leave San José's Coca Cola bus terminal at Calle 16 and Avenida 1 for the 3-hour trip to Jacó at 7:30 and 10:30am, and 1,

3:30, and 6:30pm; the fare's $2.15. **Grayline** (☎ 220-2126; www.graylinecosta rica.com) will pick you up at your hotel at 8am and 2pm and take you directly to Jacó in a little more style and comfort for $21, as will **Interbus** (☎ 283-5573; www.interbusonline.com), with buses leaving at 8:15am and 2:30pm for $19 per adult and $9.50 per child. On weekends during high season, buy tickets early or the day before to make sure you get a seat.

By Car

From San José, the quickest and most scenic route is a winding road that cuts through the mountains, dropping down to the Costanera near Orotina. Take the Interamerican Highway towards Alajuela, then make the turnoff for Atenas; you'll pass through a few hill towns as you follow the signs for Jacó or Manuel Antonio. When you reach the town of Orotina, the roads lead you right onto the Costanera, on which it's a straight shot down, with turnoffs on the right for Jacó beach. Depending on traffic, you can expect the drive to take 2 to 2½ hours. If you want to pass on the winding mountainous bit, just take the Interamerican west all the way to Puntarenas, then get on the Costanera south to Jacó. Just keep in mind that traffic can get quite heavy on the coast road, thanks to all the trucks.

Getting Around

You can walk from one end of Jacó to the other in 15 to 20 minutes, so a car is not a must unless you want to have flexibility in getting out and seeing the sights in the surrounding area (there are plenty of car-rental agencies, and you can also negotiate decent full-day rates with local cab drivers). You can easily rent bikes on the main drag for $10 to $15 per day, and a scooter at **Renta@me** (☎ 643-1809) goes for $35 to $40. Taxis are cheap and plentiful on the main strip; you can also order them from **Taxi Jacó** (☎ 643-3009).

ACCOMMODATIONS, BOTH STANDARD & NOT

Jacó Vacation Rentals

Jacó's never had all that much of a vacation home/condo rental market, but that's about to change. Developers have bought up huge tracts on the beach around town, with thousands of units slated for the rental market, if preconstruction sales are anything to go by. We wouldn't be surprised if the high-rises that are coming turn Jacó into something closer to Acapulco.

There are already a lot more rentals than there used to be, including some serious bargains. Most have a minimum stay of 3 nights, but anything longer than a week will get you pretty good discounts, making them cheaper than the "apart-hotels" around town. Anyone traveling in a group of four or more should look into these options first. At the moment these are the main agencies to call:

Beachhomecostarica.com (25m/82 ft. north of Los Amigos, downtown Jacó; ☎ 643-2222, fax in U.S. 480/247-4079) manages about 25 properties in and around town, starting from $500 a week for an air-conditioned, three-bedroom house several blocks from the beach; for $130 a night ($650 weekly), the Last Frontier House is brand spanking new, and has all sorts of updated *Little House on the Prairie* touches, like a sleeping loft that kids will love to have for their own,

$$ Owned by Germans and named after the big old pochote tree by its barbecue area, the two-story **Hotel Pochote Grande** (take the first entrance to Jacó, make a right at the crossing, cross two small bridges and make a left; ☎ 643-3236, 877/623-3109 in the U.S. and Canada; www.hotelpochotegrande.net; AE, MC, V) is right on the sand at the mellow, north end of Jacó beach. Palm trees shoot up amid lush tropical gardens, and the roomy pool area is mere steps from the ocean; an on-site snack bar serves German and Tico food. All two dozen rooms are spacious but spartan—white walls and tile, a bed, closet, small fridge, and nightstand (okay, maybe a print on the wall, depending on the room); try for the upper floor for the high ceilings and private balconies with beach, garden, or pool views. At $60 a double ($5 more for A/C) in season, this should be one of your first choices if you want to be right on the beach. Note that it's a 15-minute walk to the center of town (and that's a good thing, as Martha would say).

$$ On the other hand, for an oasis right in the thick of things, **Villas Estrellamar** (in the center of town, just next to Payless Car Rental; ☎ 643-3102; www.estrellamar.com; AE, D, MC, V) is a nifty compound 180m or so (600 ft.) from the beach, with 1.6 hectares (2 acres) of possibly the greenest, most nicely landscaped grounds in town. The 18 bungalows are boxy concrete numbers, but air-conditioned and comfy, with tiled terraces with a plastic table and chairs, simple but roomy interiors—white-painted walls, orange tile work, cheery yellow linens—and fully equipped kitchens. Guests can laze by the large pool and Jacuzzi, or in hammocks under a thatch-roofed *rancho;* there's even a full-service bar and restaurant. There are 10 standard rooms here, too, but for $59 double they're barely cheaper than the roomier $61 bungalows (two-bedroom bungalows will sleep up to six starting at $111). For privacy, centrality, and greenery, it's not bad at all . . .

$$$ Of all the hotels right on the sand, our favorite is **Canciones del Mar** ★★★ (head 500m/1,620 ft. south from the bus station and another 100m/328 ft. west; ☎ 643-3273; www.cancionesdelmar.com; AE, MC, V). An 11-apartment complex in a two-story Spanish colonial-style building, it's nice and quiet, on a secluded stretch next to the Copey River. The units are generous in size, with Indonesian-style rattan and cane furnishings, terraces, cable TV, and nice accents like candles and mood lamps; to get a private balcony, plus an ocean view, ask for the second floor. The public areas do a great job of creating another oasis-like feel away from the hurly burly: there's a large pool with a swim-up bar, a two-level open-air thatched "treehouse" for lounging and reading, and a barbecue grill area, all amid beautiful landscaping (feel like a banana, coconuts, or papaya? Feel free—they're growing all over). Oh, and about that river? You can expect the occasional surprise visitor—one morning over breakfast, we spied a crocodile climbing up from the water to laze on the edge of the grounds. Rates start at $95 a double, including buffet breakfast, and drop to $79 for stays of a week or longer.

NORTH OF JACO & PLAYA HERMOSA

Once known as a surfer's town, Playa Hermosa has been "discovered" by families and beach lovers of all stripes. As a result, developers have rushed in, throwing up condo projects, vacation homes, and, of course, hotels. While the 10km (6-mile)

A Splurge-Worthy Choice

$$$$　It may well be the honeymoon spot of Jacó, amid sumptuous surroundings 8km (5 miles) north of town, but the boutique **Villa Caletas** ✪✪✪ (between Jacó and Punta Leona; ☎ 257-3653; www.villacaletas. com; AE, MC, V) has a little something for everyone. From its perch 345m (1,150 ft.) above the Pacific, above the Jacó River, Playa Herradura, and Punta Leona, the panoramic ocean vistas seem to go on forever. The design conscious will love the French-colonial architecture, infinity pool, and the way the classical-Greek-style amphitheater frames those sunset views during dinner or cocktails on its terrace. There's a fine spa with the whole kit and kaboodle, from massages and body peels to aromatherapy, and frequent shuttle buses take you to a private beach down the mountain. The most impressive digs here are the elegant 14 villas and 7 suites, which among many other perks have great private terraces (the larger suites even have their own swimming pools). The price tag? Steep for here but a bargain by U.S. luxury hotel standards: doubles start at $165 in season and villas at $210. If you've ever wanted to try seeing how the other half lives, Villa Caletas can give you a taste at a nice little discount.

stretch of black sand has strong rip currents offshore (along with a number of totally bitchin' right and left surf breaks) and isn't ideal for swimming, we like it as a tranquil (read: crowd-free) alternative to Jacó. Lodgings here are generally more attractive, spacious, and a better value than in town. The only drawback is the limited dining and nightlife scene, but since Jacó's a 10-minute drive or taxi ride away, you can pop in and out of town pretty easily. On Wednesdays, the party people from Jacó head up here to the popular ladies' night at the surfer bar **The Backyard.**

$　There are few B&Bs in the Jacó area, so if you're looking for a cozy, intimate pad on a deserted beach, the stylish **Costanera B&B** ✪ (25m/82 ft. south of pulpería La Perla del Mar; ☎ 643-7044; www.costaneraplayahermosa.com; cash only) is a gem. You can hear the surf pound from your spacious rooms, which are tarted up with antique reproductions like dark-wood armoires and nightstands, and huge windows opening onto shaded porches. The property itself is a stylish, ochrecolored ranch house with five rooms (one of which has a kitchen), and its friendly Italian owners will cook for you, especially classic dishes and pastas from *il bel paese* ("the boot"), as well as book all your tours and get you to and from the airport. At $30 for an oceanfront room, this is one of the area's best deals. *Bellissimo!*

$$　For bargain apartment-style lodgings on a secluded beach, head a half-dozen miles south of Jacó to the intimate **Casa Pura Vida** (200m/656 ft. after the little school in Hermosa; ☎ 643-7039; www.casapuravida.com; MC, V, though you'll pay an extra 7% to use plastic). There are just three apartments for rent in this salmonhued Mediterranean-style manse, so quiet and low-key is all but guaranteed; the place is pretty to a T, with private balconies on the second floor overlooking a small pool and the ocean, and Nicaraguan leather rocking chairs in the hallways and lounge areas. The units themselves are on the simple side, with plain white walls, and basic wooden doors, bed frames, and nightstands—but they've all got air-conditioning, cable TV, decent-size windows facing gardens or ocean, and small kitchens with a table for four. Rates are $52 per night for a double, going up to $77 for five people. If you're coming with a large group (up to 18), you can even rent out the whole joint for $266 a night.

$$$ Feel like something surfing oriented but don't want to bunk in a shack or a hammock? Head 4km (2½ miles) south of Jacó to **The Backyard Hotel** ★ (3km/ 1¾ miles south of Jacó Centro; ☎ 643-7011; www.backyardhotel.com; AE, MC, V), whose eight rooms all have ocean views and deliver all the "mod-cons," as the Brits say: very good mattresses and water pressure, hair dryer, TV, A/C, and so forth. On the second floor, the rooms are larger and have private balconies, high ceilings, and nice big windows. Another on-premises perk is a nice pool complete with rock waterfall, but it doesn't get all that much use since the focus is on the waves just out front. You can get surfing lessons, packages, and a miniguide detailing when the best swells are and all the local surf breaks, with colorful names like "Roca Loca" and "Perro Fino y El Gato." The eponymous bar-restaurant here is a popular surfer's hangout; it serves burgers, pizza, steak, and such, and really heats up on Wednesdays and Fridays, when ladies drink for free. Staying here isn't exactly cheap (doubles $135), so if you're going to drop that kind of cash you might consider the Marea Brava (below)—unless of course you've just got to be where the surfer dudes and dudettes are.

$–$$$$ We hate to play favorites, but around here, we like the new **Marea Brava** ★★ (in Playa Hermosa to the right of the Jungle Surf restaurant; ☎ 643-7111, 866/727-2577 in the U.S. and Canada; www.mareabravacostarica.com; AE, MC, V), a snazzy complex steps from the beach with a colonial flavor and 22 rooms and condos on a 2-hectare (5-acre) spread of palm trees and lush gardens. The plush two-bedroom apartments sleep up to six and, besides the usual modern amenities, feature covered balconies with stunning ocean views, high ceilings with exposed beams, fully equipped kitchens, spacious sitting areas, and nice big windows. Outside there's a large pool with a swim-up bar and an ocean view. Regular doubles start at $133 and condos run $210 for up to six people, but cheaper skates can snag a bunk bed in the wood-paneled "Surfer Ranchero" for $35 a night—steep for a dorm-style set-up, but hey, at least it has A/C.

IN & AROUND ESTERILLOS

A long stretch of white-sand beach with crashing waves known mostly to surfers, Esterillos has started attracting vacationers looking for peace and quiet. Thanks to its location, 20 to 25 minutes south of Jacó and 40 minutes north of Manuel Antonio, it's a good base for launching the occasional day trip to either.

The community is split up into three zones—Este, Centro, and Oeste—spread along the coast amid pastures of grazing cows and horses. All three are ideal for those looking to drop anchor for a few days—the area's still relatively undiscovered, so prices have yet to skyrocket like in nearby Manuel Antonio, and you'll get more space for your money than there or Jacó. There are some rock-bottomish *cabinas* with cold-water showers, catering mostly to surfers, but the places we list below strike a good balance between value and ambience, and are set among private homes, giving your stay a more local Costa Rican feel. You'll want wheels here; the town of **Parrita** is a 10-minute drive away, and has a couple of grocery stores, banks, and a number of restaurants if you get fed up with of cooking or eating at your hotel.

$–$$ A beachfront find with a B&B feel, the **Pelican Hotel** ★ (right on the beach, 300m/984 ft. from the Restaurant Tulu; ☎ 778-8105; www.pelicanhotelcr.com; AE, D, MC, V) in Esterillos Este, once the Auberge du Pelican, has gone through some major upgrades and a minor expansion at the hands of owner Roberto "Oso" Pols, a former New York City resident and owner of Manhattan's Chelsea Commons bar. The dozen rooms are on the smallish side but immaculate, with hardwood floors, high wood-plank ceilings, and now A/C. The bathrooms, though, are showing their age, which may be one reason prices are pretty reasonable (another is no pool). A room with a queen bed starts at $43 (10 percent less for 4 or more nights); ask for room no. 4 or 5 on the second floor; their bathrooms have with big windows with ocean views. There's a nice open-air restaurant with a pool table, and Oso (Spanish for "bear," by the way) makes a great host, helping lend a laid-back and comfortable vibe to the Pelican.

$–$$ Three doors down from the Pelican in Esterillos Este, the **Encantada Ocean Cottages** (right in front of the airport road, 50m/164 ft. east of Hotel Xandari; ☎ 778-7048; www.encantadacostarica.com; cash only) is a dandy bevy of bungalows centered around a large rectangular pool with a view of the waves. It reminds us a bit of a Southern California low-rise apartment complex, except with barn-shaped cabins painted with tropical watercolors. Each unit has a high-beamed ceiling and a spiral staircase leading to additional sleeping areas (only the largest cabin has a view, along with a good-size terrace). A series of hammocks and an open-air restaurant complete the picture. It's all pretty laid-back and homey; most guests seem to treat the place like their condo complex away from home. High-season rates start at $40 for a room and $65 for a cabin (breakfast included).

DINING FOR ALL TASTES
Jacó

For a resort with such an international following, we're surprised at how little most of the eats in this town get us salivating. You do have your good Tico restaurants specializing in fresh seafood, but most of the international stuff, is pretty blah (there are exceptions, such as **Pacific Bistro,** below). That said, if you're a fan of mozzarella sticks, burritos, or deep-fried anything, you'll be in heaven here. Stick to the seafood whenever possible; the local tuna is good enough to export, and all the local *sodas* know how to grill a fresh piece of mahimahi and serve it up well. There are countless restaurants on the strip, but following are our top picks.

$–$$ Right off the boat and in generous portions is the big thing at **El Barco de Mariscos** ★ (main road, 50m/164 ft. from Pops; ☎ 643-2831; MC, V), almost always packed with Ticos—on our last visit, on a weekday in the low season, almost all of the 20 or so tables were taken. This is essentially a posh-ish *soda,* with a pleasing marine-blue decor and a clean ambiance (tablecloths, even!). There's a pretty chunky menu of standard Latin fare, plus a smattering of other "international" dishes—pastas ($9), sandwiches ($7), grilled chicken ($8), and so forth. The food is good, not spectacular, but what helps makes this a great experience are your fellow diners—happy Tico vacationers. In our book, it's definitely worth a stop to see the local side of Jacó.

$$ Chef and owner Kent Green opened **Pacific Bistro** ✦✦✦ (main road, towards northern end of town; ☎ 643-3771; Wed–Sun 6–10pm; MC, V) in 2001, after working in top San Francisco restaurants like Aqua and Jardinier. He doesn't do much advertising, but he doesn't need to—he's got a lot of repeat customers for his superb Asian fusion cuisine in really outrageous portions (unless you've surfed hard, you probably won't finish them). The menu changes nightly, but the perennials are the fresh tuna and mahimahi prepared with spicy green or coconut curries ($13). On our last meal there, we especially loved the succulent double chicken breast in green-bamboo-curry sauce, on a bed of rice and vegetables ($8). The decor, like the menu, is Asian-flavored minimalist, with white-paper lanterns and a warm wood-slat ceiling. Grab a seat by the window, and watch the people parade past. Reservations are a good idea.

$$ **Los Amigos** ✦ (main road, across from Pops; ☎ 643-2961; MC, V) pulls 'em in with heaping plates of Mexican and Asian favorites at good prices (quesadillas for $4.50 and superhot curries and stir-fries with rice for $8). A deep-fried innovation, mahimahi fingers, are surprisingly addictive and highly recommended ($5.75). The crowds that jam this place also like the cool ambiance—a pair of burning torches flank a nice outdoor dining patio, walled off from the street by hedgerows, and a projector beams old surf videos onto one of the walls. Cowabunga!

$$ There's more fun with finger food at **Calinche's Wishbone** (main road, across from El Galeone mall; ☎ 643-3406; Thurs–Tues 11:30am–3pm and 5:30–10pm; MC, V), where both locals and tourists really get into the stuffed pitas, mahimahi burritos, fajitas, tacos and enchiladas, and flaky-thin crust pizzas (mostly $6 or less). Bump it up several bucks and you'll also find the main courses unexpectedly well prepared; standouts include tuna steak ($11) and blackened sashimi ($9). Try to score a table under the covered wood veranda, which puts you smack at ground zero of Jacó's hopping main drag (just keep in mind you might get the occasional street vendor hawking stuff at you from the sidewalk). Another bar in the back gets busy in high season and on weekends.

$$ Ask locals what Jacó's best restaurant is, and they're likely to point you to **Tsunami Sushi** ✦✦ (main road, in El Galeone mall; no phone; hours vary; MC, V). And yeah, we'd have to agree—it's that good. Unlike a lot of the other sushi joints we've come across in Costa Rica, Tsunami's menu tends towards California fusion, with a raft of rolls that mix traditional fishy elements, with innovative ingredients like cheese or deep-fry methods (like the popular crunch roll, which is crispy outside and has shrimp, rice, and avocado inside). Make sure you also to try the *poky,* a Hawaiian concoction of marinated tuna with sticky rice, spinach, avocado, and spinach. Rolls aren't too pricey ($4 on average) but careful—that tab can add up quickly.

Playa Hermosa

Most people end up in Jacó for dinner, but there are also a few smallish eateries on Playa Hermosa's main strip. If you want to hang with the surfers, head to spots like **Jammin'**, which slings basic tico fare all day in a casual setting with reggae tunes and surf videos, or **Jungle Surf Café,** which is big on burgers, omelets, and Tex-Mex. On the lighter side, the **Goola Café** serves a vegetarian breakfast and fruit shakes, as does **Brown Sugar Café,** where you can also get juices, sandwiches, and a good banana cake. For dinner, we like the *cucina italiana* at the **Costanera B&B** (p. 148). These are such casual places that none have phones and their hours tend to be erratic, but if you head into the center of town, one is likely to be open.

$$ The quintessential Playa Hermosa surfer hotel and all-around hangout, **The Backyard** (at the Backyard Hotel, p. 149; ☎ 643-7041; daily 8am–11:30pm, the bar remains open till 2am; MC, V) is also its main purveyor of prepared comestibles. OK, maybe that's a bit too high falutin'—actually it's a burger joint which tosses in a few greasy Tex-Mex faves like quesadillas (average prices for meals: $5.75–$6.50) So it's going to be a lot of carbs and cholesterol, but the views of Playa Hermosa and its pounding surf elevate the experience a hair. And of course after dinner, the place turns into the local nightspot of choice, especially on Wednesdays and Fridays, when ladies' nights bring in the crowds out from Jacó. There's a pool table and darts near the bar.

WHY YOU'RE HERE: THE TOP SIGHTS & ATTRACTIONS

The Jacó area is essentially a fun-in-the-sun destination, so you've got some nice beaches to explore, plus the usual menu of outdoor activities (horseback riding, kayaking, and canopy tours are the most popular). And since you're an hour or so away from both the Central Valley (p. 44) and Manuel Antonio (p. 161), you've got the option of doing some of their eco-offerings as a day trip.

The Beaches

You can reach some really nice beaches on foot or a short cab ride. Our favorites are the following, listed from north to south.

PUNTA LEONA

Just south of Tárcoles, two of the cleanest and most beautiful white-sand stretches on this coast, **Playa Blanca** ★★ and **Playa Limoncito** ★★, are also among the least known. That's because both are part of the **Hotel Punta Leona** (☎ 231-3131; www.hotelpuntaleona.com), which has just over a square mile of private reserve that's a habitat for 330 migratory and native bird species; it also runs a conservation program focused on increasing the local numbers of scarlet macaws (egg-stealing poachers, you see). Brown-sand **Playa Manta** is separated from Blanca by a rock formation. All three have been awarded Costa Rica's "blue flags," with Blanca receiving the highest rating for cleanliness and so forth. And if anybody remembers the 1992 Ridley Scott flick *1492: Conquest of Paradise,* with Gérard Depardieu as Christopher Columbus, this is where it was filmed.

So what's all the fuss about? The sand is pristine, the waters are a sparkling blue, and the surf is calm and safe for swimming. And don't worry about the private reserve thing—all Tico beaches are public domain, so you can get to them by a road just south of the main entrance to Punta Leona. Consider combining a beach outing with a visit to the reserve, which has three easy trails and guided walks through lush primary and secondary forest—boffo for birding. Scarlet macaws are practically a sure thing, but you might also spot toucans, humming-birds (two feeding stations), and the endangered three-wattled bell-bird, along with the usual spider and white-faced monkeys, coatimundis, and other critters.

PLAYA HERRADURA ✸ 🧒

Easily accessible (off the Costanera's Los Sueños exit), family-friendly, and kid safe, the swimmin' is swell at this once sleepy backwater known mostly among Ticos and campers. Things changed when Marriott decided to base its mammoth, high-end **Los Sueños Resort** (☎ 630-9000; http://marriott.com/property/property page/sjols), a faux–Spanish colonial village on the northern part of Herradura Bay with a marina, yacht club, golf course, and ritzy condos galore. Still, the beach itself is still relatively crowd-free, welcoming, and popular with Costa Ricans. It's a handsome stretch of tightly packed black sand lined with palm trees, and the blue-green waters are sheltered and great for wading. It's also one of the launching-off points for boat rides out to **Playa Escondida,** known mostly to surfers for its "A-Frame" peak that breaks over a reef; you can catch a boat from Herradura for about $15 round-trip. There's a nice little patch of white sand out at Escondida, but frankly, unless you're a surfer, it may not be worth the trip.

PLAYA JACO ✸

The .8km (2½-mile) beach right in town, like most others along this shoreline, has strong rip currents (folks drown here every year), so we'd recommend it mostly for wading—or, if you're a surfing newbie, the left and right breaks over sand and small river rocks make for some interesting action (see below). Surfers tend to congregate in front of the Hotel Copacabana at the northern end, near the La Central disco in the middle, and the Cabinas Alice toward the southern end. Don't wade around in the estuaries, as the currents can be tricky, and so can the occasional crocodiles.

This is also one of few local strands where you'll get a hopping social scene. During a typical high-season day, gringo spring-breakers share the sands with families and young people from the Central Valley, with drink vendors weaving in and out. It can be kind of fun, and it's pretty easy to meet people. If you want to get away from the madding crowd, head toward the northern or southern ends of the beach (you'll likely have to wade through a shallow river or two); these zones also have rocky but flat headlands you can explore.

PLAYA HERMOSA ✸

The few folks who come to this spectacularly scenic black-sand beach are mostly surfers—and surfers who really know what they're doing. There are several famous breaks ("The Backyard," "La Terraza," "The Tree," "Corners," and "Tulín") with different types and sizes of swells; check with one of the surf websites or at The Backyard (p. 152) for more specifics. The pounding waves and strong undercurrents make it dangerous for swimming, so it's not the greatest fit for families. Plus there's very little in the way of shade, so unless you're a serious board rider, you'll probably want to just take a stroll, then grab lunch or dinner at one of the surfer joints at the northern end such as The Backyard or the Jungle Surf Café (p. 152).

PLAYAS ESTERILLOS

About 23 to 26km (14–16 miles) southeast of Jacó, this long, wide, stretch of soft gray sand is divided into three sections: Oeste, Centro, and Este. All offer decent shade and are usually pretty deserted (less so on weekends and holidays, when Ticos and surfers come out to play). Oeste, just south of Hermosa and Punta Judas, has the most restaurants, bars, and digs nearby, and its northern end more manageable for swimming. About a mile and change south, Centro has the most quiet, castaway feel, and another 4.8km (3 miles) down, Este has powerful currents but is great for exploring; the Pelican Hotel (p. 150) is down here as well.

Exploring Nature

Even in the midst of beach-resort-land, you can work in a variety of hikes and no fewer than three canopy tours. That's just around town—a little farther afield, you can get up close and personal with the crocodiles in the Tárcoles area and Carara National Park, or take a tour of the area's stunning waterfalls.

A ton of tour operators are all anxious to make a buck off you, but one of the best hikes in the area is entirely free. **Miro Mountain** ✹, the rainforested hills rising above Jacó, is something of a secret known mostly to locals and a few savvy foreigners. Its trails start in the foothills at the southern end of Jacó (on the east side of the Costanera away from the town, across from the gas station and right next to the Canopy Adventure Tour). The moderate hike takes around 2 hours, through lush rainforest where you'll probably see sloths, coatimundis, and anteaters along with birds like mot-mots, trogons, and scarlet macaws. There are a two trails, actually—one follows a stream and takes you past some waterfalls—and both lead up to the top of the ridge, from where you'll get a stellar view of the Pacific, as well as a view down to Jacó beach, Herradura, and the Nicoya Peninsula to the north.

Right next to the start of the trail up Miro Mountain, the **Canopy Adventure Tour** (☎ 643-3271; canopyadventurejaco@yahoo.com; $55) is one of three area ziplines, and its dozen-platform, 2km (11/4-mile) circuit covers much of the same area as the hike above, with spectacular views of the beach and town as you make your way through the tree tops.

We like even more the **Waterfalls Canopy Tour** ✹✹ (☎ 643-1103 or 643-3322; www.waterfallscanopy.com; $58 plus an additional $5 for round-trip transportation from the Jacó area), a 13-platform setup just up the Costanera towards the north end of Jacó. For starters, to get here you hike first to (just guess) a waterfall. And you careen around a hundred feet above the ground, there are some nifty surprises—around the halfway mark, for example, you'll stop for a drink at an elaborate three-story treehouse with a bedroom and champagne bucket. To finish up, you make the last run on a "Tarzan swing," instead of a taut cable, then rappel the 27m (90 ft.) back to the ground. Four runs are offered each day (7am, 9am, 1pm, and 3:30pm) and if you go for the transportation option, they'll pick you up from your hotel. And after you're done, you can pop down the road to the nearby **Neofauna Butterfly Farm and Serpentarium** (☎ 643-1904; $15), a 929-sq.-m (10,000-sq.-ft.) compound, which also has a *ranario* (froggery).

The third area zipline is most convenient for those in the Playa Hermosa area. It's not quite as thrilling as the Waterfalls Canopy Tour, but the **Chiclets Tree Canopy Tour** ★ (☎ 643-1879; $55) does offer 14 platforms up to 40m (132 ft.) above the forested slopes. It's one of the largest of these types of tours in the region and serves up an abundance of sweeping views. You can book the 2½-hour tour through any hotel desk.

As in other parts of Costa Rica, there's a tamer alternative to the ziplines: the **Pacific Rainforest Aerial Tram** (☎ 257-5691, 866/759-8726 in the U.S. and Canada; www.rainforestram.com; Tues–Sun 6:30am–4pm, Mon 9am–4:30pm; $55). Set in its own nature park, it has 18 gondolas hauling nine passengers each on 45-minute rides through the rainforest canopy. You can spot howler monkeys and birds, as a guide explains it all. The entrance fee also includes a guided hike. Not bad, but in our book this is best for people who really need something sedate— like seniors, those with limited mobility, and really small kids.

Probably the star eco-draw along this coast is an hour north of Jacó. Just over 52 sq. km (20 sq. miles), **Carara National Park** ★★★ (☎ 200-5023; high season daily 7am–5pm, low season daily 8am–4pm; $8 adults, $1 children 6–12) is one of the country's newest (2000), yet already among its most popular. The setting packs a double punch as it bridges the dry forest of the Pacific northwest and the humid, tropical rainforest of the southern coast, so it has wildlife common to both, from toucans and trogons to armadillos, anteaters, and wildcats such as pumas and margays (the margays are almost impossible to spot, though). The most famous residents are the 150 or so scarlet macaws that nest here, along with its crocodiles ("Carara" is taken from an indigenous word for crocodile). There are two hiking trails, and a number of outfitters in Jacó will bring you in on a guided tour for $35–$45, including park admission. But you know what? There are always birding and guided groups roaming around here; if you bring your own pair of binoculars, you can politely attach yourself to one of them without too much trouble—heck, chances are the guides or experienced birders you meet will let you have a peek through their telescopes as they describe what you're looking at.

While it's definitely a worthwhile experience, if for whatever reason you don't get to Carara, you can also see crocs and macaws right next door at the **waterfalls near Bijagual** ★ (☎ 661-8263; daily 7am–3pm; $10). In fact, many people skip the sometimes crowded park (it gets a lot of bus tours from San José, especially in the middle of the day) and opt for the 45-minute hike to one of Costa Rica's highest cascades (almost 198m/660 ft.). You see much of the same jungle and wildlife but also get to cool off in the pools near the bottom of the waterfall (not at the base—too dangerous). There's access at the top of the gorge, as well, but this trail is steep and often damp and slippery. Along the way, though, there are plenty of *miradores* (lookouts) for taking in the spectacular scenery and wildlife (you'll also see other varmints, like monkeys and poison-dart frogs). Jacó tour operators lead guided jaunts for $30 to $40, but it's easy enough to go on your own by car; just take the Costanera (Hwy. 34) for the turnoff for Bijagual near Tárcoles.

A little comfier way to go birding and croc viewing is a Tárcoles river boat tour, run by several companies up from Jacó. The best organized is the **Jungle Crocodile Safari** ★ (☎ 236-6473; www.junglecrocodilesafari.com; $25), a 2-hour covered-catamaran ride with good bilingual guides. They'll give you an illustrated pamphlet, which labels all the local species by number; the guide will announce he's spotted, say, number 27, and sure enough, there it is, sometimes just 3m (10 ft.) away in the mangroves and trees on the river banks. Of the roughly 50 species regularly spotted from the river, besides the scarlet macaws (more likely towards sunset), there are roseate spoonbills, crested caracaras, a variety of egrets and herons, and purple gallinules. Then, of course, there are the crocodiles, cruising alongside the catamaran. But the show really starts when the guide jumps onto the banks and slaps a big hunk of raw chicken on the water, then dangles it in the air. Sure enough, one will leap up to snatch the meat right out of the guide's hands. Okay, it's not really ecologically correct—not to mention a touch hokey and melodramatic—but there's no question it's a riveting crowd-pleaser (though we overheard one jaded Tica who lives nearby sniff, "Oh, these crocodiles are so overfed").

Outdoor Pursuits

In addition to the activities below, there are an infinite number of other things on which to spend your time (and money, lots of money), such as **horseback riding, ATV tours, sportfishing, scuba diving,** and most recently, **hang gliding.** You can book any of them through your hotel or any tour operator on the main strip.

If you haven't figured it out already, though, the number-one activity to do in this area is **surf.** If you're experienced, you probably won't need us to break down where the best breaks are—you've probably researched the waves and planned accordingly. Most everyone else, though—from your average spring-breaker up to a boomer not ready to let go of youth—could probably benefit from a surf lesson or two. What makes Costa Rica *pura vida* for beginners (as opposed to, say, some spots in Hawaii) is that the surf is extremely consistent, water temps are generally around a balmy 80°F (27°C), and you'll find lots of beaches, where the waves break over soft sand.

If you've mastered the basics, there are more than a dozen shops on the main strip that rent boards by the hour, usually adding up to $12 to $20 per day. You should also check with your hotel—some are "surfer" hotels with their own bevies of boards. For complete newbies, the shops also offer lessons. But don't focus just on price; ask how many students there will be per instructor (don't go with anything more than four), and make sure that they're not 19-year-old Ticos who

---

The View from the Bridge

If you don't have much time in the Jacó area or are just speeding down the Costanera, you can make a stop at the bridge over the Río Tárcoles and spot both **scarlet macaws** and **crocodiles** for free. The best time is around 5pm, when the birds fly overhead on their nightly migration from the park to the coastal mangrove swamps. Then look down from the bridge, and you'll get an eyeful of up to 20 or so large crocodiles (some of the suckers are 12-footers) sunning or swimming. To get to the bridge, watch for the police post right near the entrance to Carara; there are usually cars parked nearby, as well as birders and others taking in the view on the bridge's narrow strip of sidewalk.

barely speak English. The best bet for novices is **Playa Jacó; Playa Hermosa** is better for intermediate levels.

One way to get an immersion experience is to sign up for surf camps. Although there are tons of them all along the coast, **Vista Guapa** ✪ (take the first entrance to Jacó, drive another 300m/984 ft. and it will be the first house on the right; ☎ 643-2830, 409-599-1828 in the U.S.; www.vistaguapa.com; AE, MC, V) is a cut above as it's run by seven-time national champ Álvaro Solano and a hand-picked team of top-notch instructors. Along with providing intensive instruction, they know every inch of the coast and take guests to the best breaks in the Jacó area. There are three bungalows with private baths and wood decks, perched on a hill overlooking the countryside, downtown, and the ocean. You don't have to hang ten to stay here, but the focus really is on surfing and nature, so there are no TVs, phones, or Internet. Days start with a full breakfast, followed by a 2- to 3-hour surfing lesson, then a jaunt into town for lunch and shopping; the rest of the afternoon's free for whatever. Vista Guapa's other big thing is yoga (classes $12–$15 per person). Rates vary; a weeklong package including five surfing lessons, transfers from San José, daily breakfast and dinner, and a Manuel Antonio tour starts at $1,100 per person. There's also a B&B option: $140 for a double room, then $50 per person for each surfing lesson.

A great outdoor activity for families is to explore the beaches on an **outrigger canoe** through **Kayak Jacó** (☎ 643-1233; www.kayakjaco.com). The canoes seat up to eight, plus a bilingual guide, and glide on the water relatively easily, making it less of a workout than rafting. Tours average $60, though it's possible to bargain for less in the off season. That also includes round-trip transportation from Jacó, snorkeling (when conditions permit), a fruit buffet on the beach, and cold drinks. If you're up for more adventure (and exercise), there are also sea and whitewater kayaking options.

SIDE TRIPS FROM JACO

It's not far to a lot of stuff around the country, so you've got a lot of choices here. Some make more sense than others; for example, you'll find tour operators selling 1-day excursions to the Arenal, Poás, or Irazú volcanoes, or even Monteverde. But tempting as they might be, keep in mind you'll end up spending most of that looong day on a bus. Instead, consider a couple of more accessible jaunts. If you're into watersports like snorkeling, how about a cruise to **Isla Tortuga** ✪✪ (p. 338), a Nicoya Gulf island famous for its white sand and turquoise waters? The best option comes from **Calypso** (☎ 256-2727, 866/978-5177 in the U.S. and Canada; www.calypsocruises.com), whose white catamaran is fitted with showers, two deck pools, a full bar, and a spacious lounging area; the tour includes lunch (ceviche and a barbecue chicken) on the beach under white umbrellas, and runs $99 per person ($89 in low season), including transportation from Jacó, Quepos, or Manuel Antonio. Calypso picks you up at your hotel on an air-conditioned bus and shuttles you to Puntarenas to board the catamaran.

The other worthwhile possibility, if you're not continuing down the coast before you leave Costa Rica, is a tour of **Manuel Antonio National Park** ✪✪✪ (p. 173; closed Mon), including a look at the beach and scene there. The road from Jacó to Manuel Antonio is in good condition, so the trip should only take about an hour each way. The only snafu comes at the falling-apart bridge into

> ## All the Surf That's Fit to Print
>
> Looking for tubular waves and expert advice on boards and beaches? Surf on over to **www.surf-costarica.com**, which besides the usual tourist packages and charters serves up expert advice on all things surf-oriented, from the best time of year to visit different coastal spots to safety issues. You get a long, detailed list of the different breaks around the country, plus current forecasts of wave and wind conditions. You can even download a 42-page guide to surfing in Costa Rica, which delivers all the site's info as a printable PDF file.

Quepos from Jacó, which has been under repair for quite some time (hopefully, it will be fixed by the time you read this—but don't hold your breath).

ATTENTION, SHOPPERS!

If you're into easy-breezy tropical wear (surf shorts, batik sarongs, skimpy tops and skirts, shell necklaces, and earrings) or any of the wood crafts ubiquitous throughout Costa Rica, you'll love Jacó. The **Avenida Pastor Diaz** is a riot of shops packed with brightly covered loot; you could wander around here for hours. Just don't expect any refunds, should your hot new number fall apart after a couple of washes and wears.

Several stores, however, are a few notches above the rest, selling stuff you might actually use back home. The **El Cofre del Tesoro** (50m/164 ft. east of Calle Cocal; ☎ 643-1912; daily 9am–10pm) has a treasure chest full of crafts, furniture, sculpture, and home furnishings from all over Central America. Another good hunting ground for unique artisanal gifts is **La Galería Heliconia** ✦ (across from Pops ice-cream shop; ☎ 643-3613; daily 9am–10pm), with a nice selection of ceramics, pottery, and artwork. The ladies won't want to miss stopping by **Guacamole** ✦ (50m/164 ft. west of National Car Rental; ☎ 643-1120; daily 9am–9pm), which sells chic, nicer-quality batiks, and hand-painted clothing designed by a Tica designer.

NIGHTLIFE

Pub crawlers will be in heaven in Jacó. It has the most active nightlife on the Central Pacific. Almost all the spots are on the main road, or right on the beach, and the clientele mixes spring-breakers, surfers, and sportfishermen with weekending Ticos, and not a small number of working girls (on the last item: keep in mind that hookers hang at most of the bars, and reports of them pickpocketing or robbing drunk gringos is fairly common). Furthermore, there's a noticeable drug scene, which also tends to mean a certain amount of petty crime. But don't let it turn you off from a night out at the bars. Just keep your wits about you; plenty of happy vacationers down a few, shoot some pool, watch some videos, and have a grand old time without any hitch.

A good start to the evening is to drop in on the **Beatle Bar** ★ (main road towards northern end; no phone; daily 11am–1am) for happy hour with classic rock blaring overhead. Sports fans will definitely want to check out the latest game, beamed in via satellite TV, and there are also a pair of pool tables and a foosball machine. Though the joint gets packed early on, getting watered is usually not a hassle, since there's a large island bar in the middle and a smaller bar in the back. Most people tend to move on to other nightspots by 11pm. A lower-key, somewhat hipper alternative is the **Jungle Bar and Grill** (upstairs from Subway; no phone; daily 10pm–2am), which also has pool table and a large-screen TV.

For a place to tank up on cheap beers among a young, trendy crowd, head to **La Hacienda** ★★ (main road, at the northern end of town near Economy Rent a Car; ☎ 643-3460; 4pm–2:30am; $3 cover), a two-story open-air bar with a tin roof, palm trees, and a distinctly tropical vibe. Upstairs, the main drinking area has one long bar against the wall, and a mess of tables and chairs, pool tables, foosball, and dart boards. People start early here, packing in for the weekday happy hour (two-for-one beers until 9pm). By 10, though, there's usually a line on the sidewalk, and both upstairs and downstairs bars are wall to wall during high season. Things eventually fizzle out towards midnight when the partiers head to the discos.

Speaking of which, there are several discos in town, the longest running of which is **La Central** (southern end of Jacó beach; ☎ 643-3076; daily 9pm–2am); it also has the largest dance floor. Problem is, these days there's always a seedy element, so unless you're a diehard fan of beach discos, we'd avoid it and the area around it. Instead, try the newish **Nacho Daddy's** ★ (main road, in El Galleone mall; no phone; daily 9pm–2am; $3 cover). A Mexican restaurant until dinner ends, Nacho Daddy's turns kicks into high gear with reggae, hip-hop, pop, and house music, plus surf videos. On our last visit, Saturday's DJ Night made it the place to be in the wee hours. The crowd's a mostly 20-something mix of Ticos and *turistas*.

Itsy Bitsy Teeny Weeny, Tough-as-Nails Kick-Ass Bikini . . .

A local secret among the ladies-who-surf set is Venezuelan designer **Desiree Morffe** ★ (☎ 813-2669; desimorffe@hotmail.com; Mon–Sat 9am–5pm), who runs a small studio in an unmarked beach shack next to the Backyard Hotel/Bar in Playa Hermosa. The surf *chicas* swear by Desiree because as a surfer herself, she designs the bikinis not just to look hot—and *mamacita*, do they ever—but also to withstand the crashing waves (the last thing you need after a wipeout is to lose your top or have it fall apart, right?). Prices start at around $60 for a reversible bikini, and it takes a couple of days to stitch it together. This is also the place for other types of beach/tropical wear: smocked tops, long cotton skirts, flowy shirts with intricate embroidered patterns, or slinky, off-the shoulder mini-dresses with a black–and–white close-up of a tiger's face. Grrrrrrrrrrrrrr.

¡Vamos a Surfear!

One of Jacó's most unique experiences (and best deals) is a stay at the **La Escuela del Mundo (School of the World).** Founded in 1997 by Atlanta artist Zack McDuffie, this was the first to combine surf lessons with Spanish classes, with equal emphasis on both. Here, school's scheduled around tide tables.

Visitors come for 1-, 2-week, or month-long programs, which include combinations of art, photography, surf, and Spanish. Students are housed in a stylish two-story building, with artistic flourishes throughout, all designed by Zack. There are 12 rooms (including two apartments; baths are both shared and private) in an open, loftlike setting that melds a Zen, minimalist sensibility with tropical elements. Classrooms and offices have sliding-glass and wood doors resembling Japanese paper-screen walls; a granite waterfall flowing from the second floor greets visitors at the entrance, and there's a koi pond river running through the living/kitchen area.

Perhaps the best thing about the place is how you're instantly connected to a community. Jacó can seem like an overgrown thicket of bars, restaurants, and shops, but Zack and his young Tico instructors know most everyone in town and are totally plugged into events and happenings, from art shows to, say, an impromptu fashion show on a beach outside of town. Students socialize around a large communal kitchen and several bar/living areas. It's kinda like being on the set of MTV's *The Real World*: a bunch of cool people thrown together in a supercool loft (it's not just 20-somethings, though; ages range from 18–60).

La Escuela del Mundo (on the road in Jacó that runs perpendicular to the main road and has the ice-cream shop Pops, turn left after the Cabinas Dolphins; ☎ *506/643-2462; www.schooloftheworld.org). Prices start at $495 a week (shared room and classes), with discounts for longer stays. All programs include a tour in the area once per week.*

THE "OTHER" JACO

It sometimes feels like there's not much more to life in Jacó than tourist-filled beaches, bars, and restaurants. But one place that's been drawing an interesting crowd is the **Hotel Docelunas** ★ (from Herrradura, pass all four entrances to Jacó on the right, then continue on the Costanera main road; after the fourth entrance you will see a hotel sign from Docelunas, then you have to exit left at the first entrance of Quebrada Seca and keep going straight for 500m/1,640 ft.; ☎ 643-2211; http://docelunas.com; doubles from $140; MC, V). Maybe because it's on the other side of the Costanera, away from the regular tourist track, it's become a gathering place for a festive bunch of locals, language-school students, and dialed-in tourists. At least twice a month, you can catch cocktail-hour exhibitions of Tico or expat artists that usually draw a good 50 people mingling and enjoying the free sangria and *bocas* in this beautiful resort setting. Another great value and fun way to meet some of the locals is to drop in on the Doceluna's daily yoga classes (usually $2.90–$5.75). While yoga hasn't really hit it big with most Costa Ricans, the classes do draw a few younger Ticos, plus some local expats. Call for times on both classes and art openings.

MANUEL ANTONIO ✮✮ *Day trip from S.Jose* *BEAUTIFUL*

Even in a country full of beaches that regularly elicit rhapsodic raves, Manuel Antonio stands out—it's simply one of the most impressive and scenic stretches of coastline in the world, something like a tropical version of California's Big Sur or Carmel. The road connecting the town of Quepos with Manuel Antonio rises up into lushly forested hillside with breathtaking ocean views. The most unique thing is its 100m-high (300-ft.) tombolo ("TOME-bo-lo," from the Italian), which is a sandy buildup that connects an island to mainland. Called Punta Catedral (Cathedral Point), it's part of Manuel Antonio National Park, jutting into the Pacific 100m (300 ft.) with pristine white beaches along its sides, and when you throw in the rich flora and fauna (it's one of only two places in the world where you can spot the endangered *mono tití,* aka squirrel monkey), for us it's practically the perfect mix of sun, fun, and nature.

So not surprisingly, Manuel Antonio has been "discovered." Since the mid-1980s, hotels have sprung up all along the road to the park, now one of the most heavily visited in the country. Even in low season, you'll be sharing the trail with so many people that passersby will ask you, "Are the monkeys that way?" As for the monkeys, they're so blasé about us by now that they'll sometimes come up and snatch your stuff if you're not careful. Signs are everywhere reminding visitors not to feed them.

Now that once-sleepy Manuel Antonio is a major tourist resort with two canopy tours, scuba outfitters, fishing charters, several Spanish schools, a yoga center, and a thriving nightlife, it's also one of Costa Rica's priciest destinations, both for eating and sleeping. There are exceptions, of course (see below), but if you're on a tightish budget, Manuel Antonio might be a stretch and you might want to consider the next-door town of Quepos ("KAY-pohss"), a 10- to 15-minute bus or cab ride away.

Or better still, travel in the "green season," from April to December. Not only do prices take more of a nosedive (hotels are sometimes 30 to 50 percent less than elsewhere in Costa Rica), but you'll also get to enjoy the area more (fewer crowds, no restaurant waits). In April and May the weather is still pretty dry and sunny. But whenever you visit, it's hard not to love Manuel Antonio. Even in peak season, you'll still find spots where you can enjoy private moments and take in sublime sunsets. Yeah, yeah, we know eco-purists slam the place as overdeveloped and complain it just isn't what it used to be. But you'll see for yourself, and you'll agree with us, that what Manuel Antonio is, is pretty darn great.

GETTING TO & AROUND MANUEL ANTONIO
By Bus

From San José, **Transportes Delia Morales** buses (☎ 223-5567) leave the Coca Cola terminal (Calle 16 between avs. 1 and 3) at 6am, noon, 6pm and 7:30pm, on a 3½-hour direct run to Manuel Antonio; the fare's $4. The driver will let you off at any hotel along the way to the entrance of the national park. Buses also leave for Quepos at 7am, 10am, 2pm, and 4pm. The Quepos trip takes about 10 minutes more and costs $4.

For a little more comfort and style (think air-conditioning and seats with a bit more padding), you can get picked up at your San José hotel starting around 8am by **Grayline** (☎ 220-2126; www.graylinecostarica.com; $25) or at 9am or 2pm by **Interbus** (☎ 283-5573; www.costaricapass.com; $25).

By Car

The most popular route is the winding road that cuts through the mountains, dropping down on the Costanera (coast road), near Orotina. Take the Interamerican Highway out from San José past the airport towards Alajuela and take the turn off for Atenas. You'll pass through hilltop towns as you follow the signs for Jacó or Manuel Antonio. When you reach the town of Orotina, the road leads you right to the Costanera. From there, it's a straight shot down, passing Jacó along the way. The drive takes about 3½ hours.

By Air

The quickest way out is to fly directly into Quepos Airport. During the high season, **Nature Air** (☎ 299-6000, 800/235-9272 in the U.S. and Canada; www.natureair.com) departs daily at 9am, 1pm, and 4:25pm; the 25-minute flight will run you $54 each way. **Sansa** (☎ 221-9414; www.flysansa.com) charges $48 each way for its flights at 6, 7:25, 8:50, 10:25, and 11:35am, and 12:55, 2:40, and 4:25pm.

Getting Around

Smallish and set up on a grid, Quepos is an easy walking town, while Manuel Antonio is hillier and more spread out. You could walk from the top of the ridge down to the park in maybe 20 to 30 minutes, but getting back uphill could wind you. And the walk between Quepos to Manuel Antonio is a bit of stretch. Fortunately, cabs are cheap and plentiful hereabouts, and most trips between hotels on the main road and the park will run you $2 to $5. You can ask your hotel to call one for you or do it yourself, at ☎ 777-1695 or 777-0277, or simply hail one along the side of the road (they will pick up more than one passenger, making the ride cheaper for everyone). There are also public buses between Quepos and Manuel Antonio that depart roughly every half-hour, but schedules can vary so taxi may be more reliable.

ACCOMMODATIONS, BOTH STANDARD & NOT

In the past couple of decades, Manuel Antonio's popularity as a tourist destination and vacation home mecca have driven prices up like mad. In most other parts of Costa Rica, you might expect a fairly luxurious room for $100 a night; here that's somewhere in the average range. And many of the higher-end places, such as the large family resort **Hotel Sí Como No;** the small, lovely **Makanda by the Sea;** and the big, bells-and-whistles-crammed **Hotel Parador,** break the $200 mark. Despite the fluctuating fortunes of each high season (2006, for example, was kind of lackluster), rates continue to climb.

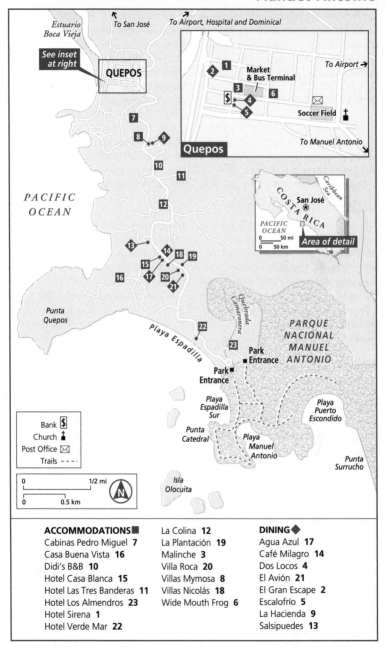

Manuel Antonio

Estuario Boca Vieja

To San José

To Airport, Hospital and Dominical

See inset at right

QUEPOS

Market & Bus Terminal

To Airport →

$

Soccer Field

To Manuel Antonio

Quepos

PACIFIC OCEAN

Caribbean Sea

San José

COSTA RICA

PACIFIC OCEAN

0   50 mi
0   50 km

Area of detail

Punta Quepos

Playa Espadilla

Quebrada Camaronera

PARQUE NACIONAL MANUEL ANTONIO

Park Entrance

Park Entrance

Playa Espadilla Sur

Punta Catedral

Playa Manuel Antonio

Playa Puerto Escondido

Punta Surrucho

Bank $
Church ✝
Post Office ⊠
Trails - - - -

0   1/2 mi
0   0.5 km

N

Isla Olocuita

ACCOMMODATIONS ■
Cabinas Pedro Miguel **7**
Casa Buena Vista **16**
Didi's B&B **10**
Hotel Casa Blanca **15**
Hotel Las Tres Banderas **11**
Hotel Los Almendros **23**
Hotel Sirena **1**
Hotel Verde Mar **22**

La Colina **12**
La Plantación **19**
Malinche **3**
Villa Roca **20**
Villas Mymosa **8**
Villas Nicolás **18**
Wide Mouth Frog **6**

DINING ◆
Agua Azul **17**
Café Milagro **14**
Dos Locos **4**
El Avión **21**
El Gran Escape **2**
Escalofrío **5**
La Hacienda **9**
Salsipuedes **13**

163

But you can still find something decent for less than $80—several B&Bs come to mind—but if you show up without reservations in advance you'll be reduced to sifting through the many "dives" (strange-smelling, run-down rooms with chipped paint and concrete floors) that abound especially in Quepos. The options we list below are among the better picks at the moderate range, but there are plenty of others, especially, again, in Quepos, where rates can be half or more of what they are in Manuel Antonio. There are also plenty of restaurants and services in Quepos, many catering to Ticos (meaning—ding! ding! ding!—Tico prices).

And especially if you're a family or group, don't rule out a vacation rental. Apart from Guanacaste, Manuel Antonio has one of the country's best organized pools of condos and villas, plus fluent English speakers (in fact, usually expats) on the other end of that 800 number. In fact, we find that these rentals are usually a better value than most of the hotels in terms of price, space, decor, and amenities.

Vacation Rentals

Manuel Antonio's stunning hilltop and ocean vistas make it a popular for vacation homes, and there are dozens of short-term rentals on the market. True, most of them are multi-million-dollar villas with infinity pools, four-plus bedrooms, and perfectly manicured grounds, at $4,000 to $8,000 or more per week (some have made the snooty likes of *Architectural Digest* and *Elle Décor*). But at almost all the rental agencies and websites, you can also snag deals from $700 a week. Most are on the smaller side—one- or two-bedroom condos, or small houses without palatial grounds—but almost all will have some nice views, either of forested hillside or ocean, plus regular maid service and soothing decor (tile floors, a bit of art on the walls, comfy couches, full kitchens, and better than decent beds). And if you're okay with something several miles away from Manuel Antonio, the deals get even better.

Most of the properties demand a week's minimum stay, with discounts negotiable for longer. During the high season, you should ideally make a reservation at least 60 days in advance, and you'll need a credit card to hold a reservation (most people prefer to pay for the rental itself with cash or traveler's checks—remember, most credit card companies charge a 3 percent fee for transactions abroad, which for a $2,000 rental would mean $60). Here's a list of real estate agencies and websites to check:

Manuel Antonio Estates (☎ 777-3339, 800/831-3770 in the U.S. and Canada; www.manuelantonioestates.com; AE, MC, V) is a development about a kilometer (half mile) past Quepos on the road to Manuel Antonio, near the Mono Azul, with eight gringo-owned properties, hiking trails, and the **Raindrop Spa.** Rates start at $800 a week for a one-bedroom hillside chalet furnished in a rustic cabin style (lots of handsome dark woods, colorful pillows and blankets) with a Jacuzzi. For $2,100, **The Tucan** is a new, 204-sq.-m (2,200-sq.-ft.) Mediterranean-style two-story house with three bedrooms, three bathrooms (one with Jacuzzi), and pool. It's perfect for a family reunion, with an oversized dining room, a living room with long cushy banquets mounded with pillows and perfect for just hanging around, and lots of artworks scattered here and there, giving the place a lived-in vibe. Though they won't advertise this, if you're booking at the last minute (2 weeks or less before arrival), you can probably negotiate a significant discount.

The **Vacation Villas Costa Rica** (☎ 777-5018, 800/867-5759 in the U.S. and Canada; www.vacationvillas.co.cr) specializes in larger homes on the luxury end, but it does have a handful of budget options. Its best deal is the **Condo Atardasol** ★, part of the Villas El Parque complex with a large pool, Jacuzzi, and patio area with great sunset ocean views. The stark-white apartment itself has high ceilings, tile floors, a fabulous covered dining area for six facing the ocean, and the usual other amenities, for $1,100 a week ($700 in low season). For more ideas, visit their website.

Beyond the rental agencies, there are a couple of individual places that are just such good values, we have to mention them. **Pete's Place** (☎ 777-2363; www.petesplacemanuelantonio.com), for example, offers two different properties on 1 hectare (2½ acres) halfway between Quepos and the national park, 2 blocks from the COSI and Escuela D'Amore language schools and Cockatoo bar, along with a convenience store and pharmacy. The larger one, **Casa Linda** ★, is an airy one-story three-bedroom with an Olympic-size pool and ocean views. We love the big windows and archways, and it can easily sleep seven, so $1,700 a week can work out to be a good deal. But if $700 a week is more your speed, you can opt for the more modest two-bedroom **Casa La Niña,** which has a good raft of amenities (A/C, good mattresses, cookable kitchen), the ocean views, and access to the Casa Linda pool.

The international website **Great Rentals** (www.greatrentals.com) lists several dozen around here at all price points, with several in the cheaper Quepos area; most fall within $1,000 to $2,000 a week. Keep in mind it's only a listing service, so it's up to you contact the owners or property managers directly. One affordable example is the **Casa Segunda Vida** (www.casasegundavida.com), a sunny white hillside duplex in a residential part of Manuel Antonio, an easy walk to services and the beach. Each floor is self-contained and can accommodate up to four, renting separately for $130 a night (3 night minimum) or $875 weekly, or together for $195 a night/$1,295 weekly. The house's best feature is its covered balconies facing the ocean, where you can laze away the day drinking in the views. A number of individual owners also list their properties in the classifieds at **Quepolandia** (☎ 777-3634; www.quepolandia.com).

Hotels
IN QUEPOS
This former banana port is now the all-purpose commercial hub for the Manuel Antonio area. Easily walkable, it has most of the local shops and restaurants, not to mention the airport and main bus station, and almost all of the area's Ticos live here. So in addition to better prices, you're also getting more local vibe by basing yourself here. Besides the digs listed below, it might be worth walking around and checking out what's on offer once you get here—especially if you're looking to drop less than $30 a night. In that price range, a pair of hotels we think particularly worth a look are the **Ceciliano** (right across from the Republic of Korea Public School; ☎ 777-0192; cash only) with 24 rooms, and the **Malinche** (75m/246 ft. west of bus terminal; ☎ 777-0093; V), also with 24 rooms. Both are pretty plain, but offer white-glove clean rooms and have friendly staffs. There's also a very social, newish hostel called **Wide Mouth Frog** (150m/492 ft. east of bus terminal;

☎ 777-2798; www.widemouthfrog.org), with a pool, pool table, outdoor hammocks, a TV room (with DVD library), and a kitchen that guests can use. Dorm beds are $9, and private doubles $27 to $34. Otherwise, check out the following:

$–$$ Just outside Quepos, **The Cabinas Pedro Miguel** ★ (1km/⅔ mile from Quepos on the road to Manuel Antonio; ☎ 777-0035; www.cabinaspedromiguel; MC, V) offers 16 recently spruced-up rooms that are unpretentious in their looks—the usual hardwood floors and white walls—but truly comfy, with such amenities as A/C, TV, and a hot-water shower for an average price of $43. So-called "ecological rooms" are self-consciously "green," with one all-screen wall (for great views), a hammock, and kitchenette for $73 (these can sleep up to four). Go with a second-floor room for water views. There's a teeny-tiny pool out front and a breakfast buffet in the high season (for an extra $5).

$$ You could do a lot worse than heeding the moderately priced siren's call to the two-story whitewashed **Hotel Sirena** ★ (50m/164 ft. from the beach; ☎ 777-0528, 800/493-8426 in the U.S. and Canada; www.lasirenahotel.com; cash only), a spot of calm right amid the town's bustle. You get 10 clean, blue-and-white rooms that are kind of nondescript but at least air-conditioned, and there's even a cute little pool if you need even more quick cooling off. The staff's a little hard to find during the day, but whatever—everything in Quepos is right at your doorstep here, so the lack of hand-holding isn't all that big a deal. Doubles go for $89 in high season.

IN MANUEL ANTONIO

To stay closer to the national park, these are the picks of the pack, located on the road to the park or a side road. Keep in mind that paying by credit card in some cases will tack 6 percent onto your bill.

$–$$ Just $50 (during high season, less otherwise) a night for a comfy double, warm pampering, and great cooking (breakfast included) in pricey Manuel Antonio? Check out the pink-villa B&B run by Ezio Laueriotti and named for his deceased wife, **Didi's Charming House Bed & Breakfast** ★★ (road to national park, next to Tuany's restaurant; ☎ 777-0069; www.didiscr.com; AE, D, MC, V). Up on a forested hillside where squirrel monkeys regularly put in appearances, its four rooms open onto a lovely, shaded, polished-hardwood terrace, a small pool, and Jacuzzi. Furnishings are simple but color-rich and tasteful (we love the sky-lit bathrooms with pretty decorative tile work). Breakfasts include organic eggs taken from an on-site henhouse, and Enzio makes Italian dinners from organic ingredients, too. If you want A/C, the rate goes up to $65—but the breezes up here, plus the ceiling fans, keep things comfortable without. There's also no charge for adding a third bed in a room for kids under 15.

$–$$ On a steep hillside *(colina)* heading down to the water, **La Colina** (halfway between Quepos and Manuel Antonio on Calle Manuel Antonio; ☎ 777-0231; www.lacolina.com; AE, D, MC, V) is an attractive place to drop your bags, with a charming little two-level pool with a little waterfall and a pleasant thatch-roof dining area. The 13 rooms are clean, with good writing desks and pretty French doors, and many have drop-dead ocean views. But we've found the upkeep here is spotty, with some rooms in need of touch-ups, paint jobs, and new furnishings (while others are just fine). But if that doesn't particularly bother you, go for it (or be ready to request a room change when you arrive). Digs range from standard garden doubles for $49 in season to an oceanview suite, with truly spectacular views, for $85 (breakfast included); we find the garden rooms can be dark, but if you don't spend that much time in them, it may not be a big deal for you.

$$ If Didi's is full, another great B&B with a view worth checking out is **Casa Buena Vista** (Punta Quepos Rd., 100m/328 ft. past Hotel Mango Moon; ☎ 777-0292; buennota@racsa.co.cr; MC, V), on the way out toward Punta Quepos, near all the top resorts. Anita Myketuk, the no-nonsense owner of a well-known shop called La Buena Nota (souvenirs, international press, sundries), rents out five rooms in his rustic-wooden-lodge-style home, and as a bonus he'll be happy to give you the local scoop, including tourist traps to avoid. Rooms ($50 a night) are split between the main house and a second, white-stucco building; we'd take the outbuilding because these rooms are a more stylish (the others look like a throwback to the '70s). There's no A/C, but again, you get good breezes through the screened windows. Also, it's a bit of a hike to the main road, so a car is a good idea.

$$ For that same $50, you can swap character for convenience: staying downhill right next to the national park, and around the corner from the strip of restaurants and bars along the beach. Okay, **Hotel Los Almendros** (on road just off Playa Espadilla, 300m/984 ft. from beach; ☎ 777-0225; cash only) has all the pizzazz of a motel on I-95, but the 21 rooms are very presentable, white-glove clean, and not tiny. Another advantage over Casa Buena Vista is the on-premises pool and dining—pretty good Argentine-Tico fare at affordable prices. *One note:* You may want to spring for air-conditioning, an extra $9 and a good idea at this low elevation.

$$ Also down here in this area but a couple of notches up from Los Almendros (doubles from $80), the two-story **Casa del Sol/Hotel Verde Mar** ✸ (200m/656 ft. from park entrance; ☎ 777-1805; www.verdemar.com; AE, MC, V) has pretty, open-air public areas, an attractive landscaped pool, and 22 spacious, cheery yellow-orange rooms with wrought-iron queen beds. They're admittedly a wee bit dim, partly thanks to low ceilings, but they do have perks like A/C and kitchenettes, and the location can't be beat for convenience—beautiful Playa Espadilla is just 50m (165 ft.) away, the park about 195m (650 ft.), and the popular Mar y Sombra restaurant and nightspot is just down the road.

$$ Spanish colonial style but Polish run (no joke), the **Hotel Las Tres Banderas** (located on the main road, halfway between Manuel Antonio and Quepos; ☎ 777-1521; www.hotellastresbanderas.com; AE, MC, V) is a two-story "luxury motel" right off the main road but tucked into the forested hills, giving it the feel of a secret hideaway. The 17 rooms are a little short on natural light, but they're spotless, large, and chockablock with pretty tile and carved woodwork. The best by far are on the upper level, thanks in no small part to balconies with rocking chairs that face the woods. Out back is a king-size Jacuzzi, a large pool with waterfall,

Where the *Chicos* Are

They don't call it "Gay-pos" for nothing.

Long before Quepos/Manuel Antonio had been "discovered" by mass tourism, it'd already been popular with *playos* (gay men), both Tico and foreign for decades. Yes, Manuel Antonio is Costa Rica's Provincetown, Fire Island, or Key West—a getaway where much of the year bars and hotels fill up on Friday and empty out by Monday, but the beat goes on all week long in high season. And Semana Santa (Easter Week)? A cast of thousands; it's raining *hombres, aleluya*.

Some stay in one of several gay hotels, with great views and pretty moderately priced. Though these are all clothing-optional, that doesn't mean orgies-a-go-go—in fact, these days, we've noticed more couples than singles in them (also, women are welcome, but much less common than men). We'd recommend the popular **Villa Roca** ✦ (on the main road to Manuel Antonio, 3.5km (2¼ miles) from Quepos; ☎ 777-1349; www.villa roca.com; AE, MC, V), on the "gay strip" near the gay bar Tutú (see below) and the other resorts. The infinity pool facing the ocean has amazing views, and the 11 rooms and three apartments are airy and spacious, with white-tile floors, A/C, cable, minibars, and terraces. Doubles start at $90 a night, including breakfast. A tad cheaper (doubles from $80) but with equally voluptuous vistas, **Casa Blanca** (on the same main road, 4.5km/2¾ miles from Quepos; ☎ 777-0253; www.hotelcasablanca.com; AE, MC, V) has two pools. But the area's first exclusively gay resort is beginning to show its age, and the decor is a bit ho-hum.

and an open-air dining room (and open-air kitchen where you can watch the owner and chefs at work) so good that nonguests often also come to get fed. Standard doubles start at $70. Heads-up to moms and dads: This may not be the best place for families. Since there's no policy against overnight guests, you may just run into, say, a bunch of rowdy anglers with their newly acquired "girlfriends" (as we did on our last visit).

$$ We're big fans of the **Villas Nicolás** ✦✦ (3km/1¾ miles from Quepos on the main road to Manuel Antonio; ☎ 777-0481; www.villasnicolas.com; AE, MC, V), which has personality to spare and some of the kindest hospitality in the area. It's a pool-equipped, dozen-villa complex on a steep hill; each individually decorated villa gets a va-va-voom view, handsome wicker and dark-wood furniture, and colorful print fabrics. Some also have A/C (not really necessary up here), separate sitting areas, and kitchenettes. But the deal closer, for us, are the ample outdoor terraces with hammocks and banquette-style sofas. And when we stayed here on the top floor of a duplex, the large bathroom had a window that opened for a tasty view of the ocean while we showered. We should also mention manager Sheryl

If you're able to spend a little more like (ahem) a queen, **La Planta-ción** ✷ (again on the main road, 6km/3¾ miles from Quepos; ☎ 777-1332 or 800/477-7829 in the U.S. and Canada; www.bigrubys.com; MC, V) is an offshoot of one of Key West's best-quality guesthouses, Big Ruby's. Down on the Plantation, you'll pay $149 in season, and yes, its design and decor are more high-end contemporary; and yes, it has the perks you would expect, including pool and Jacuzzi, plus a few more, like DVD players in the rooms. But if you're a social butterfly, there's more of a social scene at the Villa Roca. Also, the heftier rates mean mostly gringos, whereas both Villa Roca and Casa Blanca attract a good number of Ticos, too.

There are several uniquely gay sides to Manuel Antonio. Numero uno is the clothing-optional gay beach, **Playita** ✷✷. It's on the far western end of the main beach, just past some rocks that you'll have to cross at low tide. There's only one exclusively gay bar, called **Tutú** ✷✷ (above the Gato Negro restaurant/Hotel Casitas Eclipse; ☎ 777-0408; www.casitaseclipse. org/tutu.htm; Mon–Sun 4pm–2am), a great little rooftop terrace spot where everyone ends up at some point or another. It only really gets going around sunset for happy hour, or after 10pm, when the restaurants close. Also, at press time the place to go on Thursdays was the gay dance night at **Barba Roja** (main road, 200m/656 ft. north of La Mariposa Hotel; ☎ 777-0331; Thurs 8pm–2am). Check the events calendar in the local gay weekly *Playita*. It's published by Paul Sfez, owner of **Gaytours** (☎ 236-9257; www.gaytourscr.com), which runs a cavalcade of queer outings, from canopy tours and sunset sails to park excursions.

Livingston, who's lived in the area for over 20 years and is just a doll, plus very helpful with excellent local advice. The only downside is that some units show a little bit of wear and tear. Still, for as little as $95 a night in high season, for the space and the views it's one of the best values around.

$$$ While not as fetching as the Villas Nicolas, the **Villas Mymosa** ✷ (on the main road between Quepos and Manuel Antonio, 2km/1¼ miles from Quepos; ☎ 777-1254; www.villasmymosa.com; AE, D, MC, V) might be a bit better for families. A two-story complex of 10 condo-apartments with balconies and terraces, arranged around a pool, it accepts small children and units are big enough to house the whole gang. The smallest, the two-bedroom "junior villa," is almost 84 sq. m (900 sq. ft.), including a living room, fully equipped kitchen, and tiled terrace with a hammock. At $112 a night in high season ($70 in low), including breakfast, it's a little on the pricey side, especially considering no ocean views. Still, the units have a whitewashed-island charm, and in any case here the main appeal is plenty of room to spread out.

DINING FOR ALL TASTES

Most dining spots in Manuel Antonio are scattered along the main road between Quepos to the national park, with several tucked away on the side roads. With a few exceptions, we've found Quepos restaurants a better value than Manuel Antonio's, which tend to sell mediocre grub to gringo tourists at gringo prices (well, in many cases you're also paying for the view, of course); many also stay open later than the usual M-A closing time of 10pm. So even if you're staying in Manuel Antonio, a $2 or $3 taxi ride down to Quepos can pay off.

$–$$ Okay, we admit it, we love pigging out in the morning on the banana pancakes ($3) and big honkin' omelettes ($3.50) at Manuel Antonio's **Café Milagro** ★★ (across from Hotel Casa Blanca; ☎ 777-0794; daily 6am–6pm; AE, MC, V), part of a minichain with locations in Quepos and San José. You can get all your Starbucks-style coffee concoctions, hot and cold, made from freshly ground beans ($1; cappuccino is 10 cents cheaper as it does not cover refills) along with muffins, croissants, and sandwiches ($2–$6). There's also a gift shop with Costa Rican coffee, foreign newspapers and magazines, souvenirs, and a bunch of odds and ends.

$–$$ Down in Quepos, meanwhile, we're partial to the brick-oven pizzas ($4.50–$9, 40 varieties!) at the family-run **Escalofrío** ★ (Calle Central, 100m west/50m south [328 ft. west/164 ft. south] of the central market; ☎ 777-0833; 2:30–10:30pm). Being native Italians, the Catullos are whizzes with various pasta dishes, too (we think the *tagliatella pescatore* for $9 is *buonissimo*, though you can get more straightforward red-sauce dishes for just $5.50) And if you've got a sweet tooth, hie thee hither for the *gelati* (frothy Italian-style ice cream), in 25 flavors. Get it plain ($1), in a milkshake ($3), or even a banana split ($3.75)—but just get it. *Escalofrío* means "shiver," and that's just what these cold smidgeons of sin will delightfully deliver.

$–$$ The lively atmosphere and good, cheap Mexican fare packs 'em in at **Dos Locos** ★ (next door to Escalofrío; ☎ 777-1526; Mon–Sat 7am–11pm, Sun 11am–8pm; MC, V), an open-air joint owned by a San Francisco transplant. That, plus the live tunes on Wednesdays and Fridays, have turned this spot into a bit of a local favorite. Diners gorge themselves on gigantic burritos ($4–$5), beef or chicken chimichangas ($10), or chili con carne ($6.50), and if they're really famished, the house specialty, Steak Dos Locos, a shareable slab of filet mignon topped with a bacon-and-mushroom sauce ($15). Dos Locos is credited as among the first places to introduce the guaro sour, a tart cocktail made with local guaro firewater, triple sec, and lime juice ($4). If you've haven't tried one, here's your chance.

$$ For a casual lunch with some of the best views in Manuel Antonio, the open-air **Café Agua Azul** ★ (over Villas El Parque Hotel; ☎ 777-5280; www.cafe aguaazul.com; Thurs–Tues 10:30am–10pm; cash only) not only is perched on one of the highest points around, but also delivers on the grub. And after 5pm, the tasty chicken fajitas ($8) and Big Ass burgers (their name, not ours—$7 and enormous even by U.S. standards) give way to sophisticated Asian-tropical fusion à la coconut-crusted mahi-mahi with pineapple-chayote slaw ($6); we also like the coq au vin with porcini red-wine reduction ($8), though it's not always on the menu, which changes frequently. Sometimes we think Agua Azul comes across as almost too casual to be charging these kinds of prices, but still, the food is among M-A's best.

$$ At this local's hangout (whose name means "get out if you can"), the food is good but the scene is better. Near the top of the hill overlooking some forested slopes and the ocean, **Salsipuedes** (main road to park, just before Economy Rent a Car; ☎ 777-5019; Wed–Sun 4pm–late; cash only) has some nice open-air dining on its hardwood patio, along with plenty of folks dropping in for cocktails and the salsa soundtrack at the bar alongside. The menu is full of Latin-style tapas, from ceviche ($3) and *frijolitos negros con chorizo* (black-bean stew with sausage, $2.20) to *chicharrones con yuca* (fried pork chunks with cassava, $2.80). They can turn any of 'em into full-blown main courses, or you can go for couple of basic pastas ($7–$8) or a grilled mahi-mahi or tuna ($9). Dinner aside, this makes a good spot for a start to a night out on the town.

$$–$$$ The big swordfish in the middle of the dining room in **El Gran Escape** ✪✪ (Quepos beachfront road; ☎ 777-0395; www.elgranescape.com; 7am–11pm; AE, MC, V) is a dead giveaway: It's all about the seafood. A restaurant since 1981, this local institution has been getting bigger and better under the current owner, ex-Californian Marsha Bennett (now there's a sushi bar, for example). But whatever floats your boat—from tangy traditional ceviche ($4) or simple peel-and-eat "bucket of shrimp" ($7.50) to nouvelle-ish tamarind-and-pineapple red snapper ($14)—it's all about the fresh catch of the day. And the Tico paella (a gumbo of mussels, calamari, scallops, and crab, $15)? We have to skip lunch to handle that one, but it's worth it. There are plenty of nonfish dishes, too, and the bar is a magnet for Ticos and expats. We'd advise reservations, especially on weekends.

$$$–$$$$ Hands down the quirkiest eatery in the area (if not Costa Rica), **El Avión** ✪ kids (road to park, across from Hotel Casitas Eclipse; ☎ 777-3378; 3–10pm; MC, V) is, indeed, "the airplane"—specifically, an old Fairchild C-123 Army transport used by the CIA to traffic arms to Nicaraguan contras in the 1980s. Downed by the Sandinistas, the plane was at the center of Iran-Contra scandal, made a hero out of Oliver North, and somehow ended up in Manuel Antonio. Kids will love checking out this relic and its cockpit, and their parents will find the food respectable surf and turf (entrees $18–$25 on average). After dinner, there's a bar that turns fairly lively with tourists leavened by a handful of locals.

WHY YOU'RE HERE: THE TOP SIGHTS & ATTRACTIONS

It starts, of course, with Manuel Antonio National Park, unique because it has some of the country's most beautiful beaches, great hiking trails, and endangered species—all making it ideal for combining sun-'n'-fun with ecotourism. Additionally, given the rapacious rate of tourist development, almost every activity or tour imaginable is available in the area from ATV tours, horseback riding, kayaking in the mangroves, rafting, sunset booze cruises, and of course, sportfishing charters. Your hotel will likely have all the brochures for those activities and

Restaurant Worth a Splurge

$$–$$$$—Manuel Antonio has more than its fair share of restaurants featuring international cuisine, but most are fairly "so what." You won't say that after a meal at **La Hacienda** ★★★ (road to the park, Centro Commercial Plaza Yara; ☎ 777-3473; www.lahaciendacr.com; Mon–Sat 5–11pm; MC, V), run since 2004 by Canadian expats Geoff Polci and Alana Duggan. Its refined mélange of nuevo Latino, Mediterranean, and Asian is as sublime as the setting: an open-air terrace surrounded by jungle and with a 1.8m (6-ft.) stone fountain. The tables are candlelit and the curved bar is eye-candy polished coral. But the real stars are dishes like grilled beef tenderloin with chipotle-lime cilantro butter and yuca hash browns ($15), or maybe the seafood tagliatelle with jumbo shrimp, mahi-mahi, calamari, and mussels, tossed in a sinful-but-light lemon-sage cream sauce ($12). The *vino* list is also better than most hereabouts, heavy on Argentine, Chilean, and California vintages. And by the way, if you must bring the kids, there's always a safe hamburger option, served with chipotle ketchup and yuca hash browns ($8). Reservations? You bet.

can arrange them for you, so I'll outline the main highlights below—and the ones that won't put a huge dent in your budget.

The Beaches

The best known beaches around here are the four within **Manuel Antonio National Park** (daily 7am–4pm; $7), and the one right next to it; they've all been awarded Costa Rica's "blue flag" for cleanliness and eco-correctness (highest scores in the country!). But down the hill in Quepos, the in-town beach is polluted, so stroll but don't loll.

If you're looking for a lively scene and reasonably good surfing and body boarding, **Playa Espadilla** ★, outside the entrance to the park, is the longest and most convenient; a good bunch of restaurants, shops, street vendors and surf shops line the road along the beach. That means, of course, that during Christmas and Easter weeks, and weekends in high season it can be pretty crowded. But otherwise, it's a great place for sunning or hanging in the shade of the palm and almond trees. As for the waters, they look mild, but the rip currents can be dangerous at times.

Just inside the park, over a shallow stream, **Playa Espadilla Sur** is an extension of Playa Espadilla, arcing out toward and sheltered from the heavy surf by Punta Catedral. So it's better for swimming and sports a panoramic eyeful of Playa Espadilla.

The area's loveliest beach, though, is right on the flip side of Espadilla Sur, facing south. **Playa Manuel Antonio** ★★★ is a white-sand wonder, with sheltered waters ideal for swimming and snorkeling. All along you'll find a string of tide pools brimming with marine life, and at the far end, close to Punta Catedral, you'll see, at low tide, **ancient turtle decoys** carved out of rocks by the Quepoas, the pre-Columbian tribe that used to live around here (they realized early on that male green turtles would hang out in the water at high tide for the gals as they laid their eggs in the sand, so they put the decoys out to keep them in the water until low tide, when they would be trapped by the rocks). There are showers, bathrooms, and picnic tables; just come before 10am to beat the crowds.

Accessible only on one of the park trails, the next beach in is **Playa Gemelas,** an intimate little stretch named for its view of the Islas Gemelas (Twin Islands), just a bit offshore. It's a fairly easy walk on mostly flat ground, but you'll have to come at low tide, otherwise it's totally submerged.

You'll find the best snorkeling in the area at the remote **Playa Escondida** ✹✹, tucked away in a cove ringed by steep cliffs. You'll need to follow the trail in the park for about a half-hour past Playa Manuel Antonio—just make sure not to come when it's high tide, when the surf literally crashes on to the cliffs. At low tide, the beach is a decent size, and a great place to have a picnic lunch and a snorkel—you'll see iridescent fish of all shapes and shades wriggling in and out of the coral.

Outside the park, there are a few beaches known mostly to locals and a few of the savvier tourists. The most popular is secluded **Playita** ✹✹, known as Manuel Antonio's clothing-optional **gay beach.** You'll have to walk to the far north end of Espadilla and cross the rocks—do it at low tide and with shoes or thick sandals; there's a path through a jungle with a small waterfall and swimming hole. Many of the guests at the gay hotels get out here during the day, so if you're not staying in one of them, you'll be sure to catch up with people here. Like Espadilla, however, Playita has strong rip currents and isn't recommended for swimming.

Another beach popular among locals is **Playa Biesanz** ✹, and while it's not exactly a secret, we'll probably tick some folks off for publicizing it. This small, secluded stretch of sand is reached by a steep trail leading from the road to the Hotel Parador. Since the beach is located on an arc stretching from Punta Quepos, the water is sheltered and great for swimming and snorkeling. Apart from that, it's not only crowd-free, but free, period.

The last beach, **Playa La Macha** (aka Doctor's Beach) is probably the most secluded. It's not just that few folks know about it, but also because it's underwater at high tide and you can only get here on a steep trail that can be grueling on the return uphill, especially on a hot, humid day. Just take the turnoff for Hotel Villa Teca and follow the road all the way down. At the fork, go straight for another 100m (328 ft.), then you'll see the trail to the beach. There's not much to do here, so you'll likely find yourself alone with your thoughts and the beach itself, which is littered with large rocks (including a rock formation thought to be another ancient turtle trap).

Exploring Nature

Okay, back to **Manuel Antonio National Park** ✹✹✹ (☎ 777-0654; www. costarica-nationalparks.com/manuelantonionationalpark.html; daily 7am–4pm; $7). Created in 1972, the park is small (just 6.9km/2⅔ sq. miles) compared with most of the rest in Costa Rica, but it more than makes up for that with its location, beauty, the beaches (p. 172), and the wildlife (the squirrel monkey is the star attraction, but you'll see everything from sloths and coatimundis to iguanas and scarlet macaws).

The park gets very crowded in high season, so get there early in the morning, right when it opens. It certainly can't hurt to have a guide to explain some of the ecology, though you can spot a good bit of wildlife on your own (it's not as tricky as it can be in other parks), and get other info from the small open-air natural history museum here. There are also plenty of other guides and other people on the trails who can help direct your eye to the right spots.

Some of the trails lead to beaches, others into the jungle. The **Sendero Punta Catedral** ✹ loops around the tombolo and takes you 90m (300 ft.) up to the top of the point for truly dramatic panoramas of the Pacific. Just keep in mind the steep trail can get muddy and slippery during the rainy season, so bring a good pair of shoes with decent tread, and you'll thank us later.

Another good trail to explore is the **Sendero Perezoso** ✹, named after the sloths who like to hang out in the trees alongside it. Chances are you won't get to spot some of the more exotic critters known to live in this neck of the park, like ocelots and marmosets, but as it takes you along the ridge high above Playa Escondido to a *mirador* (lookout), again, the views are priceless. After the initial climb up, the rest of the hike is a fairly easy.

Canopy Tours

Of the half-dozen ziplines now in the area, one of the most established and thrilling is **Canopy Safari** 🦥 (☎ 777-0100; www.canopysafari.com), about 45 minutes away in Paso Real. The circuit's a whopping 5 hours, covering 21 platforms, 9 ziplines, 2 rappel lines, a "Tarzan swing," and a suspension bridge. At the end, sweaty visitors get to splash around in a secluded water hole on the property. The $80 cost is pricier than most, but it *is* 5 hours (which may be too many for some), and includes breakfast or lunch, plus air-conditioned van transfers to and from your hotel.

We also get a jolt out of **Dream Forest Canopy** ✹ 🦥 (☎ 777-4657; www.dreamforestcanopy.com), which is also faster to get to (in the mountains near Quepos) and less expensive ($65 per person, and you can get a $55 Internet special for during the low season, along with special group and student rates). Three hours here takes you through 14 platforms and 9 ziplines (including the longest in the area—one's more than a third of a mile long). Tours run daily at 7:30am and 1pm, and include hotel pick-ups. Kids are welcomed and nicely catered to by both Dream Forest (over age 4) and Canopy Safari (over age 5).

If you'd really rather try something a little tamer, the **Rainmaker Nature Refuge** (☎ 777-3565; www.rainmakercostarica.com), 20 minutes outside Quepos, has a half-day tour ($65) that lets you crisscross the canopy on a series of a half-dozen suspension bridges, the longest just under 300 feet. Afterward, you can finish off with a dip in one of the swimming holes on the property.

Then, of course, it just wouldn't be a Costa Rican resort town without a *mariposario* (butterfly garden). The local contender is the **Nature Farm Refuge** ✹ 🦥 (☎ 777-0850; www.butterflygardens.co.cr), part of a 12-hectare (30-acre) nature reserve run by the Hotel Sí Como No. Through several guided tours on a small network of well-tended trails, you'll get a full introduction to the life cycle of the butterfly—and get to spot various monkeys along the way. The basic 1-hour tour costs $15 per person.

ATTENTION, SHOPPERS!

There's little "quality" shopping in Manuel Antonio besides the usual beachwear, trinkets, and souvenirs which you'll find spilling out of the stalls along Playa Espadilla and in the shops in downtown Quepos. You can get all that plus international magazines, newspapers, and three rooms full of books a bit up the hill at **La Buena Nota** (road to park, 1km/⅔ mile from Playa Espadilla; ☎ 777-1002; daily 9am–6pm).

For stuff that's a little more unique and has a touch of quality, the Hotel Sí Como No's shop, **Regálame Art Gallery and Gift Shop** (☎ 777-0777; www. regalameart.com; daily 7am–10pm) has the best selection in Manuel Antonio of work by Costa Rican artists: woodwork, ceramics, prints, paintings, and glass art, and more recently a jewelry line based on pre-Columbian pieces like the ones you see at San José's Gold Museum, in silver, bronze, and goldplate, in such motifs as monkeys, birds, butterflies, and other animals. Prices start at $40 but don't be surprised to find a few items over $600.

NIGHTLIFE

The social calendar in Manuel Antonio can get very full, especially during high season. On any given night you have a choice of a few different nightspots, many featuring live music. The atmosphere's friendly and sometimes raucous, whether you're partying in the bars or the beachside disco.

Pre-raucous, some folks like to kick off the evening with a drink and a gawk at the exceptional local sunsets. One of the faves for this is **Ronny's Place** ★★ (across from Amigos del Río Rafting; ☎ 777-5120; www.ronnysplace.com), on a 36-hectare (90-acre) farm atop one of the seaside bluffs by the water. A string of stone tables and benches line the edge of the property facing the ocean to allow everybody the best unobstructed vistas possible. And might we be so bold as to recommend the strong and tasty house piña coladas, served in a pineapple ($5), or sangria served with a hibicus flower on top ($4)? You can have dinner here, too, if you want.

One of the hotter new places in town around sunset is **The Lounge** (across from Escuela d'Amore; ☎ 777-5143), with discount happy-hour drinks and a pre–**Mar y Sombra** party on Friday and Saturday nights (that's the beach disco; see below). The crowd is usually heavy on 20-something tourists.

The iconic dance palace hereabouts is **Mar y Sombra** ★ (on Playa Espadilla; ☎ 777-0510; daily 10pm–late). This laid-back beach eatery puts on its boogie shoes sometime after 10pm, doesn't charge cover, and unlike some of the other local nightspots, both Ticos and gringos tip back Imperial beers ($1.60) and mix it up on the cement open-air dance floor to the beats of salsa, meringue, and reggaetón (just be sure to wear something cool). If you still haven't had enough, head to **Arco Iris** around midnight (just before the bridge heading into town; no phone; daily 10:30pm–2:30am), with a $3 cover. It has the distinction of being the loudest disco in town—good for some, hell for others—and unleashes mist makers and dizzying spinning lights for those who dance themselves into a frenzy.

If live bands are more your thing, check out a Manuel Antonio bar-restaurant called **Bambú Jam** ★ (1km/⅔ mile from Quepos on the main road to Manuel Antonio; ☎ 777-3369; music from 8–11pm, restaurant open from 7am daily), which brings in local and Central Valley bands on Tuesdays and Fridays, and Tuesdays are Latin music nights. Here, too, it's a mix of locals and tourists, along with students from the nearby language schools. In Quepos, most everyone meets at the **Dos Locos** restaurant (p. 170) for live music Wednesday and Friday nights.

THE "OTHER" MANUEL ANTONIO

Manuel Antonio is so tourism oriented that it's hard to imagine any kind of "authentic local" scene. All the waiters and shopkeepers address you in English, even if you speak Spanish; the bars are packed with gringos in their backwards baseball caps; and you have to wonder: Do any Ticos actually live around here?

Well, the fact of the matter is they do, but most of them live in and around Quepos, and a great way to track them down (and, by the way, get groceries if you're renting a house, or have a kitchenette) is at the **Quepos farmers' market** down at the waterfront on Friday evenings and Saturday mornings. It's a treat to watch the *agricultores* in their tarp-covered trucks selling oranges, strawberries, lemons, palm trees, orchids, tubers like yucca and *ñampí*, free-range chickens, fish, eggs, homemade cheese, and more. The locals have a dandy old time, stocking up for the coming week and meeting up with friends, family, and neighbors. If you want to practice your Spanish, many of the farmers are chatty but don't speak much English. Some of the other locals do, though (plus there are a fair number of expats shopping, too), and we've found everybody's usually in a friendly mood here.

If you've got kids, a great way for them to interact with local kids (and, to some extent, you with their parents) is the **Kids Saving the Rainforest mini-camps** at the Hotel Mono Azul (☎ 777-2592; www.kidssavingtherainforest.com; $20). Every Saturday from 9am to 1pm, a number of local kids 7 to 17 (there's a core group that meets regularly), plus a few visitors, meet at the hotel's pool and tiki hut. The activities include making crafts to benefit reforestation projects; classes on rainforest ecology; field trips; and heading down to the national park to educate tourists about the monkeys (mostly about why it's a no-no to feed them). It's a friendly environment, and the kids usually mix well and become fast friends. There's also swim time from noon to 1pm, so be sure to bring a bathing suit and towel.

For something a little more grown-up-oriented, try getting twisted. Yoga's pretty popular here (well, mostly among the expats), and **Buena Vista Yoga** (in the Quepos Zona Americana; ☎ 777-0706) offers a hybrid of Ashtanga and

---

Cheers to the Chicks

Revelers tend to go where the crowds are, and nothing draws them out like ladies' nights in the Manuel Antonio bars, and almost all of them pour free drinks for the gals. On Tuesdays and Thursdays it's **The Lounge** (p. 175) after 9pm, and on Fridays and Saturdays persons of the female persuasion can get liquored up for nothing after 10pm at **Coconut's** (on Playa at Espadilla; ☎ 777-2382).

Vinyasa taught by Marc Ford in an attractive open-air studio facing the ocean. They get full, though—filled with parents from the private school in the Zona Americana, a good mix of Ticos, and expats—so reservations are a good idea. The classes run $15 and are held weekdays at 7:30am and Saturday at 8:30am; there's also a 1-hour presunset stretch at 4pm on Mondays, Wednesdays, and Fridays. Buena Vista even provides a free shuttle, which picks up in town in front of the Best Western Kamuk.

Or you can twist just your tongue (around Spanish, that is). Because of the stunning setting, there are quite a few language schools here, all offering similar courses from beginning to medical and business Spanish; some also do field trips and other classes such as dance or cooking. Choosing a homestay option with one is a great way to get hooked directly into the community; some schools will also help you find volunteer opportunities. The three most reputable to try are **La Escuela d'Amore** (☎ 777-1143, 800/261-3203 in the U.S. and Canada; www. escueladamore.com); **Centro de Idiomas Pacífico** (☎ 777-0805; cipacifico.com); and **COSI** (☎ 777-0021; www.cosi.co.cr).

And here's something fun to do with locals that's *really* off the tourist track. Over in the Zona Americana, the **Banana Club** (50m/164 ft. past El Avión Restaurant; ☎ 777-5197; daily 6:30am–10pm) is the country club used by employees of Palma Tica (the company that owns all those African palm planta-tions), complete with swimming pool, tennis court, bar, and the area's only bowl-ing alley—the old-style kind where you have to pick up the pins. Technically, you're supposed to have a club pass to enter the area, but they almost never check the passes as you drive down the private road, and we're told they regularly serve anyone who shows up.

DOMINICAL & PUNTA UVITA

Once a secret paradise known only among surfers and backpackers, Dominical and Punta Uvita are now on the map as the hottest resort areas on the Central Pacific; multi-million-dollar developments catering to European holidaymakers and North American vacationers have transformed this stretch into a new gold coast. The roads are gloriously smooth and paved (in Costa Rica terms, the coast road over here is like some Euro autobahn!), and condo complexes are sprouting all over, accompa-nied by several new hotels, B&Bs, and restaurants. And in once sleepy Uvita, there's even now a bilingual elementary school. Most of the development has at least been spread out and is still fairly low-density, but there have still been casualties; one indigenous tribe was reportedly kicked off the land it had lived on near one of the beaches, exiled to camp out in the area around the highway. Ah, progress.

Anyway, surfers still groove on Dominical's waves for their awesomely consis-tent right and left breaks. But the new tourists see the area as a high-end, more secluded and tranquil alternative to Manuel Antonio. You won't get the teeming wildlife like you get in Manuel Antonio National Park right at your doorstep (though it's only an hour's drive away), but the 40-hectare (100-acre) private **Barú National Wildlife Refuge** ★ is home to more than 300 bird species, as well as ocelots and jaguarundis. Farther south along the coast near Punta Uvita, **Ballena Marine National Park** ★★★ is superb for spotting whales and dolphins, not to mention roosting egrets along the Río Barú.

But if it's just a nice dip in calm waters you're after, Dominicalito, Playa Hermosa, and the beaches of Ballena Park are wonderful and uncrowded. Playa Uvita is the crown jewel here, 3m (2 miles) of white sand with moderate waves and sparkling blue waters; swimming conditions are ideal and watersports abound. All this is set against scenic creeks, mangrove swamps, and a tombolo that's an echo of Manuel Antonio's Cathedral Point.

Though prices have been edging up, this beautiful coastline is still accessible to all budgets (especially for larger groups, which can take advantage of the burgeoning vacation home rentals). If you're looking for more relaxed, low-key community with top-drawer amenities, this should be where you set up camp on the Central Pacific.

GETTING TO & AROUND DOMINICAL & UVITA
By Bus

The most efficient way to Dominical is via San Isidro del General. Buses leave San José (Calle Central between avs. 22 and 24; ☎ 222-2422) for the 3½-hour trip to San Isidro every hour between 5:30am and 6pm; the fare is $2.75. From San Isidro, you can catch buses (☎ 771-4744) for Dominical at 7am, 9am, 1:30pm, and 4pm (1½ hr., $1.50); to Uvita they're at 9am and 4pm (2 hr., $1.50).

If you're coming down from Quepos/Manuel Antonio, buses (300m/984 ft. south of the court building in Pérez Zeledón on Interamerican Hwy.) leave daily at 5am or 1:30pm for San Isidro, passing through Dominical 2 hours later; the fare's $1.

By Car

From San José, the most direct route is to drive south on the Interamerican Highway (Pan American) 135km (84 miles) to San Isidro, where you turn southwest on 22, which becomes 243 to Dominical. Total drive time should be around 4 hours, and Uvita is just a half-hour farther south down a smooth, paved coastal road.

By Air

The quickest way to get to Uvita is to take a flight directly to Palmar Sur airport and take a taxi north to Uvita. **Nature Air** (☎ 299-6000, 800/235-9272 in the U.S. and Canada; www.natureair.com) has daily hour-long flights leaving San José at 9am and costing $80 each way. Meanwhile, **Sansa** (☎ 221-9414; www.fly sansa.com) charges $72 and takes 45 minutes; flights leave daily at 9:30am.

Getting Around

If you're planning on basing yourself in the area for some time, you'll really want to consider your own wheels. Public transportation isn't great, and while you'll be able to call taxis or catch one around the soccer field in Dominical, the area is spread out, so it's best explored by rental car.

ACCOMODATIONS, BOTH STANDARD & NOT
Vacation Rentals

Unlike Manuel Antonio, Dominical and Uvita are only now getting the onslaught of North American and European second-home buyers. But thankfully, efforts to rein in eco-unfriendly condo complexes by locals and conservationists have paid

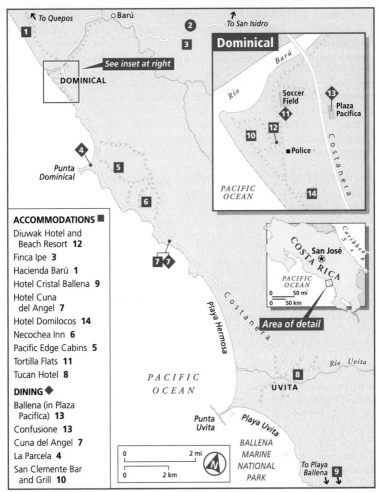

ACCOMMODATIONS ■

Diuwak Hotel and Beach Resort **12**

Finca Ipe **3**

Hacienda Barú **1**

Hotel Cristal Ballena **9**

Hotel Cuna del Angel **7**

Hotel Domilocos **14**

Necochea Inn **6**

Pacific Edge Cabins **5**

Tortilla Flats **11**

Tucan Hotel **8**

DINING ◆

Ballena (in Plaza Pacífica) **13**

Confusione **13**

Cuna del Angel **7**

La Parcela **4**

San Clemente Bar and Grill **10**

off, and there's a better balance between tourism and ecology here; most of the building here has been lower key and higher quality. There's more choice than ever among rentals, and some great deals on villas and bungalows by the beach or up in the hills. Terms and conditions vary—some want security deposits, others have you wire money to bank accounts; most have strict cancellation policies, so keep that in mind when booking. Below is a sampling of the options:

Zec Real Estate and Vacation Rentals (☎ 787-0024; www.zecrealestate.com) manages more than a dozen beachfront and hilltop properties in Dominical, Escaleras, and Uvita. They range from **La Doña del Mar,** a modest, pleasant two-bedroom beach house just off Playa Dominical ($350 a week), to **Casa Pacífico,** an eight-bedroom Mediterreanean-style estate that could make it onto *Lifestyles of* *the Ricos y Famosos* ($6,000 weekly, still cheap compared to what you'd pay in North America or Europe). Some immaculate new homes rent for as little as $75 a night (such as **Villa Las Rocas**).

Dominical Realty (☎ 787-0150; 877/309-9238 in the U.S. and Canada; www.dominicalrealty.com) is a Coldwell Banker affiliate that does mostly sales but also manages around a half-dozen rentals in the Dominical area (possibly many more by the time you read this). They're real homes for real people, not ultraluxe villas, so you'll be able to rent a standard two-bedroom house, equipped to North American standards and usually prettily decorated (colorful linens, bent-iron light fixtures, hammocks on verandas, and so forth), starting at $400 a week.

Ocean Bay (☎ 843-3706; www.oceanbay.biz) offers a pair of one-bedroom apartments with killer Pacific views in a Dominicalito white-stucco condo with A/C, a sprawling upper deck and lower patio, a spacious kitchen, and plush living-room furnishings; the manicured area just off the main road is only a 3-minute walk to the beach. They can be rented separately or together, starting at $700 per week for the upper level, $800 for the lower, and both for $1,400. It's a good option for short stays, because the minimum's only 3 days, at $140 a night.

Finally, **Uvita Realty** (☎ 743-8922; www.uvitarealty.com) is the one of the main real estate offices in the village of Uvita, and specializes in residential sales for Uvita/Ojochal but also does the odd vacation home rental. Check its website for current offerings, or if you're in the area, drop in at its office next door to the Don Israel supermarket to see if there are any last-minute possibilities.

Hotels

In general, the cheaper digs tend to be clustered around Dominical's main drag, and the higher-end hotels, condos, and houses are up in the hills and farther down the coast. Besides saving *dinero,* by staying in or near town you're in walking distance of a slew of bars, restaurants, and an Internet center; the downside is that the beach right here isn't the best for swimming or sunbathing. If you want lushly forested hills and the most dramatic views of the Pacific, head straight to **Escaleras,** perched at the top of the mountains above Dominical and reachable only by four-wheel drive.

IN & AROUND DOMINCIAL

$ Terrific for nature lovers, one of Dominical's more creative digs is also one of its dandiest deals. Scented by the blooms of its ylang-ylang trees, **Finca Ipe** ★ (main road to Playa Dominical, follow the signs and keep your nose poised for the smell of ylang yland flowers; no phone; www.fincaipe.com; cash only) is a 12-hectare (30-acre) organic farm up in the hills, which rents out a trio of freestanding wood cabins that are as charming as all get out, for $225 to $250 per week (or, $32–$36 a night). The treehouse-style "Mothership" and "Mango House," along with the thatch-roofed "Owl's House," all have *magnífico* views and private baths, but don't expect fancy amenities or A/C (the mountain breezes do the job nicely). Now, you can just hang around and use this as you would any lodging, or you can help out on the farm (and get more of a break on the rent).

$ If your ideal vacation is mainly about surfing on the cheap, you'll fit right in at **Tortilla Flats** (on Playa Dominical; ☎ 787-0033; www.tortillaflatsdominical. com; AE, D, MC, V). The unbeatable right-on-the-sand location pulls in surfers, and its 18 wood-paneled *cabinas* create a cozy cabin-in-the-woods feel, but apart from having private baths and A/C they're pretty bare-bones. If the humidity doesn't bother you, try a second-floor room with ocean views (and breezes) but no A/C for $30 instead of $39. Some rooms are newer than others, so ask to see what's available instead of taking the first thing they try to give you. There's a cute beach bar-restaurant here, too, where you can get bargain seafood, *comida típica,* and sandwiches.

$ Personally, if we were looking for the best mix of price ($43, $35 in low season), location, and amenities, it'd probably be the new Dutch-run **Hotel Domilocos** ★ (100m/328 ft. from Playa Dominical; ☎ 787-0244; www.domilocos.net; AE, MC, V). Its 25 rooms have king-size beds, TV, air-conditioning, and room enough to swing a sloth (they can sleep up to four); decor's pleasant if not hugely exciting— pinkish walls and spare, no-nonsense furnishings heavy on rattan. The best thing about the place is the open-air restaurant Confusione, which does a great job with authentic and terrific Italian fare like tuna carpaccio, mushroom risotto, and more (p. 183). The main drag and the beach are right nearby.

$$ The name ("sun people" in the indigenous BriBri language) pretty much sums up the clientele at the Castro Murillo family's **Diuwak Hotel and Beach Resort** 〔kids〕 (on main strip of Playa Dominical; ☎ 787-0087; www.diuwak.com; AE, MC, V). There they are, tanning at the big pool with its big burbling waterfall, in the Jacuzzi, in the lush gardens; and of course at the beach, just over 45m (150 ft.) away. Diuwak keeps up the BriBri theme with tribal statues and sculptures throughout, but otherwise it's basically a ranch-style complex with a rough-hewn log veranda and chairs. The 18 rooms have a funky, tropical vibe and are big enough for families, with stark white walls, brightly colored bedspreads, and exposed beam ceilings. By the time you read this, there will also be four upstairs suites with pool views, so ask for those first. In-season rates start at $65 with fans, $69 with A/C, including breakfast (if you're not a breakfast person, you can sub-tract $10 night).

$$ Another great deal for nature boys, girls, moms, and dads, **Hacienda Barú** ★★ 〔kids〕 (1km/⅔ mile north of Dominical; ☎ 787-0003; www.haciendabaru.com; AE, D, MC, V) is nestled in a 3.2–sq.-km (1¼-sq.-mile) reserve teeming with wildlife; it's a fun spot for families looking for a little beach action, a little eco, and a little adventure all in one. There are hiking trails (tours both guided and self-guided), a secluded stretch of beach, a butterfly garden, an orchid garden, even a zipline ($35). You stay in one of the half-dozen cabins with white-washed walls, plush bamboo furniture, kitchenette, and fan—but no air-conditioning, TV, or phones. The staff is great, the restaurant good, and cabins start at $60 for two, $70 for three (including breakfast; kids younger than 10 free). A top choice in the area.

$$$$ If you're looking for a little more full-service pampering, the recently opened **Cuna del Angel** ★★ (9km/5½ miles south of Dominical on the coastal road, 50m/164 ft. from the ocean; ☎ 222-0704; www.cunadelangel.com; AE, MC, V) is worth a splurge in our book. This boutique resort–cum–country club owned by a German expat 1.7km (5½ miles) south of town has a look based on Boruca indigenous ceremonial dwellings, but inside it feels a more like Italian villa meets Las Vegas; in the 16 airy, amenity-laden rooms, floors are inlaid with stone, beds have beautifully embroidered comforters, and there are floor-to-ceiling windows and balustraded balconies. The grounds are lush (you'll spot monkeys and toucans), and there's a gigantic infinity pool, a state-of-the-art spa, and a dining room that's the area's top culinary experience (p. 184). Doubles start at $153, but parents will pay $10 extra a night for children staying with them; according to management, they don't consider the resort, with its fine furnishings and terrain, "suitable" for kids younger than 16.

IN & AROUND ESCALERAS

$$ If "away from it all with drop-dead ocean and valley views" sounds like just the ticket, **Pacific Edge Cabins** ★ (Dominicalito, Km 148, just after the small bridge; ☎ 787-8010; www.pacificedge.info; AE, MC, V), 5km (3 miles) south of Dominical on a ridge of Costa Rica's highest mountain, Chirripó, may be the place for you. Lots of guests spend lots of time just drinking in the vistas (like the sunsets from your hammock or one of the oversize balcony/deck areas). You can go birding (more than 800 species have been logged on the property), take a swim in the pool, or spot howler monkeys from the observation deck. As a place to stay, it has a homier ambiance than most, thanks to chatty owners George and Susan Atkinson, who love trading tales with guests over breakfast or dinner in the open-air bamboo dining room. The four cabins are rustic but appealing, their all-wood interiors livened up with pink and purple linens and curtains in native designs (there's no A/C, but trust us, the nights are pretty cool up here); rates start at $50 a night (10 percent off if you stay more than 4 days). Only children 12 and up are welcome.

$$–$$$ Nestled in the Escaleras woods, the stylish, intimate **Necochea Inn** ★★ (2 km/1¼ miles from coast road Bella Vista exit; ☎ 395-2984; www.thenecochea inn.com; MC, V) is a B&B that's a couple of notches up Pacific Edge, amenities-wise. It's a modern hacienda-style home with five spacious guest rooms, each with a large private balcony jutting out into the rainforest (two share a bath); our favorite is the Macaw Room, with its wooden sleigh bed and big dark-wood armoire. There is a small outdoor pool and sundecks that terrace down to a beautiful natural spring. Downstairs there's a library, game room and intimate, marble-laid bar. At $75 a night for a double and $125 for the suite, including breakfast, it's an affordable, scenic slice of civility in this increasingly pricey area.

IN & AROUND UVITA

Apart from the obvious attraction of its eye-candy beaches and the Ballena Marine National Park, what we love about this area is its quiet, unpopulated feel. The village of Uvita has just the bare essentials, with one decent grocery store, a hardware store, a couple of Internet cafes, a gas station, and just a handful of restaurants. If "secluded" and "sleepy" are adjectives that speak to you, well, c'mon down. Right next door is the village of **Bahía,** a popular vacation spot for Ticos, many of whom camp near the beach. Another dozen miles down the paved road, the town of **Ojochal** has ended up with a sizable French-Canadian expat community (no, we haven't quite figured out *pourquoi*), and communications are by satellite phone or the one public phone in the town's convenience store.

In addition to the option listed below, there are over a dozen cheap *cabinas* around town that charge from $10 to $30 a night, with **The Tucan Hotel** (across from Ebais; ☎ 743-8140; www.tucanhotel.com) being the backpacker and budget favorite (dorm beds $8–$10, private rooms $18–$25). You can find more at www.uvita.biz.

$$–$$$$ Yes, it's a fancy, full-service luxury resort, but Playa Ballena's recently opened **Hotel Cristal Ballena** ✹✹ (7km/4⅓ miles south of Uvita; ☎ 786-5354, 888/790-5264 in the U.S. and Canada; www.cristal-ballena.com; AE, MC, V) also has four reduced-rate ($64–$73) "adventure lodges"—upscale-rustic units with handsome four-posters, dark hardwood floors, terraces, electricity, ceiling fans, and a mosquito-netting-draped king bed. If you want to splurge, of course, the 19 "suites" (from $159) are the way to go, with all the bells and whistles including air-conditioning, Wi-Fi, and fab Pacific views. Ringed with traveler palms, the 12-hectare (30-acre) spread is a beaut; the open-air poolside restaurant does an elegant job with both local and international fare, and just get a load of that infinity pool—a whopping 400 sq. m (4,300 sq. feet)—you could practically stage a naval battle on that sucker!

DINING FOR ALL TASTES

Yeah, things are certainly coming along in Dominical, Uvita, and Ojochal, but we've gotta say, the dining scene is only beginning to catch up. In Dominical, it's split between *sodas* and casual surfer joints on the main strip and higher-end affairs outside town. In Uvita, options are limited to *sodas* (particularly in neighboring Bahía) and hotel restaurants. In Ojochal, all those French-Canadians means a good smattering of continental eateries and bakeries; the new **La Palmeraie** (open weekends only) and **Chez-Elle** in particular have been developing foodie followings.

$ You won't need more than a bathing suit and flip-flops at the **San Clemente Bar and Grill** ✹ (Dominical main drag; ☎ 787-0055; daily 7am–10pm; AE, D, MC, V), a quintessential surfer hang-out, and also a social center for both tourists and Ticos, with a foosball and a pool table, darts, and cable TV. Decor is 1960s surf regalia, with old and busted boards lining the ceiling and walls. You eat outside at wooden picnic tables under a thatched roof, and the chow's a mix between gringo and Tico staples (can't go wrong with the fresh seafood); whatever you order, it'll never cost more than $5. Try their fresh fruit *batidos* ($1.80), as well as owner Mike McGinnis's special sauces.

$ **Ballena** (on the coastal road, in Plaza Pacifica mall; ☎ 787-0125; hours vary; cash only) is essentially an open-air bar restaurant, and your next best bet for good, cheap Tico comfort food—chicken and rice ($5), ceviche ($2), *casado* plates ($5). It's unpretentious, friendly, and quick, and sometimes that's what you need from a meal.

$$ Several cuts above most everything else in town, the open-air **Confusione** ✹✹ (☎ 787-0244; www.domilocos.net; daily 3–11:30pm; AE, D, MC, V) in the Hotel

Domilocos has wicker bistro appointments and two first-class chefs, who create an extensive and actually pretty unconfusing menu of really good and authentic Italian fare. Start with succulent mushrooms stuffed with gorgonzola and tomatoes ($5), then move on to jumbo shrimp in brandy sauce ($12), or any one of the old-country-style pizzas ($7–$8 for margherita or *quattro stagioni*).

$$ Cuna del Angel ✫✫ (off the coastal highway near Playa Hermosa, 8km/ 5 miles south of Kiana Resorts; ☎ 787-8012; www.cunadelangel.com; daily 6:30–9:30pm; AE, D, MC, V), in the resort of the same name (p. 181), Confusione's main competition food-wise. In terms of decor, however, it's the closest thing to a truly upscale dining experience in the area. From this spacious two-story traditional-style *palapa*-roof rancho with indoor and outdoor seating (try to get a balcony table), the views of jungle and beach are fabulous and so is the constantly changing nouvelle-cuisine (one of our recent favorites was robalo in a mushroom basil sauce with anchovies for $10; the tagliatelle with gorgonzola sauce and veggies was also a delight).

$$–$$$$ Ocean views over a rocky bluff and gourmet-quality grub have been the main draws at **La Parcela** ✫ (Punta Dominical; ☎ 787-0016; daily 7:30am–9pm; AE, D, MC, V) since it opened way back in 1972 at the end of a small point of land surrounded by water. It's just a perfect spot to savor the sunset and have a romantic dinner—superbly prepared mahimahi ($8) served on a white tablecloth is definitely worth a splurge. Head waiter Rodolfo, a local fisherman, has worked the dining room for more than 20 years and is an essential part of the experience. Bend his ear about what looks good, and oftentimes it'll be something he caught that morning. Entrees run $4 to $20, with a splurge dish or two at $30. Reservations are recommended.

WHY YOU'RE HERE: THE TOP SIGHTS & ATTRACTIONS
The Beaches

Wow, where do we start—whether you're here to hang ten, for a morning swim, kayaking, or just ogling the coastline, there's tons to see and do along this 10-mile stretch. As with much of the Central Pacific, surf camps and outfits are all over the place. For surf packages, lessons and rentals, the main ones are **Green Iguana Surf Camp** (☎ 825-1381; www.greeniguanasurfcamp.com) and **Costa Rica Surf School** (☎ 812-3625; www.crsurfschool.com). Okay, now here goes with the main beaches, from north to south.

In town, **Playa Dominical** is a long stretch known mostly for surfing, with consistent waist-high breaks right by the shore. At any given time you can find at least a dozen 'boarders in the water, some of whom gather toward the southern end where the larger swells are. But since the surf is so strong so close in, and the beach is narrow and unshaded, this isn't really the best spot for swimming or even sunbathing—and most certainly not a good idea for kids. Just a couple of miles or so south, **Playa Dominicalito** ✫ is 2km (1¼ miles) of sand with **impressive rock formations** and tide pools at either end—much better for families.

Playa Hermosa ✫ seems to go on forever, with miles of packed sand perfect for a jog or a stroll without another soul in sight. Its northern end is a little pebbly, but popular with beginner surfers; farther south it gets flatter and sandy. If you're coming by car, you'll need to enter towards the northern end; farther south there's a sign-posted entrance, then you'll walk 10 minutes along a trail through the vegetation.

The next beach down the coast, scenic **Playa Uvita** ✭, is known for a "whale tail" formation at its northern end, where a tombolo connects Punta Uvita to the mainland. The best time to go is of course at low tide, when the half-mile-long sandbar is exposed and waves gently lap at both sides. At the tip toward the point, you can take in layers of coral rock and the long sweep of Playa Hermosa off to the north and Uvita to the south. Depending on the water conditions, it's worth bringing your **snorkel** gear out here to float around the reef a bit.

All the beaches south of Uvita, with the exception of **Playa Tortuga,** are part of Ballena National Marine Park. The first beach south of Playa Uvita is **Playa La Colonia** ✭, a long strand ending in a rocky formation where waves break. This is one of the best beaches for **families** with small children, since there are many shallow, calm areas both on the beach and in a small stream that empties into the sea. It's also ideal for a **picnic** thanks to the stone picnic tables and chairs. Unless you're a fan of crowds or are interested in seeing how Ticos vacation, avoid Sundays and holidays, when families pack La Colonia for a day-long party with loud music and lots of kids running around. Also, on those days, there's an attendant at the park entrance gate, where you'll have to pay $6 (for locals it's $1.20).

If you're hankering for a real castaway-island feel, head to the small, slightly less than easily accessible **Playa Arco.** You can't drive to it, but need to walk along a short trail over the headland at the north end of Playa Ballena. You can almost always count on having the whole beach, which is tropical-postcard-perfect, complete with monkeys, little waterfalls, and a dramatic, almost perpendicular cliff that rises right up from the sand. The best time to visit is an hour before or after low tide; check with the park staff about tide conditions.

Playa Ballena is another stroller's paradise—long, gleaming white, its foliage teeming with wildlife, particularly birds. As you walk, you'll be able to see Isla Ballena off in the distance, but park staff tells us it's a bad idea to wade in the water past waist level because of strong riptides. Since this beach is administered by the park, you'll again have to pay $6 to get in, but an upside is that the facilities include outdoor showers, picnic tables, and trash bins.

At the southernmost end of the Ballena National Marine Park, **Playa Piñuelas** ✭ has waters so calm that it's a natural harbor. That means there are always a bunch of small fishing boats (photo op!), and it's ideal for splashing around. From the shore you'll get views of the Tres Hermanas (Three Sisters) rock formation a little ways off, as well as the Isla Ballena. Because of its popularity among fishermen, this is a good place to **buy fresh seafood,** or **charter a sport fishing excursion.** Again, it's part of the park, so that $6 applies here.

The last on this stretch of coast is **Playa Tortuga,** a breathtaking sugar-white strand where you'll occasionally sight whales, dolphins, and of course turtles (*tortugas*). The other big thing here is kayaking the mangrove-lined estuaries (see below, p. 187).

Exploring Nature

Though most visitors come to Dominical and Uvita mainly for the beaches, the lushly forested slopes and mangrove-lined waterways along the coast give a wonderful added eco-dimension to your "fun-in-the-sun" vacation. If you haven't already gotten to **Manuel Antonio National Park** (p. 173), it's a pretty easy day trip—an hour-long drive from Dominical on a bumpy dirt road.

You'll also want to head to the 54-sq.-km (21-sq.-mile) **Parque Nacional Ballena Marina** ✫✫✫ (26km/16 miles south of Dominical; no phone; www.costarica-nationalparks.com/ballenanationalmarinepark.html; park station 8am–4pm; $6), home to Costa Rica's largest coral reef. This marine-based wildlife wonderland established in 1990 stretches from Playa Hermosa to Playa Piñuela and stretches some 15km (9 miles) into the Pacific, including Ballena Island. Its beaches (see above) are still relatively pristine and secluded, and if you stay long enough you may spot a **green marine iguana** (*iguana verde*) feeding on algae in the saltwater pools.

All this water means a sterling chance to experience some super **snorkeling** (though if you have the time and are up for a splurge, I'd take the trip out to **Isla de Caño** ✫✫, which has the country's best snorkeling (see p. 225). A word to the wise: Go during the drier times of year, because rain makes the waters murky. We'd also recommend taking a boat trip, since the parts of the reef where you'll see the most interesting fish are not really reachable from shore. Many of the outfitters in the area combine both a snorkeling and whale-watching tour, and any hotel should be able to book for you; otherwise, call one of the best outfitters, **Mystic Dive Center** (☎ 788-8636; www.mysticdivecenter.com), which charges $55 for a morning or afternoon.

These waters are also breeding and calving grounds for both North American and South American whales including **humpback** (Dec–Apr) and **sperm whales,** as well as **striped** and **spinner dolphins** (Sept–Oct). Here you'll definitely need to take a boat trip out, and even so, with an experienced guide, they'll be tricky to track and there are never any guarantees, even in peak season. A typical tour will take you out reasonably far offshore, west and south, and there's a lot of down time waiting for a whale to appear. But when it finally does, it's a stunner—off in the distance, you might glimpse a blowing spurt of water, followed by the arc of a humpback. Then it might be another good while before a fin surfaces, or a

---

A Beach That Really Rocks

You won't want to miss the **impressive grottoes and natural tunnels** on **Playa Ventanas** ✫✫✫, just south of Ballena. A small, palm-ringed crescent bay with fine sand, it's nice for swimming and wading, but the star attraction is the grottoes in the soaring, forest-covered limestone cliffs (*ventanas* means windows in Spanish, so the name comes from these "windows" to the sea). These huge arches and tunnels were formed over thousands of years, and you can get to them at low tide; some take you through long, dark, eerie tunnels to the ocean. You can also take kayak tours through here, though you'll probably want to have some decent experience in sea kayaking.

Turtle Beach

Olive Ridley and hawksbill turtles come to nest on Playa Tortuga from May to October, though not in the impressive numbers you'll see on the Caribbean coast. If you want to see the turtles nest, you'll want to at least talk to the rangers at park offices to find out where to go for the best views. You may also want to check in with the volunteers you'll see helping the national park rangers patrolling the beaches so that they'll know you're not a poacher.

blowhole spouts. These encounters, however, don't come terribly cheap: one popular outfitter, **Southern Expeditions** (☎ 787-0100; www.southernexpeditionscr. com) charges $90 for its 6am to 4:30pm excursion, and most others will cost no less than $60.

Many *fincas* (farms) offer day and overnight **hikes on foot or by horseback** through forests, orchards, and along the sandy shores. Experiencing the rainforests on horseback is one of our favorite things—it lets you cover more ground and greater heights. Waterfall tours are often done by horse and usually end with a dip in the natural pools below. For example, for $45 **Bella Vista Lodge** (2km/1¼ miles up Escaleras Rd. from Dominical; ☎ 787-8069 or 877/268-2916 in the U.S.; www. bellavistalodge.com) will take you on a 6- to 7-hour outing into the Escaleras mountains on tame, surefooted Berber horses and through 90m (300-ft.) Barú Falls. You then cross the river on an aerial tram and hike briefly along the ridge for some breathtaking views. Lunch is prepared on-site by your guide.

For mounted tours of the impressive **Nauyaca Waterfalls** we'd recommend **Don Lulo's Horseback Tours** ★ (☎ 787-8013; www.cataratasnauyaca.com), run by the local Jimenez-Solis family of experienced guides. After an hour-long horseback ride, you'll get a homemade breakfast at their house and meet some of the animals at the mini-zoo next door—parrots, toucans, chickens, and large rodents. Then it's off to the falls where you spend most of your time swimming, diving into the clear pools, or just exploring the area. There's another stop at the home for lunch, and maybe some live music from the family.

A **kayaking** tour is one of the most fun ways to explore the national park's beaches and marine life. **Flying Dutchman River Tours** (☎ 786-5074), at the Hotel Posada del Tortuga, runs top-quality mangrove kayaking at the more than fair price of $30. During the 2-hour trip you'll spot boa constrictors, egrets, spoonbills, crocodiles, white-faced monkeys, and crab-eating raccoons, with commentary from guides who are terrifically knowledgeable about the area's geology and wildlife. **Rafiki Safari Lodge** (☎ 777-2250); www.rafikisafari.com) will take you up the Savegre River by kayak or for whitewater rafting. You'll snake through waterfalls and canyons, take dips (intentional or not) in natural pools, and cross the river's high-suspension bridge for treetop views. Lunch and gear are included and there are classes and tours for all levels, with prices varying depending on the package.

Just Sing, Sing a Song

Even if you don't end up seeing a humpback whale, you may just end up hearing one. If you're snorkeling, scuba diving, or swimming in the waters of Ballena Marina National Park, there's a definite chance to catch a snatch of the humpback's song—one of nature's most sublime, primordial, and unique sounds.

Only the males make these sounds, and scientists still aren't sure whether the point is to attract the gals, to ward off other dudes, or for another entirely different reason. Each "song" is usually 6 to 15 minutes of long groans, low moans, roars, chirps, and other trilling sounds, in repeating patterns. After the last in the series, the singer surfaces to breathe, before starting the song again. Sometimes it can last for hours.

At any given time, all the males in the pod sing the same song, but patterns and sequences can evolve and change over time. Though the song will likely be completely different a few years on, all the singers will still be on the same page of the choir book. It's one of nature's more amazing and moving mysteries.

If you scuba, the finest outfitter is the same one that runs the snorkel tours, **Mystic Dive Center** ✦ (☎ 788-8636; www.mysticdivecenter.com), based in the Centro Comercial Ventanas, a strip mall down near Ojochal. It offers scuba lessons and expeditions out to Isla de Caño (See p. 225 for more on the island and its pre-Columbian spheres), relaxed affairs that let you explore at your own pace (but guides will point you in the right direction when there's something neat to see). Caño is known for its teeming waters: Look out for surgeon fish, puffers, eels, rays, and the intimidating but nonaggressive reef shark. After lunch, take some time to explore the jungle island.

If you've had enough of the water, bird-watching is a year-round pursuit hereabouts, with more than 600 species logged. **Hacienda Barú** ✦✦ (☎ 787-0003; www.haciendabaru.com) and its wildlife refuge run both lowland and rainforest birding hikes at $35 each; both tours provide breakfast at La Casona, the old Hacienda Barú home. The 6-hour lowland circuit will take you through the mangrove estuary to observe shorebirds. The rainforest tour begins at daybreak and will take you through old cocao plantations deep into the jungle, serve a trail breakfast, then go on to track some of the area's more elusive birds like trogons, mot-mots, and curasows. This is not necessarily a kid-friendly activity as it requires a lot of patience and sssshhhh!

If you'd rather have your varmints served up a little more conveniently, the recently opened **Parque Reptilandia** ✦✦ 🅺 (7km/4¾ miles south of Dominical on San Isidro Rd.; ☎ 787-8007; www.dominical.biz/reptiles; daily 9am–4:30pm; $10, students $3, kids under 12 $1) gives visitors the chance to get a good close look at the local snakes, crocodiles, and amphibians like poison-dart frogs (there's a resident komodo dragon, too, even if she's an import from Indonesia). You see them in 55 glass-enclosed terrariums and ponds on a little more than an acre. Wide, flat walking paths make it wheelchair accessible, and a self-guided tour in English and Spanish means you can explore at your own pace. Night tours are also available with advance reservation.

ATTENTION, SHOPPERS!

There's not much of it in this part of the Central Pacific coast. The Plaza Pacífica mall in Dominical's main strip has a few chances to drop a few bucks, most notably at **Banana Bay Gallery & Gifts** (☎ 787-0106; daily 9am–5pm), which stocks a variety of local art, indigenous crafts (Boruca masks), wooden crafts, and the usual trinkets and toys.

Your only other option for retail therapy is to head down to the beach. Some local merchants sell things like handmade jewelry and sarongs at tables on the sand, and bargaining is expected. If you're staying in a rental or have a room with a kitchenette, you might consider stopping at one of the roadside vendors to buy some fresh seafood (just look for signs saying *SE VENDE PESCADO*).

NIGHTLIFE

With the exception of Dominical, a surfer town (and therefore party central), there's not much of a nightlife scene elsewhere. Most folks come to "chill," and the usual night out most like means a relaxing meal at a nice restaurant.

But if you do want to find a crowd, hit the popular surf bars on Dominical's main strip. The **San Clemente Bar & Grill** (next to the soccer field; ☎ 787-0055; daily 7am–10pm) is a popular Friday-night hang-out with drink specials, pool, and Ping-Pong tables, and a big-screen TV playing mostly videos and sports. Among the other surfer hangs, **Tortilla Flats** (p. 181) has a lively happy hour with cheap drinks and snacks, while **Thrusters** (30m/98 ft. south of police station; ☎ 787-0127; daily 7am–2am) is open late and has pool, darts, and a bar menu of burritos and pizzas. On Sundays there's a karaoke night at **El Coco** (across from Thrusters; ☎ 787-0235; restaurant daily 8am–midnight). For dance action, head for the **Hotel Roca Verde Bar & Restaurant** ★ (main road 1km/⅔ mile south of town; ☎ 787-0036; www.rocaverde.net; hours vary), which has the

---

Super-Duper Fly

Every hotel touts its amazing views of the Pacific, but for an unbeatable bird's-eye view—along with an adrenaline rush—**Skyline Nature Ultra Flight** (☎ 743-8037; www.flyultralight.com) runs tours of the marine park in an ultralight two-seater. You'll get to gaze down on the coral reefs and spectacular coastline dotted with rock formations like Isla Ballena and Las Tres Hermanas. Or, if you're up for it, sign up for a 20-minute thrill ride where you fly the plane (well, with an experienced pilot on tandem controls). Prices start at $65, and special tours of the region go for $150 an hour.

area's hottest disco every Saturday night; the following afternoon, it has a mariachi band with a barbecue lunch.

Fans of live tunes will want to cruise over to the rastafarian **Restaurante Guachacha** (25m/82 ft. from Playa Dominical; ☎ 787-0313; hours vary), which has live reggae. **Jazzy's River House** (on river in Dominical, next to the market; ☎ 787-0310; hours vary) also stages myriad types of live performances—reggae, Latin, jazz, blues—at least twice a week, but only on Wednesdays and Saturdays, after sunset.

THE "OTHER" DOMINICAL & UVITA

As they say, to meet the locals, do like they do. One activity that draws a great mix of both expats and Ticos is the potluck movie nights at the **Cinema Escaleras** (south from Dominical, turn left at soccer field, go around and then through the river, and up Poza Azul road to the third Marina Vista gate; ☎ 787-8065). The open-air theater, perched on a mountain 300m (1,000 ft.) above the Pacific, was started in 2003 by a pair of American transplants with a mission to "turn on all the gringos and Ticos to some of the best movies of the last hundred years." Things get rolling every Friday night at 5pm with a sunset potluck dinner. At 6pm the lights go out, and a movie plays on a 4.2m-wide (14-ft.) screen (a lot of classics, like *20,000 Leagues Under the Sea* and *Cleopatra* with Elizabeth Taylor and Richard Burton). Every other Saturday night, the theater screens a Spanish-language film, although it may just be a dubbed Hollywood flick. Admission is technically free, but contributions of 2,000 *colones* ($3.85) are encouraged, mainly to cover the cost of projector bulbs and popcorn.

Another community-oriented outing centers on the area's own English-language theater. Running out of the Hotel Roca Verde (p. 189), **The Dominical Theater** (☎ 308-8855 or 787-8007; dominical_theatre@yahoo.com) stages productions throughout the high season. In 2006 it was *The Female Odd Couple,* a twist on the classic Neil Simon play; previous years saw *The Fantastiks* and *South Pacific.* On performance nights, there's a cocktail hour at 5:30pm, with curtain up at 7pm. Ticket prices start at $5 and go up to $20 for certain reserved seats.

Jazzy's River House (above), apart from its twice-weekly live music, holds morning "Tropical Yoga" classes popular with expats, which include a blend of hatha yoga, tai chi, and aikido. They're held every Monday, Wednesday, and Friday at 6:30am, and the cost is $2. While there, you might even consider signing up for a half-day basket-weaving workshop (we're serious!) along the banks of the Barú river, taught by local fixture Ruby Kim, an organic gardener, farmer, and "plant artist" (which means she creates art from local materials like bamboo and royal palm). Ms. Kim learned her skills in the Pacific Northwestern United States, but has been living in Costa Rica for over 30 years. The cost is $30 per class and it's a lot of fun, and good for kids over 10.

Another way to connect to the local community, and experience Dominical on the cheap, is to spend a stint volunteering at the **Finca Ipe** (p. 180), an organic farm up in the mountains. Ipe offers nature lovers a chance to get their hands dirty and to earn their keep in one of the shared rooms or get discounts on the private bungalows. Volunteers come from all over, including the U.S., U.K., Canada, and Germany, and spend most of their time working in the gardens, weeding, harvesting, digging, mulching, making compost, clearing out the animal housing, helping with essential oil production, trail building, and making preps; they're provided with staples such as rice, beans, pasta, and fresh produce. You'll end up working a maximum of 5 hours a day, Monday through Friday, usually from 6:30 to 11am. One big bonus is that you'll be meeting many locals and practicing Spanish much of the time at communal dinners and out in the gardens. The cost varies; the longer you stay, the less you pay. For example, for fewer than 7 days it's $20 per person per day; for a week or more it's $15.

6 The Osa Peninsula

Way down south, Costa Rica's last frontier is its mind-blowing ultimate in ecotourism.

by David Appell & Nelson Mui

THERE ARE PARTS OF THE WORLD THAT, DUE TO THEIR ISOLATION AND lore, have achieved near-mythical status. The Sahara. The Himalayas. The Amazon. Patagonia. Siberia. All capture the imagination with visions of nature at its most extreme. Making them more all the more exotic is the fact that few of us are likely to go there.

Though much smaller, a little closer, and far from a household name, we'd say the Pacific Coast's nearly untouristed Osa Peninsula is this kind of destination. The star of Costa Rica's so-called Southern Zone, down the coast from Manuel Antonio, this remote, wet, jungled hook of land looks like a smaller echo of the Nicoya Peninsula up in Guanacaste—but much, much wilder. A few indigenous tribes whose ancestors survived the Spanish conquistadors still live here, but to this day settlement is pretty darn sparse, and a good chunk of the Osa is taken up by the Corcovado National Park, whose primeval wet rainforest offers some of the planet's best wildlife-spotting (*National Geographic* once famously dubbed the area the "most biologically intense on earth").

Yep, just 1,600 sq. km or so (625 sq. miles) are home to 2½ percent of the world's biodiversity—that adds up to more than 400 bird species (the U.S. has only half that), more than 3,100 plant species, 600 of insects, about 125 of mammals. Some of these are found nowhere else, and a few have just been recently discovered. And unlike even the most famous reserves in other parts of Costa Rica—Monteverde, Tortuguero, Manuel Antonio—you don't have to wait and squint to spot a critter or two. Here they're right in your face and come right at you: scarlet macaws swooping and squawking overhead, electric blue morpho butterflies fluttering past your shoulder as you walk; Jesus Christ lizards zipping across your path; sloths hanging from branches a couple of feet away; giant toads sitting on your ecolodge terrace. You don't even have to try.

Of course, in exchange for that, the Osa's a bit more of a schlep—and overall, a bit more expensive to visit than other parts of the country. That's changing a little, with new roads and a new airport on the way making it easier to get here, and more lodging at all price levels coming online. Naturally this means the usual growing pains for local communities, but so far they've managed to keep their eye on the ball of "sustainable" development: to avoid turning this amazing land into another cheesy coastful of golf courses and beach resorts. And a lot of that, we think, has to do with the people who call the peninsula home. Apart from being blown away by the spectacular nature here, we also came away with a deep admiration for the warmth, conservationist spirit, and sense of community of the Osa residents. For us, these folks and region really capture the essence of Costa Rica, and made us feel hopeful about its future.

DON'T LEAVE THE OSA WITHOUT . . .

TAKING A HIKE THROUGH THE TROPICAL RAINFOREST   Whether on one of Corcovado's trails or through one of the Osa's many public and private reserves, you'll likely see more birds, monkeys, amphibians, and mammals than anywhere else in Costa Rica. Not to mention a waterfall or two along the way.

GOING DOLPHIN- & WHALE-WATCHING   Go out on the Golfo Dulce or Drake Bay to get up close and personal with Flipper and friends. You can no longer swim with them, but depending on the day and season, you'll spot pods galore.

SNORKELING OR DIVING OFF THE COAST OF CAÑO ISLAND Simply Costa Rica's best snorkel and scuba spot (after the expensive Coco Island, almost 322km/200 miles offshore). Caño was a burial site for indigenous people, so you can check out mysterious stone spheres and other pre-Columbian artifacts on your way to the coral reefs.

SPOTTING A WILDCAT IN CORCOVADO   It's a trek, but if you make it to one of the rugged trails of Costa Rica's most untamed national parks, you'll be in wildcat territory. You probably won't spot a jaguar—but a puma? Here, kitty, kitty . . . .

KAYAKING IN THE MANGROVES   In the mangrove-lined waterways in the Platanares River or the Esquinas River into Piedras Blancas National Park, it's like a tropical-adventure version of Amsterdam or Venice (cue the gondola—"*O, mangrovia mia . . . .*"

A BRIEF HISTORY

Before the last ice age 20,000 years ago connected it to the mainland, part of the Osa Peninsula was literally an island, but the theme of remoteness and isolation has held all down through the millennia since. Its tough climate and terrain (plus a few other factors like yellow fever) discouraged most people from settling here, with the exception of the Diquis tribes; they managed to eke out an existence around Palmar and on the Isla del Caño before being decimated by diseases brought by the Spaniards.

The new colonizers also had a rough time of it—in fact, the Osa got a whiff of an Australia-like frontier/penal colony reputation, with exiles sent into the wilds with machetes and orders never to return. A little later, in the early 20th century, the famous (and infamous) United Fruit Company set up shop harvesting bananas, but they weren't the only new settlers at that time: It turned out there was gold in them thar jungles—a gold rush in the 1930s brought a wave of immigrants to the Osa's main town, Puerto Jiménez. But things didn't really pick up in what you'd call a "major" way until the Interamerican Highway arrived in the Southern Zone in the 1950s. In the next decade, droves of scientists and other researchers descended up on the region. Also around this time, lumber barons discovered gold in the massive swathes of virgin forestland, and enthusiastically set to hacking it down. Until, that is, conservationists banded together and pushed the government to set up Corcovado National Park in 1975. Several hundred settler families and livestock were relocated, but outside the park, the deforestation kept roaring along, so another 20 percent was added to Corcovado in 1980.

By the mid-1980s, banana prices had collapsed, United Fruit pulled out, and thousands of people lost jobs as plantations shut down. Many of them streamed into the park to prospect for gold, and the government again had to step in to get them out of there. To this day, there are still pockets around the peninsula where a few miners are still doing their thing—some even own land, and the possibility of that land being sold to developers continues to keep local conservationists on edge.

But these days, more and more Osa residents have turned to panning for green gold—that is, ecotourism. A few, mostly foreign-owned ecolodges have sprung up, and former *campesinos* (farm workers) have converted to the conservation cause and retrained themselves as nature guides. Inevitably, too, the foreign expat community has been growing—buying land, building homes, and starting businesses. Just 20 years ago, the town of Puerto Jiménez barely had electricity; today, there's an American school next to the library, across from the soccer field.

How much are Ticos benefiting from all this? It's hard to say exactly, but clearly some are—and in any case, tourism and development are still in their very early stages, meaning that at least some of the errors made elsewhere in the country might be avoided here. In the meantime, the Osa's back-of-beyond remoteness suits its fans just fine, and means that visitors can still experience the real deal: seeing unspoiled nature in the reserves, visiting some of the indigenous peoples, and getting a taste of frontier flavor from the former and current gold prospectors still knocking around these parts.

LAY OF THE LAND

The Osa Peninsula can be generally divided into several distinct areas based on terrain and how to get there.

DRAKE BAY

This rugged, remote area up north has a scenically rocky coastline and a bay teeming with aquatic critters, including at least 20 species of dolphins and whales. There are a bunch of mostly self-contained ecolodges dotted throughout the area, which serve as bases for excursions into Corcovado National Park and out to the Isla de Caño, a small forested island with crystal-clear water awesome for snorkeling and scuba. (Also out here are a few hundred mysterious stone spheres—some more than 1.8m/6 ft. around—sculpted in pre-Columbian times.) The permanent population barely reaches a thousand, and up till now the only ways in and

Osa Peninsula/Corcovado National Park

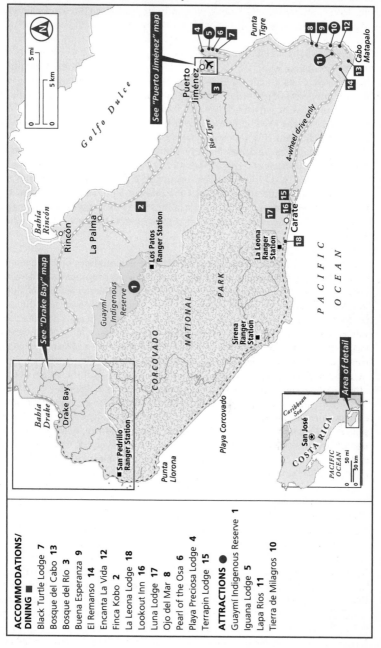

ACCOMMODATIONS/
DINING ■

Black Turtle Lodge **7**
Bosque del Cabo **13**
Bosque del Río **3**
Buena Esperanza **9**
El Remanso **14**
Encanta La Vida **12**
Finca Kobo **2**
La Leona Lodge **18**
Lookout Inn **16**
Luna Lodge **17**
Ojo del Mar **8**
Pearl of the Osa **6**
Playa Preciosa Lodge **4**
Terrapin Lodge **15**

ATTRACTIONS ●

Guaymí Indigenous Reserve **1**
Iguana Lodge **5**
Lapa Ríos **11**
Tierra de Milagros **10**

out have been by boat (as more development and infrastructure comes in, that's likely to change on the soon side).

PUERTO JIMENEZ AREA

A former gold-rush port on the Golfo Dulce—still pretty raw, not much more than a gravel-strewn main street—Puerto Jimenez is the Osa's largest town, and the primary jump-off point for exploring the peninsula, including Corcovado. As recently as 20 years ago, there was no electricity and not much else, but these days, it's turned into the local hub for everyone on down the coast to Carate for picking up supplies, running tour operations, banking, and so forth. There's an air strip here, and a *lancha* comes in every day from the town of Golfito across the gulf, disgorging people and cargo. About 5 to 10 minutes south of Puerto Jimenez is Playa Platanares, a mostly deserted beach just dandy for swimming, and now home to a number of beachfront hotels and cabinas. Some tourists make pit stops through Puerto Jiménez and Platanares, as they make their way down the coast to Matapalo and Carate, where one of the three entrances to Corcovado is located.

MATAPALO & CARATE

One to two hours south of Puerto Jiménez, the communities of Matapalo and Carate are set amid primary rainforest with spectacular mountains and valleys, waterfalls, and wildlife. Many of the guided excursions organized out of Puerto Jiménez head here, and two of Costa Rica's best-known ecolodges, Lapa Ríos and Bosque del Cabo, maintain thousands of acres hereabouts. There are no stores, services, telephones, or Internet (most everybody communicates by radio). Matapalo is the peninsula's main surfing destination, and home to a growing expatriate community. Over here, in one of the most remote parts of the country, a progressive, counterculture-flavored scene is alive and kicking—half the lodges here are into yoga, and the weekly organic food-and-crafts fair is a big deal.

Carate, in the meantime, is at the end of the coastal road, and there's practically nothin' but nothin' here except for a handful of lodges and private homes (much of the land has been put into conservation, so development has been limited). Down here you'll feel like you're at the end of the world, with nothing but miles of white sand beaches and pounding surf (swimming's not a good idea, though—killer riptides). Most people pass through here to get to Corcovado—the La Leona ranger station is just an hour's walk away, along the beach.

CORCOVADO NATIONAL PARK

Mostly virgin, primeval forest closed to development, the park is the heart of the peninsula and covers almost a quarter of it. It's the largest stretch of contiguous tropical rainforest north of the Amazon, and has no roads and no official residents. But it does have many miles of well-maintained trails; four ranger stations; lots of rivers and waterfalls; and thousands of plant and animal species, some found nowhere else in the world.

GOLFITO AREA

On the north side of the Golfo Dolce is Golfito, a banana port–turned–duty-free zone (on weekends, Ticos hit the malls here in search of appliances and other tax-free merch). The town itself is kinda run-down, with not much to see. But the hills and mountains around it are covered with lush, virgin rainforest, much of it now part of reserves including Piedras Blancas National Park. In nearby San Vito, La Cruces Biological Station runs the impressive Wilson Botanical Gardens, and farther down the coast Playa Zancudo and Pavones are surfer magnets.

PUERTO JIMENEZ

The Osa's largest town, Puerto Jiménez is the gateway to its southeastern half, which includes the tiny villages of Matapalo and Carate. It's touted as a base to explore Corcovado, but to tell you the truth, Puerto Jiménez isn't all that convenient for this—unless of course, you're planning to hire an air charter to take you straight in. There's not much of a beach, nor stunning trails nearby. So what gives with this place?

For starters, it's one of the few Tico communities involved in tourism where you can still catch a glimpse of bona fide country village life. The locals are super-friendly and genuinely want to talk to you, whether you're just walking down the street or taking a taxi. Everyone knows each other, honking and waving while passing on the roads. And though it's far from dead (there's a pretty lively and growing restaurant and bar scene, for example), people will tell you they like PJ because it's *muy tranquilo* (real quiet).

And practically speaking, Puerto Jiménez is a great place for exploring the Osa outside of Corcovado; in fact, plenty of visitors who come intending to do Corcovado end up so distracted with all the stuff to see and do right around here, they never make it.

GETTING TO & AROUND PUERTO JIMENEZ

The Osa Peninsula is located in the southeastern corner of the country, far from San José. Because of the distance and the amazingly crappy state of many of local roads (during the rainy season, you might as well just forget it), many fly directly to Puerto Jiménez from San José and other regional airports. But for those with more time than money, catching a bus is relatively straightforward.

By Bus

Blanco Lobo (☎ 771-4744) buses leave San José for the 8-hour drive to Puerto Jiménez at 6am and noon; the fare's $5.50. From Quepos, catch the bus at 5am or 1:30pm to San Isidro de El General, which takes about an hour and a half and costs $2. From San Isidro de El General, buses leave for Puerto Jiménez at 6:30 and 9am, noon, and 3pm ($4.20).

Itinerary Advice

Consider combining your visit to the Osa with a stop at the central Pacific beaches of Manuel Antonio/Quepos or Dominical, just up the coast (p. 140); that way you can avoid backtracking by driving or flying in from San José to Puerto Jiménez and back to San José from, say, Quepos.

By Air

In high season, **Nature Air** (☎ 506/299-6000 or 800/235-9272 from the U.S. and Canada; www.natureair.com) runs four daily flights from San José's Pavas airport to Puerto Jiménez, at 6, 8:30, and 10:45am, and 3:15pm. From Quepos, there's a 7:40am flight to Puerto Jiménez that connects through San José. The trip lasts 50 minutes and costs $87. **Sansa** (☎ 506/221-9414; www.flysansa.com) flights leave at 6 and 10:15am and 1:55p.m (1 hr. and 20 min., $78 each way).

By Car

The trip to Puerto Jiménez is long and tough, but relatively straightforward. From San José, the quickest route is to take the Interamerican Highway to San Isidro, where you'll turn right on to the Dominical Highway. When you reach the Costanera Highway, hang a left. Drive through Dominical and Uvita, and take a right on the Panamerican Highway at Palmar Norte. Make another right at Chacarita and follow the signs to Rincón, La Palma, and finally Puerto Jiménez. If you're planning on visiting Golfito first, you can take the 11:30am water taxi (**Boat Taxi Hermanos Atencio;** ☎ 775-1092; $3), which delivers you right to Puerto Jiménez by 1pm.

Getting Around

Puerto Jiménez is a piece of cake on foot—a small grid whose one main street has most of the restaurants, tour offices, and services on it or just off it. You'd only need taxis if you're staying in nearby Playa Platanares, or hitting a restaurant or bar just outside of town. Anyone in town can help you call a cab, or call one of the cab companies listed on the free maps given out in stores and hotels. Negotiate the fare upfront (rides within or just outside town should run no more than $3–$4, and to Playa Platanares around $10 each way).

Getting Out of Town

For day trips out to Matapalo, Carate, La Palma, or Dos Brazos, the cheapest option is to take a *colectivo*, a four-wheel-drive truck with a tarp cover and slat seats in the back. *Colectivos* leave from in front of the *soda* Carolina at 6am and 1pm, returning from Carate at 4 and 8pm (it will cost you around $7 each way for Carate, less for Matapalo). *Colectivos* for Dos Brazos leave at 5:30 and 11am and 4pm, and for La Palma at 8:30am, 12:30pm, and 4pm. Ask around town to confirm current times (schedule? What's a schedule?). You can hop on a *colectivo* by flagging it down anywhere along its route. Hitching a ride is pretty common and considered safe, as long as you're smart about it (don't go solo, use your best judgment, and remember to offer a few *colones* as a courtesy).

You can hire a taxi to take you to anywhere around the peninsula; fares can range from $50 to $70 each way depending on how far you're going. You'd probably be better off arranging for a driver for the day (the fee's negotiable, but $100 seems standard). Most lodge owners have favorite drivers, so ask them to book for you; they'll get the best rates and the most reliable drivers. Otherwise, we've found **Nago** (☎ 850-5084), **Orlando Mesen** (☎ 836-8241), and **Benito Vasques** (☎ 826-2765) to be good bets.

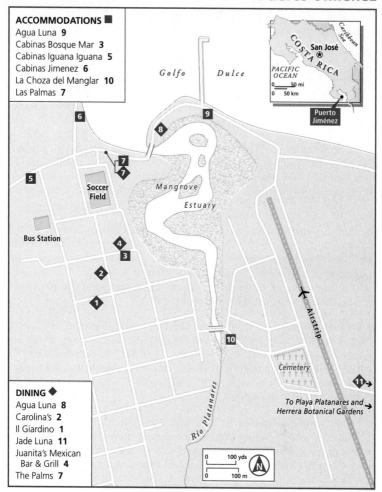

ACCOMMODATIONS ■
Agua Luna **9**
Cabinas Bosque Mar **3**
Cabinas Iguana Iguana **5**
Cabinas Jimenez **6**
La Choza del Manglar **10**
Las Palmas **7**

Golfo Dulce

Mangrove Estuary

Soccer Field

Bus Station

Rio Platanares

Airstrip

Cemetery

To Playa Platanares and
Herrera Botanical Gardens

DINING ◆
Agua Luna **8**
Carolina's **2**
Il Giardino **1**
Jade Luna **11**
Juanita's Mexican
   Bar & Grill **4**
The Palms **7**

0   100 yds
0   100 m

PACIFIC OCEAN
San José
COSTA RICA
Caribbean Sea
Puerto Jiménez
0   50 mi
0   50 km

Car Rental

Unlike other parts of the country, where the international chains hold sway in terms of car rentals (see p. 352) here, **Solid Car Rental** (35m/115 ft. west of Banco Nacional); ☎ 735-5062; www.solidcarrental.com) is the only game in town, and is therefore your de facto choice should you decide you want your own set of wheels (not a bad idea in these parts, by the way). It charges starting at $65 a day (less per diem if you rent for a week). Other rental-car companies in Costa Rica do drop-offs in Puerto Jiménez, but will charge upwards of $120 for that august privilege.

ACCOMODATIONS, BOTH STANDARD & NOT
In Puerto Jiménez

At most, Puerto Jiménez is okay for 1 or 2 overnights before moving on to other parts of the peninsula. The handful of locally owned *cabinas* in this town are mostly budget flophouses, fine on cleanliness but low on charm (for ambience, head straight to Playa Platanares, or even Matapalo or Carate). If you're on an especially tight budget, a couple of rock-bottom options worth looking into are a 5-minute stroll from the bus station. **Cabinas Bosque Mar** (198m/660 ft. from the beach; ☎ 735-5681; AE, MC, V) and **Cabinas Iguana Iguana** (198m/660 ft. west of soccer field; ☎ 735-5158; MC) are both basic but clean and with a modicum of charm (bamboo furniture, for example), along with private baths, firms beds, fans, and cold-water showers; rates start at $10 per person. There are some vacation rental opportunities on the Osa Peninsula, but none in this direct area worth recommending.

$ On the waterfront and remodeled in 2004, the **Cabinas Jiménez** (50m/165 ft. north of soccer field; ☎ 735-5090; www.cabinasjimenez.com; MC, V) offers 10 clean, motel-style rooms with tile floors, fridges, and hot-water showers, and even a deck with hammocks (from $25; $10 more if you want air-conditioning). Several have views of the water (during low tide at the end of the May–Nov dry season, though, what you'll mostly see is mud).

$ Just down the road, also on the gulf, the recently opened restaurant **Las Palmas** ✠ (10m/33 ft. north of soccer field; ☎ 735-5012; MC, V), awash in colorful hand-painted murals, also rents out nine rooms. The best deal is the "backpackers special": $39 a night for a cheerily decorated double with hot water and comfy beds. There's free Internet, too, but no H_2O views—rooms face a lush backyard instead of the beach.

$ Right near Las Palmas, the soda **Agua Luna** (in front of the public dock; ☎ 735-5034 or 735-5393; V) charges a tad more (from $45) for bath-equipped rooms that are pretty bare-bones—just a thin mattress on a wood frame, and a slatted bench—but overlooking an adjacent mangrove forest and river. You can also take in that scenery from a hammock on the nice tiled veranda.

Shouldering the Costs

To save money, plan to come around the shoulder period between high and "green" seasons. If you ask the locals, their favorite time is the early part of "green season," around April and May, since the mind-addling heat lets up when the rains come. Rates drop a good bit during this time, but avoid October and November, when it's literally a downpour each day—even the lodge owners get out of Dodge around then.

$$ The best in-town mix of comfort and value is **La Choza del Manglar** ✦ (99m/330 ft. west of airstrip; ☎ 735-5002; www.manglares.com; MC, V), several blocks off the main drag and across the street from the Esquina supermarket (hang out for a few minutes and a local will probably chat you up). La Choza's biggest pluses are a pool, a peaceful garden which attracts monkeys and birds, and free Wi-Fi. The 11 rooms are pretty spacious, but a tad grungy for the price (doubles from $51, breakfast included)—lime-green walls beginning to peel, and small, industrial-feeling bathrooms. They're comfy enough, though, and have A/C. Live music on Saturday nights bring some of the locals into the bar and restaurant, plastered with cheerful murals.

North of Puerto Jiménez

$$$ Not just one of the Osa's cheapest digs but possibly its most unique is this organic farm, the 44-hectare (110-acre) **Finca Kobo** (close to Los Patos Ranger Station/Jiménez Hwy. to La Palma; ☎ 351-8576; www.fincakobo.com; cash only). It grows more than 30 different kinds of fruits and vegetables, and its cacao bushes produce some of the best organic chocolate around, widely sold locally. The lodge offers six woody, simple rooms ($80 per person, $140 double occupancy, including three meals a day), and tours covering organic gardening and chocolate (ecotour $12, chocolate tour $25; p. 212). One minus: It's kind of far from most of the Osa's main attractions, so it probably works best as a stop for a couple of days.

$$$ The 19-hectare (31-acre) **Bosque del Río Tigre Sanctuary and Lodge** (400m/1,312 ft. southeast of school, Dos Brazos; ☎ 824-1372, but you'll get a faster response if you e-mail them at info@osaadventures.com; www.osaadventures. com; cash only) is a private reserve 20 minutes northwest of Puerto Jiménez, owned by friendly Tico-American couple Abraham Gallo and Liz Jones. The feather in the cap here is the birding. More than 300 species have been spotted on property, and guests rave about Liz and Abram's keen eyes and enthusiasm. Digs are in a two-story riverside lodge with four open-air rooms with mosquito nets and shared bath/outdoor hot shower (for a little more privacy, ask for the cabin by the river, with its own bathroom). It has the feeling of a treehouse, but a minimalistic elegant one—it's really all about the nature here. Rooms start at $103 per person per night in season, and $96 for 5 or more nights).

In Playa Platanares

About 5km (3 miles) from Puerto Jiménez, Playa Platanares is a secluded, barely developed dozen-plus-mile stretch of gorgeous sands dotted with almond and palm trees—considered the Osa's most ravishing beach, and one of the best for just taking a dip. You could probably wander around all afternoon without spotting another soul (if you do, chances are it'll be a local, not a tourist). The surrounding area is lush, with mangrove swamps fed by the Río Platanares. Savvy travelers make a point of stopping here on the way to or from Corcovado Park. But you might want to consider dropping your bags here. For about the same rates as Puerto Jiménez, it's a helluva lot nicer, and just as convenient for getting around the rest of the peninsula.

$ Affordable and right on the beach, the popular **Playa Preciosa Lodge** (about 5km/3 miles east of Puerto Jiménez; ☎ 818-2959; www.playa-preciosa-lodge.de; cash only) has four two-story bungalows with ceiling fans and private baths but no hot water (from $42 for one person, $54 for two), as well as eight tent-cabins on stilts ($30 single, $35 double); rates include breakfast. The bungalows are kind of salt-weathered and run-down, so we prefer the tent cabins—they don't have private bathrooms but are clean and open right onto the beach. The German owner, Veleska Vogt, makes yoga and massages available on request and serves hearty breakfast and dinner. But if you're looking to hang out on the beach all day or don't have a car, for lunch the only game is the nearby Península de Osa restaurant.

$$ Our favorite in the area is a few patches of sand down the road from Playa Preciosa Lodge (see above). At **Black Turtle Lodge** ★★★ (5km/3 miles east of Puerto Jimenez, 100m/328 ft. before Pearl de Osa and Iguana Lodge; ☎ 735-5005; www.blackturtlelodge.com; MC, V), superfriendly Berkeley native Nico Zimmerman and his family deliver a gorgeously laid-back, upscale experience for $95 per person per night, including all meals (the cost goes down with more people in the room, dropping to $65 per person with four sharing). The sounds of jungle life are all around you, and a mostly deserted black-sand beach is a short stroll away. There are four open-air *casitas* with mosquito-netting sides and a pair of duplex two-bedroom "treehouses" 4.5m (15 ft.) above ground; all are done up in Balinese-flavored bamboo and cane (one drawback of the *casitas* is that the private bathroom is a hundred or so feet away). What really makes this one of the Osa's best deals, though, are the tasty family-style meals (unusual for a place this small, and for the area), where Nico chews the fat, as it were, with his American and Euro guests (many of whom are repeaters).

$$$ The two-story terra-cotta **Pearl of the Osa** ★★ (about 5km/3 miles east of Puerto Jimenez, 100m/320 ft. after Black Turtle Lodge; ☎ 829-5865; www.the pearloftheosa.com; MC, V) has eight pretty-good-size rooms (four overlooking the surf) with balconies, bamboo furnishings, ceiling fans, and bathrooms with hot showers (not always guaranteed in the Osa). Join a game of volleyball in the big backyard; catch a glimpse of turtles, macaws, and dolphins along the nearby half-dozen miles of white sand; practice your tree pose or salsa moves; or take an afternoon siesta (or martini) under shady beachside *palapa* huts. On Fridays, the party in Platanares is at the restaurant and bar here—everybody comes for afternoon drinks, followed by a hugely popular pasta night; it's a great meet-and-greet, especially if you're traveling on your own (don't worry: the action usually dies down by 9pm). Room rates in season run $100 to $110, including breakfast.

In Matapalo

The thing to understand about Matapalo is that it's not a town so much as a smattering of private homes, lodges, and *fincas* (farms) set among some of the Osa's most scenic valleys and rainforests. There are no services, just one public bar and restaurant, and most communication is via radio; absolutely everything—food, supplies, hotel guests—is schlepped in from Puerto Jiménez, about an hour away. This kind of seclusion, along with the miles of hiking trails, four beaches, and

Matapalo Vacation House Rentals

Development—of the gringo gated-community kind—is a dirty word in these parts, but it does give you more affordable lodgings to choose from. At the time of this writing, about a dozen foreign-owned homes around Cabo Matapalo, mostly right off the beach, are for rent. Fully equipped with kitchens, linens, and towels, most have attractive open-air architecture and decor along the lines of bamboo, thatch roofs, hammocks, and rustic furniture. In high season, rates start at $85 a day or $510 a week for the low-key, one-bedroom **Casa Planta Niña** on Playa Carbonera or the beautiful **Casa La Luz,** which is just a few steps from Matapalo beach and sleeps up to eight (a cook/housekeeper's available for $155 a day).

Check out these and other properties on www.jimenezhotels.com, then contact the manager at **CaféNet El Sol** in Puerto Jiménez (☎ 735-5719; reservations@soldeosa.com). Also have a look at **Casa Bambú** (www.casabambu-beach-house-rentals.com), which has three different Swiss Family Robinson–style bamboo houses that sleep up to eight on Pan Dulce beach (in season, $155 daily/$1,015 weekly). Keep in mind that since there are no shops and services in this neck of the jungle, you'll have to do a lot of cooking, or at least have a car to get to the grub at the various lodges. You'll have to either stock up on supplies in Puerto Jiménez, or make regular trips back into town, an hour each way (tours, though, you can generally set up at lodges out here, like Encanta La Vida or El Remanso).

several world-class surf breaks, is what makes Matapalo so special. You'll feel like some intrepid eco-explorer for having gotten yourself so far off the beaten path.

If you stay out here, you'll have to take most of your meals at the area lodges. Several ecolodges welcome nonguests for lunch or dinner. As for the lodges themselves, some have electricity, some solar powered, so don't bring anything to plug in that you don't really need. And unless you've got a car, or don't mind hitchhiking, it's kind of hard to get around; *colectivos* run only twice a day, and taxis charge rates that include their trek out from Puerto Jiménez.

Besides the following, the **Buena Esperanza** restaurant (p. 208) also rents a couple of very simple *cabinas* out back for around $25 per person. It's very much a sideline, so if you don't expect much in the way of service or amenities you should be fine (better are the choices below).

$ The most reasonably priced pick down here is the unique, four-unit **Ojo del Mar** ✫ (Playa Carbonera, 19km/12 miles south of Puerto Jiménez; ☎ 735-5351; ojodelmar@yahoo.de; cash only), an ecofriendly B&B run by Mark, a Munich-born performance artist-cum-surfer, and his wife, Nico. The hand-built wood-and-bamboo lodge sits near a rocky beach that's better for views than swimming (surfing's another story, dude—Mark will let you take one of his boards out for

An Osa Assist

Organizing a trip to the peninsula can send even seasoned travelers running for help. With the distances and remoteness involved, trying to coordinate all the wheres, whens, and whats can be—well, trying. So allow us to introduce a pair of "old Osa hands," based in Puerto Jiménez, who can be your fixers—and do it quickly and efficiently (not always a common trait in *mañana* Costa Rica).

Isabel Esquivel runs **Osa Tropical** (50m/165 ft. southeast of Banco Nacional; ☎ 735-5692; osatropi@sol.racsa.co.cr). Perfectly bilingual and tapped into the local scene, she keeps in regular touch with most of the lodges and is a whiz at matching you with the products right for you—without pushing you to blow your budget. **Paul Collar,** a gringo who's lived here for more than 2 decades, owns **CafeNet El Sol** (10m/33 ft. northwest of Banco Nacional; ☎ 735-5718; www.soldeosa.com), a cybercafe and tour agency. His portal, which links www.jimenezhotels.com, has extensive listings of tours and hotels throughout the peninsula, and you can book with him online. He also books vacation rentals in Matapalo (p. 203). Finally, Collar runs several other local businesses, including Juanita's bar and restaurant and Osa Pen Realty, so he's a great go-to guy, especially for less standard requests.

free). Locals and guests mingle at daily yoga classes, while Mark's kung fu lessons are mostly for locals. At night you'll hear the noises of the jungle from your cabin—open-air, with mosquito netting for walls. At mealtime, guests tuck into organic goodies family-style. The $45 per-person price tag includes all meals—and that, plus a chance to hang out with the character who owns the place, makes this one remarkable deal. (Make sure to ask Mark about the chainsaw displayed in the living room—it's from a performance-art piece at the Costa Rican Museum of Modern Art where he and a few Ticos simultaneously sawed through the trees and reassembled them.)

$$ If you're into surfing, head to the funky, super-relaxed **Encanta La Vida** ★ (100m/330 ft. from Matapalo beach; ☎ 735-5678; www.encantalavida.com; MC, V), on a 3.6-hectare (9-acre) spread in Matapalo's residential area near the popular surfing beaches of Pan Dulce, Matapalo, and Backwash. The overall vibe is California relaxed and laid-back, much like its host Brian Daily, who's from Santa Barbara but grew up in Costa Rica, and has breakfast every day surrounded by parrots eating off his plate. Owing to Brian's 2 decades of roots in the area, locals drop by all the time for visits, and often linger at the bar, giving you a chance to mingle with some Ticos. The nine rooms aren't bad (the walls could use a fresh coat of paint), and the bathrooms are nice white-stone open-air numbers; there are three quality houses for rent, too (rates run $75–$85 per person, with all meals). At nearby Playa Matapalo, there are showers, a changing area, and a new swimming pool.

$$ Next to El Remanso, the **Bosque del Cabo** ✪✪✪ (23km/14 miles south of Puerto Jiménez on road to Carate; ☎ 735-5206; www.bosquedelcabo. com; MC, V) is thought by lots of folks to be the most spectacular of the Matapalo ecolodges. Perched some 500 feet over the water on more than 300 acres, the joint is both at once rustic and elegant, with 10 roomy, solar-powered bungalows and a pair of houses, all classily tarted up in hardwoods, cane, and tile. There are lots of nifty features and activities—a nice pool, of course, but also the 90m (300-ft.) suspension bridge over a deep ravine that connects to the thatched-roof open-air restaurant, bar, and birding station; ziplines; rappelling down waterfalls; and so forth. It takes an hour to get to and from the beach, but you can have the lodge cart you down and back. It's sure not cheap—starting at $95 per person in season (based on double occupancy)—but includes all your grub. Look at it this way: With all the wildlife-spotting and activities right here, you won't have to shell out for that stuff off-premises.

$$$ A 78-hectare (195-acre) spread tucked away on the Pacific side of Cape Matapalo, the charming ecolodge **El Remanso** ✪ (23km/14 miles south of Puerto Jiménez on road to Carate; ☎ 735-5569; www.elremanso.com; MC, V) has its own hiking trails, waterfalls, and a couple of small ziplines (guests can breakfast in the canopy on one platform), besides a bar/restaurant, Jacuzzi, and yoga platform. The digs consist of three freestanding one-bedroom cabins, a two-story bungalow, and a three-bedroom house that sleeps up to 10; all have screens, electricity, and great jungle and water views. If the place looks familiar, by the way, you might've caught it on MTV's *Trippin'*, when Cameron Diaz, Kelly Slater, Jessica Alba, and Kid Rock stayed here to promote saving the rainforests. One minus: It's a bit of a walk down to the beach and the main road, so a car helps a lot. Doubles start at $120, including meals.

In Carate

Next to Carate, Matapalo's a metropolis. There's nothing up here but miles of desolate beaches, thousands of acres of primary rainforest, and the occasional lodge or private home. With strong rip currents, the waves are surfable, but most surfers like them better in Matapalo. So why do people stay out here? Two reasons: to get as far away from "civilization" as possible, and to be close to Corcovado—the entrance is a 45-minute stroll away, along the beach.

What you'll find up here are mostly higher-end lodges and, in the woods on the beach next to La Leona ranger station, a couple of tent camp/lodges (see below). If you stay at either, expect to be isolated, since you're always a 45-minute

---

Watch Where You Park

Beware of the *pulpería* (grocery store) at Carate where the road turns inland. The surly gringo owner will try to charge you 2,500 *colones* ($5), to park here—and that's after he's lectured you about private property. You can park for free a few yards away, right next to the beach.

walk away from the nearest road; also, the surf's too rough for comfortably swimming, and there's only one park trail around La Leona for spotting wildlife (though the lodges have their own trails). Even so, we'd stay only 1 or 2 nights at most before venturing deeper into the park. Unless, of course, you're just looking to unwind, do a little horseback riding on the beach, or surf and boogie board.

In Carate, the dining room at **Luna Lodge** (see below) welcomes anyone for lunch or dinner, but it's quite a trek over the river and up the mountain—not exactly a casual pop-over-for-dinner kind of thing. You'll probably end up dining in your own lodge; beyond the Luna, that's your only option.

$ Right next door to La Leona, the **Corcovado Tent Camp** ✖ (2km/1¼ mile north of Carate Beach; ☎ 257-0766 or 222-0333; www.corcovadolodge.com; AE, MC, V) has 16 rustic but swanker-than-average tent-cabins on platforms right off the beach, with mosquito-net walls, comfy twin beds, and electricity (no private baths, though). The camp is part of a 79-hectare/198-acre reserve, so you can really get into nature in a big way. (Want cool? Get hoisted up to the observation platform, a hundred feet up, in the canopy—you can even spend the night in a tent up here.) Besides a thatch-roof dining and bar area, there's a hammock pavilion and a Ping-Pong table. In-season rates start at $42 per person (double occupancy), including breakfast and dinner.

$$ You can't get any closer to Corcovado than the **La Leona Lodge** (next to Corcovado entrance, a 30-min. hike along Carate Beach; ☎ 735-5705; www.laleona lodge.com; MC, V) with 16 comfy, roomy tent-cabins on platforms (roofs are thick and walls are insect-proof screening); each has a private deck, but only six have private bathrooms. There's a spring-fed swimming pool, a restaurant where guests eat by candlelight, and several trails (a couple leading through waterfalls). Rates start at $40 per person (double occupancy) without meals, $65 with the full meal plan.

$$ One of the best values in Carate, especially if you're planning to explore on horseback and/or take in a sea turtle tour, is the **Terrapin Lodge** (2km/1¼ miles north of Carate *pulpería;* ☎ 735-5719; www.terrapinlodge.com; MC, V), a 10-minute walk from Pejeperrito lagoon and the beach. Typical for a local backpacker pad, it's clean but pretty spare—the walls could really use a lick of paint and the floors a spot of varnish, plus there are no fans or hot water in the rooms. But the five basic, screen-walled cabins (two with ocean views) on raised platforms do come with electric power and their own bathrooms—both major pluses for this kind of place. You can get horses for a guided or solo ride along the beach or on local trails (one of which leads to a stunning waterfall), and from June to November you can also work with the Osa Sea Turtles Foundation, tracking nests, monitoring egg laying, and helping with the hatching. Rates start at $70 per person (double occupancy), and include all meals and the use of kayaks to paddle around the lagoon.

$$ The most breathtakingly scenic ecolodge hereabouts, **La Luna Lodge** ✖✖✖ (2km/1¼ mile up a steep road from Carate; ☎ 380-5036 or 888/409-8448 from the U.S. and Canada; www.lunalodge.com; MC, V) is as much about yoga and healing as about the nature around you. It's a helluva trek—you've got to ford the Carate River and climb up a mountain road—but you'll feel like you've arrived in

Wild About Animals

Places on the peninsula are often named after animals (in fact, the word *osa* itself means bear). The town of Carate is dubbed with the word for hookworm (charming, eh?), El Tigre means "tiger," and Corcovado's ranger stations, Los Patos and La Leona, translate to "ducks" and "lioness."

Shangri-La, 60 hectares (150 acres) atop a mountain facing the Pacific and Corcovado (doing yoga on the dramatic platform up here is a mind-blower). Owner Lana Wedmore, who's lived on the peninsula for a couple dozen years, designed the three elegant "hacienda" rooms and eight bungalows, which all have private decks and showers surrounded by a minigarden. There's a nice pool, and a pair of private trails take you into primary forest (pumas have been spotted here). The only drawback is the trek to the beach, but sometimes Lana can pick you up or drop you off. The food is health conscious and truly tasty, from quiches to grilled mahimahi. Rates start at $99 per person (double occupancy), and include meals and a waterfall tour. To really save, opt for one of the tent-cabins for $73 per person.

$$ With its charming tiki-style huts you'll feel a little bit like you've gone native at the **Lookout Inn** ★ (296m/985 ft. east of Carate airstrip; ☎ 735-543, 815/955-1520 in the United States; www.lookout-inn.com; AE, DISC, MC, V), the only digs on Carate Beach. On a steep hill facing water, this homey, rustic three-story lodge is at the center of a 4-hectare (10-acre) spread, where narrow wooden walkways lead through dense foliage to the restaurant/bar, monkey feeding stations, and pool and Jacuzzi (at the top of it all is the 227-step Stairway to Heaven, which leads to trails through the primary forest similar to Corcovado). Rooms are on the basic side but nice, with quirky ceramic iguanas and tropical wall murals. The place gets only one star, however, because you'll feel the springs in the bed when you lie down (we're hoping they'll be getting new mattresses soon; ask before booking). The rate's $94 per person (double occupancy), including all meals (half off for kids under 12). For our money, we'd go with one of the open-air tiki huts ($85 per person), each with steep roofs and all-wood interiors, a simple bed with mosquito netting, and bathrooms next door. If you want to be close to Corcovado's entrance but still have easy access to the rest of the peninsula (including the Matapalo surfing beaches), the Lookout's a winner.

DINING FOR ALL TASTES
In Puerto Jiménez

The Osa's not as up to speed dining-wise as Costa Rica's more longstanding tourist areas, partly because all the lodges feed their guests, making it tough for indie eateries. More have been cropping up anyway, mostly in and around Puerto Jiménez, which got its first high-end restaurant, **Jade Luna** (p. 209) in 2004; word around town is that more are on the way. If you're really counting your *colones,* though, it's pretty easy to grab cheap grub like burgers and sausages from street vendors on the town's main strip, or outside the disco on weekend nights.

$ In Puerto Jiménez, the best-known standby has always been **Carolina's** (main street, center of town; ☎ 735-5185; daily 7am–10pm; V), frequented by Ticos, expats, and tourists alike (they say that if you're looking for anyone around town, try Carolina's). The fare is solid, standard Latin, but there's also a pretty good choice of Yankee imperialist hits like pizza, burgers, and spaghetti. Most dishes are around $5.

$ Another long-established favorite is the **Juanita's Mexican Bar & Grille** (next to CafeNet El Sol, center of town; ☎ 735-5056; daily 6am–11pm; cash only), which also used to be *the* nightspot in town before Iguana Iguana came along (p. 213). Folks still flock to this frontier-style cantina for the generous portions of Tex-Mex burritos, quesadillas, and such. The signature dish is fajitas, with chicken, beef, fish, or veggies, and a side of *pico de gallo,* for only $5; pizza by the slice will run you two bucks. The best deal, though, is the breakfast buffet: all you can scarf down for $4 (great for fueling up before a long hike).

$ Just above the mouth of a mangrove-lined river, the *soda* **Agua Luna** (in front of the dock; ☎ 735-5033; daily 10am–11pm; cash only), is a *chino-latino,* slinging a mix of Chinese and Tico fare. The owner may be Guangdong but the Chinese food isn't what you'd call extremely authentic—spiced Latin-style as it is. But it's all fairly tasty, the price is right (most mains $4–$7, beef fried rice $3.50), and the joint's popular with locals. The best picks are the fish dishes (get the catch of the day filleted in mushroom sauce, grilled in garlic sauce, fried with tartar sauce, and such); also don't miss out on the creamy pineapple milkshakes. Grab a table out on the terrace; you'll feel like you're dining on a bridge right over the water.

$ Out in Matapalo, near Playa Carbonera, the only stand-alone restaurant is **Buena Esperanza** (18km/11 miles south of Puerto Jiménez, on the road to Carate; no phone; Mon–Fri 9am–11pm, Sat–Sun 9am–4pm; cash only), a popular open-air roadside spot that locals refer to as "Martina's," for the German owner. It's mostly a bar that brings out expats and Ticos alike after 7:30pm or so, but there are always two or three dishes available depending on what Martina chooses to whip up and what ingredients she's got at hand. On some days it'll be a simple pasta with a side of vegetables; on another, it might be a fish filet. Definitely worth a stop, if you're in the Matapalo area (and if you want to reserve one of Martina's *cabinas* for $25, e-mail her at martinatica@hotmail.com.)

$–$$ A relative newbie in Puerto Jiménez, **The Palms** ✖ (10m/33 ft. north of the public square/soccer field; ☎ 735-5012; daily 6am–10pm, in low season lunch and dinner only; MC, V) is nifty for feeding alfresco in a cool, contemporary ambiance (deep-blue walls, panoramic gulf views, fancy tropical drinks). The menu's crowd-pleasing Mexican, with your usual battery of quesadillas and enchiladas (in choice of mole, tomato-chipotle, and cheese sauces), but there are a handful of slightly more exotic choices, like the taco of pork slow-cooked in banana leaves; entree prices run $6 to $15. For your latte fix, the place also has a coffee shop cheekily christened "OurBucks."

The Osa Gets Jaded

$$$ If you want to treat yourself, or you just want a change from the usual soda fare, head for local sensation **Jade Luna** ★★★ (.5km/⅓ mile east of the Puerto Jiménez airstrip, on the road to Playa Platanares; ☎ 735-5739, Mon–Sat 5–9pm; cash only), whose owner Barbara Burckhardt did kitchen time in New York and Long Island's Hamptons before setting up shop here in 2004. Barbara tweaks her menu depending on the catch of the day, but for the most part it's a rotating cast of simple but well-prepared dishes, lightly grilled or sautéed. Vinaigrette-dressed salads are overflowing with apple and orange slices, and fried goat or Gorgonzola cheese, while the mains are surprisingly varied for way down here in the Osa. There's always a beef tenderloin or pork chop, but the best bets are the fish and shrimp (my favorite last time was the succulent red snapper sautéed in a light white wine–and–garlic butter sauce); entrée prices run $11 to $15. Desserts include a variety of homemade sorbets and ice creams (the ginger tea ice cream, $3.25, was scrumptious). Decor is a simple and elegant, with sconce-punctuated terra-cotta walls, tropical scenes painted by local artists, and fresh flowers and candles on every table. Don't forget to reserve ahead!

$–$$ For pretty good pizza in PJ, stop in at **Il Giardino** (100m/330 ft. north and 25m/82 ft. west of Banco Nacional; ☎ 735-5129; daily 5–10pm; cash only), which besides its clay-oven-baked pies also does pasta and sushi. I've heard mixed reviews—some locals say what you get depends on who's cooking on any given day (the dish you ordered might well come out different than you expected). Still, the pizzas are reliably decent, and the dining experience pretty nice, especially on the stylish back terrace with rugged wood tables and chairs under huge tropical trees. Entrees, including the pizza, range from $4 to $13.

In Playa Platanares

$–$$ A popular beach hangout in Playa Platanares, the Pearl of the Osa's **Monochingo Bar and Grille** ★ (100m/330 ft. north of Iguana Lodge; ☎ 829-5865; daily 11am–8pm; MC, V) is best known as a place to lift a few; it's also the only place nonlodge guests can chow down out here. Friday pasta nights ($6) have developed quite a following—the hungry hordes line up at the buffet table to pile on the spaghetti and salads while a local band belts out salsa, meringue, and cumbia. The regular menu, meanwhile, features local mahimahi, ceviche, and *patacones,* as well as burgers, burritos, pizza, and tacos ($4–$12).

WHY YOU'RE HERE: THE TOP SIGHTS & ATTRACTIONS

From the moment you arrive, by road or by plane, it's hard not to be moved by the Osa's staggering beauty. Here, verdant rainforests rise dizzyingly out of a deep-blue sea teeming with whales and dolphins. And in a country exploding with flora and fauna, this neck of the jungle is the richest eco-trove of all. In fact, there's so much to choose from—canopy tours, horseback riding, waterfall rappelling, kayaking, dolphin/whale-watching, snorkeling, diving, and hiking—making those choices isn't always easy. Whatever you do, whichever trail you take, you'll spot no end of animals (especially an unending variety of birds). Most people end up exploring mostly the areas near their lodge; add the mammoth and (deservedly) much-hyped **Corcovado National Park,** and it's an awful lot to tackle.

On the other hand, no matter what you do you can hardly go wrong. First and foremost, decide how important it really is for you to visit Corcovado. Unless you're a rabid nature fanatic, you'll find hiking and touring other parts of the Osa to be wonderful enough without making the effort to get out to Corcovado (it's not that it's inaccessible, but it does involve a certain amount of planning, roughing it, and expense; in fact, most visitors don't even make it out to the park). We've talked to travelers in Matapalo who were thrilled to be simply spotting white-faced monkeys playing in nearby trees and snapping photos of leafcutter ants. If you're that kind of person, someone who doesn't necessarily know the difference between a two- and three-toed sloth, you can have a perfectly fab frolic in the Osa without Corcovado.

So with that in mind, we've listed activities throughout the peninsula first, with an emphasis on what's unique to the Osa, followed by a section entirely about Corcovado. And though we've included some attractions you can do on your own without dropping a bundle, this part of the country still isn't well set up for independent travel—at least for the time being—so for a lot of it you'll need to go on a tour and/or hire a guide

Hiking, Watersports, Fishing & Ziplines

The first thing on everyone's list is a rainforest hike. Those staying at lodges with their own big reserves and miles of private trails (Lapa Ríos, Bosque del Cabo, Drake Bay Wilderness) will probably end up on an on-property tour with a lodge guide. But if you're bunking in town or at smaller lodges, you'll need to sign up for a guided hike (if you're tempted to go it on your own, keep in mind that though park trails are marked, lots of lodge trails aren't always; thus, you could end up trespassing on private property). **Escondido Trex** (inside the *soda* Carolina's, Puerto Jiménez; ☎ 735-5210; www.escondidotrex.com) is tops in this department. Owner Josh Sibley and his crew will take you on the top-of-the-line excursion for $100 per person: hiking through Matapalo-area forests, where you can spot monkeys, plus a field-guide's-worth of birds including macaws, toucans, and kingfishers. The highlight is a visit to a waterfall crashing down more than 30m (100 ft.), followed by a drink at Matapalo's only watering hole. More affordable adventures include a $50 Matapalo hike (lunch, snacks, and transportation included); kayaking through mangroves for $40; a 3-hour surfing lesson for $50; or the gold tour, where you'll explore an old mining town and try your hand at panning for gold in a river ($45). *Important tip:* Skip snorkeling in Matapalo—unlike the on-land nature, the reef here isn't doing all that great, and less likely to be full of colorful fish and corals than elsewhere in Costa Rica.

You can also watch dolphins from a kayak (Escondido Trex, see above, which also organizes a sunset dolphin-watch cruise) or a boat (**Aventuras Tropicales,** p. 211). Lots of outfits offer this option, but the sportfishing outfitter **Delfin Blanco** (☎ 358-8966; www.fishosa.com) runs probably the most luxe and comfy cruises: 4 hours on a 15m (50-ft.) boat with a bathroom and a shaded upper-deck viewing platform (out on the open water for half the day, the shade is a lifesaver). The cost is $35 per person for the tour.

Another biggie is kayaking amid the fantastic tangles of local mangroves—some reaching as much as 24m (80 ft.) out of the water—followed by post-lunch beachcombing. Because of the mangrove forests' key role filtering coastal waters, you'll see all sorts of varmints in here, like crabs, crocs, and caimans, and up in the canopy, probably monkeys. Your guides will give you the full 411, but apart from the educational side of it, this is just a very exciting experience, like paddling through the deepest parts of the Amazon. Both **Escondido Trex** (p. 210) and **Aventuras Tropicales** (☎ 735-5195; www.aventurastropicales.com) have good 3- to 4-hour excursions through the river Platanares and the gulf coast, including snacks and beach stops. Escondido's ($40) is run by expats whose guides have a better tourist perspective on the Osa and can also give advice on stuff like local real estate. Aventuras ($25) tends to use Tico guides, so you'll get some local color along the way (like trying exotic foods like cashew candy, made from cashew fruit). In any case, it's a good idea to ask at your lodge for the reps of the various guides, and before going out with guides, ask them about their experience and how long they've been doing this. Not long ago, one very young guide took a father and son out in kayaks, and when they capsized in a bad storm, he was too green and not strong enough to help (they were eventually fished out by a guide with another tour operator).

We've been threatened with bodily harm if we reveal the next bit of information, but here goes anyway: The surfing at Playa Pan Dulce, Backwash, and Matalpo is downright spectacular and not to be missed. There are three right point breaks, which get tougher the closer you get to Cabo Matapalo (where the gulf and Pacific Ocean meet), warm water, and swells that can reach 3m (10 ft.). And since it's out in the back of beyond, you don't have to share the waves with too many people. If you're staying at the **Ojo del Mar** (p. 203) or some of the lodges right on the beach, you might be able to just take out the house surfboards for free. Otherwise, you can rent them at **Encanta La Vida** (p. 204) for $15 a day. Pan Dulce's inside break is pretty calm and shallow, so this is where most beginners head, and where the instructors do their thing. Encanta la Vida gives lessons for beginners starting at $40 a pop, including board rental. Mike Hennessy's **Captain Mike's Surf School** (☎ 735-5531; www.cabo-matapalo.com) offers lessons for $50, including a money-back guarantee if you don't end up at least standing on the board by the end of the 2 hours. Veteran boarders can check with Encanta La Vida's Brian Duffy, who organizes jaunts across the gulf to Playa Pavones, the other notable surf spot in the area.

The sportfishing out here is superb, thanks to oodles of schools of snapper, grouper, snook, sierra mackerel, and rooster fish. Farther out in the deep sea, the catch includes striped, blue, and black marlin; yellowfin tuna; and dorado. It's not exactly a budget-travel thing, though—most charters cost hundreds of dollars for half a day, almost a grand for a full day. But if you're up for a splurge, and/or have a big enough group to lessen the per-head outlay, the two main sportfishing lodges are **Crocodile Bay Lodge** (☎ 735-5631, or 800/733-1115 in the U.S. and Canada; www.crocodilebay.com) and **Parrot Bay Village** (☎ 735-5180; www.parrotbayvillage.com). Besides them, **Osa Sportfishing** (☎ 735-5531; www.fishosa.com), **Aventuras Bosque Mar** (p. 212), and **Cabo Matapalo Sportfishing** (Captain Mike's Surf School, see above) offer various angles on angling.

And this being Costa Rica, the Puerto Jiménez area now inevitably has a canopy tour, run out on the Miramar road about 10 minutes' drive from town by **Aventuras Bosque Mar** (across from Juanita's Mexican Bar & Grille; ☎ 735-5681; hours vary). It's not bad, but it has just five platforms and five ziplines running just 18m (60 ft.) above the ground, and charges a relatively steep $75 a head (more with transfers). That being said, if you're heading to other parts of the country, we recommend you save your cash for those ziplines, most of which are bigger, more dramatic—and cheaper. The Osa's only other canopy tour is up by Drake Bay (p. 226), which is more extensive and less pricy than this one.

Cultural & Ecotours

During the June-through-December "green" (aka rainy) season, you might get to have the amazing experience of watching giant sea turtles nesting at Playa Platanares, usually after midnight. Four species include the Olive Ridley (the most common), Pacific green, hawksbill, and occasionally leatherbacks. Check with the **Save the Osa Turtle Project (ASTO)** (at **Iguana Lodge;** ☎ 829-5865; www.iguana lodge.com), whose patrols make sure the annual nesting and hatching go well. Turtle moms can lay up to a hundred eggs a night, and when they hatch a couple of months later, the little guys make a dash for the sea—and if you're staying at one of the lodges out on the beach, like Black Turtle or Iguana Iguana, you'll get to have front-row seats, so to speak. The Turtle Project runs organized tours between June and December, charging $15 per person for their expert commentary (and help with footing!).

Over by Matapalo, the beach in front of **El Remanso** (p. 205) is also a turtle nesting area. The lodge works with local guide Miguel Sánchez and a volunteer patrol to protect the turtles, and also runs a turtle nursery nearby on the Río Piro. In December and January, they'll let you watch the hatchlings being released into the sea, and ask for a $20 donation. You can also watch green turtles nest over at Playa Carate; check with **Terrapin Lodge** (p. 206) for more details on when and how.

If you're not an Audubon Society member, **birding** at the **Bosque del Río Tigre lodge** (p. 201) just might just turn you into one. Owners Liz Jones and Abraham Gallo are the most expert English-speaking birding guides you'll find in the Osa, and their enthusiasm definitely rubs off on their guests and visitors. The 3-hour walk costs $32 per person and includes breakfast; expect to see 40 to 50 species of birds (some have spotted twice that; there are a total of 358 in the area). Abraham has lived in Costa Rica his whole life, and has insider tips on hidden mountain trails in Corcovado Park. After your visit, you can sign up to get their birding e-newsletter.

Not far from Bosque del Rio, the **Finca Kobo** (p. 201), an organic farm that raises some 30 tropical crops such as papaya, cantaloupe, peppers, and especially cacao. Paul Collar of **CafeNet El Sol** (p. 204) can arrange a 3-hour **chocolate tour** here **($25),** covering everything from its history to its making. Along the way, you'll see loads of toucans, monkeys, and other fruit-loving critters clambering through the treetops. The tour ends, naturally, with samples: plenty of fruit (love the baked plantains), fresh baked bread, and, of course, organic chocolate, melted for dipping fruit. Diabetic coma, anyone? . . .

For a lush jolt of flower power, the 48-hectare (119-acre) **Herrera Botanical Gardens and Reforestation Project** (☎ 735-5210), about 10 minutes outside of Puerto Jimenez, is a riot of tropical hardwood seedlings (the project was founded in 2000), flowering shrubs, fruit trees, ornamentals, and a kaleidoscope's worth of *flores, flores, flores*. It's divided into themed sections—medicinal herbs, birds of paradise (heliconia), what have you—connected by well-groomed nature trails. It's all very well marked, so plunk down your $2 and stroll around on your own instead of laying out $15 for the 2-hour guided tour.

ATTENTION, SHOPPERS!

There isn't much shopping in Puerto Jiménez, apart from basic supplies and trinket stands on the main street. But a couple of exceptions are worth checking out. **Galería des Artes** (100m/330 ft. north of the bank; ☎ 735-5429; daily 8am–6pm) is great for paintings and photography by local artists, as well as prints, locally designed jewelry, sculptures, and various and sundry artsy objects. Right by the airport, **Jagua** ★★ (next to the Lapa Ríos office; ☎ 735-5267; daily 6:30am–5pm) is a boutique filled with wonderful tribal arts and crafts, including Boruca masks, Wounaan baskets woven in graphic patterns, and Guaymí dolls (made by the Panamanian tribes, not the ones from the reserve near La Palma). There's also jewelry like mother of pearl earrings. A lot of it's on the pricy side, but you'll still be able to find some original souvenirs; a small Boruca bow-and-arrow set made of *chonta* (walking palm tree), for example—a great gift for your favorite kid back home—is just $15.

NIGHTLIFE

Frankly, we'll bet you'll be too knocked out from the day's activities to go out partying. But if you get in a disco nap or second wind, you can certainly find spots to give it a shot. There's always a watering hole that's "the place to go" on a given night, and they change, so it's best to ask around when you get down here. But there are a couple of fairly reliable standbys, such as Friday's hopping happy hour at the **Monochingo Bar and Grille** at the Pearl of the Osa (p. 209); Tuesdays are salsa nights. On Saturday night, **La Choza del Manglar** (p. 201) is the place for live tunes.

Pretty much any night of the week, though, you'll catch a good crowd at the **Iguana Iguana** (50km/165 ft. west of Delfines Disco; ☎ 735-5719; daily 7pm–1am), on the edge of Puerto Jiménez. It's considered *the* place to party, especially among the 18-to-35 set of both Ticos and tourists, with dancing, darts, a pool table, pinball, and a big-screen TV. Next door is the **Delfines Disco** (no phone; Tues–Sun 8pm–1am), which gets going mostly late nights during the week. The very young and the restless come here to work up a sweat on the dance floor, and it's also where sportfishermen sometimes go trawling for working girls (don't worry, it's catch and release).

CORCOVADO NATIONAL PARK

Since it was established in 1975, the 466-sq.-km (180-sq.-mile) Parque Nacional Corcovado has been one of the Costa Rica's most famous and impressive—and one of its less visited. Way down here on this remote peninsula, it's been pretty much isolated from human ravages. Where else can you experience more than 10 microclimates in a day's hike, and come across more than 500 species of trees, 400 species of birds, 116 varieties of amphibians and reptiles, and 139 types of mammals (over a third of which are bats)? No other national park in Costa Rica is home to all four of its monkey species (white-face, howler, spider, and squirrel, the last of which can be seen only here and in Manuel Antonio). And Corcovado's the most likely place you'll ever see a wildcat outside of a zoo (well, there was that one time on Lincoln Road in South Beach . . .).

But ever more tourists are starting to "discover" Corcovado—you can see it in the number of lodges that have sprung up on both sides, in Drake Bay and Puerto Jiménez, which serve as bases to get folks in and out of the park. No fewer than a dozen flights come into the area every day, and infrastructure like roads, services, and tour operators is growing by the month. All of this makes it easier than ever to visit, and now Corcovado isn't just for high-end ecotourists or scientific researchers anymore.

Still, visiting Corcovado isn't a stroll in the park, as it were; it's an adventure that demands planning, a certain amount of fitness, and tolerance for heat, humidity, sometimes muddy trails, horseflies, mosquitoes, and sundry creepy crawlies. There are no roads into the park or even leading up to it. Of the four entrances with ranger stations, arguably the most impressive, Sirena, is the farthest into the forest. Thus, you'll have to decide if you're going to get there by (lots and lots of) hiking, by boat, or by plane (the fastest and comfiest but obviously most expensive option), and whether you have enough time to make a trip to the park worth your while. You should budget at least 2 to 3 days for getting in and exploring, plus another day or two to recover before heading back to San José or your next destination.

GUIDED TOURS

Unless you really know your stuff, nature-wise, a guide familiar with the local ecology will help you spot tons more wildlife than you'd see on your own; you also won't have to figure out tide tables for hikes, or worry about getting lost (even

---

An 8-Hour Tour?

For a hundred bucks, a few tours will take you from Puerto Jiménez to and from Corcovado in a single day. Don't bother. Unless you're flying in directly to the Sirena ranger station deep in the park (in which case the damage is closer to $650), you'll end up spending most of your time in transit: The round-trip to Carate, near the entrance, takes 4 hours, and then it's an hour-and-a-half walk to and from the park entrance. That leaves you 2, maybe 3 hours in the park itself. You'll see just as much in other parts of the Osa, without coming back completely drained.

But if you've got your little heart truly set on Corcovado, a 1-day tour makes sense only if you're already staying close to one of the park entrances, in Carate (the Terrapin Lodge, p. 206, runs dandy day trips), Dos Brazos (close to the El Tigre ranger station), or La Palma (near Los Patos station).

though, granted, the trails are relatively well marked). If you're staying in one of the many all-inclusives in Drake Bay, guided tours are part of your package (these are especially good if you don't want to spend too many hours hiking in and out, but they're also among the Osa's pricier options). Hiring a guide helps the local economy and poor *campesinos*, who'd otherwise be tempted to chop down trees to farm to make money. Rates vary, but start around $100 for a full day, including transportation and lunch. Almost all of the lodges can help you set up a guide, but you can also go through park headquarters in Puerto Jiménez (see below). If you're in the Rincón area or planning to go in at the Los Patos entrance, you can also sign up for a tour from the **Fundación Neotrópica** (☎ 253-2130; www. fascinationcostarica.com), which buys up land for conservation, does scientific research, promotes environmental education, and trains locals to be guides.

Of the tour operators, **Osa Aventura** (☎ 735-5758, cell 830-9832 or 836-4114; www.osaaventura.com) is among the most professional and experienced outfits going when it comes to Corcovado (see sidebar on Mike Boston, p. 218). A 1-day hike, which includes a meeting with one of the older gold miners in the area (he's a fascinating fellow), costs $50 per person from any lodging in Carate, $80 from Puerto Jimenez, including transportation. Multiday hikes, where you really get to whack the bush, camp out, and get dirty, start at $250 for 3 days and can go above $2,000 for an involved, and involving, 9-day tour. Check the excellent website for more detailed information.

Alfa Romeo (100m/330 ft. south of the Puerto Jiménez airstrip; ☎ 735-5353 or 735-5112; www.alfaromeoair.com; MC, V) flies Cessna and Azteca five-passenger planes directly into Sirena Station, as well as to Carate, Drake Bay, and other points on the peninsula. The fare is $650 for up to four passengers. You can also arrange private charters.

LAY OF THE LAND
General Park Info

Corcovado is open daily from 8am to 4pm. Admission is $8 for the day, or $17 for 5-day passes, which include Caño Island. Entry points are at the ranger stations, **La Leona, Sirena, Los Patos,** and **San Pedrillo** (a fifth entrance at **El Tigre** is good for day trips near the station, while the **Los Planes** station near Drake Bay has been closed indefinitely). All the stations have toilets, drinking water, and basic camping facilities ($3–$4 a night). Sirena's the most visitor-friendly, offering dorm-style digs ($8 per person) and a *soda* dishing up simple grub (a day's meal plan will run you $30). At the other stations are camping facilities but no meals (hence the three-meal minimum at Sirena). There are roads up to the entrances, but not within the park itself, so come ready to hike. You can stay a maximum of 5 days and 4 nights.

Unless you're visiting only for the day, you'll have to contact the park offices **Osa Conservation Area** (☎ 735-5036 or 735-5580; www.corcovado.org) to make reservations (ideally at least 1 month ahead, possibly more in peak season, since there's limited space at any of the stations). Especially if you're going it alone, definitely check the website, which ticks off an extensive checklist of items you'll want to bring, along with other useful stuff to know (there are sharks and crocs in the waterways, for example).

A Bluffer's Field Guide to Corcovado & Environs

Costa Rica's got wildlife up the wazoo, so what makes Corcovado truly unique? For starters, more than a 10 microclimates and ecosystems thrive inside this ravishing, bigger-than-usual chunk of primeval forest, which also supports a variety of animals. Here's a little crib sheet on Corco's most wanted:

WILDCATS   Everybody wants a glimpse, but your only chance will probably be deep in the forest, hours from Sirena station. Oh, and at night. The BCOC (big cat on campus), the **jaguar,** sits at the top of the food chain, and used to be worshipped by pre-Columbian peoples. These guys can reach 1.8m long (6 ft.) at 136 kg (300 lbs.), but are megatough to spot, even for trained experts. It doesn't help that the jag's cruising for extinction, its numbers here are now fewer than 40, down from 75 to 100 a decade ago.

Less rare but still hard to spot is the **puma,** a tawny cat with black-tipped ears (more closely related to the house cat, they say, than to the lion or cheetah; recent DNA tests say they're close to jaguarundis, too). Pumas can get even bigger—a whopping 2.4m (8 ft.)—and jump 12m (40 ft.) and, gulp, 4.8m (16 ft.) straight up in the air. Judging from recent sightings, your best chances are around La Leona Ranger station and in some private reserves bordering the park.

Smaller cats here include **ocelots** and **margays,** both spotted like leopards and not too much larger than a house cat. Neither is considered a cinch to spot, but the ocelot is one of Corcovado's most commonly seen cats. Margays, though, are skillful climbers and spend most of their lives up in trees. Despite the relatively small size of both ocelots and margays, they'll not only eat, say, fruit, but bigger things that move, like white-faced monkeys and sloths.

OTHER BIG MAMMALS   One varmint you may come across is the strange-looking **Baird's tapir,** a long-snouted cross between a wild boar and an anteater. They're actually the biggest animals in the park—adult males can weigh in at 300kg (650 lbs). They feed in water and are good swimmers, so look for them in rivers, pools, and swamps. Despite their lumbering size, tapirs are mostly harmless, gentle herbivores—although

The Trails

Because Sirena Station is a hive of scientific activity (there are some semipermanent researchers and always a handful of grad students), is deep in the park, and is close to the best trails for wildlife-spotting, any multiday trip will start off from one of the three other stations and make a stop at Sirena. There's some debate as to which is the easiest starting point, but folks in the know say that the route from Los Patos (20km/ 13 miles) is longer but less of a slog than La Leona along the coast (14km/8¾ miles); plus the terrain and animal-watching along the way tends to be better. Just get to your starting point early, because it takes hours to get from

Costa Rica's environment minister was recently attacked by a mama tapir who thought he was after her baby.

White-lipped peccaries, on the other hand, have a rep for being ornery (maybe it's the white lips, who knows). The main prey of jaguars and pumas, they look like brown feral pigs. You're more likely to spot these guys both because they're out and about in the daytime and because fewer big cats mean more peccaries. They're not dangerous except if there's a herd—sometimes up to 100 or 200—stampeding through, in which case they can run your over or surround you. Not a problem, usually—you'll hear them before you see them, and all you need to do is climb a tree and wait. But you see what we mean about being fit to visit Corcovado.

AMPHIBIANS & REPTILES   At least 40 frog species, dozens of snakes, and more than a couple dozen types of lizards live here. The **red-eye tree frog,** with its dramatic, bulging red eyes, is a photogenic favorite and this is the poster-frog you often see in magazines and on guidebook covers. Other hopping hotties include the **poison-dart frogs,** so dubbed because indigenous folks dipped their arrows in their venom. Don't touch, of course—just get an eyeful of their glossy bright combos of red, green, yellow, and black. FYI, of the many snakes, you're unlikely to come across the pair of poisonous ones: the **fer-de-lance** and the **bushmaster.** Check out the complete list (with great images) on the park's website, www. corcovado.org.

TREES   Though far from unique to Corcovado, the *ceiba* (silk cotton) tree holds a special place in the affections (and finances) of people all over Central America and the Caribbean (dating back to their widespread use for tribal dugout canoes). They sure are impressive, growing up to 24m high (80 ft.) and 3m wide (10 ft.).

HARK, A HARPY?   No one's seen a **harpy eagle** in Corcovado for years, but people still hold out hope. This magnificent bird's half the size of a human, with slate-black feathers, a pale-gray head, white underside, and a helluva penentrating stare. They fly at up to 81kmph (50 mph) and dine on sloths, monkeys, and opossums.

one to the other, and you might not even be let in after 11am (besides the following rough descriptions, make sure to get detailed updates on hiking conditions from the offices before you head in).

To reach **Sirena via Los Patos,** you'll have to head towards the town of La Palma, 25km/16 miles northwest. A *colectivo* ($4) leaves Puerto Jiménez at 5am for the hour-long drive. From La Palma, it's a 12km/7½-mile hike (about 3 hr.) to the Los Patos entrance, passing the **Guaymí Indian reservation** along the way; if you don't have time for the full tour, at least consider stopping to pick up a handicraft or two to help them out (p. 228). To avoid wearing yourself out before you

Adventures with the Osa's Crocodile Dundee

by Jenna Wortham

A tour guide in the Osa for over a decade, the guy widely known to locals and visitors as the Costa Rican "Crocodile Dundee" is 55-year-old Mike Boston. Crikey—I mean *caramba*—the bloke's come face to face with jags, crocs, sharks, vipers, raging tides, rampaging peccaries—you name it. And he hasn't lost a visitor yet. While he's always up for something wild, he tailors to a range of tastes and abilities—bird-watchers, seasoned hikers, documentary makers, and greenhorns alike.

What drew you to the Osa?

After graduating from the University of Portsmouth, England, with an honors degree in biology under my belt, I first visited Costa Rica in 1995. As I made my way on a boat down the Río Sierpe, I was completely unprepared for the remote and wild beauty of the peninsula. I couldn't resist the opportunity to move back to the Tropics (as I grew up in Trinidad and Tobago). A year later, I made the move, established Osa Aventura in 1998, and have been living here ever since.

What's your ideal trip into the Osa?

Heading out into the (relatively) unknown areas, staying at locally run lodges and campsites, where we're unlikely to cross paths with other tourists, and getting a real flavor for culture and life in the Osa—that's my ideal itinerary.

What kinds of adventures can guests expect on one of your tours?

On many occasions on the long hike from the Sirena Biological Station to San Pedrillo in the northern sector of Corcovado, my clients and I have had to construct a raft for our packs from flotsam and jetsam on the

even get to Corcovado, take a cab to Los Patos ($35–$45) or to La Palma, then the rest of the way on horseback ($25 in Guadalupe, just outside La Palma). Once in, the first 5km (3 miles) or so of trail are hilly and rugged, followed by another 15km (9.3 miles) of flat walking including several river crossings (in the wet season, the water will reach to your hips). The hike from Los Patos to Sirena can take anywhere from 5 to 7 hours.

From **La Leona to Sirena,** parallel to the Pacific Ocean, you're never far from the water. To enter at La Leona, you'll have to get to Carate, to which a *colectivo* leaves from Puerto Jiménez at 6am ($7) or you can catch a cab for about $60. From Carate, you'll have to walk on along the beach, on loose sand (and when the sun is cookin', so are you) for 45 minutes to an hour. Once past La Leona, a shady wooded trail showcases lots of monkeys, some coatimundis, and, if you're early enough, trogons, honeycreepers, white-necked Jacobin hummingbirds, and mangrove hummingbirds. Checking the tide tables is a must, to make sure you get across several rocky points at low tide (one of which, hint, hint, is called

beach. This is where the remote Río Llorona flows into the sea and the high tide is too deep to wade across. We launch the raft and begin the 500-foot swim across the river. Everyone is well aware the river is home to bull sharks and large crocodiles so you can imagine our relief when we get to the other side—life and limb intact.

What kind of characters do you encounter in the Osa?

A few years back, I got lost in the mountains while searching for an elusive bush dweller and met a gold miner. Half–Costa Rican and half-Gypsy, he was born in Germany in 1936 and was smuggled to Cuba by his father to escape Hitler. He's exactly the kind of unique character people love to meet—at 70-plus years old, he's fit and feisty, living a meager and completely liberated life. With his permission, I bring day hikers into the mountains to meet him.

So, is the park dangerous?

I do sometimes encounter potentially dangerous animals. I've had to seek safety with clients in buttress roots or atop fallen trees numerous times to avoid roving packs of aggressive peccaries, large crocodiles, bull sharks, and the fer-de-lance, a large pit-viper. But the Corcovado is a wildlife wonderland—who could pass up the opportunity to see such spectacular sights? Species endangered in the rest of the world are abundant here. All in all, the jungle is relatively benign! You're more likely to see the traces of dangerous animals rather than the animals themselves. Honestly, the climate here is the most dangerous thing you will encounter.

Tours with Mike Boston can be arranged through **Osa Aventura** *(www. osaaventura.com).*

Salsipuedes—"Get Out If You Can"—Point); from Salsipuedes, the path finally cuts inland. The whole thing should take 5 to 7 hours.

The longest hike 25km (16 miles) is from **Sirena to San Pedrillo,** about 20km (13 miles) of it along tightly packed beach, easier than the La Leona–Sirena route. There are several biggish river crossings, the deepest of which is the Rio Sirena (at high tide there's a boat to get you across). Ah, one other thing—there are bull sharks and crocodiles swimming around here, so it's best to probably go with a guide, or at least clear everything with the Sirena rangers before heading out. Anyway, this trail has the most impressive trees, as well as cool stuff like **Piedra Arco,** a rock archway carpeted with greenery, and a side trail to **La Llorona,** a 160m (100-ft.) waterfall. The trek takes 7 to 9 hours, so you'll have to camp out at San Pedrillo before moving on. From San Pedrillo, it's another 12km (7.5-mile) walk along the beach to Drake Bay (or catch a ride out from Sirena or San Pedrillo with one of the Drake Bay lodge boats; fares vary, but expect to pay $25 to $40, depending on how many in your party—ask the rangers at Sirena to radio the lodges).

From Sirena Station

There are approximately eight different trails from Sirena. You'll have your choice of terrain, from flat to steep, with great wildlife-spotting on all of them. **Night hikes** are the best for catching sight of mammals, snakes, frogs, and other amphibians and reptiles. Swimming isn't a good idea on Sirena beach, but if you take the Claro trail to Río Claro, there's a safe natural pool. On the Guanacaste or Sirena trails, you'll pass the river Sirena, where you can occasionally see crocodiles, bull sharks, and tapirs. Lots of people rent canoes and go up the Sirena River ($20).

OSA & CORCOVADO ON THE CHEAP

Despite their pricey reputations, both can be done on modest budgets—assuming you've got the time and the patience for some preplanning. Granted, you'll have to make do with basic grub and digs, plus hours and hours of hiking, but it's not quite the Herculean trek some people make it out to be. I've put together a sample itinerary that will help you cut a large swath through the region in 7 to 10 days.

Days 1–2   From San José, catch the 5am bus ($4) to **Puerto Jiménez,** which will get you in around 2pm, passing some mighty fetching scenery en route along the Interamerican Highway. Spend at least 1 night in the Puerto Jiménez area. If you're staying in town a couple of days, head out on one of them to the **Black Turtle Lodge** in nearby Playa Platanares, or even out to Matapalo.

Have lunch at the popular *soda* **Carolina** ($5 for a *casado*) and meet up with locals, resident expats, and other travelers (adventure outfitter **Escondido Rex** keeps an office here, so check in with owner John Sibley about local excursions). Explore the town and pick up supplies and rations (water, sandwiches, packages of macaroni and cheese, and so forth).

Days 3–4   Catch the 6am *colectivo* to Carate (2 hr./$7). Walk a couple of miles north along the Carate Beach's soft sand to the entrance of **Corcovado Park** (sunscreen, oh yeah—*el sol* can be way intense, and there's not a scrap of shade). You'll reach **La Leona** station in 45 minutes to an hour, where you pay $17 for a pass that allows you up to 5 days in the park. The 16km (10-mile) hike onward to **Sirena** takes 5 to 7 hours, depending on your pace. Have dinner at the ranger station and spend the night in one of the dorm-style bunk beds ($8). You could also camp at La Leona for $4 a night, by the way, but there's not much else to do there. *There are a limited number of beds at Sirena Station, so you'll have to reserve in advance with the Osa Conservation Area office in Puerto Jiménez (p. 215).*

Days 4–5   Spend 2 days **discovering the trails around Sirena.** There are canoes for rent ($3), a good way of exploring the Claro and Sirena rivers; both are home to crocodiles and bull sharks. Ask the manager of Sirena station manager when the boat comes in for Drake Bay or San Pedrillo.

Days 6–7   You can either hike to **San Pedrillo** station (29km/18 miles; 7-9 hr.) or catch a boat to San Pedrillo or **Drake Bay** (for the boat, have the group split the $100 fare; with some luck, you'll be traveling with guests from the Drake Bay lodges and won't need a group). If you stay in San Pedrillo, you'll have to camp on the beach ($4) and lug in your own provisions.

Days 6–7   Arrive in Drake Bay. Check in to the **Rio Drake Lodge** ($22 a cabin), across from the airport. From Drake Bay you can catch the 4am or 1:30pm bus back to Las Palmas and from there you catch a bus back to Puerto Jimenez. The bus from Drake Bay will cost you $4 to $6 per person.

DRAKE BAY

The Bahía de Drake (pronounced "*Drah*-kay") was named after the explorer Sir Francis Drake (pronounced "Drake"), who dropped anchor in this bay between Caño Island and the north coast of the Osa Peninsula in 1579. He found pretty much today's same picturesque coastline with jigsaw coves, and calm waters home to a variety of whales, dolphins, and manta rays. One local legend even has it that Drake left behind buried treasure on Caño Island.

Into the 20th century, Drake Bay and Caño Island were home to the pre-Columbian Diquis tribes. The island, along with the area up through the Sierpe and Terraba rivers, is the site of hundreds of centuries-old stone spheres, ranging from a bocce-ball size to some 2m (6½ ft.) in diameter. Some have been found near burial sites, but nobody's completely sure what they were for.

The Díquis eventually disappeared, and the area was only repopulated in earnest when Ticos migrated in to farm and raise cattle in the early 1970s. By the '80s, tourism began to take off, leading to high-end ecolodges sprouting up, self-contained islands with their own generators and solar-power plants, septic systems, and all foodstuffs and essentials shipped in from outside. In the rest of Drake Bay, the town of Agujitas (aka Drake Bay Village, pop. 1,000) didn't get power till 2004.

Agujitas is the main tourism hub, with a tiny main drag, a couple of restaurants, several tour operators, and food stands. A few miles up in the hills, the little town of **Los Planes** is remote even for the Osa, though homes and other development are already planned for both towns. South of Agujitas, all-inclusive ecolodges line the coast all the way down to San Pedrillo ranger station, from **Playa Cocalito** and **Caletas** to **San Josécito.** The most pricey lodges are in the Punta Río Claro National Wildlife Refuge, where you can hike to Río Claro, a natural freshwater swimming pool right next to the ocean, and on Playa Josécito, a golden beach covered with mango trees and palms.

GETTING TO & AROUND DRAKE BAY
By Bus
From San José, **TRACOPA buses** (☎ 223-7685) leave from Calle 11 at Avenida 5, at 5, 7, 8:30, and 10am, then 1, 2:30, and 6pm. The trip costs $4.75 each way and takes roughly 6 hours. The same amount of buses return to San José from 5am to 4:45pm. From Palmar, you should either arrange transportation with the lodge directly, or take a bus.

By Plane
Nature Air (www.natureair.com) has two 40-minute flights daily from San José directly to Drake Bay, leaving at 8am and 3pm, $92 each way. Sansa (www.fly sansa.com) operates three daily flights (6am, 10:15am, and 1:55pm; $80 each way). Times are subject to change and stopovers could be added along the way.

By Car

Not only are the roads not great, but you won't have much use for them once you get to Drake Bay—unless you're staying in town. But if you drive, keep in mind that you'll need a high-clearance vehicle, and it'll really only be possible during dry season (Dec–Apr). Call ahead to your hotel about road conditions.

From either San José or points along the Central Pacific coast, you'll get on the Interamerican Highway to Chacarita. From there, head towards the town of Rincón on the Golfo Dulce. There's a road from Rincón that passes through to Rancho Quemado and then on to Drake Bay Village.

If you're heading to Sierpe, you'll get off the Interamerican Highway at Palmar Sur. From there, turn south, where you'll pass through endless banana plantations before getting to Sierpe. As there are no signs and the roads fork in different directions, you will have to stop and ask for directions to avoid taking wrong turns.

ACCOMODATIONS, BOTH STANDARD & NOT

Compared with Puerto Jiménez, lodgings in Drake Bay are limited and pricey, but it helps that tours like day trips to Corcovado or Caño Island, which on their own can cost as much as a night in one of the lodges, are usually included in the rate. The cost is partly due to the fact that there's only one main road leading into Drake Bay, and most lodges aren't even near that—they can only be reached by boat or a long hike. The only digs approaching budget level are in Agujitas or Punta Marenco.

In & Around Agujitas

It's not easy to find inexpensive lodging in the Drake Bay area. Staying a bit inland in or around Agujitas can save costs without losing the views—rainforest scenes frame all of the lodges here. Agujitas is ideal for solo travelers or anyone interested in a more laid-back visit to Drake Bay. Keep in mind electricity is pretty rare around Drake Bay and Agujitas is no exception.

$$ Home to Drake Bay's oldest and most respected dive operation, **Cabinas Jinetes de Osa** (3km/2 miles from Drake Bay airstrip; ☎ 231-5806, or 800/317-0333 in the U.S. and Canada; www.drakebayhotel.com; MC, V) has been built up into a "elegant-casual" destination for serious divers and adventure-seeking tourists. On these 8 hectares (20 acres), all sorts of trails lead to deserted beaches and remote waterfalls, kayaks, and a good 20 activities programs: dive certification, ziplines, and Corcovado tours, of course, but also other stuff for pretty attractive prices hereabout, like river tubing ($10) and a sunset boat tour ($30). The rooms are done in white stucco and white tile, have ceiling fans and high wood-beam ceilings, and doubles start at $60 with all meals (including daily coffee-and-muffin delivery so you won't miss the stunning sunrises from your porch). The grub's tasty, too, like fresh snapper with mango, baked breads, rice, and beans.

$$ Run by Tico-Swiss couple David and Jolanda and their son Luca on 3.2 manicured hectares (8 acres), **Las Caletas Lodge** ★ 🌟 (3km/2 miles south of Agujitas; ☎ 381-4052 or 826-1460; www.caletas.co.cr; MC, V) is fab for families. Perched atop a cove, its five basic but comfy two-story beachfront cabinas provide

a nice bit of privacy, large rooms, porches for taking in the coastline views, and private hot-water baths (some have two). Moms and dads will especially like the mild surf here, unlike in other parts of Drake Bay. Per-person rates start at $52 a night (half off for kids under 12), including kayaking, scuba, and full board (the food here is a top-notch blend of Caribbean and European, relying heavily on fresh produce, seafood, and meat—veggie dishes, too).

$$ After a good dozen years running their four-unit **Hotel Ojalá** ✹ (20 min. north of Agujitas in Drake Bay; ☎ 223-4060, or 877/769-8747 in the U.S and Canada; www.hotelojala.com; MC, V accepted only for full advance payment) on a mangrove-lined shore, family owners Fred, Yessini, and Lily have built up a reputation for treating anglers right (such as cooking guests' catch in their wood-burning oven or barbecue grill). There are three woody rooms in the main house, with cute, quirky details along the lines of batik-printed bedspreads, vintage nightstands, and red-marble sinks (and if you like your A/C—well, c'mon down). Room and board starts at $58 per person in season (or upgrade to the *casita,* where another $16 gets you a private wooden deck with breathtaking ocean views framed by the Ojalá's lush gardens and fruit trees).

In Punta Marenco

Staying inside the **Punta Río Claro National Wildlife Refuge,** you have lots of great hiking out the back doors of lodges that are even more tucked-away feeling and endless jaw-dropping views. Pretty impressive, but on the other hand you might decide it's ultimately not worth the extra bucks. Have a look:

$$ One of the things we love about the **Marenco Beach and Rainforest Lodge** ✦ (10 min. north of Corcovado by boat; ☎ 258-1919, or 800/278-6223 in the U.S. and Canada; www.marencolodge.com; AE, MC, V) is its plum location, on 6 sq. km (2⅓ sq. miles) of private reserve and 22km (14 miles) of deserted beaches. Perhaps just as lovable is the price: Each of its seven regular doubles start at just $46 a night. The screened standard rooms are perfectly comfy in our book, but if you're honeymooning or just want the bungalows' charming extras (filmy netting draped over beds, large tropical-flower bouquets, handsome dark-wood beds), $67 is still a pretty good deal for 1 of the 18 bungalows. Yes, it's true those rates don't cover meals (for the full meal plan, tack on $30 a day), but this is still less expensive than most places in Drake Bay.

$$ For the sexiest views on the Pacific side of the Osa, **Punta Marenco Lodge** ✦✦ (3km/2 miles north of Corcovado; ☎ 877-3735; www.puntamarenco.com; MC, V) is perched on a ridge, with trails leading down the coast into the Río Claro refuge. Guides will lead you as far into the refuge as you want to go, which is pretty deep—the darn thing's almost more than 400 hectares (1,000 acres) of tropical rainforest and beaches. The 17 rooms are cute, simple, and clean, with private baths and porches but the usual cold-water showers; it's $75 to stay the night in one of them, with meals included in a *rancho*-style dining room at large wooden communal tables (multiday packages are available adding transfers and tours, and if you book on the lodge website, you can save pretty considerably). But you should probably take a pass on this if you're attached to your electrical gadgets: Electricity is available only at night, and sometimes in the mornings.

Along the Coast

$$ While the rugged beauty of the Osa can already be a spiritual enough experience, those who want it extra-crunchy—adding asanas and boning up on herbs—should give a thought to **Guaria de Osa** ✦✦ (☎ 358-9788, or 510-235-4313 in the U.S.; www.guariadeosa.com; cash only). Founded by an ethnobotanist from (just guess) California, Jonathan Miller-Weisberger, the lodge offers the usual Caño Island and Corcovado exploration. But the folks here also raise, study, and teach about endangered native plants, and run an array of programs on yoga, Tai-chi, qui gong, massage, indigenous arts, and shamanism. The pagoda-style three-story greathouse is impressive, with airy common spaces decked out in rattan hammocks, plus a wide-open wood platform great for ogling sunsets; there's even an Internet cafe. Choose between two private-bath rooms in the main building, one two-story bungalow, and five bamboo tent-cabins with mosquito nets and shared baths. Rates start at $55 per person per night with all meals but they have a variety of special packages. Keep in mind that this puppy is *out* there in more ways than one—it's a 90-minute boat ride from Sierpe, then a 20- to 30-minute walk (though you can have a porter hump your bags, for an extra charge).

Drake's Bay or Bust—Without Going Bust

Getting a wee touch of ecolodge sticker shock? A trio of tips to stop your head (and wallet) from spinning:

Don't Always Go for the Package Deal. Most lodges quote package rates that include transportation and a selection of tours, relying on the fact that most people will find it too scary or a hassle to plan it themselves. But most also offer room-only or room-board rates; it's usually a much better deal to take them, then pick and choose tours a la carte, instead of getting locked into an itinerary before you even get there. This can save you as much as a few hundred dollars per person.

Arrange Your Own Transport. If you're coming in from somewhere close to this part of the country (for example, Manuel Antonio), you can get a bus easily and pretty quickly to the lodges' usual pick-up points, Sierpe or Palmar Sur. Package prices are often higher because they include round-trip airfare from San José and/or various other transfers. Check their websites to see how much they charge to cart you in from the above towns.

Check with a Vacation Packager. It's worth comparing prices and tour options with a specialist (p. 204). Many have special relationships with different lodges, so they can snag you little discounts or perks such as free transfers, room upgrades, or tours in one big package.

Probably not the best location if you want to get out to Corcovado and other stuff independently.

$$$ The sole vacation rental hereabouts is the **Drake Bay Oceanview Chalet** (5-min. walk south of Drake Bay; ☎ 561-762-1763 in U.S.; www.drakebaychalet. com). Built in 2005 by Karen Michaud, part-owner of the Drake Bay Wilderness Resort, it's a one-bedroom, sleeping up to four, perched on a hill just above a secluded beach south of town (a cab for grocery runs would cost $10–$15 each way). It's a dandy mix of independence, amenities (kitchen, outdoor grill, TV, DVD player, washer/dryer, even A/C), and services (you can radio Drake Bay Wilderness Resort from the house to book tours or report problems; maid/cook service is optional). *Caveats:* You'll probably want a car, and you'll probably be eating in most nights, since stand-alone dining around here is very limited. There's a 6-night minimum, which runs $750 in high season, $600 in low.

WHY YOU'RE HERE: THE TOP SIGHTS & ATTRACTIONS

Most lodges have pretty similar activities for their guests—sea kayaking, snorkeling, hiking, that kind of thing. The following are additional sights and activities that are most worthwhile or unique to the area.

A top don't miss is a day trip to **Isla de Caño.** Apart from those pre-Columbian spheres I mentioned above, the warm, crystal-blue waters, coral reefs, and riotous marine life make the island one of the top spots in Costa Rica for snorkeling and diving—with pretty damn good chances of spotting needlefish, porcupinefish, diadema sea urchins, moray eels, and manta rays.

And of course you won't come all the way out here without a trip to **Corcovado,** would you now? Compared to the trickier and pricier day trips from the Puerto Jiménez side of the peninsula, getting to San Pedrillo or Sirena stations from Drake Bay is a snap. Almost all the lodges offer 1-day tours via motorboat into either station; San Pedrillo (the closer of the two, a half-hour away) runs $45 to $65, and Sirena $80 and up. If you decide to go it on your own, see p. 215 for more details on the trails and hike times.

A respectable alternative or even substitute for Corcovado is the **Río Claro National Wildlife Refuge,** 200 hectares (500 acres) at the mouth of the Claro River, just south of Agujitas. It's the same "biological corridor" as Corcovado, meaning you'll see a lot of the same species, and also a boffo birding spot. The reserve's perched above Playa Caletas and Punta Marenco, right by the **Punta Marenco Lodge** (p. 224), which can set you up for a free tour with its resident biologists. During low tide you can hike the trail to Punta Marenco in an hour, and the views of the ocean and the rocky coves make it a mighty pretty experience indeed.

Oh, the peoples, they do so *looove* the **dolphins and whales,** and Drake Bay is a fab spot for this porpoise. Seriously, it's right at the crossroads of the North and South American migrations, so it's got them all: bottle-nose and Pantropic dolphins, humpback whales, orcas, sperm whales, pseudo-orcas (aka false killer whales—dolphins on steroids that look like orcas). The main outfit running tours is **Delfin Amor Wild Dolphin Encounters** (☎ 847-3131 or 866/527-5558 in the U.S. and Canada; www.divinedolphin.com; AE, MC, V), led by Sierra Goodman. A confessed "dolphin fanatic," she also has a nonprofit foundation working on a marine sanctuary and studying the area's dolphins and whales; her websites are terrific info sources about the critters. Naturally, she knows right where to find them; she's even dubbed one pod of Pantropic spotted dolphins near the shore "the homeboys." Boats head out at 8am; it's $95 for a full day, including lunch. The nearby **Drake Bay Wilderness Resort** (☎ 770-8012 or 561/762-1763 in the U.S. and Canada; www.drakebay.com; AE, MC, V) also runs tours, as does Jinetes de Osa (p. 222). Until recently, by the way, you could dive in and swim with these guys, but whatever—seeing them in their habitat like this is reward enough.

The **Original Canopy Tour** arrived in Drake Bay recently and Jinetes de Osa (p. 222) has the franchise. It's got nine platforms, a half-dozen traverse cables that go as high as 90m (300 ft.), and an observation bridge 20m up (65 ft.) at the edge of a scenic river bend. The cost for 2 to 3 hours is $55 (you can add a jaunt to the Agujitas waterfall or a horseback ride for a little extra). It's better than the Osa's other zipline, over near Puerto Jiménez, but if you're hitting other parts of Costa Rica, you might wanna hold off—you'll probably find more impressive ones to spend your money on.

At night, bug out with **Tracie the Bug Lady** (☎ 382-1619; www.thenight tour.com). Tracie Stice and her Tico partner, Gianfranco Gómez, are biologists who take you out into the jungle with boots, walking sticks, flashlights, and hand-held night-vision gear that casts a spooky green glow but doesn't rile up the creepy-crawly-flappies (mantises, bats, tree frogs, snakes, tarantulas, lizards, and a

CIA's worth of assorted bugs). Along the way, they'll give you a primer on insectile mating habits, and with any luck you'll spot a viper or boa. A very well spent $35, we've gotta say.

THE "OTHER" OSA

Conservation is a big and ever-growing "industry" here, so there's no shortage of volunteer opportunities in the field—almost everyone needs a hand, and chances are if you come across an a commercial and/or research outfit where you think you'd like to volunteer your services, you're on. Here's a thought: The lodges themselves need help, so you might be able to wrangle room and board for free (or a nominal fee) while picking up a skill and learning about the environment. Most places expect a month-plus commitment, but with lodges you may be able to make special arrangements by contacting the owners directly.

Examples: The well-known high-end **Tiskita Lodge** (3km./2 miles south of Pavones; ☎ 296-8125; www.tiskita-lodge.co.cr), across the Golfo Dulce in Playa Pavones, has seasonal volunteer positions. Volunteers pitch in on things like monitoring sea turtle nests, teaching environmental ed to local kids, and a scarlet-macaw reintroduction project. In Drake Bay, the **Guaria de Osa** (p. 224) also has a formal volunteer/internship program ($25 a night for 1–2 weeks, $15 a night for 2–4 weeks, room and board included). Over at the **Herrera Botanical Gardens** (p. 213), volunteers work on reforestation and garden planting and maintenance (who knows, you might learn enough about medicinal plants to start your own pharmaceutical). In exchange, they get free housing, chow, and what they call the "grandfathered inclusion" in PJ's expat "in-crowd"—not to mention use of kayaks and other **Escondido Trex** gear.

MEETING LOCALS

There are so few permanent residents out here that it's not hard for tourists to mix with locals, both Tico and expat. Frankly, if like most visitors you're staying in one of the lodges, the biggest problem is getting off the nice, comfy, all-inclusive reservation. Once you do, you'll find locals are more than happy to share info on their favorite spots.

There are a few places, under most tourists' radar, that bring out the locals in their spare time. In Matapalo, most everyone from Puerto Jiménez down to Carate drops in at the **organic market** outside Buena Esperanza restaurant (p. 208), every Friday from 5 to 7:30pm or so. Ticos, expats, lodge employees, and a smattering of tourists stroll around stalls of vendors hawking produce including a lot you'd never get back home (or for that matter, you've never even seen before). Besides the mundane basil and carrots, you can get an eyeful and sometimes a mouthful of unusual local fruits, including:

- *Mamón chino.* A spiky red or yellow fruit. To eat, just hold it between your fingers, bite the top off enough to remove the hard outer shell, and enjoy. Don't let the way they look intimidate you, inside you'll find something that tastes similar to a strawberry).
- *Tomates de palo.* An egg-shaped fruit that is pointed at both ends. It can be eaten in a variety of ways but one of the most popular is by just cutting it in half, sprinkling a little sugar on it, and scooping out the flesh and the pulp.

Painting the Osa

$$$ If you're looking to take advantage of the natural inspiration surrounding you and channeling it in a creative outlet, check out the **Sombra de Lapa** art retreats (near Barrio Bonito, 25 min. north of Puerto Jiménez; ☎ 378-3013, or 508/714-0622 from the U.S.; www.michaelincostarica.com; MC, V) held by expatriate artist Michael Cranford. Part-owner of Juanita's, a popular bar and restaurant in town, Cranford's lifelong devotion to art and years of experience as a professional adds expertise to his workshops; his mentors include Frank Frazetta (a well-known fantasy and sci-fi illustrator—remember *Conan the Barbarian*?) and M.C. Escher (a graphic artist known for his distorted perspectives). From January through April, Cranford conducts 5- to 9-day workshops on a 48-hectare (120-acre) private reserve up against the lush mountain rainforests, with views of the Pacific and Barú volcano. The focus is on oil, acrylic, and watercolor painting, but Cranford customizes, and also takes students out to nearby Corcovado to work outdoors. You bunk in a beautiful private home with breezy, open-air living area and kitchen overlooking dense forest and 2 landscaped hectares (5 acres) (the two-story, atrium-style kitchen alone is worth the trek). He's also been known to rent out the house, which has three spacious bedrooms, two baths, and a Jacuzzi, for $1,100 a week. Art workshops start at $850 per person, including all meals and lodging.

♦ *Manzana tica.* A plum-size apple that's both sweet and sour.
♦ *Nance.* An orange-yellow fruit with thin skin and white, juicy, oily pulp. It is sometimes used to make wine or carbonated beverages.

If you don't make it to the **Finca Kobo** cacao farm (p. 201), you can sample its goodies here. Those hunting for gifts will find a nice selection of local handicrafts—mostly earrings and bracelets.

Round about closing time, the real party begins, with folks hanging out, gabbing, listening to music, and tipping back a few. Stay for dinner and/or drinks, and you'll meet people from all over. When there's dancing, we're told the Ticos sit back and get a hoot out of watching the crazy gringos dance alone (Ticos mostly dance in couples) or otherwise make spectacles of themselves.

You should also ask around about parties. Every so often, the community out in Matapalo will send out flyers for impromptu shindigs where everyone's welcome. An invite to one recent "full moon" bonfire party on the beach encouraged people to "come naked." Sure enough, one lodge owner showed up on his white horse, Diamante, wearing nothing. Naturally, moonlit skinny-dipping ensued.

If you're in the La Palma area, we'd definitely recommend a visit to the **Guaymi Indigenous Reserve,** a couple of hours' drive south. The reserve is just outside Corcovado Park and it is south of Las Palmas.

The Guaymi (aka the Ngobe) have lived in this area for centuries, moving back and forth across the Costa Rica/Panama border. Recently, they've settled in various reserves, including this one, where a couple of dozen families live by subsistence farming and making traditional arts and handicrafts for you to buy. These include *chacaras* (bags of all sizes woven in pita fiber, bark, and nylon), *nuñungas* (plastic bead necklaces in red, white, yellow, blue, and black), drums, maracas, and flutes.

From Puerto Jiménez, you can drive out on your own, take the *colectivo* ($4; leaves at 5am) to La Palma and then take a very, very long walk (not recommended) or catch a taxi ($45). The **Ngobe lodge,** built in traditional thatched style, takes groups on "ethno-eco" and medicinal plant/botanical tours. For details, contact San José's **Galería Namu** (Av. 7, between calles 5 and 7, San José; ☎ 256-3412; www.galerianamu.com), which also specializes in indigenous arts and crafts.

Among expats and a growing number of Ticos, yoga classes are getting pretty trendy; a good half of the lodges offer them. Out in Matapalo, there are daily classes at **Ojo del Mar** (p. 203), which welcomes drop-ins (so does nearby **Bosque del Cabo,** p. 205, but that lodge is harder to get to without a car). The yoga retreat **Tierra de los Milagros** (see below) mostly hosts private groups, but it's worth asking if you can join in when they're in between groups. Out in Carate, the **La Luna Lodge** (p. 206) also takes nonguests in its classes. For times and rates, you'll have to call directly once you're down here.

Yoga is pretty big in Matapalo in general, but at **Tierra de Milagros** ✦ (off Playa Carbonera; ☎ 735-5062, cell 360-5715; www.tierrademilagros.com) it's all yoga, all the time. On 4 lush, landscaped hectares (10 acres), artist-owners Nikki and Brad have created a gorgeous, serene retreat with creative touches such as zen-like stonework and the "Path of Truth," flanked by a curtain of rocks with eyes painted on them. You stay in one of the thatched, open-air A-frames with bathrooms a short walk away. There are three yoga decks, two of which face the ocean, and classes twice daily. Nikki and Brian mostly take in groups—booked months in advance—they also accept individuals, depending on the day or week. Prices vary, and you'll need to e-mail or call for a quote, but on average it comes out to about $90 per person. You won't have to do yoga to stay here, but it definitely helps.

7 The Caribbean Coast

Life on Costa Rica's steamy, beachy, multi-culti eastern shore follows a different rhythm—a *very* different rhythm.

by David Appell & Nelson Mui

DESCENDING FROM THE COOL CONFINES OF THE CENTRAL VALLEY highlands to the coastal lowlands, it gets hotter, soupier, and mosquito-ier. The pace slows down, and the geography, people, food, and music all change—and suddenly you feel like you could be on some old-time castaway Caribbean isle back before the era of the all-inclusive. The steamy, waterway-riddled rainforests of Tortuguero to the north have the look and feel of the Amazon—and a few great jungle lodges, reachable by boat or air only, to complete the parallel. Meanwhile, the beaches and waters along the Talamanca coast to the south are truly some of the country's most luscious; they've even become something of a mecca for hanging ten (Puerto Viejo's "Salsa Brava" break is famous throughout the surf world).

And speaking of salsa, over here you're more likely to hear ska, calypso, and reggae (or at least reggaetón) instead, thanks to English-speaking Afro-Caribbeans, especially noticeable in cities like Limón and towns like Puerto Viejo, whose ancestors (originally from Jamaica) arrived in the 1860s. It often feels more like Costa Rasta than Costa Rica. But they're not the only part of the Benetton ad: in the hills just inland from the Talamanca coast you can visit members of the Bribri and Cabécar tribes—nearly 85 percent of the remnants of the "original" Costa Ricans. Add to that a smattering of descendants of Chinese coolies, a good number of Ticos from elsewhere in the country (who themselves are of Spanish and mestizo origin), and a growing expat population from Europe and North America, and it's a funky, heady mix indeed.

As if this cultural gumbo weren't enough, the sights and activities on this underrated stretch of coast will keep you occupied even if you don't surf. Snorkelers and divers will have a ball exploring Costa Rica's biggest coral reef, in Cahuita National Park; Tortuguero and Ganduca are the sites of impressive mass nestings of sea turtles; and, of course, there are plenty of ziplines, ATV tours, butterfly gardens, and other adventures and attractions of the kind you can find pretty much anywhere else in the country. And at least for now, staying here is pretty cheap; it's hard to find a room much over $100.

Why's that? Maybe it's at least partly due to neglect by the government in San José. Electricity didn't get to Talamanca until 1986, and private phones didn't arrive until 1997. Plus, only a handful of weekly flights link San José with Limón, and the roads are awful even for Costa Rica. Even today, Ticos in other parts of the country have the impression it's a cesspool of drugs and crime. Some of this is racism, some just plain ignorance, but it's true that the biggest local city, Limón, is a gritty, not particularly appealing port that most visitors pass up in favor of Puerto Viejo and Cahuita a half-hour down the coast. Down here, by contrast, it's not as dicey—for example, crime usually doesn't amount to more than selling a little reefer.

And though this coast is still off the beaten path, given how fast the Pacific side of the country is being paved over, it's only a matter of time before the big boys turn their sights this way. The laid-back scene that is now dominated by small mom-and-pop businesses could start to change—already, by mid-2007, an investment group was on track to open a $4-million luxury villa and entertainment complex in Puerto Viejo called Camaleón 24. For now, though, it's likely you'll be the first in your neighborhood to visit Caribbean Costa Rica, and catch a glimpse of a unique way of life that may not be around much longer.

DON'T LEAVE THE CARIBBEAN COAST WITHOUT . . .

WITNESSING THE ANNUAL MIGRATION OF GREEN SEA TURTLES IN TORTUGUERO OR GANDUCA   The nesting and hatching of these amazing creatures is incredibly moving to see, and tours are designed to get you there as unobtrusively as possible.

SNORKELING/DIVING THE REEFS IN CAHUITA OR MANZANILLO
It's an aquatic jungle of coral and tropical fish in these protected waters—some of the best undersea action in the country.

SAMPLING SOME FUNKY, FLAVORFUL CARIBBEAN CUISINE   From sweet *pan bon,* a fruit-glazed bread, to the spicy, coconut-based *rondón* stew, the Caribbean coast presents a culinary side of Costa Rica that's kilometers away from rice and beans.

CATCHING A WAVE (OR LEARNING HOW TO) AT THE BEACHES NEAR PUERTO VIEJO   The surfers were the first to discover this area, thanks to Costa Rica's most powerful break, "Salsa Brava," and other great breaks in these gorgeous blue-green waters.

VISITING AN INDIGENOUS RESERVE IN THE TALAMANCA HILLS
Get a glimpse of how the Bribri and Cabécar are keeping their traditions alive while trying to adapt to the 21st century.

A BRIEF HISTORY

On his fourth and last bop over to the Americas in 1502, Christopher Columbus (aka Cristóbal Colón) splashed ashore on the spot where this coast's main city, Puerto Limón, is today. But if the rest of the region Columbus dubbed "Rich Coast" was a disappointment to the Spanish colonists thanks to little gold, silver, and Indian slaves to work their *haciendas,* the Caribbean coast proved an even tougher nut to crack. The oppressive heat, tropical diseases, and dense jungles kept settlement pretty sparse for generations.

That started changing after the mid-19th century, with the rise of Costa Rican coffee and other farm exports, and a major port was needed to ship it all out to Europe and the States. In 1870, a site was chosen and named for an old lemon tree *(limón)* growing nearby. But coffee from the central highlands still had to be shipped via agonizingly slow, meandering river boats. So in 1884 the government hired North American contractor and entrepreneur Minor Keith to build a railroad from San José to the Caribbean. And when Engine No. 15 of the "Jungle Line" pulled into San José on December 7, 1890, it meant the Caribbean coast was really and finally part of Costa Rica.

Until the 1870s, it was mostly the indigenous Bribri, Cabécar, and Kéköldi who lived around here. But to help build his railroad, Keith brought in thousands of laborers, mostly from Jamaica and other islands, along with a few Nicaraguans, and cleared huge swaths of lowland jungles to create vast banana plantations along the rail lines. The indigenous tribes retreated to the hills away from the coast, where they still live—and thus the lowlands eventually developed the Afro-Caribbean "Creole" flavor they have today.

In 1899 Keith combined his coffee venture with the Boston Fruit Company in the West Indies to form the United Fruit Company, and by 1910, bananas had caught up with coffee as a major Tico export. Problem was, growing bananas needed a bottomless pool of cheap labor and unlimited land (the tropical lowland soil wears out quickly for crops) and it wasn't pretty. The system was practically feudal, worker conditions pretty nasty, and the ecology reeled from all the pesticides that had to be used. By the 1930s, a banana blight led United Fruit to pack up and head for the Pacific, leaving poverty and chaos in its ungrateful wake. Even today, you can see banana fields owned by Dole and Delmonte, but they're a fraction of what once was.

It didn't help that many of the local blacks were subject to racist laws restricting them to the coastal lowlands as late as 1949, when Costa Rica's new constitution came into effect. Isolated, they held on to their lilting English-based patois, music, customs, cuisine (p. 264), and even religion (Protestantism mixed with traditional African religion, a little like voodoo in Haiti or *santería* in Cuba). Some finally took off, leaving for Panama and elsewhere, but the ones who stayed turned their subsistence plots into cacao farms, and rode the rising tide of cacao prices in the 1950s and 1960s. To this day, cacao is still produced here; you can even take a "chocolate tour" around Puerto Viejo and Cahuita to see how it's grown and made. Minor Keith's railroad is gone, though; the last car rattled off into the sunset in 1995. The train that's remaking the area today is called tourism, and as the infrastructure keeps getting improved, that choo-choo is picking up speed.

LAY OF THE LAND

The Caribbean coast is divided up into three distinct geographic and cultural spheres: the canals of Tortuguero, stretching past Barra del Coronado all the way to Nicaragua; the main port city and local capital Limón, for which the entire province is named; and Talamanca, in Costa Rica's southeast corner, which includes Cahuita, Puerto Viejo, Manzanillo, and the rugged hinterland.

Area of detail

NICARAGUA

COSTA RICA
San José
Caribbean Sea
PACIFIC OCEAN
0   50 mi
0   50 km

0   20 mi
0   20 km

Barra del Colorado Airport
Barra del Colorado
Boca del Río Colorado
Río San Juan
Barra del Colorado
Río Chirripó
National
Wildlife Refuge
Río Colorado
Boca del Río Tortuguero
Tortuguero Airport
Tortuguero

To Puerto Viejo de Sarapiquí
TORTUGUERO NATIONAL PARK
Tortuguero Canal
Cariari

Río Frío

Caribbean Sea

Guapiles
Río Reventazón
Río Pacuare
Boca del Río Pacuare

BRAULIO CARRILLO NATIONAL PARK

Turrialba Volcano ▲
Guayabo National Monument
Siquirres
Playa Bonita
Moín
Limón
Limón Airport

▲ Irazú Volcano
BARBILLA NATIONAL PARK
Turrialba

Paraíso
CENTRAL RANGE
Río Chirripó Atlántico

Playa Cahuita
CAHUITA NATIONAL PARK
36

TAPANTÍ NATIONAL PARK
CORDILLERA DE TALAMANCA
Hitoy-Cerere Biological Reserve
Cahuita
Puerto Viejo
Manzanillo
BriBri

Cerro de la Muerte
LA AMISTAD
CHIRRIPÓ NATIONAL PARK
Cerro Chirripó ▲
NATIONAL PARK
TALAMANCA INDIAN RES.
BRIBRI INDIAN RES.
Gandoca-Manzanillo National Wildlife Refuge

San Isidro de El General
PARK
PANAMA

TORTUGUERO

One of Costa Rica's most remote regions (accessible only by boat and small plane), this Amazon-like patchwork of jade-colored canals and lagoons, lush rainforest, mangroves, and marshlands harbors manatees and other aquatic critters galore. Apart from the scenery, birding, and wildlife-spotting, the big deal up here is the western Caribbean's biggest, most important green sea turtle nesting grounds and sanctuary. There's a small village, too, and just north along the canals is **Barra del Coronado,** which besides being a wildlife refuge has landed itself a rep as a sport-fishing magnet.

Word Up: The Creole Patois

by Jenna Wortham

Called patois, the rhythmic lilt of the vernacular English spoken in this area is still used by nearly a third of Limón's population, the afro-Caribbean *costeños*. In fact, some of the older folks know little or no Spanish (which is taught in schools and more common among people younger than 30).

The patois you'll hear around Limón and the Talamanca coast was brought in by early Jamaican and Barbadian immigrants, who infused Caribbean phrases to create a lingo called *mekatelyu* (roughly, "let me tell you"). A phrase you might hear is *"Whoppin?"* (It means "What's going on?" or "Wassup?") And instead of saying *adiós*, locals will say "all right," or "okay." *"¿Qué o'clock, mon?"* translates as "What time is it?", and *"Mi cris, mon,"* is a common way of saying "I'm fine." Keep in mind that while *costeños* use patois, it's mostly meant for casual chat among themselves. When you talk to them, you should do it in standard English (or, if you can, Spanish). Try to mimic it and you'll likely get it wrong—sounding silly at best and insulting at worst.

LIMON

Costa Rica's premier Caribbean port city is the region's capital, and bustling with biz from container and cruise ships from all over the world. We're not covering it in detail because, frankly, it's a bit of a dump that has little to offer tourists except its annual Columbus Day carnival, when the streets of downtown Limón erupt with partiers in elaborate get-ups and a parade of bands and floats. Oh, yeah—good times . . . .

PUERTO VIEJO–MANZANILLO

An hour south of Limón, the once-sleepy fishing village of Puerto Viejo de Talamanca has evolved into the main tourist beach town along this stretch of coast, and the 11km (6¾ miles) of road and gorgeous beaches between here and the tiny end-of-the-line hamlet of Manzanillo are still chockablock with funky backpacker and surfer joints, joined in recent years by a few more sophisticated spots (including one of the country's best restaurants). That's not to say Puerto Viejo has turned into, say, rollicking Tamarindo on the Pacific coast. No, the area as a whole is still charmingly low-key and laid-back, with a touch of rasta and maybe the wispiest whiff of reefer.

CAHUITA

A funky, extremely laid-back beach town just north of Puerto Viejo, it's for people who think Puerto Viejo is too urban-feeling. Actually, a big plus here is easy access to the snorkeling and diving in Cahuita National Park, which boasts some of the country's most outstanding coral reefs (with over 35 species of coral and a gazillion brightly colored fish). There are also hiking trails in the park, along with one of the most divine beaches on this stretch of coast, **Puerto Vargas** ★★: white sands, picnic tables, and great snorkeling close to the shore.

THE TALAMANCA MOUNTAINS

Nestled in the foothills of the Talamanca Mountains, close to the Panama border, are various indigenous tribal reserves and communities. The largest and best known are the BriBri; others include Keköldi, Cabécar, and Telire. They're very marginalized (some don't even speak Spanish), and mostly eke out a subsistence existence, supplementing income by turning cacao into organic chocolate and making crafts for tourists. In recent years, a few grassroots programs have sprung up to bring tourists to visit and even overnight in "native" style, learning about medicinal plants, cacao growing, and indigenous culture. It's a real National Geographic experience—not fancy, but definitely fascinating.

TORTUGUERO ★★

Tortuguero means "place of turtles"—folks around here say that when Christopher Columbus anchored near Tortuguero in 1502, he noted that there were so many of them that you could walk to shore on their backs. For the next few hundred years, green sea turtles and their eggs were plundered, their meat sent to Europe for turtle soup and their shells for baubles. The poor things had been practically hunted to extinction by 1959, when University of Florida sea turtle expert Archie Carr formed the Caribbean Conservation Corporation to study and protect sea turtles along this coast.

Regulations controlling turtle hunting were pushed through in 1963, and 7 years later a national park was created here, limiting the number that could be taken and saving the species from extinction. Even with all this protection, it's thought that poachers still grab up to 80 percent of eggs laid on the Tortuguero beach; even today, in Limón and San José, it's not uncommon to find smoked turtle meat (like a jerky) in markets and raw eggs drunk as shots in bars. So the four species that nest here (loggerhead, leatherback, hawksbill, and green) are still high up on endangered lists.

Tortuguero National Park spans 19,000 hectares (about 7⅓ sq. miles) and 11 habitats—an Amazon-style wonderland of water, flora, and fauna that's nothing short of a knockout. A labyrinth of dark-green canals crisscross swamplands, and up to 250 inches of rain a year keeps everything lusher and greener than St. Patrick's Day. Blue herons, toucans, kingfishers, great green macaws, and other feathered friends nest in the lagoons and marshlands, while manatees and river otters roam the more open waterways.

Throughout the year, though, the stars of the show are the nesting or hatching marine turtles (otherwise, there are less remote spots in Costa Rica with just as much flora/fauna, plus more to do). And when these critters return (driven by instinct from hundreds or thousands of kilometers away) to these 35km (22 miles) of black-sand beaches where they were born, tourists flock in to marvel at it all. Then, a couple of months later when the eggs hatch, the babies make a dash for the water that's both comical and thrilling. Both are sights that can melt the hardest hearts.

And here's a case where tourism helps instead of hurts. Since 1971, a good many of the folks who live in the village here have been trained as guides and researchers, and licensed to guide tourists on nightly turtle-watching safaris. Others work as park rangers, staff hotels, and run restaurants and other businesses—in the long run, all better gigs than poaching the turtles and turning them into soup and trinkets. Chances are your winsome guide's an ex-poacher, logger, or hunter turned conservationist.

So when should you come? It's always very wet and humid, so unlike elsewhere in Costa Rica there's no real "rainy" or "dry" season. Instead, it's either turtle time or it's not—from June through October (peaking in Sept), up to 30,000 female green sea turtles swim in from as far away as Cuba and Venezuela to lay eggs. Starting mid-February and stretching to July (the peak's Mar–Apr), the giant leatherbacks arrive. By July, it's the turn of the hawksbill turtles (by now you see why it's called "place of turtles"). Tortuguero is a wonderful place to explore, and worth at least 2 days.

GETTING TO & AROUND TORTUGUERO
By Bus & Boat

MEPE buses (☎ 257-8129) leave San José's Caribbean bus terminal (Calle Central, a block north of Av. 1) daily at 9am for the 3½- to 4-hour trip to Cariari ($5). In Cariari you'll have to walk 5 blocks north to the local bus terminal (behind the police station) to catch the noon bus ($2) for La Geest Casa Verde, where public *lanchas* (ferries) leave for Tortuguero at 1:30 and 3:30pm. The ferry takes 2 hours and costs $8. This is one of the toughest and least reliable ways to go.

The least expensive route is to La Pavona. Once you arrive at the local station in Cariari there will be two buses that go to different riverside docks. La Geest is the first but locals like to use La Pavona because it is cheaper and possibly safer. It turns out that the road La Geest uses is private and it goes through a planta- tion. You will be required to soak the soles of your shoes in a poison meant to pro- tect the crop. Though they claim it's harmless, pregnant women and children don't have to do it. La Pavona is a local secret and it's not on any map. You'll find info and instructions at www.geocities.com/tortugueroinfo/main.html.

The best way up here is to take the transportation package put together by the Tortuguero lodge where you're headed (that might typically run $140 by air or $50 via bus/boat).

By Car

Tortuguero isn't directly accessible by car. You can only drive as far as Limón or Moín, which is the dock from which the boats leave for Tortuguero. If you drive to Limón, you'll have to take a taxi to Moín. Make sure to park in a secure lot or hotel, since rental cars left a long time unattended make great targets for break-ins.

One other option—but it's a bumpy one, and therefore discouraged—is to take the Limón highway as far as the town of Siquirres. Take the exit to the left before the overhead bridge into the center of town and follow the signs to Tortuguero National Park. You'll drive about 35km (22 miles) before reaching the marina called Cano Blanco, where you can take a boat from there (there's secure parking at the marina).

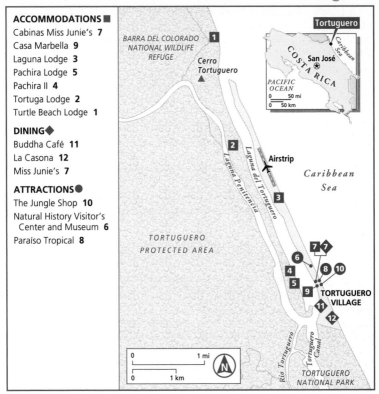

ACCOMMODATIONS ■
Cabinas Miss Junie's **7**
Casa Marbella **9**
Laguna Lodge **3**
Pachira Lodge **5**
Pachira II **4**
Tortuga Lodge **2**
Turtle Beach Lodge **1**

DINING ◆
Buddha Café **11**
La Casona **12**
Miss Junie's **7**

ATTRACTIONS ●
The Jungle Shop **10**
Natural History Visitor's Center and Museum **6**
Paraíso Tropical **8**

By Air

Flying is the quickest and easiest way to get up here. A 50-minute **Nature Air** (☎ 299-6000, 800/235-9272 in the U.S. and Canada; www.natureair.com) flight leaves San José's Tobías Bolaños International Airport in Pavas daily at 6:15am ($70 each way). **Sansa** (☎ 221-9414; www.flysansa.com) charges $63 each way for its 5:45am daily flight out of San José's Juan Santamaría International Airport.

Getting Around

Tortuguero village (pop. 550 or so) is on a narrow strip of land with the ocean on one side and the main canal on the other. If you're staying in the village, a 10-minute stroll will get you from one end to the other. If you're staying in one of the lodges across the canal, you'll need to take a ferry over here, since there are no roads. But most tours of Tortuguero throw in a stop in the village anyway. Otherwise, check with your hotel to see how much they charge for a trip to town—frankly, there isn't all that much over here, so it may or may not be worth it.

ACCOMMODATIONS, BOTH STANDARD & NOT

Tortuguero has a bit of a rep as a pricey-ish destination because most people stay at the resorts and lodges that line both sides of the main canal. Most of them only offer packages that include all meals, a couple of tours, and sometimes transfers from San José, which can bump up the cost quite a lot. But you can cut costs by checking whether your lodge will rent you only the room, and then bringing in your own groceries or eating at the *sodas* in town. You can save even more by taking a boat in from Moín on your own, staying at one of the *cabinas* in or around town, and getting your meals and tours in town as well. However, keep in mind that even though the aforementioned is a cheaper option, the lodges tend to snap up the best guides.

If you do stay at one of the lodges but want to try restaurants in town or hit a bar a couple of nights, remember that staying at one across the canal means you'll have to take a boat over each time. In that case, it's less of a hassle to stay at a lodge on the same little island as the village so you can saunter right into town on your own.

$ The only B&B in Tortuguero village, **Casa Marbella** (across from Catholic church and the Jungle Shop; ☎ 833-0827; http://casamarbella.tripod.com; cash only) offers one of the area's most complete visitor experiences. That's because friendly Canadian owner and naturalist Daryl Loth is a great go-to guy for anything you might need to know, eh? In fact, he also runs a swell website (www.geocities.com/tortugueroinfo/main.html) about Tortuguero and 2-hour turtle tours for just $10. The bright-yellow house itself faces the canal, and is centrally located along the main path through the village, with a patio and seats right by the boat dock (hearty waterfront breakfasts anybody?). The five rooms are fairly sparse— not much beyond whitewashed walls, wooden beds, tiled floors, and ceiling fans—but they're immaculate, and there's a communal kitchen if you want to whip yourself something up. Rates start at $34, including breakfast but not taxes.

$ If there were local royalty, it would be the owner of **Cabinas Miss Junie's** (north end of Tortuguero village); ☎ 709-8102; www.iguanaverdetours.com; cash only). The 67-year-old Miss Junie is the granddaughter of the village's founder, and as any local will tell you, she's the best cook in town, running a restaurant next door to her recently upgraded and expanded inn. Like Casa Marbella, it faces the canal close to the village center, but the feel is more motel-like at this block of 22 rooms in a rust-color two-story building. The rooms themselves are fairly no-nonsense but attractive, with vaguely Caribbean-pastel colors, tiled floors, large fans, and covered veranda where you can sit out and gaze at the canal. Miss Junie, too, has a trusty coterie of local guides she can call to take you around, and canoes are available for rent. Doubles generally run $30, including breakfast.

$$–$$$ The **Tortuga Lodge** ★★★ 🧒 (2km/1¼ miles from village; ☎ 257-0766; www.tortugalodge.com; AE, MC, V) was one of the first upscale resorts to set up shop hereabouts, and like a Palm Beach socialite, it keeps up with the younger gals by having a touch of work done every so often. Like the other better lodges, it's got amenities like ceiling fans, hot water, landscaped gardens—and adds a snazzy pool, a waterfront dining room (with some of the better local lodge victuals), and 20 hectares (50 acres) of grounds and jungle including a 45-minute

loop trail. The two dozen bamboo-furnished rooms are class acts (the best are on the upper floor, all sleek varnished wood, with verandas and hammocks for lazing and gazing into the jungle out back). And don't let the pricy-looking package for $300 and up scare you—you can book a la carte for $99 per double (meals included) and set up your own transfers and tours easily in town.

$$–$$$$ The **Turtle Beach Lodge** (8km/5 miles north of village; ☎ 248-0707; www.turtlebeachlodge.com; MC, V)· is the one farthest from the village, which keeps prices low. Rates range from $80 to $190 per person (double occupancy), including meals, bus/boat transfer, and tours, depending on how many nights you stay (the lower rate is for stays of 4 nights or more). Getting here, though, is part of the fun: You'll whiz up the main canal and turn off into a narrow channel that leads into the hotel's dock. The emerald scenery out here is to die for, and there's a beach right out back. There's practically nothing nearby (unlike the other lodges, which are close to each other), so you can really say you're far from the madding crowd. You can meander along miles of jungle trails to Robinson Crusoe beaches; hike up to nearby Cerro Tortuguero; take a kayak out for a spin; or just hang out in the pool or watch toucans playing in the garden's trees (if you see the gardener, ask him to chop you open a coconut for a little sweet pick-me-up). Its 25 wooden cabins, on stilts and with screen windows, are more basic than the ones at the other lodges below, but do have their own hot-water showers.

$$$ Just across from the village, **Pachira Lodge** ✿ 🄺 (.5km/⅓ mile from village; ☎ 256-7080, 800/644-7438 in U.S. and Canada; www.pachiralodge.com; AE, MC, V) is one of the largest resorts hereabouts with 80 rooms spread over 14 hectares (35 acres) of lush papaya-tree-dotted grounds. Like Tortuga Lodge, this one has a small loop trail (30–35 min.) and a good-size dining hall with the usual lodge buffets, but it's maybe a little less stylish and intimate-feeling. Still, the Pachira has enough going for it to make a good third choice if the Tortuga or Laguna (see below) are full. That includes a gigantic pool shaped like a sea turtle (boffo for families!) and poolside bar (watch it—those fruity cocktails are yummy but not cheap). Guests bed down in almond-wood rooms, in buildings connected via walkways, which are nice and spacious if a tad on the generic side. Rates for a 2-day/1-night package start at $161 per person (double occupancy), including transportation, meals, and tours; without transfers rates drop to $116.

$$$ Right next door to the Pachira Lodge is the **Pachira II** ✿✿ 🄺 (.5km/⅓ mile from village; ☎ 256-7080, 800/644-7438 in U.S. and Canada; www.pachira lodge.com; AE, MC, V), which opened in summer 2006. It's a great choice for anyone looking for a little more privacy, because its 32 *casitas* (bungalows joined by wooden walkways that're fetchingly lit up at night) have no next-door neighbors (even the Tortuga can't deliver that). The *casitas'* decor feels more contemporary than at Pachira I; it has the same amenities (including the turtle-shape pool) and then some (conference rooms, game room, spa, private terraces with rockers— sweet). Frankly, we like this new one even better than the first one. Rates start at $94 for a double, including meals but not transportation or tours.

$$$–$$$$ You can't beat the 6-hectare (15-acre) **Laguna Lodge** ✿✿✿ (1km/⅔ mile from village; ☎ 709-8082; www.lagunatortuguero.com; AE, MC, V) in terms of location. Set on the main canal right at the northern end of the same strip of land as the village, it's tucked away from the hubbub and grit, but close enough that you can saunter down for dinner. The ocean and airport are also easy strolls away. Architecture and whimsy buffs will get a huge kick out of the fact that the public areas look like the groovy, fantasmagoric stuff designed by the early 20th-century Catalan architect Antoni Gaudí. The pool, too, is simply the most stunning around—enormous, cerulean blue with a landscaped island in the middle and gardens all around. The stylishness continues in the 80 rooms, with sponge-painted earth tones, fern-filled planters, and wonderfully high ceilings. The Laguna's website lists packages from $171 per night per person (or 2 nights at $214, bringing the rate down to $107 per night), which includes transfers, grub, and tours. But you can also rent doubles without the extras from $64 per person (hey, it's right near town, so why not save by hitting the *sodas* for dinner and shopping around for tours?). Please note that you'll find different prices on the website, as this lodge (unlike most others) includes taxes in its listings. Since we wanted to compare apples with apples, we removed them from this text but as always, they're an additional 16%.

DINING FOR ALL TASTES

Most visitors end up staying in one of the lodges where all meals are included and popping over to other resorts for dinner is not encouraged (in some cases, they'd be a pain to get over to anyway). So what's left in terms of independent restaurant options boils down to a couple of *sodas* in town. In addition to the spots below, a great place to stop by for coffee and snacks—like chocolate-chip cookies, chicken pie, fab desserts like hypersweet, goopy, but oh-so-good *tres leches*—is **Dorling's Bakery and Coffee Shop** (☎ 709-8132; daily 5am–7pm, though sometimes it stays open later when full) on the main path right next to Casa Marbella.

$ At the bakery/restaurant **La Casona** (north end of the soccer field; ☎ 709-8092; daily 8am–8:30pm; AE, D, MC, V), gringo goodies like banana pancakes shine at breakfast and the dinner menu is among the best in town—not just the usual Tico *casados* (meat, rice, and beans) but also a bunch of international favorites like lasagna ($6), chicken *à l'orange* ($5), and even a few tasty veggie dishes. Decor is pure island castaway, with a smidgen of romance: sandy floors, straw roof, and flickering candles on each table.

$–$$ The onetime cook at the Caribbean Conservation Corp. (the research outfit that helped put Tortuguero on the map) now cooks for you at **Miss Junie's** (north end of village; ☎ 231-6803 or 710-0523; daily 7am–9:30pm; cash only), next to her 22-room inn and facing the canal. The menu is mostly standard *soda* fare, but with a Caribbean twist—how about a heaping plate of grilled shrimp ($12), or grilled fish and chicken with rice and beans simmered in coconut milk ($9)? As in the Caribbean, many black women name their restaurants after themselves, putting a "Miss" before their name, whether they're single or not.

$$ At the only truly somewhat-upscale restaurant in this rustic village, the **Buddha Café** ★ (main path just south of Casa Marbella; ☎ 709-8084; Tues–Sun 10am–9pm; AE, MC, V), Uruguayan owner Enrique Lopez features a chill-out soundtrack, candlelit tables, and a pretty darn credible selection of pizzas

($6–$10, though we doubt the Buddha would've okayed the pepperoni), pastas ($6–8); and mushroom, cheese, or ham crepes ($5.50). Grab a seat out in the patio facing the canal, and dive in—to the food, of course.

WHY YOU'RE HERE: THE TOP SIGHTS & ATTRACTIONS

Once you catch sight of the miles of canals sluicing through dense greenery, you'll instantly get why this area is dubbed a "little Amazon." You'll also figure out that this isn't your typical Caribbean "beach" destination—the waters are just too rough (not to mention shark-infested) for swimming, surfing, or anything too interactive.

Though the nature here is exuberant and the scenery lush, you've really come all this way for the world-class sea turtle action. However, plenty of other nature-hugging is possible—hikes through the jungles, kayaking down the canals, or simply ogling the parrots and toucans perched on the trees at your lodge.

The Turtles

The prime egg-laying seasons are March through May and July through October, when thousands of the shelled critters come ashore every night to dig nests and lay eggs. You can't just stomp out to the beach on your own, though—you'll need to sign up for a tour. If you've got an all-inclusive package at one of the lodges, this is usually included (or at least an extra option), but if you're bunking at one of the places in town or otherwise want to set it up on your own, head to the **Tortuguero Information Center** (☎ 833-0827) at the center of the village. Keep in mind that the best guides are usually snapped up by the lodges, whose tours are about twice as expensive as these, so if you have the option of taking one of the lodge tours, we'd say it's worth it. Otherwise, the cost at the center is $10, including the $7 admission to **Tortuguero National Park** ✪✪ (see below). You'll find guides hanging out here who'll be more than happy to answer any questions.

The center's **turtle tours** ✪✪✪, led by certified guides, leave at 8 and 10pm daily. Get there early (no more than 200 people are allowed onto the beach at a time); wear dark clothing; and leave flashlights, cameras, and cigarettes in your room (hatchlings in particular are sensitive to light, which mucks up their instinctive navigation toward the light reflecting off the ocean). Sometimes you'll luck out and spot mama turtles digging holes to lay their eggs, or babies pushing up through the sand and skittering toward the water. But you could also end up walking up and down the beach in vain—it's really luck of the draw.

Experiencing Nature

The number-one place everybody comes to visit is the **Parque Nacional Tortuguero** ✪ (☎ 709-8086; www.minae.go.cr; day pass $7, 3-day pass $10; daily 6am–6pm), covering 190 sq. km (74 sq. miles), including the entire beach and most of the surrounding lagoons, manatee-filled waterways, rainforests, and coastal mangrove swamps. Most people take a guided boat tour, and again, that's included in most lodge packages. If you're booking your own, though, choosing among the more than a hundred certified guides in Tortuguero can be tricky. Their quality may vary, but most are pretty good—anybody who bothers to train to be a guide is likely to be proud of Tortuguero and its history, and be good with interesting info both major and minor. One of the better ones is Canadian expat

A Mini–Field Guide to Tortuguero's Turtles

by Jenna Wortham

Tortuguero is home to four of the seven species of marine turtles: green, hawksbill, loggerhead, and giant leatherback; all are considered endangered.

Green turtles are the most common here—some 30,000 come ashore every year—and they're the largest hard-shelled sea turtles (up to 350 lbs. and 1–1.2km/3–4 ft. in length). Actually, they're not always green—the shells can vary from dark green to gray swirls and patterns. Nesting season is July to October.

Loggerheads are rarer than honest politicians, mainly because they're so migratory, so don't be disappointed if you don't see any during their mid-February through early August nesting season. And yes, they do have pretty big heads, along with powerful jaws and rust-colored shells.

The **giant leatherback** is probably the coolest to watch egg laying, if only because it is massive: up to 1.8m long (6 ft.) and well over 1,000 lbs, it's the biggest sea turtle in the world. It's called a leatherback because its shell (along with its claws) is soft. It also nests from February to early August, mostly in the southern parts of the park.

The **hawksbill turtle** has a head that tapers in a V-shape, looking kind of like birds' beaks, and a mottled brownish shell. It tends to come ashore in July. It is very rare and difficult to spot here.

Vital Stats

Each female turtle comes ashore two to six times over about 12 days, laying eggs, 100 at a time, from dusk until about 10pm (now *that's* a supermom). Sixty days later the eggs hatch and the babies make a mad dash for the ocean, where most will end up getting eaten by something or another. The turtle mother then returns faithfully every 2 to 4 years to Tortuguero—not just the same beach, but to within a few hundred yards of where she last nested. The female hatchlings who make it also return to this same site to nest. Nobody knows how or why, but one theory is that they're guided ashore by magnetic fields and phases of the moon. And you say you can't find your car in the parking lot . . . .

Daryl Loth (☎ 833-0827 or 709-8011; safari@racsa.co.cr), who owns Casa Marbella (p. 238); he does kayak rentals, canal cruises, turtle-watching expeditions, and rainforest hikes, all for around $15. Another reliable guide is **Victor Barrantes** (☎ 709-8055 or 838-6330), a SANSA agent who also arranges hiking tours to Cerro Tortuguero; he charges around $5 an hour, and most of his tours last about 3 hours.

If those guides are busy or if you need other info, the **Tortuguero Information Center** (in front of the church in the center of town; ☎ 833-0827 or 709-8011) can tell you anything you want to know about getting around and what's happening while you're here. The center can also connect you to low-cost tours, guides, restaurants, and lodges. While you're in here, check out the exhibit on Tortuguero's cultural history, covering the human settlers, where they came from, and how they've kept it going.

Finally, to explore on your own, you can rent kayaks, canoes, or *cayucas* (dugout canoes) and paddle around the 80km (50 miles) of waterways and try your hand at spotting green and blue herons, egrets, frogs, lizards, and so forth (you'll need a park ticket with you). *Cayucas* are easy enough to paddle, but not always the most stable things around—we prefer kayaks or fiberglass canoes (charm and "authenticity" are dandy, but we'd just as soon not risk authentically capsizing and becoming a caiman's lunch). You can rent from several villagers; for a *cayuca*, Miss Junie's (p. 238) charges $6 per person for an hour, $10 for a full morning. Before setting out, ask about currents and which waterway will be easiest to navigate (currents in the main canal, the Río Tortuguero, can be strong; however, a bunch of gentler channels branch off from it). If you're nervous about tackling this alone, take a 3-hour guided kayak tour for $15 per person.

What makes Tortuguero special are its waterways and the wildlife you can see in the canals (caimans, manatees, river birds). But you can also get onto dry—or at least drier—land and hike, especially if you're not planning on going to any other Costa Rica rainforest. For example, the well-maintained **Sendero Natural** begins at the park entrance's ranger station and winds around the *lomas de sierpe* (swamps). One of the more popular trails—probably thanks to its spectacular view of the swamps and coastline—the **Cerro Tortuguero** ✿ begins just north of Tortuga Lodge (p. 238) and climbs a short but steep hill to a lookout point with a rusty tower (by far the highest point in Tortuguero). Along the way, you'll see poison-arrow frogs on low-hanging branches while sloths and spider monkeys clamber through tall, dense evergreens. A water taxi to or from the beginning of the trails costs $5 a head; bring or rent boots, since the going can be a bit slippery and muddy.

Try not to leave town without visiting the **Natural History Visitor's Center and Museum** ✿ 🧒 (north end of village; ☎ 709-8091; www.cccturtle.org; $1; Mon–Sat 10am–noon and 2–5:30pm, Sun 2–5:30pm), run by the **Caribbean Conservation Corporation,** the nonprofit organization founded by Archie Carr, the conservationist whose book *The Windward Road* helped wake the world up to the approaching extinction of the sea turtles. It's only the size of a high school classroom—and that's including the souvenir shop—but pretty informative, running a 25-minute video on the turtles' life cycle, the problems that threaten their survival, and the campaign of Archie Carr and others to rescue them.

Sportfishing

Tortuguero is a fishing village at heart, and unlike other costal resorts, it won't cost you hundreds of dollars for a half-day out at sea—it averages just $50 an hour ($30 if you do it from land), which is a steal, especially for angling this good. The tarpon are found near the mouths of the Moín and Matina rivers, and you can reel in yellowfin tuna offshore.

Cruise through the waters with one of these expert guides: Longtime local fisherman **Eddy Brown** (☎ 834-3350 or 383-6097) runs day trips on foot boats out of Tortuga Lodge ($50/hr., snacks/drinks extra). For the same amount, **Elvin Gutiérrez** (☎ 709-8071 or 709-8072), locally known as Primo, will get you to the best spots for whatever you're hoping to catch. Or check with **Modesto and Fran Watson** (☎ 226-0986; www.tortuguerocanals.com), who will take you out on the river on their fiberglass-bottom *Francesca* for $40 an hour or out to sea for $50.

ATTENTION, SHOPPERS!

As you'd expect, this ain't exactly shop-till-you-drop territory. There are souvenir shops all along the main path in the village, hawking the usual crafts, wooden turtle key chains, T-shirts, and postcards. If you're headed down the coast to Limón beach towns like Cahuita or Puerto Viejo, save your cash for that—you can get the same stuff a whole lot cheaper there.

Of the gift shops, I'd stick to the **Jungle Shop** ★ (on path north of village; ☎ 709-8115) because of its sizable selection of unique handicrafts (many of them limited editions) from artisans, both local and from around Costa Rica. And every one seems to have an interesting story behind it, which owners Elvin Gutiérrez and his Connecticut-born wife Antoinette will be happy to share with you (when I last visited I was tempted to buy a fine wooden bowl created by "an ex-drug addict who's teaching others how to turn bowls"). The place has definitely come a long way since 1992, when they opened with just a single box of T-shirts on consignment.

For more boring stuff (toothpaste, whatever), or if you happen to need an extra pair of sandals, you'll probably find it at the town's largest souvenir shop, **Paraíso Tropical** (west side of village school; ☎ 709-8095), right next to the boat piers. It's nothing special, but if you really want to go trinket shopping, the selection is pretty big here.

NIGHTLIFE

For the most part, the nightlife doesn't get much hotter than the midnight sea turtle *desove* (egg laying). Yeah, the village has a handful of bars, but none is what you'd call "rockin'," and several can get a little rough. Just as long as you understand that, feel free to check them out. The **Bar La Culebra** (south end of village; no phone; hours vary), festooned with disco balls and colored lights, has great views of the canals, and live reggae some nights. Take a friend with you, if you can, because the clientele can get a little rowdy once the *guaro* (rum) gets flowing. The **Bar Brisas del Mar** (south end of village; no phone; hours vary), better known as **El Bochinche,** is a decent pick for a little open-air-dance-floor action and a pretty good sound-and-lights setup. It's on the laid-back side during the week, but on weekends half the village turns out for a romping-stomping party that goes well into the early A.M.

THE "OTHER" TORTUGUERO

In a town as itty-bitty as this, it's kinda hard *not* to bump into the locals. Many work in the tourism industry, anyway, as guides, boatmen, or shopkeepers, so you'll end up talking to one or two at some point. But one way to catch them in a more relaxed setting is to show up at the soccer field near the beach for **"Soccer Sundays,"** where practically everybody turns out to watch various teams square off throughout the afternoon. People tend to sit on the shaded sidelines, and you can chat them up—the locals are fairly friendly, and just asking a few questions about the teams and games can get a conversation going. A decent number speak English, thanks to the influence of tourism hereabouts.

CAHUITA ☆

We've always thought that if the folks in this Talamanca coast beach town were any more laid-back, they'd be horizontal. Puerto Viejo down the road has its quiet side, but it's Cancun compared to Cahuita, a proudly sleepy, somewhat counter-cultural little town of dirt roads, run-down clapboard houses, and a trio of low-key, practically deserted beaches (locals recently nixed the latest bid to pave the streets, afraid that might bring in too much development and ruin the small-town vibe). There's practically nothing to do here except hang out—well, and spend time exploring the coral reefs of **Cahuita National Park ☆☆**.

The name comes from the Miskito *cawi* (a small tree with thick red sap) and *ta* (point), but the culture here, more than in other, more mixed beach towns nearby, is black Creole. You'll see lots of dreadlock-sporting dudes, and most of the eateries and bars have a uniquely Caribbean flavor—menus are big on Creole *rondón* soup and jerk chicken, and reggae pours out of doorways every night. Because of its rasta, countercultural vibe, Cahuita has tended to attract a back-packer and surfer crowd, though for how much longer is anybody's guess, as development starts to push its way down this stretch of coast.

GETTING TO & AROUND CAHUITA

By Bus

MEPE buses (☎ 257-8129) leave San José's Carribean bus terminal (Calle Central, a block north of Av. 1) for the 3½- to 4-hour trip to Cahuita daily at 6 and 10am, and 1:30 and 3:30pm; the fare is $5 each way. Plusher **Grayline** (☎ 220-2126; www.graylinecostarica.com) buses charge $27 and leave for Cahuita and Puerto Viejo at 6:30am, while **Interbus** (☎ 283-5573; www.interbusonline.com) departs San José at 7:50am and charges $29 for the 4½-hour trip. Both companies will pick you up from most hotels in the San José and Manuel Antonio areas. Some local lodgings will also arrange transfers from elsewhere in the country. At press time there were no flights into Limón, so that's out for now.

By Car

From downtown San José's Calle 3, take the Guápiles Highway that leads to the Caribbean coast, cutting through the rainy but scenic Braulio Carrillo National Park. When you reach Guápiles, continue on the same highway, following signs for Limón. In downtown Limón, just before the railroad tracks, watch for signs for Sixaola, and make a right turn onto a paved road heading south down the coast. The first stretch south from Limón is paved but riddled with potholes, and after you take the turnoff for Cahuita/Puerto Viejo, it turns to a gravel road that can be very slow and bumpy going in spots. The drive from San José should take you 3 to 4 hours, depending on traffic and road conditions.

Getting Around

The village is laid out in a 4-block grid typical of rural Costa Rican towns, so it's easy to walk almost anywhere unless staying in one of the newer hotels on the out-skirts or just off the main road, in which case you'll want to consider renting wheels. You can also usually find taxis easily on Cahuita's main strip or have your hotel call one for you. Bicycles are available for rent in any of the hotels and shops in town, typically costing $6 to $8 a day.

ACCOMMODATIONS, BOTH STANDARD & NOT

Until the past decade, most of the digs here were simple *cabinas* catering to surfers and backpackers, and more than a dozen of them are still around; their rooms are bare-bones and the showers run cold water only, but they're dirt cheap and easy to find (just follow the signs). But midrange lodgings are both good quality and pretty affordable—in fact, you'll get more for your buck than in many other Costa Rican resort towns. And as we mentioned before, now some higher-end hotels are also cropping up just outside of town and in the hills just inland. Below we've come up with a nifty little cross section, from rustic to refined.

$ To be honest, some of Cahuita's cheaper lodgings can only be described as pretty skanky. So that's why the German-owned **Alby Lodge** (177m/590 ft. west of national park entrance; ☎ 755-0031; www.albylodge.com; cash only) is such a *wunderbar* surprise: beautifully manicured tropical gardens and four oh-so-Caribbean thatched-roof cabins on stilts with hammock-draped front porches. They're far from luxurious, mind you, but they do claim private baths, fans, and a good bit of charm (wood beams, polished hardwood floors, nicely tiled baths). There's a thatched-roof communal kitchen and dining area, and Playa Blanca beach, Cahuita's best, is just a few hundred feet away. The downside is it's right on the edge of the national park, so bands of up to a dozen howler monkeys set up camp near the cabins—adorable as all get out, but if you're a light sleeper and not an early riser, watch out. But at $35 for a cabin for two people, $43 for four, this is such a terrific value—just bring some earplugs.

$ You can't get any closer to the beach and park than the **Hotel Kelly Creek & Restaurant** (at entrance to national park; ☎ 755-0007; www.hotelkellycreek.com; AE, MC, V), run by Spanish-born artist Andrés Alcala and his French wife, Marie-Claude. There are no gardens and only four rooms, all right next to each other. But what fetching rooms: high ceilings, wraparound verandas, and a whopping 36 sq. m (390 sq. ft.) of space. Another plus here is one of Cahuita's best restaurants, serving up wonderful paella and other Spanish food with a most fetching woody ambience and water views (not to mention oils of local characters painted by Andrés). You can spot all sorts of wildlife around the eponymous Kelly Creek behind the property (sometimes *really* wild, like Roberto the caiman, fed by the owners several times a day). Again, sometimes it can be a bit of a racket when you're trying to get some shut-eye. Doubles here are $45, not including breakfast. That's the cash price; pay by credit card, and they add about $7 to the total.

$$ A short stroll from the beaches and main drag, the long-popular **El Encanto** ✹ (300km/984 ft. west of the police station in Cahuita; ☎ 755-0113; www.elencantobedandbreakfast.com; MC, V) does indeed seem to have a touch of enchantment to it. Owned by a French-Canadian artist named Pierre Leon and his Mauritius-Chinese wife Patricia Kim, this tranquil, walled compound dominated by a whitewashed colonial-style greathouse is an exotic mix of tropical (lush bromeliads, heliconias, and orchids all over), New Age (Buddha heads and Zen mediation hall), and indigenous Central American (seven rooms with colorful Guatemalan bedspreads and Panamian tapestries called moles). Mod-cons aren't ignored, though—you've got the option of splashing in the pool or feeding your

Cahuita

ACCOMMODATIONS ■
Alby Lodge **9**
El Encanto **4**
Hotel Kelly Creek **8**
La Diosa **1**
Suizo Loco Lodge **1**

DINING ◆
Cha Cha Cha **6**
Hotel Kelly Creek **8**
Restaurant Edith **5**
Sobre Las Olas **3**
Vista Del Mar **7**

ATTRACTIONS ●
Caribe Wildlife Park
Cacao Trails **10**
Sloth Rescue Center **2**

gringo TV habit in the cane/rattan-appointed lounge. In season doubles start at $65, including a hearty breakfast featuring homemade breads; there's also a three-bedroom stand-alone house renting for $175.

$$ There aren't many hotels right on the beach in Cahuita, so chalk a big one up for the new **La Diosa** ★ (4km/2½ miles west of national park entrance, ☎ 755-0055, or 877/623-3198 in the U.S. and Canada; www.hotelladiosa.net), just a couple hundred feet or so from Playa Negra. Boutiquey-feeling and somewhat yoga-oriented, "The Goddess" names its 10 bungalows for various women worshipped around the world and tarts them up stylishly with stuff like Japanese woodblock prints, modern art, and photos of local tribal folks (several also have a Jacuzzi tub on a platform). There's a nice pool overlooking the sea, a lovely garden, good *palapa*-roofed dining room, and a common room for things from meditation to movie screenings. ***Drawbacks:*** It's a little far from town and the park entrance. Doubles start at $55 ($75 with air-conditioning), including a tasty breakfast with homemade bread, made-to-order eggs, jam, and fresh fruit.

$$ A collection of 10 spic-'n'-span white bungalows amid manicured lawns and gardens, the **Suizo Loco Lodge** ★ (off main road to Cahuita, follow signs;

Cahuita Vacation Rentals

Cahuita is only beginning to take off in this area, so only a few realtors deal with rental properties. For now, check on general websites such as www.vrbo.com, www.propertiesincostarica.com, or others listed in our planning chapter (p. 341), and search under "Cahuita" or "the Caribbean." In almost all cases, you'll be dealing directly with the owner.

One Puerto Viejo agency, **Caribe Sur Real Estate** (☎ 759-9138; www.caribesur-realestate.com), handles a number of area properties, including at least one in Cahuita, a two-bedroom beach cottage that rents for $25 a day, $150 a week. With concrete walls and a corrugated tin roof, it's simple but comes with decent amenities, including a kitchen, stone garden furniture, and a tiny porch with a pair of wicker chairs. It's also worth considering renting in Puerto Viejo, Manzanillo, or in between, and driving up here for the day.

You might also try contacting the owners of the **Casa Caribe** (www.lacasacaribe.com), a two-bedroom bungalow that sleeps up to five in the middle of Cahuita's residential zone, not far from the beach. Snuggled amid tropical gardens, it's got a large front porch and a smallish living room with a sleeping loft. Luxe-a-rama it's not—you'll have hot water and a decently equipped kitchen, but no phone, TV, Internet, or air-conditioning. But the *precio* is definitely right—a week will run you just $450. (By the way, you can put the 50 percent deposit required to hold a reservation on plastic, but the balance is due in cash when you check in.)

☎ 755-0349; www.suizolocolodge.com; MC, V) is a bit away from the center of town, but it's one of Cahuita's more upscale digs—with rates to match, from $89 double in season up to $110 for the honeymoon suite. The roomy units have perks like A/C, fridges, hair dryers, satellite TV (with DVD players, even), and terraces, plus there's a huge hourglass pool right in the middle of things (the bridge that crosses it can double as a diving board). The *palapa*-covered dining room's a winner, too, not just for the Swiss and international favorites but a touch of Swiss-Tico fusion, a la *rösti* made with yucca and local *chayote* squash subbing for kohlrabi.

DINING FOR ALL TASTES

No visit to this town would be complete without sampling some of its Caribbean Creole specialties sold at stands along the street—hot and spicy, filling, and as cheap as $2 or $3 for an entire meal. Another great budget option is the heaping portions of *chino-latino* (Chinese-Latin fare—remember, there was immigration from China hereabouts, too) at **Vista Del Mar** (24m/80 ft. from Kelly Creek ranger station); most platters cost under $5. Cahuita also has a few great international choices thanks to its expats (like the Spanish restaurant at the **Kelly Creek Hotel;** p. 246).

$-$$$ Back when tourists were just starting to make their way to Cahuita, a well-known local lady named Miss Edith started serving them down-home Caribbean cooking from her front porch. Now she and her daughters run **Restaurant Edith** ✭ (off main road, near police station; ☎ 755-0248; daily 11am–10pm; cash only), which may not be long on decor but does deliver the goods, made to order. Dig in to flavorful local specialties like jerk chicken ($6) and *rondón* soup ($6–$15), which is fish, veggies, and plantains simmered in coconut milk. Keep in mind service is Caribbean slow, and during high season you might have to share a table.

$$-$$$ As its name says, glass-walled **Sobre Las Olas** ✭ 🧒 (north of town, on road to Playa Negra; ☎ 755-0109; daily noon–10pm; MC, V) is on a rocky cove "above the waves," and what a view you get here. The Caribbean-accented Italian food is pretty damn good, too—lots of seafood, with standouts like octopus in hot sauce ($13) and whole red snapper sautéed in onions, coconut, and Caribbean spices ($13). Don't worry, though, kids and other finicky eaters can count on standbys like hamburgers, fajitas, and spaghetti. The gracious, friendly owner Marco Botti is often on hand and is all too happy to provide local tips.

$$-$$$ Locals like to wryly say that lots of tourists only end up trying the other restaurants in town on Mondays when **Cha Cha Cha** ✭✭ (main road 3 blocks north of Coco's Bar; ☎ 394-4153; Tues–Sun 2–10pm; MC, V) is closed; otherwise, this joint is packed every night, especially 6 to 8pm. Why? The Canadian owners, Bertrand and Julie, sling fresh and simply prepared seafood and grilled meats, not to mention killer raspberry margaritas (nice and tangy, made with real raspberries and a big slug o' tequila). Copacetic comestibles include grilled squid salad ($6.50), curry swordfish ($10), Thai-stay tuna steak ($8), and a boatload's worth of seafood platter with huge crab cakes, tuna steak, shrimp, octopus, calamari, and mussels ($40 for two people). The ambiance in this cute clapboard house with open-air dining room also happens to be one of the nicest in town, complete with soft lighting and cheerful tablecloths.

WHY YOU'RE HERE: THE TOP SIGHTS & ATTRACTIONS

Cahuita is less a locale for "doing" as for just chilling. Hitting the highlights shouldn't take more than 2 or 3 days: exploring the three beaches (two inside the national park), hiking the park trails, and snorkeling the reefs. So you'll want to do a few tours and activities in the Talamanca region (such as ziplines or tours covering Creole and indigenous history and culture), and ideally even rent a car and explore a bit on your own, starting with Puerto Viejo, just 20 minutes south (p. 252).

The Beaches

Playa Negra, the long, uncrowded black-sand beach that runs along the north side of town tends to have rough surf, so may not make for the most comfortable swimming. But it's awesome for stretching out, strolling, and exploring the coral formations and coves.

The beaches you really shouldn't miss, though, are the two inside Cahuita National Park, especially the proverbially "postcard-perfect" **Playa Blanca** ✭ (right in town; Mon–Fri 8am–4pm, Sat–Sun 7am–5pm; entrance fee by donation)

Patí Cake, *Patí* Cake

The family that runs Sol y Mar also makes homemade goodies, snapped up in a flash on weekends round about lunchtime. On Saturday it's *patí*, a Jamaican-style spiced meat pie baked in a pie crust. Two are enough for a meal, and they're a steal at 500 *colones* (about a buck). Sundays it's *gallo pinto* in coconut sauce with chicken and salad ("much better than any-thing you'll ever get in a *soda*," one local told me). Grab some grub and sit out by the water–*pura vida*, and *pura* Cahuita.

This nearly 3km (2 miles) of gleaming white sand starts out narrow near the ranger station, with strong surf, so if you want to take a dip, head towards the middle stretch, beginning just before the Suárez River. Over here the offshore reef turns the turquoise waters into practically a smooth-as-glass lagoon. There's good snorkeling here, too, though the very best is farther offshore (for that you'll need to hire a boat or sign on to a snorkeling excursion).

The other great strand in here is down the trail behind Playa Blanca. **Puerto Vargas** ✹✹ 🅚 stretches from Punta Cahuita to the mouth of the Río Carbón, running against a backdrop of lush vegetation. Especially toward the northern end of the promontory, it too serves up bone-white sand, calm crystalline waters, and superb snorkeling. Then as you make your way south along the beach, the sand gets darker, and the surf ratchets up from mild to strong as the coast opens up to the ocean. You can reach Puerto Vargas either from the Kelley Creek park entrance and head down the 7km (4.3-mile) trail along the beach, or more directly by following the signs on the main road to the **Puerto Vargas Ranger Station** (☎ 755-0302; Mon–Fri 8am–4pm, Sat–Sun 7am–5pm; $7) and continu-ing 3km (2 miles). There are camping facilities here with showers and toilets.

Exploring Nature

Just over 10 sq. km (4 sq. miles), **Cahuita National Park** ✹ (☎ 755-0302; daily 6am–5pm; $7 at Puerto Vargas entrance, by donation at Kelly) was set up back in 1970 mostly to protect the 240 hectares (600 acres) of coral reef. Besides the aforementioned snorkeling, swimming, and turning-and-burning, a flat, sandy trail runs along the back of the beach with some pretty good wildlife-spotting. Howler monkeys, sloths, colorful crabs, and white-faced monkeys (watch it, these last little buggers can get cranky) are a dime a dozen along here, and you'll also have a good chance to glimpse iguanas, agoutis, coatis, toucans, and parrots. Keep in mind this trail is almost 6.5km (4 miles) long, and hiking the whole thing will take you a good 3 to 4 hours (including wading across streams and such). But you can always pop out to the sands for a rest and/or refreshing dip.

Wildlife Sanctuaries

Up the road apiece, the 48-hectare (120-acre) **Aviarios del Caribe/Sloth Rescue Center** ✹ 🅚 (off main road, 11km/6¾ miles north of Cahuita; ☎ 750-0075; www.slothrescue.org; $30 per person including breakfast or $15 without food, children

A Snorkel Trip in Puerto Vargas

The coral reefs off Punta Cahuita and Punta Vargas are fins-down the flashiest snorkeling spots on this stretch of the Caribbean coast, with the best conditions from February through April. Folks, we mean, fish, fish, fish! More than 300 species of 'em! Angel fish! Porcupinefish! Parrotfish! Not to mention sponges, sea urchins, lobsters! Colorful brain coral, sea fans, and elk antlers! There's even a sunken 18-century slaver ship out here (even if you can only see it on a diving trip).

To get to the best snorkeling farther off shore, hire a guide from one of the tour operators in town (it'll run you $15–$20 dollars per person), or get a local boat captain to take you (sometimes as little as $3 a head); go out in the morning to avoid the intense noon sun.

And here's a thought: after you're all snorkeled out, have the boat drop you off on the other side of the point, from where you can walk to Puerto Vargas. Then make a beeline for **Boca Chica** ★ (kids) 🐟 (at entrance to Puerto Vargas; ☎ 755-0415; daily 9am–6pm; cash only), where an Italian chef serves up Italian and Caribbean style food; a local favorite, octopus in a creamy coconut milk ($9 with rice, beans, and salad) is the house specialty. The place even has its own swimming pool, making it a popular hangout for local kids (and your kids—enjoy your feed in peace while they splash around).

under 8 pay half price; daily 6am–2:30pm) is a wildlife sanctuary specializing in those sleepy, funny-looking critters. Founded in 1992 by Luís and Judy Arroyo to help rescue by now more than three dozen sloths who've been hurt, orphaned, or displaced (mostly by humans), it's turned into one of the big kahunas in sloth research, with a clinic, education center, nursery, and more. You get to touch and sometimes hold them, and of course you'll come away knowing more than you ever dreamed you would about them (for example: they can survive falls of 27m/90 ft.; they come down to the ground just once a week, to poop; they host all sorts of algae and such in their fur to help camouflage them). You can "adopt" one of them by forking up $100, which gets you a certificate, photo, and center newsletter subscription. While you're here you can hike various trails or go on a guided canoe trip up the tributaries of the Río Estrella ($25, including a tour of the sanctuary) to check out the caimans, river otters, turtles, and lizards. You can even stay overnight at a simple six-room guesthouse ($75 for two people including breakfast and the tour, $15 for each additional person with a maximum of four people per bunk bedded room).

A fairly recent addition to the local tourist track, the **Caribe Wildlife Park Cacao Trails** (kids) (5km/3 miles south of Cahuita on road to Puerto Viejo; ☎ 756-8186; www.cacaotrails.com; daily 7am–4pm) does have a prepackaged feel to it—but what the heck, it can make for a nifty intro and overview of what the Talamanca area's all about, particularly for kids, who can roam freely and safely on its 9.2 hectares (23 acres) (the fact that it's got a pool doesn't hurt, either). There's a mini–cacao plantation, complete with some of the gadgets and tools used in making chocolate; a garden with more than a hundred plants used by local tribes to cure diseases; iguana and snake exhibits; canoe tours; and a restaurant/bar. You'll get to see some varmints in here that you might not spot on local trails (or want to—the bright yellow and majorly poisonous pit viper slithers to mind). Tours range from a couple of hours ($25) to a full day (which includes a walk through the national park, canoe paddle, and buffet lunch for $47).

ATTENTION, SHOPPERS!

Five words: nothing to write home about. Shops hawking the usual souvenirs, beachwear, and crafts line the main strip. Boutique Coco and Cahuita Tours, for example, stock an array of batiks, trinkets, and the like. You'll also find handmade crafts and jewelry sold at tables set up near the park entrance.

If you want a souvenir that's really intensely local, pick up a CD by Cahuita native **Walter Gavitt Ferguson,** a legendary calypso singer who these days lives at the Sol y Mar hotel. If you have trouble finding the CDs elsewhere, head over to buy directly from him at the hotel—a cool experience anyway, since the man's a walking history book who can tell you practically anything about the area you'd want to know.

NIGHTLIFE

In Cahuita, Bob Marley still lives. But if you're looking for variety and snap, crackle, and pop, you're better off trying Puerto Viejo (see below). Here it's all about kicking back in a down-home bar, beer in hand, and listening to reggae, calypso, or sometimes soca (dance tunes mixing calypso and Indian music). You might get asked if you wanna buy a little smoke—if not, just be cool, and it's no problem. Also keep in mind that it's mostly men hanging out in these bars, and girls on their own can expect a certain amount of unwanted attention and propositions from the locals—not dangerous, just occasionally uncomfortable.

The one joint (so to speak) that can regularly draw a crowd is **Coco's Bar** (on the main strip; ☎ 755-0437; daily noon–2am) splashed in rasta colors—yellow, red, and green—and other trappings. There's always a mix of locals (with dreads) and tourists grooving to reggae. The dance floor, complete with disco lights, gets busy late on weekend nights. Make sure to check the schedule—there's usually live calypso on Friday and ladies' night on Sunday. Across the street, the thatched-roof **Ricky's Bar** (☎ 755-0228; daily till midnight) has more or less the same clientele. There's a two-for-one happy hour from 8 to 9pm, and there are different things going on different nights—DJ, karaoke, live tunes, and so on.

THE "OTHER" CAHUITA

See the "Other" Puerto Viejo (p. 272) for info on volunteering for the ANAI sea turtle conservation project in Cahuita.

PUERTO VIEJO & MANZANILLO ✹✹

In recent years, Puerto Viejo has turned into the unofficial counterculture capital of the Caribbean coast, and even Costa Rica at large. During high season (mid-Dec to Apr), rooms are booked solid and life turns into one big party, as surfers,

Euro-hippies, and backpackers hit the beaches, get their hair braided or dread-locked, and throng the reggae bars and dance spots in a happy haze of pot smoke. While street stands elsewhere in the country are pretty much limited to local arts and crafts, you can also get plenty of other stuff along the waterfront here, including pipes, colorful rasta flags, and incense. At night, groups of young guys hang out on the dimly lit streets, lounging on car hoods and yakking the night away.

For some, Puerto Viejo is their fantasy beach party town, something like a Central American mini-Ibiza (minus the bigger, flashier discos, of course). Others have more mixed feelings, including some locals and expats who want to keep things closer to what they used to be in the "old days," when they were almost totally under the radar and off the grid (roads didn't get built until 1979, electricity came in 1986, and private phones—believe it or not—in 1997).

But eventually, inevitably, word got out about the paradisical beaches and jungles, and the barefoot charms of the town and villages. And it has never been quite the same. Still, though, even well into the first decade of the 21st century, the place still manages to hang on to a charmingly off-the-beaten-path vibe. There are still no slick condo complexes, all-inclusives, or casinos, and the barefoot charms are still there, starting with every type of beach you could want except the crowded kind—surfer-popular **Playa Cocles** ✹ gorgeous, wild-feeling **Punta Uva** ✹✹; and the white sands and turquoise waters of **Playa Manzanillo** ✹ part of the tight-knit, pretty little fishing village of **Manzanillo.** Out here, by the **Gandoca-Manzanillo Refuge** ✹, a tropical rainforest with mangrove-lined waterways, you can go watch giant leatherback turtles when they come to nest from January to April. And a few kilometers away from the coast, up in the mountains, you tour the various indigenous reserves and communities to see how the original inhabitants of these lands have lived for centuries. Snorkel the superlative reefs of **Cahuita National Park,** just north of here. Head out to a canopy tour. Take a yoga interlude at **Samasati** resort up in the hills. Or just hang out, in and around these fetching little beach communities, checking out shops, bakeries, and bars. Laid back or party-hearty—the choice is yours.

GETTING TO & AROUND PUERTO VIEJO
By Bus

MEPE buses (☎ 257-8129) leave San José's Carribean bus terminal (Calle Central, 1 block north of Av. 1) daily at 6am, 10am, 1:30pm, and 3:30pm. The trip takes around 5 hours, and costs $6 to Puerto Viejo, $7.25 down to the town of Sixaola on the Panama border (by the way, make sure the bus is heading to Puerto Viejo de Talamanca and not Puerto Viejo de Sarapiquí).

For a little more plushness, a half-hour less travel time, and pick-up from your hotel, **Grayline** (☎ 220-2126; www.graylinecostarica.com) runs a bus from San José to Cahuita and Puerto Viejo daily at 6:30am ($27). **Interbus** (☎ 283-5573; www.interbusonline.com) leaves at 7:50am ($29).

By Car

Follow the instructions on p. 245 for getting to Cahuita. From there, Puerto Viejo is 16km/10 miles farther down the road. When you come to a fork, there will be a gas station on your right; continue going straight. After a stretch of unpaved

---

Raft Your Way to the Coast

If you're coming out to the Caribbean coast and also want to run the whitewater, you can save time and money by taking one of the packages by various San José and Puerto Viejo tour operators out to the Turrialba area (with Costa Rica's best whitewater), in Cartago halfway between the capital and the coast (p. 86). You can leave in the morning, spend the day rafting, and afterward get dropped off in Puerto Viejo, Cahuita, or wherever. For details, check with **Exploradores Outdoors** (☎ 222-6262; www.exploradoresoutdoors.com).

---

road, most of the rest of your drive will be on paved road, which continues south to Punta Uva and Manzanillo.

Getting Around

If you're spending most of your time in Puerto Viejo, you'll be able to get around town on foot or by bike—and even to and from some of the lodgings, restaurants, and beaches just south of town, along the road to Manzanillo. A car is more a plus for exploring farther-flung areas like Cahuita, Manzanillo, and the tribal communities in the hills, but you can also rely on taxis, tours, and such. You can rent bikes from shops in town or at most hotels for about $4 to $5 a day, or newish Yamaha scooters from **Dragon Scooter Rentals** (at Cabinas Los Almendros; ☎ 750-0728; 8am till late) for $30 to $50 a day (if you rent for a week, the seventh day is free).

ACCOMMODATIONS, BOTH STANDARD & NOT

Like Cahuita up the road, Puerto Viejo is still a bargain compared with the rest of Costa Rica. It's hard to spend more than $100 a night on lodging, and what you can get in the midrange would be considered fancy-schmancy indeed in Pacific-coast resorts like Manuel Antonio or Tamarindo. Best of all, a ton of them are on or a short stroll from the beach—especially the ones along the road down the coast to Manzanillo. The ones in town are convenient for getting back home after a night out at the bars, but are slightly more of a hike to the sands. The digs listed below are just a fraction of what's over here; for more, check at **www.green coast.com**.

Vacation Rentals

Recent development has been busily drumming up a growing vacation rental market—not just providing more affordable options but also a dollop of fun and "going native" (a little bit, anyway). Many have been built in traditional style—how about staying in a thatch-roof house with rough-hewn logs for columns, rustic furniture, open-air living rooms, and terraces? One duplex I visited even had a Swiss Family Robinson vibe, with a big, tree-trunk-like spiral staircase connecting the floors.

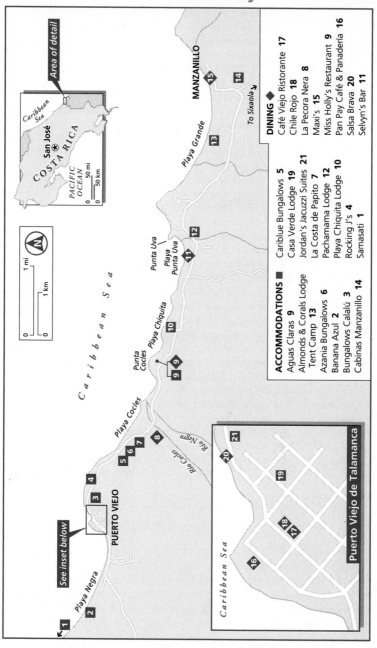

Area of detail

Caribbean Sea

COSTA RICA

San José

PACIFIC OCEAN

0   50 mi
0   50 km

0   1 mi
0   1 km

MANZANILLO

To Sixaola

Playa Grande

Punta Uva
Playa Punta Uva

Playa Chiquita

Punta Cocles

Playa Cocles

Río Negro

Río Cocles

PUERTO VIEJO

See inset below

Playa Negra

Caribbean Sea

Puerto Viejo de Talamanca

ACCOMMODATIONS ■
Aguas Claras **9**
Almonds & Corals Lodge Tent Camp **13**
Azania Bungalows **6**
Banana Azul **2**
Bungalows Calalú **3**
Cabinas Manzanillo **14**
Cariblue Bungalows **5**
Casa Verde Lodge **19**
Jordan's Jacuzzi Suites **21**
La Costa de Papito **7**
Pachamama Lodge **12**
Playa Chiquita Lodge **10**
Rocking J's **4**
Samasati **1**

DINING ◆
Café Viejo Ristorante **17**
Chile Rojo **18**
La Pecora Nera **8**
Maxi's **15**
Miss Holly's Restaurant **9**
Pan Pay Café & Panadería **16**
Salsa Brava **20**
Selvyn's Bar **11**

On the other hand, the local short-term rental market is still much less organized than over on the Pacific coast—in most cases you'll have to contact owners directly (either with the ones we've listed below or from websites in the planning chapter, p. 341). One agency we've come across, **Caribe Sur Real Estate** (☎ 759-9138; www.caribesur-realestate.com) handles a variety of rentals in Playa Chiquita, Punta Uva, and other beach communities along the coast. Its agents are friendly and know their stuff, and we were pretty impressed by the properties that I visited. A lower-end example is the two-story, two-bedroom **Casa Tranquila,** just a hop and a skip from Cocles beach, for just $70 a night, $420 a week in season; its layout is breezy and open and decor jungle-stylish, with lots of cane and wicker. A little more upscale, the luxe **Playa Chiquita Overview** sleeps up to eight on a rainforested ridge above Playa Chiquita; the two-bedroom/two-bath main house also has a couple of outlying bungalows and a nice-size pool with a thatched-roof bar and dining area. All this, plus daily maid service and a live-in caretaker, runs $150 daily, $1,000 weekly (divided by eight, that works out to $18 a person, per day).

Values in the "direct rental by owner" market are just as impressive. We checked out scads, and found this bunch to be the pick of the litter:

On the beach, have a look at **Casa Sol y Arena** (.5km/⅓ mile from Puerto Viejo, on Playa Negra; ☎ 750-0212, 800/811-5352 [enter code 750-0212] from the U.S. and Canada; www.puertoviejobeachhouse.com; MC, V), a simple concrete house painted yellow, with a corrugated steel roof, three bedrooms/two baths, full kitchen, and perks like phone, cable TV, and Internet. The friendly owners, Colin from Canada and his Tico boyfriend Roberto, also run the **Banana Azul** gay hotel just down the road, so if you need anything, they're more than happy to help. The rent is $75 daily or $450 weekly. The guys can also arrange rentals for a couple of other houses, **Casa Zorro** and **Loco Natural** (check details on their website).

You can find more hip indie properties away from the beach (some walkable to the water, others you're better off having a car for). A short stroll to Playa Chiquita is the two-story, two-bedroom **Casa Chiquita Verde** (off main road to Manzanillo; ☎ 750-0128; www.puertoviejo.net), which has 149 sq. m (1,600 sq. ft.) of open-layout living space for $75 a day, $400 a week. On 3.6 hectares (9 acres) of former cacao plantation pretty close to Playa Punta Uva, **Casa Viva** ✸✸ (off main road to Manzanillo; ☎ 750-0089; www.puntauva.net; AE, D, MC, V) has an

Skeeters & Sweat

Whether you rent a home or stay in a hotel, make sure your rooms come with screens or mosquito nets. Many of the open-air digs down here do great at supplying that George-of-the-jungle-lodge feel, but you may be less enchanted fending off the myriad of mosquitos and other bugs that are part of life here. Also, think about how big a deal air-conditioning is for you; most lodgings and houses here don't have it. At night when it's cooler, ceiling fans are usually enough, but if you're an especially delicate flower, you may find yourself wilting.

understatedly elegant vibe and landscaped botanical gardens, and three refined two-bedrooms houses for rent at $600 a week for two, $150 a week for each additional guest. Friendly owners Dave and Jeanie Waller from Chicago live on property, and have lived in the area for more than a dozen years—ask and they shall inform.

South of Punta Uva, you'll really feel like you're alone in the rainforest at **Congo Bongo** ★★ (off road to Manzanillo; ☎ 759-9016; www.congo-bongo.com; MC, V), next to the Gandoca-Manzanillo Wildlife Refuge yet right off the main road and a few hundred feet from the beach. Daan, the Dutch owner, lives on the premises and rents out four screened wooden houses (two, three, and four bedrooms); we especially love the **"Indian Rancho,"** a three-story thatched-roof, log-cabin treehouse, with a number of indigenous touches. Rates run $75 daily, $450 weekly for two, up to $160 a day, $990 a week for six.

A little farther afield (meaning a bit more of a schlep to the beach; a car is helpful), we especially like **La Finca Chica** ★ (off road to Manzanillo; ☎ 750-0643; www.fincachica.com; cash/money wire only), a 1-hectare (2½-acre) former farm (*finca*) with three homes stashed amid dense vegetation in the Playa Cocles area, ranging in rent from $55 a night/$315 a week to $120/$690. Or pull out all the stops on stylish luxury at the colorful, two-bedroom **Villa Toucan** ★★ (in hills overlooking Punta Uva; ☎ 759-9138; www.villatoucan.com; MC, V), 93 sq. m (1,000 sq. ft.) packed with amenities and awesome views (you'll want a 4×4 to get up the hill, though); it's $100 a night, $500 a week for two, or $125 a night, $625 a week for four. Finally, right inside the Gandoca-Manzanillo reserve, **The Treehouse** (198m/660 ft. south of the school, Punta Uva; ☎ 750-0706; www.costaricatreehouse.com) is a two-level, open-sided bungalow with a full kitchen and a pair of bedrooms sleeping up to six. A wooden boardwalk leads into the place, and everything has a funky *Gilligan's Island* feel to it (love the toilet, plopped—so to speak—right in the middle of a huge hollowed-out tree); rates start at $225 a night there, but another lovely house on the property (polished woods, chic tile work, massive windows) is just $650 per week.

Hotels

IN & AROUND PUERTO VIEJO

As usual, most (not all) of your cheapest choices are in the heart of town; besides price, they also have the upside of being in the thick of a slew of restaurants, shops, and bars.

$ If the countercultural party scene in Puerto Viejo has an HQ, it's **Rocking J's** (on road to Manzanillo; ☎ 750-0665; www.rockingjs.com; MC, V), kinda like a artsily done-up summer camp for college kids and recent grads, or a hippy commune–cum–beach resort for the backpacker set. There are 40 tents, with mattresses and sheets, for $6, or save a buck and just crash in the "hammock hotel" in a large open-air hall (in the mornings it brings to mind a tropical hospital ward for kids' recovering from last night's partying). You can get small private rooms for $20, too, but the fun here is the communal living—bonfire parties on the beach right out back; whipping up grub in the kitchen; downing pretty good (and cheap) burritos in the Mexican dining room; watching a movie or having a game of Ping-Pong in the rec room. The group showers are cold water only, and lockers are available for valuables. And check out the treehouse, on a big ol' tree trunk right in the middle of the compound.

$ There aren't any gay bars or restaurants around here, but the **Banana Azul** (1km/⅔ mile from Puerto Viejo, on Playa Negra; ☎ 750-0212, 800/811-5352 [enter code 750-0212] from the U.S. and Canada; www.bananaazul.com; AE, MC, V) B&B is a queer bit of business indeed (in a good way!). Colin from Canada and his Tico partner Roberto rent out three rooms in their home in a residential neighborhood right on Playa Negra, 50m (165 ft.) from the water. The decor—well, call it "Queer Eye for the Jungle Lodge." For example, check out the koi pond in the middle of the ceramic-tiled common lounge, or the "Red Frog" room with an open shower featuring a lovely frog mosaic. The guys love to share their enthusiasm and knowledge of Puerto Viejo—Roberto's a local schoolteacher, and on their website you can follow Colin's blog about the area and its people. They call themselves straight-friendly and, indeed, half their clientele is straight. Rooms run $35 to $43 a night (double occupancy), including breakfast.

$ For a mix of value, ambience, and location, I can't think of a better place to stay in town than the French-run **Bungalows Calalú** ★★ 🧒 (just south of Salsa Brava Restaurant; ☎ 750-0042; www.bungalowscalalu.com; MC, V), on the edge of town, only 90km or so (300 ft.) from the beach, its tall hedges creating a peaceful garden oasis. Five chalet-style cottages have private baths and terraces, and kitchens optional. There's a beautiful stone zero-entry pool with a little waterfall and shallow wading area for kids. You can take breakfast on a balcony overlooking a small butterfly garden with a pond and watch the butter fly (er, the butterflies). Doubles rates range from $29 (without kitchen, if paying cash) to $41 (with kitchen, paying with credit card).

$-$$ Run by Swiss René Anton Kessler and his Tica wife Carolina Jiménez, **Casa Verde Lodge** (a block from Puerto Viejo main drag; ☎ 750-0047; www.cabinas casaverde.com; AE, MC, V) has long been a budget fave for its 16 clean, comfortable rooms with fridges, verandas, and high ceilings, along with a big, beautiful pool/Jacuzzi surrounded by plants and accented with tortoise sculptures. Also on premises, you've got a cafe, a small gift shop with a pretty good selection, tour desk, a minispa, and a frog vivarium. It's a great deal for the amenities and location, but less intimate and secluded than Calalú. Double-occupancy rates in season range from $29 (with shared baths, paying in cash) to $56 (private baths, charging with plastic).

$$ At **Jordan's Jacuzzi Suites** (296m/985 ft. south of Puerto Viejo, on road to Manzanillo; ☎ 750-0232; MC, V), convenient to a bunch of beaches and restaurants, the seven suites do indeed feature Jacuzzi tubs in their large (if slightly rundown) bathrooms; besides that, they have a certain Zen-cool look, with Japanese screens, minimalist furniture, and dark-hardwood floors contrasting with white walls. But Zen-schmen—you might just find a bigger plus in the in-room air-conditioning, pretty unusual to find in these parts. Other on-premises pluses include a nice big pool set among gardens and the Lotus Garden, which serves respectable (well, for Puerto Viejo) Japanese and Chinese fare; stay 3 nights and they'll comp you an all-you-can-eat meal of sushi, miso soup, and sake. Rates start at $52 for a double, including taxes.

$$ Just north of town, there's yoga in the hills at **Samasati** (right after Cahuita National Park, about 6km/3¾ miles from the village of Puerto Viejo in the small town of Hone Creek; ☎ 756-8015, 800/563-9643 in the U.S. and Canada; www. samasati.com; AE, D, MC, V). Hugging a 195m-high (650-ft.) ridge on 100 hectares (250 acres) with voluptuous vistas of the coast, Massimo Monti's sweet retreat has been a class act around here for more than a decade (and it's not just us, okay? The *Yogi Times* is apparently just bonkers about the place). But you don't have to be a yogaholic to love this place, thanks to the gourmet veggie fare, secluded feel, and the dozen-person hot tub, with one of the best hot-tub views in Costa Rica. There are plenty of activities, too, such as Spanish lessons and guided nature walks of the property. The main digs are nine good-size bungalows with verandas, roomy baths, and an "elegant treehouse" feel (some also have lofts); they've got electricity and hot water, but don't expect phone, TV, or A/C (not that you need it up here). To save some cash, stay in on of the five doubles with shared baths, in a low building down a forest path toward the meditation pavilion. Your own 4×4 is a good idea, but there are free shuttles to the beaches, and a cab into town will run you around $20. Rates are $64 per person per day with shared bath, $99 with your own—but keep in mind, this includes all your grub.

IN & AROUND PLAYAS COCLES & CHIQUITA

Those looking for more privacy, more beach, or more rainforest should head south to Playas Cocles, Chiquita, or beyond. The area's most bodacious beaches are down here, and there are also some darn good restaurants here, as well. The first beach is Cocles, about 2km (1¼ miles) south of Puerto Viejo, popular with surfers and others; on the other side of the road you'll find a range of digs from basic, surfer-oriented *cabinas* to mid- to high-end resorts. Staying here, you'll be right by the sand but still within convenient distance of town. Just next door, Playa Chiquita has calmer waters and a more small-village-like atmosphere.

$ If there's such a thing as a "low-cost boutique jungle lodge" locally, it's **La Costa de Papito** ★ (Playa Cocles, on road to Manzanillo, 2km/1¼ miles south of Puerto Viejo; ☎ 750-0080; www.lacostadepapito.com; AE, MC, V). OK, it's right off the road, not deep in the jungle, but the feel is definitely there. On 2 hectares (5 acres) across from the beach stand eight stilt-raised wood bungalows, each individually decorated (sometimes funkily so—leopard-skin sheets, anybody?) with bathrooms done up in lovely mosaics; just outside your door are roomy, hammock-strung verandas that guests love to take breakfast on. The latest addition is a spa in a thatched-roof *rancho* where you can choose from chocolate body scrub, banana-and-cocoa butter mask, or wrap of banana leaf, frothy papaya, and honey nectar. There's also a bar and pool table, and you can get the whole local scoop from owner and recovering Brooklynite Eddie Ryan. With units starting at just $47 (if you pay cash, otherwise add 16.4 percent tax), this may be Playa Cocles' dandiest deal.

$$ In the small, laid-back beach community of Playa Chiquita, your best bet apart from renting a house is the long-established **Playa Chiquita Lodge** (5km/3 miles south of Puerto Viejo; ☎ 750-0408; www.playachiquitalodge.com; AE, MC, V), 200m or so (300 ft.) from the water. German Wolf Kissinger and his Tica-American wife Wanda Patterson run a charming compound with Wi-Fi, hiking trails to the beach, and a dozen bungalows, painted a cheery blue inside, all with solar-heated showers and verandas with leather rockers. In the 2 weeks before Easter (usually), the place hosts the annual South Caribbean music festival, an extravaganza featuring live salsa, reggae, Latin jazz, calypso, and Afro-Caribbean music. Doubles run $60 in season, including breakfast.

$$ Next door to La Costa de Papito is the somewhat pricier, more sophisticated **Azania Bungalows** ✹ (2km/1¼ mile south of Puerto Viejo on the road to Manzanillo, Playa Cocles; ☎ 750-0540; www.azania-costarica.com; AE, D, MC, V), across from the beach and snuggled amid forest and densely planted gardens. Is it worth $75 for a double, including breakfast? Could very well be—the thatch-roof bungalows have nice high ceilings, a more contemporary decor, up-to-date baths including showers where you can sit down, and lofts that let them sleep up to four. On the grounds you've got a fab little free-form pool with Jacuzzi and stone-sculpture waterfall, plus a two-level open-air *rancho* restaurant serving Argentine fare (meaning lots o' steak, *che*).

$$–$$$ Another Playa Cocles lodge, **Cariblue Bungalows** ✹✹✹ 🆔 (2km/1¼ miles south of Puerto Viejo on the road to Manzanillo; ☎ 750-0057; www.cariblue. com; AE, MC, V) is the poshest of all, with the feel of a tropical country club. The pool is the biggest around, with a thatched swim-up bar; cobblestone walkways cut through manicured lawns and gardens; and the 16 thatched bungalows are gorgeous and roomy (some sleep up to six), with showers whimsically decorated in colorful tiles. There are plenty of services, including on-site car rental, a well-stocked gift shop, a TV lounge (with satellite channels), and an Italian eatery specializing in fresh seafood. Rates are among the area's highest, starting at $86 for a standard room in the main building, $100 and up for the bungalows (breakfast included, tax is extra).

IN & AROUND PUNTA UVA & MANZANILLO

A dozen or so kilometers south of Puerto Viejo, the hotels and restaurants come fewer and farther between. Punta Uva is less a town than a diffuse community spread out along the road, while Manzanillo has a century-plus history as a small fishing village. Down here you'll want a car, unless you don't mind biking miles in the heat to get up to PU or restaurants along the main road. Many of the digs in this last stretch of coast before the Panama border are on the pricier side (a vacation rental with kitchen really makes sense here; p. 254), but there are a few *cabinas* in the town of Manzanillo if your budget is especially tight; we recommend the **Cabinas Manzanillo** (100m/330 ft. from the beach, off the main road; ☎ 759-9033), just $25 a night for a double. It's a tourism hub, as many tours leave from these areas. Other than that, they're simple, clean, and just fine.

$$ Run by an Italian couple at the edge of dense forest and a few hundred feet from the beach, **Pachamama Lodge** (road to Manzanillo, Punta Uva; ☎ 759-9196; www.greencoast.com/pachamama.htm; V) feels more like being in your own rental house since only a couple of units and a rental house are on the premises.

For relatively pricey Punta Uva, this is one of the best values around: The two pastel-painted rooms ($55 in season) have big terraces where breakfast is served, adorned with country-style furniture made by Tico artisans. The handsome house features lots of polished wood, exposed ceiling beams, and a fully equipped kitchen that opens on to an open-air dining area/deck outfitted with hammock for postprandial snooze. It rents for $75 a day, $400 a week for two people; for three to four, $110 daily and $600 weekly.

$$–$$$$ Be warned: The five gingerbread-trimmed Caribbean-style cottages at the **Aguas Claras** ★ kids (road to Manzanillo, Punta Uva; ☎ 750-0131; www.aguas claras-cr.com; MC, V) are so cute they border on twee. They come in different sizes and painted in dollhouse colors, and inside, the bedrooms have country-style plaid linens and sometimes four-poster beds. Pluses include fully equipped kitchens and shady verandas. On our last visit, the rooms were slightly worn and in need of a touch-up, but there's still a lot to recommend this place. Unlike the Pachamama, the bungalows are on the beach side off the road; a path, an inspiring stroll through old-growth forest, leads to the beach. Just off the deserted sands, the reefs form shallow tide pools perfect for kids to wade in. And after a day at the beach, guests can treat themselves to all kinds of sweet stuff (chocolate-chip and oatmeal raisin cookies, cinnamon rolls, banana muffins) at the on-premises cafe. Rates start at $60 per day, $300 per week for a one-bedroom bungalow; and up to $190 daily, $940 weekly, for a two-story, three-bedroom cottage. It's definitely on the high end for around here—you can rent your own comparable-size house for less—but it's a decent option for a family or group looking for hotel-style services and a restaurant.

$$$–$$$$ Don't let the word "camp" fool you. At **Almonds & Corals Lodge Tent Camp** ★ kids (2km/1¼ miles from the center of the town; ☎ 759-9056, 888/ 373-9044 in U.S and Canada.; www.almondsandcorals.com; AE, MC, V), despite being inside the wildlife reserve, you're most definitely not roughing it. In fact, it feels a little like an upscale jungle safari village—yes, you stay in one of 25 "tents," but they're more like tent-cabin hybrids on stilts, with screen walls, electric lamps, and private baths. Cut through the thick tangle of jungle between them are raised wooden walkways, lit by kerosene lamps at night. The lodge has lots of lounging space, appointed with tree-trunk coffee tables, swinging wood bird-cage chairs, and hanging paper lanterns. During the day, a small zipline canopy tour runs right by here, and at night after dinner, guests can sip cocktails at the tropical-style bar or shoot a few rounds of pool. The only thing missing is a pool—but Manzanillo beach is a few hundred feet away. Sure, rates are a tad steeper—starting at $130 for a double—but that includes all three meals (good thing, too, cause the pickin's on that front are a little thin right around here).

DINING FOR ALL TASTES

The Puerto Viejo food scene is a mix of Tico, black Creole, and expat imports. You've got typical rice-and-beans *sodas,* which you find everywhere in Costa Rica (here with more of an emphasis on shrimp and other seafood), plus the Creole *sodas* run by Afro-Caribbeans, where you can sample traditional Caribbean coast cookery (p. 264). Of those, **Miss Sam's** (2 blocks inland from the main drag;

☎ 750-0108) and **Miss Isma's** (on the main strip; ☎ 750-0579) are the local favorites; try their versions of rice and beans, a rich coconut milk sauce and the classic *rondón* soup/stew. If you're out by Playa Chiquita, **Elena's Bar & Restaurant** (☎ 750-0265) is a good bet.

The international offerings, meanwhile, get more varied every year, from Thai to sushi to Mexican to Spanish to Italian, the last of which is particularly tasty and authentic around here, thanks to all the Italian expats who've set up shop. In fact, the best dining spot in these parts, **La Pecora Nera** ★★★, may be Costa Rica's best Italian restaurant, period.

A goodly chunk of chow-shops are in town, naturally, but a bunch of things—from roadside breakfast spots to pizza joints to casual cafe-bakeries—have been springing up along the road south to Manzanillo at a pretty good clip, and some of the larger resorts open their restaurants to nonguests, too. One thing to keep in mind: Wherever you go, the service is probably going to be slo-o-o-w . . . .

$ Jump-start your day in town with fresh bread and other goodies at **Pan Pay Café & Panadería** (waterfront across from Cabinas Los Almendros; ☎ 750-0081; Thurs–Tues 7am–6pm; AE, D, MC, V), a beachfront hangout popular with locals and tourists alike. Get fresh-baked pastries, fruit salads, croissants (chocolate, plain, or cream-filled, just 60¢!) and wash it down with big cups of coffee (55¢) that, as they say, will grow hair on your chest (with apologies to the ladies). A rib-sticker of eggs, savory Spanish Serrano ham, french fries, and fresh bread with tomatoes and olive oil will set you back just $3.75.

$ If you're in the Punta Uva area, the go-to place for breakfast and snacks is the lovely **Miss Holly's Restaurant** ★ (main road to Manzanillo; ☎ 750-0131; www.aguasclaras.net; daily 8am–3pm; AE, D, MC, V), part of the Aguas Claras cottage complex (p. 261). It stocks baked goods like banana muffins, bagels, and cinnamon rolls, along with American-style deli sandwiches for both carnivores and veggie-types ($5–$6). Got a sweet tooth as well? You'll love their variety of cookies, from chocolate chip to oatmeal raisin.

Boy-Oh-Boy

For some spicy Caribbean soul food served by a spicy Caribbean local character, head to the center of town and look out for Boy-Boy, a sassy, statuesque Jamaican lady who one local hotelier swears is "a reincarnation of Billie Holiday". For only 75¢, she'll sell you a scrumptious patty (an Afro-Caribbean version of the empanada) filled with fruit, chicken, or meat from out of her basket. She's known around town not just for brilliant renditions of the blues but also for channeling Patsy Cline and others on open-mic night at Maritza Bar. There's no guarantee the lady will sing the blues for you, but turn up the sweet talk (or ratchet up the tip), and who knows, you might just score a few bars with your patty.

Got Lapas?

For thick, Pennsylvania Dutch–style ice cream and milkshakes, head for **Las Lapas Lechería** ★★ kids (next to Sunset Bar; no phone; daily 9am–8pm; cash only), a stand run by Susan Lapp, one of a trio of Amish sisters who moved to Costa Rica and now run a farm in nearby Siquirres. With her white apron, white hat, and vaguely Amish accent, Susan serves up the super creamy shakes for $2, along with other treats like vanilla pudding (80¢) and apple pie à la mode ($3.50).

$–$$ A hole in the wall called **Chile Rojo** (main strip, Puerto Viejo; no phone; Wed–Mon noon–10pm; cash only) is a long-time budget fave (most dishes under $8) where Thai meets Middle Eastern. Diners get shoehorned into a stuffy, claustrophobic little shack to eat off worn painted picnic tables. You're wondering, "jeez, so what's up with that?" Well, after a couple of whacks at the long cocktail menu plus a go at the spicy fare, you'll be too far gone to care. Try one of the tasty pita sandwiches (falafel plus choice of meat, $3) or the famous Thai green curries (chicken or fish, $6.25). Our top pick, though is the tuna fillet in black-bean sauce, on a sizzling platter ($7).

$–$$ In Manzanillo, most everyone ends up at **Maxi's** (end of the road in village; ☎ 759-9086; daily noon–10pm; AE, D, MC, V), a two-story beach shack with open-air dining, where seafood rules. Stars are fresh red snapper with rice, beans, and plantains ($8) and various lobster specials (try it in *caribeña* sauce, a blend of coconut, curry, and other spices); prices vary greatly by size, from $6 to $39. Upstairs you can sit outside with a nice view of the beach, but upstairs or down, the vibe is festive. Maxi's is Manzanillo's unofficial clubhouse, and at feeding time it fills up fast with both tourists and locals (who also like to hang out and play dominos).

$$ At Punta Uva's **Selvyn's Bar** ★ (at Cabinas Selvyn, on road to Manzanillo; no phone; Wed–Sun 8am–8pm in season, Fri–Sun otherwise; cash only), another local favorite, charismatic owner Selvyn Brown always draws a crowd with his tales of town life and his flavorful Caribbean-style seafood. Assuming you manage to snag one of the half-dozen tables, you'll get a choice of just two or three main dishes—he only cooks up what's freshest that day. You could find yourself chowing down on a filet of marlin ($6), whole snapper ($6.50), or a juicy lobster ($11), all accompanied by coconut-scented rice and beans, *patacones,* and a small salad.

$$–$$$ You can't miss the hip, hopping **Café Viejo Ristorante** ★ (main strip, Puerto Viejo; ☎ 750-0817; daily 6–10pm; MC, V), an Italian spot right at the crossroads of the town's center. It's mighty fetching, with candlelit tables, deep-red walls, chill-out soundtrack, and a tasty menu that crams in various pastas and almost two dozen kinds of pizza, from classic *napolitana* to prosciutto ($7–$10).

Creole Cookery 101

by Jenna Wortham

When laborers from Jamaica and other Caribbean islands were brought in to work on the Atlantic railroad and banana plantations in the 19th century, they naturally brought along their cooking traditions and favorite foods: seeds for growing oranges, mangoes, large melonlike breadfruit, and the spongelike yellow fruit ackee; and know-how for salt harvesting, charcoal making, and brewing red rum, cane liquor, ginger beer, and *guarapo*, a sugar-cane drink.

No stay on the Limón coast is complete without sampling some of the regional Creole specialties, and there are plenty of eateries in which to do it (see above). Keep in mind that more elaborate dishes are served on the weekends, while simpler staples dominate during the week.

Rice and beans (*rizanbin* in patois), simmered in coconut milk and spiced with cumin and coriander, are a big local favorite and are excellent with fresh seafood.

A *rondón* (patois for "rundown") is like a potluck stew of whatever the cook can "run down"—usually plantains and breadfruit with meat or fish, simmered for hours in a spiced coconut-milk base.

In **fresh breads and desserts,** biggies include *patí*, a flaky pastry stuffed with spicy meat and peppers; *pan bon,* glazed bread with chunks of local fruits or cheese baked into it; ginger biscuits; and plantain tarts.

The charmingly named *agua de sapo* ("toad water") is a drink of lemon juice, ginger, molasses, and a touch of *jengibre* (a secret ingredient that local cooks just ain't telling) that'll cool off your tongue after a mouthful of spicy jerk chicken.

The *penne arrabiata* ($8) and seafood carbonara ($9) are hits, but on my last visit I came back for the lasagna bolognese ($10). The slightly higher prices and the popularity of La Pecora Nera (see below) tends to keep the balance tipped more toward tourists than locals, but for quality, atmosphere, and convenient location, *non c'è problema*—we like.

$$–$$$ Run by a Spanish expat, **Salsa Brava** ☆ (on waterfront south of Puerto Viejo; ☎ 750-0241; Tues–Sun noon–10pm; MC, V) serves up something found in few Costa Rican restaurants outside the Central Valley: a juicy, tender steak ($11), a nice meaty change of pace from all the seafood hereabouts, yummy as that is. Not that you won't find plenty of fresh seafood here—grilled and simply presented in a setting pretty typical for these parts. Here, under a thatch-roof, open-air dining room, with brightly painted wooden tables, you have your choice of whole fish or fillets. The grilled calamari and shrimp are swell, as well. Most seafood entrees run $8 to $10.

$$–$$$ The biggest culinary deal on the Caribbean coast—heck, one of the biggest in the whole country—**La Pecora Nera** ★★★ (road to Manzanillo, Playa Cocles; ☎ 750-0490; Tues–Sun noon–10pm; AE, MC, V) is an elegant spot founded in 1998 by 30-something Ilario Giannoni, a roly poly bundle of energia from Livorno (and maybe "black sheep" of his family, as the restaurant's moniker implies). In a wooded setting a couple hundred feet back from the road, the open-air flagstone pavilion with thatched roof has a woodburning stove, romantic nighttime lighting, and a menu that expertly covers the waterfront, from pastas ($6–$10) to pizzas ($5–$8) and entrees ($10–$12) like barracuda and calamari. Daily specials are standouts, and if the menu doesn't quite do it for you that evening, ask Ilario to whip up something made to order.

WHY YOU'RE HERE: THE TOP SIGHTS & ATTRACTIONS

The days when people came here just to surf the **Salsa Brava** are long gone. Today, this stretch from Puerto Viejo down to Manzanillo has been discovered by beach lovers from party types who play **volleyball on the sand** during the day and hit the reggae and tequila at night to couples looking for romance and seclusion. **Snorkeling, scuba diving,** and **kayaking** are particularly popular here. If you don't plan to spend a night or two in **Cahuita** ★ (p. 245), it's worth popping up there for the day to knock around the village, the national park, and the beaches. The really ambitious might even venture down across the Panama border to **Bocas del Toro** ★★, which has developed a following of its own for sun-soaked beaches, islands, snorkeling, and party/dining scene.

The Talamanca coast also has plenty of primo nature ogling, of course, from dolphin-watching and seasonal sea turtle–nesting tours to hikes to jungle water-falls. Two excellent spots to do a lot of this are the **Cahuita National Park** and **Gandoca-Manzanillo Refuge,** a bit farther south. This being Costa Rica, there's adventure galore, too (if not always of the same caliber as elsewhere in the country): ATV tours, horseback riding, caving, kayaking, whitewater rafting, and a zipline canopy tour (the **Crazy Monkey Canopy Tour** run by Almond & Corals Tent Camp, p. 261).

Cool as this all is, what really makes the Talamanca region stand out in Costa Rica is its uniqueness as home to black Creole culture and most of what's left of the tribes that were here before the Spaniards blundered in. Several tours will get you up to the **indigenous reserves** ★ for a glimpse of their way of life. Grassroots ecotourism run by local community members is particularly strong here; the long-established **Asociación Talamanca de Ecoturismo y Conservación (ATEC)** offers wonderful half-day and full-day tours of the area (p. 272).

When to Go: Surf vs. Snorkel

When conditions are tops for surfing, it's the opposite for snorkeling. Surfing is at its best from December through March, with a minisurf season in June and July. In September and October, the Caribbean's unofficial dry season, the sea is calmer and a whole lot better for snorkeling and swimming.

The Beaches

Just north of the town, the sparsely visited **Playa Negra** is a fetching arc of black sand (as per its name), fronting a small bay. The moderate surf makes it good for wading, sunning, and strolling. We're not rabid fans of black-sand beaches, but if you're in the mood for an uncrowded strand within walking distance of town, it can be a swell spot (and speaking of swells, mornings you'll find some pretty decent surf breaks).

The string of small in-town beaches, dubbed after landmarks (El Chino, named after a Chinese-owned grocery store called Manuel León, or Playa Stanford's in front of Stanford's Disco), aren't the most attractive or great for swimming (partly because of the coral platforms just offshore), but they do have their following among folks who like hanging out by the water right in town. The gnarly standout is **Playa Pirriplí** ✸, just south of Puerto Viejo, home to the famous **"Salsa Brava"** ("hot sauce") surf break. Costa Rica's most powerful wave swells up out in deep water and comes in for both left and right breaks over a shallow reef—not for newbies, dudes. During peak surf season, Pirriplí hosts surfing competitions and can otherwise get pretty crowded. Many of the local surf shops are on or near this beach.

A bit farther south of town is one of our favorite local beaches, **Playa Cocles** ✸. Though it's also known as a surfer spot because of moderate to strong waves (in-season surf contests go on here, too), I like hanging out here just because it's a helluva looker: long, wide, gold-and-white sands, and shimmering blue water, backed by lush green vegetation and with a pretty little rock island (Isla Pirriplí) offshore. The crowd here is usually friendly, and there's a string of restaurants and bars along here, too.

A mile south of Playa Cocles, through a coconut grove, the smallish **Playa Chiquita** ✸✸ 🄺 is a boffo choice for families: the water's calmer than at Cocles, and a series of tidepools make safe, fun wading areas for the pint-size. There's often a volleyball or soccer game going on, and toward the southern end the strand arcs out into a rocky point blanketed with vegetation. The waters are calm and clear down here, too—perfect for swimming.

The next beach down is white-sand **Playa Punta Uva** ✸✸✸ 🄺, which in our humble opinion is the most ravishing on the Talamanca coast and one of the most beautiful in Costa Rica; in season it's also very popular, particularly among locals. There's good parking, and though there are fewer services than at Cocles, you'll find a grocery store at the start of the access trail. The mostly sheltered cove and no reef means it's reasonably safe to splash around and do in all types of water sports (including topnotch snorkeling and kayaking). While you're here, you can

---

Horsing Around on the Beach

If you're lucky, you might get to spot wild horses roaming up and down the beaches, munching on vegetation. In case you get any bright ideas about trying to catch them and hop on, keep in mind they're not just potentially dangerous but also protected by the law. So don't harass—just admire.

Sand Flies While You're Having Fun

Avoid walking along the beaches at low tide—that's when sand flies (aka "no-see-ums," similar to fleas) are at their worst, and out to feast on your blood. You might not notice when they bite, but you certainly will the next day when dozens of itchy welts make their appearance. Most insect repellents keep them at bay; those containing Deet are the most effective, but some oils and oil-based lotions also do the trick.

take a short hike into the rainforest hills above and check out the **Mariposario Punta Uva** ★ 🧒 (☎ 750-0245; adults $5, kids free; daily 8am–4pm;), a charming butterfly garden with a bonus: va-va-voom views of the ocean and hillside below.

You'll find the **best snorkeling and diving in the area** at **Playa Manzanillo** ★★, part of a nationally protected area that covers the rainforest along the coast and the coral reefs just offshore. While you can snorkel in the smaller reefs just off Playa Chiquita and Punta Uva, Manzanillo is home to the area's biggest reef, its aqua-green waters teeming with brightly colored fish including parrot and angel fish, blue tangs, and jack fish. The corals themselves are impressive: brain coral, boulder coral, fire coral (don't touch!), sea fans, elk horn, and lettuce coral. Rent a kayak and paddle out over the reef; once you find the fish, you'll know where to jump in.

Because there's a small town backing it up, Manzanillo beach offers more services than the beaches to its north, including restaurants, a convenience store, and dive, snorkel, and kayak rentals. Of the dive shops, **Aquamor** (50m/165 ft. east of Maxi's; ☎ 759-9012; www.greencoast.com; daily 8am–5:30pm; AE, MC, V) is the biggest and best, with everything from PADI certification courses to 2-hour snorkel tours ($12). Or you can just rent snorkel gear ($3 per hr.), kayaks ($6), or boogie boards ($3).

Finally, from Manzanillo you can reach a couple of other beaches, **Punta Mona** and **Playa Gandoca** ★, but only by hiking several hours. They're both certainly lovely, but unless you're up for quite a schlep, there are plenty of other primo stretches of sand to enjoy hereabouts. **Playa Gandoca** is known mostly as the spot where sea turtles come to nest (p. 270).

Exploring Nature

Though you can take minihikes along dozens of trails leading up the hillside from the coast, the big kahuna is the **Gandoca–Manzanillo Refuge** ★★ (end of road to Manzanillo, entrance 200m/660 ft. south of village; ☎ 754-2133; $6). Established in 1985, it protects more than 49 sq. km (19 sq. miles) on land and 44 sq. km (17 sq. miles) more offshore. Inside are forests, coral reef, mangrove-lined estuaries and swamps (home to endangered manatees as well as crocodiles and caimans), over 350 species of birds, and dolphins (including the rare tucuxí dolphin). Certain times of the year, four species of giant sea turtles swim in to nest on the beaches.

A Tip of the Hat to Panama

It'll be tempting to pop down to Bocas del Toro, another nifty beach town just over the border. After all, on maps Panama's no more than 25km (16 miles) away from Puerto Viejo, right?

Well . . . getting here isn't quite so simple. By bus, you have to get yourself to the frontier at Sixaola and wade through the red tape before crossing over in to Changuinola. There you board another bus to Bocas—and well, the whole process could take you the better part of a day. Throw in the steamy heat along with the trials and tribulations of rural third-world travel, and you get the picture.

Lately, though, getting between Puerto Viejo and Bocas del Toro has gotten a little simpler. Thanks to the ever-growing number of expats without kosher residency papers (Americans, for example, can stay only 3 months at a time), a ferry now shuttles people back and forth on day trips to Panama. Locals use it to get a passport stamp, enabling them to stay another 3 months. For you it's an easier way to spend a couple of days exploring Bocas del Toro, which, if you can believe, has even nicer beaches and snorkeling than on the Tico side of the border.

A Puerto Viejo surf shop, **Aventuras Bravas** (on the main strip; ☎ 750-2000) coordinates a 3-hour ferry to Bocas every Tuesday at 8am, returning Thursday at 3pm (keep in mind Panama's an hour ahead of Costa Rica); the fare's $35 one-way, $60 round-trip, and Aventuras will need your passport by noon Monday to get the paperwork ready.

Why go through the trouble, you wonder, just to see yet another Creole area on the same beachy coast? Well, besides just being able to say you've been to Panama, there are some differences—for one, it's even more relaxed down here (yep, amazing but true). Also, Bocas del Toro is part of a spectacular archipelago of a half-dozen bigger islands plus a bunch more smaller ones; people go everywhere by boat, and the feel is even more castaway-isle (there's a reason why various versions of *Survivor* have been shot here). The snorkeling and diving are outrageous, and wildlife is, if anything, more rampant (in a good way): humongo starfish, caimans, red frogs, dolphins, and lots more. Here's a miniguide to one of our favorite spots in Central America.

ORIENTATION

In this archipelago, the main town of Bocas, along with the airport, is on Isla Colón. Water taxis and ferries can take you to explore loads of cays, coves, and beaches on the different islands.

GETTING THERE

Apart from the above ferry, the easiest way to get to Bocas is to fly. **Nature Air** (☎ 299-6000, 800/235-9272 in the U.S. and Canada;

www.natureair.com) runs several flights to Bocas from San José and Quepos (from $62 each way). A timesaver would be take the ferry down and fly back to San José.

ACCOMMODATIONS
Your choices are mostly split between Bocas, farther up on the Isla Colón, and Isla Bastimentos. While you've got more dining and nightlife (and mingle time with locals) in town, we recommend at least a night in a resort on one of the islands. If you're here for the beaches, the best ones are far away from town. A downside to staying out on an island, though, is that unless you're on a tour, for most meals you'll have to grab a water taxi ($15–$25) or ferry ($1–$2) to town or another resort. Here are a couple of favorites; you can check out lots of others, at all price levels, at **www.bocas.com**, which also links to short-term rentals.

For a private, thatch-roof bungalow on a quiet lagoon with a tiny white beach, try the **Buccaneer Resort** ✯ (Isla Carenero; ☎ 507/707-9042; www.bucaneer-resort.com; MC, V), run by a local character, Captain Tom. Rates start at $65 per day, including breakfast.

For a memorable, get-away-from-it-all splurge, the **Punta Caracol Acqua-Lodge** ✯✯✯ (Isla Colón; ☎ 507-6612-1088; www.puntacaracol.com; MC, V) can't be beat. Stay in one of eight Caribbean style–cottages on stilts over turquoise waters and a coral reef. They're joined to each other and the dining room by a walkway, and apart from that it's just you, the sea, and the mangroves; go canoeing or snorkeling right from your porch. Granted, $265 per night per double isn't cheap, but it does include all your grub, plus transfers from Bocas town.

WHY YOU'RE HERE
In Bocas town, consider taking a 1-day tour that combines two or more of the highlights, such as **Playa Estrella,** home to dozens of bright-orange starfish, and the **Laguna de Delfines** where you can watch dolphins frolic. Another sight you won't want to miss is **Swan's Cay** (Isla de Pájaros), a big craggy rock that's a magnet for seabirds (a skilled boatman can pilot you through). The many beaches to explore include **Red Frog Beach,** a long, sandy stretch with good surf and, yes, little red frogs hopping around. Finally, make sure to stop for lunch at the **Restaurante Cayo Crawl** in **Cayo Crawl** (or Coral Key), on stilts over perfectly clear, blue-green shallows. Afterward, jump in and snorkel up to colorful needlefish, angelfish, parrotfish, and other finny phenomena.

There are two main ways of exploring here. The most obvious is to follow the trail along the beach through the coastal rainforests; 1km (⅔ mile) down, you'll have to wade across a river and hike some steep hills to reach **Punta Mona,** some 5km (3 miles) south of Manzanillo (and it can be tough going with the heat, humidity, and mosquitoes). Depending on your pace, you'll reach **Gandoca Village** in about 3 hours.

A little easier is exploring by kayak or boat with a guide. You'll get taken through the Gandoca statuary, lined with Costa Rica's only remaining red mangrove, and spawning grounds for manatees and tarpon. Outfits offering tours include the grass-roots **ATEC** ✸ (p. 272), **Aquamor** (p. 267), and **Puerto Viejo Tours & Rentals** (☎ 750-0411). From April to August, Playa Gandoca is great for observing **nesting leatherback turtles** at night; contact ATEC or **ANAI** (☎ 750-0020; www.anaicr.org), a nonprofit that runs a sea turtle conservation program. **Red Talamanca** (☎ 756-8033; www.actuarcostarica.com), another community group, arranges guided turtle-nesting expeditions for $75 per person, including transfers, dinner in a Gandoca family's home, and a couple of hours on the beach.

Don't forget, there's no guarantee of any sightings; there's always a chance you might end up taking the hour-and-a-half trek out to Gandoca and end up seeing only one turtle or even none. But if your plans don't include **Tortuguero,** where the sheer numbers and predictability of the nesting turtles make for better odds, it's worth giving it a try here.

You can get another close look at local nature at the **Finca La Isla Botanical Garden** ✸✸ (200m/660 ft. west of El Pizote Lodge, Playa Negra; ☎ 750-0046; $5 per person, guided tour $10, children 3–11 half price; Fri–Mon 10am–4pm), an abandoned cacao farm turned by Linda and Peter Kring into tropical flora a-go-go: more than 60 varieties of fruit—always in season to sample—include the stinky Asian durian; spices such as cinnamon, vanilla black pepper, and nutmeg; and gardens packed with heliconias, orchids, palms, and other plants. You'll get a look at lots of stuff you might not catch out on the jungle trails, and learn about medicinal plants and chocolate production. When we caught up with Peter on our last visit (he sells his spices at the Puerto Viejo organic market), we talked about how underrated the Caribbean has been for **birding,** and the surprising number of species he's spotted in his gardens—including three kinds of toucans and a whole bunch of trogons and manakinds. Normally, they open at 10am, but he says if you call ahead, he'll open earlier for birding tours.

ATTENTION, SHOPPERS!

If you're a fan of street fairs and stalls, welcome to heaven. All along the waterfront, vendors set up tables to hawk the usual trinkets, bracelets, and earrings made with beads, coconut shells, and other local stuff; tie-dyed T-shirts and batiks, as well as "countercultural" paraphernalia like pipes, incense, and the like.

There are also a few notable shops, starting with the **Tienda del Mar** (main strip in Puerto Viejo; ☎ 750-0355), with souvenirs but also a big selection of clothing along the lines of linen shirts and pants, men's surf shorts, and women's tops and long, flowy cotton skirts. You'll also find some of the wood and paper lanterns and other tropical decor stuff you'll see in some of the vacation homes and lodges.

The also popular **Luberlulu Caribbean Gallery** ✪ (a block inland from main strip, across from Cabinas Guaraná; ☎ 750-0394) is strong on unique arts and crafts, many cranked out locally, including colorful mosaics and watercolors, shell mobiles, decorative lamps, and sarongs; you can also get pieces made to order.

NIGHTLIFE

Reggae is a way of life here, and when night falls it's what fuels the fiesta. There is no shortage of bars and discos, and the social calendar, as in many other Costa Rican towns, revolves around live music. And unlike many other resort communities, many of the locals here go out and mingle with the tourists. Finally, Puerto Viejo's druggy, crime-prone rep is pretty exaggerated. But there are seedier elements around, so you may in fact get offered reefer or whatever, and women—particularly women alone—will inevitably get propositioned. But just be cool, take the usual precautions (such as, don't get too wasted or do anything stupid), and you'll be fine.

Keep in mind that the listings below were accurate when we went to press, but life changes, so when you get there you should ask around where the party is that night.

Let's start with a pair of reliable mainstays: **Johnny's Place** ✪ (100m/330 ft. north of ATEC office; Mon 6pm–2:30am, Tues–Sat noon–2:30am) and **Stanford's Disco** (main road to Manzanillo, just south of the main strip; ☎ 750-0608; Wed–Mon 7pm–2:30am). Chances are if there's not a crowd in one, everybody's at the other. Both are discos with smallish dance floors, featuring reggae, reggaetón, and hip-hop most nights. Of the two, Johnny's Place has a nicer and less claustrophobic feel (always nice when temps hit the 90s), with tables spilling out onto the beach. Since Stanford's is closed on Tuesdays, that's a definite Johnny's night, with live music; Thursday and Saturday nights are also popular.

Among the bars, the scene shifts based on the live music. On Monday and Friday nights, most everyone heads for the infamous reggae parties at **El Bambú** ✪ (just south of Stanford's on the main road to Manzanillo; no phone), a bar with a wee dance floor, an outdoor terrace, and steps down to a stretch of beach with plastic tables and chairs. The place is usually packed with locals and tourists, with music going till late, late into the night. During high season, the party sometimes spills out onto the street, with revelers chugging rum like coconut water and the whiff of ganja in the air. On Sunday, the scene shifts to the **Bar Maritza** (100m/330 ft. northeast of the bus stop; ☎ 750-0003), where there's live calypso and salsa from 5pm until 1am.

For a slightly tamer scene, check into the live music nights at a bar/restaurant called **El Loco Natural** ✪ (Puerto Viejo Centro, second floor; ☎ 750-0263; Thurs–Tues from 6pm). On Sunday at 7pm, and Thursday and Saturday at 8:30pm, the joint features live calypso, jazz, or reggae, which you can take in over a meal or drinks. On Wednesday, head to the open jam at the **Sunset Bar & Grill** (50m/165 ft. west of bus stop), which has a pool table; most other nights, the soundtrack's reggae. At **Hot Rocks Café** ✪ (on the water just past the main strip; ☎ 750-0525), an open-air bar and restaurant on a dirt lot, four movies a night run on a huge screen—it makes for a fun yet low-key night out. You don't have to order anything to sit down and watch, but seats can fill up quickly. It's best to find out ahead of time what's showing and when, then get there early.

Going Native at the Kékŏldi Reserve ✭

by Jenna Wortham

Unlike, say, Bolivia, Peru, and Guatemala, Costa Rica's not known for its indigenous culture (in fact, many of the "native" arts and crafts you see sold down here are imported).

Talamanca's the big exception. After fleeing the coasts centuries ago to get away from the Spanish conquistadors, peoples like the BriBri and Cabécar have stayed mostly isolated in the mountain jungles ever since, eking out a subsistence living and pretty much untouched by tourism (or anything else) at least until 1991, when a paved highway opened up the Talamanca area for more development.

Realizing that modern life was heading their way, and hoping to benefit from sustainable tourism, the Talamanca's indigenous tribes, black Creoles, and Ticos formed the **Asociación Talamanqueña de Ecoturismo y Conservación** (**ATEC;** (☎ 750-0398; www.greencoast.com/atec.htm), which began training locals to lead tours throughout the region. This way, guides can use their knowledge of the area without damaging it (either through slash-and-burn farming, turtle poaching, and so forth), and receive 90 percent of the tour price to boot.

The most personal and popular tour takes visitors to the **Kékŏldi Reserve,** set up in 1976 to protect the area's nature and culture. It's been a struggle against hunting, logging, squatting, and illegal building, though, and your signing up for an ATEC tour donates 15 to 20 percent of the take to conservation and reforestation. In these 24 sq. km (9 sq. miles) extending from the lowlands up into the Talamanca Mountains, a little more than 200 Bribri and Cabécar live in rustic communities, growing cacao and bananas, raising animals, and following a religion that binds together all the forests' inhabitants in harmony with Sibö, their god of creation.

Some of us might feel a little voyeuristic, treating ancient, primitive peoples as if they were zoo attractions, but ATEC's roots in the community

THE "OTHER" PUERTO VIEJO

Is there life in Puerto Viejo beyond reggae bars and beautiful beaches? Some people might say, who cares? But if you've been here for a few days, done that and bought the T-shirt, you might want to consider getting under the surface a bit.

Apart from meeting tipsy locals in bars, the community isn't all that easy to break into—no one really wants to invest time in transients. But there are places where you can at least *interact* with people other than tourists and partiers. A good starting point is one of the Saturday **organic markets.** Like some other areas of Costa Rica, this one attracts a certain number of folks interested in organic farming and perma-culture, and they catch up with each other at these markets. There's a Saturday-morning market across from the Panadería Elizabeth in Puerto

help make us a little less queasy. Sure, there's an inevitable touch of show-manship (look kids, here are the colorful natives making chocolate!) and prepackaging, but these 4-hour excursions manage to stay respectful, and the itineraries change, which helps keep damage to the land to a minimum. Led by reserve guides Alex Paz Balma, Herman Martinez, Maura Mayorga, or Lucas Chávez, you'll hike through lush forests (including a waterfall where you can take a dip) and pass by traditionally built homes (there are really no central villages, just individual houses and small groupings); if you're lucky, you might get invited in to meet your guide's family and sample cocoa drinks, yucca, squash, and eggs wrapped and served in banana leaves. You might also get to see tribe members thatching a roof, peeling rice, harvesting crops, or making the arts and crafts they sell these days. These woven baskets and coconut-shell carvings, by the way, aren't just a tourist shakedown—the cash does end up helping the community, and few of these trinkets cost more than a couple of bucks, anyway.

The tours also take you to an **iguana-breeding farm,** where endangered green iguanas are hatched and released to replenish the overhunted local stocks. And as you traipse alongside the gushing Yorkin River, following in the footsteps of generations of Bribri, you'll learn about the plants they use to treat everything from malaria to skin problems.

A full day will cost you about $33 per person; overnight camping jaunts are $36. Book at ATEC's office on the main road in Puerto Viejo (a day in advance to guarantee a spot). Bring shoes with traction–the forest up here is damp–and you'll definitely want to layer on the bug juice. Both ATEC and **ANAI** (p. 270) can arrange a similar trip to the village of Yorkin, another Bribri village.

Viejo and in front of the Shawandha Lodge (on the main road to Manzanillo) in Playa Chiquita. Locals buy and sell their produce, breads, and more, and you'll be able to chat them up, maybe even get some useful tips.

Another way to see a different side of Puerto Viejo is to volunteer. The NGO **ANAI** (www.anaicr.org) is a popular choice, attracting 40 to 70 people a season to their turtle-monitoring program. During the nesting season (Feb–Aug), you can help with the hatching process from about 10pm to 4am, walking the beaches to patrol against poachers. In return, you get an up-close encounter with nature: Volunteers are sometimes allowed to help collect the turtle eggs as the mothers are hatching them, which they then measure and put into a hatchery nest. Volunteers bunk in a *cabina* right by the nesting beach, and pay $16 to $20 a night for room and board. There's no minimum time commitment but most stay at least 3 days, while others end up sticking around for 3 weeks or more.

Finally, if you're interested in meeting a Bribri family or child outside of the usual packaged tour through the villages, consider contacting Barry and Nanci Stevens of **The Bridge** (☎ 750-0524, or 866/462-7585 in the U.S.; www.elpuente-thebridge.org). He's a former venture capitalist, she a wildlife artist; they founded this nonprofit to help put these dirt-poor kids through school and to provide micro-loans to help families start businesses. They welcome both donations and visitors to their home to meet some of the families and children. Sometimes you might even get to go up into the hills to one of the families' homes—very cool but not for softies, says Barry; Bribri living conditions can be pretty raw, but in exchange you'll get an experience even more authentic than the packaged reserve tours.

8 Guanacaste & the Nicoya Peninsula

From cowboys to cocktails, Costa Rica's onetime "wild west" has become the country's premier sun-and-surf magnet.

by David Appell & Nelson Mui

THE PACIFIC-COAST PROVINCE NAMED FOR COSTA RICA'S HULKING, umbrella-like national tree snuggles up against Nicaragua's southwestern border and holds a special place in the Tico psyche. Come to think of it, it's one not so different from the Old West's mystique for Americans: Much of Guanacaste is semi-arid, "big-sky" savannah, and dry forest, complete with cattle ranches, *sabaneros* (cowboys), rodeos, and a historic gold rush in its past.

And though some of that old-time flavor still lingers in the interior hinterland, a good chunk of this region has undergone a modern-day, 21st-century tourism-driven gold rush along more than 320km (200 miles) of spectacular coastline, from Salinas Bay at the border down to the Nicoya Peninsula (shared with neighboring Puntarenas province). The past couple of decades in particular have given birth to a new "gold coast" lined with multi-million-dollar resorts, condos, villas, marinas, and golf courses. The *sabaneros* have moved over for *surferos* (surfers), and English can seem almost as widely spoken as Spanish. Some old-timers in the area disdainfully refer to Guanacaste as "another Miami." Others have dissed it as Costa Rica's "second colonialization."

Despite a handful of cheesy all-inclusives and misfires, egregious development boo-boos have been largely avoided, and some parts of the coast are still home to charming little fishing villages. The mix is part of what makes the area so marvelous to visit. One afternoon you can munch on a caramel apple while taking in some bull riding at a small-town fiesta, then head out for cocktails on a catamaran at sunset. Catch a wave off Tamarindo in the morning, do lunch at a tortilla factory in Santa Cruz, and then pop over a few miles west to Guaitíl to watch local women make their distinctive pottery.

And the beaches? Well, there are dozens upon dozens to explore. From the rugged headlands and bays of the Papagayo Peninsula to the surf mecca of Malpaís, there's a fetching stretch of sand with your name on it, whether your bag is snorkeling, scuba, cavorting in the waves, people-watching, or just meandering in solitude.

While the beaches are undoubtedly the stars of the show up here, you'd be shortchanging yourself if you didn't take time out to explore the natural beauty in from the shore, along with some of Costa Rica's finest ecotouristic experiences.

If you're visiting in August and September, you can witness an *arribada,* the arrival of a million Olive Ridley turtles to their nesting grounds on Playa Ostional. Lava lovers will have a blast at the Rincón de la Vieja National Park, where you can get up close and personal with fumaroles (volcanic steam vents), bubbling mud pools, and blue-green lagoons. And if you're not claustrophobic, get yourself lowered into the caverns of Barra Honda National Park for a gawk at phantasmagoric, million-year-old stalactites and stalagmites.

Guanacaste and Nicoya are very much what you make them. Stick to the resort, the beach, and the disco, if you must. But if you do, there's a whole world of Tico culture, history, and natural beauty you'd be sorry you missed. Between the golf courses, the strip malls, and the busloads of surfers, you can still spot the *sabanero,* lasso in hand and bronzed face half-hidden behind a wide-brimmed leather hat, along the back-country road, as he gallops across the landscape.

DON'T LEAVE GUANACASTE & NICOYA WITHOUT . . .

DROPPING IN ON THE RODEO AT A FIESTA ALONG THE COAST
From late November through July, especially in January and February, Guanacaste's cowboy heritage comes alive with fiestas that feature bull riding and a county-fair atmosphere with rides, caramel apples, and costumes.

RIDING A BOARD IN TAMARINDO, NOSARA, OR MALPAÍS   If you've never hung ten before, consider giving it a shot at one of the many surf schools and instructors that have practically colonized entire stretches of beach.

GETTING AN EYEFUL OF THOUSANDS OF OLIVE RIDLEY TURTLES COMING ASHORE TO NEST AT PLAYA OSTIONAL   Between July and September, these awesome, ancient sea creatures lumber ashore and cover the sands for just the right spots to lay their eggs.

EXPLORING THE VOLCANIC MUD POOLS AND FUMAROLES OF RINCÓN DE LA VIEJA NATIONAL PARK   Feel a little like a tourist in hell when you explore this park's Las Pailas ("cauldrons") section, with its scorched landscape and sulphurous fumes.

TAKING A HIKE THROUGH A NATURE RESERVE OR TWO   From the tropical dry forests of Santa Rosa and Palo Verde national parks to the mangrove-lined waterways near Nosara and dense woodlands of the Cabo Blanco wildlife reserve at Nicoya's tip, it's a wild, wild world.

A BRIEF HISTORY

The original *guanacastecos* were sun-worshipping Chorotega Indians, descended from Mexico's Olmecs, who arrived in the 8th century and set up villages along the coast, where they fished, grew corn, and created skillful jade carvings and ceramics. Their 16th-century Chief Nicoya gave the peninsula they lived on its name, and was foolish enough to greet the conquistadors with gifts of gold when they arrived in 1523.

So the Spaniards colonized, and in fairly short order many Chorotegas were sold into slavery or decimated by smallpox and other sicknesses they had no defenses against. A few managed to hang on for another couple of centuries, but today visitors can see what their culture was like only in museums here and in San José (as well as through the pottery and other craft traditions that survive among the locals).

But most of the conquistadors didn't stick around for long, because it turned out that despite Nicoya's glittery tease, there was in fact precious little metal in these parts. So by 1531 many of the Spanish outposts had been abandoned as their inhabitants sailed off to rape places like Mexico and Peru for their gold. That's one reason you won't see all that much colonial architecture; a notable exception being some neighborhoods in Liberia, the provincial capital.

Part of the Captaincy of Guatemala under colonial rule, Guanacaste was actually linked with Nicaragua to its north until 1812 when it was transferred to Costa Rica. In 1821, however, when Central America's rulers declared independence from Spain, Nicaragua had second thoughts and started with Costa Rica over the region. The locals were divided, too: Around Liberia and the northern region they felt the tug of their Nica cattle-rancher heritage, while the Nicoyans favored the Ticos. Costa Rica narrowly got the nod in an 1824 referendum (though apparently there was some tiff about butterfly ballots or something), and the arrangement was definitively ratified by treaty in 1858.

Like the California Gold Rush in 1849, central Guanacaste had its own gold rush in the 1880s, which birthed a gold mining industry that hung on into the early 20th century. For the most part, though, the history here has pretty much been all about fishing, agriculture (especially cotton and sugar cane), and above all cattle ranching. This last was given a big boost in the second half of the 20th century by Ronald McDonald—or more generally, the ravenous maw of the U.S. fast-food chains. Between the 1960s and the late 1970s, beef exports to the United States grew 500%.

Then in 1978, a development arrived that changed Guanacaste forever after: the inauguration of a huge hydroelectric and irrigation project on nearby Laguna—now Lake—Arenal. The sudden wealth of water and electricity, combined with the coast's copious charms and sun-drenched winter and spring weather, led to a tourism-oriented building frenzy that continues, a little less frenetically, today. This development was further goosed by the 1995 inauguration of an international airport in Liberia, and big international luxury brands have started upscaling their way in, such as the Four Seasons Resort at Peninsula Papagayo in 2004 (others on the way include Ritz-Carlton, Starwood, St Regis, and Aman). The *campesinos* and *sabaneros* of yore still roam out here for now, but they're clearly the past; the future, for better or worse, lies in swimming pools, golf courses, and room service.

LAY OF THE LAND

Guanacaste province is located in Costa Rica's northwest corner, stretching from the border with Nicaragua down to the lower third of the Nicoya Peninsula; most tourism/leisure development is concentrated along the region's dramatically sculpted Pacific coastline. The best way to see it is to base yourself in one of the beach resort areas and take day trips into the hinterland.

There's a lot of ground to cover up here, so consider giving yourself at least a week if you want to see and do a decent amount. And don't be fooled by short-seeming distances on the map; in some cases, getting somewhere can easily chew up half a day. This is especially true for the beach resort areas, as there's no paved road along the coast, so getting the 40km (25 miles) from, say, Nosara to Tamarindo can take 3 hours. To keep your time behind the wheel to a minimum, I've listed national parks and attractions with the beach community they are closest to.

THE FAR NORTH

For nature boys and girls, the mostly unspoiled lands close to the Nicaraguan border are the go-to spot for a glorious grab bag of flora, fauna, and terrain. This is mostly thanks to Santa Rosa National Park (sprawling over the entire Santa Elena peninsula, with more than 11 microclimates); the Guancaste National Park (limited mostly to researchers and park officials); and the Rincón de la Vieja National Park (famous for volcanoes, bubbling mud pools, and sulfurous steam vents).

LIBERIA

Guanacaste's provincial capital and all-around "Big Apple" may be Costa Rica's most charming and historic burg (est. 1769). It's got whitewashed old adobe houses with orange-tile roofs, a neat little *sabanero* museum, and just a generally appealing vibe. Yet tourists still mostly just pass through en route from airport to beaches.

PLAYA PANAMA, PLAYA HERMOSA & PLAYA DEL COCO

Santa Rosa National Park

With a trio of horseshoe beaches a half-hour west of Liberia, placid waters, and scenic headlands rising up from the sea, this park is ideal for a romantic or family getaway. Watersports abound, and the national parks up north are only an hour away. Across the bay from Playa Panamá are the high-end resorts (including the Four Seasons) and gated communities of the Papagayo Peninsula.

Tamarindo & Vicinity

Former fishing village Tamarindo is now one of Costa Rica's priciest and most developed beach towns. Time was, people came here for the surf and to watch the giant leatherback turtles nest in nearby Playa Grande; these days, it's more for the buzzing, international beach vibe, dining, and nightlife scene driven in part by the sizable expat population. Just north you'll find the beach communities of Playa Flamingo, Brasilito, and Conchal, home to high-end residential developments and all-inclusives but with few services or attractions other than the strands.

Nosara & Sámara

Besides gnarly surfing and lush tropical scenery, Nosara has a flourishing community of progressive, often artsy Euros and Yanks, and its also one of Guanacaste's few bona fide eco-destinations thanks to reserves that have kept the joint jumping with wildlife (especially the Olive Ridley turtles that nest here by the hundreds of thousands each year). An hour south, Sámara serves up a picture-perfect tropical beach with a lively mix of Ticos and tourists. Its gentle surf makes for a fine family destination and good snorkeling and kayaking.

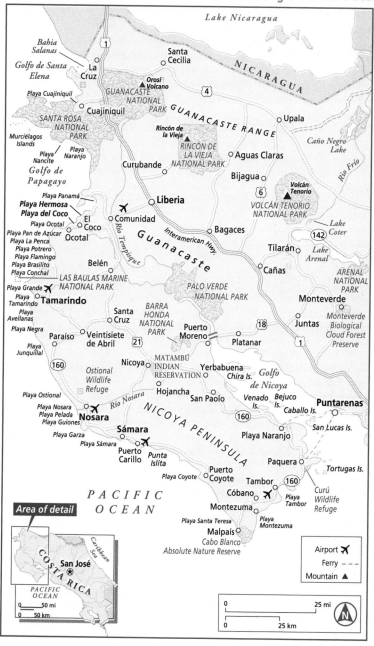

MONTEZUMA & MALPAIS

Several surfing communities sit at the southern tip of the Nicoya Peninsula, and they attract a youngish crowd, international and Tico alike. Montezuma tosses in a rep as a haven for artists, musicians, neo-hippies, and other counterculture types. And it was here, at the Cabo Blanco Wildlife Refuge, that this country's push for conservation and a national parks system was born. Though slightly off the beaten path, word has been getting out, and local towns can be packed in season.

PLAYA HERMOSA & VICINITY

Along a trio of perfectly horseshoe-shape bays, the communities of **Playa Panamá** ✹, **Playa Hermosa** ✹✹, and **Playa del Coco** are among the most eye-catching of the Guanacaste beaches—and the most accessible, thanks to direct flights to Liberia, about a half-hour away on an excellent highway. Soaring golden-brown headlands bookend beautiful gray and white sands, making the crystalline waters great for swimming and sundry watersports (families, take note). This is Costa Rica's Amalfi Coast or Côte d'Azur, and like them, a corniche road links the communities while delivering spectacular coastline and sea views. Business, as you can imagine, is booming.

Each of the three has its own flavor. **Playa Panamá** is sleepy, with a narrow 2km (1¼ mile) of gray sand that's darn near deserted during weekdays and off season. There are few services here—just a single beach restaurant (**Cangrejo's**) and a few high-end resorts. One thing I've noticed here, in particular, is the heat—it often borders on broiling, and torpor seems to grip the town on most days (even the beach dawgs seem lazier than usual).

Next door, **Playa Hermosa** is shaping up as a Tico Monaco on the bay, with ritzy villas and condos sprouting in the hills above. The crescent beach is fringed with lush greenery (which you don't otherwise see all that much of in the dusty brown local landscape) and a string of seafood eateries and hotels spilling right onto the sand. Chances are you'll dig the wonderfully relaxed vibe; on any given day, a dozen boats anchor offshore and you'll see locals batting around a volleyball by the water. The town's pretty geared towards watersports, with plenty of shops running dive trips and renting snorkel gear and kayaks—there's even a kitesurfing school.

Playa del Coco puts us more in mind of Coney Island, with middle-class Ticos thronging the strand and main drag on weekends and holidays. One of the first local beaches to be developed, Coco is beginning to show its age, and while some are into the bustling nightlife (several casinos, along with noisy bars and discos on the beach), others aren't too crazy about its seedier aspects (drugs and "working girls"). But not everyone—particularly your average Juan Tico—can foot the hotel bills in Hermosa and Panamá, so its slew of *cabinas* and moderately priced digs make Coco one of the Pacific Coast's most accessible resorts (the other is Sámara). Just south of here is the tiny enclave of **Playa Ocotal,** which features a secluded beach, a few smallish hotels, and a gated community of vacation town homes.

Given this area's quick and easy road access to Liberia, it makes a good spot to base yourself for visiting the national parks farther north (p. 289), most notably **Santa Rosa** ✹ and **Rincón de la Vieja** ✹✹.

GETTING TO & AROUND PLAYA HERMOSA

By Air

Playa Hermosa is only an hour away from Liberia's airport, so if you're planning to spend most of your vacation in Guanacaste, definitely check to see if your airline has flights directly into here. From Liberia, you can catch a bus or taxi (expect to shell out $25–$30), or rent a car and drive (see below for directions).

By Bus

From San José, buses (☎ 221-7202) leave for Playa Hermosa and Playa Panamá (Calle 20, between avs. 3 and 5) daily at 3:30pm. The trip takes 5 hours and costs $5. For Playa del Coco, buses (**Pulmitan** ☎ 222-1650) leave at 8am, 2pm, and 4pm daily from Calle 24 between avs. 5 and 7.

From Liberia, buses (☎ 666-0042) leave for Playa Hermosa and Panamá daily at 5am, 7:30am, 11:30am, 3:30pm, 5:30pm, and 7pm; the 40-minute trip costs $1.25. **Pulmitan** buses to Playa del Coco leave at 5:30am, 7am, 9:30am, 11am, 12:30pm, 2:30pm, 4:30pm, and 6:30pm.

For a smidgeon more luxury and convenience, **Gray Line** (☎ 220-2126; www. graylinecostarica.com) runs a 7am daily bus from San José to Panamá, Hermosa, and Coco, and will pick up from most hotels; the fare is $25. **Interbus** (☎ 283-5573; www.interbusonline.com) has buses leaving the San José area daily at 7:45am and 2:30pm; the cost is $29 for adults, $15 for children.

While it's possible to get from town to town along the coast by bus, schedules are erratic and the routing difficult to figure out. Your best bet, if you want to beach hop, is to rent a car (see below) or spring for a taxi.

By Car

From San José, take the Interamerican Highway west and follow the signs for Liberia and the Guanacaste beaches. When you reach Liberia, head west towards the town of Comunidad, where you'll hang a right toward the ocean. After about 11km (7 miles) you'll reach a fork. If you're headed for Playa Hermosa and Panamá, take a right; for Playa del Coco and Ocotal, go left. From San José, the whole thing should take you 4½ hours; from Liberia, only 25 to 30 minutes.

Getting Around

The road between Playas Panamá, Hermosa, and Coco is paved and easy to navigate. Only Hermosa and Coco are walkable from one end to the other (though sometimes in the daytime heat it can be a real challenge). There's decent taxi service between all three, which should run $5 to $10 depending on the distance. Always ask your hotel what you should expect to pay; once in a cab, tourists have been socked with wildly inflated fares. In fact, go ahead and use the taxis the hotel recommends, since management will usually know reliable drivers.

ACCOMODATIONS, BOTH STANDARD & NOT

Where you should base yourself will depend both on budget and tastes. Playa del Coco is most affordable, with a somewhat blah beach but a buzzy street scene and nightlife; Playa Hermosa's more laid-back, focused on fun in the water, and getting upscale; Panamá, except for a couple of small midrange hotels, is mostly about pricey all-inclusive resorts, so maybe less relevant to the independent and savings-minded.

Whichever you choose, lodgings will be split between the beachfront and the hills above town. The tradeoffs aren't rocket science—closeness to the beach and businesses instead of gorgeous views; balmier breezes and temps up high, over sometimes uncomfortable heat down by the sands. Also keep in mind that hotels and other digs in town are generally cheaper than those up in the hills—not to mention the fact that up here you'll be shelling out extra for taxis or a rental car.

Finally, definitely consider a short-term house or condo rental. Development has been skyrocketing (land in Playa Hermosa that a decade ago cost around $2 a square foot goes for $50 to $60 today), and though right now there are merely dozens of rental properties at all price ranges, the hundreds of condos and homes that have recently gone up or about to will turn these towns into a major vacation-rental destination. In Hermosa alone, more than 175 additional condos and 300 villas and town houses (many part of gated communities or resort villages) will be coming online in the near future.

Vacation Rentals

Hereabouts, gated communities rule, and there's no shortage of condos, town homes, and apartments tucked away in subdivisions much like ones all over the U.S. sunbelt. If you're in the market for a splurge, there are some knockout homes with five-plus bedrooms, infinity pools, and eye-popping ocean views (okay, for upwards of $5K a week they're far from cheap, but they'd go for three times on the coast most anywhere in the U.S., Europe, or the Caribbean).

For travelers on a budget, or who don't care about luxe living, we'd advise aiming for house or condo developments closer to town, or even in the Playa del Coco area, where prices are lower. Lodging tends to be more expensive in Guanacaste than in the rest of Costa Rica, so you should expect to drop at least $1,000 weekly for a two-bedroom, though studio apartments or one-bedrooms will run half that.

The property-management game has come of age here only in recent years, and though several real estate agencies now rep rental properties, scores of others are listed directly by owners on websites like **www.vrbo.com**, **www.vacationrentals. com**, and others outlined in the chapter on planning (p. 341). As with vacation rentals the world over, always check reservation and refund policies beforehand. Some agencies and owners let you hold a property with a credit card; others make you wire them up to half the balance in cash upfront. To boost your odds of nailing your dream rental, don't forget that Guanacaste is a hugely popular area, so it's a good idea to book 2 to 3 months in advance for high season and up to 6 months for the peak holiday weeks of Christmas and Easter.

Besides the agencies and properties below, you might also try **El Oasis,** a vacation condo complex right in Playa Hermosa managed by the hotel **Villa del Sueño** (p. 285), and the hotel **Villa Casa Blanca** (p. 288), which manages four vacation rentals in Playa Ocotal. With these two, you have fewer choices, but the convenience of having a staffed hotel nearby should you need advice from a concierge or a quick fix on a blocked kitchen sink.

In Playa Hermosa, the local **Century 21** (☎ 672-0273; www.discovercostarica. com) handles about 10 vacation rental homes, along with one in Playa Ocotal.

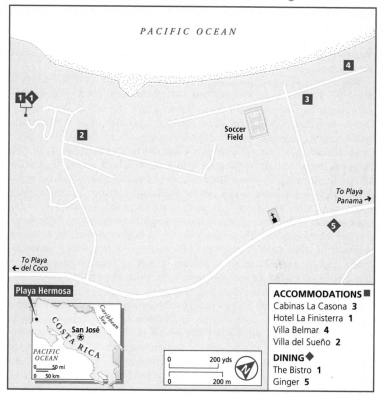

PACIFIC OCEAN

Soccer Field

To Playa Panama →

To Playa ← del Coco

Playa Hermosa

Caribbean Sea

San José

COSTA RICA

PACIFIC OCEAN

0 — 50 mi
0 — 50 km

0 — 200 yds
0 — 200 m

ACCOMMODATIONS ■
Cabinas La Casona **3**
Hotel La Finisterra **1**
Villa Belmar **4**
Villa del Sueño **2**
DINING ◆
The Bistro **1**
Ginger **5**

Italso reps a wide range of other houses, starting at $1,300 for a week in a two-bedroom/two-bath only 495m (1,650 ft.) from the beach. It's just one example, but fairly representative: Think suburban Southern California ranch house with a small lawn out front, tiled roofs, a large screened-in porch and barbecue area, and all the amenities you could need—air-conditioning and beautiful tiling throughout, and a living room with a coffee table and rattan furniture seating up to nine.

The French-run **Villa del Sol** (☎ 670-0085, 866/793-9523 from the U.S. and Canada; www.villadelsol.com) is another locally based property-management outfit, with 10 villas and 6 condos in Playa Hermosa, Playa del Coco, and Playa Ocotal; all are individual homes, not part of vacation resort complexes. A nice extra is the unofficial concierge service; the agent who comes to check you in provides a list of restaurant and activity suggestions, and will book them for you, too. At the low end among its offerings is the **Studio Braman,** a Playa del Coco efficiency that rents for $400 a week during high season. It's on the first floor of a stark white, boxy, modernist gated community on a hill overlooking the Pacific, and features a full-size bed and sofa/twin day bed in the living area, a kitchenette/dining area, A/C, TV/VCR, CD player, laundry, and access to the complex's roomy pool. If you need more space, one of its more affordable villas is the **Villa Luz de la Luna,** a three-bedroom luxury home in a development in the

Playa Hermosa hills going for $1,900 weekly in season. "Moonlight Villa" does have shiny perks, including an infinity pool with views of the ocean and headlands, a 6m (20-ft.) living-room ceiling, central A/C, and gardens. Bedrooms, on the other hand, are on the underwhelming side—tiled floors, generic blinds, and not much else—but at least they're roomy, sleeping up to seven.

Most of the 34 properties managed by **Coastal Costa Rica** (☎ 672-4114, 800/861-1482 from the U.S.; www.coastalcostarica.com) rent for $1,500 to $2,500, with almost half located in the Playa Hermosa area (the rest in Playa del Coco, Ocotal, and Panamá). One big advantage to renting with CCR is that it accepts credit cards for payment and to hold reservations. Of the few of this company's more affordable options is **Oceanview Villas del Sol,** a two-bedroom in a Playa Hermosa condo complex renting for $700 a week in high season. It comes with a living room with lofty wood-beam ceilings and sliding glass doors to a spacious terrace with ocean views; a tiny private pool; and access to the main complex pool—along with, conveniently enough, an on-site restaurant and bar. Not bad, not bad at all at this price. If you're traveling in a larger group, or just splurging, the luxe three-bedroom/three-and-a-half-bath **Casa Provence** can be a reasonable option at $2,000 a week in season ($1,500 in low). The two-story Mediterranean sports double-height living room ceilings, a curving staircase inlaid with nice ceramic tile, and a terrace and pool with bodacious views of the Bahía del Coco. Amenities are up-to-date, including flat-screen cable TV, CD stereo system, microwave, and dishwasher. And there's even concierge service. These are just two examples out of many, so surf over the CCR's well-designed website for more.

In Playa del Coco, the **Villas Mapache** (☎ 670-0239; www.mapacherental.com; cash only) is one of the large condo complexes created by the large Costa Rican developer Grupo Mapache. They're a fairly cookie-cutter couple of stories of boxy apartments with sliding doors that open to balconies overlooking a communal pool. There's not much uniqueness or personality to these one-bedrooms, but they're reasonable (at $61/night for two), only 90m or so (300 ft.) from the beach, and have an office on-site that rents out boats, jet skis, and ATVs.

Hotels

IN & AROUND PLAYA HERMOSA & PLAYA PANAMA

$ You won't find much in the way of cheap digs in Playa Hermosa, so if you're looking to save money but still be close to the beach, you'll want to head for the **Cabinas La Casona** (100m/330 ft. from the beach, facing El Velero Hotel; ☎ 672-0025; cash only). A modest, typically Tico two-story boxy wooden house with a lawn out front, La Casona's got five rooms and two efficiency-style apartments with kitchenettes a few minutes' walk from the water. Don't expect charm or character, but the units are clean and come with ceiling fans, cable TV, and private baths with cold water. A nice little garden with palm trees and stone tables is the focal point and lounging area for guests. Doubles start at $31.

$$ If views matter more than the easiest scoot to the beach, you can't do much better than the also Canadian-owned **Hotel La Finisterra** ★★ (on a hill at the end of the road at the first Playa Hermosa exit; ☎ 672-0293, 877/413-1139 from Canada; www.lafinisterra.com; MC, V). Up on a promontory over the bay (hence the name "land's end"), the Finisterra flaunts drop-dead panoramas from your

room—the kind you never get bored of—a small infinity pool, and an open-air eatery. *Muy romántico,* indeed. Gazing out at the villa-sprinkled hillside and boats (sometimes even a megayacht) anchored in cerulean waters, you'll feel like you're in some jet-set hideaway on the Mediterranean. That theme is played up by the hotel, two stories in ochre and burnt orange accented with indigenous stonework. It's just 10 rooms—nothing hugely fancy but immaculate and equipped with firm beds (even by U.S. standards), fluffy pillows, big picture windows (some with those boffo views), and up-to-date bathrooms with kicky water pressure. The dining room is a local favorite for its international menu and social scene; you'll get to schmooze not only with Finisterra owners George and Sheila but also plenty of local expats and Ticos. Doubles start at $90 in high season, $70 in low. They also have free Wi-Fi.

$$ Of all the hotels right on the beach, we prefer the new, Chilean-owned **Villa Belmar** ★ (on the beach, 50m/165 ft. north of El Velero Hotel; ☎ 672-0276; www.hotelvillabelmar.com; AE, MC, V). For the same or a couple of bucks more than its neighbors, you get a chic, boutique-hotel atmosphere at an all-white manse right on the water—tailor-made for a couple hankering for a cozy inn. The six rooms have stark-white walls, gauzy white curtains, yellow- and clay-color tile floors, and nice touches such as paintings and tropical plants (less visible but even more appreciated during torrid summers, blessed A/C). The pool and deck have to be the loveliest of any of the beach hotels, with bang-on ocean views and foliage romantically lit at night. There's secure parking on premises (handy since break-ins along the Pacific beaches have been an issue). Doubles go for $95 in high season, $80 in low (for ocean views, tack on another $15).

$$ Snuggled amid tropical gardens, the **Villa del Sueño** ★ 🄺 (89m/295 ft. from the beach, at the first exit for Playa Hermosa; ☎ 672-0026, 800/378-8599 from U.S., 888/225-3979 from Canada; www.villadelsueno.com; AE, MC, V) is a charming Spanish-colonial-style compound run by Canadians and centered around a sizable pool, *palapa* bar, and boutique. Its 45 units are spacious and stylish, with pastel walls, high wood-beam ceilings, mod artwork, wicker/bamboo desks and rocking chairs, and big picture windows in some. A big bonus: One of the area's best restaurants dishes up seafood and international faves alfresco by the pool. That, along with live entertainment and other extras, make it feel closer to a miniresort than plain old hotel, and all this plus larger rooms make a better fit for families than say, the Villa Belmar or La Finisterra (see below). If you need to spread out even more, rent a condo in the complex next door, managed by the same folks. Doubles start at $75 in high season, $65 in low.

IN & AROUND PLAYA DEL COCO & OCOTAL

Even though it doesn't have the exclusive, secluded feel of Playa Hermosa and Panamá, Playa del Coco can be surprisingly uncheap. If you're trying to stretch a really tight budget, you'll have to settle for the dozen or so cold-water *cabinas* in town; plain and offering basic amenities such as only fridges and fans, occasionally A/C. Most of these are located right by the soccer field or on the main strip. The north end of the beach tends to be quieter and more upscale; ditto the outskirts of town.

The main reason to stay in Playa del Coco is its dozens of restaurants and bars, along with hopping beach and street scenes thronged by both Ticos and gringos—dive shops, beach bars, that kind of thing. Some people find the town kind of tacky, but at least it's not totally Americanized—in fact, it's one of the few spots along the coast where you'll get to see how your average Tico family vacations.

If staying full time in the thick of it all is a bit too much, base yourself in either Hermosa or Ocotal and drive or cab in for a meal, drink, swim, or whatever. With road access only through Playa del Coco, Playa Ocotal is a cute little hideaway with a bit of a sportfishing scene that makes a fab oasis away from the hullaballoo. On a little cove a mile or so south of Coco, there's not much down here besides a gated development, a couple of hotels, and a low-key gray-sand beach.

$–$$ Our favorite among the less pretentious hotels in the area is **Laura's House** (about 250m/820 ft. east of the Lizard Lounge; ☎ 506/670-0571; www.laurashousecr.net; cash only). As friendly as the owner (yes, her name is Laura), it's a pristine eight-room inn, with rooms decorated entirely in white (white tiles, white comforters, white curtains). Several rooms have bunk beds along with a queen-size bed and a single, making them ideal for larger families or groups. Kids in the family will also enjoy the small on-site pool, and excellent monkey-spotting opportunities from the hammocks out back. Double rooms start at just $40 a night in high season ($10 more to use the A/C), with those larger rooms we mentioned a reasonable $60 per night; shave $5 off these rates when business is slow. The price includes a fruit-laden breakfast.

$$ It'll come as no surprise that the **Hotel Casino Coco Verde** (on the main strip 200m/660 ft. from the beach; ☎ 670-0112; V) began life as a Best Western. From the outside, the two green-and-white stories of the "Green Coconut" look like pretty much any middling chain motel: a bunch of windows and doors side by side, linked by an outdoor corridor. Yet underneath is a pretty good budget resort, with a surf-and-turf restaurant, a pool set amid palm trees, and a perky casino with slots and a roulette table. Another plus: It's right on the strip, so everything's at your doorstep. On the downside: It's right on the strip, so everything's at your doorstep—including any raucous partying. For a more secluded spot to drop your bags for about the same rate—and more charm, a better pool, and breakfast, to boot—I'd check the Puerta del Sol first. Doubles are $80 a night.

$$ Of the Playa del Coco hotels within strolling distance to the beach, the family-owned **Puerta del Sol** ✱ (250m/820 ft. from the beach; ☎ 670-0195; MC, V) is one of the most appealing. A bright, sunny yellow with a tropical vibe, it's got eight rooms and a pair of suites overlooking a landscaped garden and a pretty good-size lap pool that, in my opinion, can be even better for cooling off than the town strand. Ceilings in the units are nice and high, and banquette-style wrap-around sofas are attached to the walls. The bedrooms feature king-size beds perched on adobe platforms and made up with colorful linens, along with sparkling white bathrooms; other amenities include safes and cable TV. A stand-out in the common area is a small gym—unusual for Costa Rican hotels—but the jewel in the crown is Sol y Luna (p. 288), one of the best Italian eateries in a town with no shortage of them; *mangia bene* on great homemade pasta washed down

PACIFIC OCEAN

Bus Stop
(Provides service to
Liberia and San José)

Soccer Field

6

To Playa Hermosa ↗

5

7 7 8 ↗

3

† 4

← To Playa Ocotal

2

← 1

ACCOMMODATIONS ■
Hotel Casino
Coco Verde **2**
Laura's House **3**
Puerta del Sol **8**
Puerto del Sol **7**
Rancho Armadillo
Estate **6**
Villa Casa Blanca **1**

DINING ◆
Louisiana Bar & Grill **4**
Sol y Luna **7**
Tequila Bar & Grill **5**

Police 🅿
Post Office ✉

To Liberia ↓

Playa del Coco

San José
COSTA RICA
PACIFIC OCEAN
Caribbean Sea

0   50 mi
0   50 km

with a nice Chianti in a cozy garden setting. Rates start at $80 for a double, including breakfast.

$$$ It's not exactly just a hop and a skip to the shore, and a bit pricier than many in-town options, but the **Rancho Armadillo Estate** ✿✿ 🎒 (1.6km/1 mile from the beach; ☎ 670-0108; www.ranchoarmadillo.com; MC, V), on 10 flora-and-fauna-crammed hectares (25 acres) of dry forest, more than makes up for it. To its splendid sense of privacy, stir in constant wildlife sightings (iguanas, fruit bats, coatimundis), then add a generous dollop of salt-of-the-earth hospitality from owners Rick Vogel and Debbie Miesl from Detroit, Michigan. They make the experience homey to a T: They collect you at the airport, dole out tireless advice on local sights, eats, and stuff to do; and just hang out. The curvaceous pool is a keeper, and the half-dozen guest quarters are spread over three bunga-lows, the largest is a two-bedroom suite. And the grub—well, Rick's a retired chef, you see, so not only are the included breakfasts a major treat, but you've really got to ask him to cook dinner for you at least once. He's not only Mr. Friendly but also a whiz with a whisk who can do it all. Doubles in season start at $120 per diem (low season $86).

$$$ Down in Playa Ocotal—a good bit of which is taken up by a gated community of fancy villas and condos—the **Villa Casa Blanca** ✭ (Playa Ocotal; ☎ 670-0448, 877/623-3198 from the U.S. and Canada; www.hotelvillacasablanca.com; AE, MC, V) is the only game in town on two counts: It's intimate and budget-friendly. Owned by Texans and set on a hill overlooking sands a 10- to 15-minute walk away, this here's a plumb purty Spanish-style villa with elegant dark woods and Iberian floor tiles. Landscaped gardens brim with bougainvillea and yuccas, and there's a nice little pool with swim-up bar and whirlpool. The 14 rooms feature four-poster canopy beds with plush linens; the pair of honeymoon suites throw in Jacuzzis. In short, it's a pretty romantic choice for a honeymoon or a getaway. High-season rates run $90 double; $115 for honeymoon suites; and $135 for a one-bedroom condo with a double canopy bed, living room with double sofa bed, a fully equipped kitchen, and a private terrace (in low season, all the above run $20–$25 less). Also part of the deal is a hearty buffet breakfast starring homemade waffles, pancakes, breads, and jams. The owners also manage four Playa Ocotal condos; check their website for more info.

DINING FOR ALL TASTES

Though you'll find several waterfront and other options in Playa Hermosa, the largest cluster is in Playa del Coco, with dozens of restaurants and bars. A couple to keep in mind beyond the listings below: **Oku Sushi** (☎ 670-0513) is a swell spot for a sashimi-and-sake fix, and **Chile Dulce** (☎ 670-00465) hawks a nice variety of tropical-style sandwiches, salads, and drinks—and even a painting or two. The spots below are open for lunch and dinner, until 10 or 11pm.

$$ Not much to look at—just a big ol' bar and a jumble of indoor and street-side tables on the Playa del Coco strip—the **Tequila Bar & Grill** ✭ (150m/490 ft. from the beach; ☎ 670-0741; closed Wed; no credit cards) serves solid Mexican fare to a cool jazz soundtrack and a head-spinning choice of 20 margarita variations. I like the tacos and fajitas (beef, chicken, or fish), as well as the grilled pork and chicken zipped up with chipotle and tomatillo $9. It's the *chilaquiles* (meat casserole) for $9.50, though, that turn first-timers into repeat customers. Entrees run $9 to $12.

$$–$$$ Playa del Coco is big on seafood, and one of the best eateries to reel in the catch of the day (red snapper, marlin, mahimahi), cooked and seasoned just as you like it, is the main strip's **Louisiana Bar & Grill** ✭ (200m/660 ft. from the beach; ☎ 670-0400; MC, V). As the moniker suggests, the menu's crammed with Cajun, from basic gumbo to three types of jambalaya—not to mention creole shrimp and fish in any of a dozen kinds of hot salsas (the broiled grouper in Veracruz sauce will really let your *bons temps rouler*). Expect to lay out about $8 to $15 for entrees. The best seats in the house are on the open-air deck where you'll get an eyeful of both the street circus and howler monkeys cavorting in a nearby tree.

$$–$$$ There are a lot of "Italian" restaurants in Playa del Coco (and Costa Rica in general) with pastas and pizzas from dubious to downright blah, but the Hotel Puerta del Sol's garden-set **Sol y Luna** ✭ (222m/740 ft. from the beach;

☎ 670-0195; AE, MC, V) is the real deal. Though the restaurant is tucked away on a street parallel to the main strip, diners end up here via on the say-so of locals and hotel owners. An extensive Italian wine list will help you savor the homemade pastas, as fresh as the local catch; entrees run $5 all the way up to $19 (but most will cost in the teens or less).

$$$ In Playa Hermosa, another atmospheric hotel restaurant wins stellar marks for romance and creative contemporary cuisine, **The Bistro** ★★ (end of the road at the first Playa Hermosa exit; ☎ 672-0293; www.finisterra.net; MC, V). Up on the hill at La Finisterra, this breezy, softly lit, open-air space is where Chef Eduardo, a Cordon Bleu–trained Peruvian, presents an eclectic fusion of Thai, Peruvian, and Italian. Eduardo's yucca salad is a signature, his way with fish formidable (try the sea bass, $13), and on my last visit his Thai-style curry (also $13) of tender beef slices sent me to heaven. Finisterra owners George and Sheila often dine at a corner table, so feel free to chat them up or even bum some advice on what to order that day.

$$$ For sheer creativity, **Ginger** ★★★ (main road; ☎ 672-0041; closed Mon.; AE, M, V) in Playa Hermosa is probably tops. On a hillside amid a forest of feathery dark-green trees, overlooking a jagged coastline of volcanic sands, this petite spot crosses laid-back beach shack with the polished, upscale look so trendy hereabouts lately. Expansive chrome windows impart a mod feel, and ditto the Mediterranean- and Asian-influenced menu, which makes liberal use of the ravishing root for which the joint is named (ginger-glazed chicken wings, seared pepper-crusted tuna with a pickled ginger slaw, and so forth); another winner is the fresh-caught mahimahi marinated in vodka and spices. It's all served in small plates ($3–$8) perfect for grazing and/or sharing.

WHY YOU'RE HERE: THE TOP SIGHTS & ATTRACTIONS

Between the copious water-based fun along this stretch of coast and northern Guanacaste's national parks nearby, you could keep yourself going for weeks. On dry land, hike between sulfurous mud pools in **Rincón de la Vieja National Park** ★★ or through tropical dry forest in **Santa Rosa National Park** ★. On the water, take diving excursions to **Catalina** and **Bat Islands,** fishing charters out in Papagayo Gulf (best May–Sept), or surf **Witch's Rock** ★ or **Ollie's Point** ★. Or just splash, snorkel, or paddle close to the sands—not a thing wrong with that!

Watersports

This stretch of coast is known for its scuba diving excursions, and virtually every community has a few pro dive shops that run trips out to the **Catalina** or **Bat islands (Islas Murciélagos)** ★, part of the Santa Rosa National Park, 15 to 45 minutes out by boat. Hit your hotelier or concierge up for their recommendations, but I can tell you the most respected and long-established trio are Playa Hermosa's **Diving Safaris de Costa Rica** (☎ 672-0267, 877/853-0538 in the U.S. and Canada; www.costaricadiving.net), **Ocotal Diving** (☎ 670-0914), and **Rich Coast Diving** (☎ 670-0176, 800/434-8464 in the U.S. and Canada; www.rich coastdiving.com). You can't go wrong booking any of the three. A half-day trip with two-tank dive starts at around $65.

A Sand Blast

by Jenna Wortham

If you're around the last weekend in March, it's worth checking out the **Papagayo Sand Fest** (☎ 670-1522 or 670-1530). Not a big-league sand sculptor? No biggie—there are plenty of classes and amateur contests. The event kicks off with a green bang: a massive beachcombing of trash rather than seashells or bits of driftwood.

The festival in Playa del Coco includes concerts, magic shows, games, and contests. But the main event and real delight is watching master sand artists from all over the world craft intricate constructions ranging from caricatures of famous people to landscapes, incorporating details down to strands of hair or blades of grass. The awards are handed out midday Sunday—the best time to stroll down the beach and marvel at the finished artwork. Make sure you call and double-check dates before making plans.

Divers come out not to explore colorful coral like you'd see in the Caribbean, but this coast's big fish: eagle and manta rays, giant groupers, bull and other sharks. You'll probably spot them, but it may take two or three dives, partly because visibility can sometimes be a problem; the plankton and such that make these waters so fish-rich can make it harder to see them (best seasons for clearer waters are May–Nov). More common sights are puffers, various types of eels, and jellyfish. The Catalina and Bat islands are considered advanced sites (although newly PADI-certified divers are often accepted), with dive depths of 18 to 21m (60–70 ft.). If you're new to it all, you can take PADI certification courses and go on dives closer to shore, including **Monkey's Head,** a volcanic outcropping resembling a simian noggin. You probably won't spot sharks, but you will get to see a bevy of sea life, including sea horses, angel fish, bass, groupers, and rays.

If you're on the hunt for waves to surf, you've gotta get away from the developed beaches. The dive shops above will run you up by boat to prime spots like **Roca Bruja (Witch's Rock)** and **Potrero Grande** (aka **Ollie's Point,** after Oliver North, the Iran-contra spook who did his end-run around the Constitution with covert ops hereabouts in the 1980s). These are near **Playa Naranjo** and **Playa Blanca,** hard-to-reach beaches in Santa Rosa National Park, and their action (captured in the flick *Endless Summer II*), like much of the local diving, isn't really for beginners. The cost of a day trip can hit $250 to $300 for a group of six. You can get there by land, but it's rough—four-wheel drive required—and impassible except in dry season.

Exploring Nature

SANTA ROSA NATIONAL PARK

Though it's made a name for itself thanks to pristine beaches and surf breaks, 1,100-sq.-km (425-sq.-mile) **Santa Rosa National Park** ✸ (☎ 666-5051; www.costarica-nationalparks.com/santarosanationalpark.html; daily 8am–4pm; $6), covering the entire Santa Elena peninsula, is a flora and fauna powerhouse, too, with 10 distinct ecosystems—almost every type there is in Costa Rica, from the once ubiquitous tropical dry forest to mangrove swamps. To get here, take the Interamerican Highway north; it enters the park 10km (6 miles) beyond the town of Potrerillos.

Santa Rosa was Costa Rica's first national park, established in 1970 partly to protect **La Casona.** This thatched-roof ranch house overlooking a stone corral was the site of the historic 1856 battle of Santa Rosa, in which a volunteer Costa Rican army marched all the way from the Central Valley and beat down the marauding mercenaries under William Walker, an American trying to annex Costa Rica to Guatemala. Ticos revere the house so much that when it was burned down by an arsonist in 2001, they rebuilt it in a matter of months thanks to a national fundraising campaign. Today it houses a small **museum** (www.acguanacaste.ac. cr/1997/ecodesarrollo/ecoturismo/museosantarosaing.html; daily) worth a visit for a look at Guanacaste archeology, 19th-century life, and exhibits about the park itself.

But most folks come here for the white-sand beaches and to commune with nature. You can drive yourself, easy enough in the dry season if you have a sturdy four-wheel drive with a high clearance. The drive on the Interamerican Highway up from Liberia is a snap, and inside the park a paved road will take you right up to La Casona and the administration area (where you can also grab a bite to eat). Beyond that, though, the 13km (8-mile) dirt road to handsome gray-sand **Playa Naranjo** ⚝ (famed among surfers for its perfect tube) and **Playa Nancite** ⚝ (accessed via a .8km/.5-mile hiking trail from Estero Real near Naranjo) is super-steep and pothole-pitted; in the rainy season, it's impassable when the Río Nisperal swells. Wimpier four-wheel drives routinely get stuck in the roads out here, so consider yourself warned.

Both Naranjo and Nancite are major nesting grounds for the Olive Ridley leatherback and Pacific green sea turtles.Between September and November, in particular, thousands of these stately sea critters haul themselves out of the sea on moonless nights to dig nests on the beach. Unlike at Playa Naranjo, access to Nancite is restricted; only 25 people are allowed on the sands, and first have to get permits from the park office. If you're set on witnessing an *arribada,* I'd suggest heading for **Playa Ostional** (p. 318), where the viewing is easier and more set up for tourists. You can, by the way, catch *arribadas* of other marine turtles on the Caribbean coast (p. 241). There's a campsite with showers and toilets at Naranjo (as well as back near the park office).

Hanging Ten with Oliver North

Here's another neat little bit of local history that might be more of interest to Americans who lived through Ronald Reagan's Iran-contra scandal. It was on the north part of the Santa Elena Peninsula, just south of the Nicaragua border, where the CIA ran a training camp for the anti-Sandinista contras and Oliver North had a covert airstrip built to illegally smuggle arms to them. Over by **Playa Blanca,** a perfect-right surf break is named after him: "Ollie's Point."

If you're looking only to spot some wildlife, on the other hand, you don't need to haul yourself all the way out to Playa Naranjo; there are trails closer to the park office that will do the trick nicely. Just before the Santa Rosa National Monument is the **Indio Desnudo** (Naked Indian) trail, chockfull of some of the park's best animal-watching, especially in early morning or late afternoon. You can spot three of Costa Rica's four monkey species, along with white tailed deer, coatamundi, lizards, falcons, and a variety of birds. Along the way, check out the gumbo-limbo trees, sometimes dubbed "Naked Indians" for their peeling red bark.

By the way, easier but pricier ways to do Santa Rosa involve organized tours. A day trip by boat from any beach near Playa Hermosa or even Tamarindo to Witch's Rock will get you to Playa Naranjo; from there you can explore nearby trails. Or take a land excursion with an area tour operator, which includes La Casona and a short trail hike; the cost is usually $60 to $75, depending on your pick-up location (see "Local Agents," p. 356). Keep in mind, though, that there's little or no time for independent exploration.

Rincón de la Vieja

At 140 sq. km (54 sq. miles) it's a lot smaller than Santa Rosa, but it makes up for what it lacks in size with its fire power: **Rincón de la Vieja National Park** ★★★ (☎ 661-5051; www.costarica-nationalparks.com/rincondelaviejanationalpark.html; daily 8am–4pm; $6) is home to five active volcanoes, part of the Cordillera de Guanacaste. The biggest is 1,885m (6,286-ft.) Rincón de la Vieja, whose last big eruptions (earthquakes, ash clouds, the whole shebang) took place between 1966 and 1970, though there was some lesser eruptions in 1983–84, 1995, and 1998. While Santa Rosa's probably a bit better for wildlife-spotting, this park's lunar-looking cragscapes, sulfur-fume-spewing fumaroles, and boiling mud pools put on a flashier show. And actually, it's no slouch in the animal department, either—Rincón's a watershed for 32 rivers as well as monkeys, sloths, anteaters, and at least 300 bird species, including the striking, melodic three-wattled bell-bird and oropendola. So if you have time for only one park up north, this should probably be it.

Of the two entrances, we recommend Las Pailas ("The Cauldrons"), since it's both more accessible from Liberia and the beaches than the eastern **Santa María** entrance and closer to most of the volcanic action. From the Las Pailas ranger station, you'll want to start off on the **Sendero Encantado** ("Enchanted Trail"), leading toward the volcano's summit through mossy rainforest teeming with wild *guaria morada*, a purple orchid that's the national flower.

But unless you're planning on staying overnight at one of the lodges near the park, we wouldn't get into tackling the 15km-plus (9-mile) hike to the summit and back. It takes pretty much a full day—at a brisk pace; in fact, many hikers camp on the trail overnight. It's also darn windy the higher up you get, and easy to get lost (it really shouldn't be attempted without a guide in tow). At the top, your reward's a knockout view of the crater's blue-green lagoon and spectacular panoramas of mountains, Pacific, and all the way north to Lake Nicaragua (on a clear day, of course).

But a lot of what's so cool (er, hot) about this park is easy enough to reach lower down. For example, one side trail leads to **Las Hornillas** ★★ ("the stoves"),

Of Mud Baths, Rapids & Ziplines

Though you can't dip into the volcanic mud inside the national park, feel free to wallow away at the rustic **Hacienda Guachipelín** ★ (kids) (☎ 442-2818; www.guachipelin.com; doubles from $67; AE, D, MC, V), a working cattle ranch–cum–ecotourism playland on the edge of the park about .8km (½ mile) east of the village of Curubandé. Besides mud pools and thermal springs, it's got a canopy tour (ziplines, rappelling, Tarzan swing); kid-friendly canyon adventures; wall climbing; tubing down rapids; and cattle round-ups. Activities cost $15 to $75 for adults, $10 less for kids under 10.

For more of a splurge, the **Hotel Borínquen Mountain Resort Thermae & Spa** (☎ 690-1900; www.borinquenresort.com; doubles from $182; AE, DC, MC, V) is a lovely, traditional-ranch-style ecolodge built around bubbling mud ponds; an enormous pool with island and swim-up bar; and a first-class, Zen-flavored spa offering myriad treatments (many mud-centered) overlooking river and forest. There's also a canopy tour on the premises and a variety of day packages (adults $25–$100, kids $15–$50) that combine, say, a trip to the waterfalls that ends up with a spell at the Borínquen's own springs, spa, and mud baths.

a 48-hectare (123-acre) zone at the volcano's foot pitted with pools of boiling water, geysers, fumaroles, and mud pots that look like minivolcanoes. On a sunny scorcher of a day, you might get a notion you've ended up on the road to hell (paved with good intentions, of course). Just don't ignore the many signs warning you away from certain spots; the brittle surface crust can collapse, and more than a few tourists over the years have ended up lightly (or not so lightly) poached upon sliding into boiling water or mud.

Another must-do is **La Cangreja falls and its blue lagoon** ★★, some 5km (3 miles) from the Las Pailas entrance. Ask for a map at the ranger station and follow signs for **Catarata La Cangreja** ("Crab Waterfall") and **Cataratas Escondidas** ("Hidden Waterfall"). The minerals in the stones on the lagoon bed turn the water a striking blue-green, and the falls plummet dramatically from more than 40m (130 ft.); you can check out other smaller falls nearby. Bring your swim duds!

To get up to Rincón, you can rent a car (not necessarily a four-wheel drive), hire a *colectivo* taxi ($25 from Liberia for up to four people), or sign onto a day excursion (typically $75–$80). Driving yourself, you'll take the Interamerican Highway north from Liberia toward Nicaragua. After some 6km (3¾ miles), take a right at the sign for the village of Curubandé and continue on the reasonably well-kept gravel road for another dozen kilometers. From the village it's 6km (3¾ miles) to Hacienda Guachipelín, where you'll have to fork over $2 to go the final 4km (2½ miles) on its access road to the Las Pailas entrance. *A note on guides:* You can hire one from any of the area lodges, but many aren't trained naturalists—essentially what you're getting is someone familiar with the trails and park. Since trails are fairly well marked, especially in the Las Pailas sector, save your money unless the guide's a bona fide nature expert who can really add something to your experience.

Canopy Tours

Witch's Rock Canopy Tour (☎ 666-7546; witchsrockcanopytour@hotmail.com; daily 8am–4pm), near the Allegro Papagayo Resort between Tamarindo and Nosara, used to be the largest, and it's still a thrill ride. Its 2½-hour circuit involves 11 ziplines and 23 platforms over tropical dry forest; some runs are longer than 4 city blocks. Other features include a short forest hike and a stroll across three swinging bridges. Prices are $65 for adults, $55 for children under 11. A little closer, in the mountains between Playa del Coco and Playa Potrero, the **Congo Trail Canopy Tour** (☎ 666-4422; congotrail@racsa.co.cr; daily 8am–5pm) also has 11 lines (one stretch topping 394m/1,312 feet) but just 15 platforms. It's a bit more beginner level, in terms of the height of the platforms (and the depth of the thrills) but happily much cheaper, charging $45 including hotel transfers, $35 without.

To read about the region's other canopy tours, go to the section on Nosara and Samara (p. 307).

Exploring the Interior

Since the roads into and out of Playa Hermosa and Playa del Coco are paved and in excellent condition, touring the inland areas of the Nicoya Peninsula is pretty easy, and it's here, away from all the beach-blanket Bablyon that you can still experience Guanacaste's traditional heritage and flavor. For example, you can drive to the towns of **Santa Cruz** and **Guaitíl,** home to much of the region's folkloric music and pottery making, in a scenic 2 hours through valleys and rolling hills (since they're a bit farther south and closer to Tamarindo, see that section below for details, p. 295).

ATTENTION, SHOPPERS!

Apart from a few souvenir shops in Playa del Coco, there aren't that many places to shop locally, with a few exceptions such as **Toad Hall Gallery** (☎ 670-0533), which opened in 2005 on the main drag just south of the turnoff to Playa Ocotal; it sells excellent local art, books, leather goods, ceramics, and more. You might also keep an eye peeled for some of the traditional Chorotega-style pottery sold on roads and the highway on your way in or out of Playa Hermosa and Playa del Coco.

NIGHTLIFE

Playa del Coco is party central for this stretch of coast. Down by the beach, discos thump with reggaetón; gaggles of Ticos (mostly men) shuffle up and down a strip of boardwalk; and as the evening bops on, working girls make the scene in some of the bars and streets. Think Front Street in Maui, Venice Beach, that kind of thing, with plenty of street vendors, bar hoppers, and miscellaneous colorful characters.

Kick things off at the **Lizard Lounge** (150m/490 ft. south of the beachfront park; no phone; daily 5pm–2am), which features a pool table, kicky cocktails, and a mix of gringos and Ticos. Its 5 to 7pm happy hour packs 'em in for the $2 shots, and for ladies' nights (complete with go-go boyz). For all-out dance parties, **La Vida Loca** (right on the beach; ☎ 670-0180; www.costaricabeachbar.com; daily 3pm–2am) has jamming beats (along with pool tables, Ping-Pong, foosball, and darts), and is the place to go on weekdays. However, on Saturday nights, *la vida* turns even more *loca* at the **Cocomar Discoteca** (on the beach; no phone; daily 5pm–2am). Loud reggaetón spills out off the roomy concrete dance floor and videos careen across a big-screen TV overhead. Ladies, keep in mind that the clientele tends to be more guys—and Tico guys, for that matter—so it's best to venture here with a group. For something a bit more relaxed, try the recently opened, more tourist-oriented **Zouk Santana** (☎ 670-0191; www.zouksantana. com; no cover; daily 6pm–2am) over on the opposite corner. It has a nice, little seating area with couches, and serves up pub grub if you get peckish.

TAMARINDO

One of Guanacaste's first beach spots to open up to outside development, Tamarindo is in some ways a victim of its own success. Blessed with long, expansive white sands and some of the Pacific coast's best surfing, the once sedate fishing village these days feels fully Americanized and condo-ized, a la Cancún or Los Cabos.

When we first visited Tamarindo a decade ago, early signs of overdevelopment were already popping up, but the scale was still manageable, traces of its original mellowness still lingered, and locals still spoke Spanish as a first language. Nowadays, along the main strip you see hordes of spring-breakers, fast-food chains (Burger King, TCBY, Pizza Hut), and Colombian hookers (with hearts of Colombian gold, no doubt) trawling at the bars in the traffic circle where the main strip dead-ends. And these days, the folks working at all these places are more likely to be Nicaraguan than Costa Rican.

There's also no denying that all this has also meant lots more and better places to stay and eat, as well as fun stuff to do (horseback riding, ATV tours, sunset booze cruises, scuba diving, surf schools, canopy tours, and *mucho más*). Along with that, the level of service has risen, and you'll be addressed automatically in English (the next-biggest local expat group is Italians). At the same time, prices are pushing upwards toward North American levels. Budget travelers in particular will find both better deals and more of a local feel farther down the coast. Having said all that, there's no denying that Tamarindo can be fun.

GETTING TO & AROUND TAMARINDO
By Air

You can fly directly into Tamarindo; during the high season, **Nature Air** (☎ 299-6000, 800/235-9272 in the U.S. and Canada; www.natureair.com) has daily flights leaving San José's Tobías Bolaños International Airport in Pavas at 6:30am, 8:40am, 10am, and 2pm; the trip takes 1 hour and 10 minutes and costs $88 each way. **Sansa** (☎ 221-9414; www.flysansa.com) runs 14 flights daily out of San José's Juan Santamaría International Airport from 5am to 4:20pm; it's 50 minutes and costs $78 each way.

By Bus

Express buses (**Tracopa-Alfaro; ☎** 222-2666) leave for Tamarindo at 11:30am and 3:30pm from San José (Calle 14 between Av. 3 and 5) at 3:30pm. The trip takes 6 hours and costs $5.

With a similar travel time but tossing in a little more luxury and convenience, **Gray Line** (☎ 220-2126; www.graylinecostarica.com) leaves San José for Tamarindo daily at 7am and picks up from most hotels; the fare is $29. **Interbus** (☎ 283-5573; www.interbusonline.com) also has buses leaving the San José area daily at 7:45am and 2:30pm; the fare is $29 for adults, $15 for children. Coming from Liberia, there's a daily bus at noon to Tamarindo; the trip takes 1 hour and 15 minutes and costs $29 for adults, $15 for children.

By Car

From San José, take the Interamerican Highway west, follow signs for Liberia, and take the turnoff for the Tempisque River bridge. After crossing the river, follow signs for Nicoya and Santa Cruz, and continue north through Santa Cruz. Just before the town of Belén you'll reach the Tamarindo turnoff; 20km (12 miles) after Belén, take the left fork at the town of Huacas, which will take you to Villareal and then Tamarindo. The drive should take 4½ to 5 hours. From Liberia it's about an hour and 15 minutes; head west, following signs for Santa Cruz. After passing Belén, you'll see the turnoff for Playas Flamingo, Brasilito, and Tamarindo.

Getting Around

If you're staying downtown, you can stroll most anywhere. Taxis are easy to snag along the main strip, and shouldn't cost more than $5 throughout town.

ACCOMMODATIONS, BOTH STANDARD & NOT

Touristy as it is, Tamarindo frankly doesn't offer much in the way of nonstandard digs unless you count condos and villas. This is also one of Costa Rica's more expensive towns to stay overnight, and compared with, say, Manuel Antonio, the blue-chip resort area farther south, fewer hotels come with any views to speak of. Rooms can easily break $100 a night, and more than a handful top $200. Vacation rentals, too, tend to be pricier than elsewhere in Costa Rica, but one upside of Tamarindo's overdevelopment is that you've got hundreds of condos and villas to choose from—eventually you're bound to find one for the right price.

Vacation Rentals

Most of what's available tends toward the luxe variety, particularly mansionlike villas tucked into hillsides offering gorgeous views, lush vegetation, and seclusion. For the moderate to budget traveler, the best bet is one of the condos around town, which would yield, say, a two-bedroom for $700 to $900 weekly.

This area is one of the highest traveled in the country, so if you're coming in the dry season, most of the agencies listed below recommend reserving at least 6 months in advance (as much as a year for Christmas/New Year's). Expect to put down a 50% deposit, with the balance due before you arrive. You might get a price break by offering to wire cash, thereby saving them the steep credit card fees; many local agencies have U.S. bank accounts for secure and easy transfer.

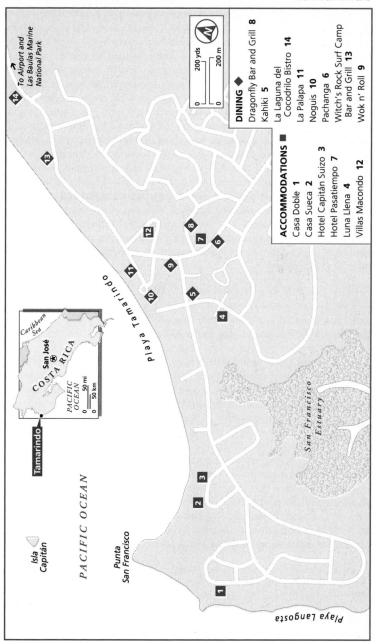

Tamarindo

DINING ◆
Dragonfly Bar and Grill **8**
Kahiki **5**
La Laguna del
  Cocodrilo Bistro **14**
La Palapa **11**
Noguis **10**
Pachanga **6**
Witch's Rock Surf Camp
  Bar and Grill **13**
Wok n' Roll **9**

ACCOMMODATIONS ■
Casa Doble **1**
Casa Sueca **2**
Hotel Capitán Suizo **3**
Hotel Pasatiempo **7**
Luna Llena **4**
Villas Macondo **12**

To Airport and
Las Baulas Marine
National Park

Caribbean
Sea

San José

COSTA RICA

PACIFIC
OCEAN

0   50 mi
0   50 km

Tamarindo

Isla
Capitán

PACIFIC OCEAN

Punta
San Francisco

Playa Tamarindo

San Francisco
Estuary

Playa Langosta

200 yds
200 m

297

By far the most extensive local agency roster belongs to **RPM Tamarindo** (☎ 653-0738 or 832-2820; www.tulin.com/costarica), which handles 120 properties. Even better, you'll never wind up more than 2 blocks from the beach, regardless of price or size. Rentals typically come with pool access—shared for condos, usually private with houses. While many of its rentals top $2,000 weekly, Eduardo Villa, who handles rentals properties, is an accommodating fellow, and quite good about finding something in your range. And here is the range, roughly: His best deal is **Villas Playa Pueblo del Mar,** where $695 gets you a week in a tiki-flavored two-bedroom condo with good-size windows and full amenities. The coral-stucco complex is appealing, with stone-lined walkways, tropical landscaping, and a nice central-courtyard pool with palm-thatched *palapa*. For more elbow room, **La Jolla del Mar,** RPM's new three-bedroom/three-bathroom house in ritzy Playa Langosta, sleeps nine for $1,750 a week. Behind a plain two-story facade it's Mediterranean-handsome, with patterned-tile floors and wrought-iron staircases down to the manicured backyard with pool. Interior spaces are roomy, ceilings high, and a second-floor outdoor patio with hardwood chairs and tables begs to host dinner parties or drinks before a night out. A cottage behind the pool doubles as a changing room or studio apartment, complete with twin beds, bathroom, and kitchenette.

Century 21's **Costa Rica Vacation Rentals** (☎ 653-0200, 866/627-5610 from the U.S. and Canada; www.gammatamarindo.com) is a close second to RPM in listings, with more than 30 lovely and "fully loaded" (landscaped yards, infinity pools, daily laundry/maid services, and so forth) beachfront homes and villas. Ask for Javier—he's lived in the area for years and can tailor your rental to suit your needs and desires (not just price but variables such as noise levels and access to stuff to do). One of its more affordable (and romantic) picks is the **Casa Tapada** (from $120 per day), a condo studio for two with a king bed and private bath, complete with its own entrance. Textured woodprints hang over cream-colored couches, and a clever backlighting system adds a warm glow to everything. And the *pièce de résistance:* floor-to-ceiling glass doors open onto its very own infinity-edge pool with two small waterfalls, surrounded by with tropical flora. Less secluded but more practical for a slightly larger group are the **Bahía Langosta** condos, starting at $875 a week for a one-bedroom with balcony overlooking both the pool and the Pacific. Thatched huts provide some shaded lounging outdoors, and oodles of chairs around the pool provide an alternative to navigating the hordes on the Tamarindo strand. These condos are not as fancy as the agency's other properties, but with these rates, along with cute touches like a cozy breakfast nook doubling as a bar for entertaining, might be just the ticket.

If you're looking to rent a beach house with a few friends, but Tamarindo rates are inducing sticker shock, check with **Pacific Coast Realty** (☎ 654-5050, 817/776-5363 from the U.S. and Canada; www.acquirecostarica.com), whose 10 oceanfront condos and houses are in Playa Flamingo, just north of Tamarindo. Quite a few are reasonably priced (as low as $700 a week), split among the four or more people they sleep. Few smaller condos are available, but the real bargains are the lovely homes. And hagglers' alert: This is one of the agencies willing to negotiate if you're willing to pay cash. Contact Sharon Franklin (sharon@flamingobeach.com) with inquiries—she'll walk you through the process as well as suggest and arrange tours. Ask about the spacious **Casa Surfside,** which comfily puts up 12 in a four-bedroom/three-bathroom, um, surfside for $3,000 per week in high season. It's got matching wraparound balconies and patios with rockers and tables on both stories, and a great swimming pool takes up most of the backyard. Bikes and kayaks are part of the deal; several restaurants and bars are walkable; and the Tamarindo tumult is a half-hour drive away. For cutting-edge luxe, have a peek at the **Villas Catalina,** a three-bedroom townhouse sleeping eight, with breathtaking views of Flamingo and nearby beaches, and costing $2,400 per week. In the living room, flat-screen TVs face a sleek suede couch; the 3½ baths are appointed with marble walls, sinks, and clear glass showers; the kitchen has a heavy, dark-wood table with elegant flatware and wine glasses; and large windows look out onto an infinity pool with a view of the lush offshore islands.

Since it's always good to have choices, we'll mention another agency, **1st Choice Realty** (☎ 653-1191, 800/858-6365 in the U.S.; www.1stcostaricarealestate.com), which has hooked up with a tour operator to offer 14 select rentals in Tamarindo, Playa Grande, and surrounding areas. While most go for a whopping $4,000 a week and more, others are less, and include some of the area's choicest rentals. One of them is Tamarindo's **Villas Mariposa** complex, with 10 tropical-hued two-bedroom, two-bath bungalows sleeping six for $595 a week. There's a great pool out back with thatched cabana, and you also get your own personal *palapa,* with hammocks and bamboo-screened walls. Or how about a 1.2-hectare (3-acre) estate on a hilltop over Playa Grande, just north of Tamarindo? The **Casa & Casitas Linda Vista** is an oasis yet an easy stroll to restaurants, shops, and the sands (swim at Playa Ventana, see mollusk-filled tide pools at black-sand Playa Carbon, or, depending on the season, watch *baulas*—leatherback turtles—nesting on Playa Grande). There are three houses, all with large windows and open-air balconies or verandas for fab views. The big Casa Linda Vista runs $980 for up to four; the **Casita Linda Vista** sleeps three for $280 a week; and the one-bedroom **Casa Azul** cottage is $700. The owners will set up local excursions for an additional fee. One drawback: no pool.

There are some independents worth checking out, too (some are cross-listed through the larger agencies, but you'll get a better deal right at the source). A good example is **The Surf House** (just off the main road to Tamarindo; ☎ 255-0448; www.thesurfhouse.com; cash only), a three-bedroom, two-bathroom gem with high ceilings and chunky wood furniture, and all the space and amenities you'd want from a beach house, plus a panoramic peek at Las Baulas National Park and the feel of a ranch set away from the road. The rate's $140 nightly for up to three.

Another, not directly on the beach, is **Casa de las Olas** (off the main road between Tamarindo and Langosta; ☎ 805/773-5738; www.houseofthewaves.com), which is great for little extras like CD players, DVD players, and kid-friendly boogie boards. The airy hacienda-style two-bedroom, two-bath unit is a great value at $125 a night, but doesn't have a pool. Or, right on the sands of secluded Playa Potrero, a half-hour from Tamarindo, **Villa Malibu** (off the main road between

Flamingo and Potrero; ☎ 816/729-7330 or 816/880-0693 in the U.S.; www.villa malibu.com) offers a pair of sleek, fully equipped studios starting at $120 per night including maid service; besides the beach there's a 12m (40-ft.) infinity lap pool with swim-up bar, and the shopping, dining, and drinking of Playa Flamingo is a hop and a skip away.

Hotels

$$ A block from the beach, the **Hotel Pasatiempo** ★ (off the road to Playa Langosta; ☎ 653-0096; www.hotelpasatiempo.com; AE, MC, V) is in the heart of the restaurant/bar district, yet surprisingly quiet thanks to a surrounding grove of trees. Starting at $79, rooms have hand-painted tropical wall murals along with perks like CD players and private terraces, and there's a nice poolside restaurant/bar (live-music Wed nights pack 'em in). Owner/surfer Ron Stewart and his wife Janet are generous with recommendations—and who knows, he might even take you to the area's secret breaks.

$$ Finding elegance in Tamarindo for less than $100 is tough, but the thatched-roof bungalows at **Luna Llena** ★ (on the road to Playa Langosta; ☎ 653-0082 or 653-0120; www.hotellunallena.com; AE, MC, V) fit the bill nicely. Centered around a charming pool and Jacuzzi with swim-up bar, the grounds are woodsy and the digs outfitted with vintage bric-a-brac, funky wall coverings, and whimsical furniture, all carefully chosen by Italian owner Simona Daniela. Seven bungalows with kitchenette go for $99, while regular doubles are $85 (check for discounts on her website).

$$ A garden oasis smack-dab amid the bustle, the **Villas Macondo** (200m/660 ft. from the beach, Playa Tamarindo; ☎ 653-0812; www.villasmacondo.com; cash or Paypal) offers a better deal (doubles $55) than others of its class because it's a bit farther from the beach. But really, big whoop—it's a steal for the charming backyard with pool and bright, cheery rooms with A/C, TV, and Wi-Fi. Owner Tom and his girlfriend Anja have a superfriendly staff, and guests missing their pets can get their fix from house dog Theo. A spacious, fully equipped one-bedroom duplex is also available for $540 a week.

$$$ Playa Langosta and budget travel are normally mutually exclusive, but **Casa Doble** (drive all the way through Tamarindo until you come to the last left hand turn; then take the dirt road left and stay on the right, through two forks in the road; after about 3.2km (2 miles), take the first right-hand turn; ☎ 653-0312; www.tamarindo.com/casadoble; MC, V), a seven-room/two-cabin B&B, can get you there for $100 a night or $600 a week (a little pricier but less hopped-up than Tamarindo, several minutes down the beach). You get a private terrace, use of a big infinity pool, and the expertise of owner Valerie Townley, a 20-year Costa Rica resident (came with the Peace Corp, never left). Here they'll even take you out to catch dinner from their 9m (30-ft.) fishing boat.

$$$ Owned by Swedes (*suecos*), the white-stucco **Casa Sueca** (50m/164 ft. to the right of Hotel Capitán Suizo; ☎ 653-0021; www.tamarindo.com/sueca; MC, V) is tucked away in a hoity-toity residential zone about a 7-minute walk from the main strip in a cul-de-sac. For $112 per night, not including breakfast, you get a suite with patio and kitchenette, sleeping four. The landscaping is gorgeous and the beach right across the street, and the rooms are comfortable, with queen-size beds and futons, cable TV, Wi-Fi, full bathrooms, and kitchenettes.

$$$$ If you can swing it, Tamarindo's **Hotel Capitán Suizo** ★★ (right side of road to Playa Langosta; ☎ 653-0075 or 653-0292; www.hotelcapitansuizo.com; AE, MC, V) is worth the splurge ($160 a night). The big stretch of sugary beach out back feels practically private, and the rest isn't shabby, either. The beautifully landscaped, hacienda-style grounds have a big free-form pool, separate kids pool, Swiss-tinged international restaurant, and handsome split-level units (22 rooms, 8 thatched-roof bungalows) with balconies and sunken bathtubs.

DINING FOR ALL TASTES

Even more than other Tico resort areas, Tamarindo's evolution from surfer hideaway to tourist hot spot has matured the dining scene from simple Latin fare to a United Nations of gastronomy. With more sophistication, of course, come higher prices. But apart from the listings below, you can maximize savings at **Nogui's** (on the beach, south side of Tamarindo Circle; ☎ 653-0029; closed Wed; AE, DC, MC, V), a 1970s holdover where fresh fish tacos or homemade meat pies will set you back less than $5. Or stock up on groceries and drinks (including wine) at the **Supermercado Tamarindo** (next to Banco Nacional; ☎ 653-1072).

$ **Wok n' Roll** ★ (50m/164 ft. east of the Conchal Mall on the road to Langosta; ☎ 653-0156; Mon–Sat 10am–10pm) is a great place to grab a Pan-Asian bite on your way to the beach or before surf class. The sashimi ($7), lettuce wraps ($6), and potstickers ($4) are all good, but if you dine in, order a wok dish ($6), where you pick the meat and vegetables and have it stir-fried while you wait.

$–$$ Friendly service makes **Kahiki** (at Iguana Surf, on the road to Langosta; ☎ 653-0148; Wed–Mon 5:30–10:30pm; cash only) a local standout partly because bartenders and servers will actually bother to remember your name. The decor's bamboo-woody and the menu's South Seas–ish: coconut ceviche ($4.50), pineapple chicken kabobs ($8), and several tropical burgers including grilled tuna ($7.50). Vegetarians will dig the likes of black-bean hummus ($4.50) and barbecued tofu ($8). For wetting your whistle, try the Kahikirita, the tasty house margarita with fresh *guanábana* ("soursop"), tamarind, blackberry, or mango juice.

$–$$ **La Palapa** (main Tamarindo strip; ☎ 653-0362; daily 5–11pm [kitchen], bar till midnight; AE, D, MC, V) is one of the best places in town for gringos homesick for Philly cheese steaks ($8), Caesar salads ($4), ribs ($11), and pasta ($4), all in generous portions. Open from breakfast onward, La Palapa sets aside its patio at 5pm for fancier candlelit dining, when you can feast on tempura, mahimahi, and lobster kebabs (most entrees are between $10 and $20 for the fancier stuff).

$–$$ Head out to the thatch-roof **Witch's Rock Surf Camp Bar and Grill** (main road into Tamarindo; ☎ 653-1138; 8am–9pm; MC, V) for lively, casual dining right on the beach. Happy hour's huge—a sign outside promises ice-cold beer and nachos "as big as your ass" (would that be Kate Moss' or J-Lo's, I wonder?) The grub is Mexican, à la fresh tortilla chips with homemade guacamole ($4), heart-of-palm salad ($6), and fajitas ($9).

$$ At the chic, open-air **Dragonfly Bar and Grill** ✹ (100m/330 ft. behind Hotel Pasatiempo; ☎ 653-1506; Mon–Sat 6–10pm; cash only) you'll find Tamarindo's top tipples, from daiquiris with a fresh mango purée to house specialties like "South of the Border," blending tequila, Kahlúa, and lime juice over ice. Choosing a booze from the extensive list and ask the bartender to just whip something up with whatever local juices he's got (that'll run you about $2, while menu drinks are $4–$5). The dinner-only food is just as tasty and creative, with such dishes as chile-garlic shrimp with grilled pineapple salsa ($7), wood-fire-cooked red snapper with plantains ($10), and fresh tuna with sesame noodles and wasabi cream ($9). Reservations for dinner are definitely recommended, since this stylish spot is pretty popular.

$$–$$$ Mediterranean cuisine is the thing at **Pachanga** ✹✹ (across from Hotel Pasatiempo, 177m/590 ft. from beach, behind Tamarindo Circle); ☎ 368-6983; Mon–Sat 6–10pm; cash only), where Cordon Bleu–trained Shlomi Koren piles the best fresh seafood and produce onto your dinner plate (a daily special might be red snapper served with sun-dried tomatoes and thyme in a white-wine sauce, $13) on a romantic, warmly lit terrace with outdoor seating and sunburst murals on tangerine walls. Just keep in mind that it'll be a little bit of a splurge, since entrees run $11 to $20.

Worth the Splurge

It's not often that you can (or even want to) dine on haute cuisine over a crocodile-filled lagoon, but at **La Laguna del Cocodrilo Bistro** ✹✹✹ (north end of the road into Tamarindo; ☎ 653-3897; Mon–Sat 4–11pm; AE, MC, V), I'm gonna throw caution to the wind and say—go for it. Crisp white tablecloths? Check. Carefully selected French pinot gris or Argentine malbec poured out of a temperature-controlled dispenser? Check.

Then there's Sebastien Courtier, a Parisian freshness fiend who prepares delicacies from *la belle France* with the ingredients and spices of *la belle Côte Riche:* duck breast with corn mousse and vanilla-mango marmalade, or delicate, herb-garnished snapper-and-shrimp cassoulet. Just to keep things interesting, you'll also come across, say, a 21-piece sashimi platter. Entrees run $13 to $22, making La Laguna one of Costa Rica's most expensive restaurants, but if you stick to the lower end of the menu, even budgeters can swing it. During the dry season, grab one of several back garden patio tables, set between tall palms and shoulder-high hedges pimped up with strings of white lights.

WHY YOU'RE HERE: THE TOP SIGHTS & ATTRACTIONS

Gone are the days when surfing (and surfers) like, totally ruled Tamarindo. But even today, the beaches and splishy-splashy sports remain the top draw. You've also got canopy tours and seasonal leatherback turtle–nesting excursions, and northern parks like **Santa Rosa** ✭ and **Rincón de la Vieja** (p. 289) are a little over 2 hours away. Closer parks are **Las Baulas** (best known for its nesting leatherback turtles, a hop and a skip up the coast) and as well as the caverns of **Barra Honda National Park** ✭✭, about an hour inland (p. 328). It's not all natural wonders—we highly recommend a visit to the even closer and totally charming inland towns of **Santa Cruz** (29km/18 miles east) or **Guaitíl** ✭✭ (42km/26 miles).

The Beaches

Playa Tamarindo ✭✭ is hands-down one of the prettiest beaches in Guanacaste—it's one long expanse of white sand. Known for surfing for a good number of years, its middle stretch is thick with both experts and beginners, many of the newbies taught by instructors from the various local surfing schools. As at many good surfing beaches, swimming and wading can be tricky due to big waves, riptides, and submerged rocks; canoeing and kayaking, though, are no problem.

Just south of here, **Playa Langosta** ✭ features black sand, rough surf, and a shore lined with gorgeous bed-and-breakfasts and million-dollar manses (thankfully out of sight behind mangroves). The kicker here is the rightly famous sunsets—rich oranges and reds melting magnificently into the horizon. We like it more for strolling than trying to swim or wade. The cove's divided by the mouth of the San Francisco River into a mangrove estuary and to its north a rocky coast. Both are swell for long walks—the scenery's spectacular and the bird-watching a treat (especially wading snowy egrets, blue herons, and pelicans swooping down for a snack).

You'll have to drive to get to **Playa Avellanas** ✭ (4.8km/3 miles south of Langosta, 9.7km/6 miles south of Tamarindo), which used to be mostly a surfer's beach (known as "little Hawaii" among locals) but is now something of a trendy hangout. Experience the relatively untouched white sands and great surf breaks while you can, because the developers, they be a-comin' with a gleam in their eyes. For the time being, people have a great time chilling at the beach, especially at **Lola's** ✭✭ (no phone; hours vary; cash only), a funky cafe and bar with rustic, sculptural furniture driftwood tables, and an eponymous mascot—an 880-pound pig. Lola's attracts both surfers and hip expats, not just for lunch or a day on the sand, but also the Saturday-night scene. Bring sunblock and/or a beach umbrella—there's not much shade out here.

To get to brown-sand **Playa Grande** ✭, just north from Tamarindo, you'll have to either drive around the large mangrove swamp that separates the beach from town, or take one of the miniferries across. It's this touch of over-the-river-and-through-the-woods inaccessibility that makes Playa Grande a refuge from the Tamarindo "scene"—folks come up here for quiet, and, of course, from October through February to see the nesting *baulas* (leatherback turtles; p. 304). Here, too, the waters are a little rough, better for surfing than swimming, but there are also a fair number of sunbathers out here during the day in addition to surfers.

Tortugas & Turistas

by Jenna Wortham

Leatherbacks used to nest on other area beaches, such as Playa Flamingo and even Playa Tamarindo. But thanks to development and human encroachment, most have been driven away, and as tourism grows, turtle populations dwindle further. In the 1980s, leatherbacks used to arrive here in the thousands, but today they number fewer than 25,000 worldwide. It's important that if you do get to observe turtles on Playa Grande that you give them, as Aretha would sing it, R-E-S-P-E-C-T—don't get too close, take photos or touch them. And remember to watch your step making your way along—tourists occasionally step on eggs or, once they're hatched, baby turtles scurrying to the ocean.

Surf Camps

Diving right into surfer culture is easy; if you're a decent swimmer, you can learn to surf. At **Witch's Rock Surf Camp** (☎ 653-1262, 888/318-7873 in the U.S.; www.witchsrocksurfcamp.com) you'll learn more than riding a board—you'll eat, sleep, and breathe surfing, and learn the history, etiquette, how to repair boards, and how to read waves. Students get unlimited access to boards, so budding surfers can head out to polish their moves and catch waves whenever they damn well please. Seven days will cost you $595 without lodging, $895 with. If that's just a little too hardcore for you, the **Tamarindo Surf School** (☎ 653-0923; www.tamarindosurfschool.com) caters not just to serious surfer wannabes but also folks who just want to dip a toe in—spend a week or just a couple of hours. Prices range from $30 for a 2½-hour group session to $500 for 3 days to $1,000 for a week with lodging.

Exploring Nature

Though their numbers have dwindled, the leatherback turtles that come to nest on Playa Grande are still a huge tourist draw. They're unpredictable, though; their numbers fluctuate between thousands and less than 100, and they're not as loyal to nesting sites as the marine turtles on the Caribbean coast. During the October-through-March season, you may spend all night waiting around on the beach yet find nothing but other tour groups.

You'll need to make reservations for a tour with a certified guide. And hop to it (at least a week in advance if you can), because the number of nightly gawkers on the beach is controlled and snagging a spot last minute is pretty unlikely. The tours, set up by no shortage of local outfits (your hotel can book it for you), usually cost around $40; admission to the **Las Baulas Marine National Park** ★★ (north of Tamarindo, across the river; ☎ 653-0470) is another $6. You hike out near the sand, then wait for guides to spot a burrowing turtle, before scurrying after them to gather quietly behind the big, bulky creature as she hollows out the sand and deposits 80 or more pool-ball-size eggs. You're not allowed any artificial lights, so you need to stay alert. Again, keep in mind that having the luck to see one on your particular outing is far from a sure thing these days.

Luck out or not, do stop at the sea turtle museum, **El Mundo de la Tortuga** (200m/660 ft. from the Las Baulas gate, Playa Grande; ☎ 653-0471; daily 4pm–6:30am, $5). Audio tours in English and other languages supplement interactive exhibits where you'll learn loads about this endangered species—life span, brain size, favorite food (jellyfish), threats they face, and more.

SIDE TRIPS INLAND

If you're planning to stay in the Tamarindo Bay area for a few days, don't miss out on an afternoon or full-day excursion to Santa Cruz and Guaitíl, in the heart of the peninsula. Santa Cruz is a fetching little ranch town a 20-minute drive inland (there's daily bus service) that makes for a nice change of pace and a chance to see a little more of the "real" Guanacaste than is left on the coast these days. Take part of a day to wander amid its brightly painted old houses, sit in the Parque de los Mangos, and check out church ruins and the monument to Costa Rica's vanished indigenous people. Definitely have lunch at **Coope-Tortillas** ★★ (in town; daily 4am–6pm; cash only), a women's collective and tortilla factory near the central park, where you can get authentic *guanacasteco* fare like large handmade corn tortillas with black beans and melted cheese, washed down with *horchata* (a rice-based drink sweetened with dark cane sugar). An entire meal will cost about $5 here. If spending the night (there are plenty of decent places to bunk), head to one of the local watering holes to listen to marimba, toss back a shot of *guaro* if you dare (this moonshine rum will knock your socks and possibly your toenails off), and keep an eye out for festive *payasos,* gigantic papier-mâché decorations. Mostly things are pretty sleepy here, but Costa Rica's official "National Folklore City" does come up with some great spectacles—traditional festivals, rodeos, music, and more—especially in January but also year-round. If you're lucky you'll get to see some *punto,* the stylized national dance of Costa Rica, invented in Santa Cruz.

As long as you're over here, do make time to push on another 11km or so (7 miles) east to **Guaitíl** ★★, where ancient Chorotega Indian pottery techniques were revived in the 1980s by the **Artesanía Co-op** (in town; daily hours vary from about 8am–7pm), which has pretty much turned much of the town into Potteryville. The pre-Columbian techniques are practiced mostly by women, who shape freshly dug clay with their hands into bowls spun on wheels propped up beneath shady trees. These are polished, painted with traditional animal designs in red and black, baked in open-hearth kilns, and sold all over town. All in all, Guaitíl is about a 40 minute drive from Tamarindo.

ATTENTION, SHOPPERS!

Most shops are inside strip malls along Tamarindo's main road, carrying the same stuff you'll find around the rest of Costa Rica, but marked up (a pound of coffee weighs in at $7, compared to $1 in San José); for most run-of-the-mill gifts, consider the Liberia or San José airports. On the other hand, there are several spots with more unique and high-quality merch. An example is **Azul Profundo** (Centro

Comercial; ☎ 653-0395), which specializes in polished semiprecious stones set in slim silver bands, designed and handcrafted by an Argentine artist. From wrists to hips, don't leave town without a brightly patterned local sarong; **Tienda Bambora** (on the beach next to Nogui's) has a great selection plus other beach duds. And at the **Green Turtle** (main road; ☎ 653-1606 or 653-1607), look for soaps with coffee, mango, and even "cloud-forest" scents, made out of creamy beeswax and rich olive oils by a women's collective in Sabalita, near Lake Arenal.

For Costa Rican fine art, head to the area's first upscale gallery, **Galería Guacamole** ✶ (across from Aster Commercial Center; ☎ 653-1214), a merciful break from endless craft shops crammed with generic wood carvings and parrot-shape jewelry boxes. The goods here include mixed-media paintings, amazing basketwork, and masks painted with wonderfully Picassoesque pre-Columbian motifs.

In Tamarindo you just can't ignore surf shops, so here goes: Many are tiny and limited, but **Iguana Surf** (first right on main road into town; ☎ 653-0148; www. iguanasurf.net) is the king of the hill, top of the heap. New, used, buy, rent—it's got boards in all shapes and sizes, plus the total scoop on the local surfer scene (rides into town, last-minute trips, surf-class slots, best digs, party happenings).

NIGHTLIFE

It's fiesta time, *muchachos*—the Tamarindo party scene may well be Costa Rica's wildest and craziest, and most folks don't come to town to catch up on their rest (for that, head down the coast). Okay, during the week things tend to be a tad slower, but weekends the kasbah rocks till dawn (a couple of years ago the town was even spotlighted on the E! network's *Wild On* series on the world's hip and/or rowdy party scenes). And if you're thinking of coming here during spring break, get ready for heaven or hell, depending which side of 25 you're on.

In general, though, you'll have no trouble finding pretty much whatever floats your boat, from traditional watering holes and hotel bars with live bands to out-door concerts and raves with bumpin' DJ sets; you've even got a couple of casinos. Check out the listings below, but keep in mind you can pretty much zero in on what you're looking for just by strolling up and down the strip.

Get the evening started with a fruity tropical potion or two at the **Crazy Monkey Bar** ✶ (at the Vista Villas resort, main road into Tamarindo; ☎ 653-0114; daily 10am–midnight), which hosts one of the biggest parties in town. Salsa rules; the outdoor deck provides gorgeous sunset views; the swim-up bar is open all night; and the bar videos run toward surfing. Depending on the night, it can get really packed and pick up a bit of a meat-market feel. Friday is ladies' night, with drink specials and reduced cover for *las chicas.*

If you're in the market for just a cool place to have a cocktail and conversation, **Restobar La Caracola** (Tamarindo Circle, next to Noguis; ☎ 653-0583; daily 2pm–1am) is lively without being over the top. Latin bands often perform here, and many afternoons you'll find tango, salsa, and merengue classes.

Finally, we're not wild about casinos, but if you are, hit the slots, roulette, and poker at the **Casino Jazz** (at El Diriá resort; ☎ 653-0406; www.casinojazz.com/landbased/tamarindo.php; daily 4pm–midnight) and down at the **Barceló Playa Langosta Resort** (☎ 633-0363; www.barcelolangostabeach.com; daily 7pm–2am).

THE "OTHER" TAMARINDO

It's actually through the over-the-top nightlife that one can best meet locals and get a taste of the flavor of local life here. Beyond the clubs mentioned above, there are a number of unique weekly parties that draw both Ticos and visitors. If you've ever wanted to front a rock band—and who hasn't?—head to **open-mic Tuesdays** ★ at **Hotel Pasatiempo** (p. 300). There you'll belt out some sort of tune live with the house band (and their repertory is large—from salsa to reggae to classic rock). This quasi-karaoke is extremely popular, so get there no later than 9pm if you want to get your name on the singing list. Can't carry a tune? No worries, the thatch roof and TV perched above the bamboo bar create a relaxed vibe to match the relaxed decor.

On Saturday nights the place to be is a massive beach party called **The Big Bazaar,** with a huge bonfire, fire dancers, and occasionally big-name DJs. It's a bit "Burning Man" to be sure, but welcoming of all, and an experience that won't fade from memory soon. If that's a little too crazed and/or crowded for you, there's a lower-key version nightly at **Hotel Capitán Suizo** (p. 301), with a lavish barbecue and cocktail hour that gives way to dancing to live music (the crowd here is a little older, you have to reserve in advance and there's a $30 cover).

NOSARA & VICINITY

If there's one place that represents the best of Guanacaste—what it all woulda-shoulda-coulda been—it's Nosara. The magic is its authenticity: true Tico, its nature minimally messed-with, its vibe *tranquilo.* Hotels, businesses, and houses aren't jammed onto a honky-tonk beachfront strip but spread out, off the beach behind a reserve filled with mangroves or nestled in the nearby hills and jungles.

Nosara's also one of the last bona fide ecotourism destinations on the north Guanacaste coast. One reason is nearby **Ostional National Wildlife Refuge.** Another is the crappy unpaved roads—getting here is dusty and bumpy in the dry season, muddy in the wet. But it helps keeps boozy beach bunnies away and draws expats and visitors (including the occasional boldface name) into a sophisticated but low-key community dedicated to hanging onto the best of the real Costa Rica. Miles of unspoiled sands are one result—you could truly imagine you've stumbled across a castaway bit of paradise. That's a selling point that has attracted the likes of Susan Sarandon and Tim Robbins, Danny DeVito, Goldie Hawn, and Woody Harrelson.

Banning hunting and development, the Ostional refuge includes three gorgeous, mostly deserted beaches (**playas Nosara, Pelada,** and **Guiones**); the mouth of the Río Nosara; and the hamlet of Ostional, home to one of world's top beaches for Olive Ridley turtle nesting. Hop in a canoe and explore the mangroves along the river, or hike through the forests and spot all manner of critters. Guiones is the place for way gnarly surfing; at Pelada, there's fascinating stuff to explore like tide pools, bat cave, and a blow hole.

There's a dot of New-Ageiness here, too; the **Nosara Yoga Insititute** is one of the hemisphere's finest and famous, hosting top yogis from around the world and several astral planes; the "spiritual eco-village" of **PachaMama** is also nearby. They're more examples of local "development" way different from the golf courses and gated-condo-mania that have taken over elsewhere along the coast.

By the way, we're using the name "Nosara" to cover all the beaches, digs, eats, and activities in this section. But the name comes from not just Playa Nosara but Bocas de Nosara, the little village 4.8km (3 miles) inland where most area Ticos live, shop, play, pray, and go to school (as they do in several other even smaller nearby hamlets). For visitors, it's where buses and flights come in and out, but if you're interested in a glimpse of real-deal Tico life and/or want the cheapest lodging and dining in the area, you might consider an overnight or at least a bite at its smattering of *sodas* and great eateries for locals such as **Rancho Tico** (p. 313). You can also sign up for Spanish lessons at **Rey de Nosara Language School** (☎ 682-0215; www.reydenosara.itgo.com).

GETTING TO & AROUND NOSARA
By Air

A sign of Nosara's growing tourism and real estate prowess is the newly constructed airport (that term is used loosely!) terminal—a gleaming brick-and-chrome building with outdoor seating situated at the end of the airstrip. It's a 45- to 50-minute flight from San José directly into Nosara, and during the high season, **Nature Air** (☎ 299-6000, 800/235-9272 in the U.S. or Canada; www.natureair.com) has one leaving San José's Tobías Bolaños International Airport in Pavas daily at 3:30pm; the one-way fare is $86. For $78 each way, **Sansa** (☎ 221-9414; www.flysansa.com) will fly you there at 8am and 11:30am daily from the main airport, Juan Santamaría.

By Bus

Express buses (☎ 222-2666) leave for Nosara from San José every day at 6am (Calle 14 between avs. 3 and 5); the trip takes 7 hours and costs $6. The cushier **Interbus** (☎ 283-5573; www.interbusonline.com) leaves later (8:15am), is 45 minutes faster, and will pick you up from most San José area hotels, but you'll have to lay out $39 ($20 for kids).

By Car

From San José, follow the signs for Sámara. Several miles before you reach Sámara beach, there's a fork with a sign for Nosara. Bear right and hold onto your *sombrero:* It's 22km (14 miles) of bumpy unpaved road.

Getting Around

There's only one road in and out of Nosara, and all the stuff below is either on this main road or its side roads. Taxis have to be ordered through where you're staying or eating, and things are so spread out that if you're staying someplace not walkable to the beach, fares can add up. For that reason, renting wheels isn't a bad idea; it will enable you to take some essential day trips. Playa Guiones offers several options, like **National** (☎ 682-0254; www.nationalcarrental.com) and **Alamo** (www.alamocarrental.com), along with bicycles (try **Juan Surfo** near the beach across from the Blew Dog Bar; ☎ 506/682-4041; or at **Solo Bueno** surf hostel near Guiones, last left exit on road from village; p. 311), off-road golf carts (☎ 682-0574; rental place in Coconut Harry's Surf Shop), and ATV/quad rentals (**Monkey Quads;** ☎ 682-1001; monkeyquads@yahoo.com). You will get mighty dusty riding a bike or an off-roader, so you may want to invest in a bandana to tie

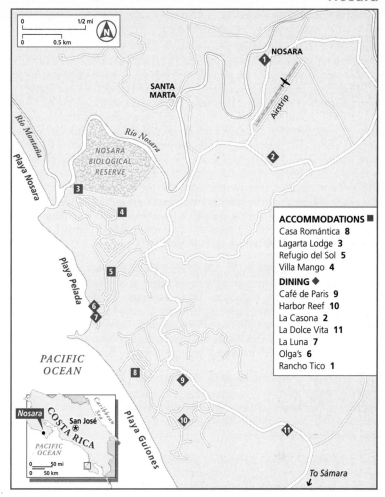

ACCOMMODATIONS ■
Casa Romántica **8**
Lagarta Lodge **3**
Refugio del Sol **5**
Villa Mango **4**
DINING ◆
Café de Paris **9**
Harbor Reef **10**
La Casona **2**
La Dolce Vita **11**
La Luna **7**
Olga's **6**
Rancho Tico **1**

around your mouth and a pair of sturdy sunglasses. ***Car-renters' caveat:*** The only place to buy gas is Bocas de Nosara, and it's just a garage where a teenager pours gas into your tank with a cut-off plastic milk jug; if you're on a day trip and see a gas station, always fill 'er up.

ACCOMMODATIONS, BOTH STANDARD & NOT

On the coast, your choices are spread out between playas Guiones, Pelada, and Nosara. To be able to walk to the beach, restaurants, and bars, go for Guiones. If it's seclusion and/or views you're after, head for the hills above Pelada and Guiones. **FYI:** several more places to stay are mentioned as part of our dining and nightlife sections below.

Vacation Rentals

Despite something of a housing boom, Nosara is still mostly flying below the radar, and therefore still offers great lodging values. In fact, it almost pains us to get the word out more. Hmmm—do us a favor, will you? Don't tell your friends.

Anyway, there's never been a better time to rent a vacation house here, many of which have been built in the last 2 or 3 years. The typical Guanacaste-coast gated condo and town-home complexes are minimal; instead you'll find mostly single-family homes sprinkled through the dry forests, from modest houses right out of gringo suburbia to palatial hillside villas with snazzy architectural details, infinity pools, and views galore. Many are very affordable (especially compared with Tamarindo or Playa Hermosa); nice two- or three-bedrooms go for less than a grand a week (some even $500 or less), and if you stay 2 weeks or more, there are discounts on top of that. Keep in mind that the closer to the beach, the higher the price. Always check the websites with direct owner listings; in the meantime, below are four agencies that represent local properties. The folks at the guesthouse **Villa Mango** (p. 312) also represent about a dozen well-maintained, lovingly decorated properties, so check with them as well.

The **Nosara Beach Rentals** (☎ 682-0153; www.nosarabeachrentals.com) is the largest of the bunch, representing a varied selection of 40-some homes, almost all requiring a 1-week minimum. Some examples: At the lower end, **Casa Hemingway** ($560 a week, $1,000 for 2 weeks) is a two-bedroom/two-bath house sleeping up to six in the hills above Playa Ostional. Overlooking Playa Guiones, the recently built **Casa Dos Gatos** has three attached houses ($600–$1,500) for two to eight people, with a big pool and great detailing but no phone or TV.

The portfolio at **Nosara Property Management** (☎ 682-0130; www.nosara propertymanagement.com) numbers just 15, but most of them are especially friendly to the budget-traveler wallet. For example, **Casa Izquierda,** a simply furnished two-bedroom surrounded by jungle, is a 10-minute walk to Playa Pelada and sleeps four for $425 a week.

For walkability to sands and services, go with **Harbor Reef Lodge** (☎ 682-0059; www.harborreef.com) in Guiones. Besides being a nice surfer- and angler-oriented hotel (doubles from $70), it reps nine nearby properties that average $1,000 per week, though some cost as little as $600 and one particularly swank one comes in at $1,995 in high season—a tad steep for Nosara—but that's the mark-up that comes with location, location, location. The Mediterranean-style **Villa La Carolina** ($1,120–$1,530 a week) may be the best of the bunch, a three-bedroom/two-bath with high ceilings, nice details, a little pool, and just a block from the beach and the Harbor Reef, where you can grab dinner or a drink.

The **Nosara Travel & Rentals** (☎ 682-0300; www.nosaratravel.com) handles more than a dozen rental properties—spacious, unique dream houses (a la hilltop villas with Spanish-style arches overlooking ocean and forest) especially great for weddings and other special events, or two or more families vacationing together. They don't come cheap, of course—rates can hit $5,000 a week in season—but if you spread it among a group, the math can work out. Besides, the agency also has studios starting at $200 a week in low season. The owners don't put prices on their website, but will usually get back to you via e-mail within 24 hours.

Hotels

This being a surfing mecca, there are several dorm-style accommodations, which are so basic (just a bed for you and wall space for your board, dude) that the **Blew Dog** (☎ 682-0080; www.blewdogs.com) proudly calls its digs a "flop house." Its dorm accommodations place strangers into rooms holding three a piece. **Solo Bueno** (www.solobuenohostel.com), has much the same vibe, looking like a big tree house, a la Gilligan's Island (tall thatched roof, simple open spaces within, lots of hammocks), with sturdy wooden bunk beds with foam mattresses and camping out back. If you're really low on cash, you can stay at one of these two for just $9 a night in a shared room, $32 a night for your own *cabina* (at Blew Dog). On recent inspection neither looked all too mildewed and grungy—a back-handed compliment, we know. Let's just say we've seen worse.

$ If you want something more civilized—*much* more civilized—but still cheap, **Refugio del Sol** ★ (300m/985 ft. from Playa Pelada; ☎ 682-0287; http://refugiodelsol.com; cash only) should be your choice. A cute little ranch-style B&B on the quiet main road to Playa Pelada, its location is perfect for those without wheels: a 5-minute saunter to the beach, dining, and bars, it has a convenience store, and Pancho's Mexican restaurant right across the road. Rooms are quite spiffy at just $40 per double ($30 for a single) with pretty sunset-colored woven throws on the beds, whitewashed walls, and spotless tile floors. All in all there are two double rooms, two triples, and an oversized double with a useable kitchen; the last is a steal at just $55. Your gracious, laid-back host José serves a mean paella from his native Spain, and locals drop in all the time for his grilled fish and squid at the informal, tiny restaurant on-site. There's no air-conditioning, but if you want to save big without schlepping all the way into town, it's not possible to do better out here by the water. José rents out surf equipment as well.

$$ Another decent value, walkable to everything, is **Casa Romántica** 🛝 (Playa Guiones beachfront road; ☎ 682-0272; www.casa-romantica.net; MC, V, but those who pay in cash get a discount). Run by a German couple, Silvia and Remo Britschgi, this Spanish-colonial-style inn isn't all that *romántica* (the 10 understated rooms are a bit plain but have nice tile work and wood-beam ceilings) but *excelente* for families thanks to the on-site pool (one of the largest and loveliest around, with a big *palapa* bar and a restaurant alongside) and the private path to the nearby beach, which keeps guests off the dusty road. Upstairs are several two-bedrooms with kitchens and verandas; a couple of stand-alone *cabinas* are recent additions. Surf and boogie boards are yours for the renting, and rates go from $55 for low-season doubles to $84 for more elaborate units in high. Rooms with A/C go for $10 more, and you're going to want A/C down here by the beach, as it does get muggy. Why no star? We always get the feeling we're bothering the staff here when we ask for anything. The service isn't exactly rude, just indifferent and a bit brusque. You'll get a warmer welcome elsewhere.

$$ Perched far above the mangrove-lined river, atop Punta Nosara, **Lagarta Lodge** ✪✪ (4km/2½ miles from Bocas de Nosara; ☎ 682-0035; www.lagarta. com; AM, DISC, MC, V) not only offers some of Guanacaste's most voluptuous views but also its very own 50-hectare (125-acre) reserve. And it's the reserve—with its mangrove swamp, its access to the Nosara River, and its well-marked trails—that's the main draw here. You can tackle it on your own or with the Swiss owners, Regina and Amadeo Amacker, who lead free nature walks to guests each morning (heavy on the flora, light on fauna). It's also a superb spot for birding as the reserve abuts an estuary where many herons, toucans, waders, and other seabirds dive bomb into the water for fish (all in all, you can eyeball a good 200 species here; there's a $6 fee for nonguests to visit the reserve). Yeah, the beach is a bit of a steep hike, but one look at the open-air dining room, lounge, and pool area, and you may not be that eager to leave the premises. Four of the seven minimalist but pretty rooms (think floral curtains, rattan chairs, and wood-beamed ceilings) are in the main two-story house; three others are in a smaller white-stucco outbuilding; and all have terraces with those socko vistas (but no A/C, just ceiling fans). Moms and dads should know that the walkways are steep, and there are open areas where you'll want to keep an eagle eye on junior. Doubles are $68 in season, less the rest of the year; breakfast is an additional $6. If you don't end up staying here, be sure to come up for cocktails around 5pm; there's no better place in town for sunsets (especially when enhanced by strong, fruity potables).

$$ Saving the best in this area for last, we come to a very, very special place, the **Villa Mango** ✪✪✪ (.5km/⅓ mile east of Lagarta Lodge; ☎ 682-0130; www. villamangocr.com; MC, V). What makes it unique? I think it all comes down to the hosts, Agnes and Jo Pinheiro, a French and Portuguese couple (who also lived in Colorado for a spell), who have lavished a tremendous amount of care and attention on this little B&B, as they do on their guests. Joe is the decorator and he has a sharp eye for detail and color, adding a little piece of sculpture here, a fanciful decorative tile or a billowing saffron curtain there, to give what would otherwise be just a simple B&B—ceramic floors, whitewashed walls—a lot of style. The bathrooms, in particular, are lovely, with a twisted, small tree trunk worked into the design of each shower, giving them an indoor/outdoor feel. Each of the five rooms has a slightly different shape and look, with those upstairs featuring spectacular views and those downstairs a bit larger with a small, semiprivate porch out front. All have A/C. By the time this book comes out, they may well have added several self-contained *cabinas* to the side, with their own kitchens (those were still in the planning stage when we visited). The *pièce de résistance* is the curvaceous open deck on the main floor, which has a glamorous treehouse feel and scattered hammocks and couches perfect for taking in the glorious views, almost the equal of the slightly higher Lagarta Lodge just up the road. The midsize pool is great for soaking in both the sun and the views, not to mention spotting the occasional monkey or coati coming by for a dip or a sip. But all of this would be mere decoration if Joe and Agnes weren't such talented, warm hosts. Breakfasts here (eggs made to order, home-baked croissants and pastries, fruit salad) is held around one long wooden table, and has the aspect of a spirited dinner party. It's such a convivial atmosphere that in the evenings, guests gather round that same table to play board games (there's no TV here) or just chat with a cocktail from the honor bar.

And for all this, prices are quite reasonable. In high season they start at $70 (two double beds) including breakfast.

DINING FOR ALL TASTES

Restaurants here also tend to be spread out, so unless you're in the Playa Guiones area (where a bunch are within walking distance of each other), expect to cab it or drive to a good number of them. Newcomers have been cropping up of late, specializing in various world cuisines. Besides the ones listed below, don't forget the **Casa Romántica** (p. 311), which serves good international fare poolside; the *paella* at **Refugio del Sol** (p. 311) or **Pancho's** (300m/985 ft. from Playa Pelada; ☎ 682-0087; www.panchosresort.com; noon–9:30pm) for pretty decent tacos, burritos, enchiladas, and fajitas (*ay, caramba,* and they even do takeout).

$ La Casona 🧒 (south of Bocas de Nosara town center, at the turn-off to the gas station; ☎ 682-0442; daily 11:30am–10pm; cash only) is the Tico restaurant of choice for *casados* (combination plates); personally, I'm a big fan of the fish with garlic and olive oil ($7). The atmosphere matches the no-frills prices (typically $4–$7)—the joint is clean, the food tasty, and it's good for kids (quick service, faves like pizza and burgers, and they can safely roam around). Note that sandwiches here and in most of Costa Rica come slathered in mayo and other condiments, which many kids hate. Be sure to specify that you want it *"sin mayo"* and anything else you don't want on it!

$–$$ Start your day with a croissant or crepe and a *café crème* at the **Café de Paris** ★ 🧒 (☎ 682-0087; www.cafedeparis.net; daily 7am–11pm; AE, MC, V), an appealing French bakery stocked with pastries, sandwiches, and baguettes. It's pretty much all good: the omelets ($6), the French toast ($5), the pastas ($8), the salads ($4–$10); parents will be sure to find something the kids will like. They'll also like the on-site pool, where they can splash around until the food comes while the adults down a cocktail. This is one of those places you'll find yourself stopping by repeatedly—now for a light snack, later to check your e-mail, maybe even shoot a game of pool after dinner.

$–$$ Arguably the area's best traditional eatery, the family-owned **Rancho Tico** ★★ 🧒 (100m/330 ft. west of Bocas de Nosara town center, next to Nature Air ticket office; ☎ 682-0006; daily 11:30am–10pm; MC, V) is housed in a large, handsome, thatched-roof *rancho*. You'll find killer margaritas and a terrific selection of tasty, superfresh choices, including some of the best steak in town and outstanding *ceviche*. You can't go wrong with any of the fish dishes. Entrees run $4 to $7.50. Leo, the English-speaking manager, will make you feel like a local and moms/dads will like that there are toys and a tiny plastic slide to keep the little darlings busy.

$–$$ Only two area restaurants actually sit on the beach in Nosara, **Olga's** (on the beach at Playa Pelada; no telephone; daily 6:30am–10pm; cash only) and La Luna (p. 314). Olga's is the budget choice, a concrete, open-air shack that, because of its locale, still serves up a dollop of charm. It's one of the few places in the area where Ticos and expats end up dining in the same room—and you can get out without dropping more than $8 or $9 a head. The fresh fish soup ($3.50, served with a bowl of rice), whole fried snapper ($6), and shrimp plates ($6) are among the top menu choices, but pretty much anything caught from the sea will be good. Try to stop in for a drop or two around sunset—you'll get to chat up a local and watch the fishing boats disappear off into the setting sun. On Sunday nights, Olga's turns into *the* Tico hotspot for dancing, karaoke, and just hanging out.

$$ For a dose of American comfort food, head to the eatery at **Harbor Reef** (100m/330 ft. from the beach at Playa Guiones; daily 7am–9pm; ☎ 682-0060; www.harborreef.com; MC, V). This massive thatch-roof *rancho* serves pretty credible burgers, quesadillas, fish and chips, and tacos, plus various sandwiches and stuff like chicken and fish fingers. Sandwiches run from $6 to $8, salads $4 to $8 and entrees can range from just $4.75 all the way up to $8. Sunday brunch is a local favorite *(una mimosa, por favor!)*. And a meal here can be mighty entertaining. Like Café de Paris (see above), there's a pool with swim-up bar, plus a tethered ring toss–type game in one corner and live music several nights a week.

$$ Handcrafted gourmet ice creams and sorbets in exotic flavors all made from the best Costa Rican ingredients (think tangy guava and mora fruits or decadent dark chocolate from native cacao plants) can be found at **Robin's Café** (25m/82 ft. west of Banco Popular in the Guiones strip mall; ☎ 682-0617; daily in high season 8am–8pm, hours vary in low season) and are the perfect post-beach treat. Sweet and savory crepes, sandwiches on bodacious homemade foccacia bread, and start-your-engines espressos and coffee drinks are all on the menu at this streetside Euro-style cafe.

$$–$$$ Though on the outskirts of town, it's worth the drive to **La Dolce Vita** ✹✹ (2km/1¼ miles south of Nosara, near the town of Esperanza; ☎ 682-0107; daily 6–10pm), one of the very finest restaurants in the area, despite its local look of thatch roof and rough-hewn logs. Roberto the owner serves the cuisine of his native northern Italy with a big emphasis on the local bounty of the sea—penne with fish ($14), large plates of prawns, grouper in butter and lemon ($14)—and other treats like spinach lasagna ($12, never easy to find in Costa Rica) and all sorts of other classic pasta dishes ($8–$9). And the wine list—*estupendo*.

$$–$$$ I can't think of a more romantic, even stunning, setting than that at **La Luna** ✹✹✹ (50m/165 ft. from Playa Pelada; ☎ 682-0122; www.nosarabeach hotel.com; daily 11am–9pm; reservations advised in high season; cash only). It's something of a splurge, but no trip to Nosara would be complete without dinner at this open-air, grass-and-sand-covered dining terrace, amid the trees and candlelight. Plunk yourself down in the funky wood folding chairs and order one of the yummy seafood salads (the shrimp with avocado for $8 is a standout), followed by an entree of snapper, tuna, or other fish—grilled filets or kabobs, in curry or green sauce ($8–$13 on average). You can get other stuff like steaks, chops, and pasta, too. Afterward, who knows, you may want to hang out longer on one of the couches in the funky bar area (the cocktails are killer and the international staff are a funny, friendly bunch) or catch a bonfire party nearby on the beach.

WHY YOU'RE HERE: THE TOP SIGHTS & ATTRACTIONS

Nosara magnificently couples sun-'n'-surf with eco-opportunities. Beyond the **beaches** and the **turtle nesting** this area's most famous for, you can take a canoe or kayak through the mangroves of Río Nosara, hike through the biological reserve (boffo for birders; see Lagarta Lodge, p. 312), go horseback riding inland or on the beach, and in season take in a traditional *sabanero* rodeo.

And you don't even need to go elsewhere for the requisite zip through the treetops: **Miss Sky Canopy Tour** ★★ kids (200m/656 ft. north of Nosara Servicentro; ☎ 682-0969; www.missskycanopytour.com; $35/children 12 and under, $55 for adults; reservations required) is one of the country's newest and highest tech ziplines and is being touted as the world's largest. Twelve runs (more are being added as we write)—most between 500 and 600m long (1,640–1,968 ft.)—provide a total of 6,400 *yeeeozah!* meters (20,992 ft.) of fantastic fly-time several hundred feet above the treetops, rivers, and waterfalls of a 1,000-hectare (2,500-acre) forest reserve. Unlike other canopy tours throughout the country, this one requires no hiking—your landing spot is your next departure point—and you are not precariously perched on a platform wrapped around a tree between runs (which, for those of us with fear of heights, is far more terrifying than the actual flight). Here you're always above the trees, moving from mountaintop to mountaintop, with landings happening on flat ground, aided by the strong and reassuring hands of a well-trained guide. Like many activities in the Nosara area, the drive to the first launching point is far more harrowing than the attraction itself.

There's also plenty more stuff to do within an hour or two's drive from Nosara. About a 45 minutes away is **Sámara** (p. 322), which has sea kayaking, diving, surfing, and swimming. Or take a 2½-hour scenic drive out to Guanacaste's **Santa Cruz** and **Guaitíl** ★★ (p. 305), towns where you can see traditional dancing, visit a tortilla factory, or watch villagers keeping ancient pottery-making traditions alive. Or are you intrigued by the thought of exploring 70-million-year-old limestone caves? At **Barra Honda National Park** ★ (p. 328) you can get lowered into an amazing stalactite-stalagmite forest.

The Beaches

Playa Guiones ★★★ kids is nearly 3km (2 miles) of soft, superb sand, with some of Costa Rica's very best surfing. The main access is off the main drag where **Coconut Harry's Surf Shop, Marlin Bill's** restaurant, and **Café de Paris** are clustered. This is the epicenter of the tourist area, but don't let that scare you off. This is laid-back Nosara, not go-go Tamarindo—you could end up driving right past it if you're not paying attention.

All your surfing needs can be met along this strip, starting with **Coconut Harry's** (☎ 682-0574; www.coconutharrys.com). Rent or buy surf or boogie boards, sign up for lessons, buy swimsuits and sunglasses—and get a snapshot with the icon himself: the ripped, longhaired, bleached-blonde Harry (assuming he's not at the beach catching a wave). Just down the road, **Nosara Surf Shop** (☎ 682-0186) has the largest selection of board rentals, including soft-top longboards for those first-timers nervous about cracking their noggins on hunks of fiberglass. We also like **Juan Surfo** ★★ (across from the Blew Dog Bar; ☎ 506/ 682-4041) because of well, Juan, who's the Tico version of Spicoli in *Fast Times at*

Theft alert

by Maggie Jacobus

Petty theft at the beach is rampant, so it's advisable to never leave things unattended. Although a guard is often posted at the main entrance to Guiones, one who is paid by area tourism organizations and who can watch your stuff, still use common sense and use this service at your own discretion. This service is free, but tips are appreciated. The guard can be found at the small rancho at the entrance to the beach.

Ridgemont High—wise cracking, super laid-back, and a superman on the board (he's also a terrific teacher). Three private lessons will cost about $40, group lessons about half that (it all depends on the size of the group).

The Guiones waves produce consistent top quality breaks nearly year-round (except the rainiest months, Oct and the first half of Nov). This makes it, like a, totally awesome experience for both beginners and veterans. Recently, "surf camps" have been on the upswing; an outstanding example is **Safari Surf School** ★★ (kids) (☎ 682-0573; www.safarisurfschool.com), which offers lessons by the day or week. Their patient teachers make them tops for families and kids wanting to learn. To flaunt your prowess to the poor schmucks back home, Safari will videotape you or get still shots from **Soul Arch** (in Guiones strip mall; ☎ 682-2006; www.soularchphoto.com). And they'll be sure to make you look good, which is so much more important than actually being good, don't you think?

Punta Guiones to the south offers a rare opportunity to walk to one of the world's few pink-sand beaches. Here you'll find tide pools perfect for snorkeling, which are protected by a small offshore barrier reef. But be mindful in your planning: You can only get here when the tide is out—and can't get back when it's in! Good shelling conditions exist throughout the year from Punta Guiones all the way to the point to the north.

For postcard scenery, stunning rock formations, tidal pools, and waves dramatically crashing through a blowhole, you'll want to head to **Playa Pelada** ★ (kids). It's small and more suited to swimming and snorkeling instead of surfing, and more popular for Tico picnics and campfires than tourists. One drawback, though, is that the beach pretty much disappears at high tide.

For that proverbial getting away from it all, it's black-sand **Playa Nosara,** where some say the surfing beats the pants off even Guiones. One reason it doesn't get as crowded is that the rocks and tricky breaks mean you've *reeeally* gotta know your stuff. Another is that the only way here is to walk across the mouth of the Nosara River at low tide. The beach attracts local fisherman, and you can watch them hand-toss enormous nets like their dads and granddads once did; come early in the morning, and you can buy the first catch of the day (this is true at Playa Pelada, too).

Nearby **San Juanillo** ★★, about a half-hour north of Nosara, is an off-the-beaten-track fishing village with an exquisite beach ideal for snorkeling and popular with the "seekers" from the nearby "spiritual eco-village" of PachaMama.

Toro, Toro Toro! A Bull's-Eye View of the Nosara Rodeo

by Maggie Jacobus

If you're here in mid-December (for the Esperanza fiesta), the end of January, or late March (for Nosara's festival), you're in for a Tico treat, Guancaste style.

The 3-day rodeos are where locals show their stuff, whether it's riding a bull, parading horses, competing in the pageant to be the fiesta queen, or shaking it up on the temporary dance floor. It's a major social event and community celebration, one for which the town spends weeks preparing. Food stands sell traditional favorites, carnival rides of possibly iffy safety, and vendors of crafts and cheap toys round out the scene.

The main event, of course, is the bull riding. You can watch safely away from the ring in the grandstands, or up close to the action, perched right on the bullring rail. A third option for the bravest of the brave (or the stupidest of the stupid, depending on your perspective) is to actually go *in* the ring. When my family and I visited last spring, we chose to join the circle of moderate thrill-seekers straddling the rail.

Over the course of a couple hours about a dozen different riders—on some nights professionals, on others total amateurs—showed their bull-riding staying power. Once a rider was bucked off, it was time for the "yahoos" inside the ring to strut. This consisted of running near, behind, or even in front of the bull (depending, possibly, on how many beers they'd had), risking catching its attention—or its horn.

The yahoos are an important part of the fiesta; the unofficial clowns. When they started their shenanigans those of us on the rail thought we must just get our money's worth and see someone get gored. This didn't happen, but we all got very excited when a yahoo would catch the ire of the bull, take chase, and, at the last moment, squeeze under the bottom rung of the ring, resulting in a fuming bull ramming the ring and, if we were lucky, running around it, hitting it several times with its head and horns. We were living on the edge, or at least the edge of the ring. All of us spectators would scream in delight and lift our legs up into the air when the bull ran past (an act much more dangerous and likely to result in injury than the bull itself).

Eventually, the real cowboys came into the ring, roped the bull, and led it out—and we all got ready to do it all over again. Midway through, the festival queen candidates took a stroll around the ring (without bulls, of course) and the local show-horse group cantered in to display its fantastic steeds and do feats of skill and daring at lightning speed. The evening wrapped up with blaring dance music that thumped away into the wee hours of the morning, turning us all into midnight cowboys.

Close Encounters of the Turtle Kind

by Maggie Jacobus

One March evening, we received *the* call: Olive Ridleys were nesting at Ostional.

My husband and I and our three boys—ages 7, 9, and 11—quickly headed off in the dark of night to witness this amazing event. The adventure began with the drive as we barreled over the bumps and splashed through the rivers in our 4-wheel-drive truck. When we arrived, we checked in at **Associacíon Desarrollo Integral de Ostional (ADIO)** headquarters, a small one-room shack on the side of the road at the entrance to the beach. There, we connected with an ADIO guide who handed us each a flashlight and a piece of red cellophane to put over it. Bright lights disturb the nesting, which is the main reason there is no development allowed near the beach; the lights from buildings would drive away the turtles.

As we walked, our guide softly shared facts about the Olive Ridleys: they are about 70cm long and weigh about 45 kilos, making them some of the smallest of the sea turtles. When she told us that this beach is one of *the* most important nesting spots in the *world* for these turtles, we felt privileged indeed to be here. After just a couple minutes of walking we were on a wide-open expanse of beach with the waves lapping gently a few meters away. Standing hushed, we could make out another faint sound, a rhythmic scratching noise and then a thump or two. Digging! A turtle was at work nearby.

The flashlights are used only when absolutely necessary, so it was up to us to play a version of blind man's bluff in the darkness to search out the turtle by its sounds. Suddenly, my youngest son noticed a lump in the sand the size of a half-inflated beach ball. Bingo! We cautiously picked our way over to a mama turtle.

Exploring Nature

Costa Rica is famous for the life-changing chance to get up close and personal with wildlife, and the most impressive example in Nosara are the seasonal synchronized nestings *(arribadas)* and hatchings of Olive Ridley turtles at **Playa Ostional** ★★★ 🧒. Though it might be tricky to time perfectly with your visit, the famed *arribadas* of up to a million of these grand creatures over just a few weeks is one of nature's most awesome sights. If you're here July through December—the peak being August and September, you can't hit the beach on your own, but you can sign up for a nighttime tour through any hotel or the **Asociacíon Desarrollo Integral de Ostional (ADIO; ☎ 682-0470; http://ostionalcr.tripod.com).** The entrance and guide fees will run $21. Contact them as soon as you arrive in Nosara, and they'll give you a call if and when it happens.

Crouching just inches away from this large, ancient-looking animal, we watched her methodically and dexterously dig a hole with her back flippers, back her behind up to it, and lay dozens of white, rubbery, Ping-Pong ball–sized eggs. We were spellbound. The guides are vigilant, making sure visitors don't disrupt the process. But as long as you're respectful, you can get right in there. And in there we were: close enough to get sand thrown in our faces while she dug, and to see the gleaming white eggs plop down into the hole.

When finished, the turtle meticulously covered her nest, taking extra care to disguise it from predators. Then she ambled off in the dark to swim thousands of miles away, never to see her youngsters hatch several weeks later.

On another occasion we had the opportunity to observe thousands of baby Olive Ridleys struggle out of their shells. It was an equally thrilling sight to behold. As the kids said, "There's a volcano of turtles exploding out of the ground!" Indeed, they seemed to be bursting out from their sandy nest just below the surface, wriggling over each other, and then racing off to the ocean, finding it by pure instinct. At times our kids even got into the act, gently guiding a few wayward wee ones toward their new, watery abode. A decade or so later, these very same turtles will return to this exact beach to lay *their* eggs, recognizing the site by its smell.

This hands-on interaction with nature is a lesson my boys would never receive in a classroom and is one they will forever remember (as will I). It's this type of "up-close-and-personal" encounter that's exactly what you dream of experiencing when coming to Costa Rica. If you "get the call"—take it! It'll be a top highlight of your trip.

Each *arribada* lasts from 3 to 10 days, and anywhere from 5 to 10 happen during the year; yielding a grand total of up to 30 million eggs annually. Depending on your luck, you might hit the jackpot and witness an *arribada* where almost every grain of sand seems to be covered by female Olive Ridley turtles (about 30 inches long with, yep, an olive-color shell) in various stages of the nesting process. These hard-shelled honeys use their flippers to burrow into the sand, deposit up to 100 eggs, then fill in the new nests. Even if you miss the main event, chances are you'll see at least a few turtles nesting.

The tour itself is a bit of an adventure, since getting to Ostional in the rainy season, when the majority of the *arribadas* happen, means either you or your driver will be splashing across the Nosara and Montaña rivers at night. The refuge office transforms into a turtle central command of sorts, with a contingent of young locals (some still in school) on hand to take tourists to turtles. Poaching by

A Local's Guide to Getting Connected in Nosara

by Maggie Jacobus

Nosara is one of those places where beguiled visitors start playing the Traveler Fantasy Game. You know the one: "I could live here. I really could. I'm going home and quitting my job . . . ." You may not pull the trigger like I did, but you can spend a few days living the dream while you're in town. Let me tell you how.

String Yourself Along What could be more Jack Johnson than playing guitar in a surfer town? Bill MacPherson (www.billmacpherson.net), a pro musician, teacher, and Nosara resident by way of the U.S. and Congo, will work with you whether you're a rank beginner or an advanced student aiming for the next level, whatever. Also known as Billy Rio, his Medicine Show band does local gigs nearly every night of the week (see "Nightlife," above), and he'll sometimes invite his students to sit in.

Try Some Nosara Hold 'Em Most Monday nights are poker night for the local gang. Game location, however, is subject to change. Check in with Coconut Harry (if he's not at his shop, he'll be on the beach at sunset). At press time, Texas Hold 'Em was the game, Tutti's Place, a bar/restaurant at Club Guiones was the name (it's just under 150m/500 ft. south and across the road from the yoga institute). Sometimes Tutti's runs Latin dance classes, but not during poker.

Box with a Champ Tiger Brenda, as she's known around town, is a former world championship boxer who now lives in Nosara and holds classes for kids and adults in boxing, exercise, and body sculpting at **The Enchanted Forest** 🧒 (682-0621; tigerboxer@hotmail.com). Personal training and massage are available as well. Kids (ages 4–6 and 7–12) get a kick out of

locals has been a problem in the past, but these kids have instead been trained to patrol the beaches; in return, they and their families get to take a small number of eggs during the first couple of nights of each nesting period (eggs that would probably not survive anyway, since turtle-moms-come-lately often end up digging up the nests of earlier ones). If you're here a couple of months later, you can enjoy a sight that's, if anything, even more moving: the same beach teeming with turtle tots wriggling out of their shells and racing to the ocean. The drill is the same for tours.

A sunset horseback ride on the beach, across the Nosara River and through the mangrove thicket and open plains is both educational and spectacular. German couple HaWe and Beata run **Boca Nosara Tours** (☎ 682-0610; 150m/490 ft. below Lagarta Lodge; $60 per person [6 max] for a 3½-hour trip, prices vary for fewer people), expertly guiding riders on their beautiful steeds, all the while providing running (er, riding) commentary on the nature all around. The horses are well trained so no riding experience is necessary, but children under the age of 8 are not accepted.

her classes because they're part gymnastics, part boxing, part circus, and led by a really fun lady with a bunch of tiger stripe tattoos all over her body. (She got one for each fight she won. Clearly, she won a lot.)

Hit the Rodeo Slip on your jeans and cowboy hat and head to a hootenanny, as authentic and local as they come. In late January and the end of March, Nosara holds its rodeo/bull riding festival, a traditional event akin to a U.S. county fair, that is a sight to behold (p. 317). In mid-December, the rodeo in the nearby town of Esperanza feels even more local (meaning fewer *turistas*).

Gab Over Groceries The Mini Super Delicias del Mundo in Playa Guiones (down the road from Blew Dog's) is the place to check your e-mail (if you must) or stock up on all those delectable indulgences you've been missing from home like organic almond nut butter (it caters to foreigners, so you'll find stuff no Tico would ever buy). And since grocery shopping in Nosara is a social event, feel free to chat up your fellow shoppers all the while.

Ogle the Sunset Around 5:30pm a magical phenomenon unfolds. Like so many Olive Ridley turtles mysteriously called ashore, people begin quietly gathering on Playa Guiones from the main access point to stare at the gorgeous sunset ★★★ 🧒. From Ticos to tourists, wave riders to retirees, pretty much the entire community makes a ritual of it.

Don't Bother with Last Names You may have noticed that few local expats have last names; at least that anybody knows. Instead, we have colorful monikers like Jungle Joe, Coconut Harry, and Tiger Brenda. Stick around long enough and you'll get one, too.

Likewise, a laid-back kayak float down the Nosara River with **Jungle Joe of Iguana Tours** (☎ 682-0450) is a relaxing way to spot monkeys, tropical birds, and iguanas—even the occasional croc sunning on the banks. Joe, an American late of Key West (and he has that Key West bonhomie to prove it), also leads easy hikes to the Mala Noche waterfalls (keep your eyes peeled for the above animals, minus the crocs, and coatimundis, armadillos, pelicans, maybe even a jaguarundi, a wild cat that looks like a mini-jaguar). And he can arrange private or semiprivate Spanish lessons with a few weeks' notice.

NIGHTLIFE

Clubbers and one-arm-bandit victims, why are you still even reading this? The scene in Nosara would probably put you to sleep, but lower-key types will dig how casual, friendly, and small town it is—when out, you're sure to recognize people from the beach that day or the bar the night before. Much of the weeknight action centers around the local cover band, The Medicine Show (Tues at the Gilded Iguana, Thurs at Blew Dog's, Sun at Casa Toucan).

A weeknight highlight is live-music Tuesdays at **The Gilded Iguana** ⭐⭐ (kids) (300m/985 ft. from the beach; ☎ 682-0259; www.gildediguana.com). The restaurant/bar/hotel of this popular, long-time Playa Guiones hotel revs up early—the older crowd and families start streaming in around 6pm for some of the best food in the area (reservations really recommended), and the folk, jazz, and rock sets get going as of 7:30. Jungle Joe is one of the star acts most nights; when he's not leading hikes, he's playing jazz and folk. Unlike Blew Dog's or the Tropicana, which cater to the 20-something set, this place is popular with practically everybody from cradle to grave.

Blew Dog's Surf Club ⭐ (down the road from the Gilded Iguana; ☎ 682-0080; www.blewdogs.com) in Guiones draws a young, hip, crowd of Ticos, tourists expats, and especially surfers. The pool table is a hot commodity, and those not sinking them are chowing down on good Mexicanoid grub and washing it down with gallons of Imperial *cerveza* or Centenario rum. The joint is at its most jumpin' Thursday nights when live music starts at 8pm (buy the band shots of Flor de Caña Nicaraguan rum and they'll play your favorite song—or kill it trying).

On Saturday night, soak up some real local flavor along with your brews at Bocas de Nosara's **Tropicana Disco** (across from the soccer field; ☎ 682-0140), where Ticos outnumber tourists by a good three to one. Visitors are very welcome, though—especially the ones willing to get down and *baila,* baby. DJs spin lots of Latin—cumbia, salsa, reggaetón—but there's also reggae and occasional live acts. Things don't get going until at least 10:30pm, and the last drunk will probably stumble out around 3am.

THE "OTHER" NOSARA

Costa Rica is fast becoming known as one of the world's big yoga meccas, with hundreds of retreats, seminars, and ongoing programs around the country each year. The main spot for karma chameleons hereabouts is the beautiful **Nosara Yoga Institute** ⭐⭐ (main road south of Café de Paris; ☎ 682-9971, or 866/439-4704 in the U.S.; www.nosarayoga.com), reached by a 5-minute stroll down a path behind Harbor Reef. One of its yoga platforms is nestled in the treetops for some awesome arboreal asanas. It's mostly a teacher training center but also hosts programs for the rest of us, typically starting around $1,000 a week, including off-premises room and board. Much less pricey, and some 11km (7 miles) north, between San Juanillo and Ostional, there's also **PachaMama** ⭐ (road to Tamarindo; ☎ 289-7081; www.pachamama.com), a "spiritual eco-village" where 2 weeks of on-premises lodging and veggie victuals runs just $560, and half that for teens (jeez, you'd think they eat 'em out of ashram and home).

PLAYA SAMARA & PLAYA CARRILLO

Much smaller than Nosara up the coast, Sámara is a zesty beach town on a long horseshoe bay with shimmering, silken sands—what many people picture when fantasizing about living the tropical life. In fact, plenty of Costa Rica beach aficionados call Sámara their top choice.

Unlike much of Costa Rica's northern Pacific coast, the clear, calm waters here are swell for swimming and kid-safe, since a lot of the surf is broken by Chora Island and a coral reef (super for snorkeling and sea kayaking). Drive up or down the coastal road and you'll come across other beaches—like Playa Carrillo 15 minutes south—made even more spectacular by the fact that they're practically deserted and untouched. You want to get far from the maddening crowd? Go for Carrillo.

For a bodacious beach plus a bit of action, Sámara's a good choice—it hasn't turned into Tamarindo but it has become one of Guanacaste's most easily reached beach areas thanks to a well-paved road (yes! A well-paved road! In Costa Rica!) and the new Tempisque River bridge across the Gulf of Nicoya. That and a respectable number of lodging and dining bargains has helped make Sámara more and more popular with backpackers and Ticos from families to party boys and girls who really kick it into gear on weekends.

GETTING TO & AROUND PLAYA SAMARA
By Air

The quickest way to get to the area is flying from San José's Juan Santamaría International Airport into Carillo (about 15 min. south of Sámara). **Sansa** (☎ 221-9414; www.flysansa.com) has hour-long flights leaving daily at 8:40 and 11:30am; the fare is $78 each way.

By Bus

Express buses (☎ 221-2666), costing $6 each way, leave for Sámara from San José (Calle 14, between avs. 3 and 5) at 12:30 and 6pm daily, taking 5 hours. A bit comfier and more convenient (picking you up at most hotels), the 7am daily bus run by **Gray Line** (☎ 220-2126; www.graylinecostarica.com) costs $29, as does **Interbus** (☎ 283-5573; www.interbusonline.com), which leaves the San José area every day at 8:15am (for kids, though, Interbus is $15).

By Car

From San José, take the Interamerican Highway west and follow the signs for Liberia. Take the turn off for the Río Tempisque River bridge, after which you'll follow the signs for Nicoya. Once you're through Nicoya, Sámara is about 35km (22 miles) southwest. The entire trip should take 4½ hours.

Getting Around

There's one main strip leading to the ocean, with a road at the end heading south and lined with a few beachfront restaurants and hotels. You can walk to most places around town. If you need to hire a taxi to reach nearby attractions or towards Playa Carrillo, you can simply flag one down along the main strip or ask one of the hotels to call one for you.

ACCOMMODATIONS, BOTH STANDARD & NOT
Vacation Rentals

Both Sámara and Playa Carrillo are very accessible when it comes to vacation rentals—you'll pretty much have your pick right on the beach, in the village, or up in the hills, and most of the time for less than $2,000 a week. Check the owner-listed websites as well as **www.samarabeach.com**, a general guide to

Sámara which lists a few properties. You can also try **Exclusive Escapes Costa Rica** (☎ 898-8640; www.exclusiveescapescr.com), an agency handling 10 area houses and 7 apartments; rates range from $300 to $1,500. Its best deal is undoubtedly the **The Beach House,** a two-house property with three bedrooms and two-and-a-half baths for only $300 a week in high season for up to two people, $600 for larger groups up to a dozen. Nice place, but the best part is the location, right on Sámara beach, close to everything (**Shake Joe's** restaurant is right next door).

Hotels

IN & AROUND SAMARA

$ On the way into town, the hillside **Entre Dos Aguas B & B** ★★ (100m/330 ft. from town and 200m/660 ft. from the beach; 656-0641; www.samara.net.ms; cash only) is cutely rustic yet surprisingly upscale-feeling considering that doubles go for as little as $35 a night in season. The seven whitewashed rooms are fresh and spacious (several sleep up to four; all have ceiling fans, not A/C), but the highlight's a private bath with artistic decor using natural stone and driftwood—definitely among the hippest bathrooms we've seen in Costa Rica. Owners Sara and Thomas make you feel right at home, as does the whole place, with its land-scaped pool area, inviting hammocks, free Internet, and resident monkey.

$–$$ Also up on the hillside, the **Hotel Belvedere** ★ (100m/330 ft. east of Pulpería San Rafael; ☎ 656-0213; www.samara-costarica.com; MC, V) is run by Michaela Landwehr and Manfred Link, who came to Costa Rica in 1991 from near Stuttgart, Germany. Several rooms have boffo views of Sámara Bay, and if you've just gotta have your A/C, this might be better than Entre Dos Aguas, since most of its 20 pleasant and spotless units on two floors have it, along with solar-heated showers and small fridges. Doubles start at $45 in season, and there are a couple of efficiency apartments for $75. We just love the breezy breakfast terrace and pool/Jacuzzi area with two pools, one of them nice and big.

$$ If you're in the market for something in a more midsize resort, the **Hotel Giada** (main street near access to Sámara beach; ☎ 656-0132, 888/790-5264 in the U.S./Canada; www.hotelgiada.net; MC, V, AE) is a *bella cosa* indeed (the own-ers are Italian, just like its popular trattoria/pizzeria, which opens onto the side-walk). This is a Mediterranean-flavored affair with a great tropical-feeling pool area and two dozen big, cheerful rooms with balconies and A/C. The walls are a mite thin and the bathrooms could be a little spiffier, but overall we can say the Giada wins on location, services, vibe, and affordability (doubles start at $65 in season, including breakfast). Parents take note: Toddlers younger than 5 stay free, ages 5 to 12 are half price.

IN & AROUND PLAYA CARRILLO

$$ A 5-minute stroll from the water's edge, the **Hotel Esperanza** (just under .5km/⅓ mile from the beach; ☎ 656-0564; www.hotelesperanza.com; MC, V) is a friendly Carrillo favorite that's gotten a bit of a revamp under new owners, Americans Dennis and Becky Clifton. New mattresses, satellite TV, phones, mini-bars, and A/C adorn its seven clean, bright rooms, and the popular El Ginger restaurant now serves all meals, with a new menu focusing on Costa Rican fare

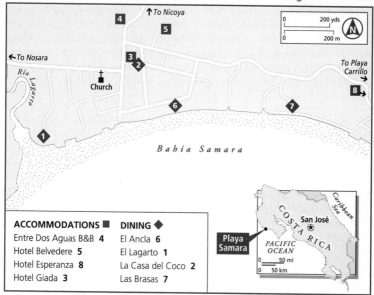

ACCOMMODATIONS ■

Entre Dos Aguas B&B **4**
Hotel Belvedere **5**
Hotel Esperanza **8**
Hotel Giada **3**

DINING ◆

El Ancla **6**
El Lagarto **1**
La Casa del Coco **2**
Las Brasas **7**

with an international twist. And best of all is the new pool, with an attached Jacuzzi cascading into it. Not bad for $93 double (including breakfast).

DINING FOR ALL TASTES

Young Ticos, families, and budget-conscious gringos love Sámara not just for the beach, cheap *cabinas,* and hopping bar scene, but the yummy stuff you can get here for just a modest clutch of *colones.* There's a lot to choose from, much of it seafood in laid-back settings. Most of the hotels have their own dining rooms, and there are plenty of inexpensive *sodas* all along the main strip.

Two particular local favorites, right on the beach, are the **Soda Sheriff Rustic** (sheriff as in police chief, the owner) and **Jardín Marino.** They're barely more than jumbles of plastic tables and chairs in front of concrete buildings, but they serve tasty, heaping *casados* (grilled fish or meat with rice, beans, and plantains) for less than $4. After dinner, the sweet of tooth should get over to **Coco Loco** (☎ 656-0820) on the main strip for homemade ice cream or a fresh-fruit smoothie.

$$ Saunter off the beach and into the thatch-roofed, waterfront **El Ancla** ★ (173m/575 ft. east of the main beach entrance; ☎ 656-0254 or 656-0716; Fri–Wed 11am–11pm; cash only) for bodacious bay views and fresh-caught mahimahi, marlin, tuna, and so forth, all cooked up in a variety of creative styles. Expect to pay between $8 and $10 for a plate. For something lighter, we'd go for the tangy ceviche washed down with an Imperial beer.

$$–$$$ A beachfront spot whose big thing is Tico-style barbecue is **El Lagarto** ★ (200m/660 ft. west of main beach entrance; ☎ 656-0750; daily 5:30–10pm or

11pm, depending on business; AE, D, MC, V). The dinner scene is pretty peppy—what with the festive music, colorful hanging piñatas, and cocktail-swilling clientele—and the spice-rubbed chicken, steak, and fish grilled in an open pit in the sand will have you drooling (assuming you aren't already there after a few margaritas). Most dishes run between $10 and $15, with a few pricier options. On weekends the place shoehorns 'em in for the live bands. El Lagarto opens at 2pm, but only serves drinks earlier in the day.

$$–$$$ Local seafood mixes with Spanish cuisine at **Las Brasas** (on main road into Sámara; ☎ 656-0546 or 656-0250; Tues–Sun noon–11pm; MC, V), an open-air spot overlooking the Sámara Bay, where the service manages to be casual and attentive. We loved the whole fish served *a la catalana* (in a thick stew of tomatoes, onions, shrimp, and parsley, $6.75), even though it was too much for us to finish; the house gazpacho ($4) is a treat, too. And the wine list of Spanish vintages is better than you'd ever imagine for a little town on the Costa Rican coast. Most entrees start at $10, though the lobster and paella can push up toward the $20 mark.

$$–$$$ For a lively tropical-garden atmosphere the **La Casa del Coco** ✹ 🧒 (main road; ☎ 656-0665; daily 11am–10pm; MC, V) is a treat at night, with its colored lights and polished hardwood-and-bamboo tables. The eclectic menu has a little something for everyone (nachos, chicken in coconut curry, whole lobster steamed with garlic), and entrees run about $9 to $16. To wash it down, order a glass of house sangria and/or a *batido* (fresh-fruit shake). Though it's best known for dinner, this is also one of few Sámara eateries where you can get American-style breakfast goodies like pancakes topped with fresh fruit.

WHY YOU'RE HERE: THE TOP SIGHTS & ATTRACTIONS

It kind of goes without saying that "it's the beaches, stupid"—I mean, as you fly or drive in, the sight of the tall palms swaying against the talcum-powdery sands and the crystal-clear, drop-dead-gorgeous waters of the Pacific is positively stupefying. As I mentioned above, Chora Island, nearby headlands, and a barrier reef make the shallow waters calm and swimmable by just about anyone—in fact, it's often been tagged as one of the safest beaches in Costa Rica, and you'll see swimmers, snorkelers, windsurfers, and kayakers all over the place. Away from the water, there's a canopy tour right in town.

Or you can take a few great little day trips (the good roads in and out of Sámara get you efficiently within an hour or two to places like the caves of **Barra Honda National Park** ✹✹ (p. 328), the cute folkloric town of **Santa Cruz** (p. 305), and **Guaitíl** ✹✹, where you can visit local artisans crafting pottery in the hundreds of years old tradition of the Chorotega Indians (p. 276). Or head north along the coast to **Nosara** ✹✹✹ (p. 307), one of Guanacaste's few real eco-tourism beaches, a lightly developed paradise teeming with wildlife (the most famous of which are the **Olive Ridley turtles** ✹✹✹ that come here to nest by the thousands; p. 318).

The Beaches

Playa Sámara ✹✹ 🧒 is a very pretty strand. Yes, in high season it can get busy, yet it rarely feels overcrowded. Five kilometers (3 miles) southeast down the coast, the next bay over from Sámara is palm-fringed **Playa Carrillo** ✪✪✪ 🧒. It's exquisite and sleepier than Sámara (sometimes practically deserted), but there's also a fishing town on the south side of the bay with some tourist services and places to stay.

And there are sandy gems along this coast that are even less touristed, such as coral-hued **Playa Buena Vista** and **Playa Barrigona** (aka **Playa Dorada**), down dirt roads just over a half-mile north of Sámara (you can drive or take a taxi, which will cost at least $10). Southeast some 13km (8 miles) past Playa Carrillo, the bay of **Punta Islita** is home to a beautiful black-sand beach a half-mile long; a village with an open-air art museum; and the fancy-schmancy **Hotel Punta Islita,** which starts at over $200 a night. Getting here is a roller-coaster of a drive, which includes crossing the Tempisque River (in the rainy season it can be impassable). But especially if you're a connoisseur of views, the sweeping vistas from the beach and the hills above are worth it. We recommend savoring both panorama and $3- to $5-a-plate Tico lunch or dinner at the **Restaurant Mirador Barranquilla** (right on the beach; Wed–Mon 11am–10pm). Sunsets out here are to die for—just be extra careful driving back at night, and also note that there's not a gas station anywhere along the way.

Watersports

Carrillo Tours 🧒 (near the Super Sámara market; second location in Carillo; ☎ 656-0543; www.carrillotours.com) is one of the best local outfitters on and in the water. These guys can take you for a **sea-kayak paddle** 🧒 out to the reef off **Isla Chora** for some great **snorkeling** ✷ (last time here I saw a startlingly vibrant purple starfish, among other things) followed by soft drinks and fruit on the island's beach. Or kayak down the mangroves of the Río Ora to spot monkeys, birds, iguanas, and more. In season, there are dolphin-watching excursions and trips up to see the nesting sea turtles.

Sportfishing is a major draw for those who fancy that action. Like Garza, there is no marina, so the experience is more *rustico,* which adds to the adventure. Best outfits: **Samara Sport Fishing** (☎ 656-0589) or **Kingfisher** (☎ 656-0091).

For Putt's Sake

Okay, it may be kind of a gringo thing to do, but if the kids are getting restless at night, one solution is to round 'em up and head to Puerto Carrillo for a round of minigolf at the **Onda Latina** 🧒 (next to the Puerto Carillo church; ☎ 656-0434; http://minigolfondalatina.bravehost.com; Thurs–Tues 8am–10pm). Set near the beautiful Playa Carrillo beach, the Onda Latina has a well-lit 18-hole minigolf course as well as a bocce court (you can even ask owners Fiorella and Gabriel to set up a tournament). After you've swung up a sweat, a cafeteria serves espresso, pastries, and ice cream, along with a few basic dishes.

Into the Wild, Blue Yonder

by Maggie Jacobus

Unique to this region, the fixed wing, ultralight flights of the **Flying Crocodile** ★★ (kids) (☎ 656-0153—call to check wind conditions and make a reservation) offer exhilarating soars over the sea and countryside.

We first tried them because my oldest son has always wanted to fly, as in, wishing he had wings. So for his 11th birthday, his wish was granted. We arrived midmorning to take advantage of a nearly windless, sunny day and he stepped into what was essentially a hang glider with a motor (you also get to sit upright, versus lying on your stomach). Experienced German-born pilot Guido operated the machine while my son just enjoyed the ride. He and the pilot flew over the beach, sighting crocodiles, turtles, and more; then over the hills where they were greeted by blustery winds that tossed them about a bit. His after-flight report was succinct: "That was COOL!!!!" he shouted. And then as an afterthought, "and a little scary." Like so many experiences in Costa Rica.

Flying lessons are also available.

Canopy Tour

If you're not wandering far afield but don't want to miss the by-now-quintessential ziplines of Costa Rica, you can find the family-owned **Wing Nuts Canopy Tour** (☎ 656-0153; www.samarabeach.com/wingnuts) right on Sámara beach. It's not the most extensive or high-flying outfit of its kind; you're not really in dense forest canopy; and it's a little pricey for what you get ($50 a head, not counting family discounts, for just a dozen platforms). The sea views are nice and the location certainly convenient, but if you're planning to stay elsewhere in Costa Rica, I'd look into other canopy tours before committing to this one.

DAY TRIPS

Top of the list is one of this country's most unique geological formations, a 1½-hour drive inland from Sámara. Originally mistaken for an active volcano—locals figured the whirring of bat wings and the pungent aroma of guano (bat poop) were telltale signs of volcanic rumblings—the intricate maze of limestone caves in the 23-sq.-km (9-sq.-mile) **Barra Honda National Park** ★★ (63km/39 miles north of Sámara; ☎ 685-5267 or 686-6760; www.costarica-nationalparks.com/barrahondanationalpark.html; daily 8am–sunset; $7) wasn't discovered until the '60s. Some 200m (650 ft.) and deeper, these caverns were formed by moving water as the peak rose out of the sea millions of years ago. Maps and info are available at the **ranger's station** near the park entrance and at an off-site park office in the town of Nicoya (across from the colonial church; ☎ 686-6760; Mon–Fri 7am–4pm).

Even today, only about half the caves have been explored, and only one is open to the public, the pretty vertical **Cueva Terciopelo** ("Velvet Cave"; daily

7am–1pm), where you get to see all manner of sometimes funkily named formations (cave grapes, rose, popcorn, sharks' teeth, fried-egg-shape stalagmites, and more). You can go down even if you don't know a maillon from an earring (though if you're claustrophobic, scared of heights, or creeped out by bats, you might want to think twice). What you need to do is at the park entrance hire a spelunking guide ($16 for up to four people); the **Asociación de Guías Ecologistas** (☎ 659-1551) rents equipment ($12) if you don't have your own.

If it all sounds a little too hardcore (or if you're under 12, the minimum age to be allowed down into Terciopelo), there's another interesting cavern here called La Cuevita, where rangers lead nature hikes. And the park trails are great for **bird-watching** and **hiking;** the Los Laureles trail to Terciopelo continues on for almost another couple of miles up to the 355m (1,184-ft.) summit plateau, where you'll see sweeping panoramas over the Gulf of Nicoya and Tempisque valley. Another hike leads to a neat-o stepped waterfall called **La Cascada,** where you can take a dip.

ATTENTION, SHOPPERS!

Typical beach-town woodcarvings, pottery, and beachwear abound in the tourist shops along the main drag. One of the more interesting beach shops is **Biolife Macrobiótica** (main street; ☎ 656-0503; AE, D, MC, V), which, besides more standard souvenirs, sells cosmetics and beauty products created from the local forests and seas of Costa Rica; organic foods; and a few watercolors of the sea and local villages.

There are also several very good local galleries. One that's right on the sand is the **Jamie Koss Art Gallery** ★ (next to Las Brisas del Pacífico Hotel; ☎ 656-0284; MC, V; daily 9am–3pm, but call first as the owner sometimes takes the day off if he's feeling creative). A well-known Tico artist for more than 30 years, Koss paints Kandinsky-esque takes on local people and their lives. The vivid oil paintings are sold unframed in three sizes.

Another local artist with a beach stand is German-born **Barbara Rieche,** who studied with Koss and other major Costa Rican artists. Her boldly colored acrylic-on-canvas pieces depict Nicoya women in tropical or traditional settings. You'll usually find her at a stand along the beach.

A couple of young guys called Leo and El Flaco ("Slim") run the snappy little **Galería Sámara Arte Dragonfly** (main street; ☎ 656-0964; AE, D, MC, V; noon–9:30pm), using driftwood and other found materials to craft all kinds of jewelry, paintings, carvings, masks, and other creations. Swing by for special exhibits, info about the local haps, or even a (temporary) henna tattoo.

NIGHTLIFE

The high season is noticeably more happening than low, but any time of the year the buzziest place in town is usually **La Góndola** (on the main street 173m/575 ft. from the beach; no phone). Live bands are usually on the roster here, and loud partying is always on the roster. If body shots on the bar aren't your style, you can always shoot pool or throw a game of darts. A similar but less hopped-up alternative is **Bar Las Olas** (on the beach 250m/820 ft. from the main street; no phone), which also stays open late and has pool and other games. Local DJs often pass through on the weekends, and midweek it's fab for a mellow *cerveza* or two.

MONTEZUMA & MALPAIS ✶

Heading toward the southern tip of the Nicoya Peninsula, it gets greener (more rainfall than in northern Guanacaste) and the scenery more dramatic, with exuberant jungle vegetation, waterfalls, rock formations, and awesome beaches. The mostly unpaved roads down here are terrible—which is one reason mass tourism hasn't moved in yet and the two coolest beach towns, Montezuma and Malpaís, have held on to their laid-back, boho vibe (think Berkeley-by-the-Beach).

At the same time, in these towns it sometimes feels like you only meet foreigners—especially Euro backpackers, surfers, and neo-hippies. There's overlap between the two, but I'd have to say picturesque Montezuma has a younger feel; it's become a practically mandatory stopover on the international wandering-slacker circuit, and crunchy New-Age cafes, surf shops, and art galleries clog the downtown. A little farther down the road, Malpaís (sometimes spelled "Mal País") covers the area including the villages of Malpaís, Santa Teresa, and Playa Carmen. It caters more toward mature types rejuvenating on luxe retreats and feels more meditative than margarita-mad. Another spot worth mentioning is Playa Tambor, but apart from a couple of big resorts, Tambor's something of a backwater, mostly a pit stop for folks on their way to Montezuma and Malpaís. Meanwhile, the main "sight" in this neck of the Nicoya is the **Cabo Blanco Wildlife Refuge** ✶, just below Malpaís at the peninsula's southeastern tippy-tip and known for its ever-green forests.

GETTING TO & AROUND MONTEZUMA

Travel down here is slow and tough and the few roads are pretty lousy, so if you can afford to fly in, you'll save tons of time and your vacation will probably go much more smoothly. But if saving money trumps all else, the bus is a good bet; plus you'll get to see some great scenery around Tambor, Cóbano, and in between. It's easier to get here via Puntarenas than Guanacaste, because south Nicoya is part of the Puntarenas Province.

By Air

The local airstrip is near Tambor, 18km (11 miles) away. During high season, **Nature Air** (☎ 299-6000, 800-235-9272 in the U.S. and Canada; www.natureair. com) runs a daily flight out of San José's Tobías Bolaños International Airport in Pavas at 12:30pm; the trip takes a half-hour and costs $69 one-way. For $63 each way, **Sansa** (☎ 221-9414; www.flysansa.com) has 14 half-hour flights leaving Juan Santamaría International Airport every day (times include 8:20am, 10am, and 4:30pm). From Tambor, you can rent a car, catch a bus, or hire a cab ($15) for the half-hour ride to Montezuma.

By Bus

From San José, an **express bus** (☎ 222-0064) runs to Puntarenas, leaving daily every half-hour between 6am and 9pm from Calle 16 and Avenida 12. The fare is $3 and the trip will take just over 2 hours. From Puntarenas, take a ferry to Paquera, which leaves every 2 hours between 6am and 9pm. **La Paquereña ferry** (☎ 641-0515) crosses the Nicoya Gulf just three times daily from the pier behind the market (6am, 11:30am, and 3pm); fares cost $2. Be careful not to take the

The Jacó Water Taxi

Get out on the water, and take an hour-long ride in a covered water taxi from Jacó right into Montezuma for $35 per person; bikes and surfboards can be carted aboard for $10 per piece. **Zuma Tours** (☎ 642-0024; www. zumatours.net) is the operator. You'll leave at 7:45am from Playa Herradura, just north of Jacó; the return crossing leaves from the center of Montezuma at 6:30pm.

Naranjo ferry since it doesn't meet up with bus connections to Montezuma. Those buses meet **La Paquereña** when it docks; the fare is $3, and the 26km (16-mile) trip to Montezuma should take about 1½ hours.

By Car

From San Jóse, take the International Highway to Puntarenas and drive onto the ferry to Paquera. Avoid the Naranjo ferry since the road from Naranjo to Paquera is a mess and will add hours to your journey. During peak season, get there early since lines can be long; if you miss one ferry, you'll end up waiting 2 hours for the next one (call ahead for schedules, which change depending on season). The two ferry companies are **La Paquereña** (☎ 641-0515) and **Ferries to Paquera** (☎ 661-2084); the crossing takes an hour and a half and costs $10 for car and driver plus $1.50 for each passenger. From Paquera, follow signs to Montezuma for about an hour until you reach the village.

These days, by the way, you can also take the recently opened Tempisque River bridge. It's less direct than the above, but during peak season with its fearsome ferry lines and sold-out crossings, it could end up actually saving time. Take the Interamerican Highway west from San José, and about 47km (29 miles) past the Puntarenas turn-off take a left towards the bridge. Once over the river, head to Quebrada Honda, then south to Route 21. Follow signs for San Pablo, Jicaral, Lepanto, Playa Naranjo, and Paquera—but be careful, since the roadway can be rugged along this stretch. From Paquera, follow signs to Montezuma and you should be there in about an hour.

Getting Around

Most people bike or hike to the surrounding beaches, a few of which are inaccessible by road. Public transportation is limited, so getting your own car is an excellent idea. But in town, you can walk to most everything; for the rest, if you don't want to rent wheels, taxis are fairly cheap; plus you can also pick up rides at a surf camp or surf shop. In the easygoing local culture, a grin-garnished pretty-please and an offer of a few *colones* for gas can get you a long way.

GETTING TO & AROUND MALPAIS

As with Montezuma, you fly into Tambor or get yourself to the Puntarenas-Paquera ferry, then catch a bus, rent a car, or cab it. This part of the peninsula is even more remote, so you're going to need patience—by road it takes at least 5 hours, and that's in halfway decent conditions. Note that as the area gets more popular, more transport options come online; check with your hotel to see if it offers transfers.

By Bus

Follow the drill above for getting to Montezuma, and when your ferry pulls into Paquera, catch a bus headed south to Cóbano, with regular departures from 6am to 6pm. From Cóbano, buses down to Malpaís and Santa Teresa leave at 10:30am and 2:30pm, though schedules can vary (if you miss your bus, a cab from Cóbano costs around $12).

Several shuttle services run down here from San José for about $30, and can pick you up and drop you almost anywhere. The most popular and economical is **Surf Costa Rica** (☎ 888/427-7769 from the U.S. and Canada; www.surf-costarica. com).

By Car

Follow the above directions to Paquera. Off the ferry, signs will direct you southward to Playa Tambor, then Cóbano, which is an hour's drive. From Cóbano, you'll see signs to Santa Tereasa and Malpaís still farther south. The whole trip takes about 6 hours (the last 7km/4½ miles to Malpaís are a rough dirt road, so at the very least you should rent a four-wheel drive; during rainy season there's a chance it might be totally undriveable, so make a call or two to check out the road conditions before heading out). As you near the end, you'll get to an intersection; for Malpaís, hang a left and go about 3km (2 miles) north (for Santa Teresa you'll turn right for the same distance, and Playa Carmen's just in front of you).

Getting Around

If you're planning to hang mostly in the villages of Malpaís and/or Santa Teresa, you can pretty much get by walking, cabbing, or busing. Renting wheels is a better bet if you're planning to head over to Montezuma or to more remote beaches.

ACCOMMODATIONS, BOTH STANDARD & NOT
Vacation Rentals

A number of agencies we've already mentioned in this chapter offer rentals in this area; one that's locally based (and therefore more expert) is **Tropisphere** (☎ 642-0345 or 640-0710; www.tropisphere.com), with more than 30 properties in Montezuma, Malpaís, Santa Teresa, and other communities like Cabuya and Playa Hermosa. The digs run from sumptuous (a couple of fancy villas with all the trimmings run a cool grand a night—but they also sleep 10 to 15, so do the division and it's not bad at all) to simple (a one-bedroom wooden beach house for $400 a month).

Hotels
IN & AROUND MONTEZUMA
Clustered around several central streets are a variety of choices from full-service resorts to simple *cabinas.* For a superthrifty standby, you can always head just out

of town to Montezuma's first lodging, the **Pensión Lucy** (200m/660 ft. south of town; ☎ 642-0273; cash only), with an on-site eatery and still run by the same hospitable family. Although the two-story landmark facing the sea was renovated several years back, prices are still among the lowest in town (doubles from $18).

$ Both hotel and Spanish-language school, **Horizontes de Montezuma** ★★ (just over 1.5km/a mile north of town; ☎ 642-0534; www.horizontes-montezuma. com; cash only) is a seven-room charmer, inside a Victorian-style hilltop manse with French doors and a wraparound veranda. You've got a nice little pool to cool off in and botanical gardens for bird- or monkey-spotting; rooms are bright white (even most of the bedspreads are white), with lovely pieces of art here and there but simple in their amenities (private bath but no TV, phone, or A/C besides a ceiling fan). Most of the year doubles run $39 to $49; if you also want to learn *español*, lessons are $15 each and multiday courses start at $390 a week.

$–$$ An upscale-resort feel comes at affordable rates at **Los Mangos Hotel** ★★ (250m/820 ft. from public park; ☎ 642-0076; www.hotellosmangos.com; MC, V): the free-form lagoon pool with waterfall and Jacuzzi; the handsome yoga pavilion; the lush landscaping; the fine decor finishes. You can opt for one of the nine Bali-flavored bungalows scattered among mango trees for $74 a night, or save a bit in the two-story main building, with one of the six rooms with verandas and rocking chairs from $62. Save really big with two double rooms sharing one bathroom ($32). Drawbacks: no A/C, no TV/phone, and no restaurant (for that last one, a quick stroll into town or to nearby Amor de Mar, below).

$$ Another away-from-it-all paradise, just a 5-minute stroll from town, Ori and Richard Stocker's 11-room **Hotel Amor de Mar** ★ (300m/985 ft. southwest of town; ☎ 642-0262; www.amordemar.com; MC,V) is perched on a spectacular rocky point where the Montezuma River drops over a waterfall into the Pacific; nothing like lazing away an afternoon in a hammock, staring down the front lawn sloping to the rocky shore (swimming beaches are right nearby). Hardwood-paneled or white-stucco doubles start at $45 in season (with private bath on the ground floor or shared bath upstairs); a couple of kitchen-equipped bungalows sleep four to six for $170. Make it the second floor if you're into sleeping in (ground-floor units get dining-pavilion breakfast chatter).

$$ At the **Hotel El Jardín** ★ (100m/330 ft. from the beach; ☎ 642-0548; www.hoteleljardin.com; AE, DC, MC, V), you'll shell out a mite more than the local run of the mill, but in exchange you get a pretty cool combo of boutique feel; very central location; rooms with A/C and fridge; and killer ocean views (it's on a hillside right on the edge of town). El Jardín means "garden," and the grounds are indeed awash in fragrant, riotous flora, with indigenous-style sculptures scattered throughout; the newish pool and Jacuzzi are a true treat. The 15 rooms have nice rustic decor heavy on wood and tile (not to mention terraces with hammocks); they start at $73 in season. If you feel like splurging a bit, there are a couple of kitchen-equipped villas for $99 to $116, depending on the number of people.

IN & AROUND MALPAIS

Cute, affordable little hotels and lodges are scattered over a couple of miles in and around this fishing village, quieter than Montezuma and even teenier Santa Teresa just up the road. But that doesn't mean they're not popular; show up without reservations and you could find yourself forced to fork over more than you might want to in the likes of the **Flor Blanca** (☎ 640-0232; www.florblanca.com), which is gorgeous but starts around $435 a night in season.

$ I'd have to say the **Ritmo Tropical** ★ (main road to Malpaís; ☎ 640-0174; rtropical@racsa.co.cr; cash only) is this town's best moderate bet. Eleven pretty, red-tiled bungalows sleep two for $45 a night and you get privacy, private bath, and hot water (still not all that common in these parts) along with a surfboard rack and a shady terrace with chairs and hammocks; be sure to ask for a bungalow with an ocean view. Perky fans cool interiors tastefully tarted up with Polynesiana; and unlike at some other casual local digs, there's daily maid service. On-premises amenities include an affordable bar and Italian restaurant, but no pool.

$–$$ Over the years the **Malpaís Surf Camp and Resort** (main road to Malpaís; ☎ 640-0031; www.malpaissurfcamp.com; AE, MC, V), local ground zero for surfers and wannabes, has gotten to be something of a local institution. The friendly, laid-back vibe is great for connecting with fellow travelers, and the 4 hectares (10 acres) are jammed with perks like pool; workout room; rec area with pool tables, satellite TV, and a mechanical bull; a hopping bar/restaurant; and of course loads of surf gear rentals, lessons, and all the rest. The look is driftwood and *palapa* roofs, and the digs are basic but various, including bring-your-own-tent campsites ($7), shared-bath rooms ($30), open-air *palapa rachos* with hammocks ($45), up to villas with kitchens (from $85).

$$$ If it is within your karma to splurge, meditate on the possibility of the Buddhism-themed, beachfront **Milarepa Hotel** ★★ (2km/1¼ miles north of the school; ☎ 640-0023; www.milarepahotel.com; MC, V). Owned by a Frenchman, it's small but classy: four open-sided bamboo cabins have stone floors and Indonesian frame beds, exquisitely carved and draped with gauzy stuff, and a private bath but no phone, TV, or A/C. Besides the carefully raked beach out back, there's a nice pool, chic restaurant (see below), massage, and yoga—but be prepared to lay out $133 to $159 a night. "Master," you will say, "that is a bit steep." But did not Gautama teach that money, too, is impermanent?

DINING FOR ALL TASTES

In this part of Nicoya, you'll find typical Tico hole-in-the-wall diners known as *sodas* alongside top-dollar upscale cuisine. Be it humble or hoity-toity, though, the emphasis everywhere is on fresh local seafood and produce.

There are plenty of little cafes and food stands where you can grab grub on the fly for less than $10. A good example on one of Montezuma's busiest corners, is the **Café Iguana** (in front of Hotel Montezuma; ☎ 642-0422; daily 6am–10pm; cash only), where the people-watching is as tasty as the house ice cream, sandwiches on fresh crusty bread, coconut coffeecake, and local fruit juices. In Malpaís, scarf down garlic shrimp at picnic tables under a tin roof at **Piedra Mar** (1km/½mile from crossroad on the road into Malpaís; ☎ 640-0069; daily 8am–8pm; cash only), one of the oldest eateries in town (don't expect to pay more than $5).

$$–$$$ Mod Mediterranean takes center stage at the **Playa de los Artistas** ★ (270m/900 ft. south of Montezuma, near Los Mangos Hotel; ☎ 642-0920; Mon–Sat 5:30–10pm; cash only), where you dine at driftwood tables right on the sand. It's plenty romantic, and the daily-changing menu and nicely chosen, Italian-dominated wine list is pretty decent. Depending on what's in season and fresh out of the water, you might get tuna carpaccio with basil leaves, steamed lobster in clarified butter, or smoked fish with aioli; a wood-burning oven also turns out great focaccia pizzas. Entrees average $15 but portions are hefty and served family style.

$$$ The shtick is all-natural, hormone-free, and organic at **El Sano Banano** (main road, Montezuma center; ☎ 642-0920; daily 7am–10pm; AE, MC, V). Vegetarians fed up with endless rice and beans will happily tuck into the likes of curried vegetables with rice, but the rest of us will be very impressed with the fish and chicken dishes, while chocoholics shouldn't miss the semifrozen "mocha chiller"; most entrees run around $15. And by the way, flicks are shown nightly on a big screen (free with dinner), and if you're planning on catching it, instead of the outside terrace, grab an inside table with a good view of the screen.

$$$–$$$$ The Milarepa Hotel's cozy **Soma** ★★ (2km/1¼ miles north of the school, near the end of town in Malpaís; ☎ 640-0023; 7:30–10:30am [breakfast], 11:30am–2:30pm [lunch], 6:30–9:30pm [dinner]; cash only) pulls 'em in from all over southern Nicoya with its Zen vibe and Latin-inspired fusion. Bamboo tables poolside with potted palms create a tranquil setting. The daily-changing menu might include sashimi, garlic papaya soup, or seared tuna with plantains. Especially for a little beach town, it's amazing stuff, and dished in ample portions. But the price tag's a little splurgey—entrees can hit $23 and a bottle of wine $30, but the majority of dishes are in the $14 to $18 range.

$$$$ **Nectar** ★★★ (2km/1¼ miles north of the soccer field, Malpaís; ☎ 640-0232; www.florblanca.com; daily noon–10pm; MC, V, AE), the Flor Blanca resort's alfresco dining room, has outstanding service and ambience up the wazoo, including winsome water views. The Asian-inflected continental fare is top notch, too, with vegetarian and pasta options ($16) crowding the menu but goodies like grilled filet mignon (6 oz., $28) or barbecued shrimp ($26) also making regular appearances (a lot of it depends on the day's catch). In season, there's a daily sushi happy hour and a barbecue buffet with live local bands each Sunday.

WHY YOU'RE HERE: THE TOP SIGHTS & ATTRACTIONS

La playa and *las olas*, of course. Both Montezuma and Malpaís are youngish communities where most everything is played out on the sand—from beach pick-up games of soccer and ultimate Frisbee to bonfire parties and strolls down along the surf. In particular, the area's biggest draw is its **world-class surfing,** and in fact nonsurfers can sometimes feel a little left out socially. It has a lot to do with how the mix of gringos and Ticos connects—all the posturing and posing that can go along with surf culture, the tattooed bod-watching, and, of course, the hottest happy hours at the various bars.

The recent tourism boom has turbocharged the tour-company population, giving you lots of options for hopping onto a bus or a horse (or into a harness) to drink in the beauty of the area from different perspectives. To get the full scoop, check out **Montezuma Travel Adventures** (main road, next to El Sano Banano; ☎ 642-0808; www.montezumatraveladventures.com), which sells transfers and tours that run the gamut: horseback rides to various rivers, reef snorkeling, fishing, and sundry forays along the coast.

The Beaches

The sands dusting the tip of the southern Nicoya Peninsula are some of Guanacaste's most beautiful and secluded, thanks to the local lushness fed by higher rainfalls and much less development to screw things up. For both the Montezuma and Malpaís areas, we'll run through the beaches from north to south.

AROUND MONTEZUMA

The northernmost area strand (a 2-hour hike up from Montezuma) is **Playa Cocolito** 🗡, and lordy is it a beaut: pristine white sands, spectacular coves, breathtaking scenery, and a colorful cast of critters (especially early in the morning, when sand crabs scurry along and howler monkeys hoot from the jungles). A couple of miles before, you'll come across the area's main attraction, the **Cascada Cocolito** (aka **El Chorro**), where water crashes over a cliff into the Pacific. A few dozen feet before the waterfall you can grab a rest and a cold one at the beach stand selling food and fruit juices.

If a 2-hour trek is pushing it, try 30 to 45 minutes, to the next beach down, **Playa Grande** 🗡. With 3 broad, soft kilometers (2 miles) of white sand, dotted by palms and tall, skinny coconut trees, it's undeveloped (no cars allowed, even), and the crowd factor low—mostly folks into sunning their buns, if you get my drift, and surfing diehards riding swells that are consistently large and low on swimmers. Swimming here is good though—lots easier and safer than at Playa Montezuma. No vendors here, so bring drinks and eats, and be ready to take your trash back with you. And what are those odd piles of rocks you see along the way? Sculptures done by a local artist.

The biggest and most popular strand hereabouts is **Playa Montezuma** 🗡, stretching out from either side of the village. Punctuated with rocky outcroppings and colorful foliage, it's fetching but naturally more peopled with tattooed surfers, Euro backpackers, and locals. Folks dive in all along this stretch, but the part to the south of town (with the fishing boats) can get polluted from nearby businesses and houses, so you're much better off north. Also, before plunging in, you might want to ask about riptides and underwater rocks.

A brisk 2km (1¼-mile) walk south from Montezuma gets you to another lovely combo of white sand and turquoise waters, **Playa Las Manchas** 🗡. What gives this place its special personality is all the Italians—hang out on the sand or pop into at one of the small hotels nearby for a *birra* and a snack and *mio dio,* it's like Pisa with palm trees. The water's great for swimming, but high tide can mean riptide, so don't get carried away (ba-*dum*-bum). Snorkeling's awesome too—fin a few toward the right and look for an underwater canyon that's like a Grand

Central Station of puffer fish, rays, parrotfish, and dozens more tropical fish); there are plenty of places to rent gear in town. At low tide, check out the fish-and-mollusk-filled temporary "aquariums" that form among the rocks.

AROUND MALPAÍS

About 3km (2 miles) up the coast from Malpaís, the long, white beaches and beautifully curved waves of **Playa Santa Teresa** ✹✹ definitely get surfers stoked. It's actually a series of beaches, and wave riding here is better at low tide; waves are big and fast, probably not the greatest for beginners. Locals can direct you to legendary breaks like "Brunnelas," "La Lora," and "Roca Mar"; they're uncrowded, but you should ask where the underwater rocks are. You can get to some of these breaks right from the road, but for some of the gnarliest, you've got to hike a bit on paths through forests thick with gigantic, thorny *pochote* trees (some more than 200 years old).

The most popular surfing spot hereabouts is probably **Playa Carmen** ✹, just south of Santa Teresa (head straight through the crossroads at **Frank's Place** (p. 340). Long, slow waves make for a longer ride, with a sandy bottom to cushion wipeouts, and at the same time beginners get a leg up from less powerful riptides and beach breaks. A popular pizza joint right on the sand also sells beer, and so naturally that's where surfer dudes and dudettes meet up after the last wave.

Finally, closest to Malpaís, you can follow the signs to **Playa Mar Azul,** a picturesque cove where I guess the *mar* (sea) is considered particularly *azul* (blue). Whatever—the waves are fun and easy, and don't barrel as much as other spots, making this a great break for long-boarders; just stick to high tide, to stay out of the way of the underwater rocks.

Exploring Nature

WATERFALL WONDERLAND

Especially on the Montezuma side of the peninsula's tip, a major part of the area's allure are a number of spectacular waterfalls—Delicias, Buena Vista, Río Lajas, Río Ario, and more; you can find them on your own, or maybe save a little time by hiring a guide. In any case, at the top of your list should be the **Cascada Montezuma** ✹✹✹. South of town, about 20 to 30 minutes on foot, head past the Lucy and La Cascada hotels until you come to a little bridge. Cross the bridge, take an immediate left, and hike upstream (the trail sort of peters in and out) along a succession of cascading falls that drop up to 24m (80 ft.) into pools. It's one of Costa Rica's most impressive sights, but if you take a dip, it's AYOR—the rocks are slippery, and divers have sometimes ended up fitted for caskets.

A bit north of here, **El Chorro** ✹, a couple of miles down from Playa Cocolito (p. 336), is a cinematic spot whose waterfall tumbles right into the ocean. Head left from the main beach access site and plan to walk for a couple of hours. A recent rainy-season landslide has left the waterfall pool unswimmable, but you'll pass seven nearby beaches with tide pools and other cool stuff to entertain you during the trek.

A bit farther south, you can hike to pretty **Los Cedros Falls,** just a little way over a bridge beyond the fork in the road from **Playa Las Manchas.** When you come to Cedros River, hike 40 minutes upstream. It's smallish, but a bonus here is coming across fossils and artifacts like ancient pottery shards, washed up by the river.

You can experience waterfalls in a unique way, plus get a taste of a Costa Rica tourism staple, by hitting the **Waterfall Canopy Tour** (head out of Cobano and take a right at the Cóbano Cemetery and then a left at the next cemetery; ☎ 823-6111 or 642-0808; $35 adults, $25 for kids 5 and up) It's smallish potatoes compared to other ziplines around the country, but how many canopy tours will give you a bird's-eye view of Montezuma's famous waterfalls? The circuit has nine cables and 11 platforms up to 300m (1,000 ft.) above the ground. Some but not all tours include a stop and a dip at the foot of the falls, so check before signing up. Their offices (Montezuma Travel Adventures) are located in Montezuma diagonally across from Bar Chicos.

DAY TRIPS

Consider a day trip to 3.2-sq.-km (1¼-sq.-mile) **Isla Tortuga,** an hour away by boat, off the coast between Tambor and Paquera: It's possibly the closest thing Costa Rica has to a virgin tropical paradise. Though you won't exactly be alone—there will be a few others snorkeling in the shallow waters; spotting dolphins; playing volleyball or Frisbee; taking the half-hour hike through forested hills to a lookout point with amazing vistas; tooling about in paddle boats, kayaks, and glass-bottom boats; or just turning and burning. Our advice: Aim for midweek to avoid the boatloads from Jacó, San José, and Puntarenas. Most local tour operators run day trips here, such as **Zuma Tours** (☎ 642-0024; www.zumatours.com), which for $50 (kids $25 or free) includes a barbecue lunch and sodas and/or a coupla brewskis.

One spot nature lovers should absolutely not miss is the **Cabo Blanco Absolute Natural Reserve** (10km/6 miles southwest of Montezuma, 11km/7 miles south of Malpaís; ☎ 642-0093; www.costarica-nationalparks.com/caboblancoabsolute naturalreserve.html; Wed–Sun 8am–4pm; $8), Costa Rica's oldest bioreserve (founded in 1963, the reserve kick-started the country's extensive national park system and launched it on the road to ecotourism stardom). These 13 sq. km (5 sq. miles) of moist tropical forest are what remains of the thick evergreens and deciduous trees that started to disappear at the beginning of the '60s; it's mostly secondary forest (meaning regrown from farm and ranch land, as opposed to primeval). Visitors were only let in starting in 1989—zero visitors before that is why the "absolute" reserve—and even today only about a third is open to the public. There's a ranger station/visitor center at the entrance.

Round about 150 species of trees have been identified here; trumpet trees, dogwoods, and cedars, some of which can get huge (one of the spiny cedars is 50m/165 ft. tall, 3m/10 ft. in diameter). Keep an eye out for sapodillas, marked by V-cuts in the bark; they're pyramid-shape with dense canopies of wide, glossy leaves, tapped for a white resin used commercially to make chewing gum. It's an example of sustainable development, as they say—letting locals tap some sap makes it less likely they'll cut the tree down altogether. There are varmints galore here, too: toucans, porcupines, gray foxes, green herons, monkeys, and parrots, among others.

You'll definitely want to hike through the forest down to the deserted, white **Playa Balsita** and **Playa Cabo Blanco.** Old hiking hands will prefer the strenuous 4km-long (2.5-mile) **Sendero Sueco** trail, about 2 hours each way, and steep in parts. The other is the 2km (1.3-mile) **Danés** loop through the patch of remaining primeval forest. Both are well maintained and well marked with directions and facts about the reserve. At the end you'll be rewarded with practically untouched beaches where you can swim and use showers, toilets, and changing rooms.

While lolling around the water, you'll be able to make out a lighthouse perched on an island—that's the **Isla Cabo Blanco.** Since early colonial times, both island and cape have been called "White Cape" because of the bird poop that covers the rocks in dry season. The island's a sea bird sanctuary for skads of brown pelicans, terns, frigate birds, laughing gulls, and the biggest brown-booby colony in the country, more than 500 strong.

ATTENTION, SHOPPERS!

The strip malls cluttering the rest of the Nicoya coast are here replaced by of loads of surf shops, most of them in Malpaís. You'll also find the usual souvenir shacks on Montezuma's main street—beachwear, banana-paper products, pottery, and wood tchotchkes. Don't bother—this area isn't known for its crafts.

Instead, one thing we like to do (during the dry season, at least) is stroll around Montezuma's downtown at sunset, when **street vendors** and **traveling artisans** set up folding tables lit by candles and paper lanterns, and lay out their knit tops, scented candles, dream catchers, and handmade leather goods (a few even play instruments to bring in buyers, creating a party atmosphere). Most Saturday mornings, an **organic fruit and vegetable market** covers the sidewalks around the Hotel El Tajalín. Need something to read for those quiet nights? Montezuma's lending library **Librería Topsy** (north end of town, across from the school; ☎ 642-0576; Mon–Fri 8am–4pm, Sat–Sun 8am–noon) also buys and sells all sorts books and magazines.

NIGHTLIFE

Boho Montezuma's got the liveliest scene in the area; most evenings you can catch street-artist performances downtown, from musicians to groups doing *capoeira* (that Brazilian cross between dance and martial arts). There's no shortage of drinking and dancing spots, but after the sun goes down (and sometimes even before) the most happening is **Chico's Bar** ✪ (next to Hotel Montezuma; daily 11am–2:30am), the local nightlife epicenter that's actually several bars popular with locals and tourists alike. Just follow the bass-heavy salsa beat inside to shoot pool or down a few streetside. For a more laid-back vibe and loungier soundtrack, head to the tiki-torchlit beachfront terrace **Chico's Playa.** Most restaurants have bars that turn into a party scene after dark; two good ones are **Cocolores** (north end of town; ☎ 642-0348) and **Playa de los Artistas** (p. 335), where you're likely to find both locals and tourists sweatily shaking booties and assorted other body parts.

For something a little mellower, the **Congo Azul** bar at the **Luz de Mono Hotel** (on the beach; ☎ 642-0090, 877/623-3198 from the U.S.; www.luzde mono.com; daily 5pm–midnight) pours great cocktails as well as locally grown "Monkey Shine" red and white wine. Try to catch one of the rotating local art shows or one of the musicians who show up impromptu knock out a few reggae or salsa sets. **El Sano Banano** (p. 335) is even lower-key, and known for its 7pm nightly movie screenings ($6, unless you're having dinner).

Over in Malpaís village, meanwhile, as with shops and such you'll find barland pretty dinky—mostly it's backpackers or travelers downing a few in little holes in the wall and weaving home on the early side. But keep an eye on the dance-party posters around town for more interesting stuff every once in awhile. And you can probably find some action at **Tabú** (on the beach; ☎ 640-0221; daily 2pm–1am) where hip-hop and dance tunes spin nightly, or the Santa Teresa dancehall **La Lora** (300m/985 ft. before Santa Teresa Surf Camp), with regular live bands and DJs. Surfer-popular watering holes include the ultra-mellow **Frank's Place** (at cross-roads on main road to Malpaís; ☎ 640-0096; www.malpais.net/franks.htm; daily 8am–9pm) and **Malpaís Surf Camp** (p. 334), which gets much rowdier and has open mic and live music on Wednesdays and Saturdays (but the mechanical bull is up 'n' buckin' every night).

THE "OTHER" MONTEZUMA & MALPAIS

Beaching and partying are all well and good, but if you're looking to combine those with something a little more meaningful, consider being an eco-volunteer. One chance to do that is in Cabuya, 2km (1¼ mile) from Cabo Blanco. Here the private **Rainsong Wildlife Sanctuary** (☎ 845-3190; www.rainsongsanctuary.com) is working to combat a downside of increasing tourism: falling animal populations. You can lend a hand to whatever interests you or needs the most help: preserving primary forest and endangered hardwood; reforestation; reintroducing endangered species; running an animal hospital; organizing a wildlife sanctuary; and studying sloths. Just show up, and there's no specific time commitment needed.

What's in it for you, besides do-gooder satisfaction? For starters, a 4-hour shift gets you a $3-a-day rate for a camp hut in the reserve, $2 meals, and use of a communal kitchen (or maybe you'd prefer the steep discounts at local ecolodges). Learning is another perk, including free Spanish classes and the chance to pick up other handy-dandy skills like tropical gardening, jungle survival, and identifying medicinal herbs. You'll get to really see what makes a bioreserve tick, so to speak, and meet some fascinating folks—fellow volunteers, local conservationists, and naturalists. It could really turn out to be one of those "life-changing" experiences you hear about.

The Essentials of Planning

by Pauline Frommer

THE HIGHLIGHTS OF A VISIT TO COSTA RICA—THE RAINFORESTS AND beaches, the hotels, restaurants, shops, and adventurous activities—have filled the bulk of this book. But almost as important is the miscellany that doesn't fit into broader categories. Those nitty-gritty details—from trip-planning essentials to tips for families and travelers with special interests and needs—are what you'll find in this chapter.

The good news is that Costa Rica is undeniably a visitor-friendly country; in fact, you'll find out a lot simply by talking with the Ticos. But anything you can't find in this book—which is hard to imagine—you should be able to find on the following regional websites:

- www.arenal.net
- www.monteverdeinfo.com
- www.tamarindo.com
- www.greencoast.com (for the Talamanca region)
- www.soldeosa.com (for the Osa Peninsula)
- www.nicoyapeninsula.com

Which websites *shouldn't* you look at? Take any information you find on the more generalized Costa Rica websites (those with the words "Costa Rica" in the name) with a grain of salt. The hotels, tours, and restaurants listed on them have coughed up big bucks to be there, whereas the websites above are community run and give a more impartial view of their subject. The booth of the official Costa Rica Travel board in San José can also be of help, although I find their website (www.visitcostarica.com) to be deficient. It's possible, however, to call and speak with a member of the staff from the U.S. and Canada (☎ 800/343-6332).

WHEN TO VISIT

That's the $40,000 question when it comes to Costa Rica. Do you save money and risk a spot (or daily deluges) of rain? Or do you choose the dry season, and ante up more for hotels and airfares? And what about the micro climates within Costa Rica that will parch one area, while flooding the area next door. And the turtles—when exactly will they be storming the beaches to lay eggs before the gazes of awestruck tourists. I'd say *when* to visit is the most important question in planning your Costa Rican holiday.

In general, Costa Rica's Costa Rica's dry season (or high season, also known as "tourist season") runs from late November to late April. This is when most tourists make their way to Costa Rica and consequently, prices and crowds hit their peak during this time, especially for the weeks of Christmas and New Year's Eve.

The so-called "Green Season" (sounds more appealing than "rainy season", eh?) takes up the rest of the year. Morning sun and afternoon storms are the classic pattern during the rainy season, but there are variations. You're almost always going to get some rain in the rain forests, even during the dry season, and often the real punch of wetness doesn't hit until several weeks into May, with the rains letting up a bit in June and July.

Is the green season so bad? Well, it depends on your taste. Some love the lushness of the plants and trees at this time of year, the lack or tourists, and, of course, the plunge in prices (by as much as 50%). And certain parts of the country are better for visitors during these months. For example, even though the rains are heaviest in September and October in most of the country, a microclimate around the Arenal volcano keeps it relatively dry; thus, you get a bit more rain than you would during the dry season then and, believe or not, a better look at the main attraction. The rains that do come tamp down the clouds that often surround the cone, and autumn volcano views are widely held to be the best of the year. Tortuguero is turtle central, and nesting time falls smack dab in the center of the green season, from July through mid-October.

But all is not sunny during the rainy season, though: Rivers often overrun their banks, splashing onto roads that then have to be forded (always go for four-wheel-drive if you're renting a car during the rainy season). Some whitewater rafting runs become too dangerous at this time of year. And if you're here to work on your tan, well, your time in direct sunlight will be limited (which might not be too bad this near to the equator; see my health and safety tips).

Costa Rica's Visit-Worthy Annual Events

It's a mistake to think of Costa Rica as simply a beach, zipline mecca, or bird-spotting destination. Cultural, sports, and culinary festivals dot the calendar and make as good an excuse for visiting as anything to be found in the trees, on the sands, or under the water.

January

Fiesta of Palmares Held during the first 2 weeks of the month, this joyously hedonistic celebration counts as one of the most famous and well attended of Costa Rica's yearly *fiestas*—the Tico equivalent of Rio's Carnaval, compete with girls in feathered headdresses, parades, carnival rides, food booths, and bands. This being a cowboy culture, rodeos and bullfights are thrown into the mix, too.

Fiesta of Santa Cruz Celebrated in honor of this Guanacaste city's patron saint, it's another bullfight, marimba, and fried-food extravaganza, nearly as popular as Palmares' shindig. This one takes place in the middle of the month.

February

Fiesta de los Diablitos Held in Rey Curé, a village near San Isidro de El General, this festival of "little devils" is an indigenous celebration, during which the battle between the Spanish forces and the Boruca Indians is reenacted. Participants wear vivid masks and costumes and native handicrafts are sold; an evening fireworks display caps the celebration.

March

Monteverde Music Festival The cloud forest is alive with the sound of music during this month-long fest, which attracts musicians from around the globe.

Dia de las Boyeros On the second Sunday of the month, a parade of elaborately hand-painted oxcarts makes it way through San Antonio de Escazú (a suburb of San José). Their destination is a church, where a priest blesses the oxen, and the participants throw a street party with food, dancing, and traditional costumes to celebrate. (Can you say "photo op"?)

Papagayo Sand Fest A Zen art fest to be sure, where even the most elaborate castles and sculptures are doomed to be washed away by the tides eventually, this 2-day fest, held in Playa del Coco the last weekend of the month, is still a heckuva lot of fun. Master artists from around the world create masterpieces in the sand; games, concerts, magic shows, and a beachcombing event round out the festivities.

April

Semana Santa (Holy Week) The entire country observes Holy Week (the week prior to Easter) with special masses and religious processions.

Juan Santamaria Day The exploits of Costa Rica's favorite war hero (see his story on p. 47), are celebrated nationwide on April 11. You'll find parades and parties across the nation, but the most elaborate ones are staged in Alajuela, where the young boy fought off American William Walker's forces in 1856.

July

Guanacaste Independence Day On July 25, 1825, Guanacaste was annexed to the rest of Costa Rica, and ever since, its capital Liberia has been the scene of merriment on that day, in the form of rodeos, parades, concerts, folk dancing, and more.

August

Fiesta of the Virgin of Los Angeles A major day of pilgrimage, in honor of the patron Saint of Costa Rica, many make a 24km (15-mile) trek from San José to the Basílica de Nuestra Señora de los Ángeles in Cartago, where a small black stone statue was found by a peasant girl several centuries ago and has been venerated ever since.

Dia de San Ramon The saints come marching in—literally—at this religious festival held on the last day of the month. About 30 statues are brought to San Ramon from surrounding villages for a terrifically colorful parade through the streets.

September

Costa Rican Independence Day Though the official celebration occurs on September 15, children parade through the streets of many towns the night before, carrying lights for an angelic prelude. Then on the day itself, the usual parades, rodeos, and folk dancing are held in cities and villages around the country.

October

Dia de la Raza In the Bahamas, they call this day "Discovery Day," in the United States it's called "Columbus Day," and in Venezuela, Cesar Chavez has changed the meaning and the name of the holiday to the "Day of Indigenous Resistance." Whatever it's called (and in Costa Rica, as in many parts of Central America it's called "Dia de la Raza"), Columbus' discovery of the "New World" is the excuse for a party on October 12, and here it has Mardi Gras overtones, especially in Limón, where fairly elaborate parades (with floats and dancers) are staged.

November

San José's Arts Festival The Costa Rican capital turns into an arts capital each November, though the focus shifts year to year. In even-numbered years, dance troupes, musicians, theater companies, and performance artists from all across the globe descend on San José for nightly performances throughout the month. In odd-numbered years, the talent is all Costa Rican, though the breadth of types of performances is nearly as wide.

Dia de Los Muertos As in Mexico, Costa Ricans spend November 2 visiting cemeteries and remembering their ancestors.

December

Fiesta de las Negritas Reminding us how much Catholicism co-opted the rituals of the people it converted, the Indian Village of Boruca throws a yearly native dance and drumming fête, during the week of December 8, to honor the Virgin of the Immaculate Conception. A fascinating meld of traditions.

Fiesta de la Yeguita The "little mare", a nickname for the Virgin of Guadalupe, is at the center of this December 12 parade and party in Nicoya. A statue leads the procession, and believers march and dance behind her.

Las Posadas and Portales Costa Rica goes all out for the Christmas season. Across the country, families and businesses display unique Nativity scenes (with prizes awarded for the best), and carolers go from door to door, starting around December 15, trading songs for refreshments.

El Tope, Carnival, and Festejos Populares The good times don't end in San José with Christmas Day. Instead, there's an impressive horse parade or *tope* through the streets the day after (Dec. 26), and a huge carnival with floats, dancers, and musicians the next day (Dec. 27). And the merriment goes on for several more days. In fact, for the entire last week of December fairgrounds are set up in the Zapote area of San José, and huge crowds gather to ride the rides, play games of chance, and watch rodeos.

ENTRY REQUIREMENTS

Visitors from the United States, Canada, Great Britain, Australia, and New Zealand need only a valid passport and a round-trip air ticket to enter Costa Rica. This holds true of most but not all European nationals, and again, most but not all citizens of Latin America, Asia, Africa, and the Middle East. Check with the Costa Rican consulate (see p. 370) for full information on entry requirements from these non-English speaking countries. Passports that are set to expire within 30 days or less from the time of entry are not acceptable, and may lead you to be turned away at the border or airport.

The initial passport stamp allows citizens of the US, Canada, and Great Britain to stay in Costa Rica for up to 90 days (citizens of Australia and New Zealand are allowed 30 days). In order to stay longer, you'll need to leave the country for several days (many go briefly to Panama) before obtaining another passport stamp, good for 90 more days. If you overstay, you'll need to purchase an exit visa for around $45 (go to any travel agent in San Jose to purchase one; buying from Immigration directly can be a hassle). Those driving into the country pay a fee of $80: $40 when they enter and $40 when they leave. If they overstay their welcome, they end up paying taxes on the car as well as fines.

The Climate at a Glance

Temperatures remain consistent year-round and are based more on altitude than how far south in the country you happen to be (a moot point as Costa Rica is just 8 to 11 degrees from the equator). The hilly central region can get quite chilly, with temperatures dipping sometimes into the 60s (upper teens Celsius) in the evenings. Down by the shore those same nights will be tropical, with temperatures often hovering in the 80s and 90s (low to mid 30s Celsius) during the day, and 70s (mid 20s Celsius) at night.

Average Daily Temperature & Rainfall in San Jose & the Highlands

	Jan	Feb	Mar	Apr	May	June	July	Aug	Sept	Oct	Nov	Dec
Temp. (°F)	73	75	77	78	78	78	77	77	76	77	75	73
Temp. (°C)	23	24	25	26	26	26	25	25	24	25	24	23
Rainfall (in.)	.25	.40	.54	3.15	10.5	11	7	11	14	13.3	5	1.3

Average Daily Temperature & Rainfall in Liberia & the Lowlands

	Jan	Feb	Mar	Apr	May	June	July	Aug	Sept	Oct	Nov	Dec
Temp. (°F)	80	79	82	83	83	79	79	78	78	79	79	79
Temp. (°C)	27	26	28	28	28	26	26	26	26	26	26	26
Rainfall (in.)	.25	.40	.54	3.15	10.5	11	7	11	14	13.3	5	1.3

For more questions on entry requirements contact any of the following Costa Rican embassies or consulates: in the **United States,** 2114 S St. NW, Washington, DC 20008 (☎ 202/234-2945; www.costarica-embassy.org for consulate locations around the country); in **Canada,** 325 Dalhousie St., Suite 407, Ottawa, Ontario K1N 5TA (☎ 613/562-2855); and in **Great Britain,** 14 Lancaster Gate, London, England W2 3LH (☎ 020/7706-8844). There are no Costa Rican embassies in Australia or New Zealand, but you could try contacting the honorary consul in **Sydney, Australia,** at Level 11, De La Sala House, 30 Clarence St., Sydney NSW 2000 (☎ 02/9261-1177).

Be sure to check with the Costa Rican Embassy or Consulate for the very latest in entry requirements, as these do shift. Full information can be found at www.costarica-embassy.org/consular/visa.

CUSTOMS

Visitors are restricted in the amount of goods they can legally bring into the country and will pay fees if they take out too much. The following chart breaks out the rules.

Customs Limits

	What you can bring in to the Costa Rica*	What you can take out of the Costa Rica*
Currency	No limit	$10,000 in U.S. or foreign currency, again with no formalities
Tobacco	500g of tobacco	*U.S. citizens:* 200 cigarettes or 100 cigars *U.K. citizens:* 200 cigarettes, 50 cigars, 250g of tobacco *Canadian citizens:* 1 carton cigarettes, 1 can tobacco *Australian citizens:* 250g of cigarettes or loose tobacco *New Zealand citizens:* 200 cigarettes, 50 cigars, 200g of tobacco (combined weight of no more than 250g)
Gifts	$500 worth of gifts	*U.S. citizens:* $800 worth of merchandise *U.K. citizens:* £450 *Canadian Citizens:* C$750, plus C$60 a day mailed back (not including liquor or tobacco). That C$750 exemption only good once per year *Australian citizens:* A$400 *New Zealand citizens:* NZ$700
Liquor	5 liters of wine or liquor	*U.S. citizens:* 1 liter of alcohol without paying duty *U.K. citizens:* 2 liters still table wine, 2 liters sparkling wine or liqueur, 1 liter spirits *Canadian citizens:* 40 imperial oz. of liquor *Australian citizens:* 1,125ml of alcohol *New Zealand citizens:* 4.5 liters or wine or beer, 1,125ml of alcohol

Please note that these amounts are only for people over 18 years of age. Different rules apply to youngsters and in many cases they are not allowed to bring goods into or out of the Costa Rica.

GETTING THERE

San José International Airport and **Liberia International Airport** are the two gateways into Costa Rica. San José, which is 3km (2 miles) from the town of Alajuela, about half an hour west of San José proper, is the best arrival point for those visiting San José and the Central Valley, the Osa Peninsula, the area around Manuel Antonio Park, the Arenal volcano, and Monteverde. Flying into Liberia is the best route if your ultimate goal is the beaches of Guanacaste. To either airport,

Timing Your Flight Right

If you're planning on driving yourself from the airport to your first night's destination, it's important to schedule a flight that arrives while it's still light out. Factoring in 1 to 2 hours for getting through customs (it will likely be closer to 1, but it can't hurt to be safe) and 1 hour to rent and inspect your car, that means that you should attempt to arrive no later than 2:30pm in the afternoon. You simply don't want to be driving in the dark; it's just too easy to get lost here (p. 349).

it will take you between 3 and 7 hours to fly from the United States, varying by gate-way (obviously). San José is much larger (it has walls where Liberia resembles more of an overgrown, concrete beach shack), but in terms of pricing for flights in and out, there's parity between the two. In fact, it's sometimes possible to fly into one airport and out the other one for nearly the same price as a round-trip ticket (great news for those who want to see large swatches of Tiquicia and don't want to backtrack).

Delta, American, US Airways, American West, and Continental all have regu-lar nonstop commercial flights to the international airport in Liberia from their hubs in Atlanta, Miami, Charlotte, Phoenix, and Houston, respectively. Liberia is the gateway to the beaches of the Guanacaste region and the Nicoya Peninsula, and a direct flight here eliminates the need for a separate commuter flight in a small aircraft or roughly 5 hours in a car or bus.

FINDING CHEAP INTERNATIONAL AIRFARES TO COSTA RICA

With the cost of flying on the rise, snagging a good airfare is more important than ever, as it's the way most English-speaking travelers arrive in Costa Rica (you can drive through Mexico from the U.S., but that's a tricky proposition). Your strat-egy for getting that low airfare should include the following steps:

- **Fly when others don't.** As with hotel rates, airfares are often a full $100 lower in the green season. See p. 342 to decide whether that's enough of a lure to go at that time.
- **Look at the low fare carriers.** Airlines such as Martinair, Spirit, COPA, TACA, Lacsa, and Mexicana fly into Costa Rica from the United States and will occa-sionally have better fares than big American carriers. But you'll find that their prices (and those of the other carries) will have booking fees attached when you purchase through the brand-name travel booking sites. So use a search tool such as FareCompare.com, Sidestep.com, Kayak.com, or Mobissimo.com, which search both the airline sites and the booking sites directly, adding no service charges and often finding fares that the larger travel-agent sites miss. If you're flying from Europe to Costa Rica, take a look at the fares from Virgin Atlantic, American Airlines, Continental, Iberia, KLM, Air Canada, and Martinair, as these carriers tend to have the lowest rates on transatlantic routes. Or you might consider finding a cheap flight from your gateway city to Miami or New York City and make a connection for there. I've always found that Mobissimo.com and CheapFlights.uk.com are best for searching fares that don't originate in the U.S. The booking engine Opodo (www.opodo.co.uk) is another good resource.
- **Book at the right time.** Sounds odd, but you can often save money by book-ing your seat at 3am. That's because unpaid reservations are flushed out of the system at midnight, and since airfares are based on supply and demand, prices often sink when the system becomes aware of an increase in supply. Also, consider booking on a Wednesday, the day when most airfare sales come out. Be sure to watch such sites as Frommers.com and SmarterTravel.com, which highlight fare sales.
- **Book through a consolidator.** Also known as "bucket shops," these compa-nies buy tickets in bulk, passing along the savings to their customers. If you reside in Europe, the best place to find one that services your area is

www.cheapflights.co.uk, which serves as a clearinghouse for all sorts of buckets shops, both large and small. Many will also advertise in the Sunday papers. The American version of that site—also a terrific resource—is www.cheapflights.com. Be careful, though: Some consolidators charge outrageous change fees, so read the fine print before your purchase your ticket.

◆ **Consider a package or tour.** I'll discuss this more in depth on p. 355, but sometimes you'll pay less when you buy both your airfare and hotel room together, or those two elements plus a tour.

◆ **Book your tickets in advance.** Last-minute discounts are pretty much a thing of the past, but there are occasionally still good deals to be had by early birds.

a good alternative to driving.

✱FLYING WITHIN COSTA RICA

Because the roads are so poor (see p. 350 for more rantings on that), many travelers choose to fly between different regions of the country, reducing what could be 4 hours on twisty, unmarked roads to a brief half-hour or so in the air. Every major tourist region now has its own airstrip, and some minor ones as well. And while flights aren't dirt cheap, they're not outrageously pricey and certainly more convenient, particularly for those who want to cover a lot of ground—but not on the ground.

In-country flights are handled, almost without exception, by two rival airlines, **Nature Air** (☎ 800/235-9272; www.natureair.com) and **Sansa Airlines** (☎ 506/290-4100; www.flysansa.com). With few exceptions, you're going to be leaving from or flying through San José to get where you're going, as this is really a one-hub country when it comes to local flights. Of the two, Nature Air tends to have better service, more daily flights, and fewer cancellations and schedule changes, and doesn't overbook as often as Sansa seems to (perhaps because of its pass system; p. 349).

Sansa has a few things in its favor, though, in that it flies out of **San José International Airport** (more convenient if you need to connect with an international flight; Nature Air often uses **Tobías Bolaños International Airport** in Pavas) and offers free shuttle service from its office downtown to the airport. Be sure to shop both, though, as they inevitably fly the same routes, though at different times of the day and often for slightly different prices.

In the box below, I've broken out the cost of some of the more popular routings, along with the tremendous time savings this type of transportation can afford. This may be one of the few times on your vacation when being a cheapskate may backfire; remember, when you're on vacation the meter's ticking. Assign a monetary value to the time you waste in a bus or car getting from place to place, or on dreadful roads, and splurging on a flight may make more sense. Also, there are ways to try and game the system. For some reason, flights *from* San José tend to be slightly less expensive than those that go *to* San José (and I have no explanation as to why), so it might be more cost effective to fly out from the capital and then wend your way back in a rental car or on a bus.

If you do decide flying's the way to go for you and you'll be traveling during the high season, be sure to book your tickets well in advance.

A warning for overpackers: Both airlines' fleets consist of "puddle jumpers"—small twin propeller planes—so you'll be limited to 25 pounds total for luggage, which really ain't very heavy at all.

Parsing the Passes

Bona fide jet-setters can hop around the country on 1 or 2 weeklong flight passes from Sansa Airlines (p. 348). How it works is simple: You book your first flight, and from then on you have either 6 or 13 days of unlimited flying. You don't even need reservations: You can simply walk up and demand access, according to the folks at Sansa. A week-long pass is $300, with 2 weeks for only $49 more.

But is it worth it? For 1 week, I'd have to say no. Even if the flights were all at the higher end of the price scale, you'd have to fly four times or more in a week to make the pass pay off. And do you really want to spend your vacation hassling with that? The 2-week pass is more sensible and cost-effective. But before you ante up, be sure to crunch the numbers and look at route maps (as you'll probably be spending a lot of time ducking into and out of San José).

For those making Costa Rica just one stop on an extended Central American Itinerary, Sansa's parent alliance, TACA (p. 347), offers passes that allow travelers to alight in Guatamala, Honduras, Nicaragua, and Panama. Prices can vary widely on these, so again, do the math before purchasing.

A note for families: Better news for those with kids. Children under 12 automatically receive a 25% discount off the cost of in-country flights.

Departure city	Arrival City	One-way fares	Driving time vs. flying time
San José	Arenal/La Fortuna	$42–$65	3 hr. vs. 25 min.
San José	Drake Bay	$92 avg.	8 hr. vs. 40 min.
San José	Liberia	$44–$88	4 hr. vs. 35 min.
San José	Limón	$21–$88	2.5 hr. vs. 40 min.
San José	Nosara	$43–$86	5.5 hr. vs. 35 min.
San José	Puerto Jimenez	$28–$92	8 hr. vs. 50 min.
San José	Quepos	$27–$54	4 hr. vs. 25 min.
San José	Tamarindo	$44–$88	5 hr. vs. 40 min.
San José	Tortuguero	$21–$87	4.5 hr. vs. 30 min.
Liberia	Arenal/La Fortuna	$33	3 hr. vs. 30 min.
Quepos	Liberia	$105	6 hr. vs. 2 hr. (indirect flight)

GETTING AROUND BY CAR

Driving in Costa Rica is an adventure, and an ideal way to get off the tourist tread-mill in a country that's increasingly overwhelmed with tourists. But it's not for the faint of heart. Here are a few things to consider before you take to the road:

esp. Monteverde area

Road Conditions. Ecosensitivity has its minor downsides. Because 25% of the land in Costa Rica is protected from development, and the rest is strictly regulated, road builders aren't allowed to blast away impediments to create straight roads. Great for the environment, but a pain for the motorists, and this is why many roads in Costa Rica twist and turn, lilting upwards for a stretch before plopping downwards for no apparent reason. Add a rainy season when a number of roads become little more than riverbeds, plus a dearth of money for repairs, and you get lunar landscape–like thoroughfares in places, with potholes the diameter of office cubicles. It makes for a driving experience that will sometime feel more like a ride on a bucking bronco. Not all roads are painful, of course; it really depends on where you're going. If you're planning on renting a car (see below), it's the better part of wisdom to get one with high clearance to avoid scraping the chassis (and possibly damaging the car) on unseen potholes.

Lack of Signage. Signs and road names would be nice, but that's not the Costa Rican way. A good 90 percent of the roads and streets here are unmarked, so it's annoyingly easy to get lost. That's the reason why so many addresses in this book read: "down the main road into town, across from the pharmacy." Luckily, there are ways to find your way about. On many roads signs will be posted telling you how many kilometers it is to the nearest town; you'll also see huge hotel billboards, advertising how far away that bed for the night is. When plotting your route, try to visualize it as a string of small towns, and write down their names. You may also find it helpful to remember the names of other hotels in the area you're visiting; that way, when you see their billboards, you'll know you're on the right track. In the cases when there is no announcement with the name of the town you're passing through (a common occurrence), look out for the names listed on the stores as they'll often be named for the town itself; so if you pass, say Farmacia (Pharmacy) San Rafael and then Ferreteria (Hardware Store) San Rafael, it's a good chance you're, drumroll please, in San Rafael.

Speed Traps. Increasingly common, speeders are now liable for fines of up to $150 for speeding (and don't try and skip the country without paying; they can charge your credit card up to a year after the incident). I'd be sugarcoating it if I didn't tell you that gringos are often a bigger target than locals. So drive within the speed limit (on highways it's between 70kmph and 90kmph/45mph and 55mph), and if you spot drivers in the other lane blinking their lights at you, slow down even further: They're warning you that a trap's ahead. By the way, don't ever try to bribe a policeman to get out of a speeding ticket; you may incur a hefty fine.

Accidents. Costa Rica has one of the worst automobile accident fatalities rates in the world. Before you panic too much, know that its stats are about on par with those of the United States (which also has a miserable record, in terms of accidents). The reasons for auto accidents, however, are a bit different in Costa Rica; they often have to do with who's using the major thoroughfares (pedestrians, cyclists, livestock), the condition of the roads, and the laissez faire attitude many local drivers take towards speed limits and traffic laws. The last point may be because so few signs are posted actually stating what the laws and limits are. As well, because the roads tend to be quite narrow and shoulderless when a breakdown occurs, the stalled car can become an accident magnet itself. Though all cars are required by law to carry small, red hazard reflector signs to place on the road, warning drivers to go around, many simply don't have them. Instead, they'll place assorted, well, stuff on the road as a warning—a beach chair, a tower, sometimes just a large branch. So keep your eyes peeled for this sort of debris, as it may mean you need to slow down.

Standard road courtesy is different here, too. Pedestrians do *not* have the right of way, blinker usage is sporadic, and it's not uncommon to see a car swerve across two lanes of traffic to make a turn. And because there are no shoulders for pedestrians to walk on, or even sidewalks in many towns, they will often be on the roads with the cars, and can behave in an even more erratic fashion than the drivers.

Can it get worse? You bet. During the wet season, landslides are a hazard in many hilly areas, some roads become washed out, and visibility can be poor (thanks to driving rain or fog).

Scams and Theft. Issues of roadside crime also need to be addressed. Vehicle break-ins are common, especially at beach areas and in national parks. Scam artists have been known to slash tires outside of restaurants, tourist attractions, and even in car-rental parking lots. They then follow their victim until the flat forces him to pull over. Posing as good Samaritans, they rob the victim. To keep yourself and your possessions safe, do the following:

(handwritten note: Broke into our vehicle in Jaco.)

* Leave valuables in a safe in your hotel room, or at worst, in the trunk of your rental car. Never leave items openly displayed on the seats or floor of your vehicle. *(handwritten note: We had bags on the seats! NOT)*
* Make a copy of your passport, including the page with the Costa Rica stamp, and carry that with you instead of the passport itself when you're out for day trips. Leave your passport somewhere safe, preferably in your hotel safe.
* If you need to stop and look at a map, get a flat, or experience some other type of minor problem with your car, keep driving until you can pull in to a well-guarded or crowded area, such as a service station or a hotel parking lot. Avoid pulling over to the side of the road in deserted areas and always keep your doors locked and your windows up when you're driving (especially in San José).
* Don't pull over if you see flashing headlights—this too may be a scam. Costa Rican police and emergency vehicles have red or blue flashing lights.

Fueling Up

Getting gas is not always easy. In remote areas, gas stations may be few and far between, so it's important to leave with a full tank of gas when you're setting off into less urban or resort-centric areas. If you do find yourself out of gas and far from a station, keep an eagle eye out for hand-lettered signs in front of private homes reading GASOLINA. These mark families who sell gas to passing motorists, 1 liter at a time.

Gas stations are all full service in Costa Rica, and gas costs about $4 a gallon (though it's sold by the liter).

Rating the Roads

Not all roads in Costa Rica are uniformly appalling. Those in the Central Valley, where 70% of the population reside, are well maintained, smooth, and sometimes even have names. The Interamerican Highway between San José and Liberia, and the roads that connect the capital and Arenal, can be a downright pleasure to cruise. And except for the hair-raising one-lane bridges, the drive from Jacó to Quepos is pleasant, too.

So where are the errant roads? Generally, those that connect the various seaside communities are problematic, which is why many travelers drive inland to the highway even if they're trying to go from one seaside area to another. And the road to Monteverde is infamous—pitted, winding, and dusty, it's known as the worst road in the country...and that's saying a whole lot in Costa Rica.

Yes, driving in Costa Rica can be a challenge and a defensive sport. But the vast majority of visitors, including myself on my visits, never encounter any problems while driving around the country. You may need a bit of patience and a sense of humor but if you possess these qualities, there's no dandier way to see the country. When you have your own set of wheels, you can head out to the deserted beaches that tour busses never come near, explore back lanes, and set your own schedule. You have freedom. And if you have a good map, such as the waterproof one created by the Toucan Guides (www.costa-rica-guide.com)—more power to you.

RENTING A CAR

Make sure you tell rental company you are going to Monte Verde → need 4WD rd

Here's where being a savvy consumer really has its upsides. Yes, weekly rentals can be steep in Costa Rica—in high season about $350 a week for a standard car, up to $500 a week for an SUV, is the norm. But prices can vary widely from agency to agency. I've seen weekly rates in off season swerve from $92 total all the way up to $189 for the same week for the same type of compact.

To get an overview of what might be available when you book, try the sites that "aggregate" such information such as **Sidestep.com** and **Kayak.com.** But don't book yet. It's also possible to get steep discounts through tour operators, so after you get the score with a quick web search of the major companies, contact a few of the companies listed on p. 355 to see if they can do better.

Other ways to cut costs include creating an itinerary that makes use of a hodgepodge of transportation methods. For example, you could take a bus from San José to your next destination, and then pick up a rental car once you're there. Car-rental agencies exist in all of the country's tourist hubs, and prices are no higher than what you'll find in San José, thus renting for shorter-distance travel can be a sanity saver. You can leave the tricky long haul trips to the pros, but have your own set of wheels to tootle around an area you'll quickly get to know. If you want to take some public transportation out to where you're going and then drive back to the airport, that's doable, too. One-way rentals are no big deal, though if

What to Do If You Have an Accident

The following sentence may well be the most important piece of information you'll get in this book: **If you get in an accident, it is crucial that you do not move until the police arrive so you can file a claim.** This is not a country where motorists can simply exchange information and be on their merry way. Leave the site of an accident where one or two cars are damaged without an accident report and you could be out hundreds of dollars.

The first thing you should do if you're involved in an accident is to call the **National Insurance Institute** (☎ 800/800-8000) and then call the **Transit Police** (☎ 222-9330 or 222-9245). An official transit police report can greatly enhance your claim. If you can't get help from either of those agencies, make sure you at least get the name and number of the insurance operator you spoke to, so that you have evidence that you called from the scene. Attempt to get written statements from witnesses on the scene, and take notes yourself, listing the model, make, color, and license plate number of the other car involved in the accident. Then call ☎ 911, which will direct you to the appropriate agency.

Dealing with the local police can be tricky. Usually they won't speak English (this is why it pays to have a good phrasebook handy, if you don't speak Spanish) and some have been known to be downright antagonistic to gringo tourists. So keep your temper and patience in check; if you blow up, you'll be much less likely to get a useful accident report from them, or any help.

Before anyone arrives, bring your car over to the side of the road. If that's not possible, take the red hazard triangles that should be in your trunk and set them up to warn other motorists of the impediment (you) in the road. If those are missing from your rental car (not uncommon), do what the Ticos do, and gather large branches or leaves to create a pile other drivers will see. Often a tow truck will arrive unannounced as many of their drivers monitor the police radios. Ask for the credentials of the driver before agreeing to use the services of the body shop they're affiliated with. Make sure it's a body shop authorized by the INS (the Costa Rica insurance institution); those that aren't won't be able to fill out the paperwork you need in order to get reimbursed for the repairs).

See p. 369 for information on medical facilities and emergency services.

you rent for less than a week, you may incur a $20 to $30 fee for drop-off (it's usually waived for longer rentals).

What type of car you need will depend on when and where you're traveling. Those traveling anywhere outside the Central Valley in the green season are well advised to rent a four-wheel-drive vehicle. Road conditions deteriorate quickly, due to torrential downpours, and a road that was paved and perfectly fine in December may be a potholed mess by June. Year-round it's advisable to go for a four-wheel drive, or at least one with a high chassis, if you're going into areas where many roads are unpaved, like the Osa Peninsula, the Nicoya Peninsula, the Nosara area, Monteverde, and many national parks, among others.

Insurance. Don't assume that you'll be covered by your own car owner's insurance when in Costa Rica. Talk with your provider **in advance** to determine whether your coverage works abroad, whether it will cover all persons who might be driving the car and all types of cars, and what your third-party liability will be. Credit cards will also offer some insurance (usually it's a secondary insurance if you have car owner's insurance), but check with those companies as well to find out what the coverage is for Costa Rica. Terms vary widely with both. If you're depending on the coverage from just your credit card, remember that credit cards never cover liability or the cost of an injury to an outside party or their vehicle. So, if you don't have an insurance policy, it's important that you buy additional liability insurance.

There's one extremely important bit of business that you'll need to do before you leave the car rental lot in Costa Rica. Be sure to **inspect your vehicle,** and if possible, **take photos** of any dings or scuffs before you leave the lot. You'll be given a damage sheet, so be sure to check the oil, fuel gauge, brake fluid, and extra tire before you sign off, making copious notes on any *rayas* (scratches) you may see. Keep a copy of that damage sheet with you until you return the car. Unfortunately, overcharging customers for damage they didn't cause is a common scam. You're less likely to encounter it if you book your car rental through a travel agent (p. 355), as the rental company will probably not want to anger an agent who sends them steady business.

GETTING AROUND BY BUS

The single most budget-friendly method of seeing Costa Rica is to hop on the bus, Gus. Travel on local buses and you'll rarely pay more than $5 or $6, even for journeys of 4 or more hours' duration. And you'll have no problem getting where you're going: Bus routes in Costa Rica are extensive, with bus service to every place listed in this book and many of the smaller hamlets too obscure for us to mention. As with air travel, many of the routes originate in San José, so you could find yourself backtracking a tad if you do decide to rely entirely on the bus for your transportation needs.

In each chapter of this book you'll find listings for the buses that service the destination in question. Some are **local buses,** which are inevitably much less expensive, but don't have air-conditioning, bathrooms, or very good shock absorbers. Still, if you want to stretch your vacation dollars and are interested in meeting local folks as you travel, these should be your pick. **Express buses** are a bit more of a luxurious option. As the name suggests, they make fewer stops and are thus much faster. And as they're newer, they tend to be more comfortable (though you won't find a bathroom on these, either). Depending on the route, this express option may only run on weekends and holidays. For information on **bus schedules,** go to www.costaricamap.com, click on "Travel Information," and then on "Local Buses."

There are also what I'll call the **private bus services,** which are run by corporations, not the government, and tend to cost about four times as much as the public buses. For that uptick in cost you get a lot more comfort, however, in the form of cushy seats, smaller buses, consistent A/C, and pick-up or drop-off at your hotel. They also tend to be significantly faster than the public buses (even the express buses, though none will have bathrooms onboard). Gray Line (☎ 220-2126; www.graylinecostarica.com), run by Fantasy Tours, is the first of the two major private companies; it offers approximately 10 departures a day to such tourist hot spots as Jacó, Manuel Antonio, Liberia, Playa Hermosa, La Fortuna, Tamarindo, and Playas Conchal. About the same number of buses return each day, and there are a number of routes that interconnect at points. Prices range from $21 to $38. Its competitor, Interbus (☎ 283-5573; www.interbusonline. com), has a much more extensive routing (the 10 destinations above, plus 28 others), but tends to be a bit more expensive (between $44 and $59 on average, sometimes less).

A word to the wise: During high season, it's a very good idea to secure advance bus reservations, especially on such popular routes as San José to Golfito.

Packages & Tours vs. Independent Travel

Dense forests, unmarked roads, active volcanoes, areas where little English will be spoken—these can be intimidating factors for travelers to Costa Rica. So rather than going it alone, they turn to packagers or tour operators to help them plan their stays. It's actually not a bad strategy, though not for those who enjoy the planning as much as the trip, or prefer to visit places that are off the beaten track as tours and packages center on the country's best known highlights.

So what are the differences between the two? Usually, the term "packages" refers to the bundling together of airfare with hotels stays and sometimes a car rental. The theory is that by buying these items together, from a company that has greater bargaining power than you, would save you money. It sometimes works out that way, but sometimes not. A key to deciphering packages is to remember that they're always based on double occupancy, so be sure to double the total price of the trip and then subtract the airfares to get the lowdown on what you're actually paying for the room and/or car.

Packagers will often offer extras such as guided tours or shows, but you're under no obligation on a package to buy these extras. Of the many packagers that specialize in Costa Rica, I've always had the best luck with Capricorn Leisure Corp. (☎ 800/426-6544; www.capricorn.net), a price leader. It regularly features a week in the Quepos area, with airfare from the U.S. and rental car for as little as $759 (this is just one of its offerings in Costa Rica). Its competitor, Gate 1 Travel (☎ 800/682-3333; www.gate1travel.com), is not quite as cut-rate, but provides good value nonetheless, with weeklong stays in Guanacaste, including airfare but not car rental, from the U.S. for as little as $749. Check both.

Guided tours offer more of a safety net, as not only the essentials of the vacation (hotel, airfare) are covered, but also daily activities are preplanned and led (hopefully) by local experts. There are two ways to approach guided tours: going with local companies or booking companies in your own home country.

Let's start with the first option, as it's the more flexible of the two in that tours can be picked up on an ad hoc basis from local agencies, or planned in advance. Literally dozens of travel agents crowd the streets off the main square in most Costa Rican towns, hawking mangrove floats, guided nature walks, horseback expeditions, and more. Since many of these tours are the exact same ones being included in the larger motorcoach tours, buying them directly from these local agents, or better yet, from the tour companies directly (see below), is almost always a money-saver. Below, I list some of the Costa Rican organizations you may want to hit up, but you'll also find listings for local outfitters in each of the destination chapters. Some of these are specialists, others offer a myriad of adventures, but all can set up in-country transportation, lodgings, and the other standard elements of a tour.

Local Agents

Bi.Costa Rica (☎ 258-0303; www.bruncas.com/bicostarica.html) Creative bike tours that get well off the beaten path (one concentrates on the Osa Peninsula, another tracks the footsteps of the conquistadores), as well as hitting a number of Tico classics, such as Arenal and Manuel Antonio. The company uses only small, locally owned guesthouses, and the tours usually include a smattering of other adventures (canopy tours, kayaking, and so forth) along with daily biking.

Birding Escapes (☎ 771-4582; www.birdwatchingcostarica.com) Overseen by Richard Garrigues, the man who wrote the book (a well-respected field guide to Costa Rica's approximately 880 species of birds), this local company provides eye-on-the-sky and forest-canopy tours of Monteverde, the Central Valley highlands, and the Caribbean lowlands, plus the southern Pacific highlands, seashore, and lowland rainforest. Average trips run 4 nights/5 days.

Costa Rica Expeditions (☎ 257-0766; www.costaricaexpeditions.com) The mother of all Costa Rica tour operators, it's been around the longest and is considered the most reliable of the bunch; in 2006, it was named "best outfitter in Costa Rica" by *National Geographic*. Whitewater rafting, canopy tours, canyoning, birding, and nature expeditions are led by experts in the field. CRE can set up all these types of experiences and more, such as snorkeling and kayaking. It even has its own highly rated nature lodges sprinkled across the country. The downside to booking here: higher prices, but many travelers feel this company is worth it.

Horizontes Nature Tours (☎ 222-2022; www.horizontes.com) A long-established (since 1984) favorite, Horizontes is known for the quality of its naturalist guides and its pioneering role in setting Costa Rica along the ecotourism path (it's a very "green" company). Along with the usual sports adventures, it offers programs that explore Costa Rican culture, including tours to rural communities, art tours (where participants meet local artists as well as taking the time to paint, photograph, and sketch as they go along), homestay programs, and more. Horizontes' birding expeditions also have a stellar reputation.

Pure Trek Adventures (☎ 866/569-5723 toll-free from U.S. and Canada or 479-9940; www.puretrekcostarica.com) Best known for its canyoning adventures that send participants rappelling down waterfalls and small cliffs, this solid tour operator also puts together adventure packages to all parts of Costa Rica and can arrange day trips from San José and the Arenal area.

Rios Tropicales (☎ 233-6455; www.riostropicales.com) Founded by an Olympic sportsman, this is one of the largest whitewater rafting and kayaking companies in Costa Rica. You'll find its participants paddling in rivers and lakes across the country (it also offers sea kayaking). It also owns three nature lodges and offers a small number of hiking trips.

Serendipity Adventures (☎ 257-4171; www.serendipityadventures.com) This outfit does almost everything that Costa Rica Expeditions does (see above), but since it has a much lower profile, its customized trips are a bit cheaper. They're particularly strong in the areas of canyoneering (rapelling down into canyons) and tree climbing (yup, that's an adventure sport here, too), and have the distinction of being the only hot-air balloon concessionaire in the country.

Nonlocal Agents

Along with the local agencies above, there are several American, Australian, and British companies that offer reasonably priced local tours. I'd recommend you compare and contrast the programs of:

Adventure Center (☎ 510/654-1879; www.adventurecenter.com) Because this company runs its tours in tandem with companies in the U.K. and Australia, groups are a heady, fun mix of nationalities and prices are kept quite low. For example, a 12-night "Family Adventure," with an itinerary geared towards those traveling with active young'uns, comes in at just $895 for lodging, some meals, and many activities (a panoply of choices is offered on some days so that participants can better customize their experience). An even cheaper program, just for adults, zips them around Costa Rica, squeezing a volcano, a cloud forest, and a fabled beach all into 1 week for the remarkable price of just $495, including hotels, some tours, and in-country transportation.

Caravan Tours (☎ 800-CARAVAN or 312/321-9800 in the U.S.; www.caravantours. com) The king of the soup-to-nuts tour, Caravan covers much of the country from the Caribbean coast to the Pacific and inward, and up to the Arenal area and Monteverde on its "Costa Rica Natural Paradise Tour." The entire she-bang takes 10 days and comes in at a little under $1,000 per person, making it one of the best values in escorted tours to Central America. That price also includes all meals, hotels, tours, and in country transportation. The downside? You'll be with a group of 30 to 40 people. Consider whether or not you want such an inclusive tour. Some find it more fun to escape the group for a meal every once in a while.

Tico Tours (☎ 800/493-8426; www.ticotravel.com) With offices both in the U.S. and in Costa Rica, and an expert, dedicated staff, Tico is an excellent choice for those who value seamless, varied itineraries, and top-notch guides. That being said, it's not a cheap outfit to travel with, and many of its tours and customized itineraries come out to about $200 or more a day per person. Still, it's not the most expensive of your choices by a long shot and this is a company that really knows Costa Rica well. A good choice for a splurgier tour.

SAVING MONEY ON ACCOMMODATIONS

Getting the best price on accommodations is an art and takes effort, even in Costa Rica. But if you consider the following steps, you may be able to game the system effectively.

◆ **Go in the off-season.** Okay, that one's obvious and not always doable, but I include it here because it truly is the best way to pay less on accommodations.

◆ **Pay cash.** Many hotels will knock 10% or so off your nightly rate if you avoid credit cards. Always ask.

◆ **Consider vacation and condo rentals instead of hotels.** You'll save money on food (since you'll have the option of cooking) and you'll often pay less or just as much for five times the space. These types of accommodations are particularly well suited to families and large groups, as the more people who bunk down in the house, the less you'll be paying per person. Because we think this is such a terrific way to enjoy Costa Rica, we've included information about local rental companies in nearly every area we cover in this book. And we don't just tell you that this option exists, we checked it out for you. Nelson and David (and I, in the Arenal area) visited a number of these rental properties so that we could eliminate the agencies with subpar offerings, and give you, the reader, a bit of an idea what kind of home awaits in each region of the country—and they do vary from region to region.

◆ **Bargain.** Never haggled? It's easier than you think and can lead to big savings, if you do it intelligently. By that I mean don't try it if it's Holy Week or New Years Eve—in fact, if the prices seem to be high across the board, it's a good sign that something's going on and all of your bargaining won't get you a bargain. And just as important, do your research first. If you're going to a major area, you'll get an idea what the more established resorts are charging at such sites as Expedia.com or Travelocity. For smaller properties or less well-known areas, you'll have to rely on the prices in this book to judge the going rate. Once you have the correct price range under your belt, call the hotel directly and ask to speak with a manager (only they have the authority to play "let's make a deal.") Be nice, be friendly, be downright charming, but don't beat around the bush. Tell them that you'd sure like to give your business to hotel X, but you can't pay more than such and such a price. Stand firm and see what happens. If you're traveling with a group of people or staying for longer than 5 nights, use those facts as well when making your case. You could end up with a group discount or a "long stay" rate.

◆ **Consider house swapping.** Remember how much fun it looked in the Cameron Diaz film *The Holiday?* Well, home exchanging is even better in real life (though I can't guarantee you'll meet your Tico true love doing it). Why? Do the words "free travel" get you as giddy as it does me? You simply pony up for a membership in a home swap organization (about $75 a year), which allows you to list your home and contact other members about their listings. Because you'll exchange a number of e-mails before your visit, you'll be able to set the ground rules for how your home is to be treated and get to feel comfortable with your "swapee." It's this personal exchange that keeps the activity safe; those who engage in it rarely have problems. And it has some hidden perks. Families can pack more lightly than usual when they exchange with other families as they know they'll be going to a place crammed with toys, cribs, high chairs, and more. And because it's common for the owner to send over friends to check up on the "swapee," this method of travel is a near-guaranteed way to meet people in the area you'll be visiting—always the highlight of a trip.

Dozens of organizations promote home exchanges nowadays, but the following two seem to have the best coverage for Costa Rica: **The Home Exchange** (www.homeexchange.com) has 49 listings in Costa Rica at the time of writing. **Intervac** (www.intervac.com) has 17 listings in Costa Rica at the time of writing.

TRAVEL INSURANCE—DO YOU NEED IT?

When purchasing a big ticket travel item—a guided tour, a cruise, a home rental—it's essential to buy travel insurance. Many unforeseen circumstances can interrupt or cause you to cancel a trip, and with these types of trips, that could spell a large financial loss. But if you're purchasing the insurance to cover lost luggage or cancelled airfare, you may already be covered by your regular insurance (check with the provider of your home owners or renters insurance). And hotel stays should never be insured as hotels will usually allow you to cancel 24 hours in advance with no penalty.

So should you insure? If you've **rented a vacation home or condo** and have had to put down a large deposit, you should be insured. Same goes for **pricey airline tickets** and **escorted tours,** as they usually require significant advance payments. You may wish to invest in insurance that will **cover medical expenses** and **medical evacuation.** It's unlikely that the insurance you carry in your home country will cover you here (though check in advance before purchasing). Insurance is advised especially if you're here on an itinerary that includes a number of potentially injury-inducing activities such as whitewater rafting or canyoneering. Outside of the major cities, emergency services can be limited and many resort areas will have only a clinic on-site, no full-scale hospital. If you get injured in more remote areas, your medical evacuation (or medivac) costs could be steep.

If you do decide to buy insurance, you can easily parse the different policies by visiting the website **InsureMyTrip.com,** which compares the policies of all of the major companies. Or contact one of the following reputable companies directly: **Access America** (☎ 866/807-3982; www.accessamerica.com); **Travel Guard International** (☎ 800/807-3982; www.travelguard.com); or **CSA Travel Protection** (☎ 800/873-9844; www.csatravelprotection.com).

PACKING

The most important item in your suitcase will be a pair of very, very comfortable shoes or sandals, because your dogs are gonna be barking! Vacations in Costa Rica are active ones, what with trekking up the sides of volcanoes, dropping onto platforms from ziplines, and trudging through cloud forests. A springy, supportive pair of waterproof footwear is essential (perhaps two pairs, in case one rubs). It's also vital to pack layers, especially if you're hitting different areas of the country. As you'll see from our weather chart (p. 345), there can be a dramatic shift in temperatures from the beach areas to the higher elevations of the Central Valley. If you're planning to visit both, you'll need to come prepared for both.

For what I'll call a "gumbo" itinerary—one that mixes beaches with rainforests with volcanoes and the city of San José—be sure to bring along the following items:

- **Sunblock**—a necessity this near to the equator. Bring it with you as prices for lotions are inflated in Costa Rica.
- **A hat**—for protection from the sun.
- **Long, quick drying pants**—required for some ziplines and horseback riding expeditions, and a good idea when hiking through buggy rain- and cloudforests.
- **Two bathing suits**—the humidity in some areas makes them slower to dry, so you'll want more than one.
- **Film and more film**—you're going to want to take pictures, and film is very expensive here. Either pack what you'll need, or go digital.
- **A sweatshirt**—for those chilly nights in the mountains.
- **Bug spray** with DEET or some other powerful repellent.
- **A rain poncho**—much easier to hike with than an umbrella and oh, so handy.
- **Binoculars**—they'll come in useful, I promise.
- **An assortment of clothing**—shorts, T-shirts, sundresses, underthings, what have you.

The key is to pack lightly if you can, as you'll likely be moving from place to place and don't want to spend your vacation in your room packing and unpacking.

MONEY MATTERS

The official currency of Costa Rica is the *colon.* There are 100 centimos to each *colon.* In spring 2006, the rate of exchange was approximately 500 *colones* to the American dollar, making it fairly easy to translate those two currencies (for those in Canada, the rate was 450 *colones* to the loonie; about 1,030 to the British pound; and 430 to the Australian dollar). That being said, you can go your entire vacation in Costa Rica without ever touching a *colon,* as American dollars are accepted in restaurants, shops, and hotels (especially true if you're traveling on an escorted tour). American dollars are de rigeur here, and you'll often find prices at hotels and restaurants listed in dollars, not *colones* (though if you pay with dollars, you'll usually get the change back in *colones,* so you will have some contact with the local bills and coins).

Because of this and because it's never advisable to travel with large amounts of cash on your person, don't go out of your way to change large amounts of money before you get to Costa Rica. Simply bring enough to last you for 1 or 2 days. Every area that has tourists will also have an **ATM or bank machine** (known here as *cajera automatica*). And the rate of exchange isn't bad, though additional fees can add up and will vary bank to bank. The **Cirrus** (☎ 800/424-7787; www.mastercard.com) and **Plus** (☎ 800/843-7587; www.visa.com) networks are common in Costa Rica; contact your network in advance for the addresses of ATMs in the areas that you'll visiting. Also, inform your bank that you'll be traveling out of the country so that it doesn't assume the card has been stolen and refuse to honor it.

Exchanging dollars for *colones:* Though you can usually change money at hotels, tourist information centers, and even some *pulperias* (convenience stores), you'll get the best rates at **banks.** These open weekdays from 9am to 3pm, with some branches not closing until 5pm. Private banks such as Banco de San José and Banex tend to be less crowded with fewer lines than the state-owned banks (such as Banco Popular and Banco de Costa Rica). Never, ever change money on the street; this is a common scam and you're more likely to be parted from your cash than have it exchanged.

Traveler's checks will elicit a confused stare from many waiters and shop clerks. With ATMs so common, hardly anyone uses these little slips of paper anymore. If you want the security of a travelers check, I'd recommend getting one of the new check cards, available from American Express. These cards have a preset limit on them, so if one gets stolen, the thief cannot wipe out your bank account or run up an ugly credit card bill. And like traveler's checks, American Express promises that lost cards can be replaced within 24 hours. Go to www.american express.com for more information.

Credit cards are widely accepted in Costa Rica, with Visa seeming to be the most used, though you shouldn't have difficulty using Mastercard, either (American Express and Discovery cards are a bit less common). They offer a safe way for the traveler to carry money as they can be replaced and/or disabled if lost or stolen. Plastic also generally offers a good rate of exchange. However, some hotels and B&Bs do charge higher rates (usually about 6%) to those who use plastic, to offset the fees they're required to pay, so angle for a discount if you can pay in cash. As well, some small shops and *sodas* (casual restaurants) will not accept credit cards. Be aware, too, that the fees attached to foreign transactions on credit cards can vary greatly, depending on your issuing bank. In general, Capital One and numerous credit unions offer the lowest fee structures for travelers.

To report a stolen **Visa** card, call ☎ 0800/011-0030; for **Mastercard,** ☎ 0800/011-0184; for **American Express,** ☎ 0800/012-3211.

Tipping and taxes: When guestimating your expenses for the trip, you should always factor in the 16.3% **hotel tax** you'll be required to pay as well as the **restaurant tax** of 13% (to that add 10% in mandatory service fees). In this book, all of the hotel rates are listed before taxes, which is why you may sometimes see a discrepancy between our prices and those of hotel websites (some hotels include the taxes in their posted rates and others don't). **Tips** are added automatically to restaurant bills (10%) and it is not customary to tip extra (though you certainly can if service has been superlative). It's also not necessary to tip taxi drivers, though porters should be given about $1 per bag.

HEALTH & SAFETY

Blazing sun, a powerful ocean, dense rainforests teeming with animals, bubbling volcanoes—Costa Rica's greatest assets, its major selling points, are also the elements that pose the greatest threat to the health and safety of the visitor. About 200 people drown here each year, mostly in riptides. Malaria and dengue fever have been found in some of the more remote, jungled corners of the country. In 1968, 78 people were killed when Arenal volcano erupted; another three perished in 2000 when an avalanche of hot gas and rocks hit a popular hiking trail (now closed).

Don't get me wrong, the vast majority of vacationers who come to this eco-paradise leave intact, with no impact whatsoever on their health or well-being. But it's important to respect Mother Nature's might, to know your own limits when you're planning an active vacation, and take the steps to keep yourself healthy.

The sun: I don't think I've ever seen as many lobster red tourists anywhere as I have in Costa Rica. The sun here is a fierce foe, as the country is just 8 to 11 degrees from the equator. My advice: Take the usual precautions against sunburn and dehydration but ratchet up your vigilance. At the beach be sure to reapply sun block every hour (a Tico joked to me that 30 SPF meant "apply every 30 minutes" in Costa Rica); always carry water with you; and invest in a good sun hat, a barrier against sunstroke. Let me repeat: The sun here is no joke (especially between 11am and 2pm each day), and a bad sunburn can really put a crimp in your vacation.

Riptides: There's a downside to those gnarly waves the surfers love: strong currents and sometimes riptides. If you get caught in a riptide (basically a viselike current pulling you out to sea), don't try and swim back to shore, as you probably won't have the strength. Instead, swim *parallel* to the shore, which will get you out of the riptide. Once you stop feeling its pull, make your way to shore, letting the force of the waves help you in. ***Important:*** Don't assume that because you're only about waist high in the water that you're not in trouble if you feel a strong current. Weaker swimmers, thinking they're just wading and being pulled out to sea, account for some 90% of those who drown in rip currents. If you're near enough to the shore for people to hear you, start yelling for help.

Tropical diseases: Nelson Mui, one of the authors of this guide, got an up-close-and-personal look at **giardia,** one of the endemic diseases here you *don't* want to get. A frighteningly strong gastro-intestinal parasite, it causes prolonged bouts of diarrhea and can be quite serious (Nelson lost 10 pounds in a month from it). Though most of the water is safe to drink in Costa Rica, this parasite is waterborne, so you may want to stick with the bottled stuff. Many locals will advise that for Limón and Puntarenas especially, both of which have had problems with water purity over the years. If you do experience severe diarrhea, its important that you take a stool sample in a clean glass jar to a clinic in the town where you are as quickly as possible (most clinics will be able to give you the results of the test by later afternoon if you get them a sample in the morning). Giardia and other intestinal *amebas* need to be treated with antibiotics (especially if you get *entomoeba histolytica,* which can do liver damage), so it's important you get a diagnosis as quickly as possible.

Malaria: This disease is endemic in certain parts of Costa Rica (near the Nicaraguan border and in the Valle de Estrella in Talamanca most notably), but as the areas are well off the tourist track, it's very, very rare for a visitor to come down with a case. If you're going to these areas, the Center for Disease Control in the U.S. suggests visitors consider taking chloroquine or some other anti-malarial prophylactic. Consult with your doctor, however, before you start any course of medication, as they do have side effects and the chances of getting malaria remain slim. **Dengue fever** is more of a concern, as there have been periodic outbreaks here over the years. Like malaria, it's spread by mosquito (hence our suggestion you pack bug spray with DEET), and seems to be a problem primarily in lowland urban areas; Puntarenas, Liberia, and Limón have all battled outbreaks. The symptoms are harsh: a sudden onset of a high fever, a rash on the lower limbs and chest and, most famously, severe headaches and muscle pains (which is why dengue is nicknamed the "bonecrusher disease" and "bone break fever"). Dengue fever will make you feel extremely ill for about a week, but is not life threatening, at least in its first infection. If you get another infection, especially of a different strain, it can lead to internal hemorrhaging and in extreme cases, death. Be sure to seek medical treatment as soon as possible if you experience any of the symptoms listed above.

Bites: Creepy crawlers, such as snakes, scorpions, black widow spiders, and tarantulas are part of the ecology of Costa Rica, but less of a danger than most visitors assume. While there are some venomous **snakes** here—rattlesnakes, fer-de-lance, eyelash vipers, and bushmasters—the vast majority are nonpoisonous. To avoid these slitherers, watch where you put your hands and don't go sticking them under fallen trees, rocks, and branches. If you do encounter a snake, don't try to touch it. Simply move slowly away and don't make any sudden movements. If you do get bitten, head immediately to a doctor for an anti-venom shot and don't waste time trying to treat the bite yourself (by sucking out venom or enlarging the wound; neither of these work and will waste time). You have 4 hours before the tissue around the bite will start to die, so stay calm and get moving. You're more likely to encounter a **scorpion** (as I did on my last visit, in my hotel room in Nosara). To avoid them, shake out your shoes in the morning and hang up your clothes at night. If you leave them in a pile of the floor, be sure to shake them out before getting dressed. As with snake bites, see a doctor if you do get bitten; generally scorpion bites are most dangerous for senior citizens and children under 6.

One other bug to look out for is **Africanized bees** (known in many areas by the macabre name "killer bees"). Usually they're not a problem unless you disturb their hive, so this is another case of look where you're putting your hands. If you do get attacked, you have two courses of action: Jump into water or run as fast as you can in a random pattern (bees don't have very good eyesight and you could lose them this way). Don't drop and try to take cover; they'll swarm you and the results can be serious. If you're allergic to bee stings, consult with your doctor before coming to Costa Rica.

Crime and safety: Theft is a problem in San José and the major resort areas that attract tourists, so it's important to be vigilant. Never carry large amounts of money on your person or a wallet in the back pocket of a backpack, where it can be easily filched. And don't lug the precious jewelry to Costa Rica; this is a laid-back country and it will be safer at home. Keep your passport and any other valuable documents in your hotel's safe rather than on your person. It's a good idea, in fact, to photocopy your passport, including the page with your Costa Rican entry stamp, so you'll have the necessary information in case it should be lost and you have to have it replaced at your consulate.

I discussed common roadside scams on p. 351. You also need to keep your wits about you when riding public transportation or walking on crowded streets. If you feel yourself being jostled, guard your valuables and get away from the jostler as quickly as possible. Keep your bags with you on public busses and if you have

If You Get Ill . . .

You've picked the right Central American country to do it in. A recent United Nations study ranked Costa Rica first among its neighbors for the quality of its health care. Many doctors here were trained in the United States and Europe, and because the dentistry is so good, it's spawned its own mini-tourist industry of people coming to Costa Rica for root canals instead of zipline tours (though some take the time to do the the canopy tours once their mouths are healed).

As in many areas of the world, the best medical care is to be found in the bigger cities. Many of Costa Rica's towns will only have a small clinic, so sometimes getting good care may be a matter of driving to a better medical facility. I list the names of the top hospitals and emergency rooms in the ABCs of Costa Rica section (p. 369)

One word on prescription medications: It is crucial that you pack your prescription medications in their original containers, and bring them in your carry-on luggage. Be sure also to bring along copies of your prescriptions in case you run out or misplace your pills. Knowing the name of the generic version of the drug you're taking is also a smart move, as the brand name of the pill you're looking for may be different in Costa Rica.

to put them in an upper rack, store them where you can keep an eye on them. Don't hang your purse off the back of your chair at an outdoor restaurant; keep it on your lap.

If you do get robbed, file a *denuncia* (theft report) at the nearest Organismo de Investigacion Judicial (OIJ); you'll find these in every major tourist area and in San José. They'll investigate and give you a document that you can give to your insurance company.

Prostitution is legal in Costa Rica, but there are scams associated with it, so be very careful if you're planning to engage in this type of activity. Also know that many of the "working girls" are actually transvestites, so if this is not what you're looking for, well, ask (many transvestites make very convincing women). Costa Rica has gained a reputation for sex tourism, with many people coming here to try and have sex with minors. This, of course, is illegal and the government is making a big push to do away with this segment of the industry. If you're caught having sex with a minor, the punishment will be severe.

SPECIALIZED TRAVEL RESOURCES

FOR FAMILIES

Your child, if over the age of 5, may very well step out of character and do the unthinkable: He or she may just *thank you* for taking him to Costa Rica. It's a destination that sparks the imagination, offering the types of challenging activities that kids who are beyond the toddler stage will eat up. For the most part, age 5 or 6 is the starting age for zipline tours, whitewater rafting, horseback expeditions, and other thrill-inducing activities. And if your kids are anything like my older daughter, they'll be buzzing from morning to night with all the adventures they're having, which sometimes can be as simple as studying the sea creatures in the tidal pools or body surfing the waves on a boogie board.

Beyond the fun in the sun (and in the rainforests, and on the rivers, and in the caves), Costa Rica is choice pick for families because of its laid-back nature. There's literally no restaurant in the country where you would feel uncomfortable taking the young ones. Even the fanciest joints welcome children warmly. And speaking of restaurants, this is a country where pizza, chicken fingers, hamburgers, and other American-style comfort foods are on nearly every menu, so if you have a picky eater in tow, you shouldn't have any problems getting him or her fed.

I'm less enthusiastic about Costa Rica as a destination for families with children age 4 and under. Why? Because you, the parents, may get jealous of other travelers and their ability to try out the really fun stuff that's verboten or very difficult for little kids. Like that volcano hike that's out of the question because it's 4 hours long and over rough terrain. Or that scenic walk to the waterfall that became an endurance test when you had to carry Junior on your shoulders up and down that 45-degree slope. Not to mention the canopy tours, the horseback rides, the canyoneering, the whitewater rafting. Yes, the wee ones will enjoy the beach, but to my mind, that's not the primary reason one comes to Costa Rica. There are easier places to get to for simple beach vacations; most come here to mix the beach and the forest and all the adventures in between. And even the beaches, many of them, aren't that little-kid-friendly, what with strong currents (great for surfers, terrible for toddlers) and unshaded patches where you can watch your child sunburn in the equatorial rays right before your eyes. If you do decide to take very small children to Costa Rica, look carefully at the safety of the beach you may be visiting; and look for soft adventures, such as mangrove boat tours, aerial trams, hanging bridges, and nature parks with butterfly gardens—these should all be the right speed for your toddler or small child.

Here are the nitty-gritty details of traveling with children:

Costs: Most hotels allow children under the age of 3 or 4 to stay for free in their parent's room, and most give a discount or a freebie to those under 12. Look for similar discounts on activities.

Entrance requirements: Children, no matter how young, will need their own passport to get into Costa Rica. If a single parent is traveling with a child, he may be required to show a notarized letter from the child's other parent approving the travel. Contact the Costa Rican embassy if this last point is an issue for you.

Tours: If you're nervous about traveling with a cranky teen or preteen, there are tours specially created for families who wish to travel with other families (and they tend to be action packed). Among the companies that offer these are **Horizontes** (www.horizontes.com); **GAP Adventures** (www.gapadventures.com); and, on the high end of the price scale, **Tauck Tours** (www.tauck.com).

Babysitting: You can usually arrange this through your hotel; prices, however, will vary from property to property.

One final note on traveling with children: Renting **vacation homes** is a cost-effective option in Costa Rica, good news for families who can take advantage of the extra space, privacy, and most important kitchen facilities this option provides. Think about it: You may actually have a door to close between you and the kids at night! And if they don't eat their dinner at the restaurant, it's not a crisis as you can whip them up something quickly at "home" (or you may skip restaurants altogether to save money, no great loss as much of the food in Costa Rica is pretty bland). You'll find write-ups of vacation home rental companies in every chapter of this book.

Finally, look out for the 🛝 symbol, which will alert you to those hotels, restaurants, and activities that are particularly good for families.

FOR TRAVELERS WITH DISABILITIES

Though a law was passed in 1996 mandating equal opportunities in education and careers for people with disabilities and some hotels are now beginning to add accessible facilities for guests, Costa Rica is for the most part a challenge for those with mobility impairments. No public buses are equipped for wheelchair use yet; when there are sidewalks they're often cracked and uneven, with curbs a full foot off the street; and when there aren't sidewalks, pedestrians find themselves dodging traffic on potholed streets. The lodging scene isn't much better, with hotels just in the past couple of years starting to adapt rooms and bathrooms for those in wheelchairs.

Nonetheless, hundreds of persons with disabilities vacation in Costa Rica each year and enjoy themselves doing it. Many turn to specialist travel agencies and tour operators to help organize the trip and set up whatever extra assistance might be necessary. You can find a number of companies through **SATH (Society for Accessible Travel & Hospitality;** ☎ 212/447-7284; www.sath.org), which serves as a clearinghouse for this sort of information, as well as lobbying for accessible travel. Or contact one of the following highly regarded companies directly: **Flying Wheels Travel** (☎ 507/451-5005; www.flyingwheelstravel.com); **Accessible Journeys** (☎ 800/846-4537 or 610/521-0339; www.disabilitytravel.com); **Los Trogones Travel Agency** (☎ 506/256-0457; www.hispanohost.com); and **Vaya Con Silla De Ruedas** (☎ 506/454-2810; www.gowithwheelchairs.com).

The last two are Costa Rican–based agencies, but all should be able to find accessible accommodations, arrange appropriate vans for accommodations, and set up tours appropriate for those with all sorts of disabilities, from mobility impairments to vision problems or hearing loss.

FOR GAY & LESBIAN TRAVELERS

While it's not Provincetown, Rhode Island, or Berlin, Germany, yet, Costa Rica has proved to be quite tolerant of gay and lesbian visitors (and residents, for that matter). Yes, the predominant religion here is Catholicism, so public shows of affection will be awkward, but Ticos have always had a very "live and let live" philosophy, and incidents of gay bashing have been few and far between in the last several years. San José has a thriving gay nightlife scene (p. 44), and Quepos, near Manuel Antonio, has earned the nickname "Gay-pos" for its many gay guesthouses and nightspots.

We've covered a number of gay guesthouses and bars in this book, but if you'd like to learn more, or are interested in current information on special events, parties, and the like, pick up a copy of *Gayness,* a newspaper for the community, found on newsstands in San José. You can also try the website the **Gay and Lesbian Guide to Costa Rica** (www.gaycostarica.com) or **Purple Roofs Gay and**

Lesbian Travel Directory (www.purpleroofs.com, click on "Central America"), which focuses on gay-friendly accommodations. **Out Travel** (www.outtraveler.com) is another solid resource for information on issues of gay travel both to Costa Rica and worldwide.

FOR SENIOR TRAVELERS

The bad news is senior discounts are not at all common in Costa Rica, and airlines no longer discount the tickets of those over 65. So should you give up entirely on the privileges you enjoy in your home country? No, it can't hurt to ask if there's any sort of discount; perhaps the question will prompt an act of generosity on the part of the person you're talking with. If you belong to **AARP** (601 E Street NW, Washington, DC, 24009; ☎ 888/687-2277; www.aarp.org), see if they have any available discounts for Costa Rican travel before you make your plans. Do your homework before booking; you want to make sure AARP's discount (which is generally about 10%) trumps that of other types of discounts you might get on your own.

In terms of meals, Costa Rica does not have the early-bird specials you'll find in U.S. cities largely populated by seniors. What it does have are heaping portions, and my father, Arthur Frommer (now himself over 70), insists that with age comes a diminishment in appetite. His advice for seniors, which I pass along here, is to share food: One appetizer and one entree is what he and his wife have when they go out to dine, and they leave perfectly satisfied.

FOR WOMEN

Get ready for catcalls, perhaps some hisses on the streets, and shouted-out compliments in Spanish. This is a macho, Latin American country, after all, and the men engage in these activities as much to egg each other on as to get to know you (in fact, I think they'd be shocked if you stopped to converse). And if you're blonde, you'll get even more attention (women who look like they could be Costa Rican tend to get a bit less of the treatment). So, square your shoulders and keep walking; the incidents of actual sexual assaults in Costa Rica are blessedly low. Of course, you shouldn't take stupid chances, especially if you're traveling alone: Don't carry a lot of money with you, stick with the more populated streets or take

Staying Wired While Away

Any Costa Rican town with any level of tourism will boast an Internet cafe nowadays. To find these cafes in advance of your trip, try **www.cyber captive.com** or **www.cybercafe.com**. As well, all of the post offices in Costa Rica are now equipped with computer stations where, for a fee, you'll be able to go online to check e-mail. You'll also find access at airports, for a fee (Boingo is a major provider here). Lately, some hotels have been getting wired, but it's important to check in advance if this is important to you, as not all will offer this service.

a taxi, and keep your wits about you. In all likelihood, you'll be just fine and have a great time, but you know that old adage: "Better to be safe . . .."

A WORD ON ECOTOURISM

A full 25.6% of the land in Costa Rica is protected from development, in some fashion. Beyond the Nation Parks (of which there are 25), biological reserves (8) and wildlife refuges (56), there are many private reserves with ecolodges doing a commendable job of protecting the nature here (while offering guests a wonderful and very private experience, akin to what they'll experience at nearby national parks, but without the crowds). You'll find recommendations for these types of ecolodges throughout the book; staying at them gives a pat on the back to the green travel movement in Costa Rica.

If you're interested in finding out whether the resort you've picked is suitably "green," you'll need to ask the right questions. Currently, the government does offer Certificates of Sustainable Tourism, but many in the ecotravel movement have argued that its standards are too lenient (allowing many of the megaresorts in without any real commitment to protecting the environment or promoting local culture), and too mired in red tape (leading many of the truly eco-friendly parks and resorts to not even try for the certification). Some questions you may want to ask would involve their use of pesticides and biodegradable cleaning products, how careful they are with waste management, and whether they recycle. Coherent answers to these questions, even if you don't fully understand them, will show that your hotel is on the green bandwagon. Be sure to ask to speak to management, though (it wouldn't be appropriate to grill the reservationist on this matter).

While there have been missteps, as we've pointed out throughout the book, such as not enough money given to the enforcement of conservation law and developing certain areas too quickly and haphazardly, the Costa Rican government and people have their hearts in the right place when it comes to ecotourism. They've seen firsthand, after all, how protecting the remarkable biodiversity of their country as well as its natural beauty can have big dividends, in terms of tourist dollars. Costa Rica has one of the highest literacy rates in Central America and a higher standard of living than its neighbors. And by choosing to spend your money here, you're sending a big message to the international travel community that ecotourism is important to travelers, and thus should be important to the industry itself.

RECOMMENDED READING

Before heading off to Costa Rica, you may want to purchase a few of the following books to help give you a better context for what you'll be seeing and experiencing in Costa Rica:

Costa Rica in Focus: The Last Country the Gods Made, by Adrian Colesberry and Brass MacLean, looks like a coffee-table book thanks to its spellbinding photos by Kimberly Parsons, but reads like an astute cultural history, giving a sometimes quirky but always intriguing overview of Costa Rican cultural history.

Costa Rica: A Traveler's Literary Companion, edited by Barbara Ras, is a great airplane or beach read, filled with tales from both the early 20th century and today that illuminate what it's like to live in Costa Rica. The book is arranged by region, which is quite helpful for the traveler.

The Ticos: Culture and Social Change, by Richard, Karen, and Mavis Biesanz, is a highly readable and portable look at what makes the country and its people tick. A fascinating read.

Costa Rica (Travelers Wildlife Guide), by Lee Beletsky, is a highly useful, portable, and brief field guide, perfect for the curious traveler who may already be carrying too many things in his backpack.

Tropical Nature: Life and Death in the Rainforests of Central and South America, by Adrian Forsythe and Ken Miatta, is really a collection of essays on different aspects of the lifecycle of the rainforest and many of the creatures who call it home. The writing is superb and though it doesn't just deal with Costa Rica, it will give visitors here, even those not usually drawn to books on scientific matters, a deep understanding and appreciation of the nature that they'll be seeing.

A Guide to the Birds of Costa Rica, by F. Gary Stiles and Alexandra F. Skutch, is the bible of bird-watching in Costa Rica (it's the one the naturalists themselves use when leading tours).

The ABCs of Costa Rica

Area codes If you're calling Costa Rica from outside the country, the 506 prefix will connect you to every area of the country. There are no real "area codes" here. You will however find several types of toll-free numbers. Some will start with 800, others with 0800, and some will have eight rather than the standard seven digits following those numbers.

Business hours Offices are generally open on weekdays between 8am and 5pm, while banks tend to close at 3pm. A scattering of banks, however, do stay open until 5pm. Typically, stores open between 9am and 10am and close at around 6pm Monday through Saturday, except for those in the modern malls, which stay open until 8 or 9pm. Many stores also close down for an hour at lunch (though not those in the malls). Bars and dance clubs tend to stay open until 1 or 2am.

Drinking laws 18 is the legal age for the purchase and consumption of any sort of alcohol and proof of age is sometimes requested at liquor stores, bars, clubs, and restaurants, so be sure to carry photo identification with you at all times. During the 2 days before Easter and the 2 days before and after presidential elections, the sale of alcohol is illegal (but other than those dates, it's usually available 7 days a week).

Electricity Costa Rica uses 110–120 volts AC (60 cycles), the same as in the United States. In Europe, Australia, and New Zealand the standard is 220–240 volts AC (50 cycles) and adaptors can be hard to find, so it's advisable to bring your own. Americans may also want to carry adaptors as three-pronged outlets can be difficult to find.

Emergencies Telephone ☎ 911 for the police, to report a fire, or get an ambulance. Ask to speak with an English-speaking operator if your Spanish is weak. Costa Rica also has individual numbers for different emergency services and these should be tried if you can't get through on 911: it's ☎ 128 for an ambulance; ☎ 118 to report a fire; and ☎ 222-1365 for the police. If you have a medical emergency that does not require an ambulance you should be able to walk into the nearest hospital emergency room (see below).

Embassies and Consulates You'll find all of the following in San José: **United States Embassy** (in front of Centro Commercial, on the road to Pavas; ☎ 519-2000; **Canadian Consulate** (Oficentral Ejectivo La Sabana, Edeficio 5; ☎ 242-4400); **British Embassy** (Paseo Colon between calles 38 and 40; ☎ 258-2025). There are no Australian and New Zealand Embassies in San José.

Hospitals The following hospitals are well regarded and have emergency rooms that are open 24 hours and a good standard of care:

Clinica Biblica Catolica (Ave. 14, calles Central and 1, San José; ☎ 506/522-1000; www.clinicabiblica.com)

Hospital CIMA San José (on the highway to Santa Ana in the Central Valley; ☎ 506/208-1000; www.hospitalsanjose.com)

Information For directory assistance call ☎ 113; for international directory assistance dial ☎ 124.

Laundry Launderettes are not common in Costa Rica, and are found almost entirely in San José. Hotels do launder clothes for guests, but the charge for this service tends to be steep.

Newspapers & Magazines There are six major Spanish newspapers and one English language publication, the *Tico Times.* You should also be able to find the major American newspapers and magazines such as *USA Today, The New York Times, Time,* and *Newsweek.*

Restrooms Ask for *sanitarios, servicios sanitarios,* or *banos.* There are public bathrooms available at most service stations and usually at the entrances of national parks. Within cities, your best bet is to use the facilities at a hotel or restaurant, though you may have to buy a soda or something else small for the privilege.

Smoking Many people smoke in Costa Rica and while restaurants are required to have nonsmoking sections, a number don't follow the law. Bars also can get very smoky.

Taxes Along with hotel and restaurant taxes (p. 361), there is a $26 departure tax that can be a sorry surprise at the airport before you depart. You pay it at the Banco Credito Agricola del Cartago on site (the lines to pay it can be epic, especially at Liberia Airport). Some local travel agencies and hotels will purchase departure tax for a small service fee, which may be worth it just to avoid that awful line.

Telephone Phone calls within Costa Rica cost approximately 2 cents (or 10 *colones*) per minute. Pay phones take either 5-,10-, or 20-*colon* coins, though most phones only accept calling cards nowadays. These can be purchased at pharmacies and gift shops. The phone cards have different ranges for use; the best are the **197** and **199** calling cards, which can be used for any phone in the country. Generally the 197 cards are for national calls, and the 199 for international (they come in assorted denominations).

You can also make international calls and send faxes from the **ICE office,** Avenida 2 between calles 1 and 3 in San José (☎ 255-0444). It's open daily from 7am to 10pm (many hotels also offer these services).

Time Costa Rica is on Central Standard Time (the same as Chicago), 6 hours behind Greenwich Mean Time. Daylight savings is not observed here, so the time difference is an additional hour April through May.

Tipping Please see p. 361.

10

Costa Rican Wildlife

By Eliot Greenspan & E. Z. Weaver

FOR SUCH A SMALL COUNTRY, COSTA RICA IS INCREDIBLY RICH IN biodiversity. With just .01% of the earth's landmass, Costa Rica is home to some 5% of its biodiversity. Whether you come to Costa Rica to check 100 or so species off your lifetime list, or just to check out of the rat race for a week or so, you'll be surrounded by a rich and varied collection of flora and fauna. The information below is meant to be a selective introduction to some of what you might see.

In many instances, the prime viewing recommendations should be taken with a firm dose of reality. Most casual visitors and even many dedicated naturalists will never see a wildcat or kinkajou. However, anyone working with a good guide should be able to see a broad selection of Costa Rica's impressive flora and fauna.

FAUNA

MAMMALS

Costa Rica has over 225 species of mammals. Roughly half of these are bats. While it is very unlikely that you will spot a wildcat, you have good odds of catching a glimpse of a monkey, coatimundi, peccary, or sloth, or more likely any number of the above.

Jaguar

SCIENTIFIC NAME   *Panthera onca*

WORTH NOTING   This cat measures from 1 to 1.8m (3¼–6 ft.) plus tail and is distinguished by its tan/yellowish fur with black spots. Often called simply *tigre* (tiger) in Costa Rica.

PRIME VIEWING   **Jaguars** exist in all major tracts of primary and secondary forest in Costa Rica, as well as some open savannahs. However, jaguars are endangered and extremely hard to see in the wild. The largest concentrations of jaguars can be found in Corcovado National Park on the Osa Peninsula.

SCIENTIFIC NAME   *Leopardus pardalis*

WORTH NOTING   Known as *manigordo,* or "fat paws," in Costa Rica, the tail of this small cat is longer than its rear leg, which makes for easy identification. **Ocelots** are mostly nocturnal, and they sleep in trees.

PRIME VIEWING   Forests in all regions of Costa Rica, with the greatest concentration found on the Osa Peninsula.

Ocelot

SCIENTIFIC NAME   *Agouti paca*

WORTH NOTING   The **paca,** a nocturnal rodent, inhabits the forest floor, feeding on fallen fruit, leaves, and some tubers dug from the ground.

PRIME VIEWING   Known as *tepezquintle* in Costa Rica, these are most often found near water throughout many habitats of Costa Rica, from river valleys to swamps to dense tropical forest. However, since they're nocturnal, you're much more likely to see their smaller cousin, the diurnal agouti or *guatusa.*

Paca

Baird's Tapir

SCIENTIFIC NAME   *Tapirus bairdii*

WORTH NOTING   Known as the *danta* or *macho de monte,* **Baird's tapir** is the largest land mammal in Costa Rica. Tapirs are active both day and night, foraging along riverbanks, streams, and forest clearings.

PRIME VIEWING   An endangered species, tapirs can be found in wet forested areas, particularly on the Caribbean and south Pacific slopes.

SCIENTIFIC NAME   *Nasua narica*

WORTH NOTING   Known as *pizote* in Costa Rica, the raccoonlike **coatimundi** can adapt to habitat disturbances and is often spotted near hotels and nature lodges. Active both day and night, it is equally comfortable on the ground and in trees.

PRIME VIEWING   Found in a variety of habitats across Costa Rica, from dry scrub to dense forests, on the mainland as well as the coastal islands. Social animals, they are often found in groups of 10 to 20.

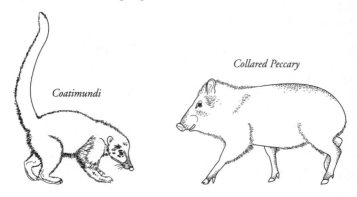

Coatimundi

Collared Peccary

SCIENTIFIC NAME   *Tayassu tajacu*

WORTH NOTING   Called *saino* or *chancho de monte* in Costa Rica, the **collared peccary** is a black or brown piglike animal that travels in small groups (larger where populations are still numerous) and has a strong musk odor.

PRIME VIEWING   Low- and middle-elevation forests in most of Costa Rica.

Northern Tamandua

SCIENTIFIC NAME   *Tamandua mexicana*

WORTH NOTING   Also known as the collared anteater (*oso hormiguero* in Spanish), the **northern tamandua** grows up to 77 centimeters (30 in.) long, not counting its thick tail which can be as long its body. It is active diurnally and nocturnally.

PRIME VIEWING   Low- and middle-elevation forests in most of Costa Rica.

SCIENTIFIC NAME   *Bradypus variegatus*

WORTH NOTING   The larger and more commonly sighted of Costa Rica's two sloth species, the **three-toed sloth** has long, coarse brown to gray fur and a distinctive eye band. It has three long, sharp claws on each foreleg. Except for brief periods used for defecation, these slow-moving creatures are entirely arboreal.

PRIME VIEWING   Low- and middle-elevation forests in most of Costa Rica. While sloths can be found in a wide variety of trees, they are most commonly spotted in the relatively sparsely leaved cecropia (see later in this chapter).

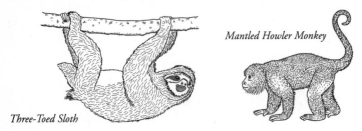

Mantled Howler Monkey

Three-Toed Sloth

SCIENTIFIC NAME   *Alouatta palliata*

WORTH NOTING   Known locally as *mono congo,* the highly social **mantled howler monkey** grows to 56 centimeters (22 in.) in size and often travels in groups of 10 to 30. The loud roar of the male can be heard as far as 1.6km (1 mile) away.

PRIME VIEWING   Wet and dry forests across Costa Rica. Almost entirely arboreal, they tend to favor the higher reaches of the canopy.

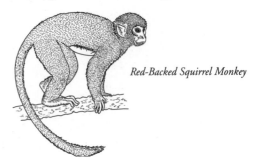

Red-Backed Squirrel Monkey

SCIENTIFIC NAME   *Saimiri oerstedii*

WORTH NOTING   The smallest and friskiest of Costa Rica's monkeys, the **red-backed squirrel monkey,** or *mono titi,* is also its most endangered. Active in the daytime, these monkeys travel in small to midsize groups. Squirrel monkeys do not have a prehensile tail.

PRIME VIEWING   Manuel Antonio National Park and Corcovado National Park.

BIRDS

Costa Rica has over 850 identified species of resident and migrant birds. The variety of habitats and compact nature of the country make it a major bird-watching destination.

Jabiru Stork

SCIENTIFIC NAME *Jabiru mycteria*

WORTH NOTING One of the largest birds in the world, the **jabiru stork** stands 1.5m (5 ft.) tall, with a wingspan of 2.4m (8 ft.) and a .3m (1-ft.) bill. An endangered species, the jabiru is very rare, with only a dozen or so nesting pairs in Costa Rica.

PRIME VIEWING The wetlands of Palo Verde National Park and Caño Negro Wildlife Reserve are the best places to try to spot the jabiru stork. The birds arrive in Costa Rica from Mexico in November and fly north with the rains in May or June.

Keel-Billed Toucan

SCIENTIFIC NAME *Ramphastos sulfuratus*

WORTH NOTING The rainbow-colored canoe-shape bill and brightly colored feathers make the **keel-billed toucan** a favorite of bird-watching tours. The toucan can grow to about 51 centimeters (20 in.) in length. It's similar in size and shape to the chestnut mandibled toucan. Costa Rica also is home to several smaller toucanet and aracari species.

PRIME VIEWING Lowland forests on the Caribbean and north Pacific slopes.

SCIENTIFIC NAME   *Ara macao*

WORTH NOTING   Known as *guacamaya* or *lapa* in Costa Rica, the **scarlet macaw** is a long-tailed member of the parrot family. It can reach 89 centimeters (35 in.) in length. The bird is endangered over most of its range, particularly because it is so coveted as a pet. Its loud squawk and rainbow-colored feathers are quite distinctive.

PRIME VIEWING   Carara National Park, Corcovado National Park, and Piedras Blancas National Park.

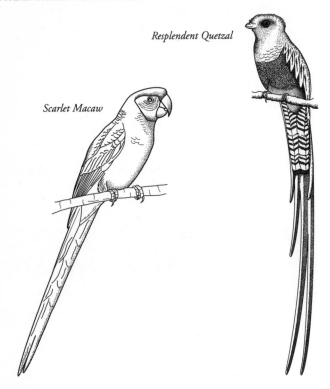

Resplendent Quetzal

Scarlet Macaw

SCIENTIFIC NAME   *Pharomchrus mocinno*

WORTH NOTING   Perhaps the most distinctive and spectacular bird in Central America, the **resplendent quetzal,** of the trogon family, can grow to 37 centimeters (15 in.). The males are distinctive, with bright red chests, iridescent blue-green coats, yellow bill, and tail feathers that can reach another 76 centimeters (30 in.) in length. The females lack the long tail feathers and a have duller beak and less pronounced red chest.

PRIME VIEWING   High-elevation wet and cloud forests, particularly in the Monteverde Cloud Forest Preserve and along the Cerro de la Muerte.

SCIENTIFIC NAME   *Fregata magnificens*

WORTH NOTING   The **magnificent frigate bird** is a naturally agile flier and it swoops (unlike other sea birds, it doesn't dive or swim) to pluck food from the water's surface—or more commonly, it steals catch from the mouths of other birds.

PRIME VIEWING   Along the shores and coastal islands of both coasts. Often seen soaring high overhead.

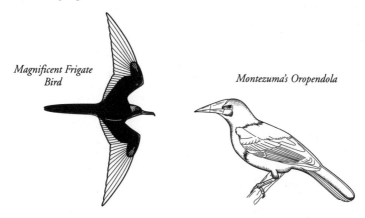

Magnificent Frigate
Bird

Montezuma's Oropendola

SCIENTIFIC NAME   *Psarocolius montezuma*

WORTH NOTING   **Montezuma's oropendola** has a black head, brown body, a yellow-edged tail, a large black bill with an orange tip, and a blue patch under the eye. These birds build long, teardrop-shape hanging nests, often found in large groups. They have several distinct loud calls, including one that they make while briefly hanging upside down.

PRIME VIEWING   Low and middle elevations along the Caribbean slope, and some sections of eastern Guanacaste.

Roseate Spoonbill

SCIENTIFIC NAME   *Ajaia ajaja*

WORTH NOTING   The **roseate spoonbill** is a large water bird, pink or light red in color and with a large spoon-shape bill. Also known as *garza rosada* (pink heron). They were almost made extinct in the United States because their pink wings were sought for feather fans.

PRIME VIEWING   Low-lying wetlands, both fresh and salt water, along both coasts.

SCIENTIFIC NAME   *Bubulcus ibis*

WORTH NOTING   The **cattle egret** changes color during breeding: A yellowish buff color appears on the head, chest, and back, and a reddish hue emerges on the bill and legs. They are usually seen anywhere there are cattle, hence the name, but can also often be found following behind tractors.

PRIME VIEWING   Throughout the country.

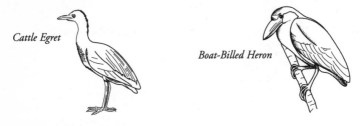

Cattle Egret

Boat-Billed Heron

SCIENTIFIC NAME   *Cochlearius cochlearius*

WORTH NOTING   The midsize **boat-billed heron** (about 51cm/20 in.) has a large black head, a large broad bill, and a rusty brown color.

PRIME VIEWING   Throughout the country, near marshes, swamps, rivers, and mangroves.

Laughing Falcon

SCIENTIFIC NAME   *Herpetotheres cachinnans*

WORTH NOTING   The **laughing falcon** is also known as the *guaco* in Costa Rica. It gets its name from its loud, piercing call. This largish (56cm/22 in.) bird of prey's wingspan reaches an impressive 94 centimeters (37 in.). It specializes in eating both venomous and nonvenomous snakes but will also hunt lizards and small rodents.

PRIME VIEWING   Throughout the country, most commonly in lowland areas, near forest edges, grasslands, and farmlands.

AMPHIBIANS

Frogs, toads, and salamanders are actually some of the most beguiling, beautiful, and easy-to-spot residents of tropical forests.

SCIENTIFIC NAME   *Bufo marinus*

WORTH NOTING   The largest toad in the Americas, the 20-centimeter (8-in.) wart-covered **marine toad** is also known as *sapo grande* (giant toad). The females are mottled in color, while the males are uniformly brown. These voracious toads have been known to eat small mammals, along with other toads, lizards, and just about any insect within range. They also have a very strong toxic chemical defense mechanism.

PRIME VIEWING   In forests and open areas throughout Costa Rica.

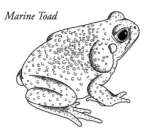
Marine Toad

Mexican Burrowing Toad

SCIENTIFIC NAME   *Rhinophrynus dorsalis*

WORTH NOTING   The bloblike, 7.6-centimeter (3-in.) **Mexican burrowing toad** will inflate like a blowfish when frightened. It often has a single red, orange, or yellow line down the center of its brown or black back.

PRIME VIEWING   Pacific lower-elevation forests and moist grasslands and farmlands.

Red-Eyed Tree Frog

Green and Black Poison Arrow Frog

SCIENTIFIC NAME   *Agalychnis callidryas*

WORTH NOTING   The colorful 7.6-centimeter (3-in.) **red-eyed tree frog** usually has a pale- or dark-green back, sometimes with white or yellow spots, with blue-purple patches and vertical bars on the body, orange hands and feet, and deep red eyes. Also known as the gaudy leaf frog or red-eyed tree frog. Nocturnal.

PRIME VIEWING   Low- and middle-elevation wet forests throughout Costa Rica. This is a very beautiful and distinctive-looking frog that you will certainly see on T-shirts and postcards if not in the wild.

SCIENTIFIC NAME   *Dendrobates auratus*

WORTH NOTING   Also called the harlequin poison-arrow frog, the small **green and black poison arrow frog** ranges between 2.5 and 4 centimeters (1–1.5 in.) in length. It has distinctive markings of iridescent green mixed with deep black.

PRIME VIEWING   On the ground, around tree roots, and under fallen logs, in low- and middle-elevation wet forests on the Caribbean and southern Pacific slopes.

REPTILES

Costa Rica's reptile species range from the frightening and justly feared fer-de-lance pit viper and massive American crocodile to a wide variety of turtles and lizards. *Note:* Sea turtles are included in the "Sea Life" section below.

SCIENTIFIC NAME   *Boa constrictor*

WORTH NOTING   Adult **boa constrictors** (*bécquer* in Costa Rica) average about 1.8 to 3m (6–10 ft.) in length and weigh over 27 kilograms (60 lb.). Their coloration camouflages them, but look for patterns of cream, brown, gray, and black ovals and diamonds.

PRIME VIEWING   Low- and middle-elevation wet and dry forests, country-wide. They often live in rafters and eaves of homes in rural areas.

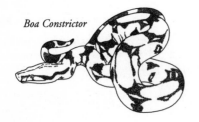
Boa Constrictor

Fer-de-Lance

SCIENTIFIC NAME   *Bothrops atrox*

WORTH NOTING   Known as *terciopelo* in Costa Rica, the aggressive **fer-de-lance** can grow to 2.4m (8 ft.) in length. Beige, brown, or black triangles flank either side of the head, while the area under the head is a vivid yellow. These snakes begin life as arboreal but become increasingly terrestrial as they grow older and larger.

PRIME VIEWING   All regions.

Leaf-Toed Gecko

SCIENTIFIC NAME   *Phyllodactylus xanti*

WORTH NOTING   Spotting the 6.8-centimeter (2½-in.) **leaf-toed gecko** is easy—it loves to be around buildings and other areas of human activity.

PRIME VIEWING   Common on the ground and in the leaf litter of low- and middle-elevation forests throughout the country.

Smooth Gecko

SCIENTIFIC NAME   *Thecadactylus rapicauda*

WORTH NOTING   The **smooth gecko**'s autonomous tail detaches from its body and acts as a diversion to a potential predator; it grows back later in a lighter shade.

PRIME VIEWING   Low-elevation wet forests on the Caribbean and southern Pacific slopes, as well as in urban and rural residential environments.

Green Iguana

SCIENTIFIC NAME   *Iguana iguana*

WORTH NOTING   **Green iguanas** can vary in shades ranging from bright green to a dull grayish-green, with quite a bit of orange mixed in. The iguana will often perch on a branch overhanging a river and plunge into the water when threatened.

PRIME VIEWING   All lowland regions of the country, living near rivers and streams, along both coasts.

Basilisk

SCIENTIFIC NAME   *Basiliscus vittatus*

WORTH NOTING   The **basilisk** can run across the surface of water for short distances by using its hind legs and holding its body almost upright; thus, the reptile is also known as "the Jesus Christ lizard."

PRIME VIEWING   In trees and on rocks located near water in wet forests throughout the country.

American Crocodile

SCIENTIFIC NAME   *Crocodylus acutus*

WORTH NOTING   Although an endangered species, environmental awareness and protection policies have allowed the massive **American crocodile** to mount an impressive comeback in recent years. While these reptiles can reach lengths of 6.4m (21 ft.), most are much smaller, usually less than 4m (13 ft.).

PRIME VIEWING   Near swamps, mangrove swamps, estuaries, large rivers, and coastal lowlands, countrywide. Guaranteed viewing from the bridge over the Tarcoles River, on the coastal highway to Jacó and Manuel Antonio.

SEA LIFE

With more than 1,290km (800 miles) of shoreline on both the Pacific and Caribbean coasts, Costa Rica has a rich diversity of underwater flora and fauna.

SCIENTIFIC NAME   *Rhincodon typus*

WORTH NOTING   Although the **whale shark** grows to lengths of 14m (45 ft.) or more, its gentle nature makes swimming with them a special treat for divers and snorkelers.

PRIME VIEWING   Can occasionally be spotted off Caño Island, and more frequently off Cocos Island.

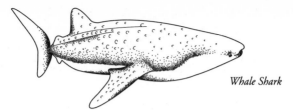

Whale Shark

SCIENTIFIC NAME   *Dermochelys coriacea*

WORTH NOTING   The world's largest sea turtle (reaching nearly 2.4m/8 ft. in length and weighing more than 544kg/1,200 lb.), the **leatherback sea turtle** is now an endangered species.

PRIME VIEWING   While these large reptiles do nest off Tortuguero, their prime nesting site in Costa Rica is Playa Grande, near Tamarindo.

Leatherback Sea Turtle

Olive Ridley Sea Turtle

SCIENTIFIC NAME   *Lepidochelys olivacea*

WORTH NOTING   Also known as *tortuga lora,* the **Olive Ridley sea turtle** is the most common and popular of Costa Rica's sea turtles, famous for its massive group nestings, or *arribadas.*

PRIME VIEWING   Large *arribadas* occur from July through December, and to a lesser extent from January through June. Playa Nancite in Santa Rosa National Park and Ostional beach are the prime nesting sites.

SCIENTIFIC NAME   *Gymnothorax mordax*

WORTH NOTING   Distinguished by a swaying serpent-head and teeth-filled jaw that continually opens and closes, the **moray eel** is most commonly seen with only its head appearing from behind rocks. At night, however, it leaves its home along the reef to hunt for small fish, crustaceans, shrimp, and octopus.

PRIME VIEWING   Rocky areas and reefs off both coasts.

Moray Eel

SCIENTIFIC NAME   *Megaptera novaeangliae*

WORTH NOTING   The migratory **humpbacked whale** spends the winters in warm southern waters and has been increasingly spotted close to the shores of Costa Rica's southern Pacific coast. These mammals have black backs and whitish throat and chest areas. Females have been known to calve here.

PRIME VIEWING   Most common in the waters off of Drake Bay and Caño Island. From December through April.

Humpbacked Whale

SCIENTIFIC NAME   *Tursiops truncates*

WORTH NOTING   Its wide tail fin, dark-gray back, and light-gray sides identify the **bottle-nosed dolphin.** Dolphins grow to lengths of 3.7m (12 ft.) and weigh up to 635 kilograms (1,400 lb.).

PRIME VIEWING   Along both coasts and inside the Golfo Dulce.

Bottle-Nosed Dolphin

SCIENTIFIC NAME   *Diploria strigosa*

WORTH NOTING   The distinctive **brain coral** is named for its striking physical similarity to a human brain.

PRIME VIEWING   Reefs off both coasts.

Brain Coral

INVERTEBRATES

Creepy crawlies, biting bugs, spiders, and the like give most folks chills. But this group, which includes moths, butterflies, ants, beetles, and even crabs, includes some of the most fascinating and easily viewed fauna in Costa Rica.

SCIENTIFIC NAME   *Morpho peleides*

WORTH NOTING   The large **blue morpho** butterfly, with a wingspan of up to 15 centimeters (6 in.), has brilliantly iridescent blue wings when opened. Fast and erratic fliers, they are often glimpsed flitting across your peripheral vision in dense forest.

PRIME VIEWING   Countrywide, particularly in moist environments.

Blue Morpho

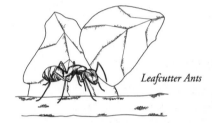

Leafcutter Ants

SCIENTIFIC NAME   *Atta cephalotes*

WORTH NOTING   You can't miss the miniature rainforest highways formed by these industrious little red **leafcutter ants** carrying their freshly cut payload. The ants do not actually eat the leaves, but instead feed off a fungus that grows on the decomposing leaves in their massive underground nests.

PRIME VIEWING   Can be found in most forests countrywide.

SCIENTIFIC NAME   *Nephila clavipes*

WORTH NOTING   The common Neotropical **golden silk spider** weaves meticulous webs that can be as much as .5m (2 ft.) across. The adult female of this species can reach 7.6 centimeters (3 in.) in length, including the legs, although the males are tiny. The silk of this spider is extremely strong and is being studied for industrial purposes.

PRIME VIEWING   Lowland forests on both coasts.

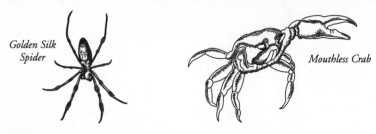

Golden Silk Spider

Mouthless Crab

SCIENTIFIC NAME   *Gecarcinus quadratus*

WORTH NOTING   The nocturnal **mouthless crab** is a distinctively colored land crab with bright orange legs, purple claws, and a deep black shell or carapace.

PRIME VIEWING   All along the Pacific coast.

FLORA

TREES

If you want to see the forest through the trees, it's often a good thing to be able to identify specific trees within the forest. We've included illustrations of the leaves, flowers, seeds, and fruit to get you started.

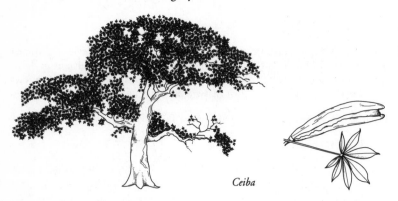

Ceiba

SCIENTIFIC NAME   *Ceiba pentandra*

WORTH NOTING   Also known as the kapok tree, **ceiba** trees are typically emergent (their large umbrella-shape canopies emerge above the forest canopy), making the species among the tallest trees in the tropical forest. Reaching as high as 60m (197 ft.), their thick columnar trunks often have large buttresses. Ceiba trees may flower as little as once every 5 years, especially in wetter forests.

PRIME VIEWING   Countrywide.

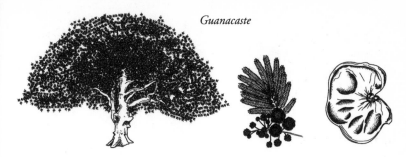

Guanacaste

SCIENTIFIC NAME   *Enterolobium cyclocarpum*

WORTH NOTING   The **guanacaste** tree is one of the largest trees found in Central America, and gives its name to Costa Rica's northwestern-most province. It can reach a total elevation of over 39m (130 ft.); its straight trunk composes 9 to 12m (30–40 ft.) of the height (the trunk's diameter measures more than 1.8m/6 ft.).

PRIME VIEWING   Countrywide.

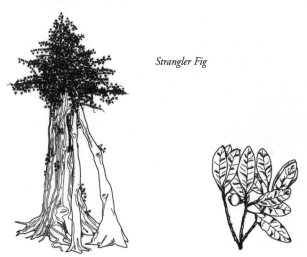

Strangler Fig

SCIENTIFIC NAME   *Ficus aurea*

WORTH NOTING   This parasitic tree gets its name from the fact that it envelops and eventually strangles its host tree. The *matapalo* or **strangler fig** begins as an epiphyte, whose seeds are deposited high in a tree's canopy by bats, birds, or monkeys. The young strangler then sends long roots down to the earth. The sap is used to relieve burns.

PRIME VIEWING   Primary and secondary forests countrywide.

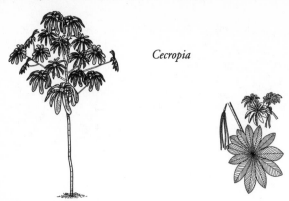

Cecropia

SCIENTIFIC NAME   *Cecropia obtusifolia*

WORTH NOTING   Several **cecropia** (trumpet tree) species are found in Costa Rica. Most are characterized by large, handlike clusters of broad leaves, and a hollow, bamboolike trunk. They are "gap specialists," fast-growing opportunists that can fill in a gap caused by a tree fall or landslide. Their trunks are usually home to Aztec ants.

PRIME VIEWING   Primary and secondary forests, rivers, and roadsides, countrywide.

Gumbo Limbo

SCIENTIFIC NAME   *Bursera simaruba*

WORTH NOTING   The bark of the **gumbo limbo** is its most distinguishing feature: A paper-thin red outer layer, when peeled off the tree, reveals a bright green bark. In Costa Rica the tree is called *indio desnudo* (naked Indian). In other countries it is the "tourist tree." Both names refer to reddish skin. The bark is used as a remedy for gum disease; gumbo limbo–bark tea allegedly alleviates hypertension. Another remarkable property is the tree's ability to root from its cut branches, which when planted right end up, develop roots and leaves, forming a new tree within a few years.

PRIME VIEWING   Primary and secondary forests, countrywide.

FLOWERS & OTHER PLANTS

Costa Rica has an amazing wealth of tropical flora, including some 1,200 orchid species.

Guaria Morada

SCIENTIFIC NAME *Cattleya skinneri*

WORTH NOTING The **guaria morada** orchid is the national flower of Costa Rica. Sporting a purple and white flower, this plant is also called the "Easter orchid" as it tends to flower between March and April each year.

PRIME VIEWING Countrywide from sea level to 1,220m (4,000 ft.).

Heliconia

SCIENTIFIC NAME *Heliconia collinsiana*

WORTH NOTING There are over 250 species of tropical heliconia, of which over 40 are found in Costa Rica. The flowers of this species are darkish pink in color, and the underside of the plant's large leaves is coated in white wax.

PRIME VIEWING Low to middle elevations countrywide, particularly in moist environments.

Hotlips

SCIENTIFIC NAME   *Psychotria poeppigiana*

WORTH NOTING   Related to coffee, **hotlips** is a forest flower that has thick red "lips" that resemble the Rolling Stones logo. The small white flowers (found inside the red "lips") attract a variety of butterflies and hummingbirds.

PRIME VIEWING   In the undergrowth of dense forests countrywide.

Red Torch Ginger

SCIENTIFIC NAME   *Nicolaia elatior*

WORTH NOTING   Called *bastón del emperador* (the emperor's cane) in Costa Rica, the tall **red torch ginger** plant has an impressive bulbous red bract, often mistaken for the flower. The numerous, small white flowers actually emerge out of this bract. Originally a native to Indonesia, it is now quite common in Costa Rica.

PRIME VIEWING   Countrywide, particularly in moist environments and gardens.

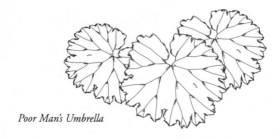

Poor Man's Umbrella

SCIENTIFIC NAME   *Gunnera insignis*

WORTH NOTING   The **poor man's umbrella,** a broad-leaved rainforest ground plant, is a member of the rhubarb family. The massive leaves are often used, as the colloquial name suggests, for protection during rainstorms.

PRIME VIEWING   Low- to middle-elevation moist forests countrywide. Commonly seen in Poás National Park and Braulio Carrillo National Park.

11 Spanish Terms & Phrases

Costa Rican Spanish is neither the easiest nor the most difficult dialect to understand. Ticos speak at a relatively relaxed speed and enunciate clearly, without dropping too many final consonants. The *y* and *ll* sounds are subtly, almost inaudibly, pronounced. Perhaps the most defining idiosyncrasy of Costa Rican Spanish is the way Ticos overemphasize, and almost chew, their *r*'s.

BASIC WORDS & PHRASES

ENGLISH	SPANISH	PRONUNCIATION
Hello	**Buenos días**	*bweh*-nohss *dee*-ahss
How are you?	**¿Cómo está usted?**	*koh*-moh ehss-*tah* oo-*stehd*
Very well	**Muy bien**	mwee byehn
Thank you	**Gracias**	*grah*-syahss
Good-bye	**Adiós**	ad-*dyohss*
Please	**Por favor**	pohr fah-*vohr*
Yes	**Sí**	see
No	**No**	noh
Excuse me (to get by someone)	**Perdóneme**	pehr-*doh*-neh-meh
Excuse me (to begin a question)	**Disculpe**	dees-*kool*-peh
Give me	**Deme**	*deh*-meh
Where is . . . ?	**¿Dónde está . . . ?**	*dohn*-deh ehss-*tah*
the station	la estación	la ehss-tah-syohn
the bus stop	la parada	la pah-rah-dah
a hotel	un hotel	oon oh-tehl
a restaurant	un restaurante	oon res-tow-rahn-teh
the toilet	el servicio	el ser-vee-syoh
To the right	**A la derecha**	ah lah deh-*reh*-chah
To the left	**A la izquierda**	ah lah ees-*kyehr*-dah
Straight ahead	**Adelante**	ah-deh-*lahn*-teh
I would like . . .	**Quiero . . .**	*kyeh*-roh
to eat	comer	ko-mehr
a room	una habitación	oo-nah ah-bee-tah-syohn
How much is it?	**¿Cuánto?**	*kwahn*-toh
The check	**La cuenta**	la *kwen*-tah
When?	**¿Cuándo?**	*kwan*-doh
What?	**¿Qué?**	keh
Yesterday	**Ayer**	ah-*yehr*
Today	**Hoy**	oy
Tomorrow	**Mañana**	mah-*nyah*-nah
Breakfast	**Desayuno**	deh-sah-*yoo*-noh

ENGLISH	SPANISH	PRONUNCIATION
Lunch	**Comida**	coh-*mee*-dah
Dinner	**Cena**	*seh*-nah
Do you speak English?	**¿Habla usted inglés?**	*ah*-blah oo-*stehd* een-*glehss*
I don't understand Spanish very well.	**No entiendo muy bien el español.**	noh ehn-*tyehn*-do mwee byehn el ehss-pah-*nyohl*

Numbers

1 **uno** (*oo*-noh)
2 **dos** (dohss)
3 **tres** (trehss)
4 **cuatro** (*kwah*-troh)
5 **cinco** (*seen*-koh)
6 **seis** (sayss)
7 **siete** (*syeh*-teh)
8 **ocho** (*oh*-choh)
9 **nueve** (*nweh*-beh)
10 **diez** (dyehss)
11 **once** (*ohn*-seh)
12 **doce** (*doh*-seh)
13 **trece** (*treh*-seh)
14 **catorce** (kah-*tohr*-seh)
15 **quince** (*keen*-seh)

16 **dieciséis** (dyeh-see-*sayss*)
17 **diecisiete** (dyeh-see-*syeh*-teh)
18 **dieciocho** (dyeh-see-*oh*-choh)
19 **diecinueve** (dyeh-see-*nweh*-beh)
20 **veinte** (*bayn*-teh)
30 **treinta** (*trayn*-tah)
40 **cuarenta** (kwah-*rehn*-tah)
50 **cincuenta** (seen-*kwehn*-tah)
60 **sesenta** (seh-*sehn*-tah)
70 **setenta** (seh-*tehn*-tah)
80 **ochenta** (oh-*chehn*-tah)
90 **noventa** (noh-*behn*-tah)
100 **cien** (syehn)
1,000 **mil** (meel)

Days of the Week

Monday	**lunes**	(*loo*-nehss)
Tuesday	**martes**	(*mahr*-tehss)
Wednesday	**miércoles**	(*myehr*-koh-lehs)
Thursday	**jueves**	(*wheh*-behss)
Friday	**viernes**	(*byehr*-nehss)
Saturday	**sábado**	(*sah*-bah-doh)
Sunday	**domingo**	(doh-*meen*-goh)

SOME TYPICAL TICO WORDS & PHRASES

Birra Slang for beer.
Boca Literally means "mouth," but also a term to describe a small appetizer served alongside a drink at many bars.
Bomba Translates literally as "pump" but is used in Costa Rica for gas station.
Brete Work, or job.
Casado Literally means "married," but is the local term for a popular restaurant offering that features a main dish and various side dishes.
Chapa Derogatory way to call someone stupid or clumsy.
Chepe Slang term for the capital city, San José.
Choza Slang for house or home.
Chunche Knickknack; thing, as in "whatchamacallit."
Con mucho gusto With pleasure.
De hoy en ocho In 1 week's time.

Diay An untranslatable but common linguistic phrase often used to begin a sentence.

Goma Hangover.

La sele Short for *la selección,* the Costa Rican national soccer team.

Macha or **machita** A blond woman.

Mae Translates as "man"; used by many Costa Ricans, particularly teenagers.

Maje A lot like *mae,* above, but with a slightly derogatory connotation.

Mala pata Bad luck.

Mejenga An informal, or pickup, soccer game.

Pachanga or **pelón** Both terms are used to signify a big party or gathering.

Ponga la maría, por favor This is how you ask taxi drivers to turn on the meter.

Pulpería The Costa Rican version of the corner store or small market.

Pura vida Literally, "pure life"; translates as: everything's great.

Qué torta What a mess; what a screw-up.

Si Dios quiere God willing. You'll hear Ticos say this all the time.

Soda A casual diner-style restaurant serving cheap Tico meals.

Tico Costa Rican.

Tiquicia Costa Rica.

Tuanis Means the same as *pura vida,* above, but is used by a younger crowd.

Una teja 100 *colones.*

Un rojo 1,000 *colones.*

Un tucán 5,000 *colones.*

Upe! Common shout to find out if anyone is home. (Used frequently since doorbells are so scarce.)

Zarpe Last drink of the night, or "one more for the road."

MENU TERMS

Fish

Almejas Clams

Atún Tuna

Bacalao Cod

Calamares Squid

Camarones Shrimp

Cangrejo Crab

Ceviche Marinated seafood salad

Dorado Dolphin or mahimahi

Langosta Lobster

Lenguado Sole

Mejillones Mussels

Ostras Oysters

Trucha Trout

Meats

Albóndigas Meatballs

Bistec Beefsteak

Cerdo Pork

Chicharrones Fried pork rinds

Cordero Lamb

Costillas Ribs

Jamón Ham

Lengua Tongue

Pavo Turkey

Pollo Chicken

Vegetables

Aceitunas Olives

Berenjena Eggplant

Elote Corn on the cob

Ensalada Salad

Espinacas Spinach

Palmito Heart of palm

Papa Potato

Tomate Tomato

Yuca Cassava or manioc

Fruits

Banano Banana

Cereza   Cherry
Fresa   Strawberry
Manzana   Apple
Naranja   Orange

Piña   Pineapple
Plátano   Plantain
Sandía   Watermelon

Basics

Aceite   Oil
Ajo   Garlic
Arreglado   Small meat sandwich
Azúcar   Sugar
Casado   Plate of the day
Frito   Fried
Gallo   Corn tortilla topped with meat or chicken
Gallo pinto   Rice and beans
Hielo   Ice
Mantequilla   Butter
Miel   Honey
Mostaza   Mustard

Natilla   Sour cream
Olla de carne   Meat and vegetable soup
Pan   Bread
Patacones   Fried plantain chips
Picadillo   Chopped vegetable side dish
Pimienta   Pepper
Queso   Cheese
Sal   Salt
Tamal   Filled cornmeal pastry
Tortilla   Flat corn pancake

Index

See also Accommodations index, below.

396   Index

400   Index

The new way to
get AROUND town.

Make the most of your stay. Go Day by Day

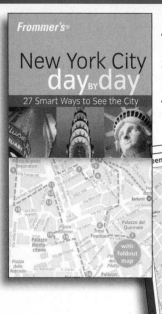

The all-new Day by Day series shows you the best places to visit and the best way to see them.

- Full-color throughout, with hundreds of photos and maps
- Packed with 1–to–3–day itineraries, neighborhood walks, and thematic tours
- Museums, literary haunts, offbeat places, and more
- Star-rated hotel and restaurant listings
- Sturdy foldout map in reclosable plastic wallet
- Foldout front covers with at-a-glance maps and info

The best trips start here.

Frommer's®

A Branded Imprint of ⓦ **WILEY**
Now you know.